# FileMaker® Pro 9 Bible

Ray Cologon, PhD
with Dennis R. Cohen

Wiley Publishing, Inc.

FileMaker® Pro 9 Bible

Published by
**Wiley Publishing, Inc.**
10475 Crosspoint Boulevard
Indianapolis, IN 46256
www.wiley.com

Copyright © 2008 by Wiley Publishing, Inc., Indianapolis, Indiana

Published simultaneously in Canada

Library of Congress Control Number: 2008922123

ISBN: 978-0-470-17743-3

Manufactured in the United States of America

10 9 8 7 6 5 4 3 2 1

No part of this publication may be reproduced, stored in a retrieval system or transmitted in any form or by any means, electronic, mechanical, photocopying, recording, scanning or otherwise, except as permitted under Sections 107 or 108 of the 1976 United States Copyright Act, without either the prior written permission of the Publisher, or authorization through payment of the appropriate per-copy fee to the Copyright Clearance Center, 222 Rosewood Drive, Danvers, MA 01923, (978) 750-8400, fax (978) 646-8600. Requests to the Publisher for permission should be addressed to the Legal Department, Wiley Publishing, Inc., 10475 Crosspoint Blvd., Indianapolis, IN 46256, (317) 572-3447, fax (317) 572-4355, or online at http://www.wiley.com/go/permissions.

LIMIT OF LIABILITY/DISCLAIMER OF WARRANTY: THE PUBLISHER AND THE AUTHOR MAKE NO REPRESENTATIONS OR WARRANTIES WITH RESPECT TO THE ACCURACY OR COMPLETENESS OF THE CONTENTS OF THIS WORK AND SPECIFICALLY DISCLAIM ALL WARRANTIES, INCLUDING WITHOUT LIMITATION WARRANTIES OF FITNESS FOR A PARTICULAR PURPOSE. NO WARRANTY MAY BE CREATED OR EXTENDED BY SALES OR PROMOTIONAL MATERIALS. THE ADVICE AND STRATEGIES CONTAINED HEREIN MAY NOT BE SUITABLE FOR EVERY SITUATION. THIS WORK IS SOLD WITH THE UNDERSTANDING THAT THE PUBLISHER IS NOT ENGAGED IN RENDERING LEGAL, ACCOUNTING, OR OTHER PROFESSIONAL SERVICES. IF PROFESSIONAL ASSISTANCE IS REQUIRED, THE SERVICES OF A COMPETENT PROFESSIONAL PERSON SHOULD BE SOUGHT. NEITHER THE PUBLISHER NOR THE AUTHOR SHALL BE LIABLE FOR DAMAGES ARISING HEREFROM. THE FACT THAT AN ORGANIZATION OR WEBSITE IS REFERRED TO IN THIS WORK AS A CITATION AND/OR A POTENTIAL SOURCE OF FURTHER INFORMATION DOES NOT MEAN THAT THE AUTHOR OR THE PUBLISHER ENDORSES THE INFORMATION THE ORGANIZATION OR WEBSITE MAY PROVIDE OR RECOMMENDATIONS IT MAY MAKE. FURTHER, READERS SHOULD BE AWARE THAT INTERNET WEBSITES LISTED IN THIS WORK MAY HAVE CHANGED OR DISAPPEARED BETWEEN WHEN THIS WORK WAS WRITTEN AND WHEN IT IS READ.

For general information on our other products and services or to obtain technical support, please contact our Customer Care Department within the U.S. at (800) 762-2974, outside the U.S. at (317) 572-3993 or fax (317) 572-4002.

**Trademarks:** Wiley, the Wiley logo, and related trade dress are trademarks or registered trademarks of John Wiley & Sons, Inc., and/or its affiliates, in the United States and other countries, and may not be used without written permission. FileMaker is a registered trademark of FileMaker, Inc. in the United States and other countries. All other trademarks are the property of their respective owners. Wiley Publishing, Inc., is not associated with any product or vendor mentioned in this book.

Wiley also publishes its books in a variety of electronic formats. Some content that appears in print may not be available in electronic books.

# About the Authors

**Ray Cologon** began using FileMaker in 1990, after having taught and worked with a number of other database tools. He subsequently used FileMaker to compile and analyze data for his doctoral thesis, as well as to design databases for a wide range of other purposes.

Ray has had a diverse career in the creative arts, education, and consulting. Over the past decade, he has developed his own business, NightWing Enterprises, which specializes in the design and development of bespoke FileMaker Pro solutions and provides consulting services to developers and clients in various parts of the world. In 2005, Ray was recipient of the FileMaker Excellence Award for Leadership and Technical Excellence in FileMaker Pro, and he has been a presenter at recent FileMaker Developer Conferences in the United States. He has also been a significant contributor to and moderator of a number of public forums on FileMaker and is a FileMaker Certified Developer.

Ray lives in Melbourne, Australia, where he is known for his sculpture and music, as well as his innovative work with FileMaker Pro.

**Dennis R. Cohen** has been developing and writing about software since the late 1970s, when he wrote and maintained the database software used at the Jet Propulsion Laboratory (JPL) to schedule which Deep Space Network tracking stations tracked which spacecraft and when. Following his time at JPL, Dennis developed and managed the development of software products and technologies at Ashton-Tate, Claris (now FileMaker, Inc.), and Aladdin Systems (now part of Smith Micro Software). For the past ten years, he has concentrated on writing and editing books and magazine articles on his favorite software and hardware products.

With over a dozen titles to his credit as author or coauthor (including the last three editions of *FileMaker Pro Bible*), he has also been the technical editor of almost 200 titles.

Dennis resides in Sunnyvale, California, with Spenser, a magnificent Boston terrier.

*Ray: To Heather, Aris, and Drue, whose patience, love, and support have been immeasurable*

*Dennis: To my friends and family, in particular, Spenser, my Boston terrier best buddy*

# Credits

**Acquisitions Editor**
Kyle Looper

**Project Editors**
Kelly Ewing
Elizabeth Kuball

**Copy Editors**
Kelly Ewing
Elizabeth Kuball
Beth Taylor

**Technical Editors**
Corn Walker
Jason DeLooze
Mark Hammer
Michael Cohen

**Editorial Manager**
Jodi Jensen

**Vice President & Executive Group Publisher**
Richard Swadley

**Vice President and Publisher**
Andy Cummings

**Editorial Director**
Mary C. Corder

**Project Coordinator**
Lynsey Stanford

**Graphics and Production Specialists**
Claudia Bell
Stacie Brooks
Carl Byers
Shane Johnson

**Quality Control Technicians**
John Greenough
Todd Lothery

**Proofreading and Indexing**
Potomac Indexing, LLC
Christine Sabooni

# Contents

**Acknowledgments** ............................................................. xxvii

**Preface** .......................................................................... xxix

    About This Book ............................................................................... xxix
    About This Book's Target Audience .................................................. xxx
    How This Book Is Organized ............................................................. xxxi
        Part I: The Fundamentals ............................................................ xxxi
        Part II: Introduction to Database Design ..................................... xxxi
        Part III: Beyond the Basics ......................................................... xxxi
        Part IV: Integrity and Security .................................................... xxxi
        Part V: Raising the Bar .............................................................. xxxi
        Part VI: Appendixes ................................................................... xxxi
    Icons Used in This Book .................................................................. xxxii
    Where to Go from Here .................................................................. xxxii

## Part I: The Fundamentals    1

### Chapter 1: Databases: The What, Why, and How ............... 3

    The Many Faces of Databases: Lists, Tables, and Forms ................... 4
        Understanding the limitations of paper-based databases ............ 4
        Entering the digital age ............................................................. 5
        Preparing to get organized ....................................................... 5
    The Concept of a Relational Database .............................................. 6
        Flat-file databases and data redundancy ................................... 6
        Opportunities for making connections ..................................... 7
    The Anatomy of a Database Solution ............................................... 7
        The data: Foundation and substance ........................................ 7
        The interface: Screens, letters, forms, and reports ................... 8
        The hidden helper: Process management ................................ 11
    How FileMaker Fits In ....................................................................... 12
        Knowing what FileMaker Pro calls things ................................ 12
        Using familiar ideas from the real world ................................. 17
        Integrating processes and information ................................... 17
        Recognizing that knowledge is power — personal and professional ........ 18

# Contents

### Chapter 2: Putting FileMaker Pro in Perspective . . . . . . . . . . . . . . . . . 19
What Makes FileMaker Pro Different from Other Database Development Tools? ............... 20
    Some common misperceptions ............................................................ 20
    A unique approach to design .............................................................. 22
The FileMaker Product Family ................................................................... 23
    Desktop and server ............................................................................... 24
    Scalability and flexibility ....................................................................... 24
FileMaker's Hidden Talents ........................................................................ 25
    The cross-platform chameleon ............................................................. 26
    Multiple technologies and formats ....................................................... 26
    Plug-ins and extensibility ..................................................................... 28
    The FileMaker calculation engine: Simplicity and power ..................... 28
Resources and Exemplars .......................................................................... 29
    Examples and brainteasers ................................................................... 30
    Other resources and opportunities ....................................................... 30

### Chapter 3: Getting Acquainted with FileMaker . . . . . . . . . . . . . . . . . 31
Getting FileMaker Working for You ........................................................... 31
    Starting and exiting from FileMaker ..................................................... 32
    Creating, saving, and closing files ........................................................ 33
    Handling files and data safely .............................................................. 35
    Earlier file formats and conversion issues ........................................... 36
Finding Your Way Around ........................................................................ 37
    The modes and their uses .................................................................... 38
    Navigating and viewing data ............................................................... 39
    Searching and the FileMaker Find/Omit puzzle ................................... 40
    Screen elements and what they're for ................................................. 42
Entering and Editing Data ......................................................................... 43
    Creating and duplicating records ......................................................... 44
    Field definitions: Validation and dependencies .................................... 44
    The significance of commitment .......................................................... 45
The Ins and Outs ...................................................................................... 46
    Importing and exporting data .............................................................. 46
    Previewing and printing options .......................................................... 48
    Send/Save as PDF and Excel ................................................................ 49
Getting to Know the Relatives .................................................................. 49
    Ways to view and edit related data ..................................................... 49
    The importance of context ................................................................... 50
    Making complexity simple in practice ................................................. 50
Optimizing the Application ....................................................................... 51
    Preference settings for your workstation ............................................. 51
    File options for the current database ................................................... 54

# Contents

## Chapter 4: What's New in FileMaker 9 .................... 59

The FileMaker Quick Start Screen .................................................................. 59
The Help Menu ............................................................................................. 60
Learn More Links on Critical Dialogs ............................................................ 61
Scheduled Software Update Notification ...................................................... 62
New Calculation Functions ........................................................................... 63
    Self .......................................................................................................... 63
    Get (TemporaryPath) ............................................................................... 64
    Get (HostApplicationVersion) .................................................................. 64
    Asin (number) ......................................................................................... 64
    Acos (number) ......................................................................................... 64
Conditional Formatting ................................................................................. 65
Append to PDF .............................................................................................. 66
The Send E-Mail Link for Database Sharing ................................................. 67
Script Grouping and Editing Tools ................................................................ 69
Automatic Resizing of Layout Objects .......................................................... 70
Enhanced Tab Control ................................................................................... 71
    Default tab selection ............................................................................... 72
    Tab width settings ................................................................................... 72
Web Viewer Feature Enhancements .............................................................. 72
    Progress indicator, location, lock icon ..................................................... 72
    Support for data URLs ............................................................................. 74
Field-Specific Enabling of Visual Spell-Checking ......................................... 74
Multiple Levels of Text Undo and Redo in Fields and ScriptMaker ............. 75
Additional Toolbar Controls .......................................................................... 76
    Save/Send as PDF or Excel, Undo and Redo .......................................... 76
    Layout alignment toolbar ........................................................................ 76
Additional Avery Label Formats ................................................................... 77
Enhanced External SQL Data Source Support ............................................. 77
Supplemental Fields for ESS Tables ............................................................. 80
    Creating supplemental fields .................................................................. 80
    Using supplemental fields ....................................................................... 80
    Considering design ................................................................................. 81
FileMaker Pro 9 Advanced ............................................................................ 82
    Script Debugger enhancements .............................................................. 82
        Launching scripts from within the Script Debugger ........................ 82
        Working with restricted-access scripts ............................................. 83
        Making multiple selections in the Script Debugger window ........... 84
        Understanding the Pause on Error and Last Error code .................. 84
        Using step buttons when a script is paused ..................................... 84
    Data Viewer enhancements .................................................................... 85
        The Current and Watch tabs ............................................................. 85
        Authenticating to view-restricted data ............................................. 86
        Identifying other usability improvements ........................................ 86

# Contents

The PHP Site Assistant ..................................................................................87
Database Design Report enhancements ..........................................................88

## Part II: Introduction to Database Design — 89

### Chapter 5: Creating a Database . . . . . . . . . . . . . . . . . . . 91

Creating a New Database File ..........................................................................92
    Adding tables and fields ..........................................................................94
        OrderLines ..........................................................................................97
        Invoices ..............................................................................................97
        InvoiceLines ......................................................................................97
        Contacts ............................................................................................97
    Working with the Field Options dialog: Validation and auto-entry ..........97
    Setting up simple calculations ..............................................................103
    Capturing simple metadata ..................................................................106
    Creating relationships between tables ..................................................108
    Adding aggregating calcs ......................................................................111
Viewing and Interacting with Data ..................................................................113
    Looking at the multiple uses of layouts ................................................114
    Creating records and entering data ......................................................114
    Editing or deleting data ........................................................................118
    Finding and sorting data you've already entered ..................................119
    Using special find symbols ..................................................................120
    Searching with the range and wildcard operators ................................120
Avoiding the Need for Data Duplication ........................................................121
    Recognizing the visual cues to data relationships ................................121
    Information has a logical flow ..............................................................122
    Anticipating the user ............................................................................123
    Making complex things simple ............................................................125
Getting Started with File Security ..................................................................125
    Working with accounts and privilege sets ............................................125
    Setting a default account and password ..............................................128
Thinking About Usability ................................................................................129
    Moving between records ......................................................................129
    Managing context ................................................................................130
    Moving between tables ........................................................................130
    Using and changing views ....................................................................130
    Using buttons for static and dynamic actions ......................................130

### Chapter 6: The Interface: Layout Mode . . . . . . . . . . . . . . 131

Initial Layouts ................................................................................................131
    A map of Layout mode ........................................................................134
        Selection then Action tools ..............................................................135
        Drag-to-Layout tools ........................................................................136
        Palette and Menu controls ..............................................................136

# Contents

Organizing the presentation of information ........................................................ 136
Applying formats to field and text objects ........................................................ 137
Setting up layouts for printing ........................................................................ 141
Understanding lists and forms ........................................................................ 144
Layout parts and their purposes ..................................................................... 145
The Importance of Visual Structure ...................................................................... 146
Adding visual pointers and aids ..................................................................... 147
Using white space ........................................................................................ 149
Ergonomics and avoiding visual fatigue ......................................................... 149
Giving information meaning .......................................................................... 150
Different Kinds of Layout Objects ........................................................................ 150
Static and dynamic objects ............................................................................ 151
Inherent object properties ............................................................................. 152
Conditional format attributes ........................................................................ 152
FileMaker as a Graphical Environment .................................................................. 154
Building graphic objects in FileMaker ............................................................ 154
Default object formats and attributes ............................................................. 155
Controlling stacking and alignment ................................................................ 156
Bringing in graphics from other applications .................................................. 157
Interacting with Layout Objects ........................................................................... 158
Keyboard control of a layout ......................................................................... 158
Setting the tab order ..................................................................................... 159
Assigning names to layout objects ................................................................. 160
Controlling visual spell-checking ................................................................... 160
The Tab Control and Its Uses ............................................................................... 160
Defining and creating a tab panel .................................................................. 161
Navigating between tab panels ...................................................................... 162
Tab panel limitations .................................................................................... 163
Displaying Related Data ...................................................................................... 163
Working within layout context ...................................................................... 163
Setting up a portal ........................................................................................ 164
The Magic of Buttons .......................................................................................... 167
Defining buttons ........................................................................................... 168
Button scope and button commands .............................................................. 170
The button as an object ................................................................................. 171
The Web Viewer: Inviting in the World ............................................................... 172
Setting up a Web viewer ............................................................................... 172
Controlling a Web viewer ............................................................................. 173
Complementary data concepts ...................................................................... 174
Reports and Data Output ..................................................................................... 174
Considerations for printed output .................................................................. 174
Using fonts ................................................................................................... 174
Page sizes and page setup ............................................................................. 175
Paper output versus PDF or Excel output ...................................................... 176
Composite PDFs from multiple layouts ........................................................ 176

ix

# Contents

### Chapter 7: The Structure: The Manage Database Dialog . . . . . . . . . . . 177
- Working with Tables .................................................................................178
  - Table concepts: A room with a view ...................................................178
  - Adding, deleting, and renaming tables ................................................178
  - Moving tables between files ................................................................180
  - Importing tables ..................................................................................180
- Specifying Fields .......................................................................................183
  - Adding, deleting, and renaming fields ................................................184
  - Understanding field/data types and their significance ........................185
  - Auto-entry options ..............................................................................187
  - Field validation options ......................................................................188
  - Storage and indexing options ..............................................................191
  - Summary and Calculation fields ..........................................................192
  - Working with global fields ..................................................................196
- Basic Calculations.....................................................................................197
  - Creating a Calculation field ................................................................198
  - Defining a calculation formula ............................................................201
  - Entering literal text ..............................................................................202
  - Referencing fields ................................................................................203
  - Understanding calculation functions and their syntax ........................204
    - The List( ) function ........................................................................204
    - The Count( ) function ....................................................................204
    - The Date( ) function ......................................................................204
    - The Round( ) function ...................................................................205
    - The Length( ) function ..................................................................205
  - Doing some simple calculations .........................................................206
    - Number of days an item is overdue ...............................................206
    - Calculating initials from a person's name .....................................206
    - Compound interest at a known rate over a given period ..............207
    - Current quarter of the calendar year ..............................................207
    - Changing ampersands to "and" in a block of text .........................207
    - Record navigation text (record n of nn).........................................208
- The Relationships Graph ..........................................................................208
  - Common misconceptions about the Relationships Graph ..................209
  - Tables versus table occurrences ..........................................................210
  - Avoiding circular references ...............................................................210
  - Named and unnamed data sources ......................................................212
  - Creating references to other FileMaker files ......................................213
- Working with External SQL Data Sources...............................................214
  - Configuring ODBC drivers: Setting up a DSN....................................214
  - Integrating SQL tables with FileMaker data .......................................219
  - Adding supplemental fields .................................................................222
- The Concept of Data Relationships...........................................................223
  - Why bother with relationships anyway? .............................................223
  - How relationships work .......................................................................224

# Contents

    Solving problems using relationships ..................................................224
    Deciding what goes where ....................................................................225
    The FileMaker relational model ............................................................225

## Chapter 8: The Processes: ScriptMaker . . . . . . . . . . . . . . . . . . . . 227

  ScriptMaker: What It Is and What It Offers You ........................................227
    Building blocks of automation ..............................................................230
    Context is everything ............................................................................232
    Doing things in sequence ......................................................................232
    Addressing objects by name ..................................................................233
  Defining and Editing Scripts........................................................................234
    Script Editor windows ..........................................................................234
    Setting up a basic script ........................................................................237
    How script commands function ............................................................239
    Changing the order of commands..........................................................239
    Assigning attributes to a command ......................................................241
  Using the Script Menu ................................................................................243
    Managing the Scripts menu ..................................................................244
    Other ways to trigger a script ................................................................244
    Using the single-threaded script engine ................................................244
    Working with the script stack and paused scripts ................................245
  Controlling Script Execution ......................................................................245
    Using conditional statements ................................................................246
    Using repetition ....................................................................................247
    Pausing for user input ..........................................................................248
  Some Notable Script Uses............................................................................249
    Navigation and view controls ..............................................................249
    Editing information via scripts ..............................................................250
    Printing and managing files ..................................................................251
  Ease of Editing in ScriptMaker ....................................................................251
    Selecting and duplicating multiple commands ....................................252
    Copying and pasting scripts ..................................................................252
    Copying and pasting script steps ..........................................................253
  Organizing Scripts ......................................................................................253
    Creating list separators ........................................................................254
    Script commenting ................................................................................254
    Creating script groups ..........................................................................255
    Reordering and grouping scripts............................................................257
    Filtering scripts by group ......................................................................257
    Searching for scripts by name ................................................................258
  Some Examples to Start With ......................................................................259
    Performing a Find..................................................................................259
    Printing a report ....................................................................................259
    Acting on user input ..............................................................................260

**xi**

## Contents

### Part III: Beyond the Basics — 261

**Chapter 9: The FileMaker Power User ................... 263**

- Making Browse Mode Work for You ................................................264
  - Using multiple windows and views ........................................264
  - Filtering portals and creating pick lists ..................................264
  - Jump buttons: Shortcut navigation ........................................270
  - Controlling one window from another ..................................274
- Performing Complex Search Operations..........................................275
  - Compound Find criteria: The AND Find ................................275
  - Stacking Find requests: The OR Find .....................................276
  - Constraining and extending the found set ............................276
  - Saving Finds and found sets ..................................................277
- Sorting Records ................................................................................280
  - Multiple sort keys....................................................................281
  - Dynamic sort techniques ........................................................281
  - Creating click-sort columns ...................................................284
  - Sorting related data................................................................288
- Understanding Formatting ...............................................................290
  - The management of formatting: A three-tiered approach .....291
  - Character-level formatting .....................................................291
  - Paragraph-level formatting ....................................................292
  - Layout format filters ..............................................................292
  - Precedence of number, date, and time formats .....................293
  - Controlling formatting programmatically .............................293
  - Creating style buttons............................................................294
- Some Notes on Variables .................................................................295
  - The three kinds of variables ..................................................296
  - Variables and memory usage.................................................296
  - Instantiating and destroying variables...................................296
  - Keeping track of variables.....................................................297
- Understanding Indexing...................................................................298
  - Text index types .....................................................................298
    - The word index ..............................................................298
    - The value index ..............................................................299
  - Indexing myths exploded ......................................................299
  - Differences between numeric and text indexing ...................301
  - Unicode and alternate language indexes ...............................301
  - Optimizing field index configurations ..................................302
- The Table of Dependencies..............................................................303
  - Cascading calculation operations .........................................303
  - The limits of dependency ......................................................303
  - Tiers of dependency ..............................................................304

# Contents

Caching Join Results......................................................................................................304
    What caching does for you ..................................................................................304
    Solving caching problems ....................................................................................304
    Gaining control of the cache ...............................................................................306
Understanding Global Fields ........................................................................................306
    The behavior of global fields ...............................................................................306
    Uses for global fields............................................................................................307
    When to avoid global fields ................................................................................307
    Using global calculation fields ............................................................................307

## Chapter 10: Building Advanced Interfaces . . . . . . . . . . . . . . . . . . . 309

Developing for Mac and Windows Users ....................................................................310
    Selecting fonts ....................................................................................................310
    Paying attention to differences in screen rendering ..........................................311
    Considering platform-specific window behavior ...............................................312
Using Dynamic Screen Elements .................................................................................314
    Disappearing/reappearing objects ......................................................................314
        The portal invisibility trick .........................................................................314
        Concealed and remotely operated tab control .........................................316
        Using conditional formatting as a visibility control ...................................317
    The hidden power of conditional formatting ....................................................318
    Multi-state buttons and objects...........................................................................319
Working with Sub-Summary Parts and Part Controls .................................................320
    Building adaptable screens .................................................................................320
    Stacking up multiple Sub-summary parts ..........................................................320
    Using multiple break fields .................................................................................322
    Controlling pagination and page breaks ............................................................324
Designing for Print .......................................................................................................325
    Non-printing objects ...........................................................................................325
    Sliding objects and reducing parts .....................................................................326
    Using Merge fields ..............................................................................................328
    Creating a letter generator .................................................................................329
Using Multiple Windows and Views............................................................................330
    Managing window placement and size ..............................................................330
    Windows as pop-ups and drill-downs ................................................................331
    Simulating modal window behavior ...................................................................332
Employing Custom Dialogs as an Interface Tool ........................................................332
    Dialogs as a data-entry device ............................................................................332
    Dynamic dialog attributes...................................................................................334
Looking at Anchors and Resizable Layout Objects .....................................................334
    Objects that move according to window size ...................................................334
    Objects that grow and shrink .............................................................................336
    Managing complex layout resizing .....................................................................336
    Resizing behavior of enclosing objects ..............................................................338
    Centering objects within the viewable area ......................................................339

**xiii**

## Contents

Implementing Shortcut Navigation ...................................................................................339
    The power of the Go to Related Record command ................................................339
    One interface, many paths ....................................................................................340
    Building Back button functionality .......................................................................340
Building Depth and Dimensionality ..................................................................................341
    Using embossing and engraving effects ................................................................342
    Spatial cues for added meaning ............................................................................342
    Delineation of element groups .............................................................................342
    Color ...................................................................................................................343
    Transparency and translucency ............................................................................343
Working with Tab Controls ..............................................................................................343
    Organizers and space savers .................................................................................344
    Tab navigation via keyboard ................................................................................344
    Scripting tab operations .......................................................................................344
Recognizing the Flexibility of Portals ................................................................................345
    Lists in many guises ............................................................................................345
    Portals as a navigation device ..............................................................................346
    Dynamically sorted portals ..................................................................................346
    Innovative portal implementations .......................................................................347
Using Advanced Web Viewer Techniques .........................................................................347
    Access to advanced functionality .........................................................................347
    Rendering internally calculated content ...............................................................348
    Scraping data from Web pages .............................................................................349
Progress Bars and Native Charting Techniques .................................................................350
    Creating script progress monitors ........................................................................351
    Native indicators and graphical displays ..............................................................352
Using Interface Elements ..................................................................................................353
    Splash screens .....................................................................................................353
    Main menus ........................................................................................................354
    About and version info ........................................................................................354
    Online Help for your users ...................................................................................354
Handling User Preferences ...............................................................................................355
    A user-centric development philosophy ...............................................................355
    Capturing state by user ........................................................................................355
    Example — a multi-lingual solution interface .......................................................356

### Chapter 11: Data Modeling in FileMaker . . . . . . . . . . . . . . . . . . . 359

Background in Relational Theory ......................................................................................359
    Set Theory in the management of data .................................................................360
    Modeling the real world ......................................................................................360
        Think about clarity of organization ..............................................................361
        Keep the big picture in view ........................................................................361
    Remembering some guiding principles ................................................................362
        Separate entities by type ...............................................................................362
        Delineate fields clearly ................................................................................363

# Contents

    Place multiples in a separate table ..................................................... 363
    Store everything once only ................................................................. 363
    Identify the major players .................................................................. 364
    Put it into practice ............................................................................... 364
FileMaker Relationships Graph Symbols .................................................... 364
    Visual cues and clues ......................................................................... 364
    The TO as a pointer ........................................................................... 365
    Understanding the graph metaphor .................................................. 366
Relationship Operators ............................................................................... 366
    Equi-joins and non-equal joins .......................................................... 367
    Comparative operators (theta joins) ................................................. 368
    Cartesian joins ................................................................................... 369
    Multi-predicate relationships ............................................................. 369
Alternative Relationship Techniques ......................................................... 370
    Multi-key fields ................................................................................. 370
    Compound keys ................................................................................ 372
    One-way relationships ...................................................................... 372
    Join tables .......................................................................................... 373
    Naturally occurring joins .................................................................. 373
Working with Data Arrays ......................................................................... 374
    Repeating fields as an array handler ................................................. 374
    Collapsing and expanding arrays ...................................................... 374
    Relationship-based techniques for managing data ........................... 375
        Allowing creation via relationship .............................................. 375
        Using self joins ............................................................................ 376
        The isolating relationship ........................................................... 376
Graph Techniques — Spiders, Squids, and Anchor-Buoy ........................ 377
    Constellations and modular centers .................................................. 377
    A satellite-based graph solution ........................................................ 379
    Segmentation on functional lines ...................................................... 379
Documenting the Database Structure ........................................................ 380
    Graph annotations ............................................................................. 381
    Naming conventions .......................................................................... 382
    Field commenting .............................................................................. 382
    Ancillary notes and documentation .................................................. 384
The Concept of Layers ................................................................................ 385
    "Back end" and "front end" ............................................................... 385
    The business or procedural layer ...................................................... 386
    FileMaker as an integrated environment .......................................... 387
    Separation anxiety ............................................................................. 387
File Architecture versus Data Structure ..................................................... 388
    Multi-file solutions ............................................................................ 388
    The modular approach ...................................................................... 389
    Interface files ..................................................................................... 389

xv

## Contents

        Approaches to separation of data ................................................................391
        Costs and benefits of separation ..................................................................392
    Separation and External SQL Sources ..................................................................393
        Understanding the rules ..............................................................................393
        Working within constraints .........................................................................393
        Supporting the user .....................................................................................394
    Implementing Separation in an Existing Solution ...............................................395
        Establishing data source(s) ..........................................................................395
        Re-pointing table occurrences ....................................................................396
        Creating separate graphs .............................................................................397
    Deployment Considerations .................................................................................398
        Your remotest dreams .................................................................................398
        The model of adaptability ...........................................................................398

## Chapter 12: Calculation Wizardry . . . . . . . . . . . . . . . . . . . . 399

    Compound Calculation Expressions .....................................................................400
        The language of logic ..................................................................................401
        Functions and schema references ...............................................................402
        Structured syntax and nesting .....................................................................404
        Putting it all together ..................................................................................405
    Order of Operations ..............................................................................................406
    Boolean Operations ...............................................................................................408
        Zero, empty, and everything else ................................................................408
        Implicit Boolean coding ..............................................................................409
        Explicit Boolean coding ..............................................................................409
    Variables — Calculation, Script, and Global ........................................................410
        Declaring calculation variables — the Let( ) function ................................410
        Understanding variables' scope ...................................................................411
        Benefiting from variables in a calculation ..................................................412
    Text Processing and Parsing Functions ................................................................412
        Substitute, Replace, and Trim ....................................................................413
        Left, Right, and Middle ..............................................................................414
        Position and PatternCount ..........................................................................415
        The xWords suite ........................................................................................417
        Parsing in practice ......................................................................................418
    Text Formatting Operations ..................................................................................419
        Applying text formatting .............................................................................419
        Removing text formatting ...........................................................................419
        Applying selective formatting .....................................................................420
        Creating a Format button ............................................................................420
    Dates, Times, and Timestamps ............................................................................421
        How FileMaker manages dates ...................................................................421
        Plotting time ................................................................................................422
        The number of seconds in 2007 years ........................................................423
        Juggling days, months, and years ...............................................................423

Summary Data ..................................................................................................424
    Using aggregate functions .........................................................................425
    The ballad of Max and Min .......................................................................426
    Referencing summary fields .....................................................................426
Lists and Arrays ................................................................................................427
    Retrieving values as a list ..........................................................................427
    Managing lists — the xValues functions ...................................................428
    Extracting one value from a list................................................................429
    Adding or inserting a list value .................................................................430
    Removing a value from a list ....................................................................430
Layers of Abstraction .......................................................................................431
    Building blocks with GetField( ) ................................................................432
    The value of Evaluate( ) ............................................................................432
Unstored Calculations .....................................................................................434
    Why and when calculations are unstored ...............................................434
    Understanding the benefits and trade-offs of unstored calculations ......435
    Discovering the hidden secrets of unstored calcs ...................................435
Calculation Fields versus Auto-Enter Calculations ........................................436
    The user over-ride capability ....................................................................436
    Auto-enter calculations and storage ........................................................438
    The Do Not Replace option .......................................................................439
Global Calculations .........................................................................................439
    The moon follows you everywhere ..........................................................440
    Managing global dependencies ................................................................440
    The freedom and efficiency of global calculations .................................442
Environment and Metadata ............................................................................442
    The Get( ) functions ..................................................................................442
    Design functions ........................................................................................443
Calculations Using Custom Functions ............................................................444
Your Code's Documentation ...........................................................................447
    Code formatting ........................................................................................447
    Code commenting .....................................................................................448

# Chapter 13: Scripting in Depth . . . . . . . . . . . . . . . . 449

Scripting the Control of Objects and Interface ..............................................450
    Addressing objects by name ....................................................................450
    Locking down the interface .....................................................................452
    Managing user interaction .......................................................................452
Trapping for Errors...........................................................................................454
    Retrieving error codes appropriately ......................................................455
    What the error codes mean......................................................................456
    Why bother with error handling? .............................................................456
    Handling errors .........................................................................................457

## Contents

Scripts and Access Privileges ................................................................................460
    Privilege-based errors ...........................................................................461
    Run script with full access privileges ...................................................461
    Determining the substantive privileges ................................................462
Automating the Automation ...................................................................................462
    Defining a script to run on file open ....................................................463
    Housekeeping practices for start-up scripts .........................................464
    Scripts that run on file close .................................................................465
Harnessing the Power of Parameters, Results, and Variables ...................................466
    Getting data into a script .....................................................................466
    Branching according to state ................................................................467
    Declaring variables ..............................................................................468
    Passing and retrieving multiple parameters .........................................470
    Specifying and retrieving a script result ...............................................473
    Storing and accumulating data as you go ............................................474
Dynamic and Indirect Controls in ScriptMaker ......................................................475
    Example – Go to Layout by name or number .....................................476
    Dynamic file paths using variables .......................................................477
    Dynamically building Find criteria .......................................................478
    Editing field data on the fly (indirection) .............................................479
Using Nonlinear Logic ...........................................................................................480
    Nested and sequential If/Else conditions .............................................481
    Looping constructs ..............................................................................481
    Specifying exit conditions ....................................................................482
Modular Script Code .............................................................................................484
    Using sub-scripts .................................................................................484
    Script recursion ...................................................................................485
Scripted Window Management ..............................................................................485
    Addressing windows by name (title) ....................................................486
    Moving and resizing windows .............................................................488
        Determining window dimensions .................................................488
    Creating windows off-screen ................................................................489
    Freezing and refreshing the screen .......................................................489
Scripting Data Import and Export ..........................................................................490
    Exporting field contents ......................................................................490
    Exporting table data ............................................................................491
    Selecting fields for export ....................................................................492
    Import options .....................................................................................493
    Data matching for import ....................................................................494
        Synchronizing and updating data ..................................................494
        Other import options ....................................................................495
    Loading and unloading container objects ............................................496
Pivoting Data between Tables ................................................................................497
    Using utility relationships ....................................................................497
    Managing related data (walking through related records) ....................498

Going over Some Practical Examples .................................................. 499
 Locating unique records ............................................................... 499
 Building a multi-part PDF report .................................................. 499

# Part IV: Integrity and Security   501

## Chapter 14: In Control with FileMaker Security . . . . . . . . . . . . . . . 503

Concepts of Security......................................................................... 503
 Balance and perspective ................................................................ 504
  Identifying threats.................................................................. 504
  Assessing value ...................................................................... 504
 Protecting your investment .......................................................... 504
 Interface vulnerabilities ................................................................ 505
  Taking things at interface value............................................ 505
  More than a semblance of security ..................................... 505
  File-based security ................................................................. 506
The Privilege Set................................................................................ 506
 Concepts of role-based security .................................................. 507
 Defining and constraining access ................................................ 508
 Schema privilege controls ............................................................. 509
Granular Security .............................................................................. 510
 Access to value lists and scripts ................................................... 510
 The two dimensions of layout access ......................................... 511
 Privileges for table, record, and field access ............................. 511
 Using and managing extended privileges ................................. 513
User Authentication ......................................................................... 514
 Creating user accounts ................................................................. 515
 Internal and external authentication .......................................... 516
Scripted Account Management ...................................................... 517
 Provision for automation of database security......................... 517
 Working with multi-file solutions ................................................ 518
 Safe scripting implementations ................................................... 519
Creating a Custom Logout Option ................................................. 520
 The locked-down database .......................................................... 520
 Structuring a solution for logging out ....................................... 521
 Security logging ............................................................................. 522
How Much Security Is Enough? ...................................................... 523
 Ways to evaluate risk .................................................................... 523
 A balanced view of threats .......................................................... 523
 A strategic model for response ................................................... 524
The Importance of Physical File Security ....................................... 524
 Layers of protection ...................................................................... 524
 Alternative forms of protection ................................................... 525
 A multi-faceted approach ............................................................. 525

## Contents

Security in Deployment: FileMaker Server ..................................................526
    Filtered display of files ..................................................................526
    Secure Socket Layer encryption ....................................................527
    Server checks and logs ................................................................527

### Chapter 15: Maintaining Referential Integrity . . . . . . . . . . . . . . . . . 529

Pinpointing Common Causes of Referential Integrity Problems ...............529
    The potential impact on your solution ..........................................530
    Costs and benefits ......................................................................530
Using Unique Keys..........................................................................530
    Key safeguards ..........................................................................531
    Keys and meaning (existence, persistence, uniqueness) ...................532
Generating Keys..............................................................................532
    Serial numbers ..........................................................................532
    Record IDs ................................................................................534
    Unique identification (UID) values ................................................535
Exploring Keys and Data Type ..........................................................536
Retrofitting Keys..............................................................................537
Deleting Redundant Records ............................................................539
    The use of cascading deletion ......................................................539
    Configuring relationships for referential integrity ...........................540
    Privilege requirements for cascade delete ......................................541
    Controlled cascading deletes at runtime ........................................542
Considering Other Integrity Issues ....................................................543
    Lookups and when to use them ..................................................543
    Auto-entry lookups and references ..............................................544
    Data design issues......................................................................544
Managing Dependencies..................................................................544
    Literal text references ................................................................545
    Indirect object/element references ..............................................545
    Filename references ..................................................................545
    Structural anomalies ..................................................................546

### Chapter 16: Making FileMaker Systems Fail-Safe. . . . . . . . . . . . . . . . 547

Expecting the Unexpected ................................................................547
    Successful backup strategies ........................................................548
        Backup frequency ..............................................................548
        An appropriate backup cycle ..............................................548
        The integrity of backups ....................................................549
        The location of backups ....................................................549
        Back up the code, not just the data ......................................549
    The hazards of copying open files................................................549
    Backing up local files ..................................................................550
    Backing up hosted files................................................................551

# Contents

A Comprehensive Approach to Error Trapping ............................................................. 551
    Dealing with record locking ................................................................................. 552
    Techniques to avoid in multi-user or multi-window environments ......................... 554
        Replace Field Contents ................................................................................. 554
        Record marking and flagging techniques ...................................................... 555
        Uses of global fields ..................................................................................... 555
Opening Remote Files ............................................................................................... 555
    Peer-to-peer hosting ........................................................................................... 556
    File sharing risks ................................................................................................ 558
    Network spaghetti ............................................................................................... 558
    Opener files ........................................................................................................ 559
    Sending an e-mail link ....................................................................................... 560
Temporary Edit Interface Techniques ......................................................................... 561
    The data viewer concept .................................................................................... 562
    The legitimate purpose of record locking .......................................................... 563
    Creating double-blind entry systems .................................................................. 563
Field Masking, Filtering, and Error Rejection ............................................................. 564
    Applying standard data formations .................................................................... 565
    Dealing with trailing spaces and carriage returns ............................................... 566
    Rejecting out-of-scope characters ....................................................................... 567
    Handling styled source text ................................................................................ 567
Built-In Logging Capabilities ..................................................................................... 567
    Making use of auto-enter options ....................................................................... 567
    Capturing and extending standard metadata ..................................................... 568
Script Logging .......................................................................................................... 569
    Infrastructure for script logging ......................................................................... 569
    Tracking script execution .................................................................................. 570
        Script-specific context variables .................................................................... 571
        Script diagnostics .......................................................................................... 571
Capturing User Edits in Detail ................................................................................... 571
    Trapping edits, field-by-field .............................................................................. 572
    Incorporating ancillary data ............................................................................... 573
    Logging record deletions ................................................................................... 574
Managing the Accumulation of Log Data ................................................................... 575
    Archiving options .............................................................................................. 575
    Generating secondary output ............................................................................. 575
Implementing Roll-Back Capabilities ......................................................................... 576
    Chronological roll-back ..................................................................................... 576
    Alternative undo and roll-back capabilities ........................................................ 577
    Using logs to roll forward .................................................................................. 578
Alternative Logging Approaches ................................................................................ 578
    Logs as Data ...................................................................................................... 579
    Scripted and triggered logging ........................................................................... 579

xxi

## Contents

### Chapter 17: Maintaining and Restoring Data . . . . . . . . . . . . . . . . . 581

Some Notes on File Recovery ........................................................................581
  Debunking common myths and misconceptions ...............................582
  The Recover process ..........................................................................582
  Salvaging data....................................................................................583
  Understanding file corruption ...........................................................584
Exporting and Importing Data .....................................................................585
  File format considerations .................................................................586
  Exporting to and importing from a folder..........................................587
  Delimiters and EOL markers ..............................................................589
Data Cleansing Operations ...........................................................................589
  Extract, transform, and load ..............................................................589
  Data format considerations ...............................................................590
    Data organization ..................................................................590
    Data presentation ..................................................................591
    Data domain ..........................................................................592
  Filtering capabilities in FileMaker.......................................................592
Synchronizing Data Sets ...............................................................................594
  Import matching ................................................................................595
  Importing selectively .........................................................................596
Handling Embedded Images and Stored Files...............................................597
  Assigning and retrieving paths ..........................................................599
  Scripted field updates ........................................................................599
Text-Handling Considerations ......................................................................600
  Export field contents .........................................................................600
  Designing a custom export process....................................................601

## Part V: Raising the Bar    603

### Chapter 18: FileMaker Pro Advanced Features . . . . . . . . . . . . . . . . . 605

Script Debugger ............................................................................................605
  Watching code in action ....................................................................606
  Debugging restricted privilege scripts ...............................................607
  Getting used to the Debugger controls ..............................................607
Data Viewer ..................................................................................................609
  Current and Watch panels .................................................................610
    The Current panel .................................................................610
    The Watch panel....................................................................612
  Using the Viewer with the Debugger..................................................613
  The Data Viewer sand pit ...................................................................613
  The Data Viewer and variables ..........................................................614
Database Design Report ...............................................................................615
  DDR capabilities.................................................................................616
  Mining the DDR for information........................................................616
  Tools and techniques for interpreting DDR data ...............................617

## Contents

File Maintenance .................................................................................... 617
    Compact File ................................................................................... 618
    Optimize File ................................................................................... 618
    The Save a Copy As / Compacted alternative ............................ 618
Defining Tooltips ................................................................................. 619
    Using conditional tooltips ............................................................. 620
    Keeping track of tooltips ............................................................... 620
Creating Custom Menus .................................................................... 621
    Defining menus .............................................................................. 621
    Editing individual menus .............................................................. 622
        Benefits of the Script Step action ........................................... 623
        Benefits of window widgets .................................................... 624
    Adding menus to sets .................................................................... 624
    Assigning menu sets throughout your file ................................. 624
        Setting the default menu set for a file ................................... 624
        Determining a menu set for each layout .............................. 625
        Controlling menu sets via script ............................................ 626
Custom Functions ............................................................................... 627
    Defining custom functions ........................................................... 627
    Custom functions as an aid to syntax readability ..................... 629
    Maximizing efficiency and ease of use ....................................... 630
Custom Functions and Recursion .................................................... 631
    Things that only custom functions can do ................................ 632
    The stack and the limits of recursion .......................................... 633
    Tail recursion in practice .............................................................. 633
    Some useful examples ................................................................... 634
        Creating an acronym from a supplied phrase ..................... 634
        Extracting a character set from a supplied block of text ... 634
        Removing an unspecified number of leading carriage returns ....... 635
Creating Runtime Applications ......................................................... 635
    Generating a stand-alone solution .............................................. 636
    Binding for each platform ............................................................. 637
    Hosting runtime files ..................................................................... 637

### Chapter 19: Efficient Code, Efficient Solutions . . . . . . . . . . . . . . . . 639

Designing for Scale: Size Considerations ........................................ 639
    The elephant in the cherry tree .................................................... 640
    Predicting what will scale well ..................................................... 640
Eliminating Redundancy ................................................................... 641
    Avoiding duplication of elements ................................................ 641
    Using portable and reusable code ................................................ 642
        Appropriate use of sub-scripts ............................................... 642
        Appropriate use of custom functions .................................... 643
Designing for Flexibility and Adaptability ...................................... 643
    Layouts and adaptable design ...................................................... 644
    Concepts of reusability applied to the Relationships Graph ... 644

**xxiii**

## Contents

Traveling the Shortest Distance Between Two Points ..................................................645
    Optimal calculation syntax ....................................................................................645
    Alternative syntax examples .................................................................................647
        Working with modifier keys .........................................................................648
        Working with Boolean values ......................................................................649
    Avoiding dependency "spaghetti" .........................................................................650
    Applying simplicity principles ..............................................................................653
Transaction Modeling ...................................................................................................654
    Live versus batch data ...........................................................................................654
    Posting edits and propagating edits to related records .......................................655
    Offline updates and processing ............................................................................655
    Robots and batch automation ...............................................................................656
    Host/server script execution .................................................................................656
Managing File Size .......................................................................................................658
    Dealing with data in chunks ................................................................................658
        Modularization strategies .............................................................................658
        Considering segmentation ............................................................................659
    Data archiving ........................................................................................................659
Images and Media in Databases ..................................................................................660

## Chapter 20: Extending FileMaker's Capabilities . . . . . . . . . . . . . . . . 661

External Scripting Calls ................................................................................................661
    Using Send Event and VBScript ............................................................................662
        Using VBScript with FileMaker Pro .............................................................662
    Perform AppleScript ..............................................................................................665
    Cross-platform solutions and external script calls ...............................................667
    Third-party helpers and macros ...........................................................................668
Rendering HTML and JavaScript ..................................................................................669
    Harnessing HTTP ..................................................................................................669
    Bringing services to your solution ........................................................................669
    Handling hypertext ................................................................................................670
Web Viewer Widgets ....................................................................................................671
    Charting with Flash ...............................................................................................671
    Applets and servlets ..............................................................................................671
FileMaker Plug-Ins ........................................................................................................672
    Installing and enabling plug-ins ...........................................................................672
    Using external functions .......................................................................................674
    Script triggering .....................................................................................................675
        Robust triggering implementations .............................................................675
        Available script triggering plug-ins .............................................................677
    Dialog capabilities .................................................................................................677
    File and media handling .......................................................................................678
    E-mail, HTTP, and FTP ..........................................................................................679
    Charting and other functionality ..........................................................................679

# Contents

Web Deployment Options ..................................................................680
    Instant Web publishing ..............................................................680
    Custom Web publishing .............................................................681
        Working with XML and XSLT ............................................681
        The FileMaker PHP API ......................................................682
        FileMaker's PHP Site Assistant ...........................................682
Finding Third-Party Tools ...................................................................683
    Developer tools...........................................................................683
    Analysis and documentation .......................................................683
    Shared information ....................................................................684

## Part VI: Appendixes     685

### Appendix A: Glossary . . . . . . . . . . . . . . . . . . . . 687

### Appendix B: Expanding Your Knowledge with Additional Resources . . . . 703
    From the Horse's Mouth ............................................................703
    Professional Consulting and Development Services ....................704
    Online Design and Development Tips and Tricks ......................705
    Online Forums and Mailing Lists ...............................................706
    Books and Periodicals................................................................707

### Appendix C: About the Web Site . . . . . . . . . . . . . . 709
    What's on the Web Site..............................................................709
    Troubleshooting .......................................................................710

### Index . . . . . . . . . . . . . . . . . . . . . . . . . . 711

# Acknowledgments

As is often the case in a project of this scope, there are too many people involved to thank all of them individually. However, we would be remiss if we didn't acknowledge the fine folks at FileMaker, Inc., on the development and testing teams who continue to improve our favorite database application without compromising its ease of use or requiring unnecessary changes to our established work habits. Additionally, we would like to thank our editors, Elizabeth Kuball and Kelly Ewing, and our technical editors, Mark Hammer, Jason DeLooze, and Corn Walker, for their attention to detail and support in making this book a work of which we're proud.

# Preface

The FileMaker database product has been around for two decades now, longer than Microsoft Excel and almost as long as Microsoft Word. Moreover, it has been cross-platform (Mac and Windows) since the days of Windows 3.1. From the beginning, FileMaker has continually evolved, adding functionality and improving performance while retaining much of the essential ease of use that thrust it to the forefront of database products from its earliest days. We've been involved with FileMaker Pro throughout most of its history, from Dennis's time in the Claris product development organization starting in 1988 and Ray's work as a FileMaker solution provider and consultant over the past decade (including winning the FileMaker Excellence Award for Leadership and Technical Excellence in FileMaker Pro in 2005).

The FileMaker Pro product family encompasses a variety of packages, including FileMaker Pro 9, FileMaker Pro 9 Advanced, FileMaker Server 9 and FileMaker Server 9 Advanced. In essence, there are two categories of FileMaker products: development/end user (Pro and Advanced) and deployment (the Server products). This book covers the development/end user products — FileMaker Pro 9 and FileMaker Pro 9 Advanced — the place(s) where you create, modify, and (most often) use your databases.

## About This Book

If you own or have read previous editions of *FileMaker Pro Bible,* you saw each edition building upon previous editions with much of the coverage identical from one edition to the next. That chain is hereby severed! *FileMaker Pro 9 Bible* is an all new, from the ground up rewrite. Although we cover some topics in much the same order as they were covered in previous editions (due to their natures and interdependencies), this book's coverage of those topics is new. This edition of *FileMaker Pro Bible* has also been reorganized to provide a more fluid progression from basic to advanced coverage.

*FileMaker Pro 9 Bible* is not a tutorial, although it does include many short tutorials. Similarly, it is not a pure reference work, like an encyclopedia, with self-contained articles on FileMaker's various features. In this book, we cover designing, creating, and maintaining databases, and we do so in the context of using the FileMaker Pro 9 product offerings. We introduce concepts, such as data validation, and then demonstrate how FileMaker Pro 9 facilitates implementing those concepts. Deeper into the book, we cover more advanced aspects of material previously introduced (but when we do so, we point you to the prerequisite material). Additionally, the detailed table of contents and index are available to help you find topics of interest.

# Preface

FileMaker Pro 9 is a cross-platform product, almost identical on Mac and Windows. On the rare occasion that a feature exists on only one platform, we make that clear. When we reference keyboard shortcuts, we show the Mac shortcut followed by the Windows shortcut (for example, ⌘+N/Ctrl+N). Similarly, when a dialog is significantly different between the two platforms, we present screenshots of both versions of the dialog the first time it is encountered. Where there are no significant differences, we show the Mac version in our screenshots.

Throughout the book, we adhere as far as possible to standard conventions and terminology. For example the tilde (~) is used to denote an unspecified object (such as one or many records in a relationship) and standard forms such as 1:n are used where applicable. When terms are used with a special meaning, you can find them in Appendix A.

In any book, there are a finite number of pages in which to address a great deal of material; in that regard, this book is no different. So occasionally we refer you to the FileMaker Pro 9 Help system for further elucidation. For example, we don't want to sacrifice dozens of pages to regurgitating the names of the various script steps and their arguments — FileMaker, Inc., does that quite well and the topics are linked so a single click can get you to the related information. Instead of reiterating information readily available elsewhere, we use the pages of this book to show you how to *use* FileMaker to make your databases better.

Any book in the *Bible* series is intended to provide self-contained, comprehensive coverage of its subject. *Comprehensive* does not necessarily imply that every aspect is examined exhaustively (there is that page-count limitation, after all). But we believe that this edition of *FileMaker Pro Bible* is the most comprehensive to date and does more to help you become productive with FileMaker Pro.

## About This Book's Target Audience

If you want to create databases and database solutions using FileMaker Pro 9 or FileMaker Pro 9 Advanced, you're the target audience for this book. Whether you're a serious amateur who's creating a database solution for your family, club, or organization; a professional managing data as part of your wider role; or a developer who's building bespoke systems or turnkey solutions to sell or license to others, *FileMaker Pro 9 Bible* can help you attain your goals.

We do make a few basic assumptions about you:

- We assume that you know how to use your computer and operating system, whether it's a PC running Windows XP or Windows Vista, or a Mac running Mac OS X.
- We assume that you have, or have access to, FileMaker Pro 9 or FileMaker Pro 9 Advanced. The book will be more useful if you have access to FileMaker Pro 9 while you read and work through the examples we present.
- The third assumption is that you want to both understand the database design process and learn how to accomplish a broad range of tasks using FileMaker Pro 9.

# How This Book Is Organized

In keeping with *Bible* tradition, *FileMaker Pro 9 Bible* is divided into parts, and each part is divided into chapters. The parts of this book are as follows.

## Part I: The Fundamentals

This part is where we cover the basics of database theory and design and provide a high-level overview of the features of FileMaker Pro 9.

## Part II: Introduction to Database Design

This part is where you learn more details of database design theory and how to use FileMaker Pro 9 to actually create a database solution.

## Part III: Beyond the Basics

In this part, you'll learn how to use more advanced FileMaker Pro 9 features in such tasks as producing more comprehensive reports, implementing fault-tolerant input forms, designing layouts for cross-platform use, designing target-specific (screen, print, Web) layouts, and automating data processing.

## Part IV: Integrity and Security

This part delves deeply into the concepts and implementation of data integrity, access control, and risk management.

## Part V: Raising the Bar

Here, we delve into the additional features and capabilities offered by FileMaker Pro 9 Advanced and explore tools and techniques facilitating professional-level database development processes.

## Part VI: Appendixes

In the appendixes, we provide a glossary of the buzzwords and buzz phrases prevalent in the discussion of database design and implementation and, in particular, in FileMaker Pro 9; a compendium of other references you might find valuable, such as targeted technical tomes, related publications, and useful Web sites; and a synopsis of what you can find on this book's companion Web site.

# Icons Used in This Book

We use a number of border icons to call attention to specific passages throughout the book. The icons are as follows:

**NOTE** Indicates useful, but noncritical, information concerning the material being presented.

**TIP** Indicates information that makes performing a task easier or describes how a feature can be utilized in a useful, but not obvious, manner.

**CAUTION** Indicates possible pitfalls or side effects arising from the use of the feature being discussed.

**CROSS-REF** Indicates where to look for additional (including prerequisite) information about the material being discussed.

**NEW FEATURE** Indicates a feature introduced in FileMaker Pro 9 or FileMaker Pro 9 Advanced.

**ON the WEB** Indicates material that you can find on the book's companion Web site at `www.wiley.com/go/filemaker9bible`.

# Where to Go from Here

If you're new to creating databases, we suggest that you start with Part I. If you're experienced at database design but new to FileMaker Pro, we suggest skimming Part I to learn the FileMaker Pro interface and feature set. If you're an experienced FileMaker Pro user, you'll probably want to check out Chapter 4 to see what's new in FileMaker Pro 9 and then bounce around the book to those areas of particular interest (so the book's index should become your good friend).

All the example files for this book are our creation and available for download from the book's companion Web site at `www.wiley.com/go/filemaker9bible`.

# Part I

# The Fundamentals

You or an organization with which you're affiliated have data to collect, consolidate, organize, summarize, and report. Moving from scraps of paper, shoeboxes of receipts, or folders and file drawers of forms to an automated system requires a plan and the understanding of some basic concepts.

The chapters in this part provide an overview of database basics for those new to computer database management systems. They also cover how FileMaker facilitates your implementation for both new database users and those experienced with other database management systems and provide a summary for experienced FileMaker users of what's been added to FileMaker Pro 9 to make database development and management tasks easier.

## IN THIS PART

**Chapter 1**
Databases: The What, Why, and How

**Chapter 2**
Putting FileMaker Pro in Perspective

**Chapter 3**
Getting Acquainted with FileMaker

**Chapter 4**
What's New in FileMaker 9

# Chapter 1

# Databases: The What, Why, and How

You see (and hear) the word *database* bandied about almost everywhere you turn. On TV, you hear it when a crime show character talks about the AFIS database (*AFIS* is short for *Automated Fingerprint Identification System*) or on lawyer shows when characters talk about LexisNexis (a searchable compendium of information collected from newspapers, magazines, legal documents, and so on). Similarly, in newspapers you might read about privacy concerns raised over various (often unspecified) government databases.

The frequency with which the term *database* is used actually pales, though, when you consider how pervasive databases are. A *database* is, basically, nothing more than an organized collection of information. Your address book is a database containing contact information regarding people and companies with whom and with which you interact. When you look at the baseball results in the sports pages, the box scores, current averages, and so forth are organized data — generated from the information stored in a database cataloging the activity in said baseball games. The tables in your newspaper's financial pages are reports of stock, bond, and mutual fund activity. The index and table of contents in this book are also database reports, telling you where to find specific information.

Peoples' memories are also databases, although some function much better than others when it comes to retrieving the stored data! Computerized databases strive to store and retrieve data somewhat like a person's mind does; however, computers have both strengths and weaknesses. Two of the weaknesses are that the garbage-in, garbage-out principle (or GIGO for short) applies and that the computer has no inherent capability to learn from experience. In short, the computer has no way of discerning the accuracy, relevance, or relative importance of the information it receives. On the other

---

**IN THIS CHAPTER**

Identifying the elements of a database

Relating data

Solving problems using a database

Looking at FileMaker's role in streamlining data management

hand, major strengths of computers are that they're incredibly fast, obedient, and consistent in performing the instructions they're given, and they're single-minded in attempting to follow their instructions.

Database Management Systems (of which FileMaker Pro 9 is an excellent example) are the digital tools that people use to design, implement, and manage their computer databases.

# The Many Faces of Databases: Lists, Tables, and Forms

When you encounter a database in the real (as opposed to cyber) world, what you see are paper-based lists, tables, forms, index cards, and the like. Like most technologies, database technology has a bit of jargon associated with it, and to make use of our (or FileMaker, Inc.'s) guidance, learning at least some of the jargon is important. Fortunately, you've probably already encountered most of the terminology. The following list provides the most elementary terms you'll need to know:

- **Field:** A discrete piece of information, such as a surname, street address, ZIP code, or date of birth
- **Record:** A collection of fields pertaining to one specific entity, such as an inventory item, a person, or a transaction
- **Table:** A set of records
- **Database:** A table or organized group of tables

## Understanding the limitations of paper-based databases

In the physical world, data is usually collected from forms people fill out, and the forms are stored in filing cabinets, while the pertinent data is transposed into ledgers or onto index cards.

When a piece of data needs to be retrieved, someone (for example, a clerk) scans through the accumulated data to find the record in question. As you can easily see, this process is not terribly efficient, leaves a lot of room for human error, and can consume a lot of physical space. Even ignoring all that, creating a consolidated report summarizing some aspects of the stored data (for example, how many male students signed up for any shop course) could pose a daunting task, also fraught with the possibility for error.

Regardless of how the data is stored, it is only organized in a single order — alphabetically is probably the most common. Taking contact information as a common example, suppose you want to send out a mass mailing. The post office gives you a price break if the data is sorted by ZIP code, so you now have to manually address all the envelopes or flyers using the data in your files and then sort the mailing by ZIP code. If time is money, the time required to do all this tedious labor makes the task incredibly expensive.

## Databases: The What, Why, and How

Modifying data is another time-consuming task in the physical world. Suppose you're keeping your contact information in a Rolodex and one of your friends gets a new phone number—you need to cross out the old number and write in the new one or replace the Rolodex card with one containing the updated information (along with retyping or rewriting all the information that didn't change).

### Entering the digital age

For a long time during the last century a debate raged based on the assumption that computers were going to replace people. By now, it should be obvious that what computers do is perform certain tasks that people performed previously, albeit much more quickly and consistently. The time freed up by computers (actually, the programs run on those computers) opens whole new sets of tasks for people to perform, tasks that aren't as repetitive or boring. For example, instead of spending hours (or days) taking inventory, you can use your sales data to track inventory levels. This data enables you to know when it's time to reorder, to identify which products are hot and which are not, and to focus on deciding which items to feature and how to promote them.

Moving your data into a computer-based system provides a couple of options right at the outset:

- You can continue to use your paper-based forms to acquire the data and then transpose it into the computer rather than to ledgers and index cards.
- You can create a digital replica of your form and acquire the data on the computer to begin with, eliminating the transposition effort for at least some of your data.

Modifying data becomes much simpler: just browse to the record, select the data that changed, and type over it—all done, without mess or superfluous effort.

Now that your data is stored electronically, you benefit from the extremely rapid searching and sorting capabilities that a computer program provides. Additionally, a task like the earlier printing example becomes faster and much less labor-intensive when you have the program print the envelopes, flyers, or labels for you, already sorted to give you the presorted mail discount.

Even if simply entering, storing, and retrieving data were the only factors, we've already shown you sufficient reason to computerize your data. However, a great database program like FileMaker Pro 9 provides additional incentives. Among other possibilities, you can summarize your data in a report, perform data analysis via calculations, share your data with others via a Web page, and automate the process of producing scheduled reports.

### Preparing to get organized

Whenever you construct something, whether in the physical or cyber realm, you need to know what you have available to work with and what result you seek. For example, you can't assemble a bicycle if you only have one wheel—maybe a unicycle, but not a bicycle.

Organization is critical to success in manufacturing, construction, and database development. In manufacturing, you need to know which components (and in what quantity) are necessary to build your product. For a database, you need to know what data your end product requires to be available. For example, to produce a product catalog, at a minimum, you'll require item names, stock-keeping numbers, and prices. You might also want (or need) images of the items, color or size information, and information on whether the item is seasonal. If you want to make the catalog available online as part of an online store, you'll also want to access inventory information (to put up a "Temporarily Out of Stock" image so the customer will be aware that the item is back-ordered).

Additionally, you need to know what you want to get from your database. For example, a company might want to generate a roster of employees in any given department, another report of all employees by seniority, another by salary range, and so forth. The reports that you want to create will determine the information that you need to store.

One useful and common approach is to prototype your output to determine the necessary input data.

# The Concept of a Relational Database

The simplest form of database is the flat-file database. A *flat-file database* is a single table containing all the fields in your database. One common implementation of a flat-file database is a spreadsheet. In database terms, each cell in a column is a field and each row of cells is a record.

## Flat-file databases and data redundancy

As the number of fields grows, a single table rapidly becomes unwieldy. Using the company personnel example, you don't need salaries or Social Security numbers commingled with the less sensitive phone extension information, especially when producing a phone roster. If you break the data into separate, more manageable tables, you wind up duplicating some of the fields from table to table. Similarly, when recording more than one piece of information about an object, such as home and work addresses, you may end up with more than one record for the same person. Such duplication makes large volumes of data difficult to track and manage.

Back in 1970, mathematician and programmer E. F. Codd introduced the idea of what he called the *relational model* to make Database Management Systems less dependent upon a specific usage. (You can find his article at www.acm.org/classics/nov95/toc.html.) Codd's work provides a mathematical model that requires an understanding of set theory and predicate logic to fully comprehend. What's important to understand about Codd's work, however, is that it led to database systems that enable you to *relate* different tables to each other based upon a common field.

If your school days were far enough in the past to pre-date teachers using computers to track attendance, test scores, homework, and the like, you've quite possibly encountered a very simple example of a paper-based relational system. In those bygone days, many teachers used grade books consisting of a master page with student names and generic data and additional, narrower pages (so that the student names still showed at the left) holding specific kinds of data — attendance, quiz scores, homework, and exams, for example. In a computerized relational database, the additional pages would each be separate tables related to the master table on the common field (student name or student ID).

## Opportunities for making connections

Databases are everywhere. Your address book, the library's card catalog, your checkbook stubs, your iTunes Library, the TV schedule, just about any place you turn to find a piece of information, you're accessing a database. Every time you double-click a document on your computer, you're accessing a database (on Macs, it's part of Launch Services; in Windows, it's called the Registry) to find the appropriate application to open your document.

Using a Database Management System like FileMaker Pro 9, you can create structure and order around your information, making data easier to retrieve and more relevant when combined with related data.

One useful example would be organizing all your personal financial data. The master table might be comprised of the names, locations, account types, and account numbers for savings accounts, checking accounts, credit card accounts, brokerage accounts, mortgages, IRAs, SEP-IRAs, 401(k)s, and so forth. Then you would create a table in which you would record all transactions — deposits, withdrawals, interest paid, interest collected, and so on. As a result, you could create reports from the master table summarizing net worth, retirement funding (IRAs, SEP-IRAs, 401(k)s, and other retirement accounts), or outstanding obligations. Additionally, you could create reports based on any selection of entries in the transactions table, detailing status and activity for just one account, for several accounts, for a specific time period, or for a specific type of transaction (for example, all interest payments).

Do you collect coins, stamps, comic books, or Beanie Babies? If you collect coins, you might create a master table listing the coinages you collect (pennies, nickels, dimes, and so on) and related tables of those coin types detailing the specific coins, their condition, and cost. Storing this data in such a way makes it easy to find gaps in your collection or coins of which you have multiples. Similarly, you can create inventory reports or valuation information for when you insure your collection. You can do comparable things with other types of collections.

# The Anatomy of a Database Solution

A *database solution* is the combination of the tables, relations, data-entry forms, reports, and everything else surrounding your database enabling you (or your clients, your customers, or your co-workers) to enter data, control access to the data, and report on the data.

## The data: Foundation and substance

If you don't have information (data) to manage, you don't need a database. The core of any database is the data *in* that database. This data is organized in tables consisting of records, with each field of a record containing a discrete piece of data.

# Part I  The Fundamentals

The way your data is organized provides your database with structure — sometimes called its *data architecture* — which provides the basis for every function and procedure you perform. The decisions you make about data structure are important because they determine what will be possible and what won't, when you're working with your data.

The model for data relationships developed in the 1970s may seem abstract; however, it provides an effective way of capturing relationships that exist in the real world and replicating them in the information stored in your database. The goal is devising a structure for your data that's a good match for the things that data represents — and the relationships between them.

An ideal database structure is one that captures information about things (people, objects, places, and so on) and also accurately represents the relationships between them. People have relationships with each other — family and work relationships, for example — but they also have relationships of ownership and association with objects and places. Your databases should provide a way to represent information and its interrelations.

## The interface: Screens, letters, forms, and reports

When you interact with a computer database, you view and manipulate data onscreen. Different views of data presented onscreen are therefore often called *screens,* irrespective of how they're organized. A screen in this sense combines data, labels, and other control elements such as menus and command buttons that enable you to interact with the data and navigate the solution. Frequently, however, the visual elements of a screen are arranged in a way that is analogous to a familiar real-world object such as a list, a form, a letter, or a report. In many cases, you'll find it helpful to refer to screens as *forms* or *lists,* as these are more descriptive terms.

The most common screen format is the digital form, which presents a selection of the fields of a single record, arranged in a logical and useful order. Emulating the real world, digital forms are used to create new records and modify existing records. Figure 1.1 shows an entry form in iTunes (a music database) where you enter information about a song.

If you are familiar with the creating of lists or using spreadsheets, you've encountered lists or tables containing so much data that they're cumbersome. When a table has too many columns, it becomes unwieldy — making the task of seeing connections and considering the data as a whole very challenging. Database forms provide a way to ameliorate this problem by allowing you to view a subset of the fields (columns) of data, arranged in a way that makes the connections clear. For example, the components of an address — street, city, state, postal code, and so on — can be grouped together and viewed as a whole. Similarly, a person's name, title, and personal details will be grouped together. When viewed in this way — rather than spread out across a row as in a conventional table or spreadsheet — you can much more easily understand what the information means and how it interrelates.

# Databases: The What, Why, and How 1

**FIGURE 1.1**

A form lets you enter information into your database and edit existing data.

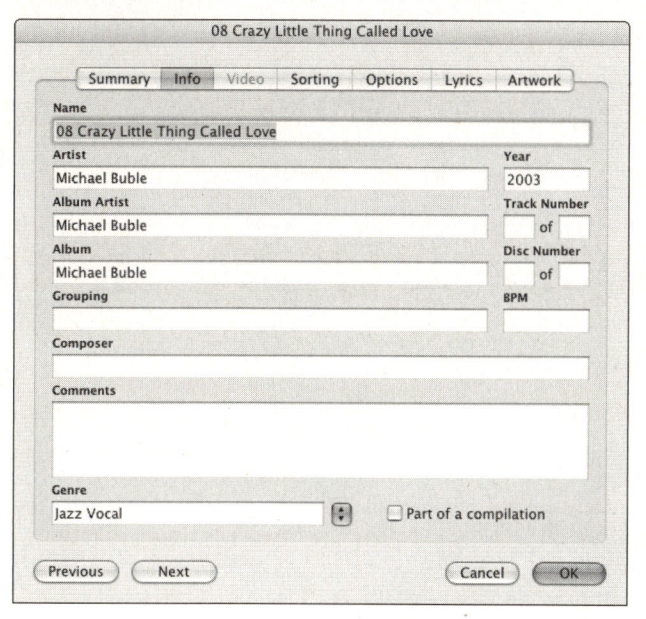

[Form screenshot: "08 Crazy Little Thing Called Love" with tabs Summary, Info, Video, Sorting, Options, Lyrics, Artwork. Fields: Name, Artist (Michael Buble), Album Artist (Michael Buble), Album (Michael Buble), Grouping, Composer, Comments, Genre (Jazz Vocal); Year 2003, Track Number, Disc Number, BPM; "Part of a compilation" checkbox; Previous, Next, Cancel, OK buttons.]

Because you can arrange a selection of fields of data onto a form, you can deal with a situation where there is too much information to fit comfortably on one screen. Just as a real-world paper form may have multiple pages, you can divide a digital form across multiple screens. In this way, the data can be broken into manageable sections — and the user will not be overwhelmed with complexity or clutter. This approach can make data entry simpler and swifter, while reducing the scope for error.

You can also use forms to retrieve your data, but that limits you to viewing one record at a time. Moreover, as noted earlier, forms frequently present a subset of a record's data. Although this may be advantageous during data entry — allowing you to deal with the data in manageable "chunks" — separate forms may not provide a comprehensive view of the record's data. That may be what you want some of the time, for example, when printing an invoice. However, one of an electronic database's major benefits is that you can quickly and easily get a consolidated report, possibly with summary information, of your data or some defined subset of that data. Figure 1.2 shows such a report — summary data from a music database created in FileMaker Pro 9.

As the example at Figure 1.2 shows, reports are frequently arranged as a list of data from successive records in rows, along with headings and appropriate summaries or totals. Although the many variations on this concept represent the most common kinds of reports required in a database, there are some exceptions.

**Part I** **The Fundamentals**

**FIGURE 1.2**

A report shows you multiple records at one time.

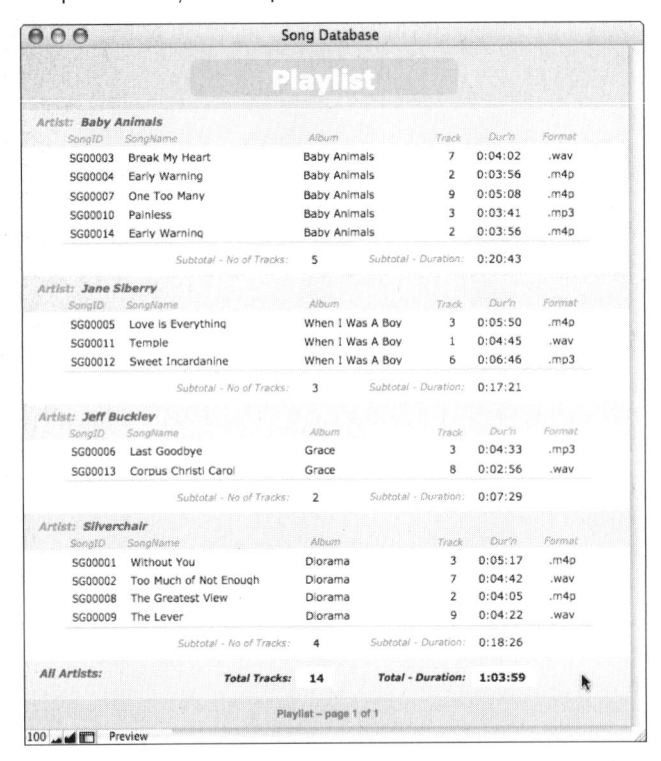

```
                           Song Database
                              Playlist
Artist: Baby Animals
      SongID    SongName              Album            Track    Dur'n    Format
      SG00003   Break My Heart        Baby Animals       7      0:04:02  .wav
      SG00004   Early Warning         Baby Animals       2      0:03:56  .m4p
      SG00007   One Too Many          Baby Animals       9      0:05:08  .m4p
      SG00010   Painless              Baby Animals       3      0:03:41  .mp3
      SG00014   Early Warning         Baby Animals       2      0:03:56  .m4p
              Subtotal - No of Tracks:  5    Subtotal - Duration:  0:20:43
Artist: Jane Siberry
      SongID    SongName              Album            Track    Dur'n    Format
      SG00005   Love is Everything    When I Was A Boy   3      0:05:50  .m4p
      SG00011   Temple                When I Was A Boy   1      0:04:45  .wav
      SG00012   Sweet Incardanine     When I Was A Boy   6      0:06:46  .mp3
              Subtotal - No of Tracks:  3    Subtotal - Duration:  0:17:21
Artist: Jeff Buckley
      SongID    SongName              Album            Track    Dur'n    Format
      SG00006   Last Goodbye          Grace              3      0:04:33  .mp3
      SG00013   Corpus Christi Carol  Grace              8      0:02:56  .wav
              Subtotal - No of Tracks:  2    Subtotal - Duration:  0:07:29
Artist: Silverchair
      SongID    SongName              Album            Track    Dur'n    Format
      SG00001   Without You           Diorama            3      0:05:17  .m4p
      SG00002   Too Much of Not Enough Diorama           7      0:04:42  .wav
      SG00008   The Greatest View     Diorama            2      0:04:05  .m4p
      SG00009   The Lever             Diorama            9      0:04:22  .wav
              Subtotal - No of Tracks:  4    Subtotal - Duration:  0:18:26
All Artists:           Total Tracks:  14    Total - Duration:  1:03:59
                            Playlist — page 1 of 1
```

When you were in school, you probably received a report card at the end of every quarter or semester that provided an overview of your achievements for the preceding period. Some schools present these reports as a simple list of the classes taken and the grades awarded. However, some school reports are arranged more like a form than a list, with classes and explanatory text arranged in different parts of the page according to the way the curriculum has been structured. Moreover, instead of listing many students, only a single student's results are included. In both respects, this is an example of a report employing the essential elements of a form rather than a list.

Another common use of information is as the basis of correspondence. Letters to colleagues, associates, customers, or clients usually contain information that is relevant and specific to the recipient. These letters can be produced from a database as a kind of report — one in which the elements of data and/or summary information are arranged within appropriate text, in a format that is conventional for correspondence. In this way, using the data that is already in your database, you can efficiently create dozens or even hundreds of different letters — each specific to the addressee. This particular type of correspondence, sometimes called a *form letter*, is a common feature of word processing applications, such as Microsoft Word. In Word, this feature is called Data Merge, and you use it to retrieve data from a separate merge data file (such as an Excel or Access file). FileMaker Pro lets you create such correspondence without involving other applications.

By enabling you to enter your data once, and then retrieve it in a variety of configurations and formats (as screens, forms, reports, summaries, lists, or letters), a database turns unwieldy tables of data into a flexible and powerful tool.

## The hidden helper: Process management

So far we've talked about putting data into computer databases via forms and getting it back out in reports of various kinds. Between the two ends of the process, however, there are many additional ways in which databases make themselves useful. Database solutions can be configured to filter information, to confirm its validity, to make connections, to calculate new data from raw inputs, to summarize sets of data, and to automate a variety of tasks involving data.

During the process of data entry, you first create a record, then enter information into the fields within the record. Database applications may allow you to specify a default value for some or all fields, so when a new record is created, some of the fields already have data in them. Sometimes the data entered automatically in this way will be *static* (always the same), but on other occasions it may vary depending on the current situation. Examples of default values that vary are a serial number, which will increment as each new record is created, or a date or time field that takes its value from the computer's internal clock and calendar.

Still more helpful is the ability to define values that will be created automatically depending on the values you enter. For example, you may enter an item's unit price and the quantity purchased into a database, and the database automatically fills in the sales tax and total price in other fields, saving you time and effort and reducing the potential for mistakes.

Database screens are often set up with lists of values for particular fields, to prompt you to select an appropriate value—and to speed up the process, enabling you to replace the work of many keystrokes with a single click or just one or two keystrokes. Moreover, databases are often configured with rules determining which values are valid and which should be rejected. The user can, thus, be alerted when making an error during data entry, and the incidence of data-entry errors is greatly reduced.

Because of these capabilities, entering data into a well-designed database solution can be much quicker and easier than typing up a table in a word processor or even a spreadsheet, and the results can be more accurate. If you have large amounts of data to manage, or if several different people are involved, using a database has many advantages. These advantages go well beyond data entry, because you can automate many other aspects of a database solution.

When you work with data, you'll frequently have to perform repetitive tasks as part of the process of managing information. For example, if you're maintaining a sales and billing system, you may need to go through the purchase invoices, marking and dating those that have been paid and mailing out receipts to the person or company that made each purchase.

## Part I: The Fundamentals

If your sales and billing are done within a database, you might instead have the database automatically cross-reference payments with outstanding invoices, update the invoices accordingly, create the corresponding receipts, and send them to the printer in the mailroom. A whole morning's tedious work can be done in the time it takes to pour your first coffee — and without the errors and omissions that are inevitable during manual processing in a busy office with endless interruptions. If implemented well, this can free you from much of the drudgery of massaging data, enabling you to do the more important work of dealing with clients, making decisions, and making things happen. Let the computer do what computers are good at, so you're freed to get on with doing the things that *humans* are good at.

# How FileMaker Fits In

FileMaker Pro 9 is a Database Management System — so are 4th Dimension, Access, dBASE, and a slew of others. Each provides its own interface and tool set to get you from the starting point — your raw data and an idea of what you want to do with it — to a database solution. Each has its own terms, techniques, and concepts, as well as its own particular strengths and quirks, with which its users become familiar. As is obvious from this book's title, we're going to show you how to use FileMaker to make that cyber-journey.

## Knowing what FileMaker Pro calls things

Earlier in this chapter we referred to database solutions, using that term's general meaning. However in the context of FileMaker Pro, a *solution* refers to a database file or a collection of database files that interact with one another to achieve a set of user-defined objectives. Whereas a file containing only a few tables might be referred to as a *database,* the term *solution* is generally reserved for the whole set of (one or more) database files forming a particular database system.

A FileMaker solution is composed of one or more files, which in turn may contain one or more tables in which data can be stored. FileMaker offers a great deal of flexibility regarding the way a solution is configured. It is possible to put many tables into a single file, to have many files each holding only a single table — or even to have some files that have no tables at all (that is, containing only code or interface). These are choices you will make depending upon the ways you want your solution to work.

The English language is rich with names, and many things have more than one name. In a word processor table or a spreadsheet, information is entered into cells. In some SQL databases, adhering to the terminology of Professor Codd (see the section "Flat-file databases and data redundancy," earlier in this chapter), the equivalent place for entering a specific item of data is called an *attribute*. However, in FileMaker these are called *fields*. Similarly, what you would refer to as a *row* in a spreadsheet is called a *record* in FileMaker.

In most cases, FileMaker uses standard database terminology: table, relation, field, and record. However two notable exceptions are screens and searches. FileMaker employs windows in which you design forms and reports, called *layouts* (because you lay out the fields, labels, and adornments you want on your form/report in the window's drawing surface), as shown in Figure 1.3. Moreover, a search or query is referred to in FileMaker as a *find,* and the result of a find is termed the *found set.*

# Databases: The What, Why, and How    1

**FIGURE 1.3**

A new layout form, all ready for record creation (top) and after record creation (bottom).

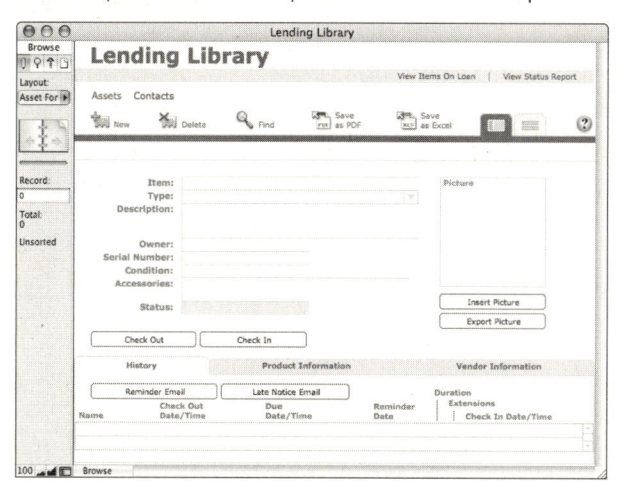

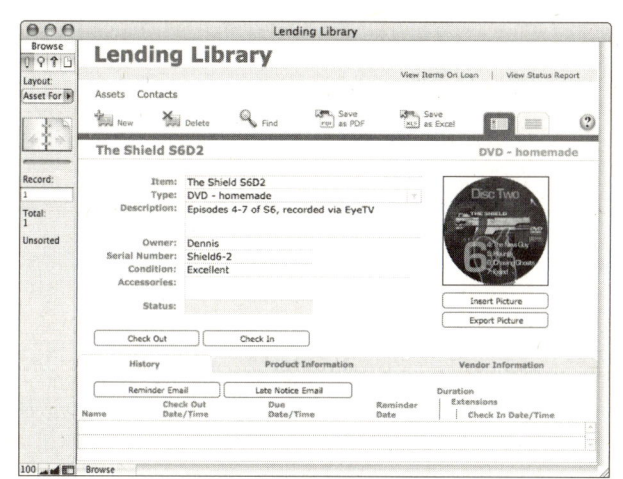

> **NOTE** Purists might quibble that *join* is the technical term for a relation. Similarly, they might argue that *tuple* is the correct term for a record. We argue that the use of *record* and *relation* is so pervasive as to render that argument moot. If you decide to delve through Codd's work, you'll discover many such terms — originating from a branch of advanced mathematics called set theory, employed to describe the underlying theory of relational databases. However, for the most part, to use FileMaker Pro all you'll need is common, descriptive terminology.

The use of the word *layout* is significant for two reasons. First, FileMaker provides a set of tools for building screens and reports, which are not unlike those you would encounter in a graphic design program — its interface builder is a *layout* builder. Second, layouts are vehicles for creating all different sorts of display and print output and can even create multipurpose screens that can be presented as a form or a list or printed as a report. Rather than provide separate objects and toolsets for building each different kind of display or output (for example, a form builder and a separate report builder), FileMaker provides a single highly flexible object — the layout. With the exception of dialogs, borders, and the Status Area (the gray band at the left), everything you see in a FileMaker window is a layout.

FileMaker tries to make things easy for you in many ways. One such convenience is the Find request, where you fill in one or more fields on a layout with data you're trying to match, as shown in Figure 1.4. Many databases require that you construct textual *queries,* conforming to a specific syntax usually employing a standardized language called SQL (short for *Structured Query Language*). A fairly simple query might be

```
SELECT * FROM Contacts WHERE LastName="Smith"
```

to retrieve all fields of the records in your Contacts table where the LastName field holds "Smith" as its value. If you only wanted specific fields retrieved, you would cite them, separated by commas, where the asterisk appears. As you can see, more conditions can make queries quite long, complicated, and prone to typographic errors, especially compared to the simple graphical method of performing finds that FileMaker provides.

> **NOTE** As you can see in Figure 1.4, other than the tools provided in the panel on the window's left side, there is virtually no visual difference between a new, empty record (as shown in Figure 1.3) and a Find request's layout area.

**FIGURE 1.4**

FileMaker provides a fill-in-the-blanks alternative to textual queries.

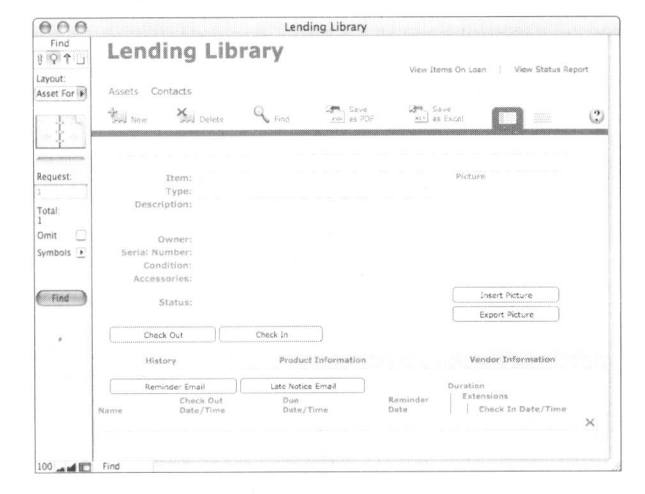

# Databases: The What, Why, and How

In FileMaker, to find records that match given criteria, you go into Find mode, whereupon the current layout is presented with blank fields. You fill in the blanks with your search criteria (in a layout that has the fields you want retrieved) and FileMaker locates the records that match what you've entered. A simple example would be a layout that prints address labels. You now have one-stop shopping to retrieve all the label information for the records you want, and you just print the result.

**CROSS-REF** We cover Find requests in Chapter 3 and delve more deeply into them in Chapter 5.

Just as searches or queries are made easy via Find requests, retrieving data from related records is made simple. In cases where only a single related record is to be displayed (for example, the name of the school a student is attending), FileMaker allows you to simply place the relevant field from a related table directly onto a layout. The first related value will then be displayed. However, in cases where there is a need to display data other than the first related record or to display a list of related records, FileMaker enables you to achieve this via the use of *portals,* groupings of fields on your layout from tables related to the table on which the layout is based. The name derives from the portal object being a window (or doorway) into related tables — maybe a little trite, but descriptive and easy to remember.

**CROSS-REF** We cover portals in detail in Chapter 6.

In FileMaker, the process by which default values — both static and varying — are assigned to fields is referred to as *Auto-Entry,* and the automatic checking of data input against predefined criteria for completeness and consistency is termed *validation.*

Derived values and dependent variables can be generated in FileMaker in several ways, but one of the most common is via the use of special kinds of fields in FileMaker: *calculation fields* and *summary fields*. To support its extensive abilities for logical, textual, and mathematical manipulation, FileMaker provides a sophisticated built-in capability for interpreting and applying your instructions, which is often termed the *calculation engine*. Moreover, in order to keep its calculation results consistent with your data, FileMaker keeps track of which fields depend on the values in other fields. This is done behind the scenes in what is sometimes referred to as FileMaker's *table of dependencies.*

**CROSS-REF** Look for additional details about auto-entry, validation, and calculation and summary fields in Chapter 7.

In database programs, there is sometimes a need to store a group of values as a cohesive set applying to a single data attribute. Value sets are often known as *arrays* — however, in FileMaker fields designated to hold data arrays are referred to as *repeating fields* and must be predefined for a specific maximum number of *repetitions.* Both data fields and memory variables in FileMaker can have repetitions.

**CROSS-REF** We discuss memory variables in depth in Chapters 9 and 12.

In general, the information held in a field, in a variable, or in a given repetition of a field or variable is referred to as a *value*. However, a text field may hold multiple lines separated by carriage returns — for example, a list — and in such cases, the content of each line is collectively regarded as a value in its own right. In that respect, a single (nonrepeating) FileMaker text field may hold multiple values.

Fields that are used to define *joins* (relationships) between tables are referred to as *Key fields* or *Match fields* in FileMaker, with the default relationship type (an *equi-join*) being one requiring a matching value in the key fields of both tables being joined. However, if the key fields are text fields and may be expected to hold multiple values, each value is separately indexed and used to establish a pluralistic relationship. In FileMaker, fields used in relationships in this way are referred to as *MultiKey fields*.

**CROSS-REF** Relationships and key fields are explored in detail in Chapters 7 and 11.

Many computer programs and programming environments provide the ability to create stored procedures or *macros* (collections of instructions, actions, or commands that can be performed automatically or called on at will by the user). In FileMaker Pro, these sets of stored instructions are referred to as *scripts*, and the environment in which they are created is called *ScriptMaker*. Scripts are made up of sequences of *script steps*, sometimes also referred to as *script commands*. When scripts are required to interact with fields, buttons, or other elements on one of the layouts in your solution, the elements they target are referred to as *objects*.

FileMaker provides support for storage of binary objects — movies, images, sounds, and even files — in fields within the database. The type of field that provides this capability is called a *container field* and is capable of displaying the contents of a range of supported media (images, movies, and sounds in a range of supported formats). Alongside this, FileMaker is able to render HTML and other Web-related technologies within designated layout objects called *Web viewer objects*.

When multiple database files are designed to operate together and interact as part of a solution, individual files will be programmed to locate and use data or call scripts within other files in the solution. Links and references to other files that allow this interaction to occur are called External Data Sources in FileMaker 9 and can include FileMaker files and also supported SQL databases.

**NOTE** In previous versions of FileMaker Pro, External Data Sources were referred to as *File References* and included only FileMaker database files.

We've provided you with a quick overview of the central concepts and terms used in FileMaker, with particular emphasis on areas where the terminology or its application differs from that found in other databases. As you read on, you'll encounter many other terms that are either in common use or that we will explain within the text. You'll also find a glossary of terms in Appendix A, which will be of help if you encounter anything unfamiliar while browsing through the chapters.

## Using familiar ideas from the real world

From its very first versions in the 1980s, FileMaker has provided a rich graphical interface that operates as a metaphor—mimicking familiar objects and ideas from the world around us. One of the clearest illustrations of this is FileMaker's ubiquitous navigation icon, which appears in the Status Area at the left of each window and represents a Rolodex or flip book. Clicking the right page of the Rolodex moves you forward one record; clicking the left page moves you back one record. This sets the scene for a program that makes extensive use of visual metaphor and that has powerful graphical capabilities.

FileMaker provides a toolset for creating layouts allowing you to mimic, with incredible fidelity, the appearance of your real-world forms and reports. In addition to a basic suite of drawing and text tools with which you can assemble the layouts that provide screens and printed output, FileMaker supports direct import of image files (including PNG, JPEG, and GIF formats) for display on layouts along with other layout elements. The combination of these elements lends itself to the creation of graphically rich database applications. Moreover, layout elements can be defined to be interactive so that clicking them performs a specific action or gives the user access to a particular record, field, or screen. These capabilities have seen FileMaker used to build a startlingly diverse range of applications, from children's games to boardroom presentation viewers—as well as the many more conventional database exploits.

It would be a mistake, however, to assume that FileMaker's strength lies primarily in its chameleon-like interface capabilities. The real power of any database is in its ability to model information and its relationships in the real world—to find order within complexity. FileMaker responds to this challenge in a very particular way, by providing an extensive palette of tools and capabilities that can be combined in many ways to solve a given problem. In this respect, FileMaker provides an environment in which to model both the problems and the solutions of the real world.

## Integrating processes and information

The real value of databases—and FileMaker is no exception—is not in their ability to store and retrieve data, but in their ability to empower you to use your data more effectively. If all you hope to do is store your information, a database is a good way to do so—but most information is part of ongoing processes and is not static.

One of the simplest examples of the power of a database solution is the ability to enter your data in one format (such as a form layout) and then retrieve subsets of it in another format, perhaps in a different sort order and with totals or summary values added. These are everyday feats for a computer database, yet they may be inordinately time-consuming to achieve using traditional record-keeping techniques. This alone is empowering.

Even more valuable is the ability to create screens and data views that support a process and follow it through from commencement to completion. This requires that data be viewed as an essential part of a larger process or project, and that the database be commissioned as a facilitative tool. When viewed in this light, it is clear that the role of the database is significant and can either guide or hinder the progress of a project, depending on its design.

## Part I: The Fundamentals

If your aim is to gain a greater command of data and the processes it supports, you have chosen wisely in exploring the capabilities of FileMaker Pro. In the following chapters, we will show you how truly flexible and powerful a modern desktop database can be.

## Recognizing that knowledge is power — personal and professional

Contrary to the old maxim, what you don't know *can* hurt you. It is indisputable that good decision-making requires having as much accurate, pertinent information as possible upon which to base your conclusions. FileMaker Pro allows you to collect, organize, and filter your data, whether it's the inventory of your comic books or the sales figures for your business. With FileMaker's statistical tools, you can perform some analyses that were once the province of spreadsheets, or you can export the pertinent data to Excel and leverage its power in creating and evaluating scenarios.

FileMaker can't make thoughtful decisions about the data you enter. However, it can help you prevent most basic data-entry errors, such as entering an invalid part code, a Social Security number with the wrong number of digits, or a date lying outside a specified range. It's a lot like computer spell checkers in that regard, telling you whether a word is in its dictionary, but not whether it is the *correct* word — that's up to you.

FileMaker Pro offers you the tools to enter, store, and reference your data so that you can make informed decisions.

# Chapter 2

# Putting FileMaker Pro in Perspective

FileMaker Pro is the dominant (in other words, best-selling) database in the Macintosh market; simultaneously, it is a strong contender in the much more crowded Windows market. In this chapter, we discuss what differentiates FileMaker Pro from many other database managers and the user and developer community surrounding it.

FileMaker has been around since the mid-1980s and was one of the first database products available for the Mac. In fact, the first version of FileMaker was the wedding of a DOS-based database engine called Nutshell with a new graphic user interface (GUI). Originally, it was a nonrelational product, but even in those early days a nod was made toward multi-table capability with the inclusion of a feature called *look-ups,* where a field could reference a field contained in a different database file (in those days, it was one table per file). FileMaker continued to evolve and, in 1990, added Pro to its name. In the autumn of 1992, FileMaker Pro went cross-platform with FileMaker Pro 2, where a single database could be shared by Mac and Windows users. The very next year, FileMaker Pro 3 added relational capabilities, a second watershed moment in a very short time frame. FileMaker continued evolving through versions 4, 5, and 6. The release of FileMaker 7, in 2004, marked another revolutionary change, significantly increasing the amount of data a single field or file could contain and removing the one-file/one-table coupling.

Throughout its history and all the power and capability enhancements, though, one aspect has remained unchanged: FileMaker's ease of use and basic interface have remained intact.

---

**IN THIS CHAPTER**

Understanding what sets FileMaker Pro apart from other database environments

Introducing the FileMaker Pro product family

Identifying some surprising capabilities in FileMaker Pro

Finding outside resources and information about FileMaker

# What Makes FileMaker Pro Different from Other Database Development Tools?

The major difference, at least in our opinion, is that FileMaker Pro integrates the screens and the database engine far more than any other product we've encountered. Additionally, FileMaker Pro is scalable, coming in versions ranging from FileMaker Pro 9 for general users and FileMaker Pro 9 Advanced for developers and solutions providers, through FileMaker Server 9 and FileMaker Server 9 Advanced for enterprise customers and online data systems. Throughout the entire product line, however, essentials of the user interface and database engine are consistent.

> **NOTE** FileMaker, Inc. has also introduced Bento, an unrelated single-user database product exclusively for Mac OS X Leopard users. Bento does not integrate with other FileMaker products and is best suited for personal rather than business or enterprise use. For modest data requirements on Mac OS X 10.5, Bento is an attractive option. Because this text focuses on meeting demanding database requirements, Bento is outside the scope of this book.

## Some common misperceptions

First impressions can be misleading, and FileMaker Pro's ease of use and the simplicity with which you can use it to perform basic tasks have led many people to dismiss the product as being too simple or limited in capability. FileMaker conceals its power, however, revealing it as you find a need for it. A fundamental FileMaker precept is that operational complexity should be restricted to those tasks or features that are inherently both complex and advanced — that is, keep simple things simple. Taking that one step further, the engineers and human interface folks at FileMaker, Inc., work very hard to simplify the complex. One aspect of this simplification is the Specify Calculation dialog, shown in Figure 2.1. Rather than introduce different interfaces for constructing a URL, specifying file references, determining arguments for script steps, and a myriad of other operations, the Specify Calculation dialog is used throughout the product, whenever the solution developer needs to specify a result. One consistent interface for many similar tasks and operations means less complexity.

> **NOTE** In some situations, you can establish a simple argument to a function without delving into the Specify Calculation dialog. For example, you can enter a static URL for a Web Viewer object or a simple decision for conditional formatting without involving Specify Calculation; however, the dialog is always available for the more complex decisions and computations.

Similarly, planning your database's tables and the relations between them often frustrates people who are new to assembling a system. Rather than give in to the impulse to just "throw everything into one humongous table," take a deep breath — determining and defining separate tables and the relationships between them involves a little extra upfront work, but you'll be glad you did so a little farther down the road. Keeping your tables focused allows you to repurpose them in other solutions, facilitates implementing access control, and improves performance of layouts that don't require access to all your fields. FileMaker Pro provides a graphical interface for defining and modifying relations between your solution's tables called the *Relationships Graph,* as shown in Figure 2.2 (taken from the Lending Library starter solution). Each *table occurrence* in the graph is a view into a specified table, and you can have multiple occurrences in the graph pointing to a single table. FileMaker Pro doesn't allow recursive or cyclic relationships and will automatically instantiate new table occurrences to avoid such conflicts. For example, in a genealogy database you're likely to have a table of people that includes information about their parents and offspring — these parents and offspring will also be records in your people table, and FileMaker creates new occurrences of the people table so that you can resolve these relationships. In one case, the view will be of children and in the other of parents — regardless, they will be separate views into (that is, occurrences of) the people table.

### FIGURE 2.1

The Specify Calculation dialog is employed in multiple contexts within FileMaker Pro.

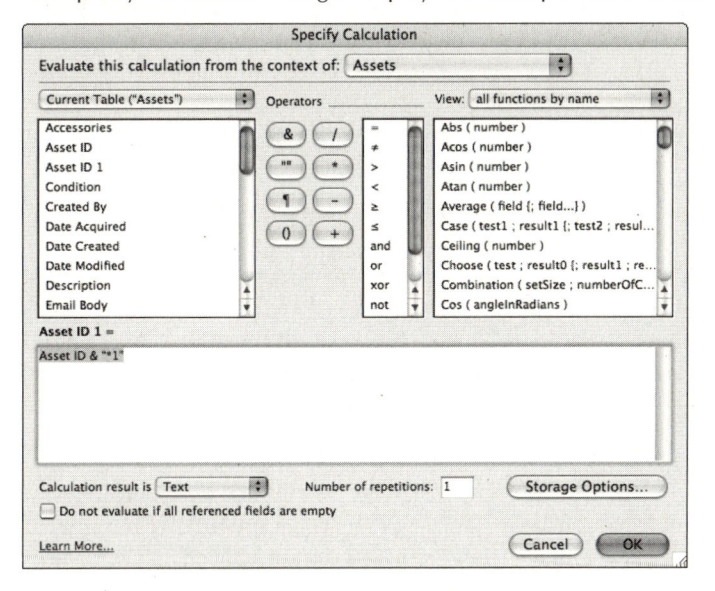

Although the Relationships Graph has some similarities to an Entity-Relationship Diagram (a tool used to model a data set and define the relationships between the various data elements), the modeling portion is separated into the Manage Database dialog's Fields tab. Another significant difference arises from the need to represent tables multiple times on FileMaker's Relationships Graph to avoid circular references (direct or indirect) and to support various navigation and interface requirements — neither of which is required in an Entity-Relationship Diagram. Thus, the similarities are mostly superficial and are not generally helpful for understanding how best to use the Relationships Graph in FileMaker.

Another misconception is that all Database Management Systems, including FileMaker Pro, are pretty much alike. Although database systems have similar goals, the methodologies they employ differ greatly. Just as cargo trains and 18-wheelers both haul freight, but with different constraints and capabilities, Database Management Systems manage data by using different processes and interfaces.

## Part I  The Fundamentals

**FIGURE 2.2**

The Relationships Graph depicts the relationships between the tables in your solution.

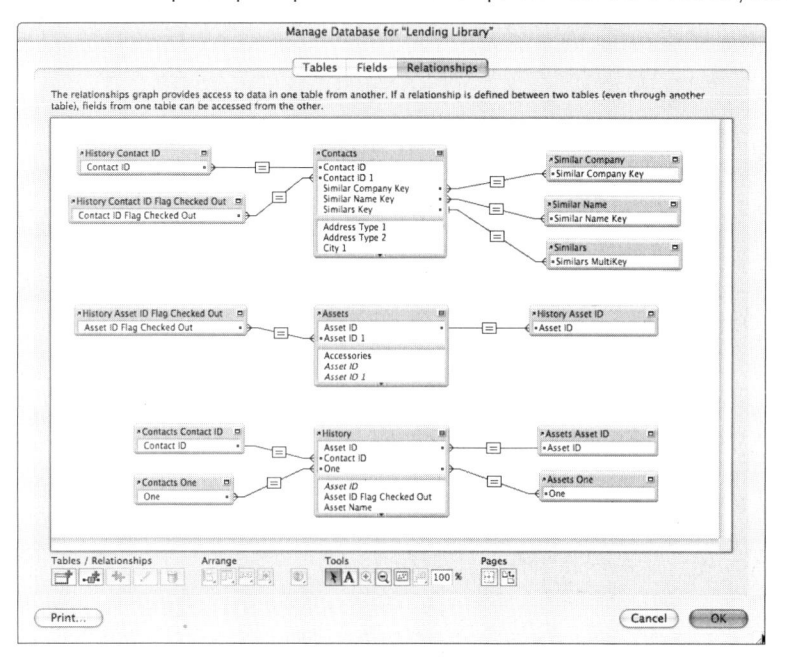

As with any flexible and powerful application (Photoshop comes quickly to mind), there isn't one "right" way to achieve most goals. FileMaker provides you with many routes to your destination; it's up to you to determine which avenue or avenues to follow when constructing your solution. We'll discuss these decision points throughout this book; sorry to say — there just aren't enough pages available to cover every alternative we've encountered or can conceive. One consequence of the incredible flexibility of FileMaker Pro is that neither the FileMaker Pro manuals nor this book can begin to describe all the ways in which you might use FileMaker's features to achieve your goals — we can only show you a selection of methods we and others have found useful and then point you toward outside resources that discuss differing or new techniques. We're making one more assumption about you that we didn't list in the Preface — we assume that you're intelligent (after all, you *did* purchase this book!) and that you can extrapolate from the examples we cite to your specific situation.

## A unique approach to design

FileMaker offers you great flexibility in constructing your solution. One paramount example of flexibility is the layout. In addition to forms and reports, your layouts can display help text or instructions on how to use your solution. The demonstration files provided by many solution developers include instructive layouts like the one shown in Figure 2.3. This figure shows the Information layout of the free Calendar View Demo from NightWing Enterprises.

## Putting FileMaker Pro in Perspective | 2

#### FIGURE 2.3
Including an informational layout (or layouts) is a common practice when providing a solution.

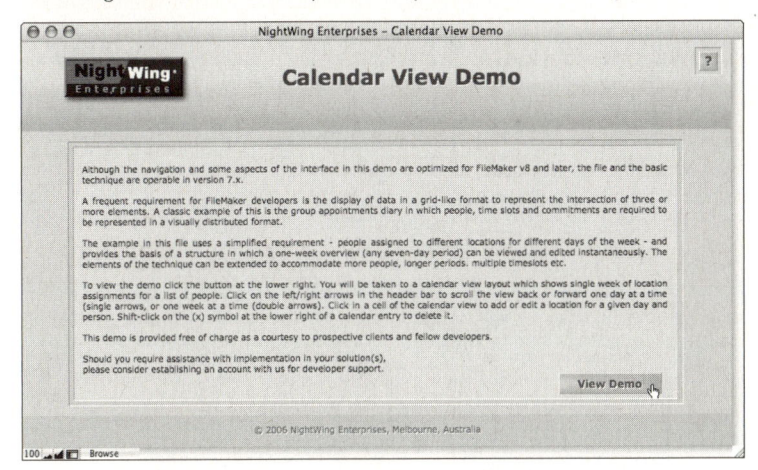

When offering the user a choice from a predetermined set of alternatives, you can use radio buttons, pop-up menus, drop-down lists, or text boxes. You can require that your users enter a value into a field, or you can place an initial value in that field that the user can replace (useful when one value is most likely to appear or when the value from the immediately prior record is likely to be repeated, such as a state in a contacts list). You can use separate, but similar, layouts for different types of data (such as one for cars and one for trucks in an automotive database), or you can use one layout with a tab object where the common fields are outside the tab object and the genre-specific fields are on their respective tabs. These are just a few examples of how FileMaker enables you to customize your solution to fit your end user's requirements or your aesthetic vision.

In addition to the flexibility in creating and designing your layouts, FileMaker lets you separate your data from the layouts. For example, you can keep all your tables in one file with no layouts at all and implement your interface in a separate file from the data. In this manner, you could, for example, implement multiple interfaces to the same tables, each customized to a particular client's needs.

**CROSS-REF** For an in-depth discussion of alternative file configurations, including the use of separate files for data and interface, see Chapter 12.

## The FileMaker Product Family

Although this book focuses (almost) exclusively on FileMaker Pro 9 and FileMaker Pro 9 Advanced, FileMaker, Inc., offers other related products to fill out its product line. There is considerable integration between the main products in the range, so transition from one to another is straightforward.

## Desktop and server

FileMaker Pro 9 is a self-contained application that enables you to develop, maintain, and use databases by employing a broad-based set of essential tools for designing, programming, and deploying databases large and small. Included in FileMaker Pro are the layout design tools, relationship and schema editing capabilities, ScriptMaker, and a comprehensive suite of commands and functions. Moreover, FileMaker Pro enables you to share databases from your workstation to up to nine concurrent client connections and access them via a Web browser by using built-in Instant Web Publishing for up to five simultaneous sessions.

With FileMaker Pro 9 Advanced, you get an application that includes all the capabilities of FileMaker Pro, plus some key extra powers enabling you to develop more rapidly, access extended capabilities such as custom functions (for example, building a custom calculation function), custom menus (for example, changing the contents and behavior of menus), and other powerful developer features. Moreover, FileMaker Pro 9 Advanced lets you create *runtime solutions* — completely self-contained single-user desktop databases that do not require the user to have a copy of FileMaker Pro. You can configure such solutions to work as kiosk implementations for customers to check on product availability in your store or to sign in or out at the front desk of a business, including the printing of a visitor's badge. Runtime applications can also operate as stand-alone desktop applications serving a wide variety of purposes and needs.

**CROSS-REF** We provide a more detailed exploration of the additional features and capabilities of FileMaker Po 9 Advanced in Chapter 18.

In addition to the main desktop products — FileMaker Pro 9 and FileMaker Pro 9 Advanced — the FileMaker suite includes two FileMaker Server products that offer enterprise-level distributed database usage, Web publishing capabilities, and integration with remote ODBC client applications. FileMaker Server 9 enables you to securely and efficiently make your solutions available to up to 250 simultaneous FileMaker Pro users over a network and to make data available via PHP or XML to an appropriately configured Web site.

When you install FileMaker Server 9 Advanced, you gain access to all the features of FileMaker Server 9, plus two key additional capabilities: the ability to make FileMaker data available to remote client applications via ODBC or JDBC protocols, and the ability to publish your databases to as many as 100 simultaneous Web users via Instant Web Publishing (IWP).

## Scalability and flexibility

FileMaker's ability to adapt to the task at hand is sometimes surprising. Performing a quick analysis of a few hundred records or sorting the invitations for a party are not too trivial a task for this tool to accomplish. And yet, in some cases, FileMaker has been used to build applications of vast complexity, accommodating millions of records in hundreds of tables. Everything in between these two extremes can be encountered in schools and universities, business, government, and industry the world over.

Despite the breadth of capability and extent of scalability that FileMaker offers, it's nevertheless fair to state that FileMaker is ideally suited to applications accessed by as many as 100 to 200 users that typically handle tens of thousands of records. Moreover, the way a solution is designed is a significant determining factor in its capability to scale. Features or designs that are acceptable in single-user or small-scale solutions may be inappropriate for large or complex server-based implementations.

> **CROSS-REF** For a detailed discussion about designing for scale and solution efficiency, refer to Chapter 21.

A key component of FileMaker's strengths is its networkable and multi-user capability. A single FileMaker solution hosted on an appropriate database server can be accessed simultaneously by several hundred users or can be configured to provide the basis of a data-driven Web solution. At its upper limits, FileMaker is capable of integrating with third-party technologies to synchronize multiple servers so as to provide increased security, performance, or extensibility.

As well as providing for both large- and small-scale solutions, FileMaker incorporates a surprisingly diverse feature set, supporting everything from powerful text formatting to workflow automation and document management, to multimedia presentation, playing digital video and sound directly from fields in the database. Moreover, FileMaker provides built-in support for external scripting protocols, such as AppleScript on the Mac and VBScript in Windows, so your solution can interact with other scriptable applications, such as Microsoft Excel or iTunes, to retrieve data or even to control the other application.

## FileMaker's Hidden Talents

FileMaker is available in multiple language versions and supports multilingual functionality, using Unicode as the technology for managing character sets. Text values can be indexed according to the conventions of more than 26 languages and variants, and techniques are available to create multilingual interfaces within a single solution (see Figure 2.4).

Additionally, FileMaker's ODBC (Open Database Connectivity) support and its ability to handle multiple different data formats (text, number, date, time, image, movie, sound, file, and so on) provides virtually unparalleled interoperability. Realizing that different subsets of the user base are going to want additional features, FileMaker, Inc., chose the same solution for FileMaker as Adobe did for Photoshop, providing a rich plug-in architecture so that developers can extend FileMaker's reach into targeted markets. And we shouldn't forget the calculation engine with its incredible flexibility and power.

## Part I  The Fundamentals

**FIGURE 2.4**

The Field Options dialog showing language indexing options for text fields in FileMaker Pro 9.

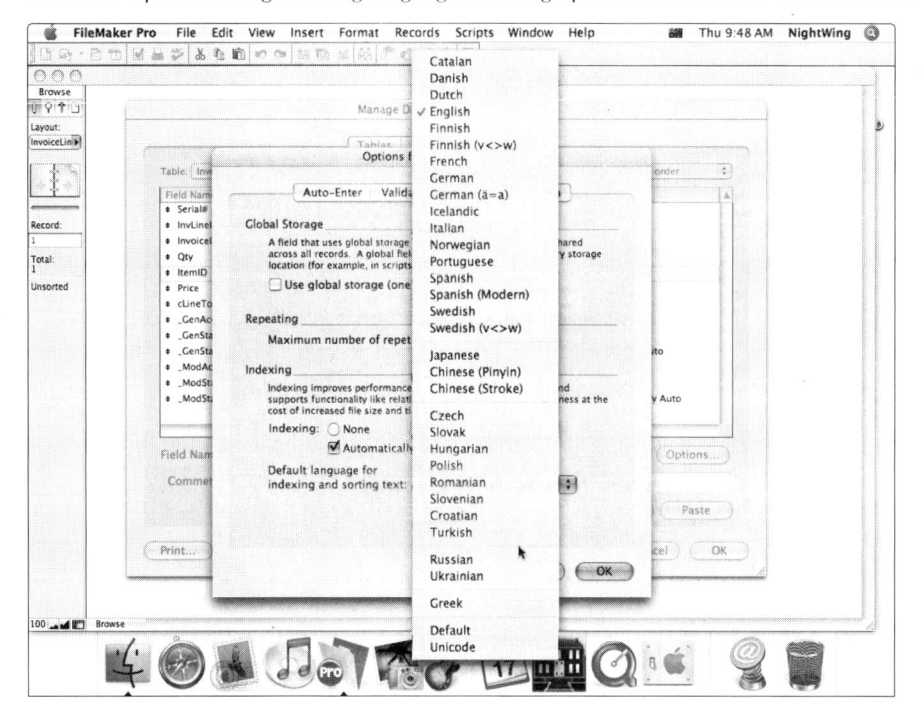

## The cross-platform chameleon

Unlike other Database Management Systems, FileMaker Pro provides an almost-seamless cross-platform experience, dealing with most platform differences behind the scenes. The file format is the same on Mac OS and in Windows, and, with very few exceptions, the application controls, menus, dialogs, and features are consistent between platforms. Consequently, you can create a solution on one platform and have it work the same way on the other platform.

**CROSS-REF** For an in-depth discussion of techniques and considerations for cross-platform development, refer to Chapter 10.

Equally attractive is the capability to have a mix of Mac OS and Windows client computers accessing a single served solution simultaneously. In mixed-platform work environments, this alone is an outstanding benefit.

## Multiple technologies and formats

FileMaker has a long history of working alongside a variety of other applications. First and foremost, it includes the capability to import and export data in a variety of formats. This includes

## Putting FileMaker Pro in Perspective

common interchange formats such as comma-separated values (CSV), tab-delimited files, dBase and Microsoft Excel files, and a number of other common desktop database formats (see Figure 2.5).

Instead of importing, if you simply drag a Microsoft Excel file (or various other supported file formats) onto the FileMaker Pro icon, the file will be converted automatically and presented to you in FileMaker database format. It really is that easy.

Equally significant is FileMaker's ability to import and export eXtensible Markup Language (XML) data, including from online XML data sources, and using parsing via eXtensible Style Language Transformation (XSLT) style sheets. Again, this provides broad-based support for data exchange and interoperability.

Similarly, FileMaker's ability to read and write seamlessly to data tables in supported versions of MySQL, Oracle, and Microsoft SQL Server give you extensive options and capabilities from desktop to enterprise systems. Moreover, you can mix and match the formats and technologies using FileMaker as the conduit. For example, a FileMaker database that uses one or more remote SQL data sources can seamlessly generate reports or data outputs (Excel, PDF, and so on) containing data from any one (or a combination) of the available sources. It is therefore not unrealistic to use FileMaker as the report generator or analysis tool for data that resides in other systems.

**FIGURE 2.5**

The available formats for data import from desktop files in FileMaker Pro 9.

## Plug-ins and extensibility

FileMaker doesn't restrict you to data entered into a layout via the keyboard or by importing a file from disc. With its plug-in architecture, you can access data from scanners, digital cameras, bar code readers, and other such devices — but FileMaker doesn't stop there.

When the engineers at FileMaker, Inc., first envisioned a plug-in Application/Programming Interface (API) for FileMaker, the primary intended purpose was adding the capability to perform complex math and calculation operations outside the core feature set. However, ingenious third-party developers have been devising unexpected uses of the API ever since.

Shortly after the plug-in API was first released in 1997, third-party products began to emerge with such diverse features as e-mail client capabilities, drawing and graphics tools, file manipulation tools, charting capabilities, Internet telephony, serial port controllers, custom dialog generators, encryption tools — the complete list is much too long to include here (and would likely be outdated by the time this book made it to the shelves). Developers found that, via the API, they could pass data from a FileMaker calculation to a compiled application (in the form of a plug-in) and then return a result — and despite some early limitations, this has provided the basis of an enormous variety of plug-ins from vendors all over the globe.

Although many plug-ins serve a very specialized purpose — interfacing with specific hardware (such as a TWAIN scanner), or exchanging data with a proprietary application (such as the elegant accounting software suite from Cognito — www.cognito.co.nz) — a number of plug-ins have focused on extending the core feature set of FileMaker itself. As a result, these plug-ins have become widely recognized and used by FileMaker developers the world over. Examples include SecureFM from New Millennium Communications (www.securefm.com), Troi File from Troi Automatisering (www.troi.com), and xmCHART from X2max Software (www.x2max.com/en/products/xmCHART/info.html). These and other plug-in-based products have found a place as part of the mainstream of FileMaker development.

**CROSS-REF** You can find a more complete discussion of plug-in extensibility in Chapter 23.

## The FileMaker calculation engine: Simplicity and power

Starting from promising beginnings in the 1980s, FileMaker's calculation capabilities have been steadily extended to the point where their diversity and scope is considerable. Although FileMaker 9 provides approximately 250 native calculation functions, each designed to accomplish a specific range of objectives, you can combine these functions in compound calculation expressions in myriad ways to solve a wide range of problems.

FileMaker's calculation interface is consistent throughout the application. Additionally, the calculation expression syntax is straightforward and follows consistent rules. Defining simple calculation formulas, therefore, requires no special expertise — it works intuitively and elegantly, so if you enter 2 + 2 into the calculation engine (or `quantity * price`), you'll get the expected results directly and effortlessly. With a little effort and experience (and with the aid of this book), considerably more challenging tasks can be made easy.

**CROSS-REF** We explore the uses of FileMaker's calculation engine in depth in Chapters 7 and 13.

FileMaker Pro Advanced also provides a developer interface for creating custom functions. Using the building blocks of the calculation engine, you can define new functions within a file, which perform complex operations with a single function call. Significantly, custom functions can be defined to use recursive capabilities, further extending their scope and power.

**NOTE** Even though FileMaker Pro Advanced is required to create custom functions, once they are in the solution FileMaker Pro is all that's required to use the functions.

**CROSS-REF** We discuss custom functions in greater detail, providing examples of their application, in Chapter 20.

## Resources and Exemplars

The first and most important thing to know about FileMaker Pro is that a thriving global developer community exists, made up of consultants and developers with considerable expertise and backgrounds in an extraordinarily diverse range of industries. Although FileMaker Pro is an application that you can use straight out of the box—and we encourage you to do so—be aware that, if you want to extend your reach beyond what you can easily achieve on your own, there is no shortage of professionals available to provide assistance or support.

The FileMaker developer community is vital for a number of other reasons as well. It is frequently within this community that new ways to use the application and new insights into its capabilities emerge. An ongoing discourse between active and gifted developers in various parts of the globe frequently results in new and ingenious approaches to puzzling or elusive problems. Just such a network exists in the FileMaker community, and many have benefited from the resourcefulness and generosity of its many members.

A secondary consequence of the thriving developer community's existence is that the community spawns a plethora of diagnostic tools and development aids, and many such tools and aids exist for FileMaker. Examples such as the analysis tools Inspector from FMNEXUS (`www.fmnexus.com/products/inspector`), FMDiff from Huslik Verlag GmbH (`www.fmdiff.com`), BaseElements from Goya (`www.goya.com.au/baseelements`), and various others provide extensive additional capability and insight to what is already a powerful core product base.

In a further signal of the FileMaker development environment's maturity, recent years have seen the introduction of a worldwide developer certification program by FileMaker, Inc. This certification program increases the visibility and viability of FileMaker as a platform for professional application developers, as well as providing users and business clients with an indication of the skills and credentials of professionals working in the field. Along with annual developer conferences in several countries around the world, this bodes well for an ongoing wealth of support and expertise in all things FileMaker.

As an important adjunct to its other activities, FileMaker, Inc., offers several support programs and assistance programs to companies and developers working across the FileMaker product range. Foremost among these is the FileMaker TechNet (www.filemaker.com/technet)— a membership-based network of developers and users who participate on a technical mailing list/forum hosted by FileMaker, Inc. Similarly, FileMaker, Inc. makes FileMaker Business Alliance membership (www.filemaker.com/fba) available to businesses that have a substantial interest in or involvement with FileMaker support, sales, or development.

## Examples and brainteasers

Flowing directly from the fertile developer community are many thorny questions concerning the best ways to approach particular problems or solve difficult development problems. As part of their participation in this ongoing discourse, a number of developers in various parts of the world publish examples, samples, tips, and tricks that provide insight into novel or elegant solutions to various development challenges.

Some of the many professional quality examples, tips, demos, and other resources made available free by participants in the FileMaker developer community may be found at the Web sites of companies in various parts of the world, such as Database Pros (www.databasepros.com), Excelisys (www.excelisys.com), Onegasoft (www.onegasoft.com), The Support Group (www.supportgroup.com), and (shameless plug) NightWing Enterprises (www.nightwing.com.au/FileMaker). Moreover, online forums such as FMForums (www.fmforums.com) and resources such as the inimitable user group network at FMPug (www.fmpug.com) provide both depth and breadth of expertise as well as a host of information and resource directories.

## Other resources and opportunities

In addition to the many resources we've already mentioned, FileMaker, Inc., maintains a network of training partners who are ready and able to provide high-quality support and training to end users and aspiring developers.

Although we believe that FileMaker is remarkable for its easy learning curve and the way it enables new users to ease into the realm of database design, don't underestimate how much more there is to know. Even after working through the many examples and explanations we provide in this book, you'll find value in exploring the wealth of training and support options available.

# Chapter 3

# Getting Acquainted with FileMaker

There is no substitute for experience when it comes to using a computer application, so if you haven't already done so, it's time to get in front of a computer and begin to use FileMaker. You can take the book with you if you wish (in fact, we encourage you to do so).

For the purposes of following the descriptions in *FileMaker Pro 9 Bible,* you'll need a copy of FileMaker Pro 9 or FileMaker Pro 9 Advanced, installed on a supported version of either a Windows or Macintosh operating system. In most respects, the Pro and Pro Advanced applications look identical, although there are a few additional menu commands and features in the Advanced version. Our screenshots are generally applicable to both versions and to both Mac and Windows systems, though the appearance of window frames and dialogs differs slightly between platforms.

If this is your very first use of FileMaker, you may need to first run the installer to get the software set up and ready for use. After FileMaker is installed, launch it from the Dock (Mac) or by choosing Start ➪ All Programs ➪ FileMaker Pro (Windows).

### IN THIS CHAPTER

Starting to use FileMaker

Navigating your database

Entering data in your database

Importing and exporting data

Dealing with related data

Configuring FileMaker

## Getting FileMaker Working for You

The first time it's launched, FileMaker Pro 9 may require that you activate your software license. This confirms that your copy is legitimate and has been installed within the terms of the purchased license. Normally, activation is required within 30 days and is completed automatically over an Internet connection.

**Part I** **The Fundamentals**

**CAUTION** If your computer is not connected to the Internet in the first 30 days after installation, you may need to contact FileMaker, Inc., to obtain an activation code. FileMaker, Inc., provides 24 activation support telephone numbers around the world, with support for 11 languages. You can find full details of activation phone numbers under the heading "Activating your FileMaker software" in the FileMaker online help by choosing Help ⇨ FileMaker Pro Help.

On subsequent launches, FileMaker presents the Quick Start screen, providing access to three options, as follows:

- Create Database
- Open Database
- Learn More

Clicking the Create Database icon provides access to any of several dozen starter templates that provide basic preprogrammed functionality for a range of various types of business, education, and home databases. The templates provide a rapid way to get started with a file that has some of the basic elements already created for you; however, as you build your knowledge of the application, you'll want to customize the files to meet your own requirements.

The Open Database icon at the left of the FileMaker Quick Start window provides a convenient list of recently opened files. You may also add favorite files under either the Favorite Files (local) or Favorite Files (remote) subheadings.

**NOTE** The term *local* refers to FileMaker files that are located on disk drives attached to the computer you are working on, or shared drives accessed from the current computer. *Remote* files are those that are hosted on another computer (that is, opened in FileMaker Pro 9, FileMaker Pro 9 Advanced or FileMaker Server 9) and accessed using FileMaker's built-in networking.

In addition, the Quick Start screen includes an icon labeled Learn More that provides access to links to the product documentation and various different sites for online information, feedback, and guidance. This gathers together, in one location, a number of resources of interest to you as you become acquainted with the application.

**TIP** The Quick Start screen is optional. You can click the Do Not Show Quick Start Again checkbox that appears at the bottom of the panel. If you do this, you can still create new files and open existing files using commands on the File menu.

## Starting and exiting from FileMaker

Your computer operating system provides numerous ways to launch FileMaker Pro. Here are several common methods:

- During installation, an icon for the application is installed (at your option) in the Dock (Mac) or (by default) in the Start ⇨ All Programs menu (Windows). Clicking the program icon in the Dock or choosing it in the Start menu starts FileMaker Pro.

### Getting Acquainted with FileMaker

- You may have an alias (in Windows, it's called a shortcut) on your computer's desktop and/or in the Quick Launch toolbar (Windows). Double-clicking an alias/shortcut icon starts FileMaker, as does selecting FileMaker from the Windows Quick Launch toolbar.
- You can locate the application itself and double-click it, or double-click a FileMaker file anywhere on your desktop or within the disk directories on your computer.

**NOTE** The default path to the FileMaker Pro application on the Mac is Macintosh HD/Applications/FileMaker Pro 9/FileMaker Pro.app. In Windows, it's C:\Program Files\FileMaker\FileMaker Pro 9\FileMaker Pro.exe.

A few seconds after the application launches, you see the Quick Start screen — or if the Quick Start screen has been disabled, a standard Open File dialog appears. You are then ready to create a new database file or to locate and open an existing file.

When you've finished using FileMaker Pro for the moment, you may end the current application session by choosing FileMaker Pro ➪ Quit FileMaker Pro (Mac) or File ➪ Exit (Windows). If you have any database files open when you choose to end the application session, the files are automatically saved and closed before FileMaker exits.

## Creating, saving, and closing files

The first step in the process of creating a new database file depends on whether FileMaker is already running and whether your computer is configured to use the Quick Start screen.

**CROSS-REF** Details about how to change the configuration of FileMaker on your computer, including enabling and disabling the Quick Start screen, are included in the "Preference settings for your workstation" section, later in this chapter.

If FileMaker is not yet running, after you launch it you see a dialog with the option to create a new database. If the Quick Start screen is enabled, you can choose whether to create a new empty file or to use one of the starter templates that ship with the application. Otherwise, you're presented with a File dialog. On the Mac, the dialog includes a New button at the lower right; in Windows, you must first enter a filename and then click the Open button, in order to be presented with a dialog confirming that you want to create a new file.

If FileMaker is already running, you can begin creating a new database file by choosing File ➪ New Database.

**NOTE** FileMaker database files for all versions from 7 to 9 inclusive use the filename extension .fp7. Using this extension on all your database filenames is important because the operating system uses it to associate the file with the FileMaker Pro application.

When you choose a folder, enter a suitable filename, and confirm the creation of the file, a new database window is displayed. If you selected a template, the new file appears, ready to use or modify. However, if you choose to create a new empty file, a blank layout window appears and the

## Part I  The Fundamentals

Manage Database dialog automatically opens. Because a database file cannot hold any data until there are some fields in which to store the data, a default table (with a name corresponding to the file name) is added, and you're prompted to create fields for your new database.

To create one or more fields, enter a name in the Field Name box of the Manage Database dialog, as shown in Figure 3.1, and click the Create button. Then click OK to close the dialog. At this point, FileMaker generates a single default layout containing the fields you've created, plus a single record. The cursor appears in the first field, ready for you to enter some data.

You now have a very simple database file, and you can begin to use it. It doesn't yet have many useful features, but those can follow. For the moment, try entering a few values into the field (or fields) on the layout. If you have several fields you can use the mouse or the Tab key to move between them.

Unlike many other computer applications, FileMaker saves data at two levels. When you change a record or a layout, the change must be saved before you can go on to do anything else. By default, FileMaker handles the saving of records automatically without asking you to confirm — so, when you exit a record, its contents are saved. Similarly, the file must periodically be saved to disk and this, too, is handled automatically. As data is entered and accumulates, FileMaker writes data to disk progressively.

**FIGURE 3.1**

Creating the first field in a new database, using the Manage Database dialog.

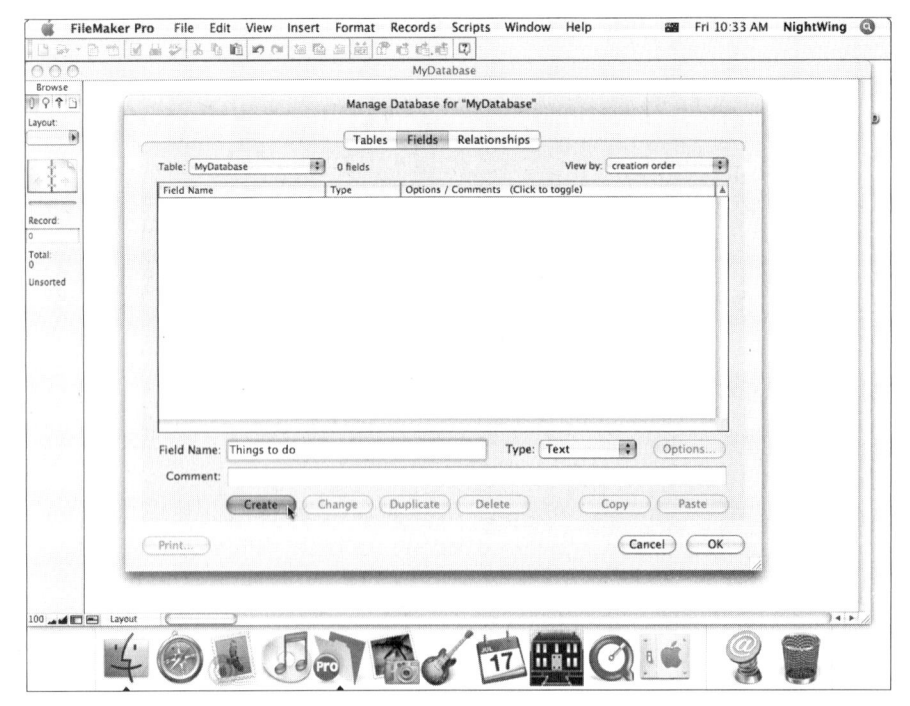

FileMaker handles the saving of data behind the scenes, so normally you don't have to worry about it. However, one consequence of this automatic operation is that, when a file is open, it's in a fluid state where, at any point, some parts of the file may not yet have been transferred to disk. When the file is closed, any remaining unsaved portions are saved to disk before the file closes.

To close a file, select its window (if you have more than one file or window open in FileMaker) and then choose File ⇨ Close (⌘+W or Ctrl+W). You may also close a file by closing all its windows.

> **TIP** A database file cannot be closed while it's still in use. In particular, a file that is a data source for another open file cannot be closed. If you choose File ⇨ Close in this situation, the file is hidden rather than closed.

## Handling files and data safely

FileMaker reads data from disk into memory when a database file is opened. The contents of the *cache* (data not yet written to disk) are then maintained as fields and records are updated. Cached data is written back to disk periodically, keeping the cache's size within a defined range.

> **CROSS-REF** You can find instructions for setting the cache size and the frequency with which data is saved to disk in the "Preference settings for your workstation" section, later in this chapter.

While FileMaker has a database open, the current state of the file includes some data that resides on disk and some that is held in cache. Neither the disk nor the cache holds a complete copy of the file. It isn't until the file is closed that FileMaker reconciles the data held in cache with the data on disk and thereby ensures that the copy on disk is complete and current. Consequently, in the event that FileMaker quits prematurely — without first closing the files it has open — it is possible that some data held in cache may not have been written to disk.

> **CAUTION** If a FileMaker database file is closed improperly (for example, a forced quit) some recent changes may be lost. It is possible, however, that an untimely end to the application session (for example, a power outage) may occur at a moment when FileMaker is updating the disk and some parts of the record structure — or other file elements — may be only partially written to disk. In such a case, there is a risk that the file may be damaged and may no longer work properly. Fortunately, this is an extremely rare occurrence; however, you should avoid situations where FileMaker is stopped when files have not first been properly closed.

Occasionally, you'll encounter situations where you can't avoid improper closure of files. Hardware failures or power outages do occur, so despite your best efforts, there may be occasion mishaps. In most cases, if a mishap occurs, the file opens again and no data has been lost. If you have difficulty opening a file, refer to Chapter 19, where we discuss the recovery of files.

Unlike other applications, databases manage many different pieces of information, so they require ready access to data from all parts of a file. This is in contrast to an application, such as a word processor, that typically accesses only one or two sections of a file at a time. This, along with the fact that FileMaker holds part of the file in cache, means that it is wise to open files from a reliable hard disk that is directly and permanently connected to your computer, instead of opening files from a network drive. This approach not only improves performance, it also reduces the risk of the network connection to the disk being lost during the session, perhaps compromising the integrity of the file.

**TIP** No matter how careful your file handling, or how reliable your computer hardware, we encourage you to make frequent backups of your files. That way, if you run into a problem, you have a recent copy of your database files to go back to and you won't lose much work. The more important your data, and the more intense the rate at which data is added or changed, the more frequently you should make backup copies.

**NOTE** Don't use the Macintosh Finder or Windows Explorer to make duplicates of a file while it is open. (You won't get the whole file, because some of it is residing in cache when open.) Either close the file first and then copy it, or in FileMaker choose File ⇨ Save a Copy As to make a backup copy of your file.

## Earlier file formats and conversion issues

FileMaker 9 opens and works directly with files created with versions of FileMaker Pro from version 7 onward. All these files should have been saved with the `.fp7` extension as part of their filenames. Because the file format is the same, you can expect all `.fp7` files to work in FileMaker 9 in the same way that they worked in the prior version of FileMaker in which they were created.

**CAUTION** FileMaker 9 includes some capabilities that aren't supported by previous versions. If you make structural changes to a file in FileMaker 9, be aware that some of the features you add may not work as intended if the file is reopened in an earlier version of FileMaker. For example, Web viewer objects aren't recognized by FileMaker Pro 7 or 8, but they are recognized by FileMaker Pro 8.5 and 9.

If you want to open a FileMaker file that was created with a version of FileMaker prior to version 7, you first have to convert the file to the `.fp7` file format. The first time you attempt to open a file that was created in FileMaker versions 3 through 6, you're prompted to convert the file, and a new file in `.fp7` format is created.

**NOTE** If you want to convert a file from a version of FileMaker earlier than version 3, for use with FileMaker 9, you must first convert the file to either the `.fp3` or `.fp5` format by using a copy of FileMaker Pro 3.x, 4.x, 5.x, or 6.x. The resulting `.fp3` or `.fp5` file can then be converted to the `.fp7` format by FileMaker 9.

Because versions of FileMaker prior to 7 differed in a number of respects (as well as using a different file format) from more recent editions of FileMaker, some calculations and other functionality may no longer work as intended after conversion. In general, FileMaker does an excellent job of anticipating many of the adjustments that must be made, and it applies them for you during the automated conversion process. Consequently, if the file you're converting is relatively straightforward in function and scope, it may require little or no further adjustment in order to operate to specification in FileMaker 9. Nevertheless, you should test the operation of the file carefully before proceeding.

In the case of complex multi-file solutions that were originally designed to operate in FileMaker version 6 or earlier, some additional preparations for conversion may be warranted. Moreover, a more thorough period of testing and revision to ensure that the solution functions effectively in the `.fp7` application environment is advisable. This process may be more or less time-consuming depending on the design and coding approach used in a given solution.

A detailed examination of the intricacies of migrating legacy solutions is outside the scope of this book. However, if you find yourself faced with this challenge, we recommend that you acquaint yourself with resources that are freely available from the downloads area of FileMaker, Inc.'s Web site. These include a comprehensive white paper entitled *Migration Foundations and Methodologies* (`www.filemaker.com/products/upgrade/techbriefs.html`), which provides extensive information and advice concerning issues that should be addressed to ensure a successful migration of a pre-`.fp7` solution.

# Finding Your Way Around

When you launch FileMaker Pro 9 and open a file, you immediately encounter two things: a menu bar that includes familiar menus (File, Edit, and so on) and some database-specific menus, and a database window with a title and a few controls at the lower-left corner.

The contents of the window depend almost entirely on the particular database file (or collection of files) you have opened. FileMaker windows show the contents of a layout, and their appearance may vary widely. However, you'll likely see a screen containing some mix of data, labels, buttons, and/or images.

Basic FileMaker housekeeping operations (Open, Close, New Database, Print, and so on) are located on the File menu. In Windows, the File menu also includes an Exit command; however, on the Mac, the equivalent command is named Quit and it resides in the FileMaker Pro menu, conforming to the OS X standard. Meanwhile, a list of open windows appears in the Window menu. If you're new to FileMaker, many of the commands in the remaining menus may be unfamiliar to you. The following pages help you to understand how FileMaker works and why, and assist you in locating the commands you seek.

First, you should familiarize yourself with the standard window control, as shown at Figure 3.2. These appear at the lower left of every FileMaker database window.

The gray area that can be seen spanning the left side of Figure 3.2 is the Status Area and includes basic contextual information and navigation controls. At the lower left, immediately below the Status Area, are the window zoom controls. The zoom percentage appears at the far left. Clicking the percentage returns it to 100% (normal size) from whatever setting it may have. The buttons adorned with close-up and distant horizon icons next to the percentage button are the zoom out and zoom in buttons—their function is to reduce or enlarge the contents of the window.

The Status Area control is beside the zoom controls at the lower left of Figure 3.2. Clicking this button hides or shows the Status Area at the left of the current window. Finally, to the right of the Status Area control is FileMaker's Mini Mode menu, which indicates the current window mode and can be used to change modes. These basic controls are present at the lower left of all FileMaker database windows at all times.

**Part I** | **The Fundamentals**

**FIGURE 3.2**

The standard controls at the lower left of a FileMaker window.

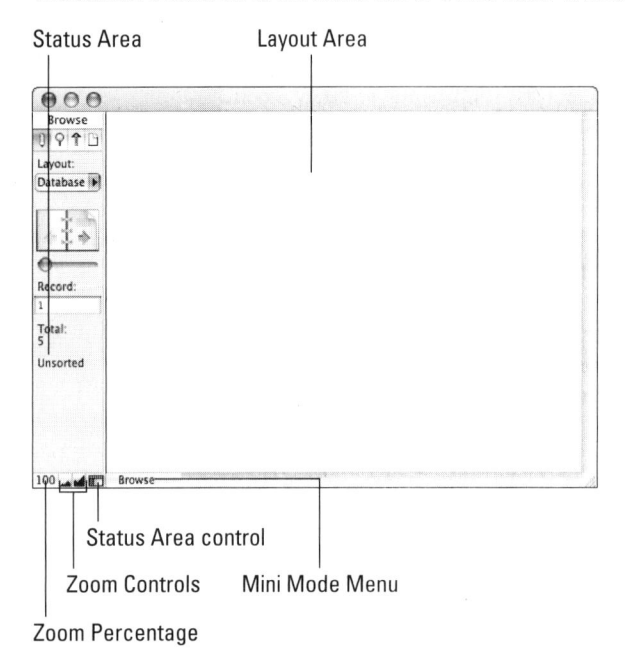

Status Area — Layout Area

Status Area control
Zoom Controls    Mini Mode Menu
Zoom Percentage

## The modes and their uses

The first and most important thing to know about FileMaker Pro is that it has several modes of operation. What you can do in each mode is different, and how the application responds to commands is also different. Until you grasp this essential concept, you may find FileMaker a little mystifying; however, the modes actually simplify matters when you understand their functions.

There are four operational modes in FileMaker. They are listed at the top of the View menu as well as in the Mini Mode menu. A row of icons at the top of the Status Area indicate the current mode and can also be used to change mode. The four operational modes are

- **Browse:** The mode used for viewing, entering, and editing data in your databases is called the Browse mode. By default, databases open in Browse mode, and much of your day-to-day database work is performed in Browse mode — you can think of it as the normal operational mode. The keyboard command to reinstate Browse mode from any other mode is ⌘+B or Ctrl+B.

- **Find:** So that you can search for records, FileMaker provides a Find mode (⌘+F or Ctrl+F). In Find mode, layouts appear as they did in Browse mode, but all the fields are devoid of data. This enables you to enter criteria for FileMaker to use in a search operation. When the database enters Find mode, the Mini Mode menu changes to read "Find" and the Status Area controls change to provide support for the Find process.

# Getting Acquainted with FileMaker

- **Layout:** The third FileMaker mode is called the Layout mode (⌘+L or Ctrl+L) and it is in this mode that FileMaker becomes a screen- and report-building environment. In Layout mode, all the objects within the window take on the behavior of elements in a drawing program, and the Status Area populates with graphical tools you can use to change the size, color, and placement of objects within the layout, and to add and remove objects at will. In Layout mode, instead of changing the data in the database, you're changing the database's interface.

- **Preview:** FileMaker provides a Preview mode (⌘+U or Ctrl+U) to display page images that demonstrate how the current layout, using the current data, looks if printed on the currently selected printer (and with current page size and printer settings).

## Navigating and viewing data

Data in your database files can be viewed in Browse mode, using an appropriate layout in a database window. With a new file, or a file relying on FileMaker's built-in interface controls, you can use the Status Area to locate a layout and move around among the records within a table.

At the upper left of the Status Area, as shown in Figure 3.3, is a label indicating the current mode and a row of four icons that can be used to switch between modes (as well as providing a graphical indication of the current mode). In Browse mode, the pencil icon at the left is shown as selected (shaded).

Immediately below the mode icons, near the top of the Status Area in Browse mode, a menu of viewable layouts is provided. From this menu you're able to select different layouts, to provide different views of the data available to the file. The layouts listed may relate to a single table of data, presenting different views or extracts of it, or to a variety of different tables. Layout names ideally should give you some guidance about the contents of each layout.

**FIGURE 3.3**

The Status Area controls in Browse mode.

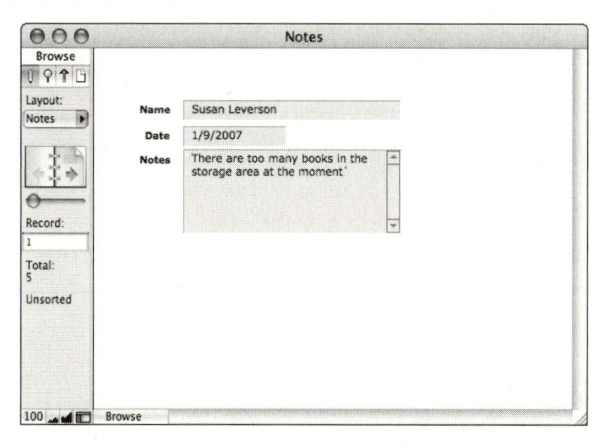

39

**Part I**    **The Fundamentals**

> **NOTE** The menu of available layouts, as with menus in many dialogs, conform to the User Interface standards of the platform on which you're working. Thus, on a Mac, the menu will be implemented as a pop-up menu; in Windows, the menu will be shown as a drop-down list. We just refer to them as *menus* rather than the more cumbersome *pop-up menus/drop-down lists*.

When you select a layout, the Status Area controls below the Layout menu reflect the state of the records in the table with which the layout is associated. In the example shown in Figure 3.3, the Status Area indicates that you're viewing record 1 of a total of 5 records on a layout called Notes. FileMaker provides a Rolodex (book) icon and a slider immediately below the Layout menu, providing a means to navigate through the records in the table being viewed. Clicking the right page of the Rolodex takes you to the next record; clicking the left page of the Rolodex takes you back to the previous record. Similarly, the position of the slider control below the Rolodex represents the current location among the available records. Dragging the slider to a new location takes you to the corresponding record in the current table.

> **NOTE** More precisely, dragging the slider takes you to the corresponding record in the currently available records from the current table. Find mode, as we discuss in the next section, can restrict the available records to a subset of the current table's records.

Finally, you can move between records in three other ways:

- If you want to go to a specific record — say record 3 — you can enter the number 3 into the Record field below the slider in the Status Area, and then press the Enter (or Return) key on your keyboard.
- You can choose Records ➪ Go to Record ➪ Next, Records ➪ Go to Record ➪ Previous, and Records ➪ Go to Record ➪ Specify.
- You can move to the next and previous records by pressing Ctrl+up arrow and Ctrl+down arrow.

## Searching and the FileMaker Find/Omit puzzle

When you have just a few records in a FileMaker table, scrolling through them and looking for the information you need isn't too difficult. However, when your records accumulate to the point where there are hundreds or even thousands of them in a table, a more efficient method of searching is needed. That's where FileMaker's Find mode comes in.

On entering Find mode, the current layout remains in view, but all the fields that displayed data in Browse mode appear empty, waiting for you to supply search criteria. Moreover, the Status Area changes its appearance when you enter Find Mode.

As you can see in Figure 3.4, when you place the database window into Find mode, the mode buttons and layout menu remain at the top of the Status Area; however, the text underneath the slider now refers to requests rather than records. Moreover, an Omit checkbox, a Symbols menu, and a Find button are included.

### Getting Acquainted with FileMaker

**FIGURE 3.4**

The Status Area controls in Find mode.

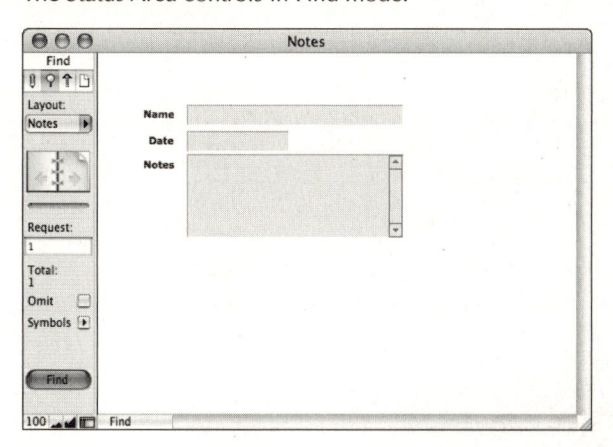

If you want to locate all the records in the current data table referring to a person whose name starts with the letters *Jo*, you can simply enter Find mode, type **Jo** in the Name field, and click the Status Area's Find button. If any records in the current table contain the name Jo — or a name starting with Jo, such as Johnson, Joan, or Joseph — those records are found.

When records are returned as the result of a Find, they are termed the *Found Set* and FileMaker temporarily presents the found records to you in Browse mode — isolated, as though they're the only records in the table. The rest of the records are not lost at this point; they've simply been omitted (ignored) for the moment.

When a Find has been conducted, the Status Area indicates the number of found records as well as the total number of records in the table. As is shown in Figure 3.5, the five records that were indicated in the Status Area in Figure 3.3 are still present, though only two are presently "found." Just as there is a found set of two records in this situation, there is also an omitted set of three records, bringing the total up to five.

At any point, when the view of a table is split into a found set and (by implication) an omitted set, you can bring the table back into a unified whole by choosing Records ➪ Show All Records (⌘+J or Ctrl+J). Alternatively, you can exchange the found and omitted record sets by choosing Records ➪ Show Omitted Only. Moreover, choosing Records ➪ Omit Record (⌘+T or Ctrl+T) and Records ➪ Omit Multiple (⌘+Shift+T or Ctrl+Shift+T) make it possible to manually fine-tune the found set, isolating a specific group of records of interest.

The found set principle gives you a mechanism to split up the records according to any criteria (or even arbitrarily or manually), isolating any subgroup of records. This is an important feature that provides support for producing extracts, summaries, and analyses of groups and subgroups of your data set.

**Part I**    **The Fundamentals**

**FIGURE 3.5**

Records returned as a result of a Find for *Jo* in the name field.

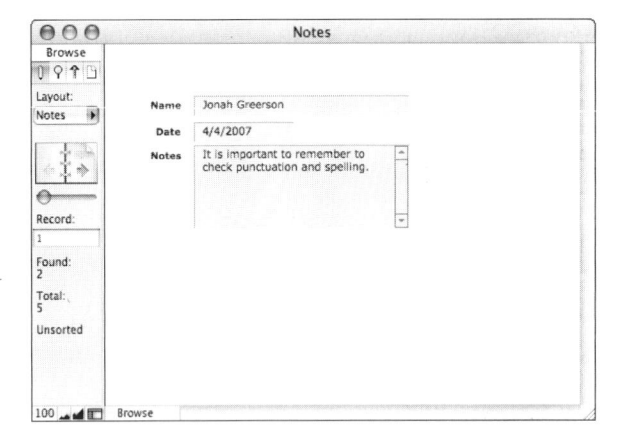

## Screen elements and what they're for

So far you've seen the window and Status Area controls for Browse mode and Find mode and you know how they work during navigation and Find procedures. However, much of the action when you're working with a database file takes place within the layouts themselves.

FileMaker database layouts include a variety of elements, some of which are purely visual. For example, text labels, headings, shaded areas, lines, and even images may be included in a layout to provide a frame of reference for the data or to contribute to the appearance of the layout. However, other layout components perform a function in the database and are part of the way users interact with the data. For example, field boxes, such as those in the white layout area in Figure 3.5, dynamically display the data within the current record — and users may click into the field boxes to enter or edit data within them.

The elements that make up layouts, in addition to static text and graphical elements, include fields, buttons, portals, tab controls, and Web viewers. In addition, layouts may be subdivided into defined horizontal areas such as Header, Body, Footer, and so on, and these are referred to as *parts*.

A *field*, or *field box*, is a rectangular object drawn or placed (pasted) onto a layout in Layout mode that is attached to a data field within a table of the database. Fields may be sized and positioned and given other graphical attributes (color, outlining, embossing, and so on). In addition to their graphical appearance, fields provide direct access to data when the layout is viewed or used in Browse mode. The cursor may be placed into a field and the data inside that field selected, formatted, deleted, or supplemented.

Layout buttons are objects having an action or command assigned to them in Layout mode. When an object has been defined as a button, clicking it in Browse or Find modes causes the assigned

## Getting Acquainted with FileMaker

action to be performed. FileMaker provides a special type of graphical object (an embossed rectangle with an attached text label) to be used where buttons are required; however, in Layout mode, you can assign button attributes to almost any object. Thus images, lines, rectangles, text objects, or even fields themselves can be defined to act as buttons.

Portals are rectangular layout objects that provide a virtual window into the data in another (related) table. So, for example, in a table of kitchen ingredients, you might add a portal to display a list of recipes that use a given ingredient.

Tab Control objects are collections of panels that operate like file index cards with labeled tabs protruding at the top. Clicking the tab of a particular panel brings it to the front. Tab Controls provide an efficient method of organizing layout elements so that groups of related layout objects can be brought forward and accessed as needed. One example might be in an automobile dealership database, where passenger cars and trucks each have their own tabs containing fields specific to that type of automobile (for example, trunk space and number of doors for cars, tow weight and capacity specifications for trucks).

The FileMaker Web Viewer is a powerful object capable of retrieving and rendering hypertext and other related Web content, directly on a database layout. This allows your database users to access browser capabilities from within the screens and reports of the database. Moreover, the content of a Web Viewer can be controlled directly from the data available within the database.

**CROSS-REF** We cover Layouts in detail in Chapter 6 and explore interface design in depth in Chapter 10.

The layouts appearing in FileMaker's database windows present you with collections of the various elements mentioned here, organized to provide you with the means to view, interpret, and interact with the data stored within your database files.

## Entering and Editing Data

So far we've talked about how you can view records and search for specific data. In many cases, your database usage is not merely as a spectator, but as an active participant, adding data and making changes to data, extending its usefulness or keeping it current.

If you need to make changes to existing data, you first need to locate the data to be changed. First, you should use the layouts menu to go to an appropriate layout — one displaying records from the table in which you want to make changes. Then you should locate the record or records that you want to change — either by navigating through the records or by conducting a Find.

When you've located a record you want to edit, the first step is to place the cursor into a field. You can do this by pressing the Tab key once to enter the first field and then repeatedly to move through the fields, or by clicking directly on the field with the mouse. In either case, the field becomes active and a text cursor appears within it. You can then enter, delete, or modify the data in the field.

If you have changes to make or data to add to several fields in the same record, you can move directly from field to field via the mouse or the Tab key, changing or adding information in each. The changes are not committed (saved) until you exit the record.

**NOTE** At any time until you commit the data by exiting the record or invoking a script with a Commit command, you can return the record to the state it had upon entry by choosing Records ⇨ Revert Record.

## Creating and duplicating records

To add a record to the current table, choose Records ⇨ New Record (⌘+N or Ctrl+N). A new record is added and the cursor is automatically placed into the first field, ready for you to enter some data.

In some cases, you may prefer to copy an existing record (for example, a record that has similar data to one you want to create). You can achieve this by choosing Records ⇨ Duplicate Record (⌘+D or Ctrl+D). As with the New Record command, the cursor is automatically placed into the first field, ready for you to begin editing the newly created record.

**NOTE** When a new record is first created, it initially exists only in memory — it has not yet been stored. If you've made a mistake and want to discard the new record, you can do so by choosing Records ⇨ Revert Record.

Some layouts show related records (for example, as a list in a portal). An example of such a layout would be an invoice where multiple purchases are shown, one per line — where an invoice table is used to store invoice details, but a separate table stores the details for each line. With a layout designed to include the display of related records, you may be able to enter new related records by typing them directly into the portal, dependent upon the relationship specification.

**CROSS-REF** For additional details concerning relationships and the creation of related records, see Chapter 11.

## Field definitions: Validation and dependencies

Databases often include fields designed to hold specific values, or fields that are dependent on the values in other fields. Frequently, such fields are set up to acquire a value automatically when the values they depend upon are entered. In other cases, the database is programmed to confirm that values entered are valid before accepting them and saving the record.

An example of a dependent value is the name of the state, as it can be determined automatically (by linking to a reference table) once the ZIP code for a location or address is entered. Similarly, a total value may be computed for each line of an order, based on the quantity and item price entries.

You can access options for the creation of dependencies between fields, for defining rules for acceptance of valid data, and for setting a variety of default or automatically entered values for each field by choosing File ⇨ Manage ⇨ Database.

**CROSS-REF** In Chapter 7, we look in detail at the uses of the Manage Database dialog.

In some cases, default values or values dependent on other inputs can be overwritten if you want. However, fields created using the explicit calculation field type cannot be overwritten (they always display the result of the calculation with which you have defined them).

## The significance of commitment

When you create a new record, duplicate a record, or make changes to the data in a record, the changes are visible only on the current workstation, even if other users are sharing the file. It is not until you finish making changes and exit the record that the new contents are saved as part of the database and may be seen by other users.

The process of exiting a record is called *record commit* — the changes to the data are committed at this point and can no longer be undone or discarded (though of course you can always go back into the record and change it back to how it was).

Because exiting a record commits its contents, there are several different ways to save a record you have been working on. One is to press the Enter key on the numeric keypad. Another is to click in an open area of the layout, outside the field boxes. In some cases a script, button, or menu item (attached to the Commit Records/Requests command) may also be available. When you commit the record, by whatever means, the record is exited (the cursor focus is removed from the fields) and any changes are saved.

A record can also be committed in less direct ways: by navigating to a different record, a different table (that is, a layout that is based on another table), or by closing the file. In each case, any changes made to the immediately preceding record are stored and the record becomes available for editing by others (only one user can edit a record at a time).

Prior to the commit point, changes to a record have not been saved and can be reverted. This is done by choosing Records ➪ Revert Record. When a record is reverted, all changes made since the previous time the record was committed are discarded — so if you've changed the value in several fields, all the changes are reversed if you revert the record.

**NOTE** After a record is committed, the changes made to it are permanent and cannot be undone. At this point, returning the record to its previous state would require that it be edited again to reverse the changes.

When your solution is available to multiple users simultaneously over a network (that is, a multi-user database), the process of committing a record has additional implications. While changes to a record are being made by one user, the record is locked and other users are unable to make changes to it — although they can see it — and can edit *other* records. The commit point releases the lock and the record becomes available for other users to edit. Moreover, it is at the commit point that changes you have made can be seen by other users viewing the record — that is, they see your changes appear when you exit the record.

# The Ins and Outs

Manually accessing, entering, and editing information in your solutions is a key part of maintaining your data, but it is labor intensive and can also be error prone. Occasionally, the data you require is already available in computerized form, so you may prefer to avoid entering the data by hand.

Similarly, there are occasions when the best solution to a problem is to take some data from your FileMaker database and view, analyze, or print it in another application. There are a variety of reasons you may choose to do this — to make use of existing chart templates in a spreadsheet application, to submit information for publication in a word processing format, to examine your data in a statistical analysis tool, and so on.

In any case, FileMaker's powerful data import and export capabilities provide you with options covering a broad range of requirements and support a wide variety of standard formats.

## Importing and exporting data

FileMaker Pro makes it extremely easy to get data from text files (comma- or tab-separated data) or Excel spreadsheet files into database files. In its simplest form, you drag and drop such files onto the FileMaker icon and they are automatically converted into databases (you're given the option to use the first row of data in the source text file to provide field names in the resulting database file). In just a few minutes you can start using the powerful searching, sorting, and organizing capabilities of a database, to work with your text or spreadsheet tables.

In cases where you already have a database file into which you want to bring data from existing files in other formats, choose File ⇨ Import Records ⇨ File. When you choose this command, you'll first be prompted to locate the file holding the data you want to import. Then you'll be presented with a dialog prompting you to map the columns or cells in the file you've selected with the fields in a table of the current database file, as shown in Figure 3.6.

In the Import Field Mapping dialog (see Figure 3.6) the data elements found in the selected file are displayed in a column at the left of the window. Navigation buttons below the column of incoming data allow you to move through the rows of data to ascertain what content the file holds. Meanwhile, the right side of the dialog provides a menu for selecting a table in the current database and displays a list of fields in the selected table.

Between the columns of fields in the Import Field Mapping dialog are two rows of symbols — a horizontal arrow and a vertical handle symbol. The arrow can be clicked to enable or disable import into a particular field, while the handle icon can be used to drag Target fields in the column at the right up and down to position them adjacent to appropriate incoming data elements.

**NOTE** On selecting a field in the right column of the Import Field Mapping dialog, you may press ⌘+up arrow or Ctrl+up arrow and ⌘+down arrow or Ctrl+down arrow to move the field up and down in the list. Similarly, when you select a number of fields in the right column (by pressing Shift+Click or ⌘+Click or Ctrl+Click), clicking an arrow symbol adjacent to any selected field toggles the import state for all selected fields simultaneously.

# Getting Acquainted with FileMaker   3

**FIGURE 3.6**

The Import Field Mapping dialog — matching incoming data to database fields.

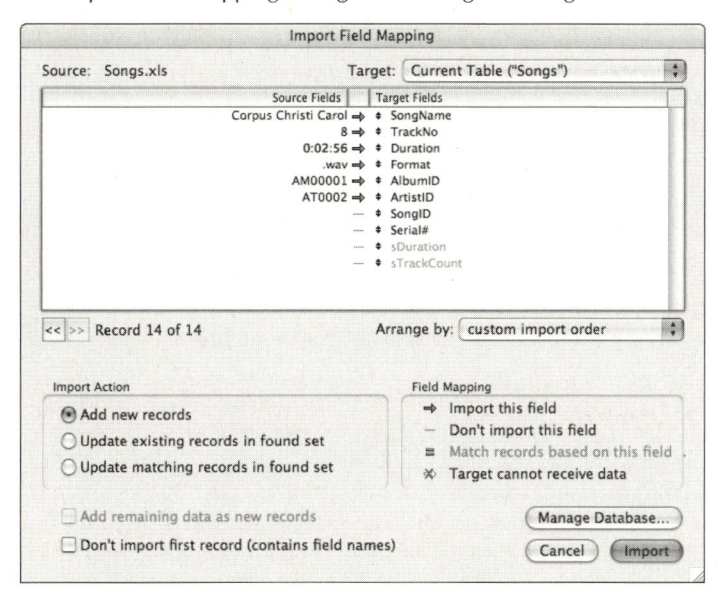

```
                         Import Field Mapping
Source:  Songs.xls           Target:  Current Table ("Songs")

               Source Fields      Target Fields
         Corpus Christi Carol  →  ♦  SongName
                            8  →  ♦  TrackNo
                      0:02:56  →  ♦  Duration
                         .wav  →  ♦  Format
                      AM00001  →  ♦  AlbumID
                       AT0002  →  ♦  ArtistID
                           —     ♦  SongID
                           —     ♦  Serial#
                           —     ♦  sDuration
                           —     ♦  sTrackCount

<<  >>  Record 14 of 14       Arrange by:  custom import order

Import Action                    Field Mapping
 ● Add new records                →  Import this field
 ○ Update existing records in found set   —  Don't import this field
 ○ Update matching records in found set   =  Match records based on this field
                                  ✶  Target cannot receive data

 ☐ Add remaining data as new records              ( Manage Database... )
 ☐ Don't import first record (contains field names)   ( Cancel ) ( Import )
```

The lower part of the Import Field Mapping dialog provides additional options relating to the import process — including the capability to add records to the selected table, or to synchronize the data with existing records in the found set. Also included is a key to the meaning of the alternate field mapping symbols.

In a procedure comparable to the import process, FileMaker enables you to export data into a variety of supported file formats by choosing File ➪ Export Records. After you choose this menu option, you're prompted to choose a file format, provide a filename, and indicate a location for the file to be created.

After you click the Save button in the Export Records to File dialog, you're presented with a dialog in which you specify and order the fields to be included in the export (see Figure 3.7). The menu above the list of fields on the left enables you to select the context from which fields are located, and the buttons in the middle of the dialog enable you to add fields to the export.

**NOTE**  The data exported is sourced from the current layout context and includes only the current found set in the frontmost layout. If you add fields from other tables, the values for inclusion depend on their table's relationship to the current layout's table.

If the data in the current found set is sorted, the grouping options at the upper right of the Specify Field Order For Export dialog becomes active. When a group-by-field option is selected, records with matching values in the selected field result in only a single entry in the exported file. This provides a means to export data summaries.

47

> **TIP** Because exports are based on the found set in the current layout, you can easily perform a Find then Export to create summaries and batch exports of subgroups of records.

**FIGURE 3.7**
The Specify Field Order for Export dialog is where you determine which fields are to be exported and in what order.

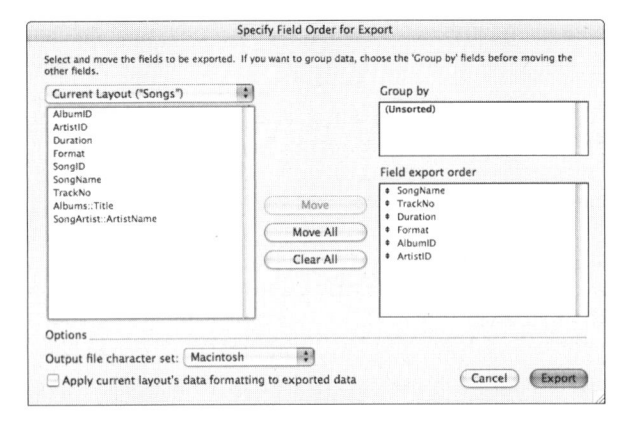

## Previewing and printing options

One of the most common requirements when it comes to getting data out of your database is the production of printed output. By default, FileMaker layouts operate on the WYSIWYG (what-you-see-is-what-you-get) principle, so, for the most part, if you choose File ➪ Print (⌘+P or Ctrl+P), what comes out of the printer closely resembles what you see onscreen.

Before printing, however, it's best to check the File ➪ Page Setup (Mac) or File ➪ Print Setup (Windows) settings to check the current print driver settings and confirm page size and orientation settings. Before proceeding to print, we also recommend that you pay a visit to the Preview mode (⌘+U or Ctrl+U) to ensure that the way the output is going to be rendered matches your expectations. It's always best to find out there is a problem *before* you've used up the last ream of paper printing the contents of your database.

> **TIP** The available options and the accuracy of the match between the Preview mode display and the actual printed output depend on the installed/selected printer driver, the printer itself, and the match between the two. When constructing the preview image, FileMaker interacts with the printer driver to arrive at a rendering of the instructions the driver prepares to send to the printer. While this is generally accurate, some combinations of drivers and printers produce results that vary slightly from the preview images. If you encounter this, it may signal that an update of the printer driver is required.

## Send/Save as PDF and Excel

In addition to its comprehensive printing and data export options, FileMaker Pro 9 provides two special-purpose output options — one to directly generate PDF files from the current found set (using the current layout to format the data) and one to efficiently create an Excel spreadsheet file from the current found set, including fields that appear on the current layout. You can access these options by choosing File ➪ Save/Send Records As ➪ PDF and File ➪ Save/Send Records As ➪ Excel, respectively.

The Save/Send Records As commands provide an elegant and immediate way to capture the current context in a form that can be archived, viewed, or shared with others (for example, as an e-mail attachment). The two supported file formats can be opened/viewed in a variety of applications on contemporary operating systems — so these options make your data very portable.

**TIP** The Save/Send as PDF option operates in much the same way as the Print command — it reflects the appearance of the current layout and also the current print driver settings — and it requires database access with printing privileges. By contrast, the Save/Send as Excel option operates along the lines of an export of data and requires database access with exporting privileges.

**CROSS-REF** The setting of database access privileges, including privileges for printing and exporting, is described in Chapter 14.

## Getting to Know the Relatives

In FileMaker solutions containing multiple tables connected via relationships, you require ways to view and edit data from related tables. For example, if you have a customer table and an invoices table, when viewing a customer record, you may want to be able to see details of that customer's invoices — and when viewing an invoice, you need to see the name and address of the customer for whom it was created.

### Ways to view and edit related data

You can see a single record from a related table, such as the name of the customer for a particular invoice, by simply placing the Customer::Name field directly onto the invoice layout. FileMaker locates and displays the first matching customer name. Moreover, the data in the corresponding customer record is editable directly from the invoice layout, just as if it were in the invoice table.

In situations where there are multiple related records, viewing just the first is usually inadequate, so FileMaker provides a layout Portal object supporting the display of a list of related records. Thus, in order to display a list of invoices for the current customer (for example, on the Customer layout), you should place a portal based on the Invoice table on the Customer layout. If desired, invoice data can be entered or edited directly in the portal, without visiting the Invoice layout, and any such changes are stored in the Invoice table and displayed on the Invoice layout when you next visit it.

Relationships in FileMaker work in both directions, so a single relationship between the Customer and Invoice tables should be sufficient to enable the relevant invoices to be displayed on the customer layout and the customer details to appear on the invoice layout.

Although the capability to view related data directly on the current layout makes FileMaker's interface powerful and flexible, it's also possible to jump directly to related records in their own table and layout. FileMaker's built-in Go to Related Records functionality (for example, via a button command or a script) can be used to achieve this efficiently.

**CROSS-REF** We cover advanced interface techniques using the Go to Related Records command in Chapter 9.

## The importance of context

Everything you do in FileMaker works from the current context. The current mode, the layout displayed in the front-most database window, and the found set and the current record in that window, determine the context from which data in the solution as a whole are viewed. The effect of any action, therefore, varies depending on context.

When you change records, the values in the match fields for relationships to other tables also change. This means that the sets of related records that are available to view and edit (from the current context) also change. If you navigate to a layout based on a different table — or on a different graph representation (Table Occurrence) of the same table, then the relationship views alter accordingly

**CROSS-REF** For a discussion of the workings of FileMaker's Relationships Graph, see Chapter 7.

Likewise, summary and calculated data may vary according to the found set, so what you see when viewing all records in a table may be different from what you see after performing a Find to isolate a subgroup of records.

## Making complexity simple in practice

On your first encounter with a relational data system, you may be tempted to throw up your hands, thinking that it's all too complicated. Surely it would be much easier to keep things in one large table than to divide the data among multiple tables?

It's important to realize that the purpose of setting up appropriate relationships within your data is to simplify matters — to let the computer handle many trivial operations so that you don't have to. So, while it may be true that setting up relationships in your data structure takes a little more thought, planning, and configuration at the outset, the resultant operational simplicity more than justifies the effort.

# Optimizing the Application

Many aspects of FileMaker Pro's operation automatically adjust to your working environment. For example, the settings for date, time, and language that are in place on the computer you are using are automatically reflected in the FileMaker interface and in the ways that your solution files operate.

Nevertheless, a number of aspects of the FileMaker feature set are user-configurable via two preference settings dialogs. The first of these dialogs sets application preferences applying to all FileMaker work done on the current computer. The second dialog sets preferences specific to the current database file, regardless of the computer it's used on.

## Preference settings for your workstation

The Preferences dialog allows you to control the behavior of FileMaker on the current workstation. You can access it by choosing FileMaker Pro ➪ Preferences (Mac) or Edit ➪ Preferences (Windows).

As you can see in Figure 3.8, the Preferences dialog is arranged into five panels, each selectable via a tab at the top of the dialog panel. The General tab allows several interface options — in the upper section, drag-and-drop text editing functionality, the Quick Start screen, and the recent files submenu are enabled or disabled. Below that, the General tab allows you to assign a custom name to the current workstation. Although this is termed the *User Name,* it refers to the workstation rather than to an individual and isn't to be confused with the login account name. Finally, the General tab allows you to enable or disable automatically checking the FileMaker, Inc., servers for application updates.

**FIGURE 3.8**

The General tab of the FileMaker Pro 9 Preferences dialog.

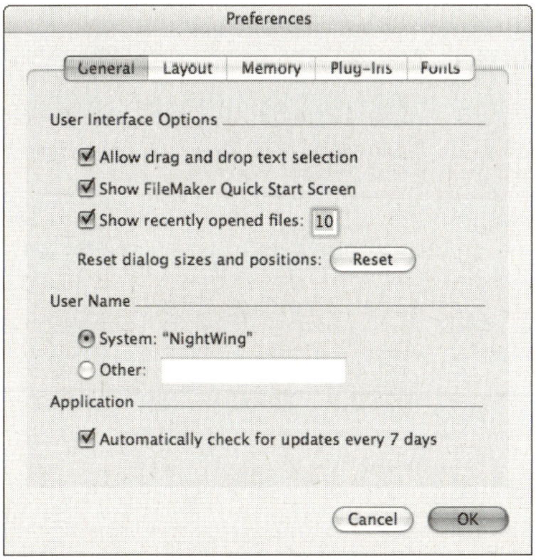

## Part I  The Fundamentals

The Preferences dialog's Layout tab, shown in Figure 3.9, provides access to options affecting the way the application works in Layout mode. The Always Lock Layout Tools setting alters the behavior of the drawing palette in the Status Area in Layout mode so that when a tool (for example, the Line tool or the Text tool) is selected, it remains active until another tool is selected; whereas, by default, a tool only remains active for a single action, unless its icon is double-clicked. Additionally, the Layout tab provides an option to add new fields to the current layout, and to save layout changes automatically.

> **TIP** If you're doing complex or exacting layout work, you may be well advised to disable the option to add new fields to the current layout (it's on by default) because creation of a new field otherwise results in changes to layouts that you may have spent many hours perfecting. You may also prefer to leave the Save Layout Changes Automatically option disabled so that you have an option to discard changes when leaving a layout (or when leaving Layout mode) after making modifications.

Finally, the Layout tab of the Preferences dialog enables you to constrain or extend the color palette available in Layout mode. The settings you choose here may depend in part on your personal tastes, but should also take account of the color support of the systems (both hardware and software) via which users are to access the interfaces you create in Layout mode.

The Preferences dialog's Memory tab, shown in Figure 3.10, provides controls for the cache size and save cycle of the application. When FileMaker is installed, a cache setting adequate for most situations is set. Unless you encounter specific problems that may indicate memory management issues, we recommend that you leave the cache setting at the default value. Similarly, the default save setting During Idle Time is best for the majority of users.

**FIGURE 3.9**

The Layout tab of the FileMaker Pro 9 Preferences dialog.

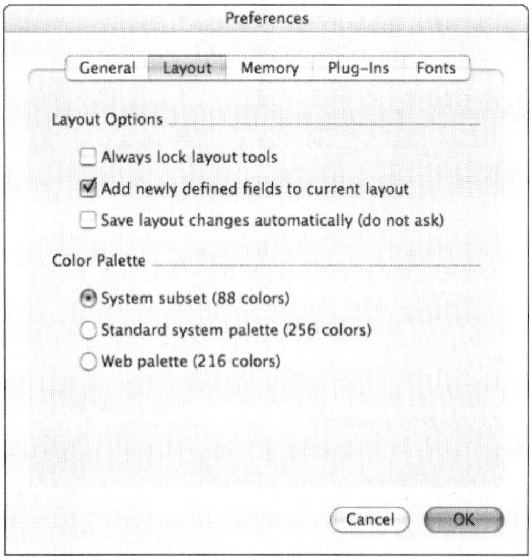

## Getting Acquainted with FileMaker 3

### FIGURE 3.10
The Memory tab of the FileMaker Pro 9 Preferences dialog.

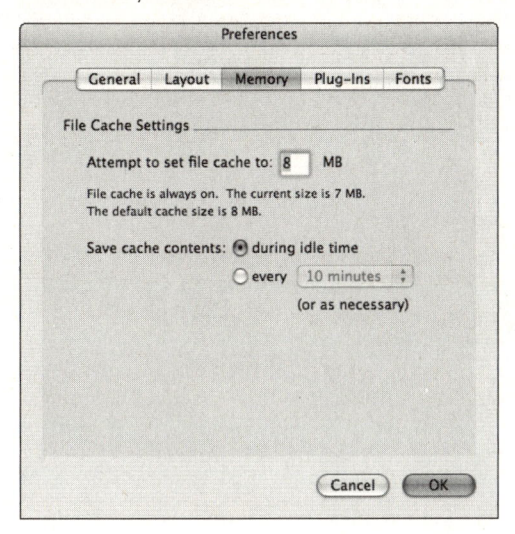

The Plug-Ins tab of the Preferences dialog (see Figure 3.11) allows you to enable/disable and configure third-party plug-ins and the Auto-Update utility (configurable to automatically load plug-in updates from FileMaker Server over a local network).

### FIGURE 3.11
The Plug-Ins tab of the FileMaker Pro 9 Preferences dialog.

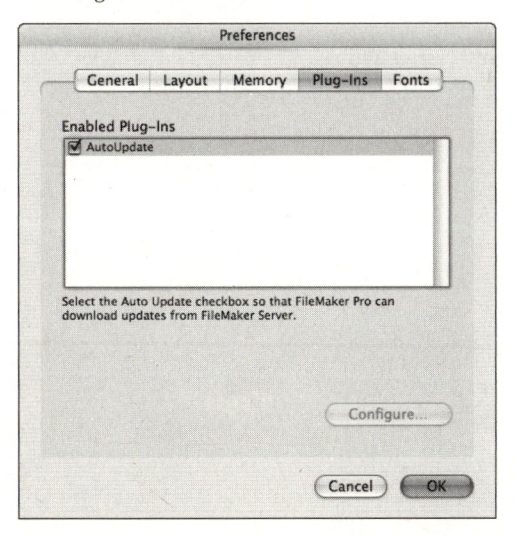

53

## Part I  The Fundamentals

**CROSS-REF** In Chapter 23, we provide a more detailed exploration of the use of FileMaker's plug-in architecture.

At the right of the Preferences dialog is the Fonts tab (see Figure 3.12). It provides access to configuration options for default fonts for each supported character system, as well as synchronization and font locking options (controlling the behavior of fields defined for a specific character system when characters from outside that system are entered — for example, Roman characters entered into a field defined to accept Kanji text).

**FIGURE 3.12**

The Fonts tab of the FileMaker Pro 9 Preferences dialog.

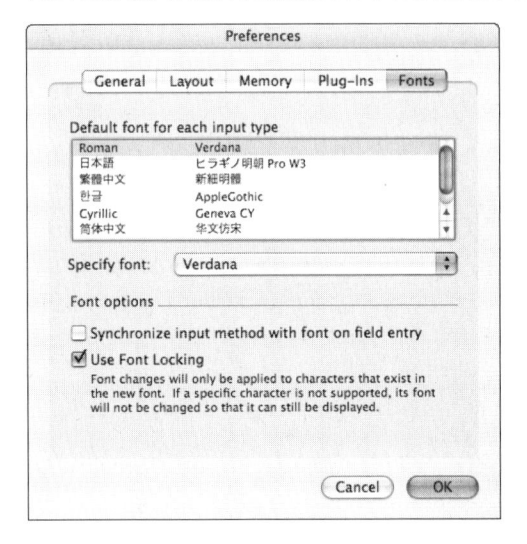

## File options for the current database

For each database file, you can access a range of additional configuration options by choosing File ➪ File Options. Settings defined in this way are saved with the file and affect its behavior whenever, wherever, and however it is opened.

The File Options dialog presents a range of controls grouped within three tab panels in Windows, and with a fourth appearing when the file is open on a Mac (as in the case of the screenshot in Figure 3.13). The first panel, shown in Figure 3.13, provides default settings for the behavior of the file when it's opened, allowing you to specify a default log-in account, specify a default layout, and specify a script to run automatically when the file is opened. Similarly, an option is provided to have a script run automatically when the file is closed.

# Getting Acquainted with FileMaker 3

**FIGURE 3.13**

The Open/Close tab of the FileMaker Pro 9 File Options dialog.

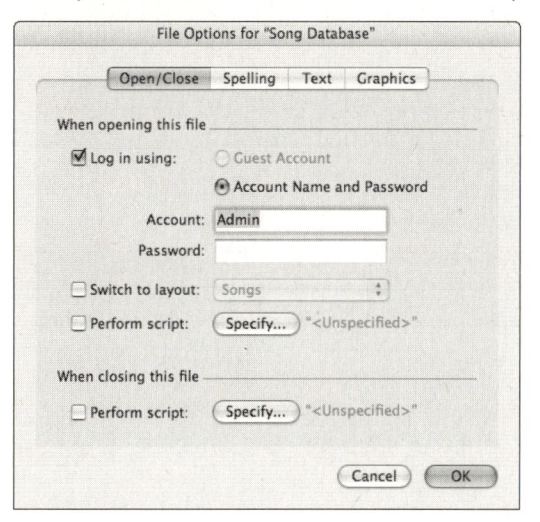

The Spelling panel, shown in Figure 3.14, provides access to settings for visual and audible alerts when the spelling of a word during data entry appears questionable (that is, when it is not in the installed FileMaker dictionary).

**FIGURE 3.14**

The Spelling tab of the FileMaker Pro 9 File Options dialog.

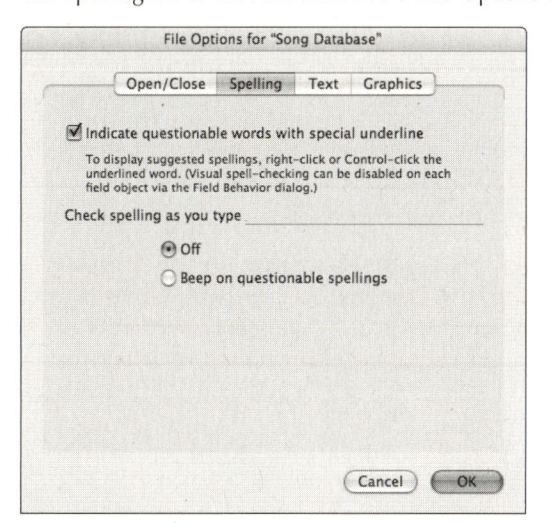

55

## Part I   The Fundamentals

> **TIP**
> When visual spell checking is enabled, you can override it on a field-by-field basis by choosing Format ▷ Field Control/Behavior in Layout mode.

The Text panel of the File Preferences dialog (see Figure 3.15) includes a setting for the use of smart quotes within the file (where straight quotation marks are automatically substituted with curly typesetting quote marks oriented forward or backward, depending on their position with respect to adjacent text). Also included are controls for the specification of line breaking (automatic text line wrapping) for Roman and Asian lettering systems.

Surprisingly, the Text panel also includes a control to set the behavior of the file with respect to localization settings for number, date, and time (including timestamp) formats. It is perhaps counterintuitive that such a control is located on a tab called "Text," since its effects apply to the storage and display formats data-entry field types *other than* text and container fields, but you do enter them as text before FileMaker (re)formats them to match the system-set representations. These controls are important and provide the ability to configure a file to operate consistently on all systems (Always Use File's Saved Settings), to adapt to changing contexts (Always Use Current System Settings), or to require the user to make a choice every time the file is opened on a system with settings that differ from the environment in which the file was created (Ask Whenever Settings Are Different).

By default, FileMaker Pro 9 applies the Always Use Current System Settings option, which works well in many cases.

> **TIP**
> We advise against choosing the Ask Whenever Settings Are Different option, since users — unless they programmed the file themselves — are unlikely to appreciate the implications of the choice when it is offered to them. Consequently, in addition to the tedium of being repeatedly presented with a dialog they don't understand, the option frequently forces the user to make an arbitrary rather than informed choice.

**FIGURE 3.15**

The Text tab of the FileMaker Pro 9 File Options dialog.

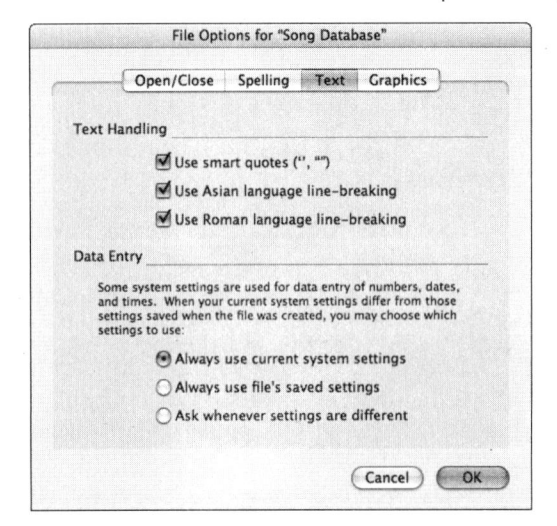

# Getting Acquainted with FileMaker 3

Finally, on the Mac, a fourth tab titled Graphics appears at the right of the File Options dialog, as shown in Figure 3.16. The Graphics panel includes a single control that enables/disables the automatic initiation of photo import when a camera is plugged in on the Mac. Because this automation option is not supported in Windows, the option is not displayed when a file is opened in Windows.

**FIGURE 3.16**

The Graphics tab (Mac only) of the FileMaker Pro 9 File Options dialog.

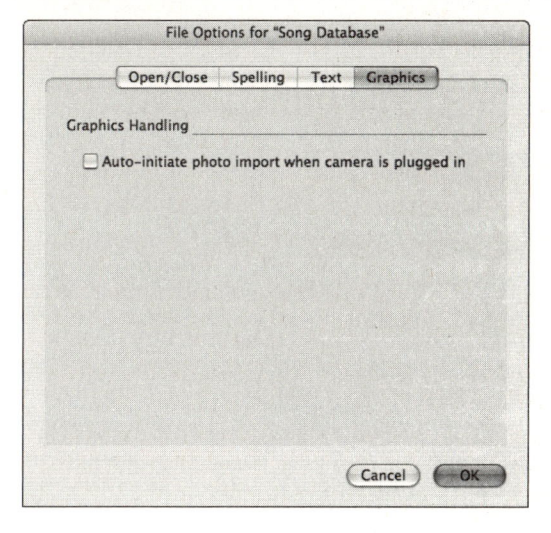

57

# Chapter 4

# What's New in FileMaker 9

FileMaker 9 is a substantial step forward in the evolution of the application—one that breaks new ground and adds depth and power to existing features. It brings many changes, both small and large, which will make life easier for users and developers. This release introduces entirely new functionality, which will introduce FileMaker to new users and give it a new role among corporate data and reporting tools.

In the following pages, we provide you with a speedy introduction to key new features, giving you an overview of the things that have changed and new possibilities that have emerged.

## The FileMaker Quick Start Screen

When FileMaker Pro 9 is launched, by default you are presented with the Quick Start screen (see Figure 4.1). The Quick Start screen brings together a number of useful features and resources, grouped into three sections:

- **Create Database:** Clicking the Create Database icon gives you access to options for creating an empty database or selecting from any of several dozen starter solutions grouped into nine broad categories.

- **Open Database:** Clicking the Open Database icon presents options for selecting from a list of recently opened files or from lists of Favorite Files (both local and remote).

> **TIP** When a file is selected in the Recent Files list, a button at the lower right can be used to add it to the relevant favorites list.

- **Learn More:** Clicking the Learn More icon provides you with access to sources of information, support, and documentation—including online resources, e-mail lists, technical data, and interactive Web sites.

### IN THIS CHAPTER

Getting familiar with the FileMaker Quick Start screen and enhanced Help menu

Reviewing new calculation functions and conditional formatting

Grouping and editing scripts

Resizing layout objects

Using FileMaker 9's enhanced tab control

Enabling field-specific visual spell-checking

Using External SQL Data Sources

Exploring new features in FileMaker Pro 9 Advanced

**Part I**    **The Fundamentals**

### FIGURE 4.1

The FileMaker Pro 9 Quick Start Screen with Create Database selected.

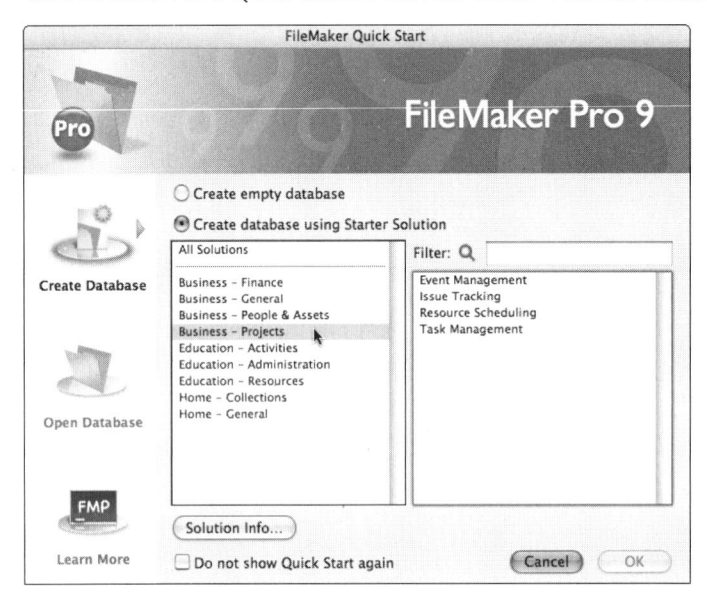

The Quick Start screen will be particularly helpful to new users. But if you'd rather go straight to a standard file dialog when you open FileMaker Pro 9, you can disable the Quick Start screen. Just click the Do Not Show Quick Start Again checkbox, near the bottom of the screen.

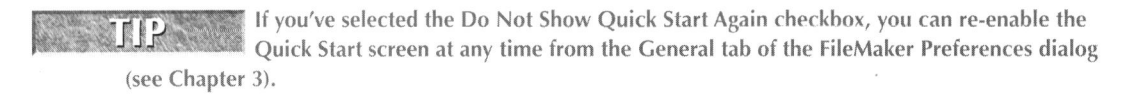

> **TIP** If you've selected the Do Not Show Quick Start Again checkbox, you can re-enable the Quick Start screen at any time from the General tab of the FileMaker Preferences dialog (see Chapter 3).

## The Help Menu

The Help menu in FileMaker Pro 9 has been enhanced to include several additional options and features. Most notably, a new category of options called Product Documentation has been added. As you can see in Figure 4.2, selecting the Product Documentation menu reveals a submenu of six options, each providing a direct link to either local or Web-based information. When selected, the relevant document loads into an appropriate application (for example, a Web browser, a PDF viewer, and so on).

What's New in FileMaker 9 | 4

#### FIGURE 4.2

The FileMaker Pro 9 Help Menu, showing the Product Documentation submenu.

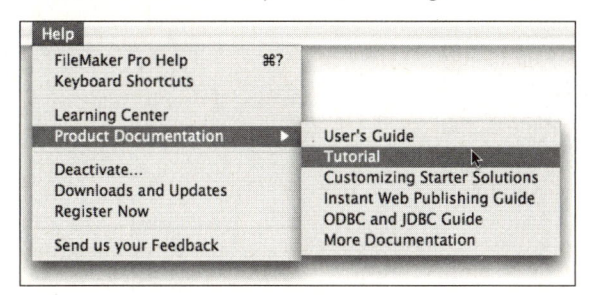

In addition, the Help menu includes an Activate/Deactivate command, which allows you to control the assignment of your user license to the permitted number of copies of FileMaker Pro, in line with the user license agreement. For example, when you replace your old computer with a shiny new model, you can deactivate the FileMaker Pro copy on your old computer so that a FileMaker installation on your new computer can be activated.

Also new in FileMaker Pro 9 is a Help menu command called Send Us Your Feedback, which provides a direct link to the relevant feedback forums on the FileMaker.com Web site. The Downloads and Updates menu command now operates dynamically, tracking updates as they become available, rather than providing a static link to the relevant Web page, as in previous releases.

**NOTE** For additional information on the operation of the Downloads and Updates menu command in FileMaker 9, see the "Scheduled Software Update Notification" section, later in this chapter.

## Learn More Links on Critical Dialogs

Extending the focus on providing access to information where you may need it, FileMaker 9 includes links in the lower-left corner of several dialogs: the Button Setup dialog and the Specify Calculation dialog (both shown in Figure 4.3), as well as the Viewer Setup dialog and the New Layout/Report dialog. If you click the Learn More link, you're taken directly to the relevant entry in the online Help file, which in turn provides a direct pointer to the Web-based Learning Center.

### FIGURE 4.3
Learn More links on the Button Setup and Specify Calculation dialogs.

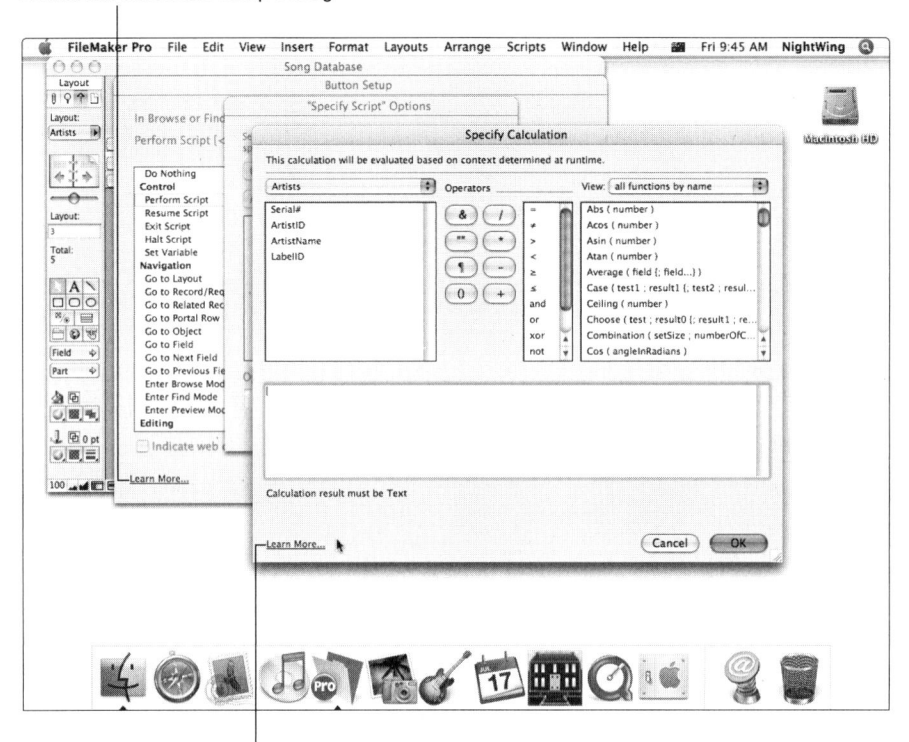

## Scheduled Software Update Notification

On FileMaker 9's first launch after installation, an automatic check for more recent versions of the application occurs, and if the installed version is not the most recent revision, you are prompted to download and install the update.

Starting at installation, by default, a check for updates is scheduled to occur automatically every seven days. FileMaker won't automatically install an update for you — it's still your decision whether to do that — but it will let you know if an update is ready to download.

If you would prefer that FileMaker not check for updates every seven days, you have the option to disable automatic notifications. To access this setting, choose FileMaker Pro ➪ Preferences (Mac) or Edit ➪ Preferences (Windows). In the General tab of the Preferences dialog, shown in Figure 4.4, the Automatically Check for Updates Every 7 Days checkbox lets you disable or re-enable software update notifications at any time.

**FIGURE 4.4**

The option to disable scheduled update notifications in the Preferences dialog.

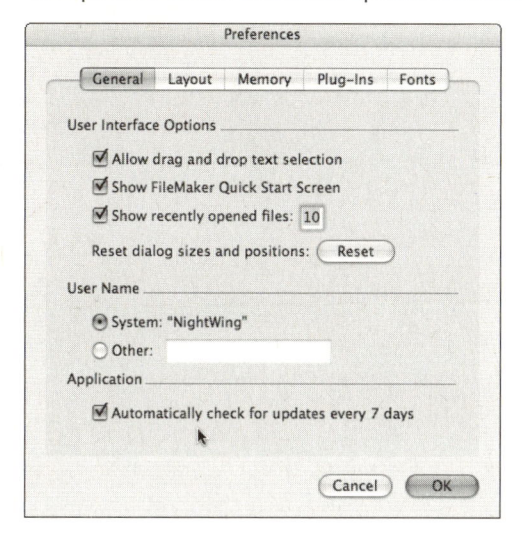

# New Calculation Functions

To extend existing functionality and provide support for the new features in FileMaker Pro 9, five additional calculation functions are now available. We outline them in the following sections.

## Self

The `Self` function accepts no parameters and is designed to return the value (if any) of the object containing the expression it's used in. The function is particularly useful in situations where you may want to reuse the same code in a variety of contexts (without updating each instance of the code to reflect its own context).

This new function is well suited to conditional formatting calculations (see the "Conditional Formatting" section later in this chapter) and for use in tooltip calculations. In either case, it allows the calculation to reference the value of the object to which it is assigned. So, for instance, a tooltip attached to a field defined as `Self` will return the contents of the field to which it is assigned.

Other uses of the `Self` function include calculation field formulas, auto-enter and validation calculations, where it returns the value of the field in which it is defined. However, it should be noted that the `Self` function is not accepted in scripts, button definitions, or other calculation expressions.

## Get (TemporaryPath)

The `Get(TemporaryPath)` function returns the operating system file path to the temporary folder used by FileMaker on the current user's workstation.

The format of the path returned by `Get(TemporaryPath)` on Mac OS will typically be along the lines of

    /Macintosh HD/private/var/tmp/folders/501/TemporaryItems/FileMaker/

and in Windows

    /C:/Documents and Settings/UserName/Local Settings/Temp

> **NOTE** The location of the temporary folder identified by the Get(TemporaryPath) function may vary depending on the configuration of your workstation.

## Get (HostApplicationVersion)

FileMaker Pro 9 includes a `Get(HostApplicationVersion)` function to enable client computers to retrieve the application version details of the host computer for the current database. On the host computer itself (or in a database that is not being hosted) the function returns an empty string.

## Asin (number)

The `Asin( )` function accepts as its parameter any expression providing a numeric result — or field containing a numeric value — in the range from –1 to 1. It returns the arcsine of the supplied number.

Arcsine is the inverse function of the `Sin( )` function (sine) — that is, the arcsine is the arc (in radians) corresponding to the angle that has a sine equal to the value (number) supplied to the `Asin( )` function. The value returned will be between $-\pi$ and $\pi$.

## Acos (number)

The `Acos( )` function accepts as its parameter any expression providing a numeric result or field containing a numeric value in the range from –1 to 1. It returns the arccosine of the supplied number.

Arccosine is the inverse function of `Cos( )` — that is, the arccosine is the arc (radians in the range between zero and $\pi$) corresponding to the angle that has a cosine equal to the value (number) supplied to the `Acos( )` function. The value returned will be between $-\pi$ and $\pi$.

> **NOTE** If you need to retrieve the value of an arcsine or arccosine in degrees rather than radians, you can achieve that by enclosing the expression or its result within the Degrees( ) function.

## What's New in FileMaker 9

# Conditional Formatting

Many databases developed using previous versions of FileMaker include calculations to display graphics or change the appearance of text based on data in the database. You may have used techniques of this kind for purposes as diverse as highlighting a portal row, dimming an inactive button, displaying overdue amounts in bold red text, and so on. FileMaker 9 provides direct support for many requirements of this kind by allowing you to apply conditional formatting attributes to layout objects.

To apply conditional formatting, first select an object in Layout mode; then choose Format ➪ Conditional (see Figure 4.5) to invoke the new Conditional Formatting dialog (shown in Figure 4.6). Alternatively, you may access the dialog by choosing Conditional Formatting from the contextual menu that appears when you right-click the selected object.

**CROSS-REF** The procedures for applying conditional formatting are explored in greater detail in Chapter 6.

**FIGURE 4.5**

The Layout mode command for conditional formatting.

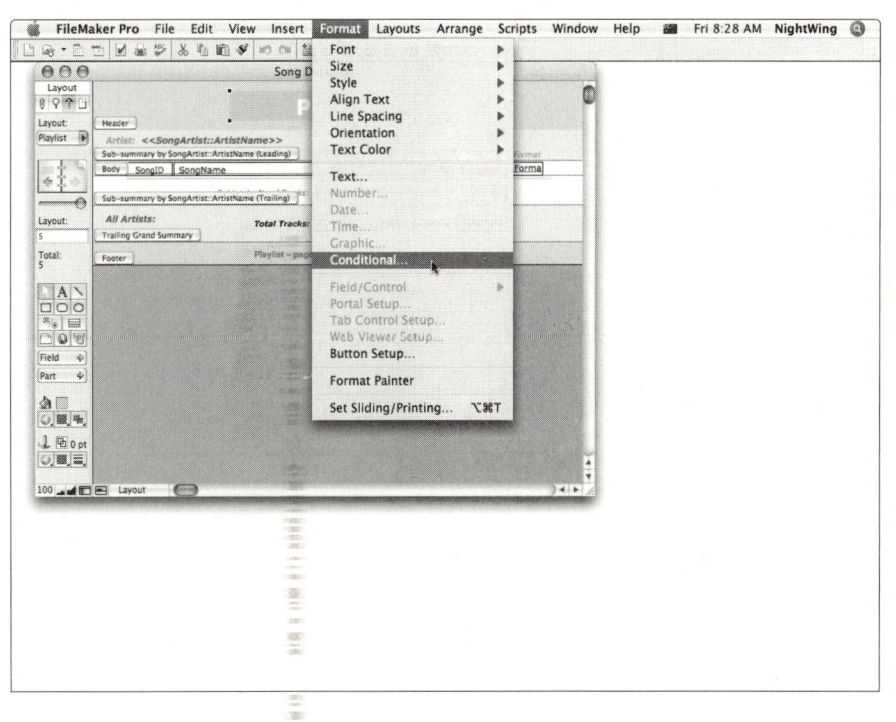

## Part I  The Fundamentals

### FIGURE 4.6
The Conditional Formatting dialog.

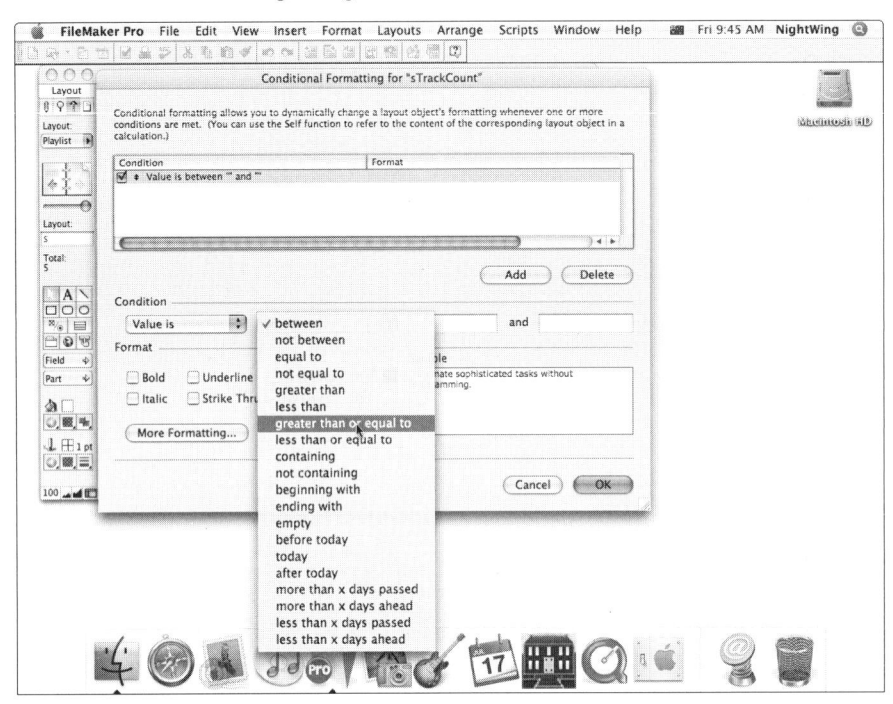

The Conditional Formatting dialog enables you to specify one or more rules and associate them with custom text and fill formats for the selected object. If the selected object is a field, the dialog enables you to define formatting rules based on the value in the field. Alternatively, you may select the option to create your formatting rules using a calculation formula.

Using the Conditional Formatting dialog, you can associate any mix of formats comprising text styles, font, size, color, and fill color with a given rule. Rules, once created, are listed in the panel at the top of the dialog and can be selected and edited or deleted in the list. The capability to define multiple rules to deal with different conditions — and to apply different formats accordingly — makes this feature powerful and extensible. Moreover, the capability extends to all layout objects that can accept text or fill formatting attributes, so graphical objects, portals, Web viewers, and tab controls can also take on a dynamic appearance, changing according to the state of the data.

## Append to PDF

Since the release of version 8, FileMaker has included the capability to create a PDF of the records and layouts being viewed. This feature has been scriptable using the Save Records as PDF [ ] command.

# What's New in FileMaker 9 | 4

As shown in Figure 4.7, the Save Records as PDF [ ] command in FileMaker 9 includes an additional configuration option. When the Append to Existing PDF checkbox is selected, as long as the name of an existing PDF file is supplied, the result is a composite PDF in which succeeding output is added as additional pages within the specified PDF file. With this powerful new feature you can create PDF reports consisting of pages generated from more than one layout or in more than one size or orientation, within a single file.

**FIGURE 4.7**

The additional Append to Existing PDF option for the Save Records as PDF [ ] command.

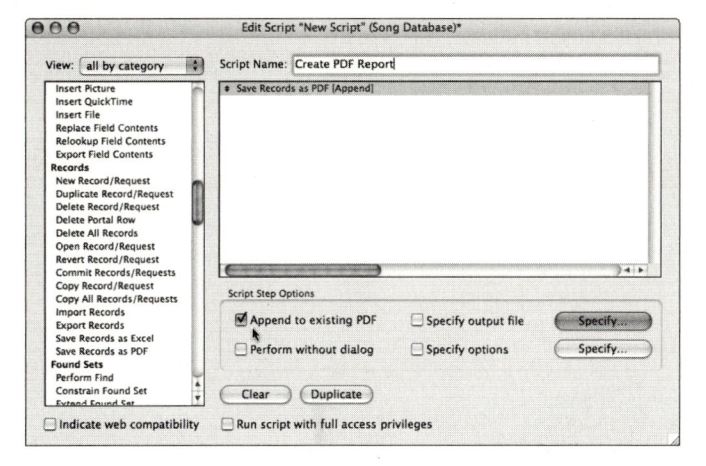

## The Send E-Mail Link for Database Sharing

One challenge to solution providers in the past was to supply users with the detailed instructions about how and where to find a hosted database on the network, so that they can log in. This was particularly problematic in cases where multiple users required occasional database access. The job of writing detailed instructions and providing IP addresses is not just tedious but requires some knowledge of the network setup and is subject to being outdated when the network topography changes, altering IP assignments.

FileMaker 9 solves this problem by providing a built-in feature streamlining the process, allowing users to send an e-mail containing a URL pointing directly to the current hosted file. You do this by choosing File ⇨ Send Link (see Figure 4.8). FileMaker then directs your default e-mail application to create a message containing details of the connection requirements and a network address for the database.

Recipients of the e-mail created using this feature (see Figure 4.9) can click the link contained in the e-mail or copy and paste it into a browser address bar. The remote database then opens in FileMaker Pro on the recipient's workstation.

**Part I**    **The Fundamentals**

### FIGURE 4.8

The Send Link command in FileMaker Pro 9.

### FIGURE 4.9

An example e-mail created automatically in Apple Mail using the Send Link command.

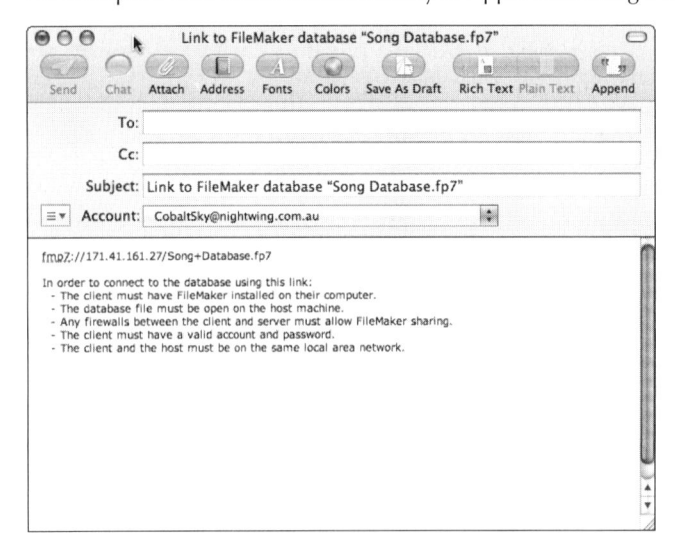

## Script Grouping and Editing Tools

A frequently requested feature over a number of years has been a way to organize scripts into groups to improve manageability, especially in files that contain many scripts. FileMaker 9 addresses this by providing script groups, which appear as folders in the new Manage Scripts window (see Figure 4.10).

**FIGURE 4.10**

Script Groups appearing within the Manage Scripts window.

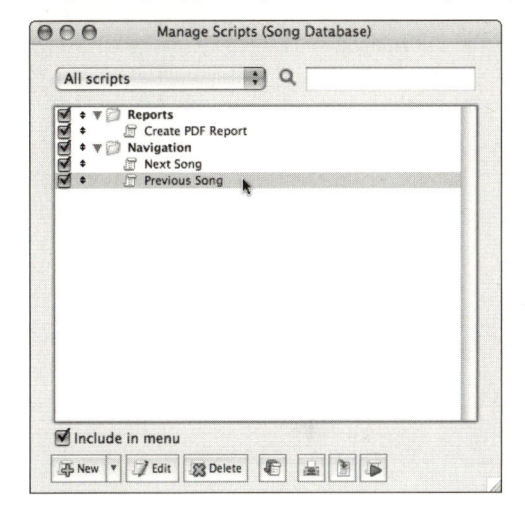

To move scripts into and out of groups, you drag them (using the handle at the left) to the bottom of an open group, and then to the right to place them into the group. Groups may be created within groups (or moved inside another group) to create a hierarchy of scripts.

When a script that is located within a group is set to appear in the Scripts menu, it appears within a submenu representing the group, as shown in Figure 4.11. When there are multiple levels of groups, the Scripts menu represents these as cascading submenus.

In FileMaker 9, the Manage Scripts window is no longer presented as a dialog, so you can access database windows and work in Browse mode while the Manage Scripts window remains open. Moreover, the Edit Script windows are non-modal, so you can open multiple scripts simultaneously, each in its own window; this makes it easy to compare scripts or to copy and paste script commands (or groups of commands) between open scripts.

**CAUTION** When a script has been edited, on closing the Edit Script window you must choose to save (or revert) changes to the script. This decision is not reversible—there is no further opportunity to cancel and discard changes when closing the ScriptMaker window. Significantly, this means that only scripts that are being edited are locked, making it possible for multiple users to edit different scripts at the same time in the same (hosted) file.

## FIGURE 4.11

Grouped Scripts available as submenus on the Scripts menu.

## Automatic Resizing of Layout Objects

New in FileMaker Pro 9 is the ability to instruct layout objects to move or resize when the window they are in is enlarged above its minimum size. By *minimum size*, we mean the dimensions required to display the contents of the layout.

So that you can control how objects will behave when the window is enlarged, FileMaker 9 includes additional settings on the Object Info palette.

> **NOTE** The Object Info palette can be displayed by choosing View ➪ Object Info while in Layout mode.

In the past, FileMaker layout objects have always remained in the same position with respect to the top-left corner of the layout. In FileMaker 9, this is their default behavior and is represented by anchor points at the top and left of the Autoresize controls, as shown in Figure 4.12.

## FIGURE 4.12

New Autoresize controls on the Object Info palette.

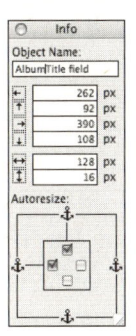

Changing the anchor points for a selected layout object modifies its behavior in the following ways:

- Disabling all the anchor checkboxes causes the object to retain its position with respect to the center of the layout area.

- Disabling both vertical or both horizontal anchors causes the object to retain its position with respect to the center of the screen on the corresponding (vertical or horizontal) axis.

- Enabling only the right or bottom anchor checkboxes results in the object maintaining a fixed position with respect to the right or bottom sides of the window, if the window is enlarged above the minimum dimensions of the layout.

- Enabling both the left and right anchor settings or the top and bottom anchor settings causes the object to resize (on the relevant axes) if the window is resized above the minimum dimensions of the layout.

By manipulating these controls, you can modify the behavior of layout elements so that they will selectively grow or reposition with changes in the window size. A particularly useful aspect of the way this feature works is that portals, when resized vertically, acquire additional rows.

**CROSS-REF** For a more in-depth discussion of the use of the layout resizing capabilities of FileMaker Pro 9, refer to Chapter 10.

# Enhanced Tab Control

The *tab control* object introduced in FileMaker Pro 8 radically changed the rules for layout design and was welcomed by users and developers alike. FileMaker 9 brings several important enhancements to the ways in which tab controls can be set up and how they behave.

## Default tab selection

Within the Tab Control Setup dialog (see Figure 4.13), you can now specify a default front tab. When a layout is first displayed, the selected tab appears at the front of the tab control. This is a significant improvement over the provision in previous versions. In the past, the default tab was whichever tab was frontmost when the layout was last visited in Layout mode.

**FIGURE 4.13**

The FileMaker Pro 9 Tab Control Setup dialog.

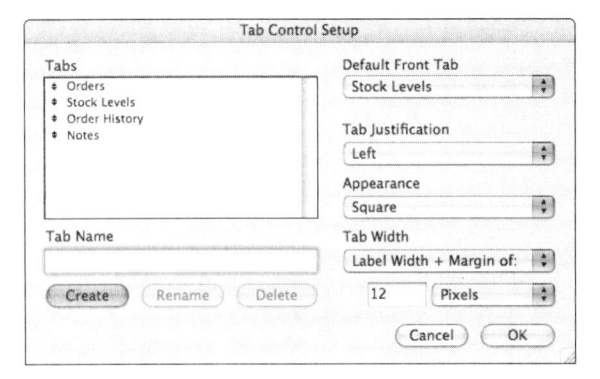

## Tab width settings

Equally significant is the inclusion of a new set of controls that provide options for tab widths to be based on individual tab label widths, with or without a margin, the width of the widest label, or fixed or minimum width settings.

You can see the new controls for tab width in the lower right of the dialog featured in Figure 4.13.

# Web Viewer Feature Enhancements

If you've worked extensively with the *Web viewer* object since its introduction in version 8.5, you will have noted several respects in which familiar browser experience of the Web was not available to users via the Web viewer. A number of these key limitations have been addressed with the release of FileMaker Pro 9.

## Progress indicator, location, lock icon

To provide users with a visual indicator that shows the progress of loading content from a URL, you should select the Display Progress Bar checkbox at the lower left of the Web Viewer Setup dialog (see Figure 4.14). The resulting indicator appears as a horizontal band across the bottom of the Web viewer, as shown in Figure 4.15.

## What's New in FileMaker 9 | 4

**FIGURE 4.14**

The FileMaker Pro 9 Web Viewer Setup dialog.

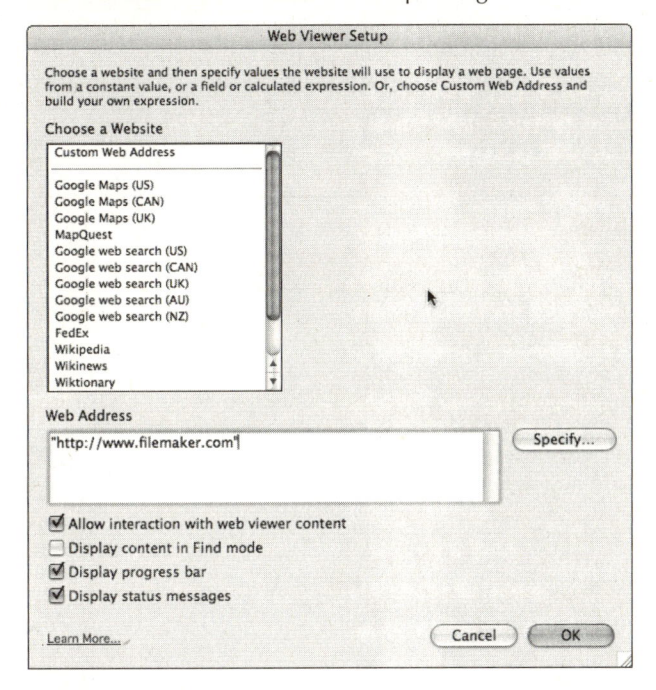

**FIGURE 4.15**

The lock icon, progress bar, and location displayed on a Web viewer.

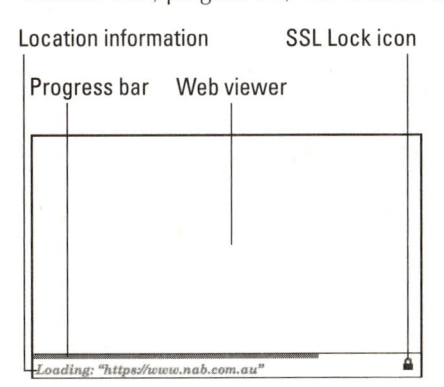

In addition, by selecting the Display Status Messages dialog, you can provide an additional band below the progress indicator to display the location of the page being loaded. This additional band also displays a lock icon when a site providing SSL security is loaded.

## Support for data URLs

A further Web viewer object feature available in FileMaker Pro 9 is support for data URLs. What this means is that source code formed as HTML or other Web-compliant technologies (JavaScript, CSS, and so on) can be passed to a Web viewer directly, instead of being sourced from a network location. This means that you can define calculations that determine what appears in a Web viewer — and the Web view updates dynamically when the calculation is re-evaluated. Although limited use of these techniques was possible in FileMaker 8.5, this capability is now fully supported in version 9.

**CROSS-REF** You can find additional detail about the use of data URLs in Chapter 10.

# Field-Specific Enabling of Visual Spell-Checking

The capability to set up your solution files to underscore questionable spellings automatically within database fields has been a useful interface option. Until now, however, this option has applied on a per-file basis — all or nothing. Since many database text fields hold names, addresses, codes, or other values that don't appear in conventional language dictionaries, the feature has not been suitable for all cases.

FileMaker 9 includes an option within the Field Behavior dialog (see Figure 4.16) to disable visual spell-checking for individual fields.

**FIGURE 4.16**

The Do Not Apply Visual Spell-Checking checkbox in the Field Behavior dialog.

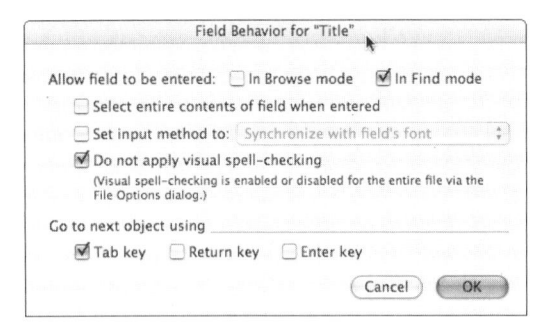

To access visual spell-checking, follow these steps:

1. Choose File ➪ File Options.
2. Select the Spelling tab.
3. Enable the Indicate Questionable Spellings with Special Underline option.
4. Enter Layout mode, and select a field in which you don't want underlines to appear.

## What's New in FileMaker 9   4

5. Choose Format ⇨ Field Control ⇨ Behavior.
6. In the resulting dialog, enable the Do Not Apply Visual Spell-Checking checkbox.

# Multiple Levels of Text Undo and Redo in Fields and ScriptMaker

Bringing FileMaker into line with many other desktop applications, version 9 introduces multilevel undo and redo capabilities within the constraints of a field (in Browse mode) or text object (in Layout mode).

FileMaker 9's undo capabilities work independently of the record revert and commit options and are available during the editing of a specific text element (field or layout text object). After you leave the text object — for example, by tabbing to another field, navigating to a different record, or selecting another object — the edits can no longer be undone using this facility.

The multilevel undo and redo capability in FileMaker 9 is integrated within the Edit menu functionality (as shown in Figure 4.17) and associated keyboard shortcuts ⌘+Z and ⌘+Shift+Z (Ctrl+Z and Ctrl+Shift+Z in Windows).

**FIGURE 4.17**

Accessing multiple levels of undo and redo from the Edit menu.

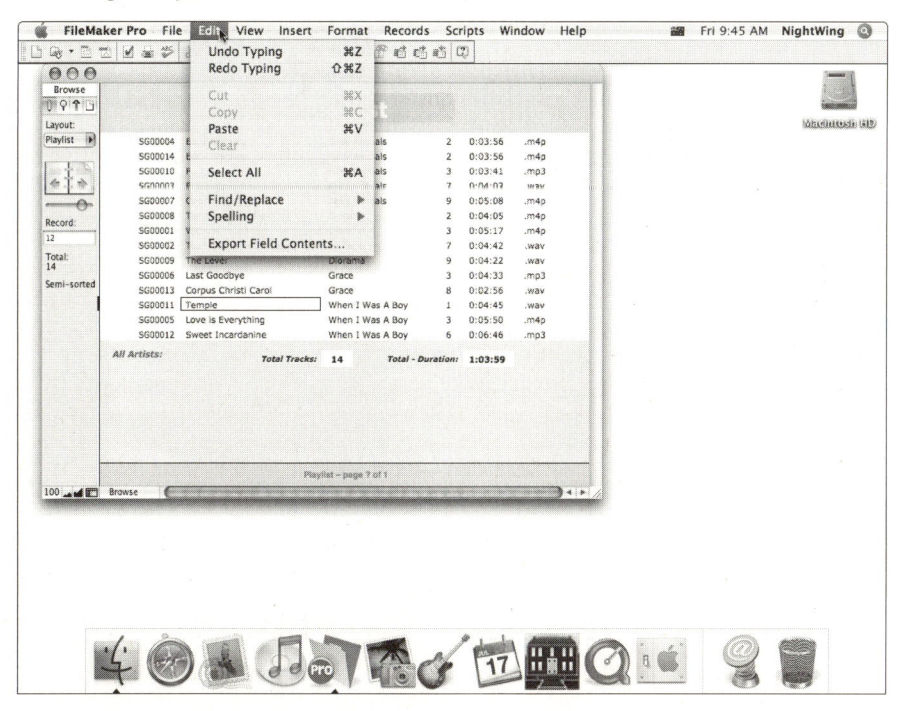

**Part I**    The Fundamentals

# Additional Toolbar Controls

With the release of previous versions of FileMaker, a number of new commands and features were added; however, the available toolbar icons did not provide access to all the new capabilities. In FileMaker 9, the toolbars have been updated to reflect the current feature set.

## Save/Send as PDF or Excel, Undo and Redo

The Standard toolbar in both Layout mode and Browse mode includes three additional command buttons, as shown in Figure 4.18. The new buttons invoke the commands to save the current found set as an Excel or PDF file, plus the new Redo command. Both the Undo and Redo buttons provide access to the multilevel undo and redo features of FileMaker 9.

## Layout alignment toolbar

In Layout mode, FileMaker 9 includes an additional toolbar called Align. The Align toolbar is shown in Figure 4.19 and includes a number of new command buttons, along with six of the buttons that formerly appeared on the Arrange toolbar.

**FIGURE 4.18**

Additional buttons on the Standard toolbar in FileMaker Pro 9.

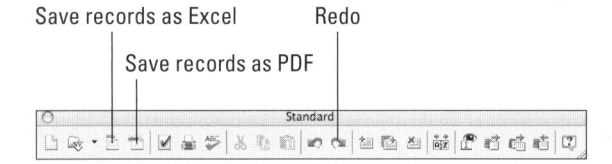

**FIGURE 4.19**

The Align toolbar in FileMaker Pro 9.

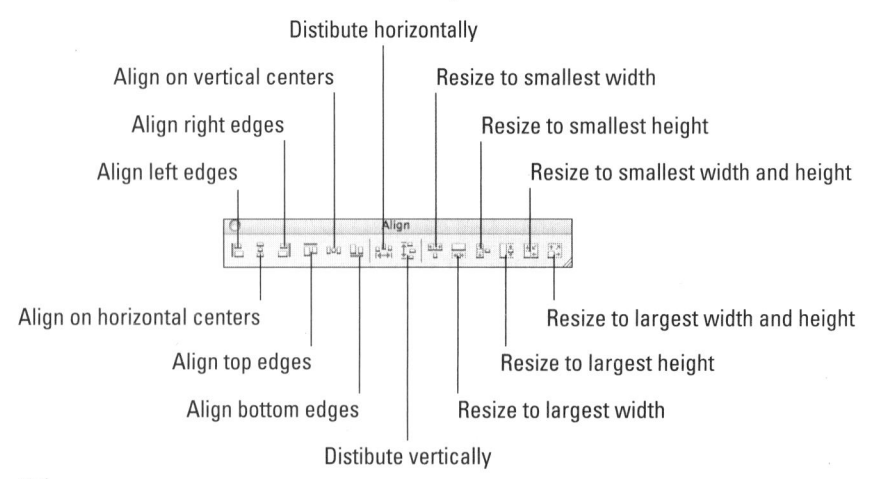

The eight new buttons that complete the complement of tools on the new Align toolbar provide convenient access to the powerful new commands such as Resize to Largest Width, Resize to Largest Height, Resize to Smallest Width, and Resize to Smallest Height — great timesavers during development.

## Additional Avery Label Formats

When you create a new layout in FileMaker, one of the available options is to format the layout to produce labels in any of a range of standard formats. In particular, FileMaker provides preformatted options for many of the popular stock label formats from Avery.

FileMaker Pro 9 includes layout options for the following new Avery label stock formats:

- Avery 5126
- Avery 5263
- Avery 5264
- Avery 6572
- Avery 6578
- Avery 8161
- Avery 8164
- Avery 8167

With the inclusion of these additional layout options, the number of supported formats for label layouts has been increased to 131.

## Enhanced External SQL Data Source Support

Perhaps the most radical innovation in the FileMaker 9 release is the inclusion of support for External SQL (ODBC) Data Sources. Although some ODBC capability has been available in previous versions, the FileMaker 9 implementation is significantly different. FileMaker 9 enables you to place tables from supported SQL databases onto the Relationships Graph in your solution and work with them in FileMaker as you would with any external table. Previously, this kind of external data functionality was available only for tables that were located within external FileMaker files.

Because external data in FileMaker 9 can come from various places, not just from other FileMaker files, the links to external data that were previously called File References are now called External Data Sources and may include any mix of tables located in FileMaker (`.fp7` format) or in any of the supported SQL applications, as shown at Figure 4.20.

**Part I** **The Fundamentals**

### FIGURE 4.20

The Manage Data Sources dialog, showing a combination of FileMaker and SQL data sources.

For the initial release of this functionality, the officially supported External SQL Data Sources are

- MySQL 5.0 Community Edition (free)
- Oracle 9g
- Oracle 10g
- SQL Server 2000
- SQL Server 2005

**NOTE** Before you can add a supported ODBC data source to your FileMaker solution, you must first install an appropriate ODBC driver and create an ODBC Data Source Name (DSN). The DSN will then enable you to access tables located in the selected SQL application.

## What's New in FileMaker 9

After you've defined external data sources via the Manage External Data Sources dialog (refer to Figure 4.20), you can select them when adding table occurrences to the Relationships Graph within your solution. You can use SQL tables — that have been added to the graph in this way — in relationships and as the basis of layouts and portals throughout your solution, just as you use external FileMaker tables.

With an external SQL table added to the Relationships Graph in your solution, as shown in Figure 4.21, live data from the remote system will integrate seamlessly with your FileMaker data. Users will be able to perform finds, sort, and print. If access privileges to the remote SQL database permit, users can add and delete records and edit values in the same way they can when the data resides within FileMaker.

**CROSS-REF** For additional details about configuring and working with External SQL Data Sources, refer to Chapter 7.

**FIGURE 4.21**

An External SQL table added to the FileMaker Relationships Graph.

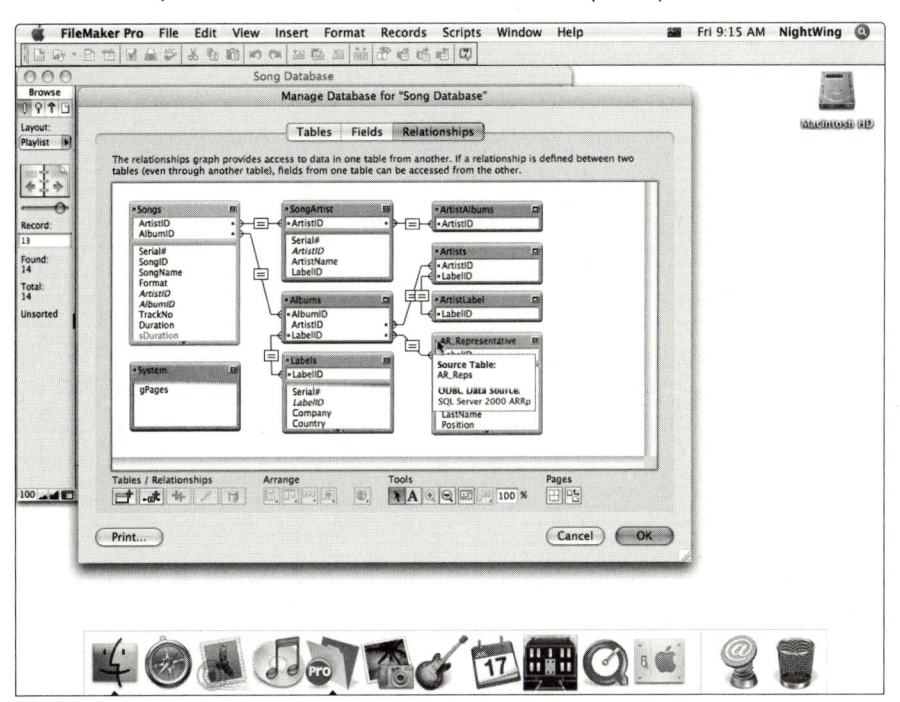

# Supplemental Fields for ESS Tables

When users work with tables located in external SQL databases, FileMaker's capabilities are available. Users can interact seamlessly with data regardless of its origins. A few notable differences between the behavior of SQL data and FileMaker data exist, however. For instance, field indexes in the SQL database may not operate in the same way as FileMaker indexes — it is common for indexing in SQL systems to be case sensitive. Finds and relationships that target SQL data are constrained by the indexing systems in operation in the SQL database.

Frequently, SQL databases you work with may be administered by someone else, so you may not have access to make changes to the schema (field and table definitions, and so on). Moreover, SQL databases do not provide the same calculation and summary field functionality that is available in FileMaker — the essential elements that you can use to create reports and display derived data values. To address this, FileMaker enables you to define unstored calculations and summary fields within your solution, to extend the capabilities of external SQL data tables you're using.

## Creating supplemental fields

When you add a SQL table to the Relationships Graph of your solution, the table automatically also appears in the Tables tab of the Manage Database dialog. When you select the table within the Manage Database dialog's Fields tab, you're presented with a list of the remote SQL table's fields (name, type, and other details appear in italic font in the list). You aren't able to make changes to fields located in an External SQL Data Source — you can delete them so that they no longer appear in the FileMaker solution, but this does not remove them from the external table.

**NOTE** For tables that reside in an External SQL Data Source, the Fields tab of the Manage Database dialog includes a Sync button (see Figure 4.22), which can be used to update the representation of the table in FileMaker to match the current SQL table definitions. If you've deleted fields from the FileMaker view of a SQL table, the Sync button will restore them.

Although, as noted earlier, you can't make changes to a remote table; you can define auto-enter or validation options, which will be applied when creating or editing records in the remote table via FileMaker. This is done from the Manage Database dialog's Fields tab in the same way as for fields within FileMaker tables.

From the Fields tab, you can also add supplemental fields to a table sourced from a SQL database. As shown in Figure 4.22, the available field type options are unstored calculations and Summary fields and, when added, they can be configured in the same way as for a local FileMaker table.

## Using supplemental fields

In any situation where you use unstored calculations or summary fields in a FileMaker table, you can use supplemental fields in an External SQL Data Source table. You can you use supplemental calculations to perform math operations and text calculations on data within the SQL table, or to aggregate data from other tables (either SQL tables or FileMaker tables) via relationships you've added to the Relationships Graph in your solution.

## What's New in FileMaker 9   4

**FIGURE 4.22**

Adding supplemental fields to an External SQL Data Source table.

Summary fields added as supplemental fields in an External SQL Data Source table will perform their aggregating action on the found set within the SQL table, just as they would if you created them in a local table. On layouts based on a table occurrence that is based on a SQL table, you can use summary fields within sub-summary parts. When the SQL data is sorted appropriately in your FileMaker window (choose Records ➪ Sort Records), the data will be summarized in subgroups in conventional FileMaker fashion.

## Considering design

It is important to recognize that the support for External SQL Data Sources operates within some clearly defined limits. FileMaker does not provide a full-featured front end for SQL systems, because it lacks the ability to create or modify SQL schema — moreover finds, sorts, and relationships are managed using FileMaker conventions rather than SQL statements.

One of the key considerations when building a FileMaker solution is performance. FileMaker can store and process large quantities of data, but it does so efficiently only if you design appropriately. Similarly, when you're working with SQL data, some reasonable limits should be placed on the use of features that will limit performance. For example, summary fields are well suited to operations

## Part I  The Fundamentals

on found sets of moderate size; however, in a table holding 30 million records, you should expect it to take a long time to return a result, regardless of whether the table is located within FileMaker or an External SQL Data Source. Comparable constraints apply to find and sort operations, as well as evaluations of calculations or relationships involving large record sets.

We recommend that you approach solution design when working with SQL data with the same expectations for performance as you would any FileMaker system. That is, the ability to connect to large-scale SQL databases should not be viewed as an opportunity to operate a FileMaker solution beyond the reasonable limits for which it is designed. However, with careful implementation, FileMaker's new capabilities will open up many opportunities for integrating systems and solving data problems.

# FileMaker Pro 9 Advanced

Many of the changes and additions in FileMaker 9 apply equally to the FileMaker Pro 9 and FileMaker Pro 9 Advanced editions of the application; however, there are several significant changes and new capabilities that are specific to FileMaker Pro Advanced. The following provides a brief overview of the main Advanced-specific additions.

## Script Debugger enhancements

The first thing you'll notice about the Script Debugger is that, when it's invoked, the Script Debugger window is always visible (although when no script is running it will be empty). If you click the Close button on the Script Debugger window, the Script Debugger option is automatically disabled. Thus, you'll always know whether the Debugger is active or not according to whether its window is on display. Moreover, the Script Debugger menu item remains accessible even when no files are open so you can now enable the debugger before you open a file (for example, to debug the startup script).

A further significant change to the Script Debugger's behavior is that if its window is closed before a script has completed, the script will run to its conclusion after the Debugger window is dismissed. Previously, closing the Debugger window terminated the script immediately. Conversely, the Debugger may be invoked even while a script is running — in which case the script will be paused and the next step (the step about to be executed) will be selected in the Debugger window.

### Launching scripts from within the Script Debugger

Scripts may be opened for viewing or editing from the Active Scripts list (by double-clicking their entry in the list), and they will open without terminating the currently running script. Multiple script editor windows can be open simultaneously while the script is still in progress in the Debugger. Changes may be made to the open scripts; however, *saving* a change to any of the active scripts will halt the currently running script.

## Working with restricted-access scripts

When a script is designated to run with login accounts that don't have full access privileges (that is, it's set as "executable only" for the privilege sets assigned to those accounts), you'll nevertheless need to use the Debugger to view it in operation under the access privilege conditions in which users will encounter it. In the past, the Debugger only worked when you were logged in with a [Full Access] account, so debugging under restricted access conditions was not possible.

As shown in Figure 4.23, the Script Debugger in FileMaker Pro 9 Advanced presents an option to authenticate with a full-access password in order to debug while logged in with restricted access. Clicking the padlock icon near the upper left of the window presents you with a login prompt. After authenticating with a [Full Access] login and password, you will be able to observe how the script operates under restricted access.

**FIGURE 4.23**
The Script Debugger option to debug a restricted access script.

Debugger authentication applies only for viewing/using the Debugger and the Data Viewer — it does not modify your access privileges elsewhere in the file, or change its behavior in any other respect.

The authentication is valid only for the current file for the duration of the current debugging session — if you close the debugger and reopen it, you'll have to authenticate again in order to debug restricted-access scripts. Alternatively, the authentication can be terminated without closing the Debugger window with a further click on the lock icon.

> **NOTE** If you de-authenticate — by clicking the lock icon, or by closing the Debugger window — all open files that are currently authenticated will be de-authenticated.

## Making multiple selections in the Script Debugger window

In FileMaker Pro 9 Advanced, you can select multiple script steps in the Script Debugger window by Shift-clicking or, for noncontiguous selections, ⌘+clicking on a Mac and Ctrl+clicking in Windows.

Because you can make multiple selections in the Script Debugger window, as shown in Figure 4.24, you can set or clear multiple breakpoints simultaneously.

**FIGURE 4.24**

Multiple selections are supported in the Script Debugger window.

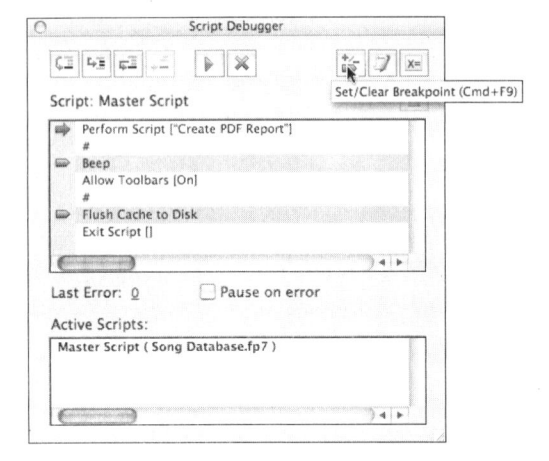

## Understanding the Pause on Error and Last Error code

The Script Debugger window in FileMaker Pro 9 Advanced automatically displays the error code returned by the most recently executed script step. This can be seen at the left immediately below the Script panel in Figure 4.24. The error value displayed updates with the execution of each command as you step through a script in the Debugger.

Additionally, the Script Debugger window provides a checkbox option to automatically pause the script when an error is encountered. If you close the Debugger window with this step enabled, the script will execute and, if an error is encountered, the script will pause and the Debugger window will reopen.

## Using step buttons when a script is paused

If a script includes a pause step, you no longer have to interrupt debugging to click the Continue button in the Status Area. In FileMaker Pro 9 Advanced, simply clicking one of the step buttons in the Script Debugger window (Step, Step Into, Step Out, or Run) advances the script past the pause command.

## Data Viewer enhancements

The Data Viewer in FileMaker Pro 9 Advanced includes some powerful new functionality, making it more agile, more useful, and more efficient. Supporting these changes, the Data Viewer now sports a tabbed interface, as shown in Figure 4.25. Its floating modeless window operation remains unchanged, however, and as in the past, the Data Viewer window may be opened and closed from a button in the Script Debugger as well as by choosing Tools ➪ Data Viewer.

With this evolution of its interface, the Data Viewer provides key additional features. We describe these new features in the following sections.

**FIGURE 4.25**

The Data Viewer Current tab in FileMaker Pro 9 Advanced.

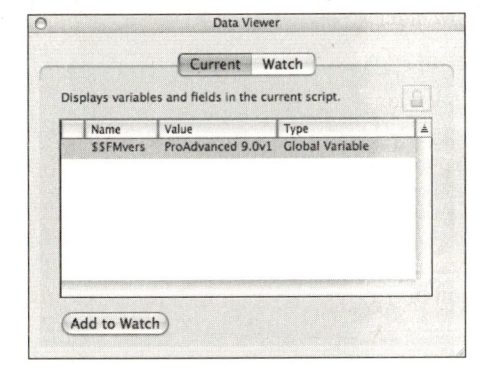

### The Current and Watch tabs

The Data Viewer's Current tab automatically loads the full complement of values (both fields and local variables) referenced in a currently running script, plus the value of any declared global variables. The fields displayed will include those that are referenced by calculation expressions throughout the script being executed, as well as fields upon which the script acts.

Values displayed in the Current tab will refresh as the script progresses and will automatically be replaced with different values — according to context — when a new script runs or when the current script concludes its run. Where a repeating data field or repeating variable is loaded into the Current tab, only those repetitions currently containing a value will be shown. However, calculation repetitions (other than the first) will not be shown until or unless they are explicitly referenced by the active script.

**NOTE** Even when no scripts are running, Global variables with a current value in the active file will be listed in the Current tab of the Data Viewer.

A button labeled Add to Watch is provided at the lower left of the Current tab. When you select an item in the Current tab and click the Add to Watch button, the value is included in the list of values being tracked in the Watch tab.

The Watch tab of the Data Viewer (shown in Figure 4.26) retains the Data Viewer functionality of previous editions of FileMaker Pro Advanced. You can manually add or remove values or expressions at will. Additions to the Watch tab persist until you remove them.

**FIGURE 4.26**

The Watch tab of the Data Viewer in FileMaker Pro 9 Advanced.

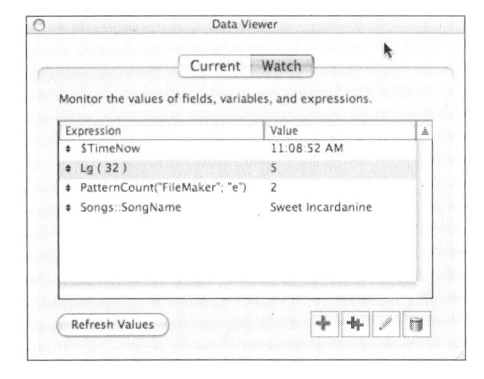

### Authenticating to view-restricted data

On the Current tab of the Data Viewer, as with the Script Debugger, you can now authenticate the Data Viewer and have it display values with full access even while running a script to which your access is restricted under current user access privileges. A lock icon appearing at the upper right of the Current tab controls the authentication option.

**NOTE** Authentication or de-authentication in the Script Debugger window also automatically authenticates/de-authenticates the Current tab of the Data Viewer — and vice-versa.

### Identifying other usability improvements

There are several additional enhancements to the Data Viewer's operation:

- You can now sort columns in both tabs of the Data Viewer by clicking their column header.
- Hovering the mouse over a line in either tab of the Data Viewer invokes a tooltip displaying its value in full.
- Double-clicking a line in the Current tab of the Data Viewer exposes its value without truncation in a further dialog (see Figure 4.27).

## What's New in FileMaker 9

**FIGURE 4.27**

The Current Value dialog exposes a Data Viewer value without truncation.

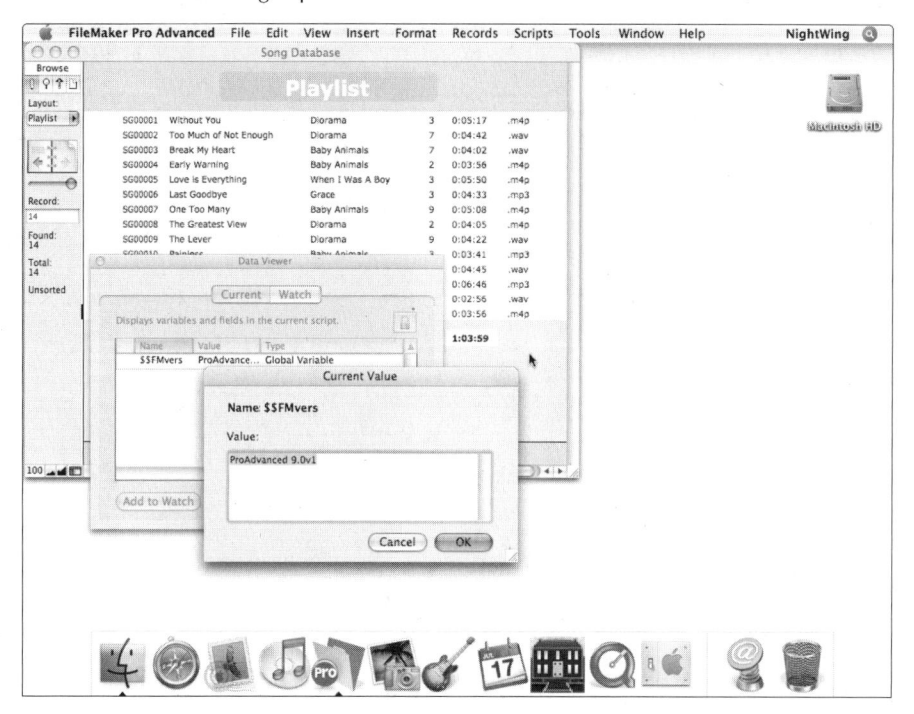

### The PHP Site Assistant

Bringing a new level of integration with Web-enabling tools, FileMaker Pro 9 Advanced includes a menu command to directly launch the PHP Site Assistant utility.

> **NOTE** The link to the PHP Site Assistant requires that the file be hosted with FileMaker Server 9, and the file must have the PHP (fmphp) extended privilege (also new in FileMaker 9) enabled.

To access this feature you must open the remote file using FileMaker Pro 9 Advanced and choose Tools ➪ Launch PHP Assistant, as shown in Figure 4.28.

87

**Part I** — **The Fundamentals**

### FIGURE 4.28

The Tools menu provides direct access to the PHP Assistant utility.

## Database Design Report enhancements

The Database Design Report in FileMaker Pro 9 Advanced has been updated to accommodate the range of additional capabilities introduced in version 9. Design specifications now document the following additional elements:

- External SQL data tables
- New calculation functions:
  ```
  Get(TemporaryPath)
  Get(HostApplicationVersion)
  Self
  Asin(number)
  Acos(number)
  ```
- Supplemental fields
- Script groups
- Default tab and width properties
- Conditional formatting
- Auto-resizing layout objects
- New Web Viewer setup options
- The Append to Existing File option for the Save Records as PDF script step

# Part II

# Introduction to Database Design

In this part, you dig in and get your hands dirty creating a working database. Throughout this book, we describe the development of an example Inventory system; this part is where we begin the project.

Starting with a fairly simple shell, our Inventory example grows as we develop it by adding new input and search capabilities, enhance the interface, automate repetitive tasks, and add powerful security and reporting features. Although this part lays foundations for the later chapters in this book, at the end of this part, you'll have the essentials of a usable solution and a collection of techniques to employ in your own solutions.

### IN THIS PART

**Chapter 5**
**Creating a Database**

**Chapter 6**
**The Interface: Layout Mode**

**Chapter 7**
**The Structure: The Manage Database Dialog**

**Chapter 8**
**The Processes: ScriptMaker**

# Chapter 5

# Creating a Database

In Part I, we provide a range of background information concerning databases, their uses, and FileMaker Pro and its role. We introduce you to many of the terms and concepts that we feature throughout this book. Much of the information thus far has been theoretical rather than practical — but that's about to change, so roll up your sleeves.

As we indicate in Chapter 3, the Quick Start window that appears when you first launch FileMaker, or when you choose File ⇨ New Database, includes lists of Starter Solutions. These Starter Solutions provide ready-made files for a range of common purposes. However, the real strength of FileMaker Pro is that it gives you the ability to custom-build a solution to meet your own needs. If a ready-made, one-size-fits-all solution were all you needed, then you could probably have found a suitable shareware solution for a few dollars and you wouldn't be reading this book.

Starter Solutions, then, are what you might use on occasions when you don't want to create a new database file (that is, when you're happy to simply use or adapt a solution that somebody else has created for you). Here, however, we lead you through the process of creating your own database from scratch, working through several stages of development to arrive at a workable and useful solution.

The example we've chosen for this exercise is the creation of a simple system to keep track of inventory. Although this is only one of the many situations where databases are useful, it clearly illustrates many of the challenges you'll encounter when building your own solutions. In fact, an inventory system that tracks products and sales has a lot in common with many other kinds of solutions, such as a school solution that tracks students and courses or a research laboratory database that tracks samples and test results.

---

**IN THIS CHAPTER**

Creating a new database file

Viewing and interacting with data

Avoiding the need for data duplication

Getting started with file security

Thinking about usability

**Part II**  Introduction to Database Design

Consequently, the techniques we cover in this chapter and throughout this book are applicable to many of the challenges you'll encounter when creating your own solutions, even though the names of the things you're tracking may be different.

## Creating a New Database File

To get started, follow these steps:

1. Launch FileMaker Pro 9 and wait until the Quick Start screen appears. If FileMaker is already running, choose File ➪ New Database to begin.

2. In the Quick Start screen, confirm that the Create Database icon is selected at the left, select the Create Empty Database radio button (see Figure 5.1), and click OK.

3. You're prompted to select a location to save the file and to supply a name. We suggest that you name the file **Inventory.fp7** and that you save the file to the Documents folder on a Mac or the My Documents folder in Windows. The database is created, its window appears, and the Manage Database for "Inventory" dialog (shown in Figure 5.2) appears.

**FIGURE 5.1**

Creating an empty database from FileMaker's Quick Start Screen.

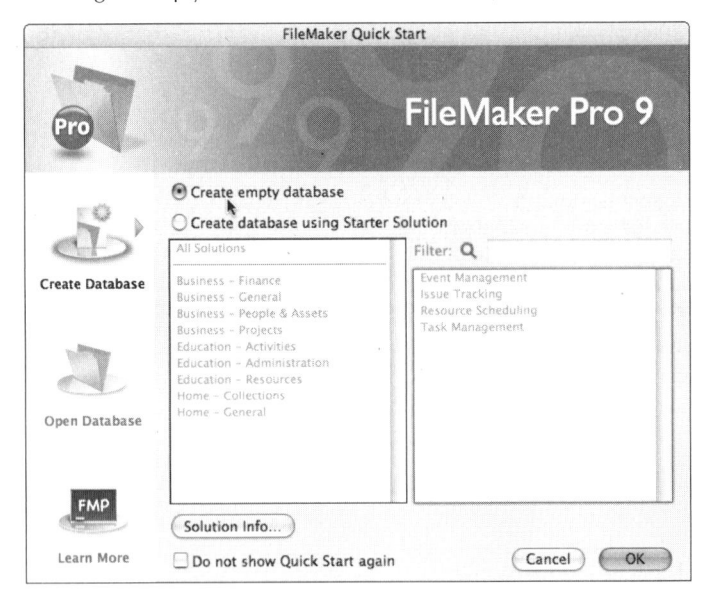

**Creating a Database** 5

**FIGURE 5.2**

The new file, showing the Manage Database for "Inventory" dialog, ready to begin.

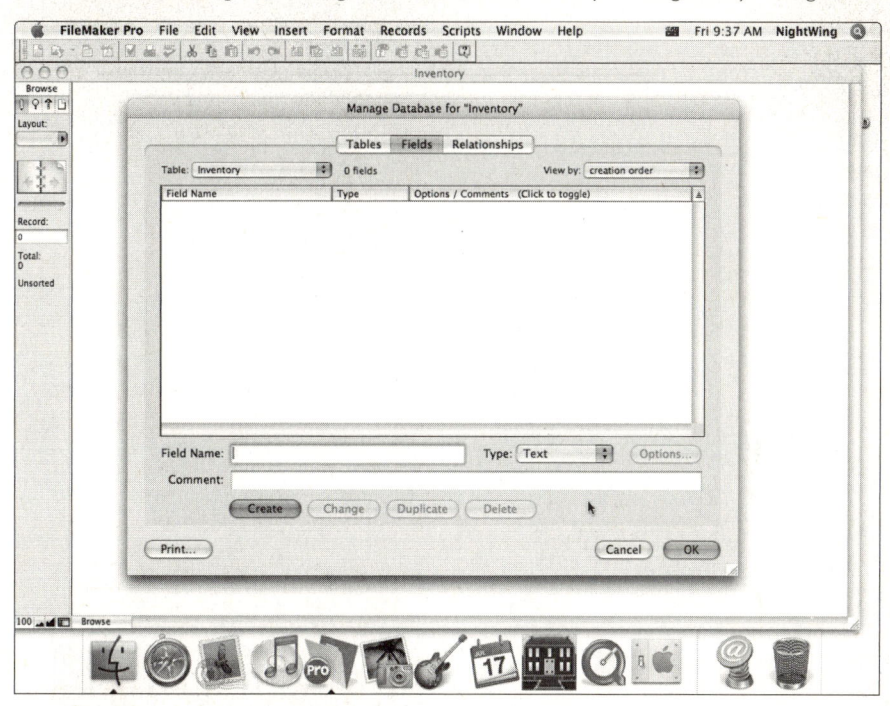

> **NOTE** All the files you create should be given an `.fp7` suffix because that's the extension used by your computer's operating system to associate files with the FileMaker Pro application.

When you create a new file in the manner just described in the preceding steps, FileMaker creates a single default table with the same name as the first part of the filename — in this case "Inventory." It then opens the Manage Database dialog to the Fields tab with the default table selected, ready for you to begin adding fields to this new empty database. (A database is not much use without fields in which you can store your data.)

93

## Adding tables and fields

Your new file is ready and waiting for you to create some fields — and nothing could be easier. To begin, follow these steps:

1. Check that the cursor is in the Field Name box, and type the name **Serial#** for the first field.

2. From the Type menu (at the right of the Field Name box), select Number, and click the Create button near the lower left of the dialog. A line appears at the top of the list of fields showing the field that you've just created.

> **TIP** You can use the keyboard to choose the Type for a field: ⌘+T or Ctrl+T for Text, ⌘+N or Ctrl+N for Number, and so forth, as you can see when the Type menu is open.

3. Repeat Steps 1 and 2 to create four additional fields, setting each as Text in the Type menu and naming these additional fields: **ItemID**, **Name**, **Description**, and **SupplierID**.

4. Create two Number fields called **Cost** and **SalePrice**, respectively. The dialog should now resemble the one shown in Figure 5.3. Above the list of fields, it shows the name of the table (Inventory) and number of fields (7), and the list of fields displays the name and type of each field in the order in which you entered them.

**FIGURE 5.3**

Creating fields in the Fields tab of the Manage Database for "Inventory" dialog.

# Creating a Database 5

> **TIP** We recommend that you leave spaces out of field names and, instead, start each new word with a capital letter. This practice is sometimes known as *camel case,* because of the shape of the word forms it produces, or as *intercapping.* Alternatively, if you prefer, you can use underscore characters instead of spaces.

Although FileMaker permits spaces in field names, some other technologies don't (Web and ODBC, for example). So one reason for omitting spaces is that you may need to pass data to another application or environment at some point. Omitting spaces also makes field names slightly shorter, which may be visually convenient in some situations.

After you enter the first few fields, you've created the basis for a single table in your new file — a place to store some data. However, to make this into a useful solution, you need additional tables to store information about what happens to each of the items listed in the main table. Because this is an inventory solution, its purpose is not simply to list the various kinds of items on hand, but to allow you to record where they come from and when, where they go to, and how many of each you have.

Therefore, to provide the basic framework for tracking inventory items, you need to record arrivals of items, departure of items, and their source and destination. At this stage, we propose that you add five more tables to start this example file. To create the additional tables, follow these steps:

1. Navigate to the Tables tab of the Manage Database for "Inventory" dialog by clicking the leftmost tab along the top of the dialog. In the Tables tab, a single table named Inventory appears in the list — as noted earlier, this is the default table (named according to the name of the file) that FileMaker creates with a new file. The Details column of the Tables list shows that the Inventory table has seven fields (these are the seven fields you've just created on the Fields tab) and zero records.

2. Check that the cursor is in the Table Name box (at the lower left of the Tables tab), and type the name Orders for the second table.

3. Click the Create button. Two lines are displayed in the list of tables — the original Inventory table, plus the Orders table you've just created.

> **TIP** If you make an error — for example, misspell a table name — simply select the table in the list, edit the name in the Table Name box, and click the Change button.

4. Repeat Steps 2 and 3 to add four more tables to the file, naming them **OrderLines**, **Invoices**, **InvoiceLines**, and **Contacts**, respectively. The dialog now resembles the one shown in Figure 5.4, with the annotation above the tables list reading "6 tables defined in this file."

95

## Part II    Introduction to Database Design

**FIGURE 5.4**

Adding tables on the Tables tab of the Manage Database for "Inventory" dialog.

Now that you have six tables, it's time to add some appropriate fields to each of them. To accomplish this, you need to select each of the new tables in turn on the Manage Database dialog's Fields tab. From the Tables tab, you can select a table and view the corresponding Fields tab by double-clicking its entry in the list of tables. When you're on the Fields tab, you can move between different tables by selecting them from the Table menu at the upper left of the Fields tab.

Follow these steps:

1. Select the Orders table on the Fields tab, using the same procedure you followed when adding fields to the Inventory table (as described earlier).
2. Add a Number field called Serial#, a Text field called OrderID, a Date field called OrderDate, a Text field called SupplierID, and a Number field called Shipping.
3. Move through the remaining four tables creating fields with name and field type as outlined in the following tables.

# Creating a Database 5

**OrderLines**

| | |
|---|---|
| Serial# | Number |
| OrdLineID | Text |
| OrderID | Text |
| Qty | Number |
| ItemID | Text |
| Price | Number |

**Invoices**

| | |
|---|---|
| Serial# | Number |
| InvoiceID | Text |
| InvoiceDate | Date |
| BuyerID | Text |
| Shipping | Number |

**InvoiceLines**

| | |
|---|---|
| Serial# | Number |
| InvLineID | Text |
| InvoiceID | Text |
| Qty | Number |
| ItemID | Text |
| Price | Number |

**Contacts**

| | |
|---|---|
| Serial# | Number |
| ContactID | Text |
| Title | Text |
| FirstName | Text |
| LastName | Text |
| Organization | Text |
| AddressLine1 | Text |
| AddressLine2 | Text |
| City | Text |
| State | Text |
| PostalCode | Text |
| ContactType | Text |
| SupplierID | Text |
| BuyerID | Text |

You've now created a basic set of data fields in each of your tables. These data fields will provide places to enter information that will accumulate, providing you with a history of items. However, there are still several additional steps to complete before your new file's data structure will be truly useful.

**TIP** If you want to take a break and continue at a later time, simply click OK to dismiss the Manage Database dialog. Then, you can close the Inventory file and quit FileMaker Pro. When you reopen the file to continue, choose File ⇨ Manage Database to take up where you left off.

## Working with the Field Options dialog: Validation and auto-entry

Some of the information required in each record in the tables you've created is routine enough that FileMaker can create it for you. The first field in each table is a serial number—a good candidate for automatic data entry. To begin setting up some automation of this kind, use the Table menu

## Part II  Introduction to Database Design

near the upper left of the Fields tab in the Manage Database dialog to return to the list of fields for the Inventory table. Then follow these steps:

1. In the Inventory table field list, select the first line — the one showing the Serial# field — and then click the Options button. The Options for Field "Serial#" dialog appears.

> **TIP** You can also invoke the Options for Field dialog by double-clicking a field in the list or by selecting the field and then using the ⌘+O (Ctrl+O) keyboard shortcut.

When the Options for Field dialog appears, it displays the first of four tabs, showing a group of controls under the heading Auto-Enter (see Figure 5.5). The Auto Enter options available on this panel include the capability to generate data in various ways; however, on this occasion, the option you require is an automatic serial number for each record.

2. To set automatic serialization of the Serial# field, follow these steps:
   - Select the Serial Number checkbox.
   - Leave Generate set to the default On Creation.
   - Make sure Next Value and Increment By are both set to 1.
   - Select the Prohibit Modification of Value during Data Entry checkbox.

Once configured, the dialog should resemble the one pictured in Figure 5.5.

**FIGURE 5.5**

The Auto-Enter tab of the Options for Field dialog.

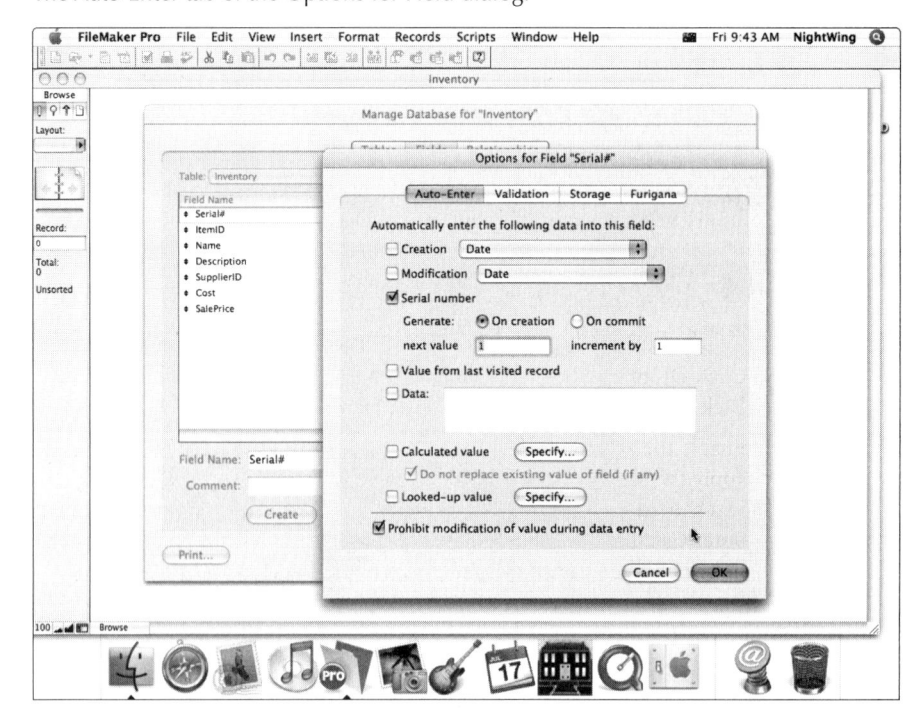

3. Click OK to accept the settings and dismiss the dialog. When the Options for Field dialog is closed and you're back in the Manage Database for "Inventory" dialog, the Options/Comments column of the field list includes the details of the settings you've applied to the Serial# field. If you completed this step correctly, beside the Serial# field it will say Auto Enter Serial, Can't Modify Auto. If it doesn't say this, you've missed a step, and you need to return to the Options for Field dialog to rectify it.

The next field in the Inventory table is named ItemID and has been defined as a text field. At this point, you may be wondering why we have suggested that you create both a serial number field and a separate ID field. Our reasoning is that for some purposes a numeric serial is useful, while for other purposes a text identifier is preferable. So as a matter of course, it's good practice to create both at the outset for each table. Doing so gives you choices and flexibility later on.

**CROSS-REF** For a more detailed discussion of the use of serial and text values as primary record identifiers (keys), refer to the section on alternative relationship techniques in Chapter 11.

To tie the values of the first two fields together, we recommend that the ID field be based on the Serial number field. That way, you can be confident that the two will never fall out of step — and knowing one, you'll be able to infer the value of the other. Follow these steps:

1. Select the ItemID field, and click the Options button. The Options for Field "ItemID" dialog appears.

2. Select the Calculated Value checkbox in the Auto-Enter panel. Another dialog appears, prompting you to specify what the calculated value should be. Shortly, we discuss the use of this dialog in more detail. For now, just place the cursor in the main text area in the lower part of the dialog, and enter the following formula:

   ```
   SerialIncrement("ITM00000"; Serial#)
   ```

   With the formula in place, the Specify Calculation dialog should look like the one shown in Figure 5.6.

**CROSS-REF** For in-depth explorations of the creation and use of calculations, such as the one shown here, refer to Chapters 7 and 13.

**NOTE** What this particular calculation does is create IDs consisting of "ITM" followed by the serial number, with the serial number padded, if necessary, by leading zeroes to guarantee ItemIDs of at least eight characters in length.

3. Click OK to accept the formula and dismiss the Specify Calculation dialog. You're now back at the Options for Field "ItemID" dialog.

4. Enable the Prohibit Modification of Value during Data Entry checkbox and click OK to apply the selected options. In the list of fields showing in the Manage Database dialog, you should now see, in the Options/Comments area adjacent to the ItemID field, Auto Enter Calculation, Can't Modify Auto. If you don't see this, retrace your steps to ensure that you've completed the procedure we've outlined.

### FIGURE 5.6

Specifying the Auto-Entry calculation formula for the ItemID field in the Inventory table.

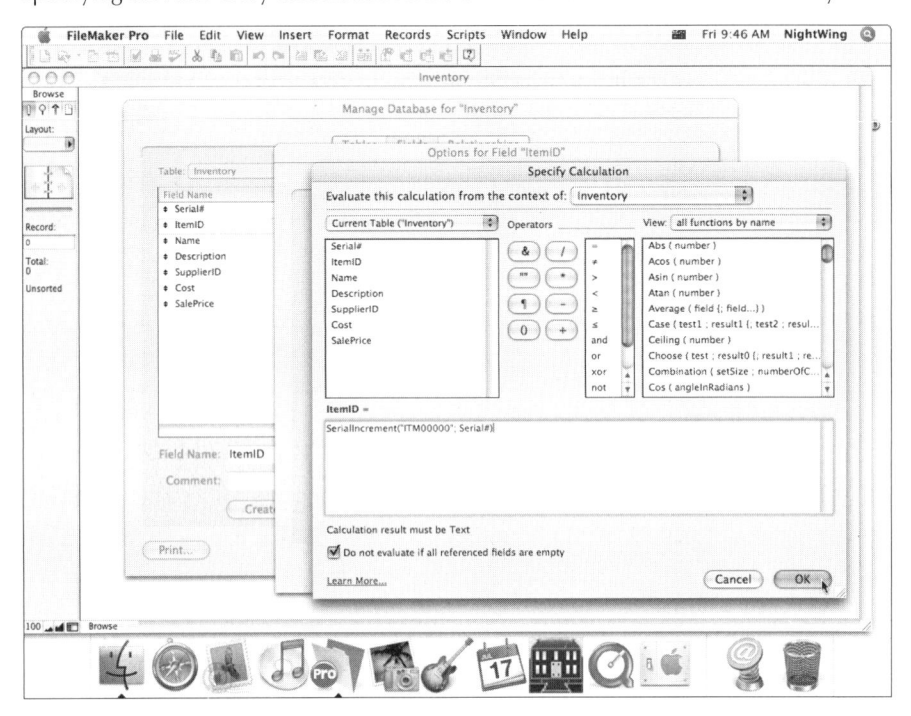

> **TIP** If you haven't entered the formula exactly as it is shown in Step 2 of this list, or if your field names don't match the ones we've indicated, an error dialog will prevent you from closing the Specify Calculation dialog. If that occurs, check the formula and make sure the field names used match the names of the fields as you entered them in the Manage Database dialog.

When you've successfully completed the preceding set of steps, repeat the process for the first two fields of each table you've created. In each case, however, vary the prefix appearing at the start of the formula for the ID field to provide an appropriate mnemonic for the table in question. We suggest using the following formulas:

| Field | Formula |
| --- | --- |
| OrderID | SerialIncrement("ORD00000"; Serial#) |
| OrdLineID | SerialIncrement("OLN0000000"; Serial#) |
| InvoiceID | SerialIncrement("INV00000"; Serial#) |
| InvLineID | SerialIncrement("ILN0000000"; Serial#) |
| ContactID | SerialIncrement("CT00000"; Serial#) |

## Creating a Database    5

> **NOTE** Although some of the tables include more than one ID field, only the first ID field in each table — the primary key for the table — should be configured as outlined here.

Now that you've set up the serial and ID fields, the next step is to add validation rules. For example, it makes no sense to add an inventory item without providing a name for it, so it would be appropriate to make the Inventory::Name field a required value.

> **NOTE** The standard convention for referring to a field in FileMaker is to provide the table name, followed by a pair of colons, and then the field name. The table name used for this purpose is the name given to the relevant table reference (usually called a *Table Occurrence* or TO) in FileMaker's Relationships Graph. In a new file, however, the table occurrence names default to the same names as the corresponding table (as in the instance cited earlier).

To set up suitable validation for the inventory table's Name field, follow these steps:

1. Select the Inventory table on the Fields tab of the Manage Database dialog (for example, by selecting Inventory from the Table menu at the upper left of the dialog), and then double-click the Name field. The Options for Field "Name" dialog appears. You want to guarantee that the user enters a name for every item carried in inventory.

2. In the Options for Field "Name" dialog, select the Validation tab and select the Not Empty checkbox.

3. Select the Display Custom Message If Validation Fails checkbox and enter the following message into the text area below it:

   `You are required to enter a name for this item!`

   The dialog should match the one shown in Figure 5.7.

4. When you're satisfied that the configuration is complete, click OK to accept the settings and dismiss the Options for Field dialog. In the Manage Database dialog, you should now see that the Options/Comments column adjacent to the Name field displays the legend Required Value, Allow Override, Message. If you don't see this, retrace your steps to ensure that you haven't omitted anything.

5. Navigate to the field list for the Contacts table, select the ContactType field, and click the Options button. The Options for Field dialog appears.

6. Click the Validation tab and select the Member of Value List checkbox.

7. Select the Manage Value Lists option from the Member of Value List menu.

8. In the Manage Value Lists for "Inventory" dialog, click the New button. The Edit Value List dialog appears.

9. Enter **ContactType** in the Value List Name box at the top of the dialog.

101

### Part II  Introduction to Database Design

#### FIGURE 5.7
Specifying validation rules for the Name field in the Inventory table.

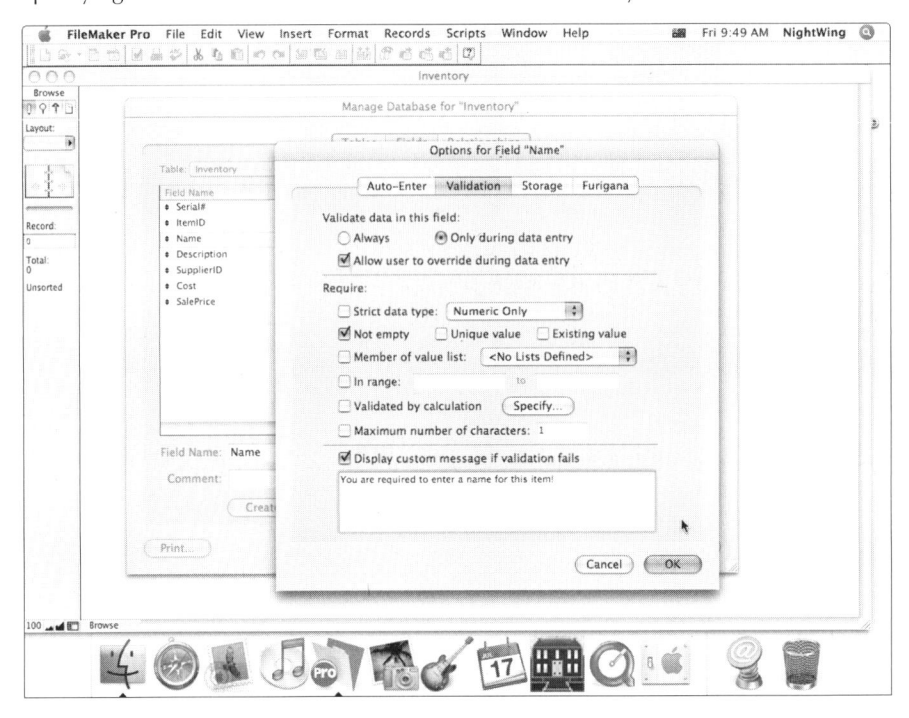

10. Enter the words **Supplier** and **Buyer** on separate lines within the custom values area at the lower left of the dialog. Figure 5.8 shows how the Edit Value List dialog should now look.

> **TIP** Do not press Return/Enter after the final entry in your list of values, or FileMaker will include an extra, empty value in the list.

11. Click OK to accept the settings and dismiss the dialog.
12. Click OK in the Manage Value Lists dialog to accept and dismiss it.
13. Click OK in the Options for Field "Contact Type" dialog to return to the Manage Database dialog.
14. In the field list adjacent to the ContactType field, the text By Value List, Allow Override should now be showing.

## Creating a Database 5

**FIGURE 5.8**

Creating a value list for validation of the ContactType field.

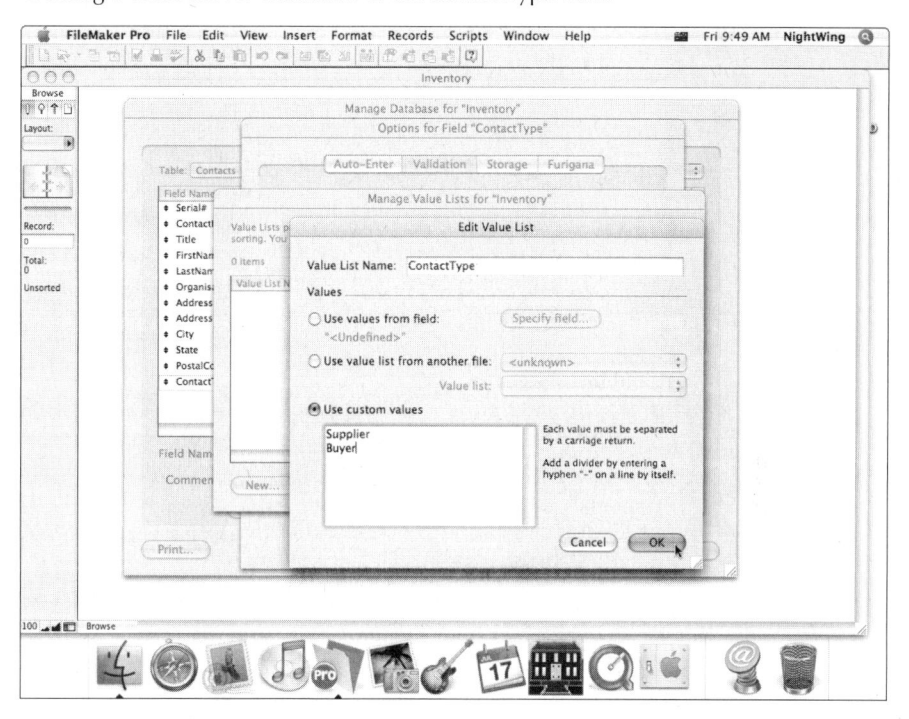

You've now established some initial auto-entry and validation configurations for the new database. However, some additional settings will depend on creating relationships between the tables, so they can't be added yet. We'll provide you with instructions for the remaining auto-entry options after describing some basic calculation and relationship configurations.

## Setting up simple calculations

In addition to automatically entering data into some of the fields, you'll want some data to be calculated from the information you enter. To create such a calculation, follow these steps:

1. Select the OrderLines table from the Table menu at the top left of the Manage Database dialog's Fields tab.
2. In the Field Name box, enter **cLineTotal**.
3. From the Type menu select Calculation (⌘+L or Ctrl+L).
4. Click the Create button. The Specify Calculation dialog appears.

103

**Part II**  Introduction to Database Design

> **TIP** We have prepended a lowercase *c* to the field name so that we'll be reminded at all times that the field is a calculation field type (that is, it can only acquire information via internal calculation, not by data entry, import, or any other means). Although prepending the lowercase *c* is not essential, conventions of this sort can prove helpful as your databases become more complex. (In programming circles, this convention is called *Hungarian notation*—the use of leading characters in an identifier name to convey data type information.)

In the Specify Calculation dialog, you see a list of fields at the upper left, a list of functions at the upper right, and, between them, buttons showing mathematical symbols and operators (add, multiply, divide, and so on).

5. Double-click the Qty field in the fields list. It appears in the calculation formula box in the lower part of the dialog.
6. Click the multiplication symbol button (*).
7. Double-click the Price field in the fields list. You should see a complete formula in the calculation area, as follows (see Figure 5.9):

   ```
   Qty * Price
   ```

8. When you've confirmed that the formula is correct, click OK to accept and dismiss the Specify Calculation dialog. The Type and Options/Comments columns adjacent to the new cLineTotal field should now show:

   ```
   Calculation = Qty * Price
   ```

**FIGURE 5.9**

Specifying a calculation formula for the cLineTotal field in the OrderLines table.

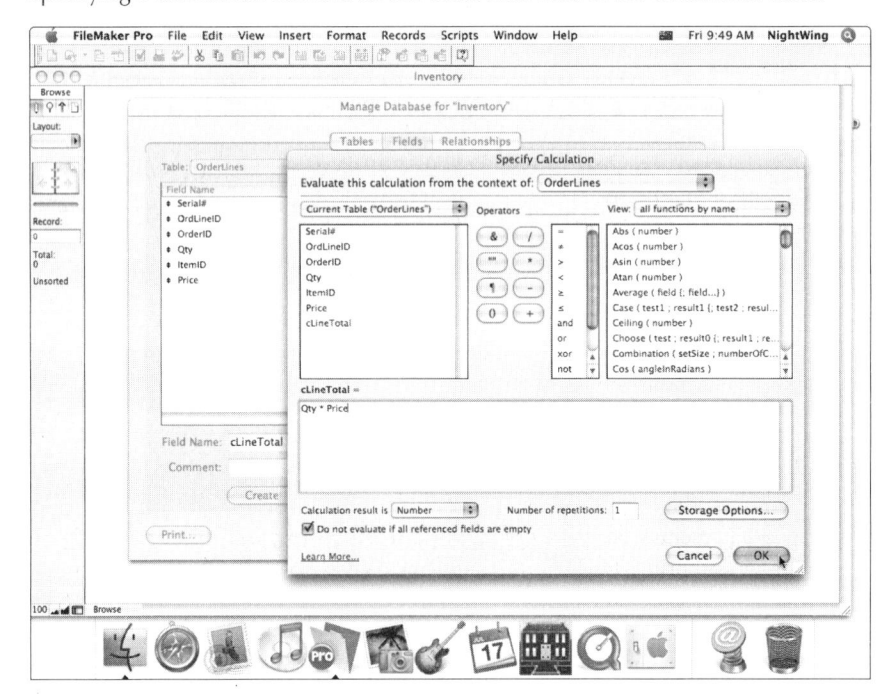

104

## Creating a Database — 5

**NOTE:** The calculation you've just created is an instruction to multiply the quantity by the price. In other words, the number found in the quantity field will be multiplied by the number found in the price field on each record to return a total for that record. Although you selected the field names from a list, you could have typed them in if you knew what they were.

Although this is a very straightforward computation performing a very simple math operation, the calculation capabilities of FileMaker are extensive, as you'll discover in later chapters. Many forms of manipulating and formatting numbers, text, dates, times, and other data types are possible.

9. Now repeat Steps 2 through 8 to create a cLineTotal field along similar lines (same field name and same formula) in the InvoiceLines table.

**TIP:** If you're using FileMaker Pro 9 Advanced, you don't have to repeat the procedure to create a line total calculation in the InvoiceLines table. Instead, you can copy and paste the field from the OrderLines table. Copying and pasting of fields in the Manage Database dialog is not available in FileMaker Pro 9.

10. Using a variation on the technique described earlier, go to the Contacts field list, select the SupplierID field, and call up the Options dialog.

11. On the Auto-Entry tab, select the Calculated Value checkbox. The Specify Calculation dialog appears.

12. Enter the formula

    `If(PatternCount(ContactType; "Supplier"); ContactID)`

    and click OK.

13. Uncheck the Do Not Replace Existing Value of Field (If Any) checkbox, and click OK. This ensures that the Supplier ID value will only exist if the contact is listed as a supplier.

**NOTE:** In FileMaker Pro's calculation syntax, a conditional expression is of the form `If (condition; then-clause; else-clause)` where the `then` clause is executed when the condition is true and the optional `else` clause is executed when the condition is false. Therefore, in the foregoing example, if the character string `"Supplier"` is present in the `ContactType` field, the `ContactID` is placed in the `SupplierID` field; otherwise, the field's value is left unchanged.

14. Repeat Steps 10 through 13 for the BuyerID field, this time entering the formula

    `If(PatternCount(ContactType; "Buyer"); ContactID)`

    With both of these formulae in place, a contact can be either a supplier or a buyer, depending on the value entered into the ContactType field.

15. Create a calculation field called cFullName in the Contacts table with the formula

    `FirstName & " " & LastName`

16. Set the calculation result type for the cFullName field to Text using the Calculation Result Is menu near the lower left of the Specify Calculation dialog, and click OK. This calculation brings together the text elements of the name on each record, for convenient display in lists and reports.

**Part II**    Introduction to Database Design

## Capturing simple metadata

As part of the process of tracking what's happening with your data, it's often helpful to have some additional fields that store reference information. This information can assist you in troubleshooting a problem, if you need to compare two versions of a database file, or if you need to synchronize two copies of your data.

To facilitate such tracking, follow these steps:

1. Return to the field list for the Inventory table (on the Fields tab of the Manage Database dialog) and create a new text field called _GenAccount. This field will be used to track the account associated with the genesis (or generation, if you prefer) of each record. Note that we are suggesting an underscore prefix for your metadata fields to ensure that they're easily separated visually from other fields in your tables.
2. Double-click the _GenAccount field. The Options dialog appears.
3. Select the Creation checkbox, located near the top left of the Auto-Enter tab.
4. Using the menu to the right of the Creation checkbox, choose the Account Name option.
5. Select the Prohibit Modification of Value during Data Entry checkbox, located at the lower left of the dialog. The dialog settings should match those shown in Figure 5.10.

**FIGURE 5.10**

Configuring a field to automatically capture the creation login account for each record.

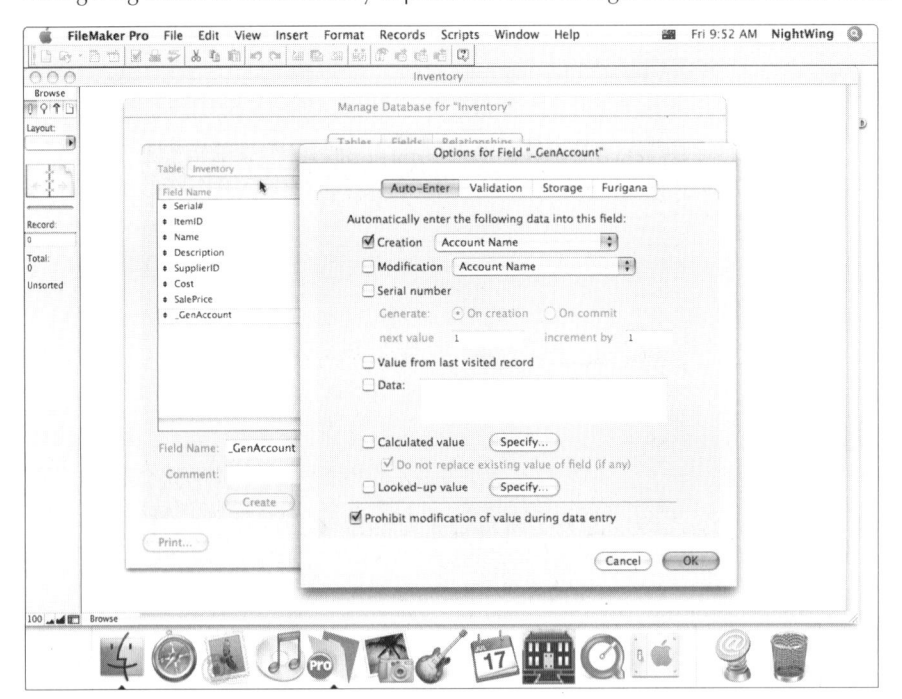

106

## Creating a Database 5

   6. Click OK to accept the settings and confirm that the Options/Comments field adjacent to the _GenAccount field says Creation Account Name, Can't Modify Auto.

   7. Create two more fields—a text field named _GenStation to capture the name associated with the workstation where each record is created and a timestamp field named _GenStamp to capture the date and time of record creation. Configure options for these two additional fields similarly to the _GenAccount field; however, when selecting from the Creation menu, choose the Name and TimeStamp options, respectively.

> **NOTE** A timestamp is a value generated by FileMaker, combining both date and time in a single value. It is a compact and efficient way to track sequences of events spanning days or even years.

   8. Now that you've defined your three _Gen fields in the Inventory table, proceed along similar lines to create three fields capturing the modification account name, workstation, and timestamp. We suggest you name these fields _ModAccount, _ModName, and _ModStamp, respectively. When setting the options for each _Mod field, select the Modification checkbox and choose the associated value from the adjacent menu. When you've completed this process, the field list for the Inventory table should match the one shown in Figure 5.11.

   9. Repeat the process outlined in Steps 1 to 8 to add a basic complement of metadata fields to each of the tables in your new database.

### FIGURE 5.11

The Inventory table field list, including six metadata fields.

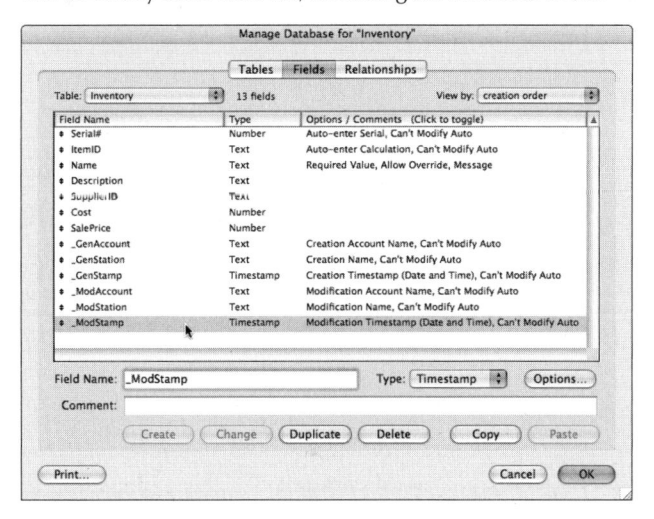

## Creating relationships between tables

Although you've added six tables and defined a number of fields in each table, they aren't yet connected in any way. In practice, you'll employ a simple mechanism to associate each record with its related records in other tables. That's where relationships come in — links created in a visual environment referred to as the *Relationships Graph*.

To access the Relationships Graph for your Inventory file, click the Manage Database dialog's Relationships tab. You're presented with a series of boxes — one for each table — containing lists of the fields you have defined. These boxes are referred to as Table Occurrences (TOs). Each TO has a header area containing the name of the table to which it refers. You can drag the TOs around by their header bars to position them more conveniently.

In order to create relationships between tables, you point the mouse at a field in one TO, click and drag to a corresponding field in another TO, then release. A line representing the relationship is created.

One of the relationships you'll need is an association between order lines and their corresponding order. To create this relationship, locate the TOs for OrderLines and Orders (if necessary, reposition them so that they're adjacent to each other) and then drag a line between the OrderID field in each, as shown at Figure 5.12.

By default, when you create a relationship in this manner, FileMaker sets up the simplest kind of relationship — one where records will be related if the value in the two fields used for the join is the same in both tables. This kind of relationship is called an *equi-join* and is represented by the = sign that appears on the box that bisects the line between the two tables.

**CROSS-REF** A detailed discussion of different kinds of relationships and their uses can be found in Chapter 11.

**FIGURE 5.12**

Using the mouse to "drag" a relationship between the Orders and OrderLines TOs.

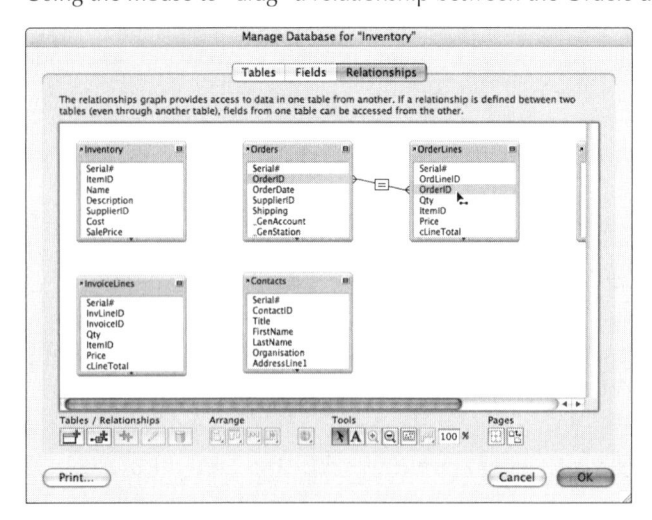

# Creating a Database

The default equi-join relationship is suitable for the join between Orders and OrderLines; however, an additional setting is required. Double-click the box containing the equal sign to bring up the Edit Relationship dialog. As you can see in Figure 5.13, the two tables that the relationship joins are listed on either side of the dialog, with corresponding settings and options listed below. On the side of the dialog where the OrderLines table appears, select the Allow Creation of Records in This Table via This Relationship checkbox.

**FIGURE 5.13**

Configuring the relationship to allow creation of related records in the OrderLines table.

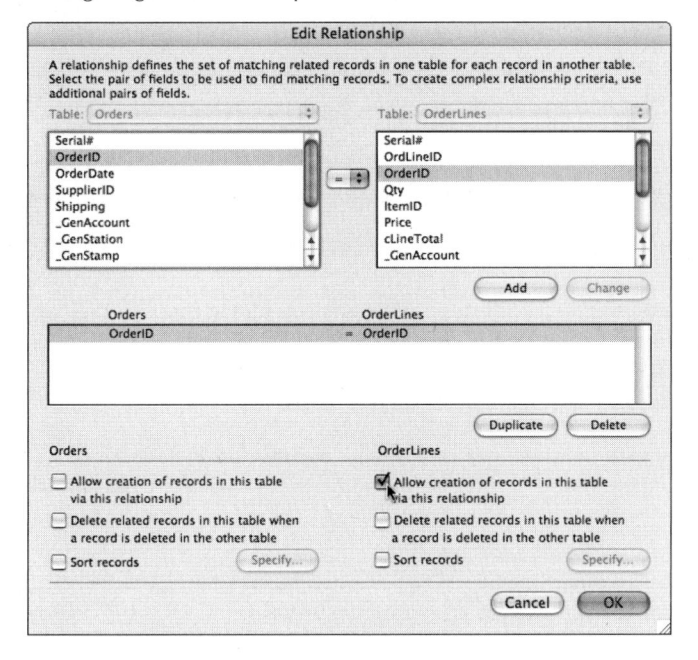

Similarly, you'll require a relationship between the Invoices and InvoiceLines TOs, so drag a line between the InvoiceID fields in those two TOs and edit the relationship selecting the checkbox option allowing creation of records in the InvoiceLines table via the relationship.

So far, we've only been working with the default TOs for the six tables in the file. At this point, we need to ensure that the graph reflects the fact that Contacts can be suppliers or buyers — and a way to do this is to represent the Contacts table multiple times on the Relationships Graph. To implement this, proceed as follows:

1. Select the Contacts table's TO and click twice on the third button from the left below the Graph window (the button bears a double plus symbol in green). Two duplicates of the Contacts TO, called Contacts 2 and Contacts 3, respectively, are created.

2. Double-click the Contacts TO. The Specify Table dialog appears.

109

## Part II  Introduction to Database Design

3. In the Name field, change the name to **Suppliers**.
4. Repeat Step 2, changing the Contacts 2 TO to **ItemSupplier** and then changing the Contacts 3 TO to **Buyers**.
5. Drag a line from the SupplierID field in the Orders TO to the SupplierID in the Suppliers TO. Similarly, drag a line from the BuyerID field in the Invoices TO to the BuyerID field in the Buyers TO.

> **NOTE** If the fields you are dragging relationship lines between are not visible in the TOs, you can either scroll the field view in the TO by clicking the arrow at the bottom center of the TO, or enlarge the TO by dragging its bottom border downward until the desired fields are visible.

6. Drag a line from the SupplierID field in the Inventory table to the SupplierID field in the ItemSupplier TO.
7. Select the OrderLines and InvoiceLines TOs and click the double-plus button to duplicate them.
8. Repeat Steps 2 through 3, renaming the OrderLines TO duplicate to **ItemsPurchased** and the InvoiceLines TO duplicate to **ItemsSold**.
9. Draw lines from the Inventory TO's ItemID field to the ItemID field in the ItemsPurchased TO, and from the Inventory TO's ItemID field to the ItemID field in the ItemsSold TO.

After completing these steps, we have enlarged the Manage Database dialog and arranged the TOs so that it's easy to see at a glance what's going on. The result is shown in Figure 5.14. As you can see, there are now three separate groups of related tables supporting distinct functions (inventory, ordering, and invoicing).

**FIGURE 5.14**
Arrangement of the Relationships Graph into three distinct Table Occurrence groups.

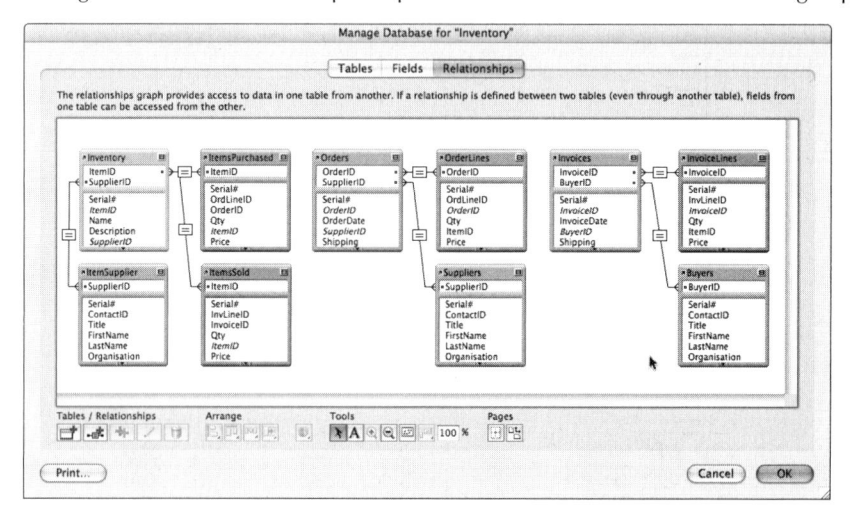

# Creating a Database  5

## Adding aggregating calcs

When your file has a suitable relationship structure, some additional calculation capabilities become available, enabling you to draw on data from related tables.

To begin setting up aggregating calculations, navigate to the Inventory table on the Manage Database dialog's Fields tab and create a calculation field called cStockLevel, entering the formula

```
0 + Sum(ItemsPurchased::Qty) - Sum(ItemsSold::Qty)
```

Make sure that the Calculation Result Is menu, at the lower left of the Calculation dialog, is set to Number and that the Do Not Evaluate If All Referenced Fields Are Empty checkbox is deselected, and then click OK to accept the calculation settings. With this calculation in place, FileMaker compares the total number of orders for a given item with the total number of sales of the item to automatically determine how many of each item remain. The Specify Calculation dialog for this procedure is shown in Figure 5.15.

**NOTE** The leading zero in the calculation provided in the preceding formula may appear redundant, but its inclusion ensures that FileMaker is able to return a value even if there are no records in either the ItemsPurchased or ItemsSold tables.

**FIGURE 5.15**

A calculation using relationships to determine aggregate stock levels.

111

## Part II  Introduction to Database Design

Next, navigate to the Orders table on the Fields tab of the Manage Database dialog and add a calculation field called cOrderTotal, entering the formula:

```
Sum(OrderLines::cLineTotal) + Shipping
```

Again, confirm that the calculation result menu is set to Number, then click OK to confirm the settings and dismiss the dialog.

Similarly, navigate to the fields list of the Invoices table and add a calculation field called cInvoiceTotal with the formula:

```
Sum(InvoiceLines::cLineTotal) + Shipping
```

Check that the result is Number, and click OK to accept the dialog.

Next, you instruct FileMaker to retrieve pricing information for the OrderLines table from the Inventory table as follows:

1. Choose the fields list for the OrderLines table.
2. Double-click the Price field. The Options dialog appears.
3. Select the Auto-Enter tab and select the Looked-Up Value checkbox near the bottom of the dialog. The Lookup for Field "Price" dialog appears.
4. From the Starting with Table menu, choose the ItemsPurchased TO.
5. From the Lookup from Related Table menu, choose Inventory.
6. Select the Cost field from the list at the lower left.

The completed settings for this dialog are shown in Figure 5.16. When the settings are in place, click OK to accept the Lookup dialog and click OK again to confirm the settings for the OrderLines::Price field.

Choose the field list for the InvoiceLines table and repeat Steps 2 to 6 for the InvoiceLines::Price field, configuring the lookup to start from the ItemsSold TO. From the list of fields to copy, select the SalePrice field.

> **NOTE** With these lookups in place, when you select an item for an order or invoice, FileMaker automatically enters the price for you, saving time and increasing the accuracy of your work.

At this point, the initial structure of an inventory system is in place, so click OK to save your work and exit to the new file. When you do, FileMaker creates an initial default layout for each of the tables you created in the file, plus a record in the first (Inventory) table. On first leaving the Manage Database dialog (if you followed our instructions regarding field validations), because the Inventory table has been set to require a name for each item, you'll be prompted to enter an item name before leaving the first record. Enter the name of an item (for example, CD-ROMs) so that you can exit the record and take a look around the file.

# Creating a Database 5

### FIGURE 5.16

Configuring a lookup to retrieve the cost price of items from the Inventory table.

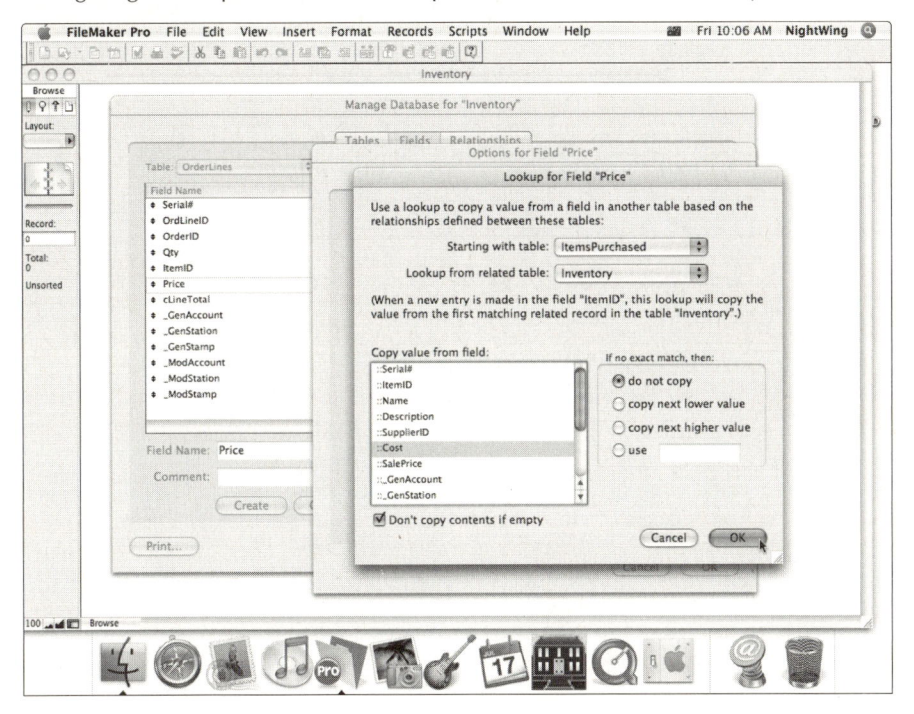

## Viewing and Interacting with Data

When you first exit the Manage Database dialog, the layouts created by default are very basic — they simply present a list of the fields created, table by table, arranged one above the next in the order in which they occur in the table's list of fields. There is no logical grouping of similar elements (for example, the parts of an address); the layout is unadorned white-on-white and the only visual cues are field names positioned to the left of the fields. Nevertheless, you have a sufficient basis to begin entering some initial data and testing the auto-enter fields, validation criteria, and the defined calculations.

Before proceeding, you might find it helpful to take a quick tour of the layouts in the file (selecting each in turn from the Layout menu at the top of the Status Area). Note that the Status Area indicates that there are presently no records in any of the tables but the first (Inventory).

113

## Part II  Introduction to Database Design

### Looking at the multiple uses of layouts

It is worth pausing again to note that FileMaker layouts are a multipurpose tool. They provide screens for viewing, entering, and editing the data within records, but they also provide options for list or table views and can be configured to provide printed output. Moreover, layouts serve equally well as the query interface when you employ FileMaker's Find mode.

While doing initial tests and familiarizing yourself with the default layouts in the Inventory file, you might find it helpful to consider ways in which the information could be arranged to increase clarity and usability. It won't be long before you begin the process of organizing the information and building the interface for this file.

**CROSS-REF** You can find additional details regarding the development of the solution interface in Chapter 6.

### Creating records and entering data

In order to test the basic structure that the Inventory file has in place, the first step is to enter some data and observe how the file responds.

Start by navigating to the layout based on the Contacts table (for the moment it will be called Suppliers or Buyers, based on the TO of the same name). Before creating any records, go to the overhead menus and choose View ➪ Layout Mode and then choose Layouts ➪ Layout Setup. The Layout Setup dialog appears, providing access to the layout settings. Change the Layout Name to Contacts, as shown in Figure 5.17, and click OK to save the change.

**FIGURE 5.17**

Editing the layout name in the Layout Setup dialog.

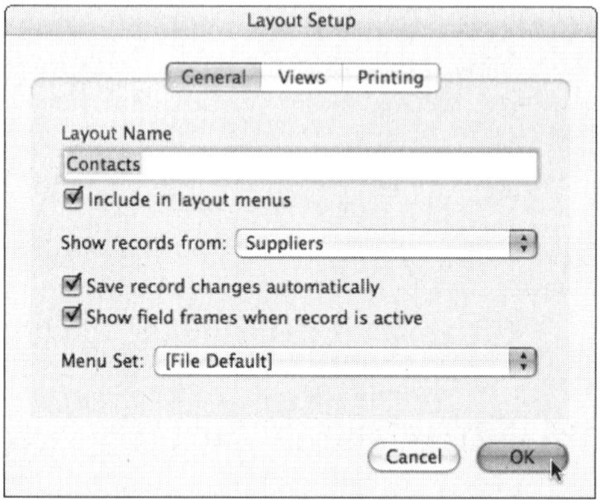

## Creating a Database 5

While you are still in Layout mode, double-click the ContactType field. The Field/Control Setup dialog for the ContactType field appears. At the upper left of the dialog, choose Checkbox Set from the Display As menu. Choose ContactType in the Display Values From menu, as shown in Figure 5.18. This provides layout access to the value list you defined when setting up the ContactType field's validation rule.

After setting the control style settings for the ContactType field, as indicated above, click OK to save the change and exit the dialog. Then choose View ➪ Browse mode to see the effects of the changes you've made.

Once in Browse mode, choose Records ➪ New Record and, using the Tab key and/or the mouse to move between fields, enter data into the empty fields. Note that the AddressLine2 field will not need to be used for most addresses, and that the SupplierID and BuyerID fields cannot be filled in directly — they acquire a value based on the selection in the ContactType field.

For testing purposes, the data you enter can be purely fictional — so stretch your imagination and enter four or so records into the Contacts layout (using the Records ➪ New Record command to create each new record in turn, and then typing information into the fields). An example Contacts record that we entered as described earlier is shown in Figure 5.19. When entering your test records, add a mix of suppliers and buyers.

**FIGURE 5.18**

Attaching the ContactType value list to the corresponding field via the Field/Control Setup dialog.

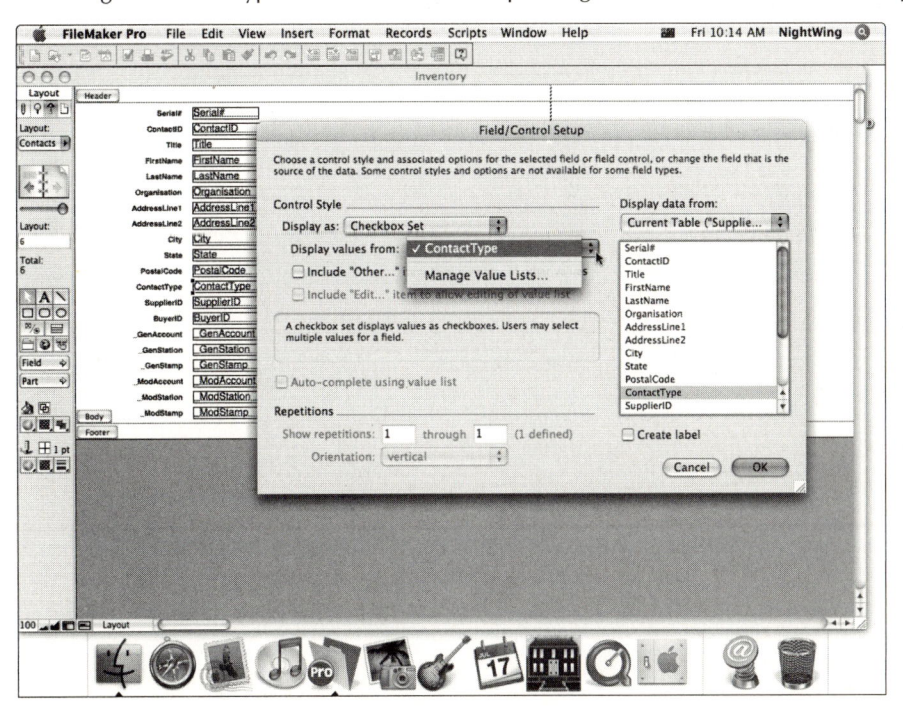

115

## Part II  Introduction to Database Design

### FIGURE 5.19

Entering some initial test data into the Contacts layout.

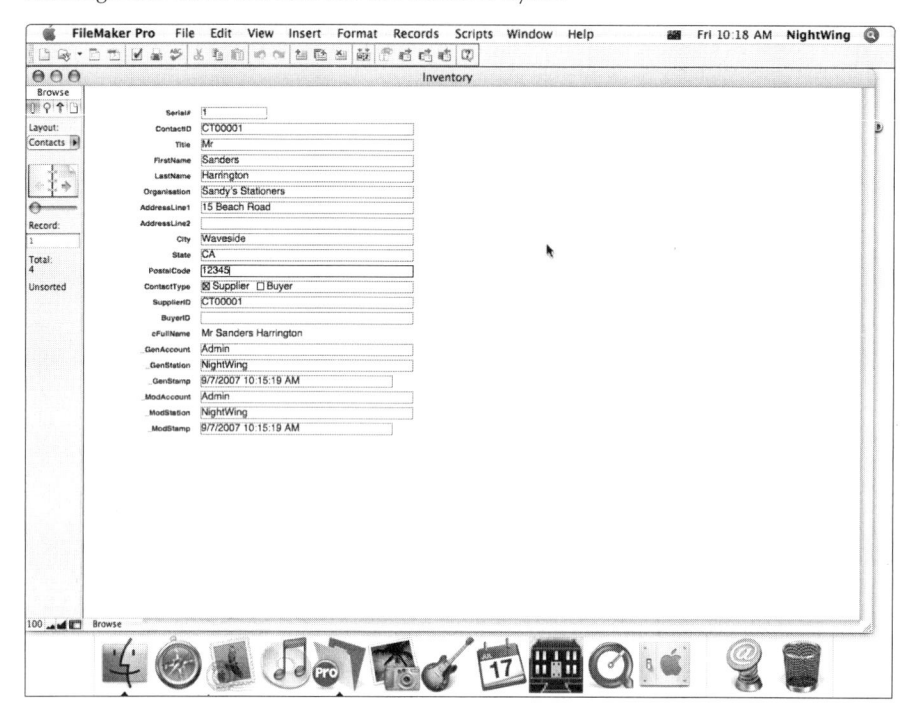

Now that you have some Data in the Contacts table, you need to be able to refer to it from elsewhere in the solution. One available option is to create value lists of suppliers and buyers that can be attached to fields on other layouts. To do so, follow these steps:

1. Choose File ➪ Manage ➪ Value Lists to display the Manage Value Lists dialog.
2. Click the New button at the lower left of the dialog. The Edit Value List dialog appears.
3. Type Suppliers into the Value List Name box.
4. Click the Use Values from Field radio button. The Specify Fields for Value List "Suppliers" dialog appears, ready for you to configure it, as shown in Figure 5.20.
5. In the Specify Fields for Value List dialog, choose Suppliers from the Use Values from First field menu at the upper left. Then locate and select SupplierID in the list of fields that appears in the box at the left of the dialog.
6. Select the Also Display Values from Second Field checkbox and locate the Suppliers cFullName field, as shown at Figure 5.20.
7. When these settings are complete, click OK to exit the Specify Fields for Value List dialog, and click OK again to exit the Edit Value Lists dialog.

## Creating a Database   5

**FIGURE 5.20**

Setting up a value list to display suppliers from the data in the Contacts table.

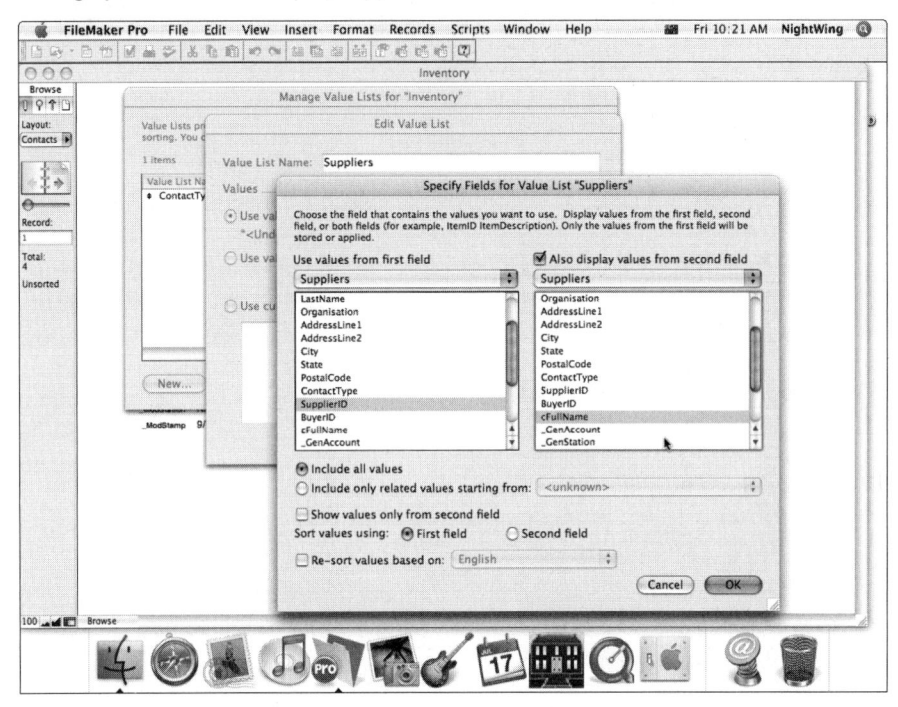

8. Click the Manage Value Lists dialog's New button again and repeat Steps 3 through 7 to create a Buyers value list, choosing the BuyerID field from the Buyers TO for the first field and the cFullName field (also from the Buyers TO) as the second. When you've created both value lists, click OK to dismiss the Manage Value Lists dialog, saving the changes you've made.

9. Navigate to the Inventory layout, choose View ➪ Layout Mode, and double-click the SupplierID field to invoke the Field/Control Setup dialog.

10. From the Display As menu, select the Drop-Down List option and from the Display Values From menu, select the Suppliers Value List.

11. Click OK to dismiss the Field/Control Setup dialog, and choose View ➪ Browse Mode.

**NOTE** FileMaker provides field control options for lists, menus, checkboxes, and radio buttons, giving you alternative methods for selecting field values from a value list. We chose to display the values in a drop-down list in this instance because a drop-down list offers maximum user flexibility, works well with lists of differing lengths, and allows you to type a value *or* choose from the list of already existing values.

117

**Part II**    **Introduction to Database Design**

12. Complete your initial Inventory record by entering values in the Description, SupplierID, Cost, and Sale Price fields. Note that the sale price may include a markup, in line with the practice of buying wholesale and selling at retail prices.

13. After completing the first record, choose Records ➪ New Record to add several additional Inventory records for testing purposes, completing each with data — either real or fictitious — it doesn't matter for the purposes of the test.

14. Navigate to the Orders layout and create an order record; then go to the OrderLines layout and create a corresponding record, entering OrderID of the order you have just created, the ItemID for your first inventory item, and entering a quantity of 20. After you've completed these two records, return to the Orders layout to confirm that the cOrderTotal field is correctly showing the combined price of the 20 items plus shipping.

15. Return to the corresponding Inventory item record in the Inventory layout and confirm that the cStockLevel value is showing 20, which reflects the stock purchase for which you have just entered an order.

16. As a final check, navigate to the Invoices and InvoiceLines layouts and create a record in each, completing them with details for a sale of 5 of the same item for which you have entered an order above.

After completing the InvoiceLines entry, check that the correct total (including shipping) is showing in the Invoices::cInvoiceTotal field, and that the Inventory::cStockLevel field for the first inventory item is now showing 15, reflecting the number of items remaining after you have purchased 20 and sold 5.

During the preceding process, you copied values from layout to layout — not a very efficient way to work — so some additional value lists and interface tools are needed. However, if the various tests have worked, then you've confirmed that the basic structure is operable, and that's enough at this stage. If anything *didn't* work as expected, look back over the process to see what you missed.

## Editing or deleting data

Now that you have some data accumulating in the Inventory solution, you need to be able to efficiently navigate it and update where necessary, adding, editing, and deleting record and field data. Moreover, you need to know that when you make a change in one part of the solution, it will be reflected elsewhere.

**CROSS-REF**    For an introduction to basic FileMaker navigation techniques, refer to Chapter 3.

Navigate to the test record you entered on the InvoiceLines layout, click in the Quantity field, and change its value from 5 to 3. As you tab or click out of the field, watch to confirm that the InvoiceLines::cLineTotal value updates to reflect the change. Similarly, click in the Shipping field in the Invoices layout, select its value, and make a change — again checking that when you leave the Shipping field, the Invoices::cInvoiceTotal updates to the appropriate new value.

Now that you've changed the number of items sold to 3, the stock level should be 17 rather than 15. Pay a visit to the Inventory layout to confirm that the cStockLevel field is accurately reflecting this change. You might also try switching to the InvoiceLines layout and choosing Records ⇨ Delete Record (you'll be prompted to confirm), and then verify that the stock level appearing on the Inventory layout has returned to 20.

## Finding and sorting data you've already entered

In Chapter 3, we describe the workings of the FileMaker Find mechanism. If you haven't already done so, now is a good time to experiment with performing finds on your test data set.

In the Inventory layout, choose View ⇨ Find Mode, and enter the first few letters of the name of one of the inventory items in your test data into the Name field. Click the Find button in the Status Area and confirm that FileMaker has located the record matching the Find criteria you entered. If more than one record in your test set included a word in the name field starting with the same characters, confirm that it was also returned as part of the found set after you clicked the Find button.

Because you have a found set in place, try choosing Records ⇨ Show Omitted Only and confirm that the records you're viewing are now the group of items that were *not* found. Choose Records ⇨ Show Omitted Only again and you'll have swapped back to the original found set. Now choose Records ⇨ Show All Records to cancel the find and bring all the available records back together, noting that as you do so, the Status Area text updates to reflect the state of the records you're viewing.

When you're viewing multiple records, you may want to sort them so they display in a predictable order. Unless sorted, records will appear in the order of their creation.

To sort the current found set of records (or all records, if there is no found set at present), choose Records ⇨ Sort Records. The Sort Records dialog appears. Select a field in the list of fields at the upper left and click the » Move » button to add it to the Sort Order list panel at the upper right. If you want to sort by multiple fields, repeat the process to add other fields to the sort order list.

**NOTE** When sorting by multiple fields, FileMaker sorts the records in the current table by the uppermost value in the sort order. Only if there are multiple records with the same value in the field that is first in the sort order is the next field in the sort order used and then only to determine the presentation order of the records that have the same value in the prior sort field(s).

When sorting by multiple fields, you can alter their precedence in the sort order by dragging them up or down in the list at the upper right. To drag an item, position the mouse pointer over the handle icon appearing to the left of the field name in the sort order list, click and drag it to a new position in the list.

By default, the sequence of values for each field in the sort order will be ascending—for example, from 0 to 99 for numeric values or from A to Z for text values. If you want to modify the presentation order for a particular field in the current sort, select it in the sort order list at the upper right and use the controls in the lower half of the dialog to select an alternative sort method.

When you've finished establishing the desired sort order, click the Sort button at the lower right of the dialog to start sorting. When the sorting process is complete, the Status Area will indicate that the records are sorted.

> **TIP** To return the records to their default (creation) order at any time, choose Records ➪ Sort Records and click the Unsort button at the lower left of the dialog.

## Using special find symbols

Searching for a word or number value, as you've just done, is useful but somewhat limited. However, FileMaker presents a range of Find options that extend the scope of searching in various ways.

Choose View ➪ Find Mode and place the cursor in the Inventory::cStockLevel field. Now locate the reveal button for the Symbols menu in the Status Area and click it to bring up FileMaker's menu of built-in Find operators. These symbols alter the way your Find criteria are interpreted. Select the first item (less than) from the symbols list, and note that a less-than character (<) is placed into the selected field. Now type the numeral 1 into the field after the < symbol. You are requesting that FileMaker locate any inventory items where the stock levels are below 1 (in other words, out of stock).

Click the Find button in the Status Area and confirm that FileMaker locates all test inventory item records for which you have not yet created orders, or for which the number of invoices is equal to or greater than the number of orders for the corresponding item.

## Searching with the range and wildcard operators

Among the special Find operators included in the Find mode's Status Area Symbols menu are four worth mentioning of here. The first of these is the Range operator, represented by an ellipsis (. . .) character.

> **TIP** If you prefer, you can simply type the special Find symbols from the keyboard. In the case of the ellipsis, FileMaker will accept a string of either two or three periods in its place.

Try entering the Find criterion **1...20** into the Inventory::cStockLevel field, and note that when you perform the find (for example, by clicking the Find button in the Status Area), FileMaker locates all records that are showing stock levels greater than 0 but less than 21.

Similarly, FileMaker supports the use of wildcard operators in Find mode. Wildcards are special characters that can be used to represent an unknown or unspecified character. The three wildcard operators available in FileMaker's Find mode are

- @ One character (either alphabetic or numeric)
- # One digit
- * Zero or more characters

## Creating a Database    5

As an example, if you enter the criterion Jo*n into a text field, FileMaker will locate records that have words such as Joan, John, or Jon Jordan in that field. If you supply the criterion as Jo@n, FileMaker will locate records containing John and Joan, but not Jon or Jordan. We encourage you to experiment with these and other special find operators to become comfortable and practiced with their use.

# Avoiding the Need for Data Duplication

If you use paper-based record-keeping systems, or even if you use a spreadsheet or word processor to create and manage invoices, you'll enter the customer details on every invoice — a duplication of effort that is inherently error prone (as well as mind-numbingly tedious and time-consuming).

By contrast, the structure of the inventory system under development allows you to store each contact only once in the Contacts table, and then reference that one record by its ID whenever an item record or a transaction involves that contact. In its present state, however, the database does not show you the related data — you have to take it on faith that when you enter the ID CT00001 on an item record, it creates a link to the corresponding contact record.

## Recognizing the visual cues to data relationships

A solution is much more useful if you can see the relationships working and if the data are presented to you in ways that make sense of the connections and data flow. One example of this usefulness is that once you select a contact ID for an item record in the Inventory layout, you can see brief details of the relevant contact record.

To make the connection between Inventory and Contact visible, follow these steps:

1. Navigate to the Inventory layout and enter Layout mode (click the Layout button in the Status Area or choose View ➪ Layout Mode).

2. Click the SupplierID field to select it (it will acquire black selection boxes at each corner) and drag the lower-right corner left, reducing the size of the box. It only needs to be about an inch wide to accommodate the ID values it's designed to hold.

3. Place the mouse pointer over the Field button in the Status Area and click and drag it onto the layout, releasing it to the right of the SupplierID field. When you release the mouse button, FileMaker draws a new field in the current position and displays a Select Field dialog.

4. Click the menu near the top of the Specify Field dialog to access a list of available TOs from which to retrieve data for the field you're adding to the layout.

5. Select the ItemSupplier TO, as shown in Figure 5.21. With the ItemSupplier TO chosen in the Specify Field dialog's menu, the fields from the Contacts table appear in the main body of the dialog (each preceded by two colons to indicate that they're located in a different table from the layout's primary table).

121

#### FIGURE 5.21

Selecting a field from a related table to add to the Inventory layout.

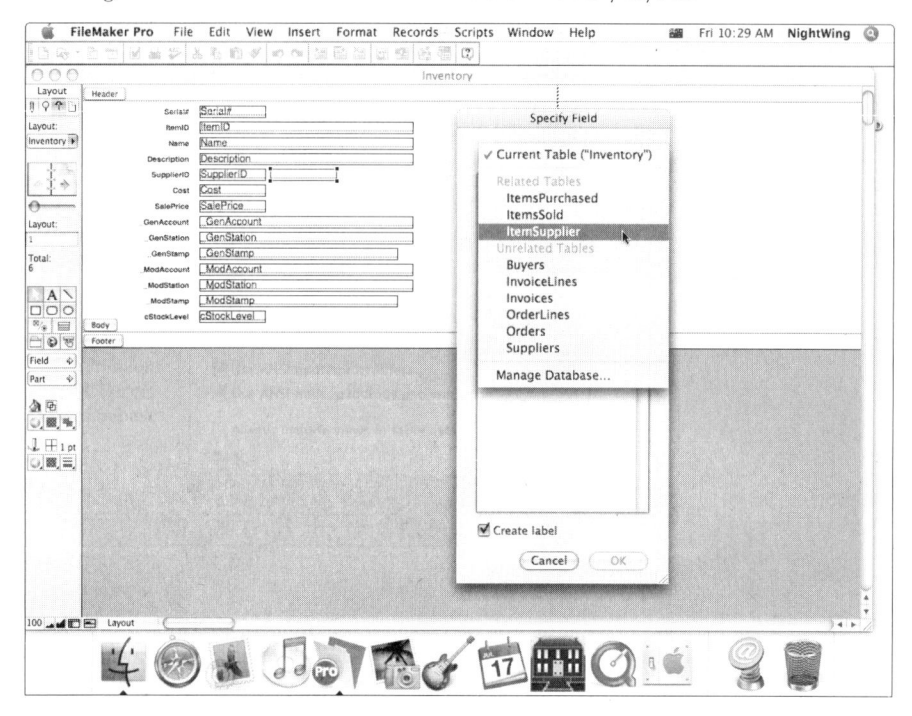

6. Click the cFullName field to select it, deselect the Create Label checkbox, and click OK to accept the selection.
7. Choose View ➪ Browse Mode to return to Browse mode.

You've now added the supplier name field from the related record, so that selecting a SupplierID value immediately displays the corresponding supplier's name. It is important to note that the field you've added simply displays the data located in the corresponding record in the Contacts table. If the Contacts record is edited, the change is automatically reflected on every other record referencing it. Instead of having to manage multiple copies of the same information, keeping them in sync whenever there is a change, the database now manages that for you.

## Information has a logical flow

What you've seen so far is that it's possible to create clean demarcations between different types of data, placing each in its own logical group, so that contacts are stored in an ordered way in the Contacts table, items in the Inventory table, and so on. Yet you're able to use the relationships to bring the data together in endless combinations, wherever you need to.

# Creating a Database 5

The capability to combine data from different tables without duplicating the data (that is, simply using the relationships to enable you to see the data in its original record) has many advantages and many implications. For example, if a related field is editable, any changes you make when viewing the field from a related table will be stored in the table of origin and will, therefore, be visible everywhere that field appears. If you correct a spelling error in a contact's name, you won't have to find all the items, invoices, or orders referring to that contact and repeat the correction, because the name is only stored once.

The underlying concept driving the approach employed here is one of keeping everything in its proper place. The information about individuals belongs in the Contacts table. You refer to it from other places, via relationships, but the information itself stays put in the part of the data structure designed for it.

The key to understanding how you can make the necessary connections is that the relationships you create provide the logic for all information flow in a solution. When setting up relationships, you're defining one or more logical connections between different kinds of "things."

## Anticipating the user

When setting up the Inventory file, you defined several auto-entry options for fields throughout the structure. In doing so, you are enabling the solution to anticipate the required data in some of the fields. In some cases, the auto-entry options are creating information that is not directly useful to the work the user is undertaking — serial numbers, creation timestamp, and so on. However, these have an essential role in supporting the structure of the database and allowing you to keep track of changes to the data.

The auto-entry lookup options you set up for the OrderLines::Price and InvoiceLine::Price fields don't merely manage solution data; they anticipate the user by looking up and entering the current wholesale or retail price for the item the user has selected. By setting default values and calculated values wherever appropriate, your solution can anticipate users, reducing effort and likelihood of error.

Similarly, the data and relationship structure can anticipate the user by grouping information about different kinds of entities and ensuring that each piece of information need only be entered once. This means that you can edit a name or address in the Contacts table (or any of the layouts that point to it) and be confident that all references to it are updated. Similarly, it means that you can enter a single value such as SupplierID and all the information on the related Contact record becomes available to the current Item or Order record — no need to enter the address or any other details, they're already there!

To make the relevant contact details visible on the Inventory layout, follow these steps:

1. Return to Layout mode on the Inventory layout.
2. Select the cFullName field and type ⌘+D or Ctrl+D to duplicate it. The Specify Field list dialog appears.

123

## Part II  Introduction to Database Design

3. Using the pull-down menu at the top of the dialog, choose the ItemSupplier TO, then from the list select the Title field.

4. Repeat the process in Steps 1 to 3 to place copies of the ItemSupplier::Organization, ItemSupplier::AddressLine1, ItemSupplier::AddressLine2, ItemSupplier::City, ItemSupplier::State, and ItemSupplier::PostalCode fields onto the layout.

5. Arrange the fields into an orderly group, as shown in Figure 5.22.

6. Click the Text tool (the one labeled with a capital A) in the Status Area, and then click above the group of fields you've just added and type **Preferred Item Supplier Details:**.

7. Click a blank area of the layout (or press the Enter key on the numeric keypad) to conclude text entry.

8. Choose View ➪ Browse Mode to view the results of your work.

**FIGURE 5.22**

An organized group of ItemSupplier fields added to the Inventory layout.

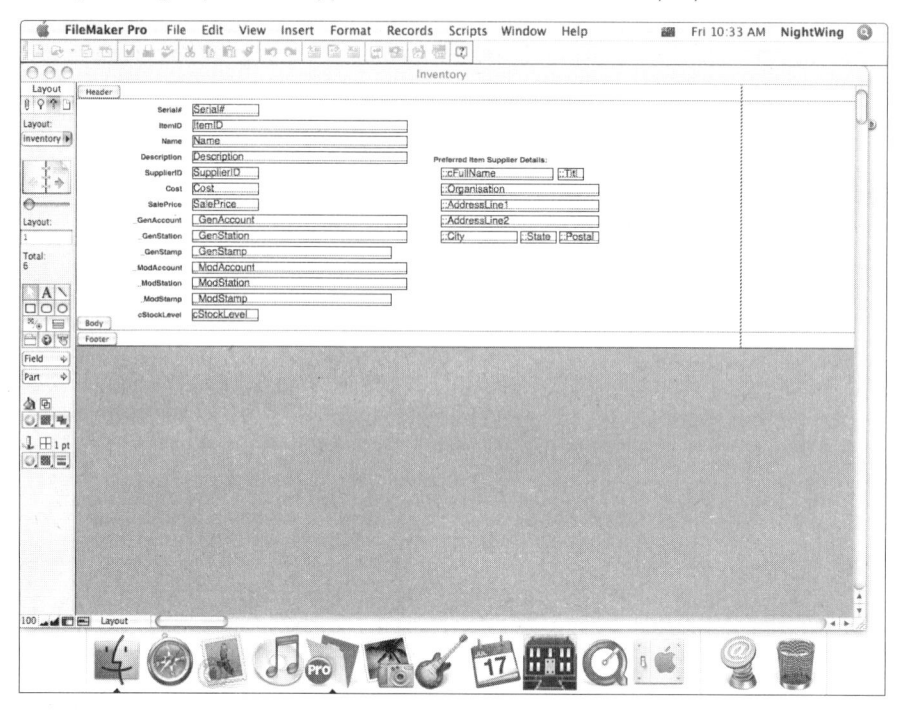

## Creating a Database 5

With the preceding steps complete, it's time to perform some tests. First, try selecting different values in the SupplierID field and confirm that the fields you've added update to show the corresponding details from the Contacts table. Now, try editing the AddressLine1 entry for the supplier address, using the field appearing on the Inventory layout, and navigate to the corresponding record on the Contacts layout to confirm that the change has been stored there. Finally, edit the same address on the Contacts layout and return to the Items layout to confirm that the latest change is visible there, as well.

### Making complex things simple

If you're new to working with databases, the structure we've proposed for the inventory example, may at first have seemed unduly complex. As you can now see, however, its purpose is to introduce both order and simplicity, enabling many data management and organizational tasks to occur automatically or with minimal effort.

A question to ask when considering a data structure — or indeed any aspect of solution design — is "Will this ultimately make things simpler?" It's clearly worth wrestling for a few hours to get a seemingly complex structure in place if it saves you hundreds or even thousands of hours a year by linking up data consistently, fluently, and automatically.

## Getting Started with File Security

Before proceeding further with the development of a solution, it's important to pay some attention to file security. If your work is worth doing and/or your data is worth organizing, then both are worth protecting. Just as you would be unwise to leave your house wide open when going on vacation, or leave your car with the keys in the ignition while attending the theater, you'd be unwise to leave your solution or the data it contains unsecured.

### Working with accounts and privilege sets

FileMaker enables you to define different levels or kinds of access that can then be assigned to one or more user accounts. These are called *privilege sets,* and they group together a range of settings that define what the user can and cannot do in your solution.

Additionally, FileMaker supports creation of multiple user accounts, each having a user name and password and assigned to a privilege set. Both accounts and privilege sets are defined on a file-by-file basis and apply to all elements, layouts, records, value lists, records fields, and so on within the file.

By default, a FileMaker file is created with three privilege sets — [Full Access], [Data Entry Only], and [Read-Only Access] — and one active account named Admin, which has no password and is assigned to the [Full Access] privilege set. Take a moment now to put some more useful and appropriate settings in place, as follows:

125

## Part II  Introduction to Database Design

1. Choose File ➪ Manage ➪ Accounts & Privileges. The Manage Accounts & Privileges dialog appears.
2. In the Accounts tab of the dialog, double-click the line identified as Admin. The Edit Account dialog appears.
3. In the Password box, enter **BibleExample**.
4. Click OK.

> **TIP** FileMaker passwords are case-sensitive (though account names are not).

5. Navigate to the Privilege Sets tab of the Manage Accounts & Privileges dialog.
6. Click the New button. The Edit Privilege Set dialog appears.
7. In the Privilege Set Name box, enter **Regular User**.

**FIGURE 5.23**

Specifying a password for the default Admin account.

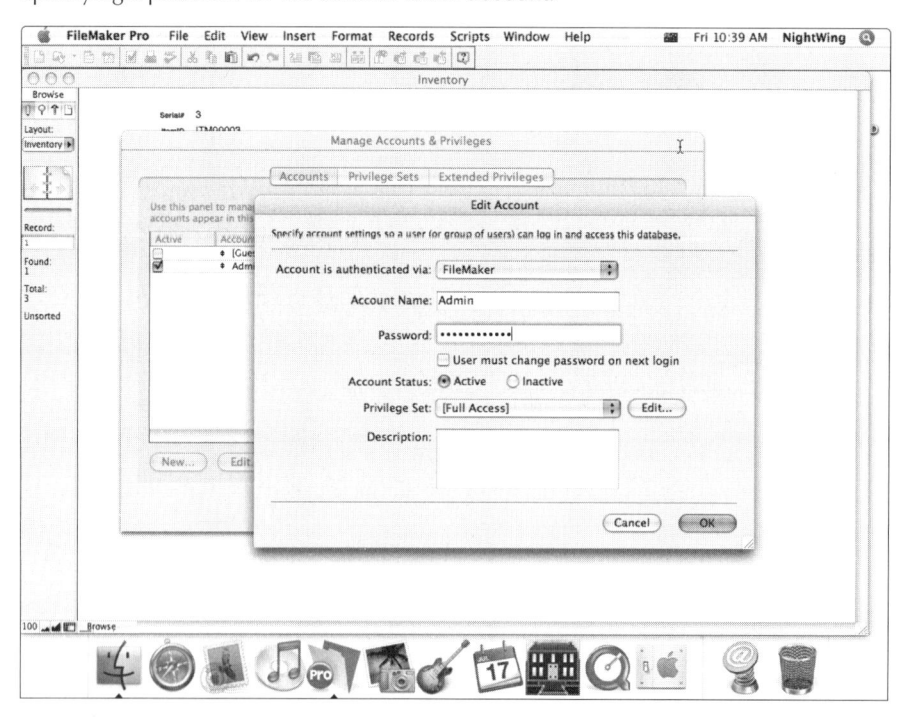

# Creating a Database

8. Under the Data Access and Design heading, use the menus to choose the following settings (see Figure 5.24):
   - Records: Create, Edit, and Delete in All Tables
   - Layouts: All View Only
   - Value Lists: All Modifiable
   - Scripts: All Executable Only
9. Under Other Privileges, select the Allow Printing checkbox and the Allow Exporting checkbox.
10. Click OK.
11. Navigate to the Accounts tab of the Manage Accounts & Privileges dialog.
12. Click New.
13. In the Account Name box, enter **User01**; in the Password box, enter **mypassword**; and from the Privilege Set menu, select Regular User.
14. Click OK to close the Edit Account dialog; then click OK again to save and close the Manage Accounts & Privileges dialog.

### FIGURE 5.24

Creating access settings and options for a new privilege set.

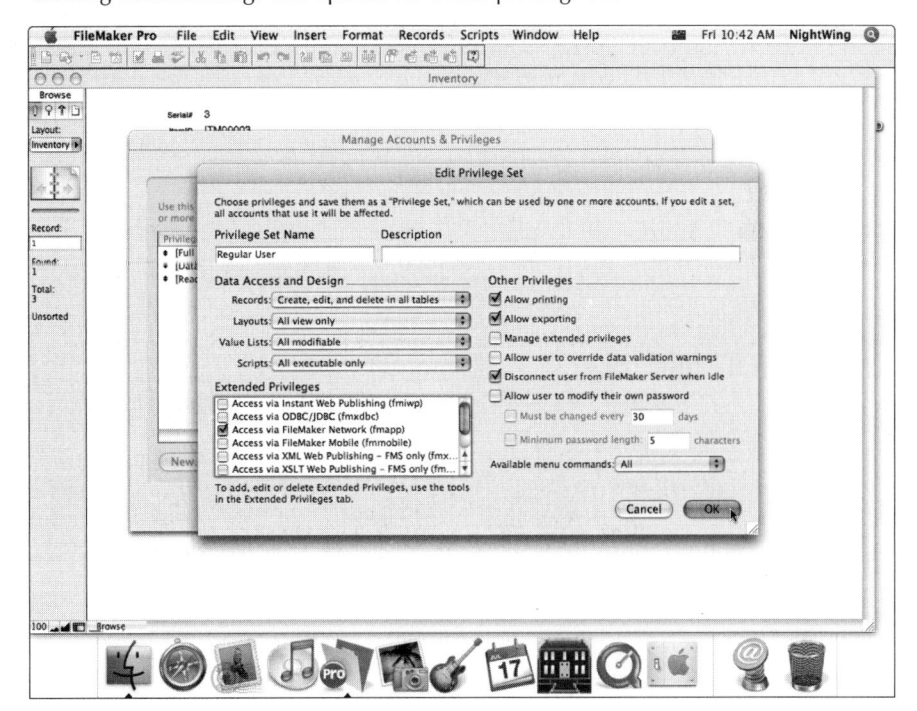

127

**Part II**    Introduction to Database Design

> **NOTE** Before closing the Manage Accounts & Privileges dialog, FileMaker will prompt you to enter a full access account and password. This is to prevent a situation where you have set a full access password inaccurately and could, therefore, permanently lock yourself out of the file.

## Setting a default account and password

After you complete the steps outlined in the preceding section, FileMaker prompts you to enter an account name and password every time the file is opened. This provides a way to reserve access to the file for those you determine should have it — and to protect the structure of the file from inadvertent or inappropriate changes by users whose purpose in using the file is limited to data entry or access to the data (who will, therefore, log in using an account assigned to the Regular User privilege set).

In some cases, defining a default privilege set is helpful, so that the file opens automatically with a particular account (without prompting the user for account name and password). For instance, to set the User01 account as the default, choose File ➪ File Options; then, in the upper area of the Open/Close tab of the File Options dialog, ensure that the Log In Using checkbox is selected and enter the account and password into their corresponding boxes.

When you click OK to close the File Options dialog after specifying a default account and password, an alert will appear, as shown at Figure 5.25, confirming that the settings have been accepted.

**FIGURE 5.25**

Specifying a password for the default Admin account.

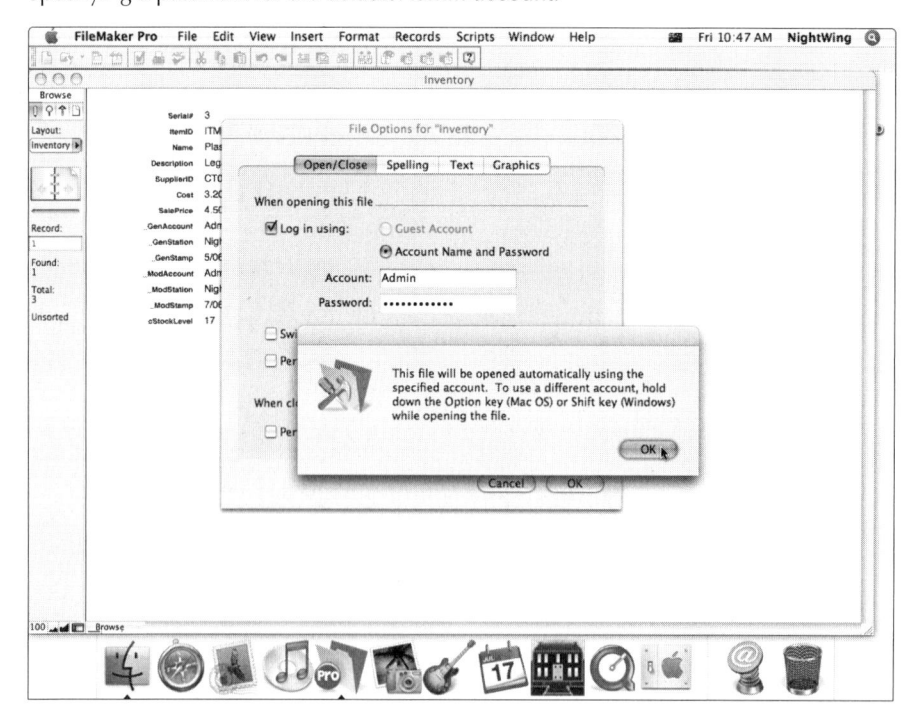

**NOTE** As the alert message indicates, once a default account/password has been set, you can still open the file using a different account by holding down a modifier key as you're opening the file. On the Mac, you use the Option key to perform this function; in Windows, you use the Shift key.

**TIP** In most circumstances, except during development, when you choose to set a default password for a file, you should select a restricted-access password as the default. In the previous example, the password with Regular User privileges is assigned as the default. If you choose an account with [Full Access] privileges as the default in a deployed file, you're effectively negating all security in the file. (Anyone can then open the file and do anything to it.)

## Thinking About Usability

After working through the example described in this chapter, you have a basic file containing data and capable of performing some essential operations. It has passed a few basic tests along the way, but in most respects it isn't yet very useful.

**ON the WEB** A copy of the database, as constructed through this chapter, is available on this book's companion Web site.

In particular, the file lacks a suitable interface — everything is pretty much wherever it fell and the only visual or functional aids are those that are provided by default by FileMaker itself. Such a minimal interface is restrictive and inconvenient. In Chapter 6, we examine some of the techniques you can use to build a more suitable interface.

Meanwhile, it is important to begin thinking about how the solution should operate, look, and feel. Most important, this will be determined by the ways you want to use the solution, the order and frequency you'll need to perform different tasks, and the range of processes you need the solution to support.

### Moving between records

In this example, you're presently moving between records using the controls in the Status Area or perhaps the corresponding keyboard or menu commands (as outlined in Chapter 3). However, there are many other ways to move around your data — lists to select from, buttons to automatically take you to particular records, and so forth.

As a central part of designing the interaction model for a solution's interface, you need to determine how users will move around the solution and what kinds of support the interface should give them to facilitate this navigation. When considering navigation, think about other computer applications you're familiar with — from music players to photo viewers — all of which provide ways of moving around that may provide models upon which you can draw.

## Managing context

When creating the Relationships Graph for the inventory example, you connected TOs into groups. As shown in Figure 5.14, the file presently has three separate "islands" of interconnected graph objects. Sets of TOs of this kind are often termed *Table Occurrence Groups* (TOGs) and operate as separate contextual "environments" — each TO within a group is able to "see" data from the other TOs in its group, according to the rules you set up for the relationships in the group.

When you're using the solution, you navigate to layouts attached to a specific TO and, therefore, present a view of data from the perspective of that TO. This is referred to as *Layout context*. The data you see and interact with depends on the current layout context and on the relationships radiating from the underlying TO.

Because context determines what you see and when, one interface design challenge is ensuring that the user can understand context and know how to interpret what they see on different layouts. Layout headings, colors, and other design cues can all be applied to facilitate clarity.

## Moving between tables

When you navigate from one layout to another, you may be changing context or not, depending on whether the layouts you're moving between are displaying records from different TOs. If the layouts are displaying records from the same TO, you may be accessing a different view of the same data. Similarly, if the layouts are based on different TOs within the same TOG, you may be accessing alternate views of the same data. Consistent visual themes or elements on layouts based on TOs within a functional group can help the user make these connections when using the solution.

In other situations, navigating to another layout may take you to a vantage point that's underpinned by a TO in a different TOG. For example, moving from the Orders layout to the Inventory layout in the example solution you've been building takes the user to a different TOG context. Both you and other users who may use the solution must be able to determine the operative perspective at all times.

## Using and changing views

Instead of changing context or perspective, it is occasionally preferable to view the same data in an alternate presentation format. FileMaker provides options to view a given layout in Form, List, or Table presentations. Frequently, however, it is preferable to provide separate layouts optimized for a specific view and provide the user with an efficient means to switch between them.

## Using buttons for static and dynamic actions

A key to making usable solutions is the addition of control elements that guide and support you. To achieve this, you can add screen devices (that is, layout objects) that perform actions or commands. These provide you with signposts, shortcuts, and other forms of assistance when using your solution.

With all the preceding considerations in mind, Chapter 6 examines a number of key techniques for developing the interface and beginning to build an appropriate user interaction model of your solutions.

# Chapter 6

# The Interface: Layout Mode

So far, we've discussed various aspects of Layout mode's role, and you've seen a few of its basic capabilities; however, our primary focus has been elsewhere. In this chapter, you come to grips with the practicalities, working through a hands-on tour of the tools and techniques for building interfaces.

In many respects, a solution is only as good as its interface. Users do not understand information if it's presented in opaque or confusing ways, they don't use features they don't know about, and they avoid working with solutions that are perplexing or tedious to use. By contrast, a thoughtfully designed solution interface makes everything easier and leads the user through the processes that the solution is designed to support. Fortunately, FileMaker Pro provides excellent tools for creating interfaces of the latter kind.

FileMaker's Layout mode exemplifies two of the central concepts of the application — simplicity and common sense. You need to be able to build a variety of screens and reports, so FileMaker gives you a flexible environment and a broad set of tools for your work. Each of the elements and each of the tools is straightforward in itself — and once you understand how they can be pieced together, the power of FileMaker's Layout mode becomes clear.

## IN THIS CHAPTER

Setting up Initial layouts

Appreciating visual structure

Working with layout objects

Leveraging the FileMaker graphical environment

Interacting with layout objects

Using Tab controls

Employing navigation options and techniques

Exploring the magic of buttons

Inviting the world in via the Web viewer

Generating reports and data output

## Initial Layouts

As you saw in Chapter 5, when you create a new database file, FileMaker adds default layouts for each of the tables in the file. The default layouts are arranged in a simple form presentation with the fields appearing in a list with their names shown as labels on the left. Both the fields themselves and the labels beside them appear in a default font, with black text and no fill, and the layout's background is white with no other adornments.

Although the initial layouts get you started and enable you to see the fields and (in due course) data in the file, they don't present or group information in meaningful ways, nor do they aid the user in comprehension, navigation, or use of the solution. Before you begin to change and enhance the layouts, however, we recommend a couple of adjustments to FileMaker's preference settings:

1. Choose FileMaker Pro ⇨ Preferences on the Mac or Edit ⇨ Preferences in Windows to display the Preferences dialog.
2. Click the Layout tab.
3. Ensure that the Add Newly Defined Fields to Current Layout checkbox is deselected and the Save Layout Changes Automatically (Do Not Ask) checkbox is selected, as shown in Figure 6.1.

   These recommended settings allow you to work more efficiently when building the interface in a new file. The option to add fields to the current layout is useful in some situations, but when you're designing custom layouts, a change of schema results in undesired changes to the layout if this option is in force. Similarly, when starting a new file, it's generally most convenient to have layout changes save automatically. When the layouts are taking shape and are complex, however, the safety net of a save prompt or the option to revert or reject layout changes can be pretty convenient.

**FIGURE 6.1**

Adjusting settings in the Layouts tab of the FileMaker Preferences dialog.

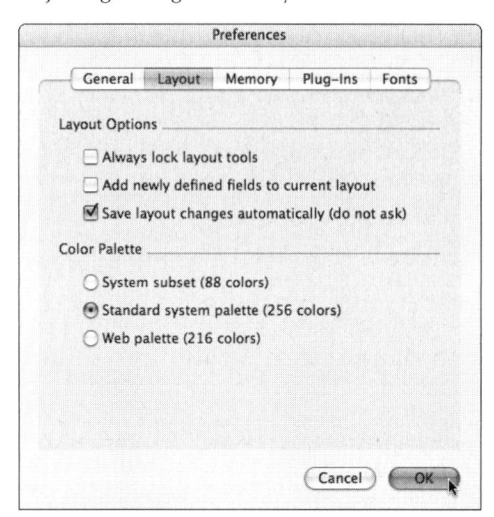

# The Interface: Layout Mode

4. In the lower part of the Preferences dialog's Layouts panel, select the Standard System Palette (256 Colors) radio button. This ensures that you have a diverse selection of stock colors available in the Status Area line and fill color palettes.
5. Select the Fonts tab.
6. Choose the Roman input type and select a default font from the menu below the list of input types. The dialog should match the settings shown in Figure 6.2.

**FIGURE 6.2**

Choosing a default font for the input and display of Roman characters.

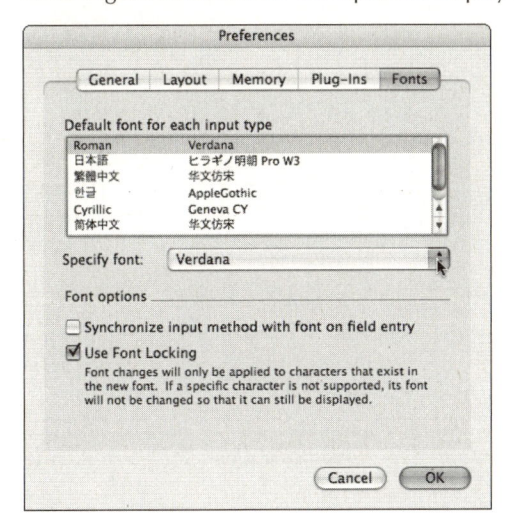

**NOTE** We recommend Verdana as the default font because it's installed by default on both Mac and Windows operating systems and renders well at a number of sizes both onscreen and in printed output.

7. Click OK to save the settings and dismiss the Preferences dialog.

If you haven't already done so, open the copy of the Inventory solution discussed in Chapter 5.

**ON the WEB** You can download the Chapter 5 Inventory solution from this book's companion Web site to use as your starting point.

**CROSS-REF** For additional details about setting preferences and file options in FileMaker, refer to Chapter 3.

133

## Part II  Introduction to Database Design

If you made a change to the font input preference, before proceeding you should go into Layout mode and select all objects on each layout and change their font to the newly selected default font. To accomplish this, follow these steps:

1. Navigate to the Inventory layout using the Layout menu at the top of the Status Area.
2. Choose View ➪ Layout Mode. (⌘-L or Ctrl+L) or click the Layout button in the Status Area.
3. Choose Edit ➪ Select All.
4. Choose Format ➪ Font ➪ Verdana (or whichever alternate font you chose as your default).

## A map of Layout mode

Before you begin serious work in Layout mode, take a moment to acquaint yourself with its various tools and features. When you choose View ➪ Layout Mode, FileMaker's Status Area populates with a number of controls and tools that, at first glance, may appear daunting. If you have any experience with a drawing or presentation application, some of the tools may seem a little familiar.

As you can see in Figures 6.3 and 6.4, many of the operations you perform in Layout mode can be accessed via the tools, palettes, and controls located in the Status Area. The Status Area tools work in three distinct ways.

**FIGURE 6.3**

The controls of Layout mode.

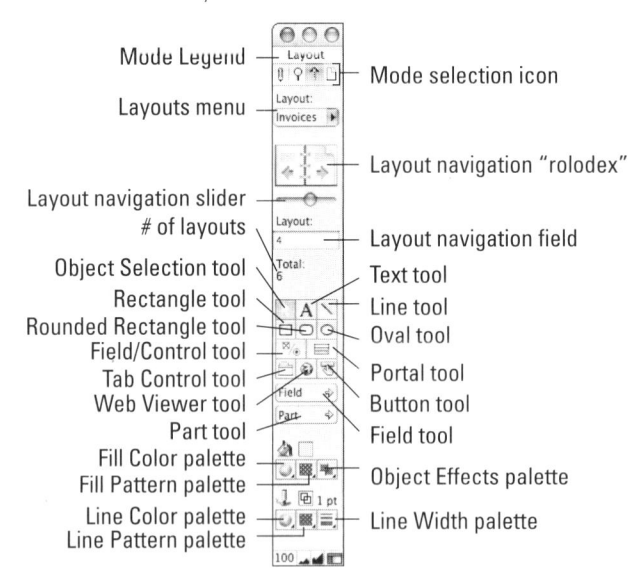

- Mode Legend
- Layouts menu
- Mode selection icon
- Layout navigation "rolodex"
- Layout navigation slider
- # of layouts
- Layout navigation field
- Object Selection tool
- Text tool
- Rectangle tool
- Line tool
- Rounded Rectangle tool
- Oval tool
- Field/Control tool
- Tab Control tool
- Portal tool
- Web Viewer tool
- Button tool
- Part tool
- Field tool
- Fill Color palette
- Fill Pattern palette
- Object Effects palette
- Line Color palette
- Line Width palette
- Line Pattern palette

# The Interface: Layout Mode 6

## FIGURE 6.4

The indicators and parts of Layout mode.

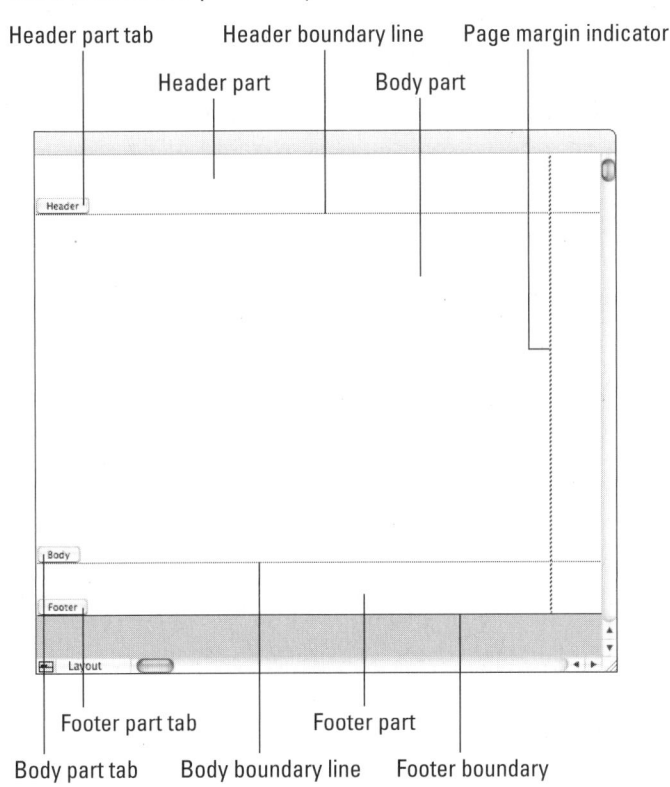

*[Figure showing a Layout mode window with the following labels: Header part tab, Header part, Header boundary line, Body part, Page margin indicator, Body part tab, Body boundary line, Footer part tab, Footer part, Footer boundary]*

### Selection then Action tools

The upper block of 11 tools starting with the Object Selection tool and ending with the Button tool can be selected with a single click (the tool becomes shaded to indicate that it's active). A subsequent mouse click/drag action in the main layout area creates an object of the corresponding type. For example, when you click the Web Viewer tool, and then drag across a section of the layout, a Web Viewer object is created in the area where you drag the mouse. Similarly, when you click the line tool and drag between two points in the layout area, a line is created between those points. All 11 tools in this group operate in a similar manner.

> **TIP** By default, after each use of any of the 11 select/act tools, the Selection tool becomes active. However, if you double-click a tool, the tool is locked as the active tool until you choose a different tool. You can change the behavior to leave tools selected in Layout Preferences (by selecting the Always Lock Layout Tools checkbox; refer to Figure 6.1).

135

### Drag-to-Layout tools

Below the first group of layout tools are two tools labeled Field and Part, respectively. When the cursor is positioned over either of these tools, it takes the shape of a hand, indicating that you must click and hold the tool and drag from the tool to the layout area to add the corresponding element (field or part) to the current layout. When you release the mouse button over the layout, a field or part will be added at the location of the mouse coordinates.

### Palette and Menu controls

The final two rows of Layout mode controls in the Status Area give you access to palettes of color, pattern, and appearance settings for the line (border) and fill attributes of selected layout objects. These controls work like menus — click once to reveal the corresponding palette of options, and then click a second time on the option (color, pattern, or line/fill attribute) you want to apply to currently selected objects.

## Organizing the presentation of information

One of the keys that people use to understand information is its position relative to other information. For example, if the name Martha has the name Samuel immediately to its right, you may conclude that you're seeing the first and last names of an individual. Conversely, if the name Martha has the name Samuel appearing immediately below it, a more likely conclusion is that you're viewing a list of names and that Martha and Samuel are two individuals who belong together in a group of some kind. Simply by positioning information according to conventions of this type, you provide intuitive cues to suggest meaning and relationships. When employing such techniques, labels become a secondary aid, confirming what object placement has already suggested.

As an example of the way information can be grouped to make its meaning clearer, we have made some initial changes to the previous chapter's Inventory layout. You can see the result of these modifications in Figure 6.5.

At this stage, the only things that have been altered in the Inventory layout are the relative sizes and placement of the elements. None has been added, removed, or otherwise altered. Yet the layout already makes more sense and is easier to scan.

To make comparable changes in your Inventory layout, follow these steps:

1. Click the Body tab at the lower left of the layout and drag it downwards, enlarging the layout area.
2. Click on field and label objects and drag them around the screen to new positions.

**TIP** You can Shift+click objects to make multiple selections, and then drag a group of selected objects to reposition them simultaneously. We recommend moving the labels and fields simultaneously.

3. To resize field boxes, click them once to select them — corner handles appear — and then drag the lower-right corner handle and release when the box is the desired size.

## The Interface: Layout Mode | 6

> **TIP**
> To make fine adjustments to the position of an object or group of objects, first select the objects, and then use the arrow keys to move them. They're nudged one pixel at a time in the direction of the arrow key you press.

**FIGURE 6.5**

Reorganizing the information in the Inventory layout into logical groupings.

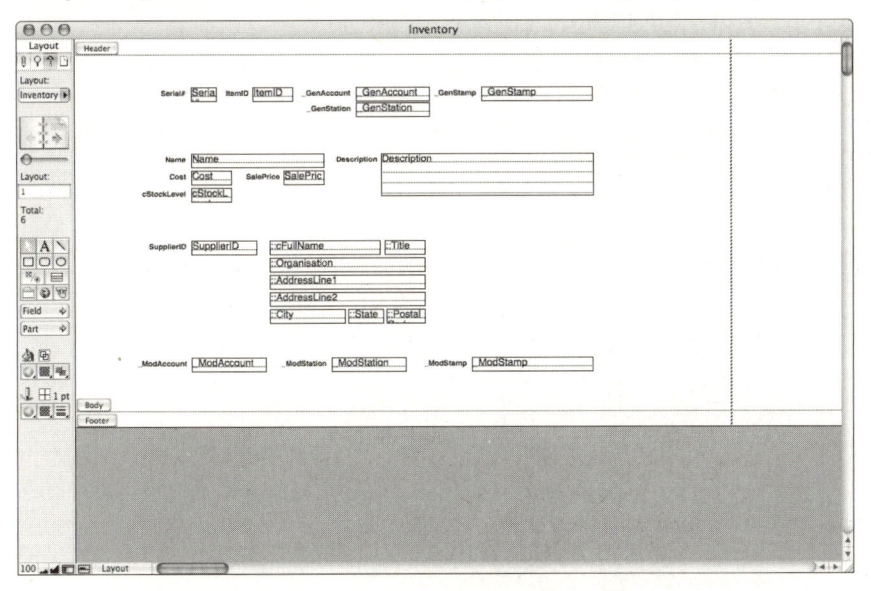

## Applying formats to field and text objects

You can apply a variety of formatting changes to selected layout objects, including text format (font size, style, color, and so on) as well as graphical effects such as line and fill color, embossing, and drop shadow. You can use combinations of effects to reinforce the groupings and distinctions between elements on your layouts. The following steps walk you through such a process:

1. In Layout mode in the Inventory layout, select the auto-entry fields (Serial#, ItemID, _GenAccount, _GetStation, _GenStamp, _ModAccount, _ModStation, and _ModStamp).

2. Click the Fill Color palette in the Status Area and select the lilac fill color, as shown in Figure 6.6.

3. With the auto-entry fields still selected, choose the object effects palette (at the right of the row of controls that includes fill color and pattern) and from the resulting menu, select the Engraved option, as shown in Figure 6.7.

> **NOTE**
> The engraving effect creates an illusion of depth, giving the impression that you're looking into a shallow depression in the layout. This effect imparts the idea of looking into something and is therefore useful for fields or other objects containing information (that is, one is "looking into" the database to see the contents of a field, so the engraving provides a useful visual analogy).

137

**Part II** Introduction to Database Design

**FIGURE 6.6**

Setting a lilac fill color for selected fields in the Inventory layout.

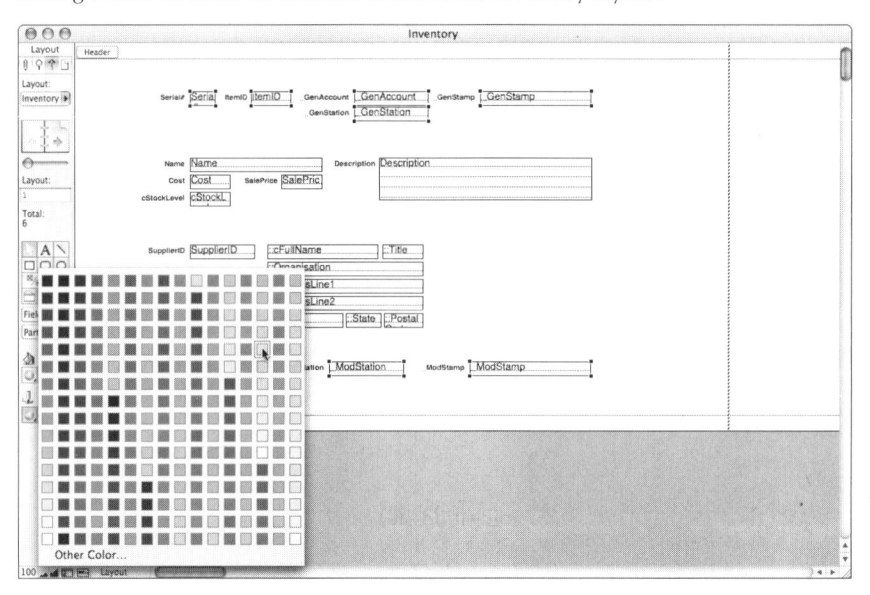

**FIGURE 6.7**

Applying the Engraved effect to selected fields in the Inventory layout.

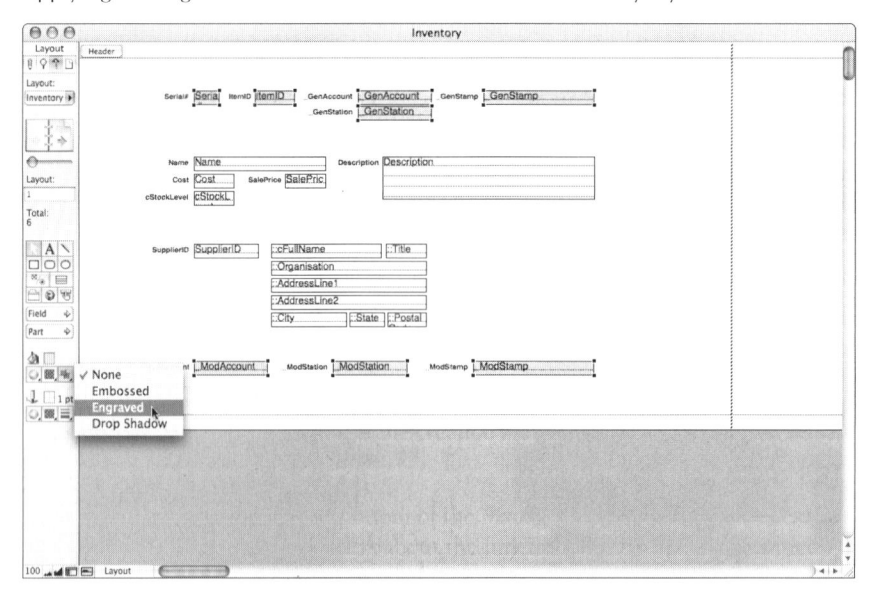

## The Interface: Layout Mode    6

4. Choose Format ➪ TextColor and select a medium dark gray from the submenu color palette, as shown in Figure 6.8.
5. Choose Format ➪ Field/Control ➪ Behavior. The Field Behavior dialog appears.
6. Deselect the In Browse mode checkbox in the section labeled Allow Field to be Entered.
7. Select the Do Not Apply Visual Spell-Checking checkbox, as shown in Figure 6.9.
8. Click OK.
9. Select the Name, Description, Cost, SalePrice, and SupplierID fields and apply the lightest gray fill and the Engraved fill effect to them.
10. Select the remaining fields and apply the second gray shade (one shade darker than the lightest gray) fill to them and, again, apply the engraved fill effect.

**NOTE** The slightly darker fill effect applied to the final group of fields differentiates them from the light gray data entry input fields. The remaining fields acquire their values automatically when the input values are entered.

11. Select the Serial#, ItemID, Cost, SalePrice, cStockLevel, State, and PostalCode fields and choose Format ➪ Align Text ➪ Center.

**FIGURE 6.8**

Setting a dark gray text color for selected fields in the Inventory layout.

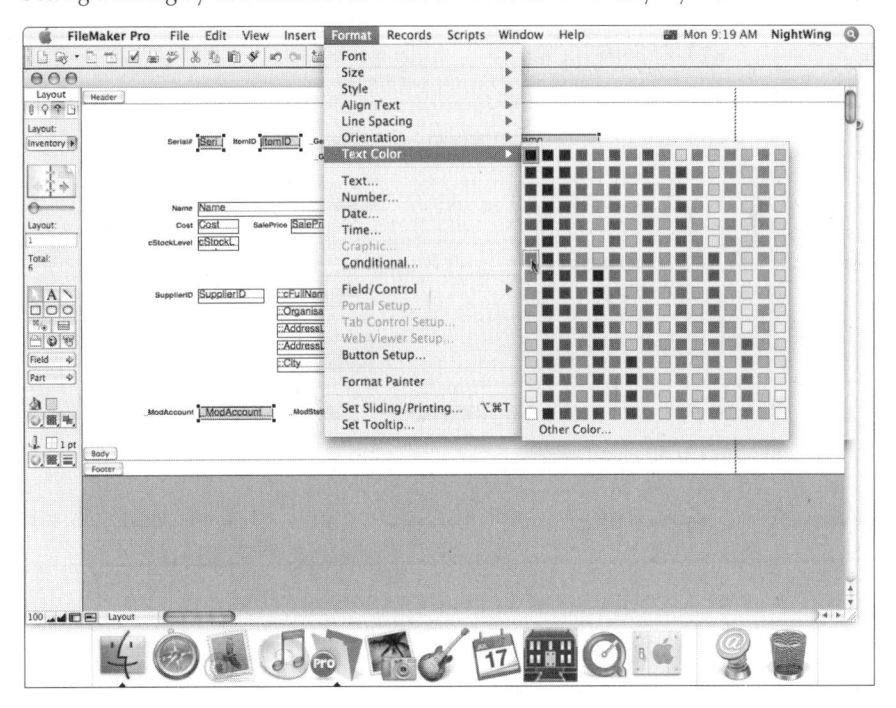

139

## Part II  Introduction to Database Design

**FIGURE 6.9**

Configuring field behavior settings for a group of fields.

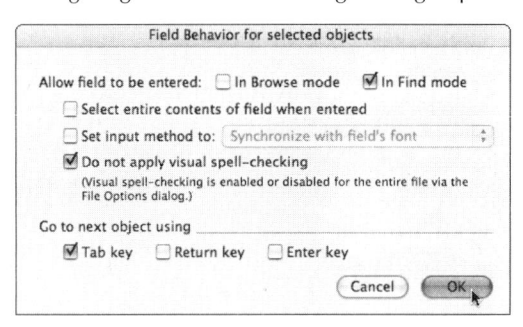

12. Select the Cost and SalePrice fields.
13. Choose Format ➪ Number. The Number Format for selected objects dialog appears.
14. Select the Format as Decimal radio button, the Fixed Number of Decimal Digits checkbox (make sure the adjacent number is 2), and the Use Notation checkbox (making sure that Currency Leading/Inside is selected in the adjacent drop-down list and that the correct currency symbol appears at the right), as shown in Figure 6.10.

**FIGURE 6.10**

Setting number display options for decimal currency.

## The Interface: Layout Mode

15. Click OK.
16. Choose View ⇨ Browse Mode to view the results of your work. Your inventory layout should now resemble the one shown in Figure 6.11.

**FIGURE 6.11**

The Inventory layout in Browse mode with basic field formatting applied.

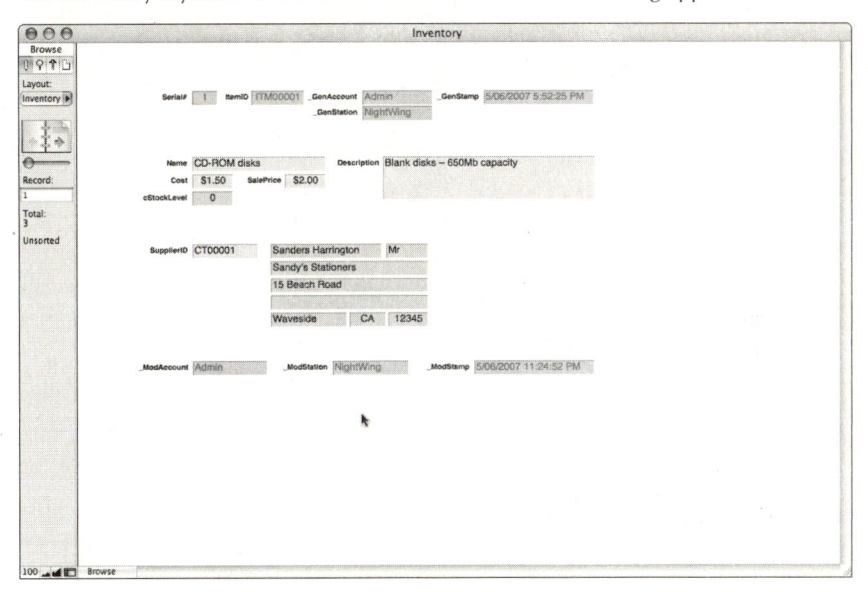

The preceding process is a first step toward providing an interface for the Inventory layout, but already its appearance is transformed — it's now easier to see what different elements are, and the layout is already more usable.

## Setting up layouts for printing

What works well onscreen is not always ideal when the document is sent to a printer. One aspect of this is the use of color. Careful and tasteful use of color can make screens more attractive and more readable, but many printers require black and white or grayscale, and, even when color is available, ink can bleed, making text against a color background harder to read. Moreover, the orientation and arrangement of elements you want onscreen may not match printed output requirements.

One answer to this dilemma — sometimes the easiest or cleanest solution — is to create separate layouts for printing. It's certainly an option, and for some purposes — such as printing onto irregular or special-purpose paper such as labels or envelopes, or matching preexisting forms or letter

141

formats—it is necessary. For relatively simple requirements, however, FileMaker provides you with techniques to control the way things print.

> **NOTE** Print settings (orientation, scaling, page margins, and so on) also affect the output FileMaker produces when you create PDF documents, such as when you choose File ⇨ Save/Send Records As ⇨ PDF.

Before making adjustments to a layout's printing configuration, choose File ⇨ Page Setup (Mac) or File ⇨ Print Setup (Windows) to choose an appropriate printer and page orientation. Next, go to Layout mode and choose Layout ⇨ Layout Setup and click the Printing tab of the Layout Setup dialog that appears. Here you can set column printing and set fixed margin widths for the current layout.

On first entering the Layout Setup dialog's Printing tab for a particular layout, the Use Fixed Page Margins option is disabled, and the margin widths are default values based on the current print driver and page setup configuration. As shown in Figure 6.12, after selecting the Use Fixed Page Margins checkbox, you can enter alternative margin widths. Bear in mind when doing so that if you specify fixed margins less than the minimums for the selected printer, the page is nevertheless cropped (that is, you can't use margin settings to extend the printable area outside your printer's hardware limits).

> **NOTE** For exacting printing requirements, you should set fixed page margins to ensure that page dimensions and placement are not dependent on the printer and driver selections. Note. however, that the paper size and orientation settings still impact the layout dimensions.

In Layout mode (refer to Figure 6.5), a vertical dotted line appears to the right side of the main window area. This line identifies the edge of the printable area, based on the current printer, page setup (orientation, scaling, and so on) and the margin settings for the current layout. If you make a change to any of these settings, the line appears in a new position, indicating the new width of the layout that can be printed on the selected paper size.

**FIGURE 6.12**

Setting fixed page margins via the Printing tab of the Layout Setup dialog.

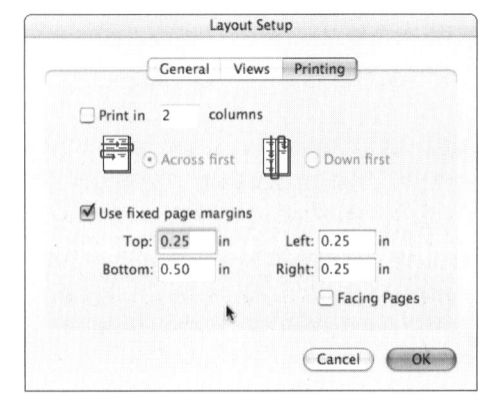

## The Interface: Layout Mode     6

> **NOTE** You can position objects outside the printable area of the layout. If you do, they nevertheless appear onscreen and behave normally, with the exception that they don't appear (or are cropped, depending on placement) in the printed output.

After setting the Page Setup configuration and specifying margins, choose View ⇨ Preview Mode to view the placement of the current layout within the area of the printed page. With settings in place for U.S. letter and landscape orientation, the preview should resemble Figure 6.13.

An invaluable feature when setting up pages for printing enables you to exclude particular layout objects from the printed image (that is, the printed output can optionally present a subset of the layout objects). In the Inventory layout example shown in Figure 6.13, it may be desirable to print only the data fields and their corresponding text labels, without the ancillary (metadata) fields showing record generation and modification details.

**FIGURE 6.13**

Preview mode shows how the current layout appears on the printed page.

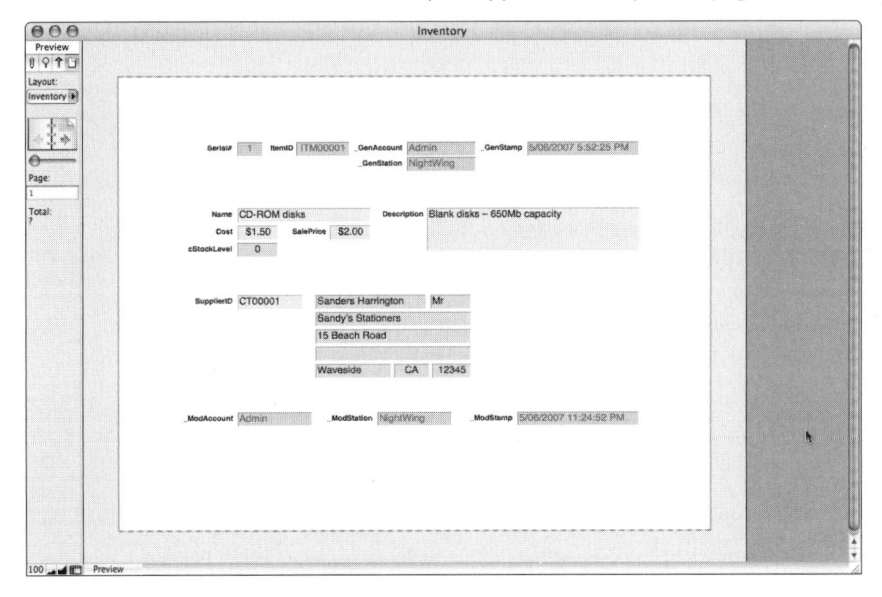

To use this subsetting, go to Layout mode and select the metadata fields and their adjacent text labels; then choose Format ⇨ Set Sliding/Printing. In the Set Sliding/Printing dialog that appears (shown in Figure 6.14), select the Do Not Print the Selected Objects checkbox in the lower left and then click OK to dismiss the dialog.

[0] After applying the Do Not Print setting, return to Browse mode and confirm that the fields and their labels still appear and display their data. Now return to Preview mode and note that the metadata fields no longer appear there. If you want, try a test print to confirm that the printed output corresponds to the preview image.

143

**Part II**    **Introduction to Database Design**

> **CROSS-REF**    For a more in-depth discussion of the options for setting up layouts for print, refer to Chapter 10.

**FIGURE 6.14**

Setting selected objects as non-printing (so that they are not included in printed output).

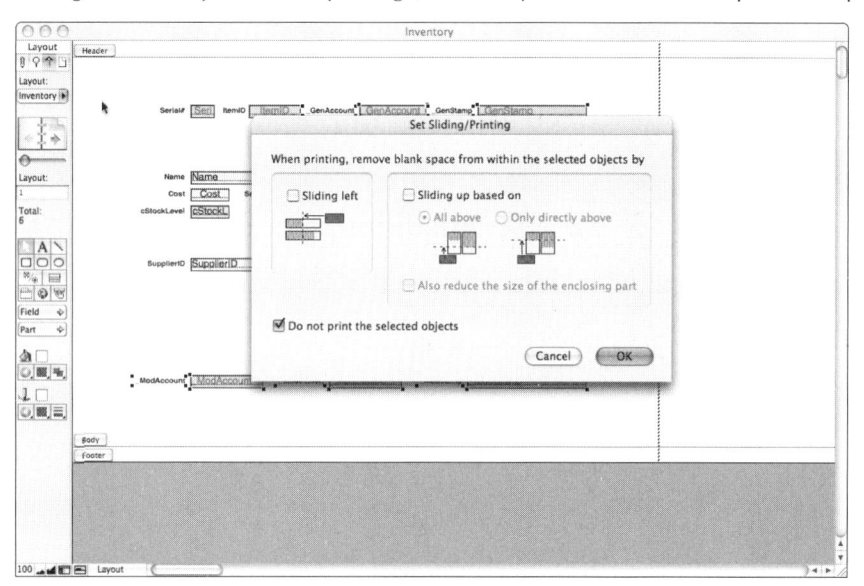

## Understanding lists and forms

FileMaker allows you to view a layout in a Form, List, or Table format.

- **Form view** presents the data one record at a time in a manner analogous to paper forms. In order to view a different record, you must navigate forward or backward (for example, using the Rolodex tool in the Status Area).
- **List view,** as the name suggests, presents multiple records (assuming there is more than one record in the current found set), one below another, allowing you to scroll down through the records.
- **Table view** also shows the records as a list but ignores the appearance of the current layout, instead showing records in a display format resembling a spreadsheet.

To see the current layout in different views, enter Browse mode, check that you're viewing a found set of two or more records, then (sequentially) choose the View ➪ View as Form, View ➪ View as List, and View ➪ View as Table commands. As you can see, FileMaker gives you a lot of control over how your layouts are presented.

Commonly, your layouts are designed with a particular presentation format in mind. Form layouts generally take up most of the screen and don't work so well when viewed as List, whereas list layouts are frequently designed to be wide and shallow so that many records fit on the screen. Consequently, you may want to constrain users to view each layout only in the formats for which you have designed them.

To specify the layout views available for selection by the user, navigate to the layout, enter Layout mode, choose Layouts ⇨ Layout Setup to display the Layout Setup dialog. Select the Views tab, as shown in Figure 6.15. By deselecting one or more checkboxes on the Views tab, you prevent users from choosing to display the current layout in the corresponding presentation format (the menu commands for the disabled views are dimmed and unavailable when the layout is displayed).

**FIGURE 6.15**

Constraining the available (user selectable) views for the current layout.

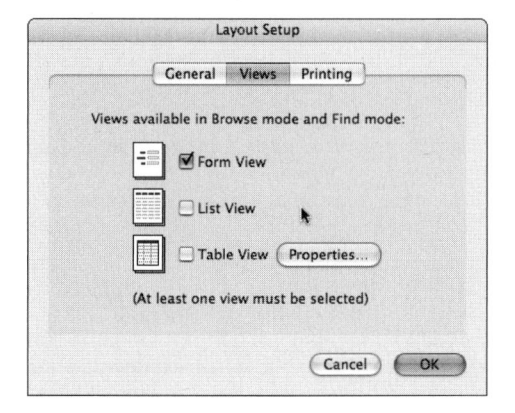

**NOTE** When constraining a layout to a single view, you should consider providing an alternate means for users to see data in a variety of appropriate formats. For example, it may be desirable to provide two or more layouts — one or more to show records from a table in a summary list view and another to show more extensive detail of the same records in a form view.

As a general principle, list views are more useful when they include a relatively small number of essential fields — providing a summary of the data in a table, whereas form presentations are better suited to the display of larger numbers (a dozen or more) fields. There is no hard rule about this, but appropriate use of forms and lists reduces clutter and confusion in your solutions.

## Layout parts and their purposes

The default layouts generated by FileMaker when you create a new file — or when you choose Layouts ⇨ New Layout/Report (in Layout mode) to generate a new blank layout — are subdivided vertically into three parts identified as Header, Body, and Footer. At the left side of the boundary of each part is a tab bearing its name. Clicking a part tab selects the part, and dragging a part tab up or down changes the corresponding part's size.

The purpose of a layout's Header and Footer parts is to provide a reserved area for layout elements that are to appear only once at the top or bottom of each screen or page (regardless of the number of records displayed). These parts are useful for the display of headings, page numbers, logos, or design elements, and anything else of a general nature (that is, applying to all records).

A layout's Body area is repeated for each record in the layout's table, giving all the detail that is particular to one record. In List view or when printed, multiple instances of the body part (one for each record) may appear between each occurrence of the Header and Footer parts, depending on the size of the body part, the size of the page, the part settings, and the number of records being displayed.

When required, you may include additional layout parts to support summary information. You do this by dragging the Status Area's Part tool to the place in the layout where you want to add a part. In addition to the Header, Body, and Footer, FileMaker supports the following layout part types:

- **Title Header:** Enables you to create a different header to appear on the first page
- **Leading Grand Summary:** Provides a place to include summary information that should appear only once, at the top of a screen or start of a printout or report
- **Sub-Summary When Sorted By:** Enables you to include summary details before and/or after each group of values in a sorted set
- **Trailing Grand Summary:** Provides a place to include summary information that should appear only once, at the bottom of a screen or end of a printout or report
- **Title Footer:** Enables you to create a different footer to appear only on the first page

You may create layouts containing many parts; however, with the exception of sub-summary parts, each part type may only appear once in a layout. You can create up to two sub-summary parts per field — one leading (that is, preceding the Body part) and/or one trailing.

> **NOTE** A sub-summary part is not displayed in Browse mode, only in Preview mode and print (or PDF) output. You may create multiple sub-summary parts, each coming into play only if the current found set is sorted by an associated field.

A layout must have at least one part; however, that part may be of any kind. Thus, it is possible to define a layout with sub-summaries but no body, for instance, to display summary data about groups of records without including details of the records themselves.

> **CROSS-REF** The creation and use of sub-summary parts is explored in greater detail in Chapter 10.

# The Importance of Visual Structure

Earlier in this chapter, you moved the fields on the Inventory layout into organized groups to lend order and meaning to the data they present. This provided a first step toward an intuitive interface — one leading the eye to the relevant data in an ordered fashion.

## The Interface: Layout Mode

To assist in the interpretation of information, you should arrange it in a sequence that users find easiest to comprehend. Frequently, this entails moving from the general to the specific (for example, users generally need to know what something is before learning about its history or other attributes, so name and ID fields should generally come before descriptive details).

## Adding visual pointers and aids

In addition to the placement of fields on your layouts, a variety of graphical elements can help to communicate the relationships between the elements and reinforce the visual effect of grouping and placement. These elements may include text, lines, borders, boxes or panels, arrows, logos, or other graphical indicators.

Using the Inventory layout as an example, in Layout mode, add a rectangle around the first group of fields. To implement this, proceed as follows:

1. Select the rectangle tool in the Status Area.
2. Draw a rectangle around the first group of fields (initially, the rectangle may obscure the fields).
3. With the rectangle selected, choose Arrange ⇨ Send to Back.
4. Apply a light gray fill using the Fill tool in the Status Area.
5. Select and apply the Engraved effect from the Object Effects palette in the Status Area.
6. Locate the Line Pattern tool (next to the Line Color tool in the Status Area; see Figure 6.16), and choose the transparent line option at the upper left of the palette of line patterns.

**FIGURE 6.16**

Selecting the transparent line attribute from the Line Pattern tool in the Status Area in Layout mode.

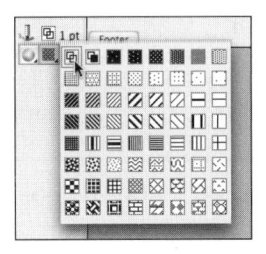

After completing the above procedure, the layout should include an engraved rectangle positioned behind the group of five fields nearest the top of the screen, as shown in Figure 6.17.

## Part II — Introduction to Database Design

### FIGURE 6.17

Adding a rectangular box behind the first group of fields on the Inventory layout.

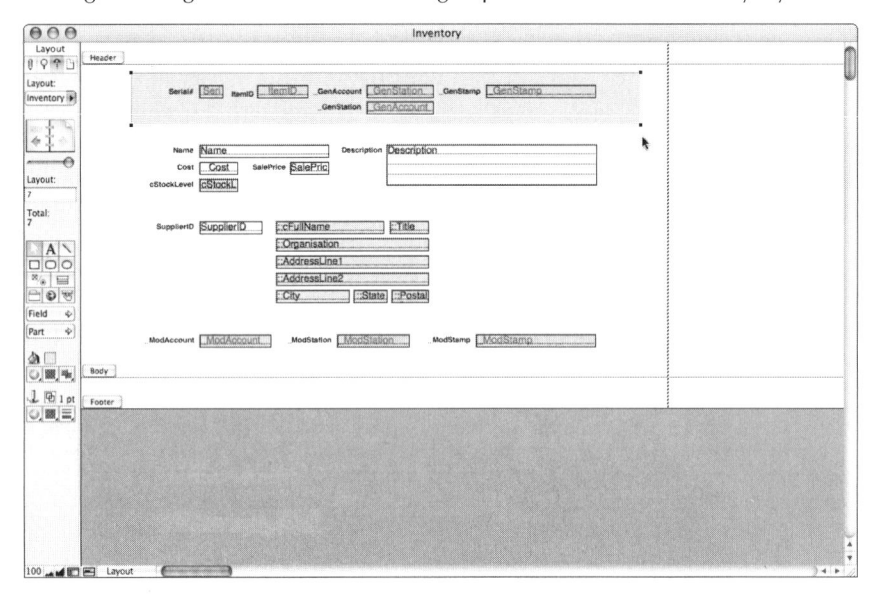

Repeat the preceding steps to add boxes behind each of the remaining three groups of fields. Apply the same shade of gray to the box behind the group of fields near the bottom of the layout, but choose a lighter shade for the data fields in the middle two groups. Then proceed as follows:

1. Click the Header part's tab to select it
2. Select the lightest gray fill color from the Fill Color tool in the Status Area. This changes the Header part's background color to light gray. Select the Footer by clicking its tab and again, apply the lightest gray fill to it.
3. Select the Text tool in the Status Area (the one labeled with an A), click near the top left of each rectangle, and type a text label to identify the group of fields.
4. Using the Text tool, click the field labels and (as appropriate) edit their names to conventional English labels for clarity.
5. Using the text tool, click in the Header area and type the word **Inventory**.
6. With the heading text selected, choose Format ⇨ Text Color and apply a mid gray,
7. Choose Format ⇨ Size to enlarge the heading and Format ⇨ Style to apply a bold type setting.
8. Increase the height of the header area (by dragging the Header tab downward a short distance) and drag the heading label text into a central position above the layout contents.

After completing these steps, return to Browse mode to view the effect of your work. Your Inventory layout should resemble the one shown in Figure 6.18.

### FIGURE 6.18

The Inventory layout, showing added visual cues to improve readability.

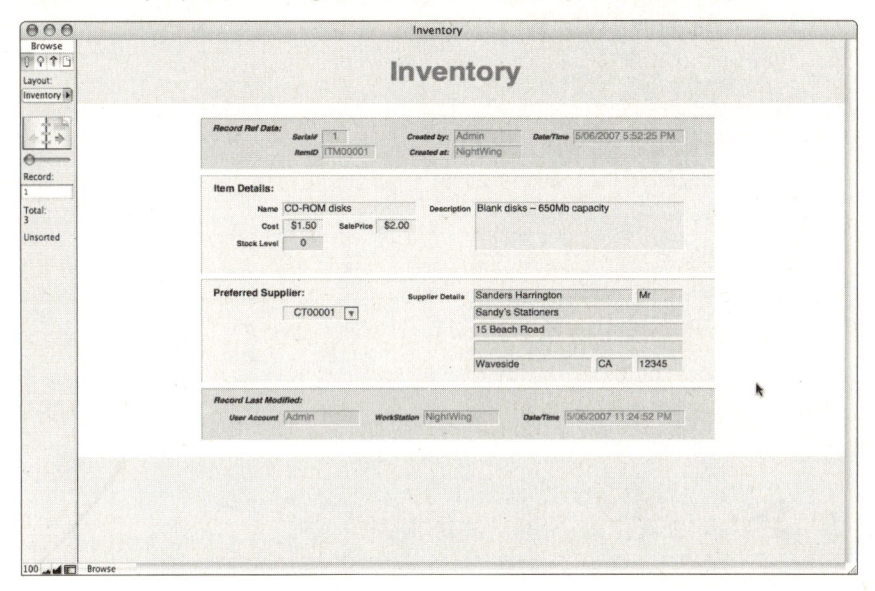

## Using white space

The proximity of layout elements is one of the cues indicating relationships between them, so grouping elements is important. To achieve the desired effect, it's equally important to leave space between the groups of elements. In other words, the spaces you leave are as important as the elements you add, when it comes to the user interpreting the screen (or page) content.

It's equally important to avoid clutter. If your table has many fields, consider showing only a manageable number of fields or groups of data on any one screen — use multiple screens or multiple panels of a tab control to create separation between groups of fields. Aim to present the user with clear and striking ideas, allowing them to focus on the essential elements that are important at each step.

## Ergonomics and avoiding visual fatigue

One of the reasons you should avoid clutter is that it's stressful and fatiguing for the user. As information is processed, mental connections are made and held in memory. It requires much more work and concentration to hold ten connections in mind than four or five. If you're able to present users with no more than a handful of interconnected ideas at any one time, your solutions become much easier to use.

Consider the essential ideas presented by the Inventory screen in its present form. In broad terms, the flow of ideas can be expressed as:

- There is an item record created by a certain user at a certain time.
- The item has a name, description, and price.
- We have a certain quantity of the item in stock.
- There is a preferred supplier with an associated address.
- The record was last modified by a certain user at a certain time.

With screen data grouped in this way, your users have a manageable group of ideas to digest at any one time.

Just as a screen's clutter or complexity affects the amount of user effort required, so do various other design aspects. Rich, or bright, colors make a strong impression and grab the user's attention, so if you want to draw attention to important items, you may want to use strong colors. However, if you overuse bright or strongly contrasting colors throughout a layout, the user is torn between many items all shouting for attention, which is also fatiguing.

We recommend that you choose subtle and relatively gentle shades for the majority of your layout areas, reserving strong or bright elements for those things that you want your screens to "shout" about.

## Giving information meaning

Most of the information you enter into the fields of a database means little on its own. The number "42" may be a profound answer — if we know what the question is. A fact such as "17 Priory Lane" may solve all our problems — if we know where it fits or to whom it belongs. The table and record structure of your solution provides a means of storing information in an ordered way, but users rely on the interfaces you design to make the order clear.

While the techniques shown earlier help your users understand the immediate connections between fields within a single record, they have to be able to comprehend the wider context. One aspect of the wider context is the overall data set encompassing the data subset displayed on the current layout. Another is the solution process or processes that the current screen supports. To add cues for these larger purposes, some additional techniques are required.

# Different Kinds of Layout Objects

In your work so far on the Inventory layout, you've dealt with three kinds of layout objects — field boxes, text labels, and graphical rectangles. Of these, the field boxes are the only ones that interact with the user or change their appearance from mode to mode or record to record. The text labels and graphical rectangles serve their purpose in a more passive fashion.

# The Interface: Layout Mode 6

When using a database, you need a variety of ways to interact with the data and the interface. To this end, FileMaker provides a number of additional object types, as represented by the main group of 11 tools in the Status Area (refer to Figure 6.5).

Among the tools, the Object Selection tool is used to choose one or more objects in the layout; you can also use it to drag objects (or groups of objects) to new locations in the layout. The remaining ten tools in the first block of tools represent various kinds of layout objects, as follows:

- Text objects
- Graphical line objects
- Rectangular (or square) objects
- Rectangles (or squares) with rounded corners
- Elliptical (or circular) objects
- Field controls (checkboxes, radio buttons, menus, and lists)
- Portals
- Tab controls
- Web viewers
- Buttons

In addition to the ten layout object types listed here, two more types of object are supported by FileMaker. The first of these, the field box, can be created using the Field tool immediately below the main group of tools. The final object type is any supported object (for example, a picture or illustration) created in another application, which you can paste into a layout or add by choosing Insert ⇨ Picture.

**NOTE** FileMaker supports more than a dozen common image formats, enabling you to place pictures and graphics from other applications directly onto FileMaker layouts. Supported formats include `.jpg`, `.gif`, `.tif`, `.png`, `.eps`, `.fpx`, and `.pdf` image files.

## Static and dynamic objects

Six of the 12 types of layout objects in FileMaker can be described as static—they add to the appearance of the layout, but you can't interact directly with them. In that regard, such objects serve their purposes passively. Inherently static layout objects include text objects, lines, squares/rectangles, round-cornered squares/rectangles, circles/ellipses, and inserted graphics/images.

By their nature, the remaining six layout object types support user interaction and can, therefore, be characterized as dynamic objects. In brief, their properties are as follows:

- **Field controls** are dynamic—when you click them, a value in the field they are attached to changes.
- **Portals** display lists of related records that you can (optionally) scroll, select, add, delete, or edit (depending on the portal and relationship configuration).

# Part II  Introduction to Database Design

- **Tab controls** let you click alternate tabs to view different layout content.
- **Web Viewer objects** display content from a remote (or local) Web site; they can be configured to enable you to click hyperlinks and interact directly with the content.
- **Field boxes** enable you to "enter" a record and directly add, edit, or delete data within the fields of the database.
- **Buttons** can be configured to execute any of 124 commands when you click them.

Now that we've told you that some objects are static and others are dynamic, we're going to risk confusing the issue by telling you that all but one type of object (a tab control) can *also* be formatted to act as a button. So even objects that are by nature static (such as lines, circles, imported images, and so on) can be given button properties so that a command is executed when the user selects them (for example, by clicking them).

## Inherent object properties

Each of the different kinds of objects has a number of inherent attributes, according to its intended function. For example, you can assign color, style, size, and font attributes to text objects, and line objects can have color, pattern, and thickness attributes. Additionally, you can assign a name to each object you place on a layout, change its size and position, and apply a variety of other formats and properties.

> **TIP** Object names, coordinates, and auto-resize properties are assigned using the Object Info palette, accessible in Layout mode by choosing View ⇨ Object Info.

According to its different appearance and behavior, each object type accepts a different range of properties and attributes. In the case of dynamic layout objects, each has a configuration dialog letting you specify its behavior. Double-clicking dynamic objects in Layout mode causes the corresponding configuration dialog to display so that you can edit the object's properties and parameters.

In addition to properties particular to their function, all objects can be assigned a variety of appearance attributes such as line and/or fill color, engraving or embossing effects, and so on. These attributes can be applied efficiently using the tools and controls in Layout mode's Status Area.

> **NOTE** The effect of applying graphical attributes to different kinds of objects varies according to the nature of the object. For example, fill/line color or transparency does not affect an inserted picture (because the picture's appearance and transparency attributes are set in the application in which it was created), but 3-D object effects can still be applied.

## Conditional format attributes

When you create an object, adding it to a layout, you establish its appearance as well as its size and placement on the layout. As you assemble the layout's components, the layout's overall appearance emerges. Moreover, FileMaker 9 provides you with the ability to link the appearance of various kinds of objects to the data within the database.

## The Interface: Layout Mode

**NEW FEATURE** In the Inventory layout for example, you may want to alert users when the stock level of an item falls below a certain level. One way to do that is to apply conditional formatting, introduced in FileMaker 9, so that the text is displayed in a different color when the stock level is low.

To apply conditional formatting, follow these steps:

1. Enter Layout mode with the Inventory layout active.
2. Select the cStockLevel field.
3. Choose Format ➪ Conditional. The Conditional Formatting dialog appears.
4. Click the Add button to create a condition.
5. Using the menus in the Condition area of the dialog, enter a value for the condition (for example, "Value is . . . less than . . . 5").
6. In the Format area of the dialog, choose the formatting attributes to be applied when the condition is met. Figure 6.19 shows the settings for a condition that changes the text color of the cStockLevel field to red when the stocking level of an item drops to fewer than five.

**FIGURE 6.19**

Settings to apply conditional text color to the cStockLevel field.

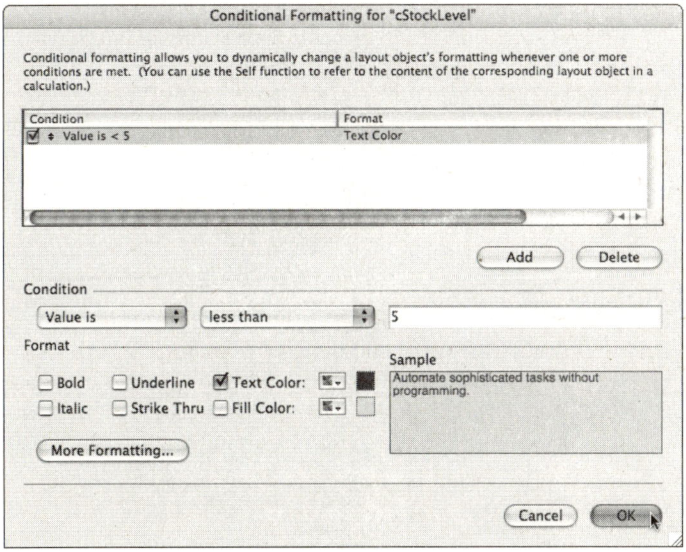

Conditional formatting can be applied to textual objects, including fields, buttons, and Web viewers, and can be used to control the text style, color, size, font, and background fill of the object.

153

Moreover, multiple conditions can be specified for an object, with conditions being evaluated in the order in which they appear in the list at the top of the dialog.

**CROSS-REF** For a more detailed discussion of the uses of conditional formatting, see Chapter 10.

# FileMaker as a Graphical Environment

FileMaker's Layout mode provides you with a drawing environment, enabling you to create graphical objects and assemble them into layouts. You can create designs, pictures, stationery, forms, slide presentations, and many other visual displays using Layout mode — with or without displaying data from FileMaker's database tables. The ability to insert images created in other applications further enriches FileMaker's interface building environment's creative possibilities.

Layout mode's flexibility is such that FileMaker has been used to create everything from boardroom presentations to store window advertising displays, shopping mall kiosks, and children's educational games. FileMaker enables you to arrange some pictures, shapes, and text and make them "do stuff" — the rest is up to your imagination.

## Building graphic objects in FileMaker

Using the Inventory layout as an example, try creating a graphical logo to appear in the header part, as described in the following steps.

1. Enter Layout mode for the Inventory layout.
2. Select the Oval tool and draw an elliptical shape approximately 2 inches wide and 0.75 inch high.
3. Using the fill color control, choose a dark mauve color, apply a dark blue line color, and, as shown in Figure 6.20, select the embossed option from the Object Effects palette.

**FIGURE 6.20**

Applying a 3-D embossed effect from the Object Effects palette.

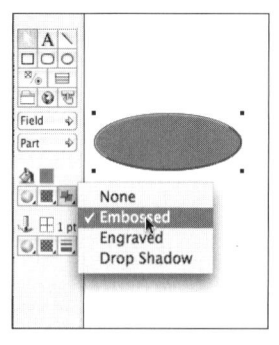

# The Interface: Layout Mode

4. Create a slightly smaller ellipse, giving it a lighter shade (of a similar hue), apply the Engraved effect, and position it centered on top of the first ellipse.

   To create a (fictitious) company name for the logo, the process is as follows:

   **a.** Choose the Text tool and type **xyz** as the logo name for this example.

   **b.** Using the Selection tool (arrow), click the text.

   **c.** Choose Format ⇨ Font ⇨ Courier New.

   **d.** Choose Format ⇨ Size ⇨ Custom and, in the resulting dialog, enter a custom size of 32 points. Click OK.

   **e.** Choose Format ⇨ Style ⇨ Italic.

   **f.** Click the text and drag it to the middle of the smaller oval shape.

   **g.** Choose Format ⇨ Text Color and select white from the submenu palette of text colors.

   **h.** Choose Edit ⇨ Copy and then Edit ⇨ Paste to create a duplicate of the xyz text.

   **i.** Choose Format ⇨ Text Color and select a dark purple color from the submenu palette of text colors.

   **j.** Position the dark purple text object exactly on top of the white text object in the middle of the two oval shapes.

   **k.** With the dark purple text object still selected, press the up arrow key (on the keyboard) to nudge it upward by one pixel, and then press the left arrow key to nudge it left by one pixel.

   When you've completed these steps, your completed logo should resemble the one shown in Figure 6.21.

5. Select all the logo parts at once by dragging a selection rectangle to encompass the entire logo and then choose Arrange ⇨ Group to lock the elements together.

### FIGURE 6.21

A logo image assembled in FileMaker from four graphical objects.

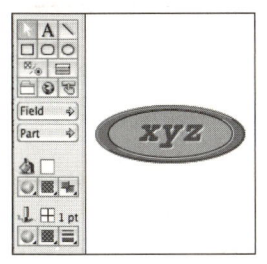

## Default object formats and attributes

When you create an object in Layout mode, it appears with default formats including style, font, color and line, although you can subsequently make alterations, if desired. If you're creating a number of similar objects, however, you'll find it advantageous to set default formats before you begin.

To set the default formats, first click with the Selection tool in a blank area of the layout to ensure that no objects are selected. Then choose the formats you want to use as defaults for objects you're about to create (for example, text color, font, style, and size — and, for fields and graphical shapes, fill, effects, and line attributes).

Now, when you select an object tool and create an object, the settings you've stored are used to determine the initial formats and attributes of each object. You can, of course, still select the objects and apply other settings if you want — setting default attributes simply saves you time by allowing you to determine the initial appearance of objects.

> **TIP** If you want to change the formatting on multiple items at once, first select them all (for example, by shift-clicking each in turn). Formatting and other attributes are then applied simultaneously to all selected items.

## Controlling stacking and alignment

When creating the xyz logo in the preceding example, each of its parts was created in order so that each new part lay in front of the previous one. In this process, graphical objects are being stacked up in a certain order to achieve the final effect. Each new object added to a layout goes on top of the stack (in front of any other objects already on the layout).

In FileMaker, you have control over the stacking order of objects, so you can change it if necessary to achieve the effect you desire.

To continue the developing visual theme of the Inventory layout, follow these steps:

1. Choose the Rounded Rectangle tool and draw a rectangle approximately 8.5 inches wide and a little less than 1 inch high (remember, you can use the Object Info palette — View ➪ Object Info — to check the size and coordinates of selected layout objects).

2. With the rectangle selected, use the Object Effects palette to apply the Embossed effect, the Fill Color palette to apply a pale lilac color, and select the transparency option from the Line Pattern palette.

3. Drag the resulting rectangle to a central position in the header. With the rectangle in the header, you can no longer see the header text because the rectangle obscures it. The next step addresses this.

4. Move the mouse to a blank area at one side just below the header area and drag a selection rectangle that encompasses the area where the heading text object is located (but not large enough to fully encompass the new rectangle you've placed in the header). When you release the mouse after dragging the selection rectangle, four selection boxes should appear to indicate that the text object in the header is selected, even though it is presently out of sight.

5. Choose Arrange ➪ Bring to Front to alter the stacking order, bringing the selected text object forward so that it appears in front of the colored rectangle.

## The Interface: Layout Mode    6

6. Select the logo object and drag it to a position within the left end of the rectangle in the header. Because the logo was created before the rectangle, it disappears behind the rectangle.

7. Click the rectangle to select it and choose Arrange ⇨ Send to Back (⌘+Option+] or Ctrl+Alt+]) to place it behind the logo.

After you adjust the placement and stacking order of the logo, heading text, and embossed rectangle, the Inventory layout should resemble the one shown in Figure 6.22.

**FIGURE 6.22**

The Inventory layout with logo and header band stacked and positioned.

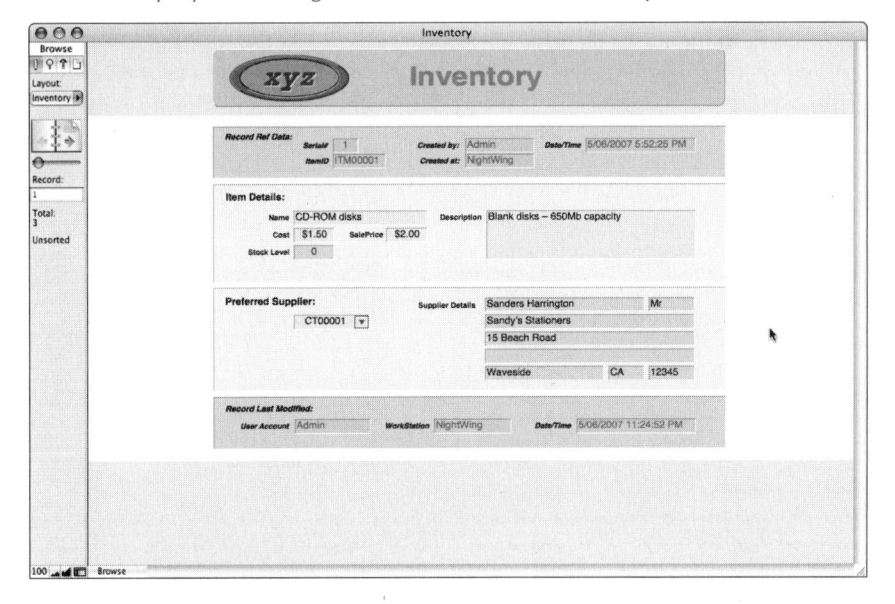

## Bringing in graphics from other applications

Instead of building graphics such as logos in FileMaker, you may prefer to create them in another application — or it may be appropriate to use photographs or other images you have on hand. In that case, you can use the images as objects in FileMaker's layouts.

Although you can copy images from other applications and paste them into FileMaker layouts, this does not always produce optimal results, depending on the attributes of the original image. We recommend that you save the image to disk in a standard format (such as .png, .gif, or .jpg) and then bring the file directly into FileMaker.

To place a picture stored in a supported file format directly onto a FileMaker layout, go to Layout mode, choose Insert ⇨ Picture, locate the file you want to add, and then click OK. The file is inserted and displayed on the layout and you can move it, resize it, and position it within the stacking order along with other layout objects.

157

# Interacting with Layout Objects

The work you do in Layout mode creates layouts for you to use in other modes, when interacting with your solution via its screens and reports. An important consideration when you build a layout is how efficiently you're able to use the layout in Browse mode and Find mode.

## Keyboard control of a layout

Controlling the behavior of layout objects (fields, buttons, tab controls, and so on) in Browse mode by clicking them with the mouse isn't always the most efficient way for your users to work. When entering data, many users prefer to perform common actions using keyboard commands.

With appropriate preparation, you can ensure that your layouts can be navigated and controlled using the keyboard. Using the Field Behavior dialog (select a field and then choose Format ➪ Field/Control ➪ Behavior) you can specify to go to the next object using the Tab key, the Return key, and/or the Enter Key. Figure 6.23 shows the Field Behavior dialog, displaying the settings for Go to Next Object Using near the bottom.

**FIGURE 6.23**

Setting the keystrokes for Go to Next Object Using in the Field Behavior dialog.

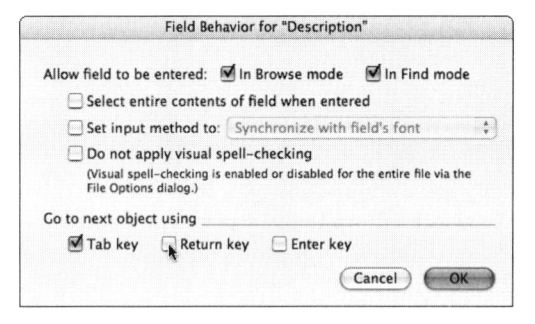

**NOTE** The Return key is the carriage return key at the right of the alphabetic section of the computer keyboard (even though on some keyboards, especially those common to Windows systems, it's labeled Enter). In FileMaker, the Enter key refers specifically to the numeric keypad's Enter key.

By default, navigating layout fields follows a sequence that goes from left to right and then top to bottom. By using the keystrokes defined in the Field Behavior dialog, you can move from field to field through the layout in Browse and Find modes. The navigation sequence that enables you to move around the layout in this way is referred to as the *tab order*.

**NEW FEATURE** Specifying the Return key as one of the Go to Next Field keystrokes for a field prevents users from typing a carriage return into the field. (However, users are not prevented from pasting carriage returns into the field from the clipboard.)

## The Interface: Layout Mode    6

This can, of course, be a useful technique for fields where the inclusion of carriage returns is not desired or may present problems.

## Setting the tab order

In many cases, you'll find it beneficial to predetermine the order of navigation through fields in your layouts, perhaps excluding some fields from the tab order. Moreover, you may want to include any tab controls, buttons, or Web viewers on your layouts in the tab order so they can be controlled from the keyboard.

To edit a layout's tab order, go to Layout mode and choose Layouts ➪ Set Tab Order to display the Set Tab Order dialog. As shown in Figure 6.24, fields (and any other keyboard-controllable objects) are displayed with adjacent arrows. The arrows attached to fields shown in the tab order include numbers indicating the field's position in the tab order sequence. Clicking the Clear All button in the Set Tab Order dialog removes the tab order numbering throughout the layout. Clicking the arrows in sequence enables you to edit the tab order or apply a new tab order.[0]

**FIGURE 6.24**

Specifying a custom tab order for fields on the Inventory layout.

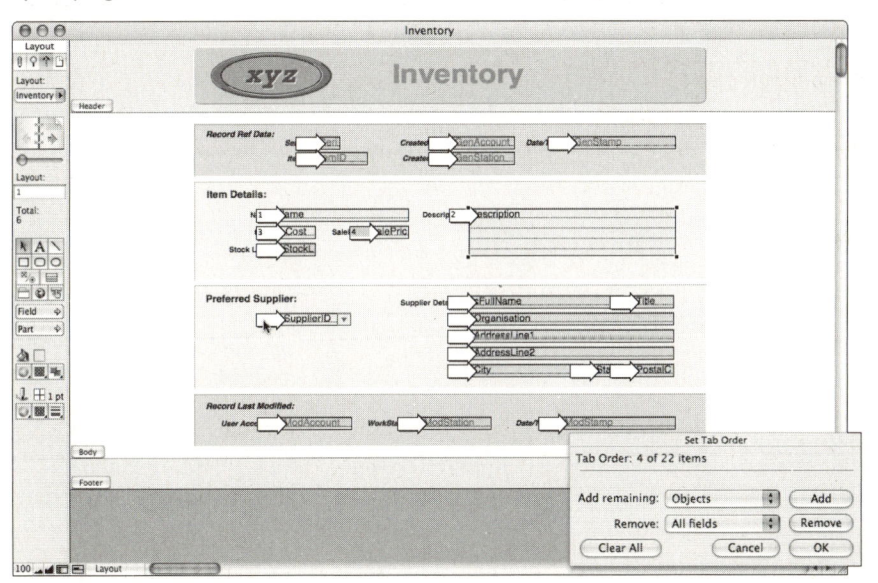

**NOTE** If a Tab Control object is included in the tab order, after you navigate to it using the keyboard, you can use the left and right arrows to select a specific tab and either the spacebar or the Return key to bring the selected tab to the front. Similarly, if a button object is included in the tab order, after selecting it using the keyboard, you can execute the button operation using the spacebar or the Return key.

159

## Assigning names to layout objects

FileMaker 8.5 introduced the ability to name objects on your layouts. Naming objects opens many possibilities — including letting you control or reference an object by its assigned name when you're defining a script or button command.

As an example, if you create a button object assigned to the Go to Object command and supply the object name of a field on the same layout, the button, when clicked, places the cursor into the corresponding field. You can use the same procedure to place focus on (or modify the behavior of) portals, Web viewers, tab control panels, and so on.

## Controlling visual spell-checking

A key usability feature in FileMaker Pro is visual spell-checking — automatic underscoring of questionable words in the active field throughout a FileMaker file. However, it is the nature of databases that some fields are designed to hold values that don't benefit from spell-checking (IDs, codes, names, and so on). In these cases, visual spell-checking is an annoyance and a distraction.

**NEW FEATURE** FileMaker Pro 9 introduces the option to disable the visual spell-checking feature for specific field objects on your layouts. Figure 6.25 shows Layout mode's Field Behavior dialog for the SupplierID field (Format ⇨ Field/Control ⇨ Behavior) with the Do Not Apply Visual Spell-Checking option enabled.[0]

**FIGURE 6.25**

Excluding a field from visual spell-checking via the Field Behavior dialog.

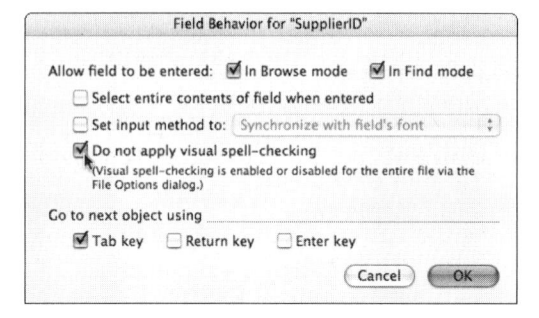

## The Tab Control and Its Uses

In complex solutions, layouts can rapidly become cluttered and the clarity of the interface impaired. FileMaker provides a useful organizational tool letting you put groups of objects away out of sight until you need them: the tab control.

## The Interface: Layout Mode

One of the best uses of tab controls is to provide locations for alternative and low-use views of data. A single click takes you to the data when you need it, but the rest of the time it's not cluttering up your view of the data.

Here is one such example: Our Inventory layout shows the preferred supplier for each item, but it may occasionally be useful to be able to view a list of buyers for the item. Because that's a secondary purpose of the layout, it would be better included on a concealed panel until needed.

## Defining and creating a tab panel

To add a tab panel to the Inventory layout, perform the following steps:

1. Enter Layout mode for the Inventory layout.
2. Delete the rectangular background behind the Preferred Supplier field.
3. Click the Status Area's Tab Control tool and then drag across the area of the Preferred Supplier fields. The Tab Control Setup dialog appears.
4. Enter **Preferred Supplier** into the Tab Name field and click the Create button.
5. Enter **List of Buyers** into the Tab Name field and click Create again.
6. In the dialog settings at the right, choose Left from the Tab Justification menu, Square from the Appearance menu, set the Tab Width menu to Label Width + Margin of:, enter **55** in the following field and choose Pixels from the bottom menu, as shown in Figure 6.26.

**FIGURE 6.26**

Adding a tab control to the Inventory layout.

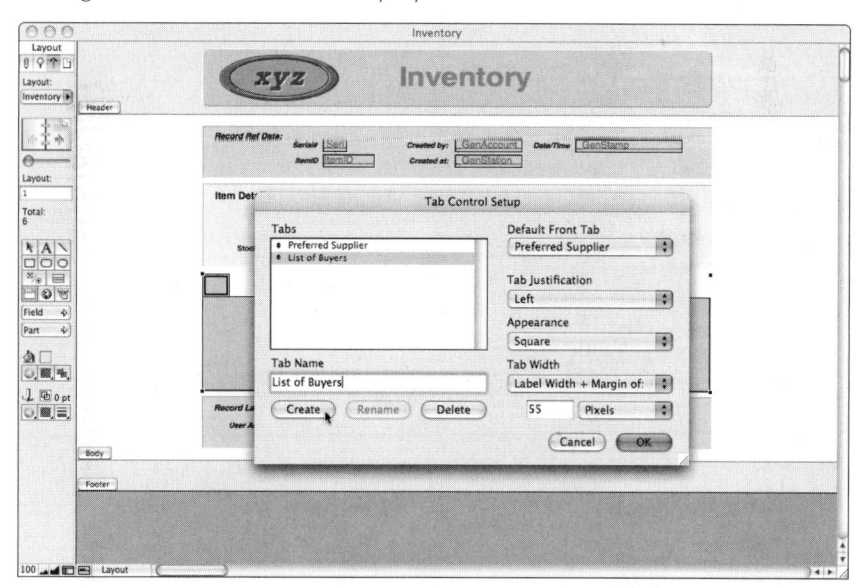

161

## Part II — Introduction to Database Design

7. Click OK to accept the Tab Control settings.
8. Choose Arrange ➪ Send to Back to place the tab control behind the existing supplier fields.
9. With the tab control still selected, choose lightest gray fill color, mid-gray line color, and select None from the Object Effects menu. If necessary, adjust the sizes and positions of the tab control and other elements on the layout to achieve appropriate spacing between objects.

After completing these steps, return to Browse mode to review the effects of your work. If all is well, the modified layout should be similar in appearance to Figure 6.27.

**FIGURE 6.27**

The appearance of the Inventory layout tab panel when viewed in Browse mode.

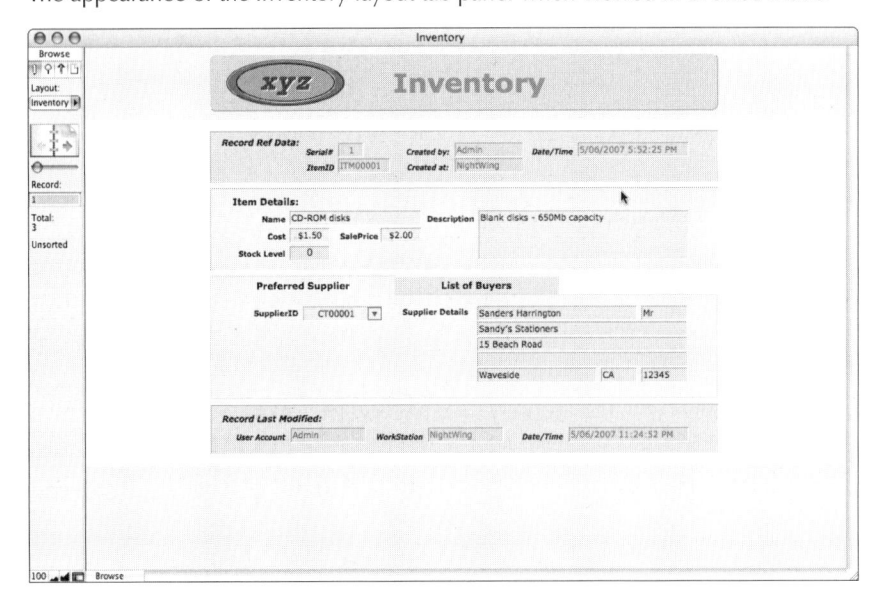

## Navigating between tab panels

In Browse mode, the default tab panel (Preferred Supplier) appears at the front, displaying the fields previously enclosed by a static rectangular panel. The tab for the second panel (List of Buyers) appears dimmed.

Click with the mouse on the List of Buyers tab and note that it comes to the foreground, obscuring the Preferred Supplier tab and its contents (the Preferred Supplier tab is now dimmed). Now click the Preferred Supplier tab and it returns to the front, reinstating your view of the supplier fields.

## Tab panel limitations

Although tab controls are powerful and flexible, an essential feature of their operation is that they provide a view of the data in your database from the same vantage point (TO on the Relationships Graph) as the layout where they're placed. Tab controls, like everything else on your layouts, are context-dependent.

In cases where you need to take the user outside the current layout context, there are two options you should consider:

- Place a portal in the tab control and build a supporting relationship structure enabling you to display the appropriate data from elsewhere in your solution.
- Create a separate layout based on an alternative TO that serves in place of the tab. To provide comparable functionality, provide a button on each layout that the users can click to move back and forth seamlessly between the two layouts. (If you set it up with care, the user experience is comparable to the use of a tab control.)

**CROSS-REF** For a more detailed exploration of the uses and advanced options available for tab controls, refer to Chapter 10.

# Displaying Related Data

The Inventory layout is based on the TO named Inventory and, by default, fields you place on the layout are sourced from the current record in the Inventory table. In some cases, however, you need to show fields from other tables so, as in the case of the Supplier Details group of fields, you choose an alternative (related) TO as the fields' source.

When you're working from a different layout (one based on a different TO), your view of the data in your solution is from a different vantage point. When sourcing data from another table, you must ensure that the TO you use to access fields from the other table is appropriately related to the current table. If in doubt, consult the Relationships Graph.

During the course of this chapter, we've described in detail processes for initial refinement of the Inventory layout. Before proceeding, take a few moments to work through the same processes on the remaining layouts in the file, using the same techniques to bring them into line with the layout and appearance of the Inventory layout.

## Working within layout context

When making adjustments to the second layout (Orders) in the file, as well as defining the SupplierID field as a drop-down list (choosing Format ➪ Field/Control ➪ Setup) and setting it to display the Suppliers value list, you need to add relevant fields from the Contacts table.

Whereas, on the Inventory layout, related suppliers fields were sourced from the ItemSupplier TO (related to Inventory), on the Orders layout, supplier fields must come from a TO that is appropriately related to the Orders TO. If you consult the Relationships Graph (in the Manage Database dialog, accessible by choosing File ➪ Manage ➪ Database), you'll see that the TO named Suppliers is directly related to the Orders TO.

On the Orders layout, when adding related fields to show the supplier details, you should source the fields from the Supplier TO, as shown in Figure 6.28.

The Supplier fields, once placed on the order layout, do their job of showing related data. There is one supplier for each order, and the relevant supplier details appear in the related fields (on the Orders layout) when a value is selected in the Orders::SupplierID field.

**FIGURE 6.28**

Using the Specify Field dialog to source fields from the related Supplier TO for inclusion on the Orders layout.

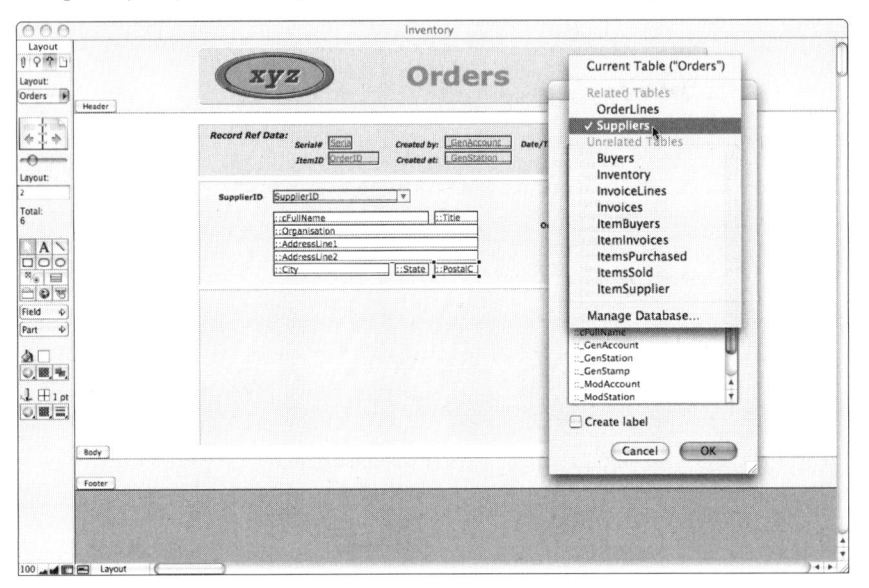

## Setting up a portal

Each order has only one supplier; however, a single order may consist of a number of items. Simply adding fields from the OrderLines TO is not adequate — you need a method to show a list of related records from the OrderLines TO. For this purpose, FileMaker provides the Portal object.

To add a portal to the Orders layout, enter Layout mode, click the Portal tool in the Status Area, and drag the mouse across the area of the layout where you want to add the portal. The Portal Setup dialog appears.

As shown in Figure 6.29, use the Show Related Records From menu near the top of the Portal Setup dialog to choose the OrderLines table from the group of related tables appearing in the list. Then select the Allow Deletion of Portal Records checkbox, and enter 8 into the Number of Rows

# The Interface: Layout Mode

field. Also, select the Alternate Background Fill checkbox and choose the second lightest gray from the adjacent color palette. When you've done this, click OK to accept the portal setup.

Immediately upon dismissing the Portal Setup dialog, you're presented with the Add Fields to Portal dialog. In the column at the left, select the OrderLines::Qty field and click the button labeled » Move » button to include it in the column at the right of the dialog. Repeat this procedure to include the OrderLines::ItemID field, the OrderLines::Price field, and the OrderLines:cLineTotal field (as shown in Figure 6.30). When complete, click the OK button.

### FIGURE 6.29

Adding a portal object (based on the OrderLines TO) to the Orders layout.

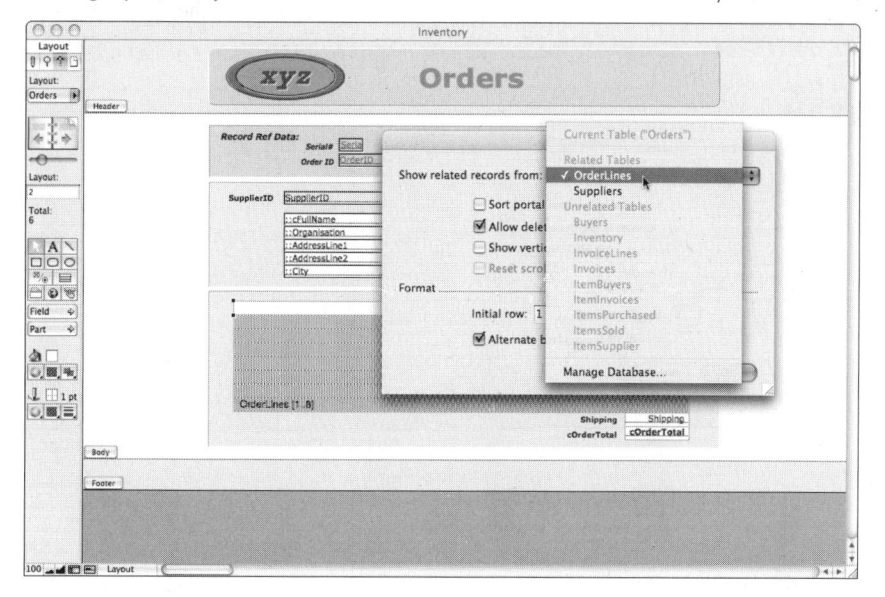

### FIGURE 6.30

Adding fields to the OrderLines portal.

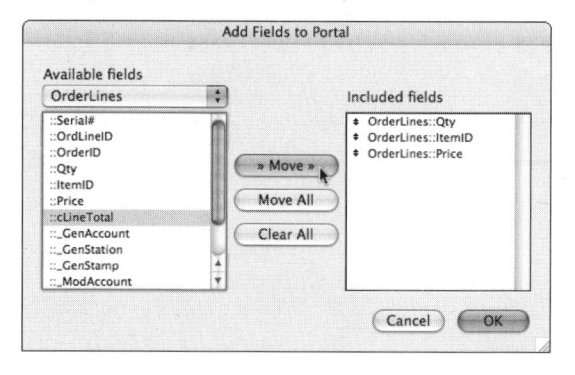

165

## Part II    Introduction to Database Design

You now have a portal on the Orders layout, but it needs some further configuration before it's ready for use. To complete the process, proceed as follows:

1. Select the ItemID field in your new portal and choose Format ➪ Field/Control ➪ Setup (⌘+Option+F/Ctrl+Alt+F).
2. In the Field/Control Setup dialog, choose Pop-up Menu from the Display As menu at the top left of the dialog.
3. Choose Manage Value Lists from the Display values from menu (immediately below the Display As menu).
4. In the Manage Value Lists dialog, click the New button at the lower left.
5. In the resulting Edit Value List dialog, enter AllItems into the field labeled Value List Name. Then select the Use Values from Field radio button. The Specify Fields for Value List "AllItems" dialog appears.
6. Choose the Inventory TO from the menu above the column at the left of the Specify Fields dialog.
7. In the list in the left column of the Specify Fields dialog, select ItemID.
8. Above the column at the right of the Specify Fields dialog, select the Also Use Values from Second Field checkbox, and then select the Name field in the list in the right column.
9. Near the bottom of the dialog, select the Show Values Only from Second Field checkbox.
10. Click OK to accept and dismiss each of the dialogs in turn.
11. In the portal, select all four fields and apply transparent line and fill attributes.
12. Resize the OrderLines::Qty field to approximately 0.5 inch wide and move it to the far left of the portal.
13. Resize both the OrderLines::Price and OrderLines::cLineTotal fields to approximately 1 inch wide each, and move them to the right side of the portal.
14. With the OrderLines::Price and OrderLines::cLineTotal fields still selected, choose Format ➪ Number, and select the options to Format as decimal, fixed number of digits 2, use currency notation, and use thousands separator. Then click OK to accept the number format settings.
15. Choose Format ➪ Align Text ➪ Right.
16. Reposition and resize the portal appropriately, applying a white fill and gray line attributes to it.
17. Immediately above the portal, add text labels for Qty, Item, Price, and Extended Price.

After you've completed these steps, return to Browse mode to view the results of your efforts. The Orders layout should now resemble Figure 6.31.

Try adding some items to the portal (by entering them into the first blank line). The portal accepts and displays up to eight lines, calculating the price, extended price, and order total values automatically. Of particular note is the way the value list operates in this case, automatically retrieving a

## The Interface: Layout Mode

list of available items from the Inventory table so that you can select them when adding a line to an order. In conjunction with the use of a portal to add OrderItems records, the value list in this example provides powerful and flexible support to the user.

Before proceeding, take a little time to look over the other layouts in the file and bring them into line with the changes you've made to the Orders layout. In particular, the Invoices layout should be developed to closely resemble the Orders layout, including the use of a portal to display invoice lines. The Contacts layout is simpler, and its presentation will more closely resemble the Inventory layout.

### FIGURE 6.31

The Orders layout in Browse mode showing the completed OrderLines portal.

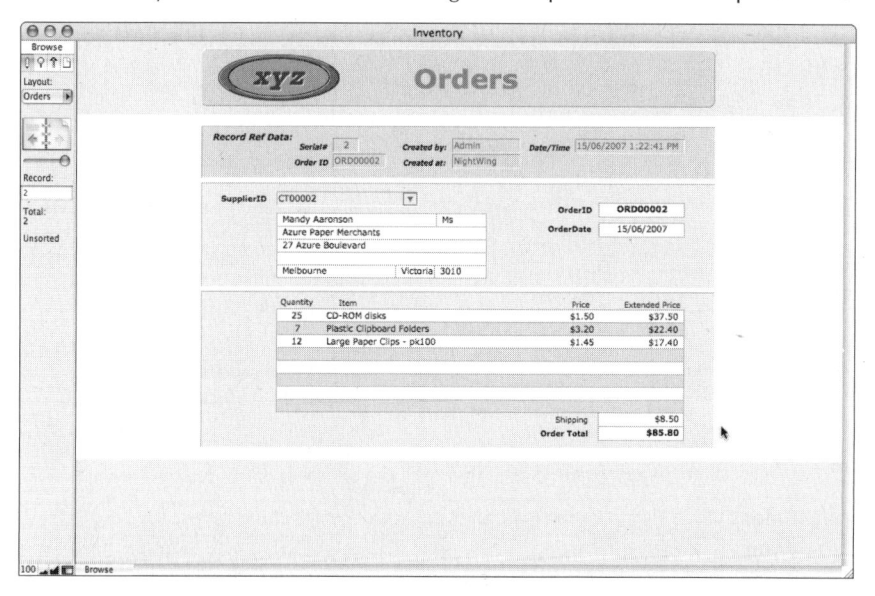

## The Magic of Buttons

FileMaker provides a special tool in Layout mode's Status Area for the creation of buttons. Buttons created with the Button tool are embossed rectangular text objects with a command attached.

There are two things you should know about buttons:

- The Format ⇨ Button command can be used to attach a command to any layout object (with the exception of a tab control) — not just objects created with the button tool. So almost anything can be a button.

167

- One of the commands you can attach to a button is more important than all the rest combined. It is the Perform Script [ ] command, and it's important because it enables a button to run a script containing many commands, capable of performing complex operations.

**CROSS-REF** For further discussion about advanced uses of buttons, refer to Chapter 10

## Defining buttons

In the Inventory database, go to Layout mode on the Orders layout. To add a button to the layout, follow these steps:

1. Select the button tool
2. Drag a rectangle approximately 2 inches wide in the footer area. When you release the mouse button, the Button Setup dialog immediately appears.
3. Choose the Go to Layout option in the list of commands at the left of the Button Setup dialog, as shown in Figure 6.32.
4. Use the Specify menu in the panel at the upper right to choose the Inventory layout.
5. Click OK to accept the settings and dismiss the dialog.

**FIGURE 6.32**

Creating a button in the footer area of the Orders layout.

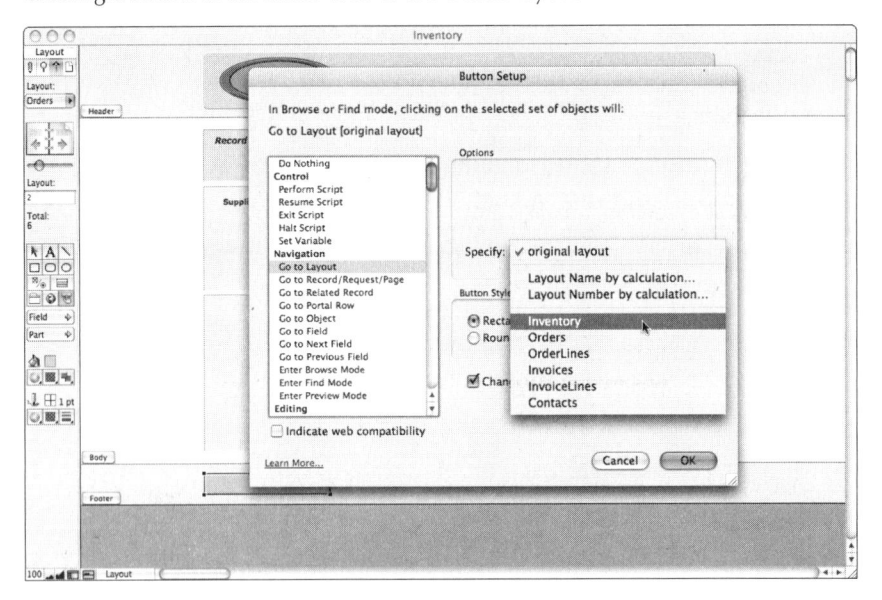

## The Interface: Layout Mode

6. After you close the Button Setup dialog, the cursor flashes in the new button you've created, waiting for you to enter a button label — type **Inventory**.
7. Press the Enter key (on the numeric keypad) or click in a blank area of the layout to exit the button.

Now you have a button in the footer area of the layout, and it is assigned to the Go to Layout [ ] command. Further work is required, however, to bring its appearance into line with the design of the layout. To style the button, proceed as follows:

1. With the button selected, choose View ➪ Object Info. The Object Info command acquires a tick and the Info palette appears.
2. Click the scale values at the right of the palette (the ones that read "in," "cm," or "px") to toggle the scale until it displays measurements in px (pixels).
3. Type **153** as the horizontal dimension and **22** as the vertical dimension.

> **TIP** The horizontal and vertical dimension parameters in the Object Info palette are grouped together and identified by double-ended arrow symbols oriented horizontally and vertically, respectively.

4. Choose Format ➪ Size ➪ 12.
5. Choose Format ➪ Style ➪ Bold.
6. Choose Format ➪ Color ➪ [white].
7. Select a medium gray from the Fill Color palette and the transparent option from the Line Pattern palette.

After you complete these steps, your button has both form and function and is ready for duty as part of the interface of your solution. To create a second button, select the Inventory button and follow these steps:

1. Choose Edit ➪ Duplicate (or type ⌘+D or Ctrl+D). A second button appears.
2. Position the duplicate button immediately to the right of the original button.
3. Click the text tool in the Status Area and then on the duplicate button and edit the text to **Orders**.
4. Change the text color of the duplicate button to match the background color of the logo, and change the fill color to two shades lighter gray.
5. Double-click the Orders button. The Button Setup dialog appears.
6. From the Specify menu in the upper-right area of the dialog, choose the Orders layout.

With both buttons complete and functional, the next task is to create corresponding buttons on another layout so that you can navigate back and forth using the buttons in the footer. To replicate the two buttons you've created so far, and to complete the navigation button set, follow these steps:

1. Select both buttons
2. Note the left and top coordinates shown in the Object Info palette.

> **TIP** The left and top coordinates in the Object Info palette are identified by an arrow symbol pointing left and an arrow symbol pointing up, respectively.

3. Choose Edit ➪ Copy.
4. Navigate to the Inventory layout.
5. Choose Edit ➪ Paste.
6. Enter the left and top coordinates (as noted before leaving the Orders layout) into the Object Info palette and press the Enter key (on the numeric keypad). This results in the pair of buttons being positioned identically in both layouts.
7. Edit the colors of the text and fill for both buttons on the Inventory layout so that the lighter gray fill is on the Inventory button, the mid-gray fill on the Orders button, the text on the Inventory button matches the color of the logo background, and the text on the Orders button is white.
8. Make two duplicates of the Orders button.
9. Change the text on the duplicate buttons to **Invoices** and **Contacts**, respectively.
10. Edit the button setup of the duplicate buttons to go to the layouts corresponding to their names.
11. Position the Invoices and Contacts buttons side-by-side to the right of the first two buttons on both the Invoices and Orders layouts.
12. Copy the four buttons and paste them at the same location in the footers of the Invoices and Contacts layouts.
13. Ensure in each case that the button corresponding to the current layout has lighter gray fill and colored text and that all the other buttons have mid-gray fill and white text.

With the above steps complete, return to Browse mode and click your new buttons. You can now navigate to the four main areas of your solution using simple mouse clicks in the footer, as shown in Figure 6.33.

## Button scope and button commands

As you saw in the preceding exercise, creating buttons is not difficult. Moreover, although all four of the buttons you've created so far use the Go to Layout command, you've seen that the Button Setup dialog provides access to a great variety of commands.

FileMaker buttons are an interface tool and have no meaning outside the layouts where they reside; they always act from the context of the layout where you place them. For some button commands — such as the Go to Layout command — context is not critical, and the command could be executed from anywhere in the file. Other commands, however, require access to the data structure of the file and are therefore constrained to operate from the perspective of the layout (and the TO associated with the layout).

### FIGURE 6.33

The Inventory layout complete with navigation buttons in the footer to provide direct access to the other main screens in the file.

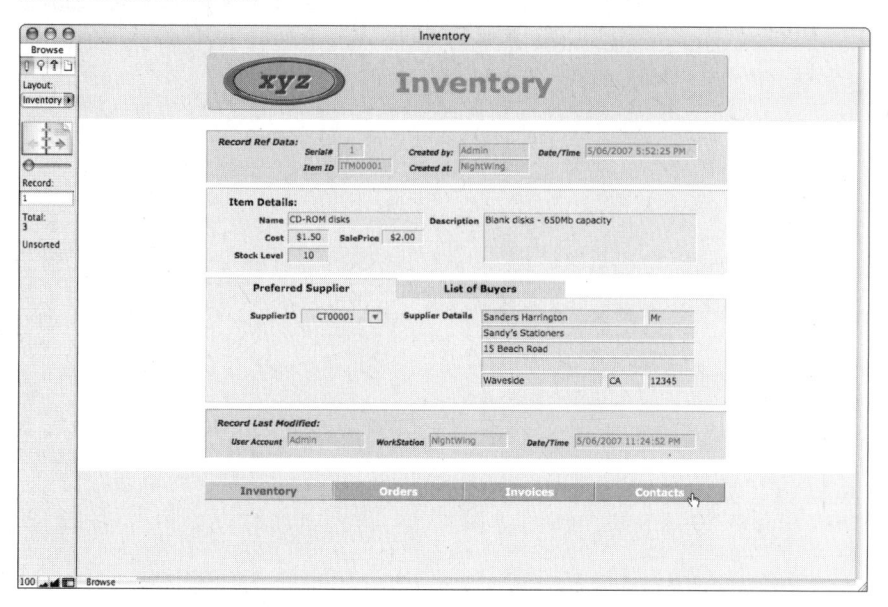

## The button as an object

Like other objects, buttons can be assigned an object name. The object name is separate from the label you type onto the button and is only seen in the Object Info palette when the button is selected in Layout mode.

> **TIP** Object names for buttons and all other objects are entered and edited via the Object Name field at the top of the Object Info palette.

When you've assigned a button's object name, scripts or buttons can select it automatically by executing the Go to Object command (supplying the relevant object name as the command parameter).

Similarly, you can include buttons in the layout tab order, along with fields, tab controls, and Web viewers. When you add a button to the tab order, you'll be able to select it using the keyboard command(s) assigned to Go to Next Object for the object preceding the button in the tab order.

When you've selected a button — either via the Go to Object command or via the keyboard — you can execute it by pressing either Return or Space.

# The Web Viewer: Inviting in the World

FileMaker's Web Viewer object enables you to incorporate Web browser capabilities within defined areas of the layouts of your solution. In FileMaker 9, a Web viewer can be deployed to retrieve online content from the World Wide Web, to render HTML content stored on your computer's drives or on a local network, or to display content directly from your database.

## Setting up a Web viewer

Implementing a Web viewer on your layout is neither difficult nor time-consuming. Simply click the Web Viewer tool in the Status Area in Layout mode, and drag across an empty area in your layout. When you release the mouse button, the Web Viewer Setup dialog appears.

The Web Viewer Setup dialog provides automated setup options for a number of useful Web resources. If you know the URL of the location you want to display, however, you can select the Custom Web Address option in the Choose a Website list and enter the desired URL directly into the Web Address field in the lower part of the dialog (see Figure 6.34).

**FIGURE 6.34**

Specifying an internet location (URL) in the Web Address field of the Web Viewer Setup dialog.

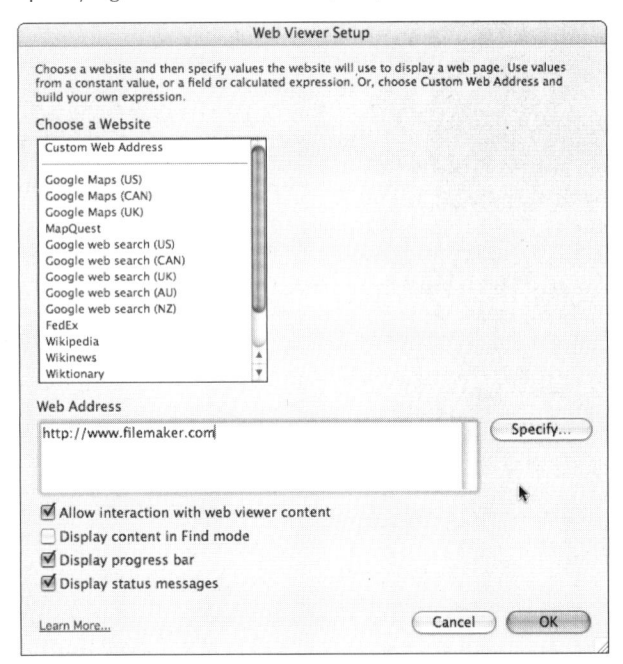

After setting up a Web viewer in this way, you can view the Web page content in your layout in Browse mode. Clicking hyperlinks enables you to navigate to other sites, download files, and so on, just as you do in a browser.

> **CROSS-REF** You can find additional information about alternative configurations and uses for Web viewers in Chapter 10.

## Controlling a Web viewer

Although a Web viewer, as outlined earlier, provides the direct Web surfing capability such as you experience in a Web browser, it does not automatically provide the various standard controls for operations such as back, forward, refresh, and so on. If you require additional functions of that kind, you have to build your own controls.

FileMaker provides a button and script command — Set Web Viewer — configurable in various ways to provide either manual or automatic control of a Web viewer. To direct FileMaker to control a specific Web viewer (it's possible to have more than one on the same layout), you must first assign an object name to the Web viewer. You can then enter the Web viewer's name into the Object Name field when configuring the options for the Set Web Viewer command, as shown in Figure 6.35.

**FIGURE 6.35**

Setting options to control a Web viewer with the Set Web Viewer command.

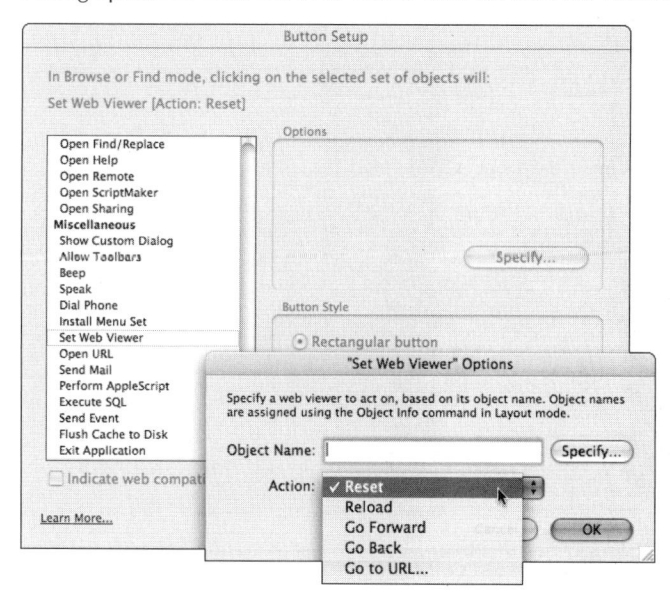

## Complementary data concepts

The value of including Web content within your databases is greatest when it directly supports and extends the core functionality of your solutions — such as providing you with maps to your supplier's dispatch stations or retrieving catalog entries and prices for new products. In other words, data and images from the Web can complement and enrich your solution.

If you have your own organization or business, you're probably publishing key information on a public Web site of your own, keeping your clients, customers, students, patients, or constituents informed. Web viewers provide you with an excellent opportunity to view your organization's public information and your internal data side-by-side, placing the information you need at your fingertips. For example, you may want to show a picture (from the Web) of each product in your inventory system.

# Reports and Data Output

This chapter has focused primarily on ways to make your solution functional and its interface operationally efficient. Consequently, the layouts and examples provided have been directed toward creating screens rather than useful printed output. However, while databases must first enable you to add data, it is equally essential that you retrieve and present data efficiently.

We encourage you to consider making separate screens for printing information from your solution. That way, you don't have to compromise screen designs to accommodate the limitations of paper sizes and printer capabilities — and your letters, lists, and summary reports are not constrained by screen ergonomics.

## Considerations for printed output

Most printed matter — from business correspondence to boardroom reports — is printed in black (or dark) ink on white (or at least light) stationery. With a few exceptions, business documents are preferred in portrait orientation, and efficient use of space on the page (packing a lot of information in) is mandated.

In each of these respects, the requirements for printed output are at odds with the things that make good and useable screens. Screens are typically landscape in orientation; judicious use of color is beneficial, and it's preferable to avoid packing the information too densely.

Creation of good reports is frequently an exercise in efficient organization of large amounts of information into compact formats, using clean lines and simple (but elegant!) presentation.

## Using fonts

Modern printers are capable of much higher resolutions than computer monitors. So, although many people begin to complain of eye strain when reading screen lettering at sizes of 10 points or less, smaller font sizes are readily accepted in most printed formats. Moreover, the most readable screen fonts are well spaced, rounded, and generally sans serif, whereas compact serif fonts work best for printed output.

We've previously suggested Verdana as a good font for general purpose use, and it's well suited to onscreen data display. For some kinds of reports, Verdana also works well, but substitutions with Trebuchet, Times, or other comparable fonts may be appropriate for more densely packed report formats.

Whatever your choices of font, we offer two essential rules:

- **Be consistent and moderate.** Try to keep to one or two fonts throughout a solution (logos and occasional special headings aside) and make sparing and judicious use of alternate faces and weights (italic, bold, and so on).

- **Ensure that whatever fonts you choose are available on every computer that the solution is to be used on.** If a font is not available, font substitution occurs and its effects can make an appalling mess of your carefully constructed layouts and reports.

Finally, be aware that fonts (even the same font family) are rendered slightly differently (including different size) on different operating systems and can even vary depending upon the font supplier. Typically, fonts appear slightly larger on Windows than they do on Macintosh, so you may need to allow for this in your screen designs.

**CROSS-REF** We discuss issues related to developing for cross-platform deployment in greater detail in Chapter 10.

## Page sizes and page setup

In most parts of the world, page sizes are standardized — unfortunately, to different standards. In Australia, in Japan, and throughout Europe, the International Standards Organization (ISO) A4 standard is customary, while in the United States, the American National Standards Institute (ANSI) letter format holds sway. With globalization and the increasing use of the Internet, it's no longer safe to assume that all users of a solution have access to the same kinds of stationery. We recommend that you make a margin allowance to ensure that your reports and letters can be accommodated on an alternative page format should the need arise.

Meanwhile, FileMaker Pro is accommodating with regard to the many printers, printer drivers, and stationery formats — it provides you with options to save page specifications and other settings in scripts that automatically generate your reports.

**TIP** If you frequently switch among different paper sizes or orientations while printing manually, consider making buttons to restore the settings for particular situations (save sets of Page Setup settings in a button command configuration). In this manner, a single mouse-click can (re)set the appropriate configuration for you.

## Paper output versus PDF or Excel output

We're not about to break into song about the dream of the paperless office — but we would nevertheless like to encourage you to save a few trees by taking advantage of FileMaker's excellent support for generation of data and reports direct to widely used formats such as Excel and PDF.

The capability to index and store documentation in electronic form is not only fast and eco-friendly, it also saves you money, effort, and storage space. An entire filing drawer of text documents can be compressed and stored on a single DVD. Terabytes of information can be stored in economical and reliable hard drives. Further, when the inevitable time arrives where you need to update your documentation, even more trees survive.

If you need any more encouragement, we note that FileMaker enables you to create a document and automatically attach it to an e-mail — all as part of a single process. With a little thought and planning, you can design your solutions to take fullest advantage of these capabilities.

**CROSS-REF** More detailed coverage of techniques for generating reports and summaries in FileMaker is provided in Chapter 10.

## Composite PDFs from multiple layouts

Layouts are the face of your data. When printing or viewing data, you're accessing the underlying tables through a layout. Although layouts are very flexible, they constrain you to a specific perspective or vantage point within the structure of your solution. In some cases, you want a report to combine content from several different vantage points, so you produce reports that combine pages or sections from different layouts.

**NEW FEATURE** FileMaker Pro 9 introduces the capability to append pages to an existing PDF file via script — so you can produce compact documents combining elements from any part of your solution.

**CROSS-REF** You can find a detailed discussion about the process of generating composite PDF reports using FileMaker's scripting engine in Chapter 14.

In the last two chapters, you've seen and used most of the basic solution-building techniques, including creating relationships to bring data together from different tables. You've seen some indications of the power at FileMaker's core. Now it's time to delve more deeply into the heart of the database and take a closer look at the workings of the Manage Database dialog, where the structure of your solutions takes shape.

**ON the WEB** The example database we've been developing, as it exists at this point, can be found on the companion Web site at www.wiley.com/go/filemaker9bible.

# Chapter 7

# The Structure: The Manage Database Dialog

People using your solution will spend almost all their time in Browse mode, Find mode, and Preview mode. While developing your solution, you will also spend a little time in each of these areas, testing your solution's implementation. However, you'll spend the bulk of your development time in Layout mode (see Chapter 6), in ScriptMaker (see Chapter 8), and in the Manage Database dialog (see Chapter 5). Just as an architect's office is where a building is planned and designed, the Manage Database dialog is the nexus where you define and refine your solution's tables, fields, and relationships. Without tables, fields, and relationships, the layouts and scripts are pointless, and the user has nothing to work with.

A building's blueprint constrains both the type and quantity of materials used in construction, but it also affects the time and labor involved. Similarly, the decisions you make defining your fields, tables, and relationships affect the layouts you create and the scripts you write.

Chapters 5 and 6 demonstrated an iterative approach to building solutions. FileMaker Pro is especially suited to this iterative style, known as *rapid application development* (RAD), a methodology developed and popularized during the 1980s. Here are some examples of FileMaker RAD behavior:

- Defining a table (and its fields) causes FileMaker to create an initial layout.
- Endowing a field definition with auto-entry criteria means that FileMaker seeds the field with an automatic initial value whenever a new record is created.
- Validation criteria cause FileMaker to verify that a field's values are appropriate before committing a record.
- Defining a relationship tells FileMaker how and when to retrieve and enter data to tables related to the layout's table.

## IN THIS CHAPTER

Working with tables

Specifying fields

Doing basic calculations

Understanding the Relationships Graph

Looking at data relationships

Working with External SQL Data Sources

## Part II   Introduction to Database Design

All the decisions you make in the Manage Database dialog impact the solution in both obvious and subtle ways, and that's what this chapter is all about.

# Working with Tables

A FileMaker table exists in two contexts:

- As a structure consisting of field definitions
- As a repository for the records (data) the user adds to the database

Your database, as an entity, consists of your tables and the relationships you define connecting them.

## Table concepts: A room with a view

Drawing upon our architectural analogy, if the database corresponds to a house, the tables are the rooms and the table occurrences (TOs) are the doors and windows through which you see into rooms and pass between rooms. How you set up your TOs determines what content is accessible from your various tables and which relationships you employ to access that data — just as the placement of rooms, doors, and windows in your home constrains how you get from one room to another.

## Adding, deleting, and renaming tables

As we demonstrate in Chapter 5, TOs are views into your tables, and you can create as many different TOs as necessary or desired to facilitate data access, just as you can put multiple doorways and windows in a room, each providing a separate perspective. Regardless of how many Contact TOs you create, there is still only one Contact table. You create, delete, and modify tables in the Manage Database dialog's Tables panel, but you create, delete, and manage TOs in the Manage Database dialog's Relationships panel.

**NOTE** You can find out how many TOs of each table appear in the Relationships Graph by counting them in the Occurrences in Graph column on the Tables tab of the Manage Database dialog. If there are numerous occurrences, you may need to enlarge the dialog to see them all. Alternatively, you can select one of the table occurrences in the Relationships Graph and type ⌘+U or Ctrl+U to select all TOs with the same source table and then count the selected TOs.

Figure 7.1 shows the Manage Database dialog's Tables panel for our Inventory example database. If you haven't been following along previously or you just want to start where we are, you can download the Inventory_Ch6.fp7 file from this book's companion Web site.

Of the three Manage Database dialog panels, the Tables panel is the least packed with controls, but it displays a lot of useful information. Of particular import, you can see in the rightmost column (Occurrences in Graph) how many TOs for a table appear in the Relationships Graph, and the names those TOs bear, information not readily apparent in the Relationships Graph or any of your

# The Structure: The Manage Database Dialog  7

layouts. Additionally, you can view the more mundane aspects for each table: the table's name, the table's source (FileMaker or, if external, the DSN via which the table is accessed), and how many fields and records the table contains. Although much of the information gathered together here can also be found in other places in the application, having an overview of your solution's structure is convenient.

### FIGURE 7.1

Create, remove, and rename your tables in the Manage Database dialog's Tables panel.

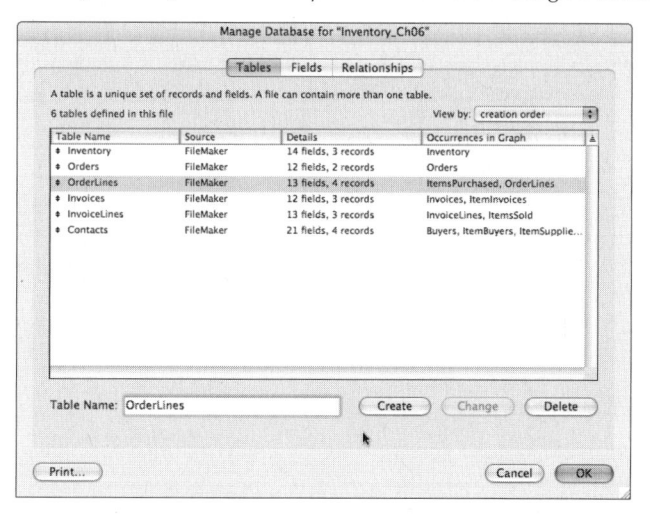

**NOTE** If you're using FileMaker Pro 9 Advanced, you also have a Database Design Report (DDR) available to you. The DDR collects all the information about your solution — tables, fields, relationships, scripts, and so on — into one consolidated report (see Chapter 18 for more information).

In the Manage Database dialog's Tables panel, you can resize the columns' widths by positioning the cursor over the column joins. The View By pop-up menu lets you choose between a creation order listing, an alphabetically sorted listing, or a single user-defined listing of your tables. Use the handles to the left of the table names to drag the table names into your desired sequence (when you do so, the View By menu automatically switches to custom order). You saw how to create a new table in Chapter 5 (type a name in the Table Name text box and click Create). To remove a table, select it in the table list and click Delete. Finally, to rename a table, select it, edit the name in the Table Name text box, and click the Change button. (The Change button is disabled when inapplicable.)

FileMaker Pro takes follow-up actions on your behalf when you change a table's name. Associated TOs with matching names (either with the same name as the table or the same name with an appended number) will be updated to match the new table name. Moreover, any layouts associated with those TOs that have names exactly matching the TO name will be automatically updated to match the new TO name. Along with these changes, references to the renamed TOs and layouts in calculations and scripts will automatically reflect the new names.

> **NOTE** In some cases, you may not want cascading name changes throughout elements in your solution. If you edit the names of the TOs so that they no longer exactly match the source table name, FileMaker doesn't apply any automatic changes when you change a table name.

## Moving tables between files

Frequently, solution providers discover that some of the tables they create for a solution would also prove useful in other solutions (for example, lots of solutions require a Contacts table). Similarly, within a multi-file solution, occasions may arise when you want to move a table between two files in the solution.

If you're using FileMaker Pro 9 Advanced, you can simply open both files, select the table you want to duplicate in the source file's Manage Database dialog Tables panel, and choose Edit ➪ Copy (⌘+C or Ctrl+C). Then, selecting the Manage Database dialog Tables panel for the target file, choose Edit ➪ Paste (⌘+V or Ctrl+V).

FileMaker Pro Advanced also provides a table import capability in the Tables panel of the Manage Database dialog. This feature adds the table structure (fields and all their calculations validation options and so on) but does not import data, relationships, or any other associated elements.

Whether or not you're using Advanced, you have the option of importing a table from one solution into another, as an additional option when using the File ➪ Import Records ➪ File command, as described in the following section.

## Importing tables

Although nowhere near as quick and convenient as copy-paste, importing a table achieves the desired goal and offers a few options not present in copy-paste. When importing a table via the File ➪ Import Records ➪ File command, you simultaneously add the entire table structure and the data it contains (or a subset of the data, if you first perform a Find in an open source file, or if you deselect some fields in the Import Mapping dialog).

> **NOTE** FileMaker always imports all fields from the source table when adding a table to the destination file. However, using the Import mapping process, you can choose whether to import data to the fields

> **CAUTION** As with any irreversible action, especially one that alters your solution's structure, we recommend that you perform the import into a copy of your solution or make a backup prior to implementing the change.

# The Structure: The Manage Database Dialog   7

In the following steps, we import a table from the Photo Catalog starter solution into a new solution:

1. Create a Photo Catalog solution by choosing File ➪ New Database, clicking the Create database using Starter Solution radio button, and choosing Photo Catalog from the Home — Collections category. Accept the default Photo Catalog name and click Save to proceed.

**NOTE** The option to select a Starter Solution when you create a new file is available via the FileMaker Quick Start screen. The Quick Start screen is enabled by default, but can be disabled. If the Quick Start screen doesn't appear when you choose File ➪ New Database, you can re-enable it in the General tab of the FileMaker Pro Preferences dialog, as described in Chapter 3.

2. Create your new solution by choosing File ➪ New Database, selecting the option to create an empty database.
3. Name the new database **MyCollections.fp7** (for the sake of this example). When you click Save, the Manage Database dialog appears. Note that by default, FileMaker has also added an empty table with the same name as the file (MyCollections).
4. Click OK to dismiss the Manage Database dialog.
5. Choose File ➪ Import Records ➪ File, choose the Photo Catalog solution created in Step 1 in the Open File dialog that appears, and click Open. The Import Field Mapping dialog (see Figure 7.2) appears.

**FIGURE 7.2**

Specify what fields to import data from (if any exist in the source file) here.

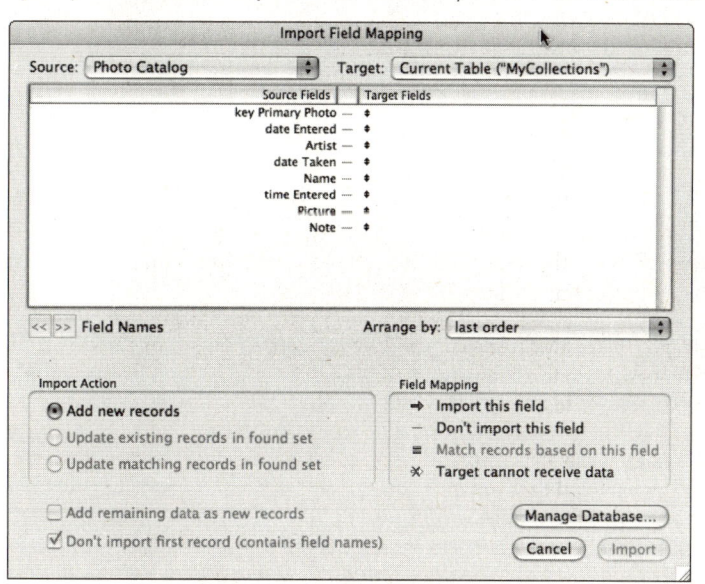

181

## Part II  Introduction to Database Design

6. Choose New Table ("Photo Catalog") from the Target pop-up menu. The Target Fields column now includes all the fields from Photo Catalog, and each source field is pointing to its same-named destination field.

7. Click Import. The Import Options dialog (see Figure 7.3) appears.

   When you click the Import button in the Import Options dialog, FileMaker imports your table and displays an Import Summary dialog, as shown in Figure 7.4.

8. Click OK.

### FIGURE 7.3
Set your import options here.

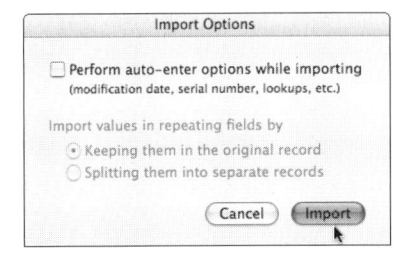

### FIGURE 7.4
FileMaker summarizes the import results.

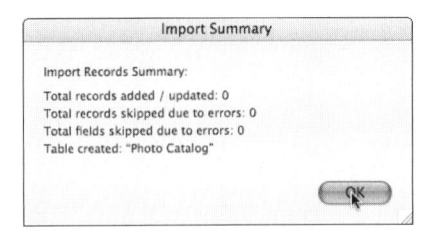

Optionally, as in the case of the creation of the MyCollections.fp7 file in the preceding example, you can now delete the empty placeholder table (MyCollections) created by default in Step 3. Your newly inserted table is a clone of the original table, including all the data types, field options, calculations, and so forth. Unless you modified the default settings in Step 4, the import process will also have brought any data existing in the source table into the new table in the destination file — however, in this example, the source file was new.

Figure 7.5 depicts the Fields panel for the new Photo Catalog table in your MyCollections solution, indistinguishable from the original. If the original table was designed to operate in relative isolation, as in this case, the preservation of all field attributes means the table is usable in your new solution exactly as it was in the original solution — you don't have to modify calculations or internal references.

## The Structure: The Manage Database Dialog   7

### FIGURE 7.5

Voilá! A duplicate of the original table appears in your solution.

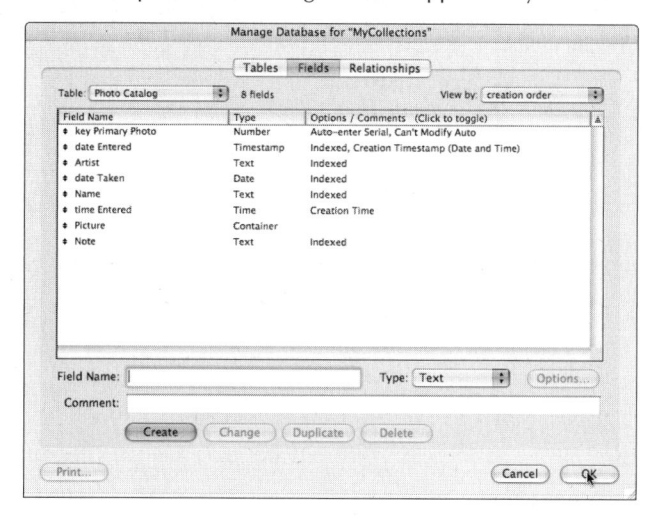

If a table you import includes references to other TOs and fields, FileMaker looks for corresponding (that is, identically named) elements in the current file and, if it finds them, references them. However, any unmatched references are automatically enclosed in code comment braces (commented out) and must be corrected manually.

**CROSS-REF**   For a detailed discussion of code commenting and the use of comment braces, refer to Chapter 12.

An important aspect of the Copy/Paste and Import Table features is the preservation of the internal IDs that FileMaker uses to track associations between elements (see the following section, "Specifying Fields"). When you add a table from another file as described earlier, the hidden IDs are preserved; whereas if you manually re-create equivalent fields, it is unlikely that internal IDs will match — making it unlikely that references to the table (for example, from other files) will resolve as expected.

## Specifying Fields

One of FileMaker's strengths, shared with many other modern databases, is your ability to add new fields to a table at any time. Not all Database Management Systems are quite so flexible. For example, xBASE and many other systems employ fixed-length fields and records, where adding a new field requires rewriting the file, extending each record as necessary. Similarly, in such databases, significantly modifying a field definition or deleting a field requires rewriting the file with the time and disk space penalties attending such operations. FileMaker imposes no such penalties.

183

**TIP** FileMaker assigns IDs to each field you create internally. These IDs are allotted sequentially, just like the Auto-Enter ID fields we created in our Inventory example. In general, you don't need to worry about Field IDs, because FileMaker manages them behind the scenes; however, when accessing data from outside the current file, all references and relationships are resolved by FileMaker using internal IDs.

## Adding, deleting, and renaming fields

Adding, removing, and renaming fields follows the same paradigm as just described for adding, deleting, and renaming tables. To add a field, open the Manage Database dialog's Fields panel, enter a field name and set its type, then click Create. To rename or delete a field, select it in the list of fields and either type the new name in the Field Name text box and click Change to rename, or click Delete to remove, the field.

**NOTE** You can't add or rename fields in an External SQL Data Source (other than adding fields, such as summary and calculation fields, that exist only in your solution and not in the external file). Moreover, if you delete fields appearing in a SQL table in FileMaker, they are removed from the FileMaker view of the table, but not from the external database (fields deleted from a shadow table can be reinstated by clicking the Sync button that appears above the shadow table field list in the Manage Database dialog).

As is the case when you rename a table, FileMaker helps you out when you rename a field. All references in the Relationships Graph, scripts, calculations, and even the noncustomized text labels on your layouts are updated to reflect the new name (if you've edited the field's label in Layout mode, deleted the field box, or moved the label and its associated field box to different parts of the layout, FileMaker doesn't modify the label).

Field Deletion occurs in three main situations, as follows:

- You delete a field from a table in the current file.
- You delete the table (and, thus, all its fields).
- You delete a field from a related table in another file.

When you attempt deletion of a field in the current file, FileMaker disallows the deletion of any field referenced in a calculation or summary field within the same table, or within a calculation determining privileges for the table. In such cases, in order to delete the field you must first modify or delete the referencing calculation(s) and/or summary field(s). When the reference is no longer present, you can successfully delete the field. If a field you want to delete is referenced in a script or used as a key field for a relationship, FileMaker posts a warning dialog (citing the first script or relationship depending in the field) but nevertheless allows you to proceed, if you want. If you disregard the warning and delete a field used in one or more scripts or relationships, the relevant script(s) or relationship(s) will not work as intended until you manually repair them. Finally, if a field you delete is referenced in a calculation in another table or file (including within a script in another file), FileMaker will neither prevent deletion nor post a warning, but external references to the field will be rendered inoperable.

Both the second and third bullet situations can occur without FileMaker trying to stop you beyond an alert asking whether you really want to perform the requested action. However, any instances of the deleted field on a layout, or in a calculation or script that referenced it, will be replaced by the placeholder flag `<Field Missing>`. More significantly, calculations referencing missing fields will (typically) return null or inaccurate results (the same is true for summaries) and scripts referencing deleted fields may produce undesired and perhaps unpredictable results.

## Understanding field/data types and their significance

FileMaker Pro fields have a number of attributes, probably the most significant being the type of data the field can contain. Specifying the appropriate type for a field impacts how FileMaker accepts, presents, indexes, and stores the data, as well as what you can do with the data. For example, if you designate a ZIP code field as being numeric, some calculations referring to the field may lose any leading 0 character(s) on ZIP codes (such as ones from New Jersey) and you may encounter similar problems with postal codes in use outside the United States, such as the six-character alphanumeric codes in Canada.

The Manage Database dialog's Fields panel includes a Type pop-up menu at the right below the fields list (as shown in Figure 7.5) where you specify a field's data type. Depending upon your perspective, either six or eight data types are available. The ambiguity arises because there are six types for storage of data and two derived data field types, as follows:

- **Text** is the most generic type and can include anything you can enter directly via the keyboard (up to 1,000,000,000 characters).

- **Number** fields can also store alphabetic characters, and these may be referenced in some text calculations. However, numeric indexing protocols are applied, so searching for alphanumeric strings will present difficulties. Although number fields can store up to a billion characters, numeric values comprising up to 800 digits on either side of the decimal point (up to 1,600 digits in total) are supported and indexed. Moreover, to be indexed and referenced appropriately, values stored in number fields must be all on one line.

- **Date** fields are stored internally as numeric data and can therefore be employed in calculations to determine the number of days between events. Date fields are restricted to values between 1 January 0001 and 31 December 4000 CE. Values stored in Date fields will sort chronologically, as opposed to dates stored in Text fields, which are subject to alphanumeric sorts. By default, Date fields display according to the date format you have on your system (Date & Time System Preferences on a Mac or Date and Time in the Windows Control Panel), but you can specify other formats (for example, by choosing Format ⇨ Date in Layout mode). Data entry, however, must be in the default date format.

**NOTE** FileMaker makes certain assumptions concerning date entries that aren't fully specified (that is, those that have fewer than eight digits and two separators). The first assumption is that entering only a single number is invalid, however, two numbers separated by a forward-slash or period (provided they fall in the 1..12 and 1..31 ranges, respectively — or vice versa in most countries outside the United States) are interpreted as specifying a date in the current year.

185

- **Time** fields contain a time of day (or a duration) in hours, minutes, and seconds, separated by colons. Times can be stored with a resolution of up to one microsecond. To have a time field display a duration greater than 24 hours, choose Format ➪ Time in Layout mode for that field and specify either Leave Data Formatted as Entered or 24-Hour Notation. FileMaker stores times internally as numeric data (in seconds since midnight) so they, too, can be used in calculations (for example, to determine the interval between two times).

> **TIP** If you enter a single number, FileMaker treats the entry as an hour value; two colon-separated numbers are treated as hours and minutes. To enter a minute value, the leading 0 for hours (and separating colon) is required — and to enter a seconds value, the leading 0s for both hours and minutes are required.

- **Timestamp** fields combine a date and time, separated by a space. You saw examples of Timestamp fields in the Inventory database begun in Chapters 5 and 6. The respective parts of a Timestamp value follow the Date and Time input requirements (except that the time portion must be between 00:00:00 and 23:59:59.999999). FileMaker stores timestamps as a numeric value representing the number of seconds elapsed since 12:00:00 a.m. on 1 January 0001, so these values too can be used in computations to determine the duration between two times on given dates.

- **Container** fields are the catchall for a variety of types of non-textual data. You can store graphics, movies/multimedia (QuickTime supported file formats), sounds you record in FileMaker Pro, or an arbitrary disk file. On Windows machines, you can also store Object Linking and Embedding (OLE) objects.

- **Calculation** fields, the first of two derived data field types, consist of a formula specified to returning one of the first six data types (including Container). Calculations are defined in the Specify Calculation dialog (see the "Basic Calculations" section, later in this chapter).

- **Summary** fields bear some similarities to Calculation fields, but instead of acting on values in a single record, they perform their calculation on a group of records (that is, records in the current found set, or the current related set when evaluated from a layout based on another table) in the table where they reside. Summary fields return aggregate results over the current record set (found or related), such as sum, average, count, or standard deviation.

FileMaker supports indexing of text, number, date, time, and timestamp field types; however, the indexing protocols differ according to type. In particular, text fields are indexed and sorted according to conventions that are not applicable to other field types. Number, date, time, and timestamp fields are all numeric in basis, but FileMaker translates date, time, and timestamp values into appropriate formats for display.

> **CROSS-REF** For additional detail regarding field indexing, refer to the section titled "Storage and indexing options" later in this chapter.

## Auto-entry options

As demonstrated in Chapter 5, situations arise where you want some fields to automatically acquire a value when new records are created — serial numbers, account names, and creation/modification dates are the examples we presented. In each case, we chose to invoke the Prohibit Modification of Value during Data Entry option because a user-override of such values would compromise the integrity or purpose of the data. Another common example benefiting from auto-entry is establishing a default value for a field — for example, initializing the State value in a contact record where most of your customers live in the same state. In this situation, you want users to be able to override the initial value, so the Prohibit Modification option is not appropriate. FileMaker Pro offers you great flexibility when specifying auto-entry values through the Field Options dialog's Auto-Enter panel (shown in Figure 7.6). You access the Field Options dialog by selecting a field in the Manage Database dialog's Fields panel and clicking Options (or by double-clicking the field entry).

**FIGURE 7.6**

The Options for Field dialog's Auto-Enter panel.

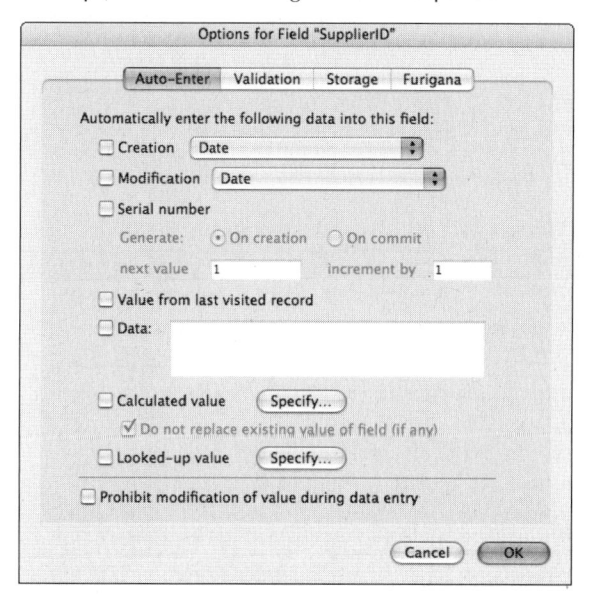

**NOTE** Okay, we'll state upfront that, although we love the flexibility offered by the Auto-Enter panel, the user interface bothers us. When you look at this panel, you see seven checkboxes grouped together and, in both Mac OS and Windows, a checkbox grouping implies that you can select multiple items. That's not the case here; the first five checkbox options are mutually exclusive, as are the last two (that is, you can select up to two options — one of the first five and/or one of the last two).

You can configure FileMaker to auto-enter values pertaining to the record's creation or modification, generate a serial number, seed a field with the value from the last record visited, seed a field with a static initial value, calculate a default value, or retrieve a value from a record in another table. The checkboxes, and their uses, follow:

- Select the **Creation** checkbox and choose from the associated pop-up menu to have FileMaker automatically place the date, time, timestamp, *user name* (a name assigned to the instance of FileMaker on the current workstation), or *account name* (the user's login credential for the current file) active at the time the user creates the record.

- Select the **Modification** checkbox to have FileMaker enter the date, time, timestamp, user name, or account name active when any field in the record is modified.

- Select the **Serial Number** checkbox to have FileMaker generate automatic, incrementing numeric, or alphanumeric serial values. When an alphanumeric serial format (that is, a serial number incorporating both letters and numbers) is specified, only the right-most numeric portion of the value is incremented.

- Select the **Value from Last Visited Record** checkbox to have FileMaker initialize the field with the previously viewed record's value for the field. For the purposes of this feature, *visited* means entering a record (for example, by placing the cursor into a field — merely scrolling past a record or viewing it does not qualify). Moreover, when a file is closed, the last record visited is not saved, so if a record is created on first opening a file (before visiting any records) the value from last visited record's auto-entry option will return a null result.

- Select the **Data** checkbox when you want to start each record with a default value in the field — for example, when entering customer data for a store in Los Angeles, you probably want the State field to default to California. Type the default value in the text box next to the Data checkbox.

- Select the **Calculated Value** checkbox when you want FileMaker to derive a value based upon other field values, system variables (for example, current computer's IP Address), constants, or any mix thereof, as in the Inventory example's various ID and line total fields.

**NOTE** By default, the Do Not Replace Existing Value of Field (If Any) checkbox is selected. When this option is selected, changes the user makes to the auto-entered value persist; whereas, if the checkbox is deselected, the field value will be overwritten if values it depends on change.

- Select the **Looked-Up Value** checkbox when you want FileMaker to retrieve and store a value from a related TO.

## Field validation options

Your design goal may be to guarantee that a field's data meets specific criteria, such as validating that a Social Security number be nine digits (with separators after the third and fifth digits), that department names are legitimate (and consistently spelled), or that price values are numeric and fall within a set range.

## The Structure: The Manage Database Dialog   7

The FileMaker Options for Field dialog's Validation panel offers ways to achieve all of the above, and more. The Validation panel is shown in Figure 7.7.

**FIGURE 7.7**

Specify a field's validation criteria in this panel.

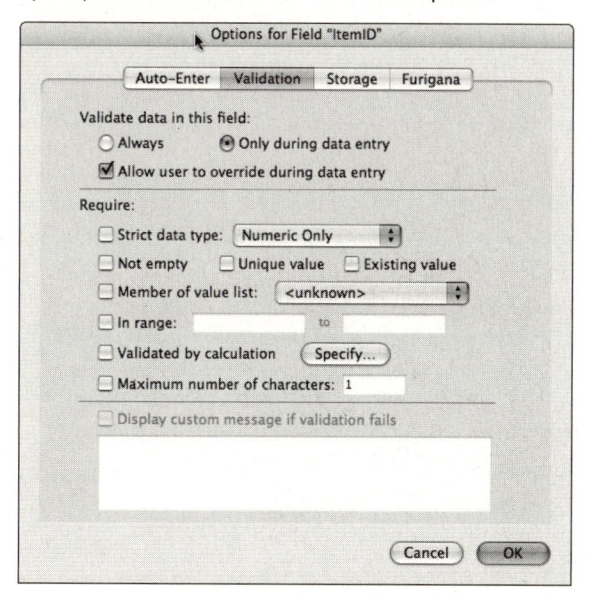

Here is a brief description of the options you'll find on the Validation panel:

- The **Validate Data in This Field** section offers two radio buttons and a checkbox that you employ to specify when validation occurs and how strictly it is enforced.
  - Select the **Only during Data Entry** radio button (the default) when you want FileMaker to validate the data only when the data is entered by the user (but not, for example, when data is imported or changed by a script).
  - The **Always** radio button tells FileMaker to also validate imported data and scripted field updates. When this option is selected, imports will ignore records that do not satisfy validation criteria, and scripts will be prevented from committing records with invalid data (and may fail or otherwise malfunction unless appropriately coded to deal with this condition).
  - The **Allow User to Override during Data Entry** checkbox (selected by default) specifies whether enforcement is absolute (that is, FileMaker won't commit the record if the criteria aren't met) or conditional (that is, FileMaker warns the user but permits the user to tell FileMaker to ignore the criteria for this record).

189

- The **Require** section is where you actually specify the validation criteria.
  - Select **Strict Data Type** when you want the data to be **Numeric Only** (useful with Number fields), a Date field to only allow entries having a four-digit year value, or a Time field to only be a time of day (that is, no durations, or at least none of 24 hours or greater), as specified by choosing from the associated pop-up menu.
  - Select **Not Empty** to require that a value be entered in the field. The Name field in our Inventory solution's Inventory table is an example of a required field.
  - **Unique Value** and **Existing Value** are mutually exclusive, self-explanatory options. Note that both these options use the field's index to determine that the requirement is satisfied during data entry.
  - Select **Member of a Value List** (and choose the value list from the associated pop-up menu) when you've defined a list of legitimate values from which you want the user to choose. (You can choose **Manage Value Lists** from the pop-up menu to alter your existing value lists or create a new value list.)
  - Select **In Range** and enter the minimum and maximum values allowed for a field. This is most useful with Number, Date, Time, and Timestamp fields; however, it also works with text values (according to their position in the collating sequence for the field's language — so you can define a field to accept only names that begin with A to M, for example).
  - Select **Validated by Calculation** or click the associated Specify button to present the Specify calculation dialog, where you can computationally validate data. One example would be to check that salaries fall within the ranges specified for different job classifications.
  - Select **Maximum Number of Characters** to constrain the length of a field.

> **NOTE** The Not Empty and By Calculation validation criteria are evaluated at record commit. All the other criteria are evaluated when you leave the field.

- Whenever you have one or more requirements specified, the **Display Custom Message if Validation Fails** checkbox and associated text box are enabled so that you can create a message for the user as to why his entry failed to validate (and what he might do to fix the entry). Note that, although multiple validation options may be specified, only one custom message can be defined and must serve for all cases.

For most purposes, the custom message option suffices; however, it is also limited, providing only two alternative presentations, dependent upon the state of the Allow User to Override during Data Entry option. Examples of those two presentations appear in Figure 7.8. In short, you don't have control over the size of the dialog or the content of the buttons, and the displayed text is limited to 255 characters. Note also that the Revert button may or may not appear, depending on the state of the record and the validation options in place.

> **CROSS-REF** Chapter 16 covers using scripts to validate field contents and provide more flexibility in communicating with the user.

## The Structure: The Manage Database Dialog | 7

**FIGURE 7.8**

If the current user is allowed to override validation criteria, an alert similar to the one on the top appears; otherwise, FileMaker displays an alert similar to that on the bottom.

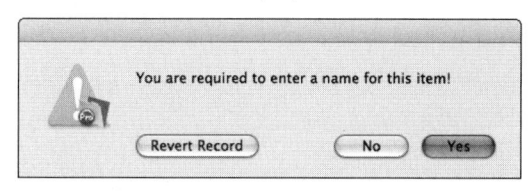

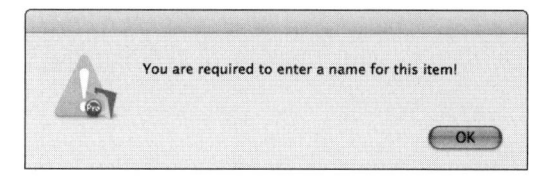

## Storage and indexing options

FileMaker has a remarkably no-fuss way of handling indexes — so much so that many basic operations can take place without requiring you to do anything. Indexing is controlled from the Storage panel of the Options for Field dialog and defaults to Automatically Create Indexes as Needed.

Unless you specifically modify the index settings, each field you create will initially be unindexed. Indexes will then be created on demand when any event requiring (or significantly benefiting from) an index for a given field occurs. Examples of events prompting creation of a field index are as follows:

- Performing a Find on the field
- Accessing records from the table where the field resides via a relationship for which the field has been used as a key (that is, a match field)
- Creating a value list defined to use values from the field
- Setting up unique or existing validation for the field
- Displaying the View Index dialog by choosing Insert ➪ From Index (⌘+I or Ctrl+I)

Additionally, the language option you choose for the indexing of a text field determines the sorting conventions that FileMaker will apply to it, though the index itself is not directly used for sorting.

For databases that you access in stand-alone mode, as well as for solutions of moderate size, you generally need not concern yourself with indexing. Let FileMaker handle it. If your solution becomes large and size and network performance are of concern, the details we provide in later chapters about optimizing indexes will be of interest to you.

191

When indexing numeric data (that is, number, date, time, and timestamp fields) FileMaker creates a sorted list of values in the field, with the IDs of the records where they occur.

For text fields, FileMaker manages two different types of indexes — a word index that's used to support Finds and a value index that's principally used to support relationships and value lists. However, FileMaker creates either type of index only when needed, so text fields may acquire only one index. This is not evident in the Options/Comments area of the Fields tab of the Manage Database dialog (which simply lists the fields as indexed) but is indicated in the Storage panel of the Options for Field dialog, where text fields that have only one type of index are shown with the Minimal indexing setting.

**CROSS-REF** For a discussion of indexing in greater depth, including format and optimization options, refer to Chapter 9.

## Summary and Calculation fields

There are times when you're going to want a field's value to be generated on the fly. For example, when creating an invoice, you want the line total to be the quantity multiplied by the per-unit price, the sales tax to be the tax rate multiplied by the sum of the line items, and the billable amount to be the sum of the line items and the sales tax minus any coupons or discounts. FileMaker provides Calculation and Summary fields to meet these needs. In less evolved Database Management Systems (and in the bygone days of file cabinets and manually created invoices and reports), filling in a report's calculated fields was the time-consuming job of a clerk using a calculator and transposing figures, with all the additional opportunities for human error. Similarly, manually sorting, aggregating, and processing data to be summarized (totaled, averaged, and so on) exacerbated the time consumption and probability of error.

When you declare a field to be of type Calculation in the Manage Database dialog's Fields panel, FileMaker presents the Specify Calculation dialog, shown in Figure 7.9 (you first encountered this dialog in Chapter 5). A calculation's result must be specified as one of the six basic data types.

**NOTE** In early FileMaker versions, the Specify Calculation dialog's raison d'être was to define Calculation fields. Over time, FileMaker, Inc. has expanded the Specify Calculation dialog's role to other parts of the product, such as ScriptMaker (for example, setting a new value into a field, specifying which layout to display based upon the value in a specific field), Web Viewer objects (for example, constructing a URL based upon values in the current record and related records), validating user input, creating custom menus for turnkey solutions (requires FileMaker Pro 9 Advanced), and conditional formatting. In fact, calculations are used almost anywhere that a solution is required to make a runtime decision based upon the current state of affairs.

At the very top of the Specify Calculation dialog, you encounter the Evaluate This Calculation from the Context Of pop-up menu. FileMaker *context* refers to the TO that should be in effect during evaluation. Obviously, when a table has only one TO, this pop-up is moot; however, when you have multiple occurrences, context determines which of several possible evaluation paths will be used. For example, our Inventory example's OrderLines table has two occurrences: OrderLines and ItemsPurchased. The OrderLines TO relates through the OrderID field to the Orders table and then

## The Structure: The Manage Database Dialog    7

to the Suppliers table via the SupplierID field. Thus, all the suppliers referenced on an invoice are available in this context; however, the ItemsPurchased TO retrieves just one SupplierID because its path to the Suppliers table is through the ItemID and then to the SupplierID in the ItemSupplier TO (for the Suppliers table).

**FIGURE 7.9**

The Specify Calculation dialog is a powerful and ubiquitous tool used for much more than just defining Calculation fields.

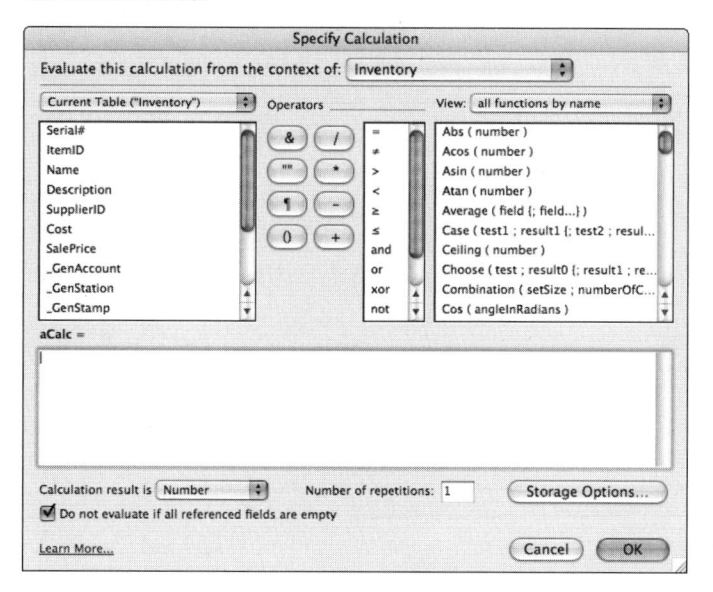

A Calculation field is said to be *dependent on* all fields referenced in its specification (meaning that if the value in either of those fields changes, FileMaker reevaluates the calculation). For example, our OrderLines table includes the cLineTotal Calculation field, defined as = Qty * Price — this makes cLineTotal dependent upon the Qty and Price fields. Re-evaluating the calculation when a dependent value changes is called *dependency triggering*. In general, dependency triggering suffices; however, you might create situations where indirect dependencies don't propagate. For example, if your calculation is dependent upon a lookup field, a change to the lookup value made by another user or in another layout after the lookup is performed in your layout means that your calculation result is based on the previous value. Sometimes this is what you want, such as when cost is based on the price in effect when the order is initiated, and sometimes this is not what you want, such as when current inventory determines availability.

**CROSS-REF** In the latter case, alternative mechanisms would be required to achieve the desired outcome. Examples of different approaches to problems of this kind are discussed in subsequent chapters, including Chapter 19.

193

## Part II  Introduction to Database Design

Calculation fields offer incredible flexibility and power within the context of a single record (and related records), but sometimes you want a summary made across a set of records within the current table (or within the current found set), such as the highest (or average) sales total in a department. Summary fields fill this role. To create a Summary field, proceed as follows:

1. Type a name in the Manage Database dialog's Fields panel's Field Name text box and choose Summary (⌘+S or Ctrl+S) in the Type pop-up menu.
2. Click Create. The Options for Summary Field dialog appears, as shown in Figure 7.10.

**FIGURE 7.10**

The Options for Summary Field dialog.

3. Select the desired summary function's radio button from the group on the left.
4. Select the field to summarize in the Available Fields list.

**NOTE** Only Number, Time, Date, and Timestamp fields (or Calculated fields returning one of those types) are available for summarization.

(Optional) Some Summary functions (all but Minimum and Maximum) present checkbox options below the Available Fields list. For example, **Total Of** offers the option of providing a **running total**. This means that if the Summary field is placed in a layout's Sub-Summary part, the value displayed will reflect the total for that group of records and all previously reported records. You can further refine a running total to reset based upon another sort field. An example of this would be in a sales report where you want a running total for all sales reps in a branch office, but you want the running totals to reset when you start reporting the results for another branch office. Table 7.1 lists the various Summary functions and their options, if any.

5. If you're summarizing a repeating field, select the Summarize Repetitions radio button appropriate to how you want the field summarized.
6. Click OK to accept the Summary field definition.

## TABLE 7.1
### Summary Functions, Descriptions, and Options

| Name | Description | Option | Option Description |
|---|---|---|---|
| Total of | Sums the values in the found set | Running Total | If placed in the Body part, returns the cumulative total for the found set up to and including the current record. |
| Average of | Provides a simple arithmetic mean of the field's values | Weighted Average | Returns the average relative to (weighted by) another field's value. For example, to return an average per-unit price across a range of purchases given only the total for the purchase and the number of items in each purchase, you would use a weighted average for the purchases weighted by the number of items in that purchase. |
| Count of | Returns the number of records where the count field is non-empty | Running Count | (See Running Total) |
| Minimum | Returns the numerically least or chronologically earliest value | N/A | |
| Maximum | Returns the numerically greatest or chronologically latest value | N/A | |
| Standard Deviation Of | Returns the statistical value indicating by how much the values in the found set differ from the *mean value* (square root of the average of the squares of the set of deviations) | By Population | Adjusts the calculation to better predict standard deviation of a population where only a subset of the population's results are involved in the calculation. |
| Fraction of Total | Returns what fraction of the total the given record (or group in a sub-summary part) is reflected | Subtotaled | Returns the fraction of a group of records (rather than all records) represented. An example would be to sort by department and return the portion of that department's payroll that is comprised of individual salaries. |

Summary fields produce live statistics reflecting the current state of data in your solution — and this is both their strength and, potentially, their weakness, depending on how you choose to use them. When data sets are relatively small (a few hundred records or less), recalculating complex summaries every time anything changes will be efficient and, in most cases, useful. However, in solutions where the quantity of data is large — or will become large over time — users will tire of delays introduced while summary data is recalculated with every small change.

## Part II  Introduction to Database Design

For extensive data sets, therefore, alternative approaches may be preferable. Because summary fields are recalculated each time they appear onscreen, one solution is to exclude them from most screens so they are only evaluated and displayed when the user specifically requires them. Alternatively, you may consider a scripted approach, which computes summary data either progressively (via transactional modeling) or on demand.

## Working with global fields

Occasionally, you want a value to be accessible to all a table's records, such as the current sales tax rate. You could, of course, define a field, initialize it with a constant Auto-Enter value, and disallow user modification. This approach is somewhat wasteful of storage space, however, because the field must be replicated in every one of your table's records. And, when the tax rate changes, you have to update the value in all the table's records. FileMaker lets you define a field and, in the Options for Field dialog's Storage panel, specify that it should use global storage (as shown in Figure 7.11). Values in a global storage field contain, as stated in the dialog panel's preface text, "only one value that is shared across all records." Presto! One-stop shopping and conservation of disk space. Some developers refer to global storage fields as *record zero* of the table.

**FIGURE 7.11**

The Options for Field dialog's Storage panel lets you declare a field to use Global Storage.

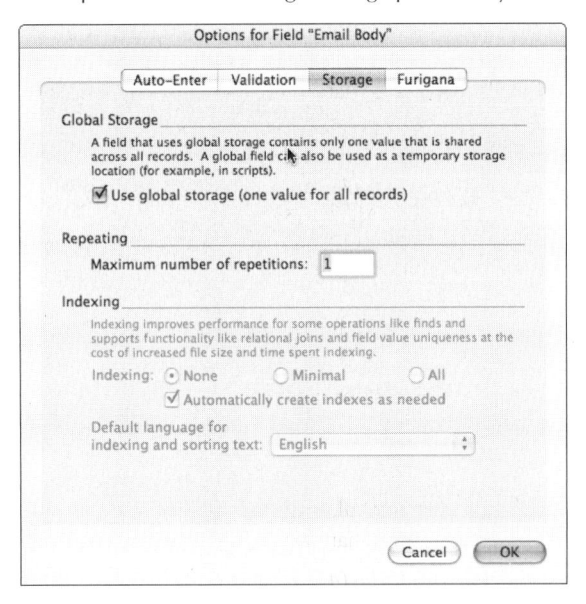

Prior to FileMaker Pro 8's introduction of script variables, global fields were heavily used to provide temporary storage of intermediate results, to provide loop variables, and for a wide variety of other purposes in support of scripting. While still usable for such traditional purposes, global fields are less convenient than script variables, so their use is waning in that area. However, global fields serve an important purpose as repositories of information across all of a table's records. For example, you could create a global container field with six repetitions containing pictures of zero to five stars. Then, you could have a listing of movies index into the field to display the image corresponding to a movie's "star rating" (0 through 5) or you could create a text field to contain the body of a form letter to be emailed—the Lending Library starter solution uses just such a global field in its Assets table. In each case, a single reference copy of the required information (star images, letter template, and so on) is stored, but it may be referenced and viewed from any record in the table.

Another useful aspect of global fields is that their value is specific to each user when a database is shared over a network. This means that if a global field is used to store temporary information (for example, while a script is running), two users may use the field simultaneously without either "colliding" with the other. However updates to global field values made by clients of a hosted database are lost when the client session concludes.

**CROSS-REF** Refer to Chapter 9 for coverage of script variables and a more in-depth discussion of the roles and uses of global fields.

## Basic Calculations

Lest the name *Calculation field* alarm the math-phobic among you, performing arithmetic and statistical operations is only a small part of a Calculation field's repertoire. You define calculations in the Specify Calculation dialog, FileMaker's all-purpose tool for manipulating and massaging data: It's used to evaluate logical alternatives, extract subsets of textual data, combine text field contents, return system status information, construct URLs and HTML source, plus perform a variety of other tasks bounded only by your imagination and resourcefulness.

Discussing calculations involves some jargon, almost all of which has its roots in mathematics or programming. Fortunately, most of the terminology is so straightforward and common that it has entered mainstream conversation; but there are some notable exceptions. Some key terms (with special meanings) you will encounter are as follows:

- **Result:** The value returned from a calculation.
- **Function:** A predefined, named operation that, given 0 or more input values, returns a single result.
- **Argument:** An input value to a function.
- **Operator:** A symbol used to denote an arithmetic, textual, or logical operation to be performed — + (plus), – (minus), * (times), & (concatenate) are examples of operators.
- **Literal:** A precisely specified (and predetermined) value (4 and "Hello" are literals).
- **Variable:** A placeholder name for a value.
- **Constant:** A placeholder name for a literal value.
- **Syntax:** The order in which FileMaker expects to receive functions, arguments, and operators within a calculation (essentially, grammatical rules).

## Part II  Introduction to Database Design

- **Expression:** A sequence of literals, constants, variables, and operators that, when evaluated, returns a result. For example, 1.0825 * (Qty * Price) is an expression that, when evaluated, returns the amount due for a purchase in a locale with an 8.25 percent sales tax rate. In FileMaker parlance, *expression* is sometimes used a little more loosely to refer to sequences including functions and fields references.

- **Formula:** The entire content of a calculation combining elements described above to produce a result — sometimes used interchangeably with *expression*.

These terms need to be part of your vocabulary, because calculation parlance pops up at almost every turn in FileMaker.

## Creating a Calculation field

Creating a Calculation field is really straightforward, and you've already seen it done in Chapter 5. The Specify Calculation dialog (see Figure 7.12) provides all the tools and flexibility you need to specify a Calculation field.

**FIGURE 7.12**

The Specify Calculation dialog and its many parts.

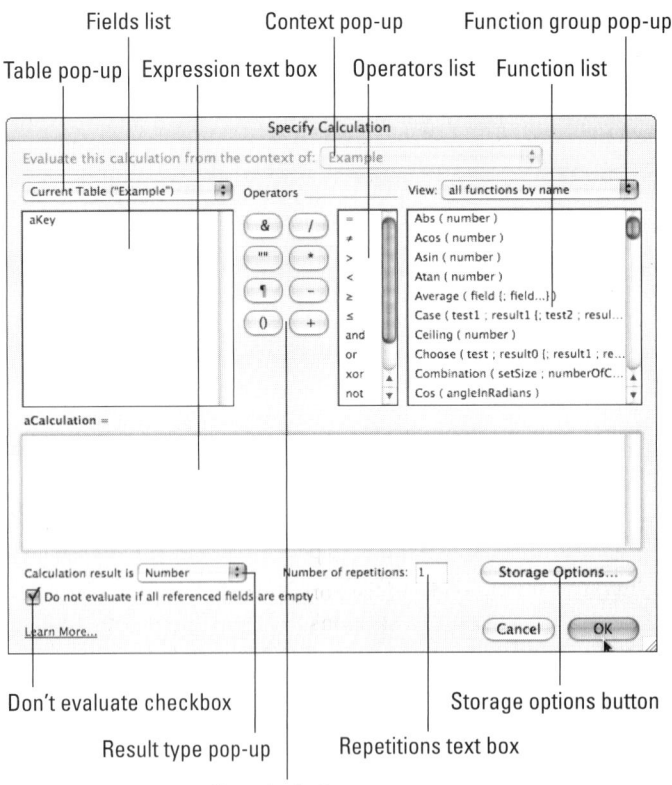

## The Structure: The Manage Database Dialog

The Specify Calculation dialog's parts are as follows:

- **Context pop-up:** Where you specify from which TO to evaluate. When there is only one table and just one TO in your graph, the pop-up is disabled.
- **Table pop-up:** Where you choose a TO to source fields you want to reference in the calculation. (The terminology here can be a little confusing — the table pop-up *only* ever lists TOs.)
- **Fields list:** Lists the fields of the TO chosen in the Table pop-up.
- **Operator buttons:** Comprise the eight arithmetic and text operators.
- **Operator list:** A scrolling list with the other 11 operators (logical and comparison) that FileMaker recognizes.

> **NOTE** We're using FileMaker's description as to what the buttons and list represent, but we have a quibble with their description. FileMaker places the exponentiation operator (which is arithmetic) in the list of what they refer to as logical and comparison operators.

- **Function Group pop-up:** An organizational aid that lets you specify which group of FileMaker functions you want to view and work with — or how you want the functions grouped in the function list. You can see the pop-up in Figure 7.13.

**FIGURE 7.13**
Organize or limit the functions from which to choose with the Function Group pop-up menu.

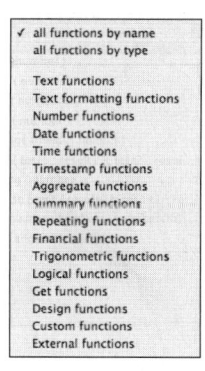

- **Function list:** A scrolling list of the available functions, as per the Function Group pop-up.
- **Expression text box** (FileMaker Pro's Help calls it the Formula box): The heart of the Specify Calculation dialog. This is where your calculation's expression appears as you select functions, operators, and fields and type.
- **Result Type pop-up:** Where you specify what data type your calculation returns as a result.

## Part II — Introduction to Database Design

- **Repetitions text box:** Lets you specify whether your calculation is a repeating field (that is, returns multiple results) and, if so, how many repetitions it comprises.
- **Don't Evaluate checkbox:** Lets you tell FileMaker not to perform the calculation if none of the referenced fields contains a value (such as in a new record). Note that if even one of the referenced fields contains a value, FileMaker will attempt to evaluate the calculation.

If you feel comfortable with expression syntax and the names of all the functions and fields your expression references, you can simply type the expression in the formula box (and, we'll admit, that's what we do most frequently). When in unfamiliar territory (obscure or lengthy field names or working with infrequently encountered functions), however, we employ the mouse-driven shortcuts the Specify Calculation dialog offers, as follows:

- To use a function, double-click the function's name in the function list. The function's skeleton appears at the cursor location in the formula box with the argument list preselected. Replace the placeholders in the argument list (called *parameters*) with field names and literals.
- To reference a field, double-click the field's name in the fields list. The field name appears at the cursor position (replacing a selection, if there was one) in the formula box.
- To enter a literal value, type it into the formula box (remembering that numeric literals don't require enclosing quotes, but text literals do).
- To enter an arithmetic or text operator, click its button.
- To enter a logical or comparison operator, double-click it in the operator list.

**TIP** If your calculation references fields in related tables and the current table has multiple occurrences in the Relationships Graph, make sure that you select the appropriate context for your calculation, as described earlier in this chapter.

Specifying the correct result type for your calculation is important for several reasons. Perhaps most important, some calculation functions and operations produce different results depending on the data type of the result, as FileMaker determines whether to treat ambiguous elements as text strings or numeric values. Moreover, FileMaker Pro references the result type when performing many operations, such as indexing and sorting. If you specify that a Calculation field (or a regular field) is a text field rather than a number field, 29 appears before 3. Similarly, with dates in a text field, December sorts before November.

**CROSS-REF** A more detailed discussion of indexing and sorting issues and conventions is included in Chapter 9.

**TIP** If you occasionally want to present data as a type other than its natural type, you can use Calculation fields to convert formats through the many type-conversion functions, such as `GetAsDate( )`, `GetAsText( )`, and `GetAsTimestamp( )`.

As a reminder, we strongly encourage the use of descriptive field names, including the use of Hungarian notation (or some similar, consistent scheme) when naming calculation fields, global fields, and summary fields to make their nature clear while developing, working with, and maintaining your solution.

## Defining a calculation formula

Calculations can be considered a form of programming. Because computers interpret everything literally, formulæ must conform to syntax rules to be parsed correctly, and, because humans reference the same formulæ, some basic stylistic conventions facilitate our comprehension.

The first rule of calculation syntax is that evaluation follows an order of precedence. Among the arithmetic operators, exponentiation has the highest precedence, followed by multiplication and division, then addition and subtraction. Operators of equal precedence are evaluated from left to right, with expressions in parentheses performed first (from inside out and then left to right). The following examples illustrate the impact of operator precedence:

8 + 5 * 4 returns 28, because the multiplication is performed first, followed by the addition

(8 + 5) * 4 returns 52, because the operation in parentheses is performed first

((8 + 2)^2 * 4) + 1 returns 401

( 8 + 2^(2 * 4)) + 1 returns 265 (8 + 256 + 1)

((8 + 2^2) * 4) + 1 returns 49

The first convention is that white space helps humans parse an expression. In other words, we find it easier to comprehend

```
If(Qty > 10; GetRepetition(gStockIndicator; 1);
        GetRepetition(gStockIndicator; 2))
```

than

```
If(Qty>10;GetRepetition(gStockIndicator;1);GetRepetition(gStockIndicator;2))
```

and the readability distinction becomes even more pronounced in longer formulæ.

Another syntactic rule is that function arguments are separated by semicolons (as demonstrated in the preceding example on white space).

One especially interesting function is the Case statement. A Case statement is equivalent to an `if...then` statement followed by a series of `else...if` clauses and a final (optional) `else` clause. For example, if you had a global field containing images for "Sold Out," "Limited Availability," and "Available," you could use the following Case statement to display the sold out image when the quantity on hand was zero, or else present the limited availability image when only one or two items are left in stock, and the available image when three or more items are in stock:

```
Case( Qty = 0; GetRepetition ( gStatus; 1);
      Qty < 3; GetRepetition (gStatus; 2);
      GetRepetition (gStatus; 3))
```

A Case statement's conditions are evaluated from left to right and top to bottom, and evaluation ceases upon a test returning true. Thus, if there are zero items on hand, the second test (`Qty < 3`) is not performed.

> **NOTE** This early termination of evaluation is called *short-circuited* evaluation and has implications. For example, tests can call functions that reference related data requiring calls to a remote server, introducing a brief delay; however the cumulative effect of a series of such effects is dependent upon how many of the tests are performed. Thus, the order in which tests are performed can impact the time FileMaker takes to determine a result.

## Entering literal text

You will encounter numerous situations involving literals when constructing a calculation formula (and elsewhere). For example, when testing whether a text field contains a specific text string, you would employ a test involving a literal. For example `If( PatternCount( GetField(Name); "Smith") > 0; "Found"; "N/A")` returns the text "Found" when the Name field contains Smith, Smithers, or Gabon-Smith and the text "N/A" otherwise. In this calculation, `Smith`, `Found`, and `N/A` are all literals.

As noted previously, textual literals are enclosed in quotation marks, allowing FileMaker to distinguish between a literal and a (possible) function, table, or field reference. Some functions, in particular the `Evaluate( )` function, process the contents of literal strings and the textual results returned from other functions. To ensure that a literal or the text value returned by a function not be processed, you use the Quote function. For example: `Evaluate("Pi")` returns the string "3.1415926535897932"; however, `Evaluate (Quote("Pi"))` returns the text "Pi."

When working with literal strings in a calculation, keep in mind whether functions you will use to process the text are case-sensitive. For example, `Substitute( )` is case-sensitive but `PatternCount()` is not. Furthermore, the uses to which your calculation might be put can be case-sensitive (for example, constructing a URL to be sent to a server — some Internet servers are case-sensitive).

Within text in calculations, several characters are reserved — they have a special meaning as text operators. Notably, the quote character is used to indicate the start and end of literal text and the pilcrow (¶) signifies a carriage return. So the question arises — what can you do if you want to include quotes or pilcrows within your literal text?

To deal with this problem, FileMaker lets you use a prefix character (called an *escape character*) to instruct the calculation engine to read the following character as written. The character used to escape quotes and pilcrows is the backslash. So anywhere you want to insert a quote in literal text, you must use \". For example the calculation

    "You're the kind of girl\¶that \"fits in\" with my world."

returns

   You're the kind of girl¶that "fits in" with my world.

With those two problems (" and ¶) solved, there remains the issue of how to deal with the backslash itself, which now has a special meaning as an escape character for the other reserved characters. Oddly enough, the answer is the same: You can escape the backslash character with itself, if you want FileMaker to interpret it as a backslash rather than an escape character for what follows. So, to summarize:

1. \" = "
2. \¶ = ¶
3. \\ = \

## Referencing fields

It's worth noting that when you create a formula referencing fields and tables, FileMaker simply accepts the names you type (or select from lists). But if, after creating a calculation formula, you go and change the name of one of the fields the calculation references, the next time you open the Specify Calculation dialog, the new field name is already there staring back at you. The first time you see it, it's kind of spooky—though after the thrill wears off it's just mildly geeky. Either way, it's very cool. Even if you've referenced a field in dozens of places, when you change its name, they are all instantly updated without your having to lifting a finger. The same thing is true of many things that have a name in FileMaker (for example, scripts, tables, layouts, and so on).

FileMaker achieves this feat by storing and tracking everything (behind the scenes) by an ID. When you open a dialog such as the Specify Calculation dialog, FileMaker simply looks up and displays the current names for the tables and fields referenced there. This gives you a lot of freedom to change your mind and modify your solution as you build it.

However, some words and characters are off-limits when it comes to field and table names. Function names and various *reserved words* (words that have a special meaning as an argument for a function) don't make good choices for field names. Moreover, field names should not start with a number or include any of the symbols used as operators.

In the event that you do use an inappropriate name for a field or table, FileMaker deals with the problem by enclosing references to the offending field (or `table::field` combination) within prefixed braces as follows: `${ }`. So, for example, if you have a field named Average, when you include it in calculations, it will appear as `${Average}` so as not to be confused with FileMaker's `Average( )` function.

When you create calculations within a table and reference fields in the same table (from the same TO selected in the table pop-up at the upper left of the Specify Calculation dialog) FileMaker accepts references to the field without a preceding TO name. However, in all other cases, fields must be referenced in the form `TOname::FieldName`.

Finally, it is worth remembering that FileMaker manages calculation dependencies only within the current record. If a calculation references another field in the record it will automatically update when the referenced field is edited. However, if you create a calculation referencing a field outside the current record, such as a field from another TO, FileMaker will make the calculation unstored and it will be evaluated only when a screen it appears on is displayed or refreshed (or when the calculation is otherwise referenced). Similarly, calculation fields referencing global fields (even those defined within the same table) are required to be unstored.

## Understanding calculation functions and their syntax

The FileMaker calculation engine includes close to 400 native calculation functions. They can be combined in many interesting and useful ways. One function can be placed within another so that its result becomes one of the inputs (arguments) for the function enclosing it. Functions work rather like building blocks, letting you fabricate answers for all sorts of problems.

With so many functions, each able to be used in various ways, we could devote an entire book the size of this one to exploring each in turn. Fortunately, that's not necessary — FileMaker provides the basic syntax for functions in the function list at the upper right of the Specify Calculation dialog; moreover, when you get started you'll discover that the process follows some straightforward predictable patterns. Here are a few examples.

### The List( ) function

The List( ) function accepts one or more fields (separated by semicolons) and returns a carriage-return separated list of all values it finds there on the current record (if the supplied fields are in the current table) or on all related records (if the supplied fields are sourced from a related TO).

If the List( ) argument includes only one field, the function will look for multiple instances of the field either in the current record (if it is a local field) or in multiple related records (if it comes from another TO) and will list any values it finds, one per line.

If, in the Inventory solution, you wanted to compose an e-mail confirming the contents of an order, you would need a list of the order's item stock numbers to include in the e-mail. From the Order record, the expression List(OrderLines::ItemID) returns a list of stock numbers on the current order — for example:

- ITM00001
- ITM00003
- ITM00002

### The Count( ) function

For the same Inventory example and e-mail of order details, the e-mail needs to include a summary line stating how many types of items are being stored. In the same way as you create a list of items, you can create a count of items: The expression Count(OrderLines::ItemID) for the above order returns the number 3.

### The Date( ) function

To convert a human-readable date into the internal numeric format that FileMaker uses to perform computations with dates, FileMaker provides the Date( ) function, which accepts month, day, and year as its arguments. So to supply FileMaker with New Year's Day in a calculation, we can enter **Date(1; 1; 2008)**.

Among many other date and time functions, FileMaker provides the function `Get(CurrentDate)` to let you retrieve the current date from the computer's internal clock and calendar. Thus, to determine how long it is to (or since) January 1, you use the following expression:

```
Date(1; 1; 2008) - Get(CurrentDate)
```

FileMaker returns a result which is the number of days between now and New Year.

## The Round( ) function

In cases where fractions or percentages have been multiplied — for example when adding tax or deducting discounts from a total amount — you need to round the result (because most people don't deal with fractions of a cent) before displaying it in a letter or report. FileMaker's `Round( )` function accepts two arguments; the amount to be rounded and the number of decimal places to round it to. Thus the expression:

```
"$" & Round(37.25297; 2)
```

returns a result of $37.25. In practice, however, it is likely that the first argument for such a calculation will either be a field holding the value to be rounded, or a calculation — or perhaps a combination of the two. If the amount is in a field in the Orders table, you can achieve the desired result with expressions such as the following:

```
"$" & Round(32.822 * 1.135; 2)

"$" & Round(Orders::cFinalTotal; 2)( )

"$" & Round(Orders::cFinalTotal * 1.135; 2)
```

Note that the arguments (in this case the first argument) can be supplied in any form which will resolve when evaluated to pass the necessary input value to the `Round( )` function.

## The Length( ) function

FileMaker calculations work with all kinds of data — and in fact many calculations are designed to manipulate text for a wide range of purposes — locating a relevant word or phrase, extracting an e-mail address from a paragraph of text, checking that an address will display correctly in an envelope window, and so on.

The building blocks that FileMaker provides so you can work with text in calculations are just as straightforward as the other examples we've cited above. For example, to determine the number of characters (including all punctuation, spaces, and carriage returns) in a field, you use FileMaker's `Length( )` function. For example:

```
Length(OrderItems::Name)
```

will return a number representing the length of the text in the indicated field.

## Part II   Introduction to Database Design

All the examples listed in this section have several things in common. They start with a function name that is plain English and gives a clear and simple indication of the purpose of the function. You could probably guess many of the function names correctly. In parentheses after each function are one or more values (separated by semicolons) to determine what the function will work on and what it will do — for example, what number is to be rounded, to what precision, and so on.

Although initially the building blocks will be unfamiliar, the process is consistent and follows straightforward and largely intuitive principles.

## Doing some simple calculations

Having covered the technical and mechanical aspects of creating calculations, what's left is to provide you with some example calculation formulas — ones that you might well use or which can form the basis of a formula you need.

### Number of days an item is overdue

Many business operations require a method of evaluating late fees or triggering a follow-up bill based upon how long overdue an item or payment is. These calculations are conceptually fairly simple. Assume that your table has a Date field named `DueDate` and that you charge a fee based upon how many days late an item is returned. You could create a Calculation field named `DaysLate` with the following formula:

```
If((Get(CurrentDate) - DueDate) > 0; (Get(CurrentDate) - DueDate); 0)
```

Although this is an obvious solution, you are invoking the `Get(CurrentDate)` function twice, which is unnecessary and can slow things down when processing thousands of records. A slightly more elegant solution is:

```
Max(0; Get(CurrentDate) - DueDate)
```

### Calculating initials from a person's name

Another somewhat common practice is to construct reference codes (to appear on forms and documents from initials of the person (or people) who initiate the document. For example, in a legal office, you might annotate client briefs with the initials of the attorney handling the client and the initials of the clerk preparing the brief. Assuming that you have a table of the firm's staff, with `FirstName`, `MiddleName`, and `LastName` fields, and a Briefs table with fields holding the StaffID of the attorney and clerk responsible for the brief, and with a relationship from each ID field to a TOs of the Staff table called Lawyer and Clerk respectively, you might construct the `RefCode` calculation as:

```
Left(Lawyer::FirstName; 1) & Left(Lawyer::MiddleName; 1) &
   Left(Lawyer::LastName; 1) & ":" & Left(Clerk::FirstName; 1) &
   Left(Clerk::MiddleName; 1) & Left(Clerk::LastName; 1)
```

Although this calculation works just fine, so long as every staff member in the firm has a first, middle, and last name, not everyone has a middle name. The following adjustment keeps all `RefCodes` at seven characters by inserting an underscore when there is no middle name.

… The Structure: The Manage Database Dialog

```
Left(Lawyer::FirstName; 1) & Left(Lawyer::MiddleName & "_"; 1) &
    Left(Lawyer::LastName; 1) & ":" & Left(Clerk::FirstName; 1) &
    Left(Clerk::MiddleName & "_"; 1) & Left(Clerk::LastName; 1)
```

**CAUTION** While the practice of adding initials to documents as handy mnemonics is reasonable, it should never be relied upon as the definitive method of identifying a document's origins (lest, for example, more than one individual with the same initials enters the company). The separate StaffID field should provide the basis of an authoritative link to the related records identifying the subject or originator of the record.

## Compound interest at a known rate over a given period

Calculating compound interest is such a common operation that schools start teaching it very early on in a student's math curriculum as it provides a concrete example of exponentiation and the use of decimal fractions. Fortunately, with the advent of slide rules, calculators, and now computers, we no longer need do the arithmetic either on paper or in our heads — we just transfer the answer provided by our hardware and software. The formula for compound interest was the principal multiplied by the quantity 1 plus the periodic interest rate raised to the power of the number of periods. Thus, if we had a 6 percent annual interest rate, compounded monthly for ten years, we would have the initial investment times $1.005^{120}$ (no, we don't want to do that math on paper, either). Fortunately, FileMaker lets us take the easy way out. Create Number fields named `InitialInvestment`, `PerIntRate`, and `Periods` to hold the values suggested by the names and a Calculation field returning a number named `CompAmt` with the following formula:

```
InitialInvestment * (1 + PerIntRate) ^ Periods
```

Now, if you enter 1000 into `InitialInvestment`, 0.005 ($\frac{1}{12}$ of the annual 6 percent is the monthly rate) into `PerIntRate`, and 120 into `Periods`, we get the result of 1819.40 (assuming we format the `CompAmt` field to display two decimals).

## Current quarter of the calendar year

Financial results are often grouped by calendar quarter. Therefore, you might find need to create a calculation field named Quarter on which to sort your records. You could make this a Number field, but custom dictates that such results be alphanumeric, such as Q1 (for Quarter 1), CQ1 (for Calendar Quarter 1), or FQ1 (for Fiscal Quarter 1). One way to approach this requirement is to create a list with the four values that your nomenclature requires — our example uses a literal string with values of Q1, Q2, Q3, and Q4 (separated by pilcrows) and a date field named `TransactionDate`. A compact definition for a calculation field named Quarter could be:

```
GetValue("Q1¶Q2¶Q3¶Q4"; Ceiling(Month(TransactionDate) / 3))
```

The rationale behind applying the `Ceiling` function to the quotient is that values in the value string enumerate starting with 1, and we need to bump the quotient up to the next integer if the result has a fractional part.

## Changing ampersands to "and" in a block of text

Replacing abbreviations or symbols with the corresponding formal word or form is a common requirement. In this example, we're going to demonstrate replacing occurrences of the ampersand

**207**

(&) character in a text field with the word *and*. FileMaker offers two functions facilitating text replacement: `Replace( )` replaces a specified number of characters at an also-specified index into the text with the replacement string, whereas `Substitute( )` replaces all occurrences of a search string with the replacement string. Obviously, `Substitute( )` is our choice for this example.

```
Substitute(TextField ; "&"; "and")
```

> **TIP** You can use the `Substitute( )` function to perform multiple substitutions simultaneously, as exemplified by the following example, which replaces ampersands with *and* and vertical bars with *or*.

```
= Substitute(TextField; ["&"; "and"]; ["|" ; "or"])
```

### Record navigation text (record n of nn)

Occasionally, you'll encounter situations where you or your clients need to know what position in the table a record is and, possibly, how many records are in the table so as to facilitate locating the record again at a later date or to document the information for evidentiary purposes. FileMaker provides a wide variety of what are termed `Get( )` functions — functions that retrieve status information about the current database (and its parts) as well as the operating environment in which it is being used (for example, the FileMaker version and the system platform on which you're running). We're going to employ two `Get` functions to create a text calculation field that reports which record in a found set is displaying as well as how many records are in that found set.

```
= "Record " & Get(RecordNumber) & " of " Get(FoundCount)
```

This sort of calculation field is often displayed in a report's Footer or Header parts.

## The Relationships Graph

The Relationships Graph in FileMaker Pro is both a visual metaphor to aid your understanding and a tool through which you manipulate your solution's data model. It seeks to provide you with a single, all-encompassing view of your solution's structure. An ambitious aim, particularly as a solution becomes complex — yet the Graph is undoubtedly a powerful tool — albeit one peculiarly well-suited to visual thinkers.

A number of divergent approaches to working with the Graph have appeared in the years since FileMaker Pro 7 was introduced — one testament to the flexibility of the model it encapsulates. In reality, however, a solution is multi-dimensional and the Graph is two-dimensional, so a certain amount of awkwardness is inevitable. Perhaps the most significant contribution to complexity arises because FileMaker relies on the graph not only for underlying data frameworks but also for direct support of the interface. TOs that provide data filtering, portal displays, or script support mingle unfettered among core data dependencies defining the data structure fundamentals. Keeping both in an orderly perspective is both the joy and the challenge of the Relationships Graph.

## Common misconceptions about the Relationships Graph

Where the Relationships Graph is concerned, various myths and misconceptions abound. Foremost among the misconceptions is the impression that those boxes you see on the graph *are* tables — rather than merely pointers to tables. It's a crucial distinction; grasping it is essential to ease of understanding of all that flows from FileMaker's context management model. The way the interface is grafted to structure via the layout-TO-table pathway places the Graph at the heart of everything.

Confusion surrounding the distinction between tables and TOs is not helped, perhaps, by the fact that, throughout FileMaker's own interface the distinction is blurred, with numerous dialogs displaying TO names with labels such as "Current Table," "Related Tables," and so on distributed among them. Figure 7.14 shows one such example.

### FIGURE 7.14

The Specify Field list dialog is one of many that exclusively lists TOs, yet refers to them throughout as "Tables."

The blurring of the distinction between TOs and the tables they point to is unfortunate because it makes grasping the pivotal importance of context more difficult. Further, it makes the necessary existence of multiple TOs for a given base table appear perplexing or even incomprehensible. This leads to a second misconception about the Relationships Graph — that it is essentially an Entity Relationship Diagram (ERD). In glossing over the distinction between TOs and tables, fundamental differences between the Relationships Graph and a conventional ERD are obscured, and inappropriate patterns of use appear both feasible and viable.

**Part II** Introduction to Database Design

> **NOTE** We've yet to see a FileMaker solution of any complexity with a graph resembling an ERD, though we've seen a few hopelessly mired projects where it seems that the developers tried to envision the graph in this way.

Whereas an ERD serves to outline defining structures to tie operations to essentials — the database equivalent of a floor plan — the Relationships Graph exists in curved space around a process better understood as analogous to fission. You solve problems in FileMaker not by referencing back always to a unified core, but by a more organic process of branching and enclosing structures; alternate paths meet only within the substrata (that is, the underlying tables). If you try to work with the Relationships Graph as though it were really an ERD with a different name, you'll encounter the frustration of circular reference errors as a constant frustration — that is simply not how FileMaker works.

## Tables versus table occurrences

It is a defining strength of FileMaker that the nexus between process and structure is chameleon-like in its flexibility. TOs, as the building blocks of the Graph, operate as tokens — that is, they are analogous to shortcuts or aliases to tables in the underlying database structure and can be multiplied and repurposed at will to perform a variety of major and minor roles spanning the data layer, the process layer, and the interface layer of your solutions.

Although tables are the central structural element in a FileMaker database's data layer, TOs are the conduit between the data and the process and interface layers. The structure of the Relationships Graph is, therefore, dictated as much by process and interface considerations as it is by entity relationships.

Key to the distinction between tables and TOs is that you can have many TOs associated with a single table, each named however you choose (none of the TO names need to resemble the underlying table name). For example, a college database may have a table called "People," which may have spawned TOs named "Students," "Faculty," "AdminStaff," "Alumni," and "BoardMembers" — each having a distinct and essential role in the solution, each related differently to various other TOs in the graph.

You can easily tell which table each TO is attached to by moving the mouse pointer over the reveal arrow at the left of the header bar on a TO in the Relationships Graph. As Figure 7.15 shows, an info panel appears indicating the source table, the data source, and (if applicable) the location of the file in which the table is stored. When you have multiple TOs attached to a base table, this feature becomes especially useful.

## Avoiding circular references

When you create a relationship between two TOs, you can reference related data via the relationship by prefixing the name of a field with the name of the related TO. For this to work, you must have only one path (direct or indirect) between any two TOs. Consider a sales force database with a relationship between the customer and sales staff tables and also a relationship between customer and bill-of-sale tables. Figure 7.16 shows what happens when you try to create a relationship between the sale and the cashier who made the sale.

## The Structure: The Manage Database Dialog | 7

#### FIGURE 7.15

Creating multiple TOs pointing to a single table and viewing the info panel that reveals the source of data for a TO.

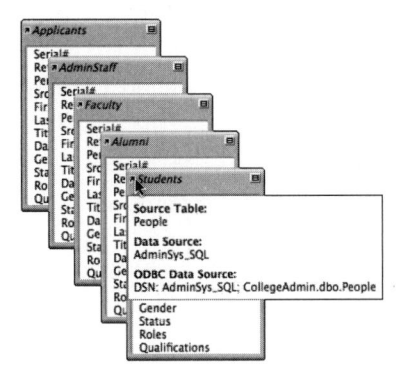

#### FIGURE 7.16

The Add Relationship dialog prompts you to create an additional TO if a relationship you are creating would result in more than one path between two existing TOs.

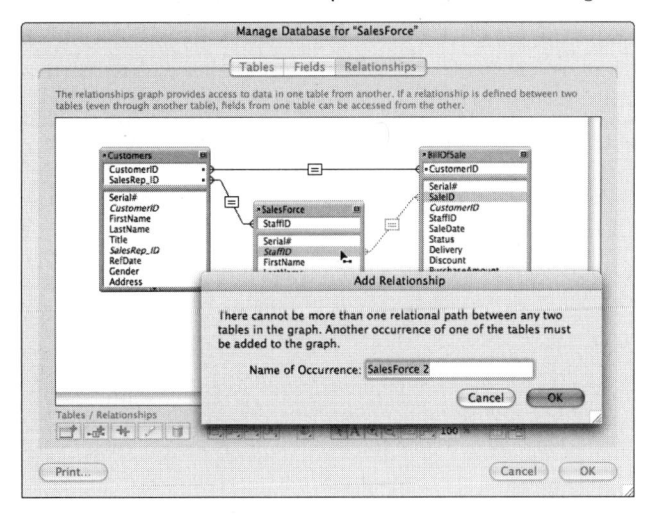

If FileMaker permitted you to add a relationship between the BillOfSale and SalesForce TOs, a reference to either of the other tables from any of the three would create confusion, because the direct path or the indirect path (via the third table) would be equally valid, yet may produce different results. For example, the cashiers for a customer's purchases may not always have been the sales rep assigned as their contact — so from a Customer layout, the assigned contact would be returned via a direct link to the SalesForce TO, but a link that passes via the BillOfSale TO may return the name of the cashier who sold the customer an appliance last week.

Instead, FileMaker requires that an additional TO be created, providing an alternate (and distinct) path to the sales staff table, so that confusion is avoided. The result, as Figure 7.17 shows, is an additional TO associated with the SalesForce table, supporting the desired logic, while avoiding conflict. Rather than being a circular reference, this might be thought of as a spiral form, because it returns to the same point yet a displaced location.

The requirement to avoid circular references and the consequent displacement of points of connection to the underlying table structure are central to grasping the way the graph works. Unlike a two-dimensional floor plan, it is best thought of as an exercise in multi-dimensional modeling.

### FIGURE 7.17

A typical spiral formation in the FileMaker Relationships Graph.

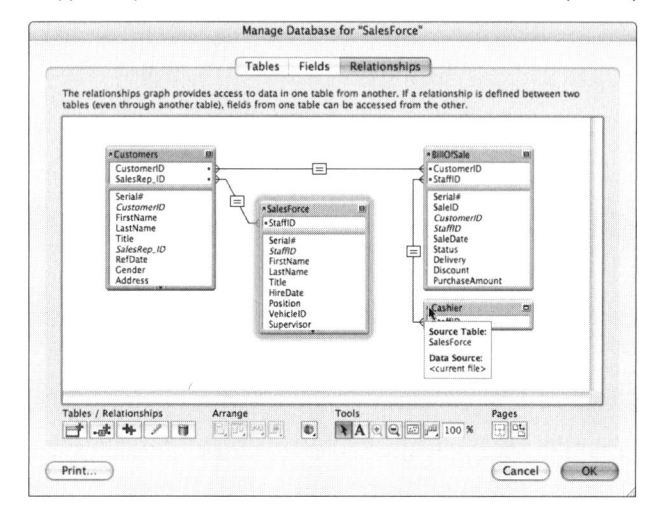

## Named and unnamed data sources

FileMaker keeps track of the locations of files you're using. These include files containing the tables associated with TOs on the Relationships Graph, files from which you are importing data, and also files your solution will create (files containing exported data, PDF files of database content, and so on).

When storing details about the identity or location of a file that your solution uses, FileMaker differentiates between data sources (files containing one or more of the tables referenced on the Relationships Graph) and all other files. A key aspect of this distinction is that files containing tables referenced on the Relationships Graph are given a name and are stored for reuse. You can view and edit a list of these named data sources by choosing File ➪ Manage ➪ External Data Sources. Named Data Sources can include any mix of FileMaker files (both local and hosted) and SQL databases sourced via ODBC (from hosts running supported versions of SQL Server, MySQL, or Oracle).

Referenced files not containing tables you've associated with TOs on the Relationships Graph include files designated in script or button commands, such as `Open File[ ]`, `Import`

## The Structure: The Manage Database Dialog

`Records[ ]`, `Insert File[ ]`, `Save Records as PDF[ ]`, and the like. In these cases, the location of the file (its path or server address) is specified and saved as a property of the command to which it relates. This is done via the Specify File dialog shown in Figure 7.18.

Whereas named data source references can be reused, unnamed file specifications are specific to a single command. Even if you've referenced the same file several times in one or more scripts, each instance is specified and stored separately.

**FIGURE 7.18**
The Specify File dialog that FileMaker provides for entering or editing unnamed file specifications.

### Creating references to other FileMaker files

FileMaker presents the Specify Table dialog showing, by default, a list of the tables in the current file when you add TOs to the Relationships Graph. At the top of the dialog is a pop-up menu of available data sources (see Figure 7.19).

If you want to use a table in another FileMaker file as the basis for a TO in the current file and the file is not already present in the Data Source list, you can choose to add it to the list by choosing Add FileMaker Data Source (within the group of options at the bottom of the menu). Choosing this option presents the standard Open File dialog, so you can choose a local or remote file. After selecting a file, as long as you have appropriate access privileges to the file, it is added to the menu and a list of available tables appears in the dialog.

As you add a FileMaker data source (as described earlier), its name and location are stored so that you can later view or edit them (after leaving the Manage Database dialog) by choosing File ➪ Manage ➪ External Data Sources. When you choose this command, FileMaker displays the Manage External Data Sources dialog, listing each external data source referenced by the current file, its type, and its location.

**FIGURE 7.19**

Adding a TO to the current file in the Specify Table dialog.

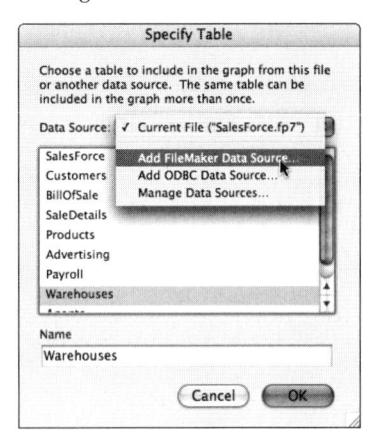

## Working with External SQL Data Sources

FileMaker Pro 9 provides you with seamless access to data from a variety of sources — and the ability to combine data from disparate sources. In doing so, it delivers new power and simplicity. When your connections are configured, you can work with remote data from one or more SQL systems in the same ways in which you work with FileMaker data. In many cases, users need not even be aware of the source of the data they're accessing.

Support for External SQL Data Sources (ESS) not only lets you integrate data from FileMaker, MySQL, SQL Server, and Oracle systems — allowing you to search, view, create, edit, and delete records in the remote systems — but also enables you to output data from any mix of these systems to a variety of formats. You won't need to write a single line of SQL to make it all work.

In many cases, systems to which you'll connect using ESS will be managed by others and you may have little influence over the form of the data or the nature of access available. Nevertheless, you'll be able to create calculations and summaries using SQL tables, while working entirely within the familiar environment of FileMaker.

### Configuring ODBC drivers: Setting up a DSN

FileMaker Pro 9 lets you work directly with tables stored in supported SQL databases. Prior to doing so, however, you need to configure your computer's connection to the relevant ODBC host. This requires creating a data source name (DSN) that points to the location of the external database.

**NOTE** ODBC stands for Open Database Connectivity and is a widely supported protocol allowing data exchange between enterprise data systems. FileMaker uses ODBC as the technology that enables its connections to supported SQL database hosts.

## The Structure: The Manage Database Dialog

If you intend to use the database as a stand-alone solution, you'll need the appropriate ODBC drivers and DSN configuration on your workstation. However, when a FileMaker file is hosted using FileMaker Server 9, the ODBC drivers and DSN configuration are required only on the server, not on individual workstations accessing the solution.

To begin, you'll need appropriate ODBC drivers for the versions of SQL you'll be accessing, which, when installed, will be available for selection in the ODBC Data Source Administrator utility on your computer.

> **TIP** **If you're working on a Windows computer, you can expect that the required drivers are already installed (they ship with the operating system). On the Mac, however, you'll need to purchase and install the required drivers, which are available from Actual Technologies (www.actualtechnologies.com).**

To access the ODBC Data Source Administrator in Windows XP, go to the Start menu and navigate to Control Panel ➪ Administrative Tools ➪ Data Sources (ODBC). On Windows Vista, go to the Start Menu and navigate to Control Panel ➪ Additional Options ➪ Data Sources (ODBC). After selecting this option, the ODBC Data Source Administrator control panel appears. Choose the System DSN tab (see Figure 7.20).

**FIGURE 7.20**

The ODBC Data Source Administrator control panel in Windows XP.

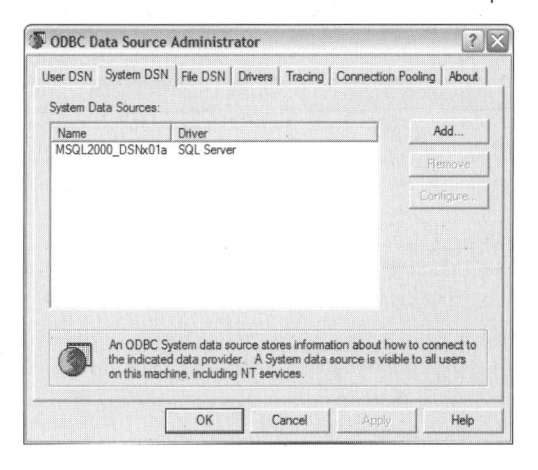

To access the ODBC Administrator on Mac OS, open the Applications folder on your system disk and locate and open the Utilities folder. Inside Applications/Utilities you'll find an application called ODBC Administrator. Double-click it, and the ODBC Administrator utility window appears. Click the padlock icon at the lower left and authenticate as an administrator for the computer. Choose the System DSN tab to show the panel in Figure 7.21.

215

### FIGURE 7.21

The ODBC Administrator Utility in Mac OS.

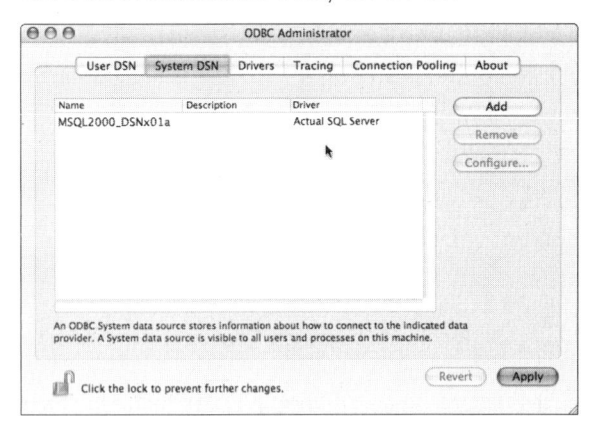

After you've accessed the ODBC Administrator on your computer (as described earlier), click the Add button at the upper right of the window. You'll be prompted to select a driver. Choose the driver appropriate to the source to which you're connecting — MySQL, SQL Server, or Oracle. (If the appropriate driver is not present in the list, you'll first have to obtain and install it.) Accept the driver selection and you'll be presented with the driver configuration panel. Although there is some variation between drivers and systems, the process is similar, requiring you to enter a name, a server address, and authentication details.

In the following steps, we show the process for creating a new DSN to connect to SQL Server from Mac OS using the Actual SQL Server driver:

1. In the first configuration panel (shown in Figure 7.22), enter the name for this connection (we chose to call the connection AdminSys_SQL, but any recognizable name will do) and the connection type (System), along with the address of the server, which may be in the form of an IP address or a domain pointer (for example, `data.yourdomain.com`). The description field, if available, is optional.

   After you accept the settings on the first panel, a second panel is presented that requires authentication details, as shown in Figure 7.23.

2. The login and password you enter here must match a valid account in the host system you're accessing. In this panel, you can click the Client Configuration button to change the network protocol or the connection's port assignment. In our case, the default settings (TCP-IP, port 1433) were appropriate. As long as your login ID and password are valid (and the server address, port, and protocol are correct), the connection is established and you're taken to a third screen (shown in Figure 7.24) that displays settings specific to the server.

3. If necessary (that is, if your login provides access to more than one database on the selected host), choose a database as the default.

# The Structure: The Manage Database Dialog  7

**FIGURE 7.22**

Configuring the DSN, Part 1: Connection name and server address.

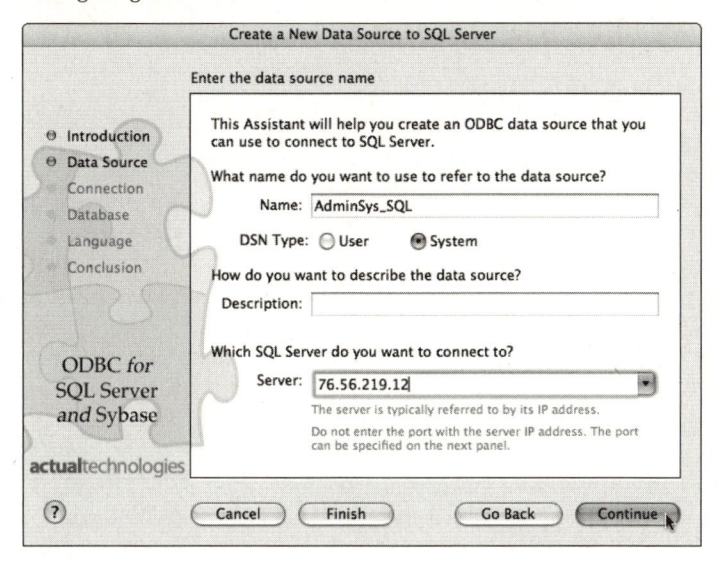

**FIGURE 7.23**

Configuring the DSN, Part 2: Authentication.

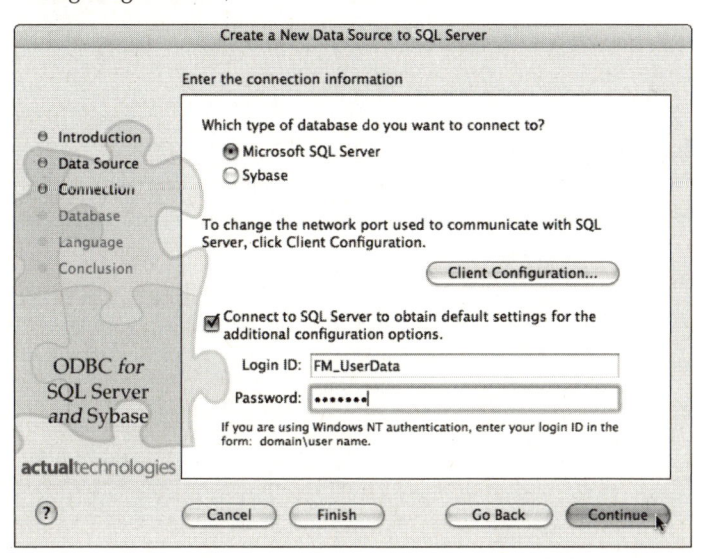

217

## Part II  Introduction to Database Design

**FIGURE 7.24**

Configuring the DSN, Part 3: Server-specific settings.

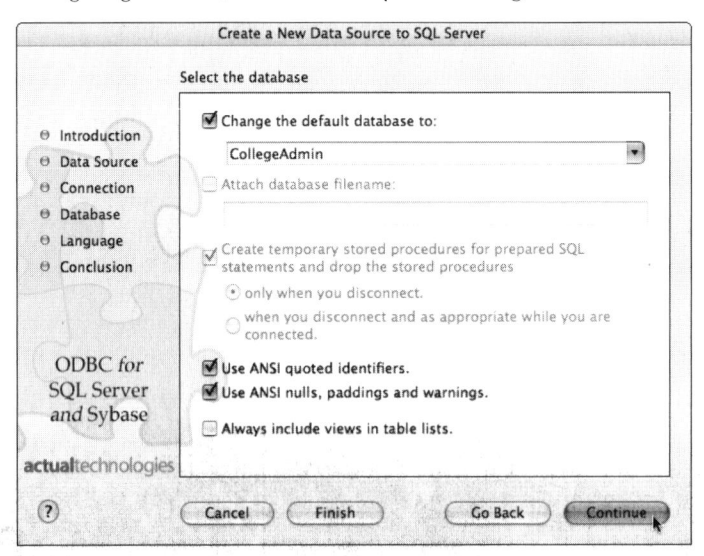

Options to change the default language and regional settings and log file locations, plus a confirmation screen, appear.

4. We accepted all the default settings. On dismissing the confirmation panel of the driver configuration panel, a new DSN was added to the ODBC Administrator panel, as shown in Figure 7.25.

**FIGURE 7.25**

The resulting DSN appearing in the ODBC Administrator Utility, after configuration of the ODBC Driver.

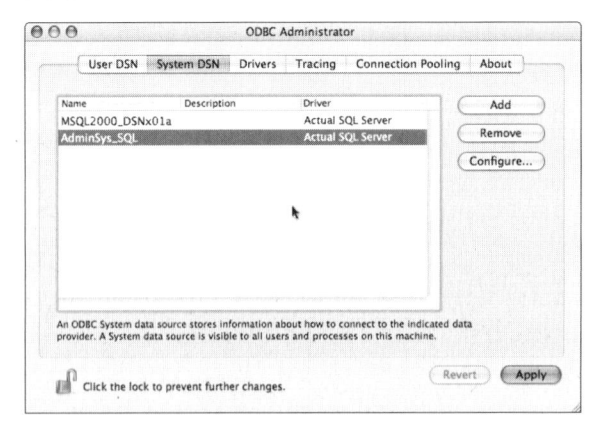

## The Structure: The Manage Database Dialog | 7

Although the configuration process described here and the accompanying images are on a Mac using the Actual SQL Server driver, we repeated the process on Windows XP (using the default SQL Server driver on Windows) and the process was identical.

## Integrating SQL tables with FileMaker data

After establishing a DSN as described earlier, you can add SQL tables directly onto the Relationships Graph in FileMaker Pro 9. To do this, follow these steps:

1. Choose File ⇨ Manage ⇨ Database and navigate to the Relationships panel.
2. Click the New TO icon at the far left of the tools along the bottom of the dialog. The Specify Table dialog appears, as shown in Figure 7.26.

**FIGURE 7.26**

Adding an ODBC Data Source via the Specify Table dialog.

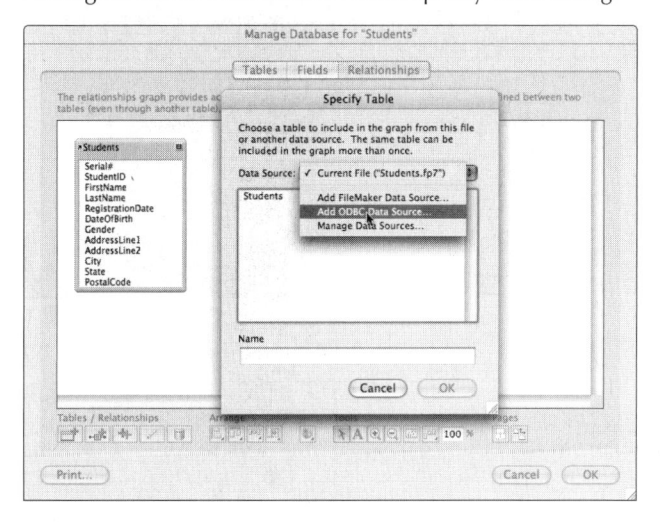

3. Select Add ODBC Data Source from the Data Source menu.
4. You're prompted to choose a DSN (from a list of previously configured DSNs). Select the appropriate DSN and click Continue. FileMaker displays the Edit Data source dialog, as shown in Figure 7.27.

   The only essential settings when configuring your connection to a SQL database are a valid System DSN and a name to identify the external source within FileMaker (it can be the same as the DSN name if you want). You will, of course, need a valid user name and password to access the SQL host; however, you have the choice of being prompted to authenticate for every connection or to save the authentication details when creating the connection.

219

## Part II   Introduction to Database Design

**FIGURE 7.27**

The Edit Data Source dialog for configuration of an external SQL connection.

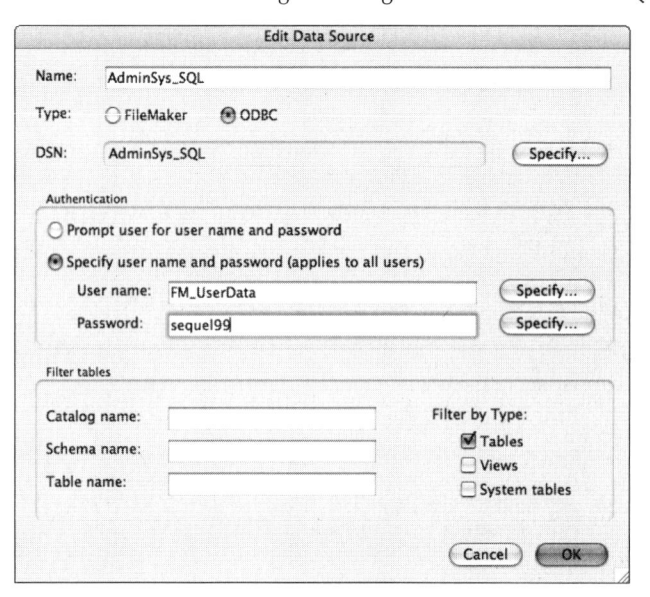

> **CAUTION** If you store authentication details for an SQL Host in your FileMaker file, ensure that your solution is appropriately secured with its own account and password authentication (see Chapters 5 and 14).

For most purposes, the Filter options at the bottom of the Edit Data Source dialog can be left with the default settings, but this may vary depending on the nature and configuration of the SQL database and the settings of the DSN on your computer. If you're unfamiliar with the database to which you're connecting, you may want to confer with the database administrator to ensure that you have an appropriate account and other configuration details.

On accepting the Data Source settings, you're returned to the Specify Table dialog, and a list of tables available in the selected SQL database is displayed, as shown in Figure 7.28.

5. For the purposes of this example, we've added three SQL tables to a file alongside a FileMaker table called Students. With SQL tables appearing as TOs on the Relationships Graph, as shown in Figure 7.29, you are able to drag connections between the tables to create relationships, exactly as you do when working with FileMaker tables.

## The Structure: The Manage Database Dialog   7

#### FIGURE 7.28
Selecting from a list of SQL Server tables in the Specify Table dialog.

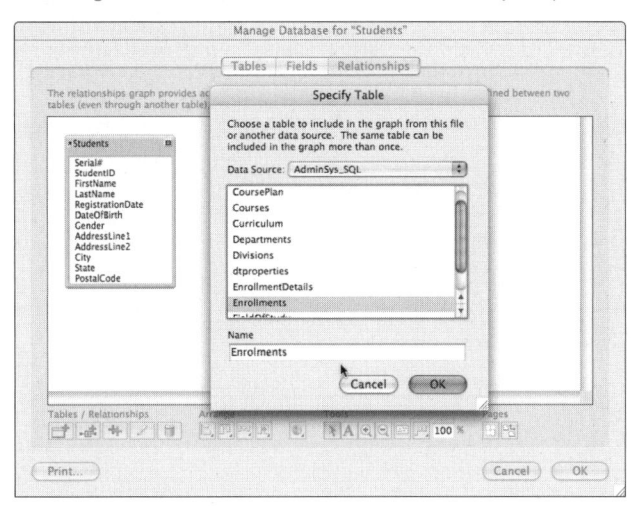

#### FIGURE 7.29
Creating relationships to join FileMaker tables and SQL tables.

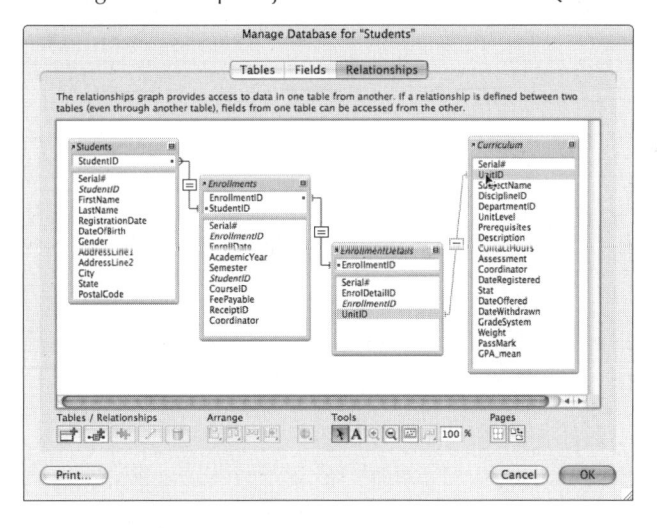

**221**

## Part II  Introduction to Database Design

> **NOTE** The names of TOs based on external tables (both FileMaker and SQL) appear in italics in the header band of their boxes on the Relationships Graph.

With relationships in place, you can work with your solution, incorporating SQL data alongside FileMaker data, performing Finds, and creating and editing records (subject to privilege restrictions, if any, of your account to the SQL host).

Because some of the tables in your solution are created and hosted elsewhere, you'll be constrained by the available fields and their formats. SQL fields do not always behave in the same ways as FileMaker fields. However, you'll be able to define auto-enter options (default values, serial numbers, auto-enter calculations and lookups, and so on) and data validations for the fields in the SQL tables in your solution. To facilitate this, FileMaker creates shadow tables representing the content of the SQL tables you've referenced, as shown in Figure 7.30.

**FIGURE 7.30**
Shadow tables created by FileMaker to support SQL TOs added to the Relationships Graph.

## Adding supplemental fields

In addition to specifying auto-enter and validation options for fields within shadow tables, FileMaker lets you add summary and calculation fields (for use only within FileMaker).

Using the example shown at Figures 7.29 and 7.30, data can be added to create and update student enrollment records in the remote SQL Server database. As subjects are added to a student's enrollment, the total attendance hours increase; however, there is no facility in the SQL database to calculate the total. You can resolve an issue of this kind by adding a calculation field to the Enrollment table, exactly as you would if it were a FileMaker table.

## The Structure: The Manage Database Dialog

Figure 7.31 shows the FileMaker calculation field added to the Enrollments table. Supplemental fields added in this way are re-evaluated as data is displayed in the same way as unstored calculations within native FileMaker tables.

**CROSS-REF** For further discussion of the use of SQL data, you may want to consult the discussion on the use of separated data in SQL sources in Chapter 11.

**FIGURE 7.31**

A FileMaker supplemental field added to the SQL Enrollments table that calculates the sum of course hours by using a FileMaker relationship between two SQL tables.

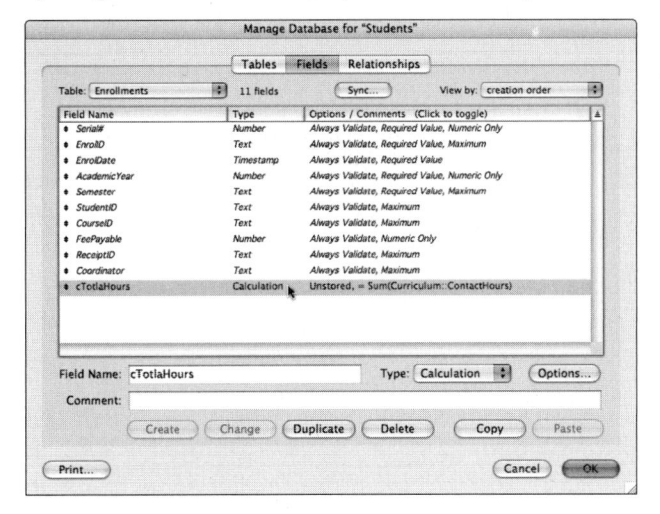

# The Concept of Data Relationships

Previously, we've mentioned the value of investing time and effort in setting up appropriate data relationships in your solutions. Establishing a comfortable and "natural" fit between the information itself and the structures where you store it greatly simplifies effective information management.

As well as mirroring reality, relational data systems make practical sense because they allow you to store each piece of information once and connect it to other relevant information. The reduced duplication not only saves labor but also reduces the scope for error.

## Why bother with relationships anyway?

In a solution such as the inventory example from the previous chapters, each kind of item has a single corresponding record in the Inventory table. Wherever the item is purchased or sold — or included on a list of acquisitions for a customer in the contacts table — the name and description of the item, as stored in its Inventory record, is displayed. If you correct an error in the description of an item, the change instantly propagates to every place in the system referencing the item.

Similarly, each buyer and supplier has a single record in the Contacts table. If a contact's address is updated, the change will be seen throughout the system without further effort on your part.

The time and money you invest designing and implementing an appropriate structure (and solution to support it) for your databases will pay off many times over in the improved accuracy and accessibility of your data and the time saved in coming years.

## How relationships work

Relationships use one or more key fields, which are matched to corresponding values in another table. There are three guidelines for the values used as keys — they should be unique (duplicates cause instant confusion), persistent (not changing periodically), and not empty.

Using an attribute such as a person's name or initials (or some other data about them) as the key to his record is generally unwise — the information may not be unique (people can have the same name) and it may not be persistent (people occasionally change their names). For these and similar reasons, it's often safer to use serial numbers or code values as keys.

When you've chosen key values, FileMaker builds value indexes for the key fields so that relationship matching can be undertaken efficiently. When your solution retrieves data from another table, it is the other table's index that is used. The value of the key field in the current table is referenced against the index of the related table to instantly locate matching records. For this reason, a relationship will work as long as the "other" table's key field is indexed.

In FileMaker, most fields can be indexed, so most relationships work in both directions (from the perspective of layouts associated with TOs at both ends of the join). However, in cases where a global field or an unstored calculation has been used as the key field on one side of a relationship, the relationship will work in one direction only.

## Solving problems using relationships

A useful feature of FileMaker relationships is that they match field values. In text fields, a value is one line of text. Because text fields can hold multiple lines, however, a text field can hold multiple key values. When you place multiple values (separated by carriage returns) into a text field that you've defined as the key field for a relationship, matches to any of the values will be valid. A key field used in this way is referred to as a *multi-key field* (or sometimes, just a *multi-key*). By employing multi-key fields you increase the possible matches, creating an OR relationship condition (that is, records will be related to the current record if they match one value *or* the other). Multi-key text fields can be used on either side, or both sides, of a relationship (in the latter case, the join is valid if any of the values on one side matches any of the values on the other).

FileMaker also lets you narrow the scope of a relationship by specifying additional pairs of key fields, Relationships of this kind are called *multi-predicate relationships*. When more than one pair of key fields has been assigned to a relationship, both criteria are applied, returning an AND condition (the first pair of keys must match *and* any subsequent pairs must match in order for the relationship to be valid).

By far the most common kind of relationship is one in which values on either side of the relationship must exactly match. This kind of relation is called an *equi-join* and is symbolized by the = relationship operator. However, FileMaker provides a number of alternative operators that can be used to control the behavior of relationships.

**CROSS-REF** For additional detail about relationships and relationship operators in FileMaker, refer to Chapter 11.

## Deciding what goes where

A central principle of relational design is that of separating entities and describing their attributes. From a data design perspective, each kind of entity warrants a table and each attribute of an entity warrants a field in the entity's table.

In practical terms, tables are used to store information about a class of items. Whenever an item has independence from another (with which it is associated) you should consider treating them as separate entities and giving them separate tables.

Persons are entities and they live at addresses. Because persons are not inseparable from their places of residence, however, it often makes sense to store addresses in a separate table from persons. Similarly, employees occupy jobs for periods of time, but they are not inseparable, so it makes sense to have separate tables for them and relationships to show who is in which job and when.

**CROSS-REF** We provide a more extensive discussion of relational modeling and data design in Chapters 11 and 15.

## The FileMaker relational model

FileMaker offers you a very appealing combination of elements. It provides coverage for a wide range of requirements from stand-alone systems to major server-based installations. It is a stealth weapon, concealing its power behind a demure interface and apparent ease of use.

A defining characteristic of FileMaker has been its integrated approach — wherein data, logic, and interface are combined within a unified format. But in reality, FileMaker's extraordinary flexibility gives you many choices. The ability to work seamlessly with SQL data in FileMaker 9 further extends FileMaker's scope as an all-purpose tool.

However, powerful relational tools and good data modeling aren't the only things that make FileMaker an instant asset. Its capability to automate your work processes adds another dimension. In Chapter 8, we delve into FileMaker's capabilities as a process management tool.

# Chapter 8

# The Processes: ScriptMaker

People, especially people who use technology, want and expect that technology to perform as much of the grunt work as possible. In fact, utopia would be for the software to read the user's mind and just provide the results. Well, we've not quite reached utopia, but FileMaker's built-in scripting capabilities let your solution appear to have at least a little ESP.

In the preceding chapters, you've become acquainted with the tools and techniques for building database structures and interfaces. ScriptMaker provides a third essential element that makes everything work together. When you need your solution to take a more active role, you have to provide it with a script. That's where ScriptMaker comes in. ScriptMaker enables you to store instructions about tasks to be performed with your data — then ScriptMaker performs those tasks for you!

Any series of database tasks you need to do repetitively may benefit from being scripted and performed on demand. ScriptMaker performs this essential automation role, with the potential to take much of the drudgery out of your digital days. The best thing is that you'll find it very easy to get started using ScriptMaker — and, when you do, you'll wonder how you ever got by without it!

**IN THIS CHAPTER**

Getting acquainted with ScriptMaker

Defining and editing scripts

Using the Script menu

Controlling script execution

Identifying some notable script uses

Organizing your scripts

Getting started with some examples

## ScriptMaker: What It Is and What It Offers You

At its inception, ScriptMaker was analogous to a macro environment — its focus was to perform a number of simple tasks in the same ways in which the users would perform the tasks. That was a couple of decades ago, however, and ScriptMaker's capabilities have been growing and evolving version by version ever since. Nevertheless, ScriptMaker retains those original capabilities, and these make it easy for you to get started.

ScriptMaker typically performs a series of actions in the same sequence in which you would perform those actions if you were stepping through a task manually. When the actions are set out in a script, however, you can perform them as though they were a single action or command. A simple example would be a customer database that, when you retrieve a customer record, offers a button to retrieve the status of pending or recent orders. More complex scripted operations might include automated archiving of quarterly or annual data and preparing the solution for a new period.

Discussing FileMaker automation requires a little terminology. The mini programs (or stored procedures) you create with ScriptMaker are called *scripts*. You create, modify, and delete scripts using FileMaker's ScriptMaker feature (Scripts ⇨ ScriptMaker or Shift+⌘+S or Ctrl+Shift+S). Individual ScriptMaker commands are often referred to as *steps* or *script steps*. ScriptMaker organizes script steps into 12 function-based categories, as follows:

- **Control steps** direct a script's operation and include conditional execution, looping, termination, calling other scripts, and so forth.
- **Navigation steps** direct your solution in such areas as which field should have the cursor, which layout should be in front, which record(s) should be displayed, and which mode should be active.
- **Editing steps** provide a procedural interface to the commands found in FileMaker's Edit menu, such as Cut, Copy, Paste, and Undo.
- **Fields steps** let you programmatically set or modify a field's value and export a field's contents.
- **Records steps** let you manage the records (and Find requests) in your solution, including such operations as creating new records, duplicating existing records, deleting records, committing records, and exporting records.
- **Found Sets steps** let you perform Finds and manipulate found sets resulting from a Find operation.
- **Windows steps** have nothing to do with Microsoft. They let you manage the display of your solution's windows, including such operations as creating a new window and positioning or resizing an existing window.
- **Files steps** let you create, open, and close files. They also let you perform programmatically many of the actions manually accessible via FileMaker's File menu, including Print Setup and Print.
- **Accounts steps** provide a programmatic interface to managing your solution's accounts. This includes adding and deleting accounts, managing account passwords, activating and deactivating accounts, and controlling account login.

## The Processes: ScriptMaker    8

- **Spelling steps** provide a programmatic interface to the Edit ⇨ Spelling submenu options.
- **Open Menu Item steps** provide you with a mechanism to display various FileMaker dialogs, such as Preferences, Manage Database, Help, and even ScriptMaker itself.
- **Miscellaneous steps** comprise a variety of useful but not easily categorized commands, such as setting a Web Viewer object and the operation to perform on it, installing a custom menu set, displaying a custom dialog, and sending e-mail.

ScriptMaker differs from traditional programming environments, where you write your code in a text editor and you need to be careful about syntax and spelling. Building a script in ScriptMaker is more like setting type. You choose the command (step) you want from a list and then click checkboxes and choose from lists and pop-up menus in subsequent specification dialogs to establish the step's parameters. For example, Figure 8.1 shows the "Move/Resize Window" Options dialog that appears when you click the Move/Resize Window step's Specify button. Those five Specify buttons down the right side of the dialog all invoke the Specify Calculation dialog, allowing your script to determine the values to be used conditionally when the script is running. Or, you can enter constant values as the parameters for any or all of the corresponding text boxes. (We told you that the Specify Calculation dialog was ubiquitous!)

#### FIGURE 8.1
Clicking a step's Specify button(s) presents dialogs where you select the step's arguments.

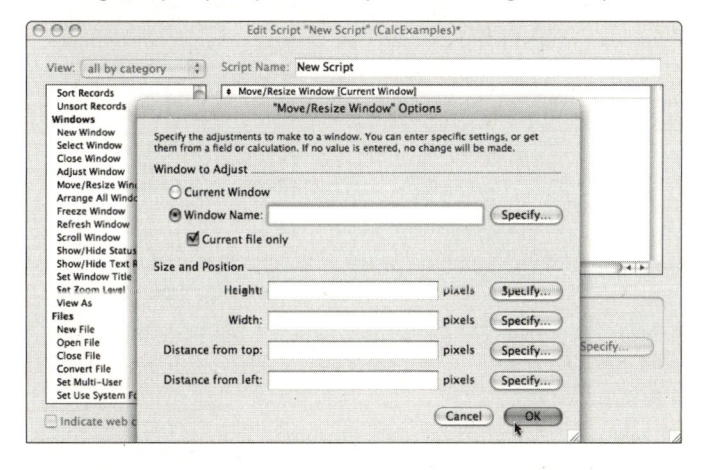

**TIP**    If your solution may be Web-hosted, make sure to select the Indicate Web Compatibility checkbox in the Edit Script dialog's lower-left corner. Knowing which steps won't function in a Web-hosted environment allows you to adjust your approach or disable specific functionality when running on the Web.

229

## Building blocks of automation

ScriptMaker offers 14 Control steps, 11 Navigation steps, 8 Editing steps, 15 Fields steps (Mac) or 16 Fields steps (Windows), 14 Records steps, 10 Found Sets steps, 14 Windows steps, 10 Files steps, 6 Accounts steps, 7 Spelling steps, 10 Open Menu Item steps, and 15 Miscellaneous steps (Mac) or 14 Miscellaneous steps (Windows) for a total of 134 script steps on either platform; however, 2 steps (Perform AppleScript and Speak) are Mac-only and 2 (Update Link and Send DDE Execute) are Windows-only, with 1 (Send Event) being present on both but having different syntax on the two platforms.

We don't propose to give a detailed description of the 134 steps here. Listing and describing them all here would consume whole chapters without contributing much, since that is something the FileMaker Pro 9 Help system covers quite well. (Also refer to Appendix B for links to free and comprehensive resources detailing the operation of each script command.)

Unlike the Specify Calculation dialog, where you can type your calculation expression, the Edit Script dialog leads you to create and edit scripts by selecting items from lists and configuring their predefined options. Some users start out performing these selections and manipulations entirely via the mouse, but you'll quickly find that there are keyboard commands to control the whole process efficiently. You select script steps (using the mouse, the tab and arrow keys, or type-ahead selection) in a list box at the left of the Edit Script window. After you've located/selected the step you want, you can (with a double-click or by pressing Return) add it to the current script. By default, new steps are added at the end of the current script, but if you've selected a step in the current script, any new steps will be added immediately after that step.

In the main working area of the Edit Script window, you use the same methods to select a script step to configure, reposition, or delete. You can select options for a selected script step from checkboxes (occasionally with adjoining Specify buttons) in the Script Step Options panel, as seen in the lower portion of the dialog shown in Figure 8.2.

> **TIP** You can press the Tab key to move focus from the Script Name text box to the Script Step list box and then to the Script Definition list box (Shift+Tab moves in the opposite order).

When one of the two list boxes in the Edit Script window has focus (a blue border), you can use the keyboard to select items/lines by typing the first letter(s) of the entry. For example, in Figure 8.2, typing *en* would select the End If script command line.

When a line is selected in the list box, press Return (or Enter or the space bar) to add it to the current script, and when a line in the script definition window is selected, press Return (or Enter or the space bar) to open a configuration dialog.

Selected script step options are summarized in brackets ([ ]) in the Script Definition box. These selected options are usually called *arguments* or *parameters*. You'll quickly learn to read a script definition and understand the arguments — but you're still reading a programming language listing, and the code will be terse and stilted as ScriptMaker balances readability by the developer with efficient parsing by the script engine.

## FIGURE 8.2

The Edit Script window with a step in the current script selected.

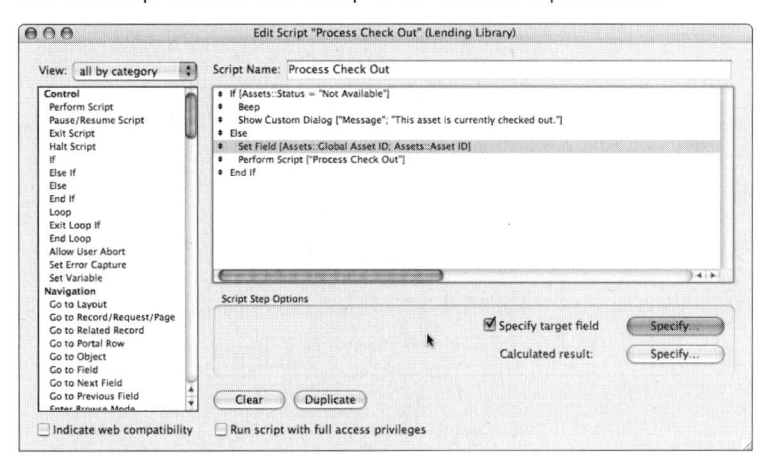

Some script steps are straightforward and have no parameters to be configured. Perhaps the best example is the Halt Script command, which stops the script dead in its tracks. Another example is the New Record/Request step, which requires no parameters and always simply creates a new record (if the database is in Browse mode at the time) or a new Find request (if the database is in Find mode).

Many script commands have multiple options and can perform a variety of different actions depending on the options you select. A simple example is the Undo/Redo command, which provides a menu of three options: Undo, Redo, or Toggle. In effect, the Undo/Redo command can provide three different behaviors depending on the parameter you select.

At the opposite extreme, however, are some commands that have many options and can be configured to do a variety of different tasks within a single script step. One such command is Go to Related Records [ ]. It can be configured to

- Select records from a related table
- Choose an appropriate layout to display the selected records
- Create a new window
- Give the new window a custom title
- Size and position the new window
- Constrain the found set of records in the selected table

With all these capabilities available simultaneously, this one particular command can do work that would otherwise require a number of steps. In this manner, many of the available script commands may be viewed as "packages" of functionality.

Similarly, when you create a script, you're assembling a number of steps into a particular order (and with particular options selected), such that the script itself becomes a package of functionality in your solution. In other words, you can call your script with one action (for example, from a menu or with an assigned keystroke) and it responds, delivering the full functionality of its sequence of steps, at a single stroke.

## Context is everything

FileMaker scripts act as though they're the user — they temporarily take over control of your solution and perform a sequence of actions. In doing so, scripts are constrained to work with the solution's layouts and windows (though they can be programmed to switch layouts or create new windows if desired). Just like the user, a script must be focused on the appropriate screen before it can act on the data that's accessible from that screen.

The way your scripts depend on context is similar to the way you, as a user, depend on context when using your solutions. From a particular layout, you can see data from the associated table and also from related tables (for example, in a portal). Similarly, scripts can act on the current record or on related records, based on the currently active layout and record as each script command executes.

Many script steps require not only that the correct layout be active but that the field or object they are programmed to act on be present on the layout. For example, when your script includes the command:

```
Paste [Select; Contacts::ContactName]
```

the step will fail if you remove the ContactName field from the current layout.

**NOTE** Although scripts act from the context established via the interface, some script commands such as `Set Field [ ]` work directly with the data structure available from the current layout context, regardless of the presence of fields on the layout.

To ensure that your scripts work as intended, you should code them to manage context. Doing so entails establishing the correct context before taking context-dependent actions (such as changing data), testing for context where appropriate, and returning the user to a familiar context after completing their operation.

## Doing things in sequence

Because scripts control the interface and act on your solution as a user does, they're constrained to perform actions in the same logical sequence that a user would. If you want to create a record in the Invoice table, you have to make sure you're in Browse mode, navigate to an invoice layout, then select the New Record command. To script the same procedure, you would require three commands as follows:

```
Enter Browse Mode [ ]
Go to Layout ["InvoiceList" (Invoices)]
New Record/Request
```

# The Processes: ScriptMaker

A script is a list of instructions to be performed in the order in which they appear. In this respect, your scripts are a detailed and sequential documentation of a specific process. If you're able to clearly document all the steps required to perform a specific task, then you'll be able to script the task by assembling the commands that represent each user action, in the order in which the actions are to occur.

## Addressing objects by name

Many script commands act directly on the solution interface, whether entering data into a field on the layout or setting a URL into a Web viewer. To do this, scripts must move the cursor to the appropriate field, select the appropriate Web viewer, and so on.

Some layout objects types have a special command to place the focus on them. For example, the commands

```
Go to Field [ ]
Go to Portal Row [ ]
```

are specially designed to move the focus to a specific field on the current layout or row of the current portal. However, objects of other types can be addressed by first assigning an object name (via the Object Info palette) and then using the command:

```
Go to Object [ ]
```

For example, if you have more than one portal on a layout called InvoiceSummary, in order to place the cursor into a particular field in the last row in one of the portals, you could use a script sequence such as:

```
Enter Browse Mode [ ]
Go to Layout ["InvoiceSummary" (Invoices)]
Go to Object ["AvailableItems"]
Go to Portal Row [Last]
Go to Field [Items::QuantityAvailable]
```

By naming the portal in question AvailableItems and then addressing it explicitly by its name in the script, you ensure that the script will locate the desired portal and the correct instance of the Items::QuantityAvailable field.

In any situation where more than one instance of an object may be present on the layout, the Go to Object [ ] command provides a way to ensure your script will target the desired object. Moreover, the Go to Object [ ] command can be used to place the focus on a variety of different object types including tab panels, buttons, and Web viewers as well as fields and portals.

> **NOTE** An added advantage of the Go to Object [ ] command is the ability to determine the name of the object it is to target by calculation. This enables you to program your scripts to behave more intelligently (for example, taking the user to the first empty field, or selecting a field if it has a value in it, but if not, going to a different field).

# Defining and Editing Scripts

In the sense that script commands and scripts themselves can be considered packages of functionality, ScriptMaker can be viewed as analogous to an object environment — where larger objects can be assembled from smaller ones — and then, in turn, used as components in the assembly of still other objects. Just as parameters (or *arguments*) can be supplied to a script command to determine its behavior, a script parameter can be passed to a script and referenced within the script to control the behavior of the script.

**CROSS-REF**  The use of script parameters is explored in detail in Chapter 9.

We encourage you to think about scripts as reusable objects — maps of action and process — and to strive for a mix of simplicity and versatility. As you develop your skills with ScriptMaker, you may come to view a script as operating like the roll of a player piano — encapsulating detail while re-creating artistry.

## Script Editor windows

When you choose File ➪ ➪ Manage ➪ Scripts (⌘+Shift+S or Ctrl+Shift+S), FileMaker displays the Manage Scripts window for the current file.

**NOTE**  An alternative way to invoke the Manage Scripts window is to choose Scripts ➪ ScriptMaker, as in previous versions of the application. Both commands take you to the same window.

As shown in Figure 8.3, the Manage Scripts window provides a list of scripts in the current file, along with basic search and selection tools at the top of the window and a selection of controls along the bottom.

The Manage Scripts window in FileMaker 9 is nonmodal, so you can leave it open (off to one side of your monitor) while you continue to work with your solution in Browse mode, Layout mode, and so on. Moreover, if you have more than one FileMaker database file open, it is possible to display the Manage Scripts windows for both files simultaneously. This is particularly useful for comparing different versions of the same file, or copying and pasting scripts between files. The title bars of the Manage Scripts windows show the name of the file to which each belongs.

**NOTE**  The Include in Menu option adds the selected script(s) to the Scripts menu. However, if you have access to FileMaker Pro 9 Advanced, you can create custom menus adding script calls to other menus throughout your solution.

**CROSS-REF**  For a more detailed discussion of the creation and use of custom menus in FileMaker Pro Advanced, refer to Chapter 18.

Although only three of the controls at the bottom of the Manage Scripts window have text labels, mouse-over tooltips provide reminders about the function of the remaining four icon-only buttons.

**The Processes: ScriptMaker** | 8

**FIGURE 8.3**

The Manage Scripts window and its controls.

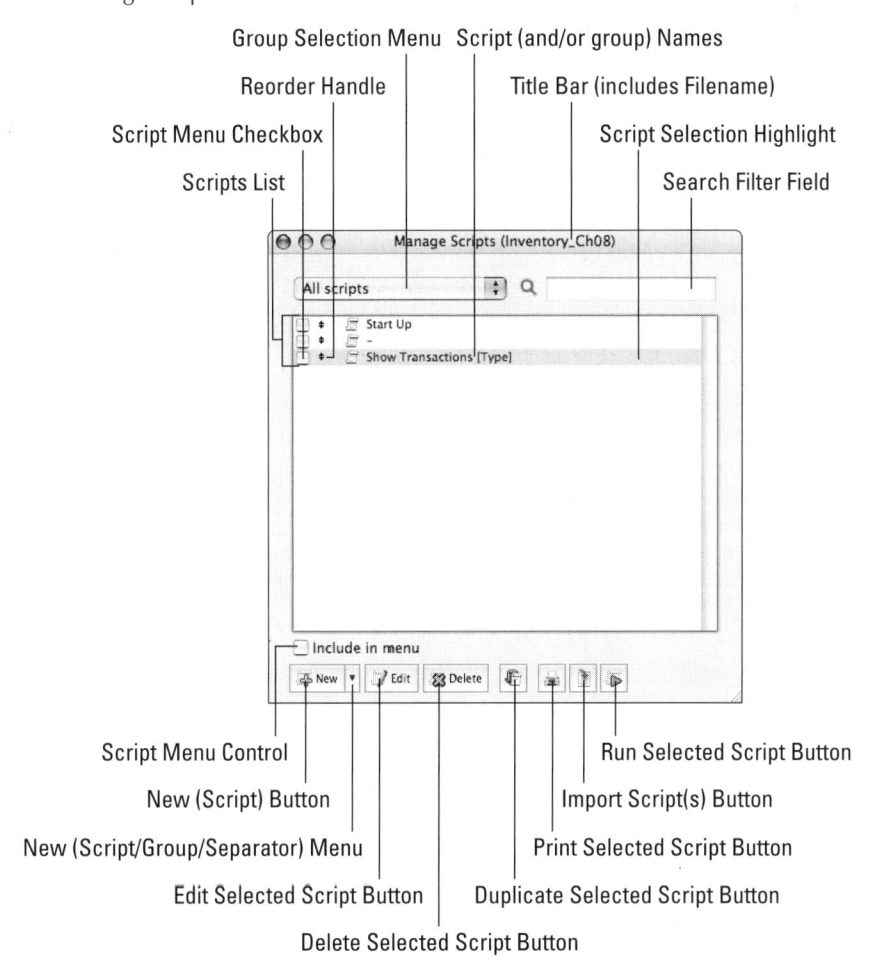

- Group Selection Menu
- Script (and/or group) Names
- Reorder Handle
- Title Bar (includes Filename)
- Script Menu Checkbox
- Script Selection Highlight
- Scripts List
- Search Filter Field
- Script Menu Control
- Run Selected Script Button
- New (Script) Button
- Import Script(s) Button
- New (Script/Group/Separator) Menu
- Print Selected Script Button
- Edit Selected Script Button
- Duplicate Selected Script Button
- Delete Selected Script Button

To create a script, click the New button at the lower left — or to edit an existing script, select it in the list (it will highlight, as shown in Figure 8.3) and click the Edit button (or simply double-click the script). In either case, an Edit Script window will be displayed for the script in question, as exemplified in Figure 8.4.

Like the Manage Scripts window, the Edit Script window is nonmodal in FileMaker 9, meaning that you can open the Edit Script window for multiple scripts (from the same or different files) simultaneously. For comparison and also for copying and pasting commands (or groups of commands) between scripts, this is advantageous.

235

## Part II   Introduction to Database Design

When you've opened multiple Manage Script or Edit Script windows, they'll each be added to the list of windows appearing at the bottom of the Window menu. Selecting a window from the Window menu will bring it to the front.

To save changes to a script in an Edit Script window, choose Scripts ➪ Save Script, or to discard all changes since the script was last saved, choose Scripts ➪ Revert Script.

To close an Edit Script window, or the Manage Scripts window (while either has focus), choose File ➪ Close (⌘+W or Ctrl+W) or click the close button in the window's title bar. If you have made changes to a script in an Edit Script window and the changes have not been saved, you'll be prompted to save (or discard) the changes when closing the window.

**FIGURE 8.4**

The Edit Script window and its controls and parts.

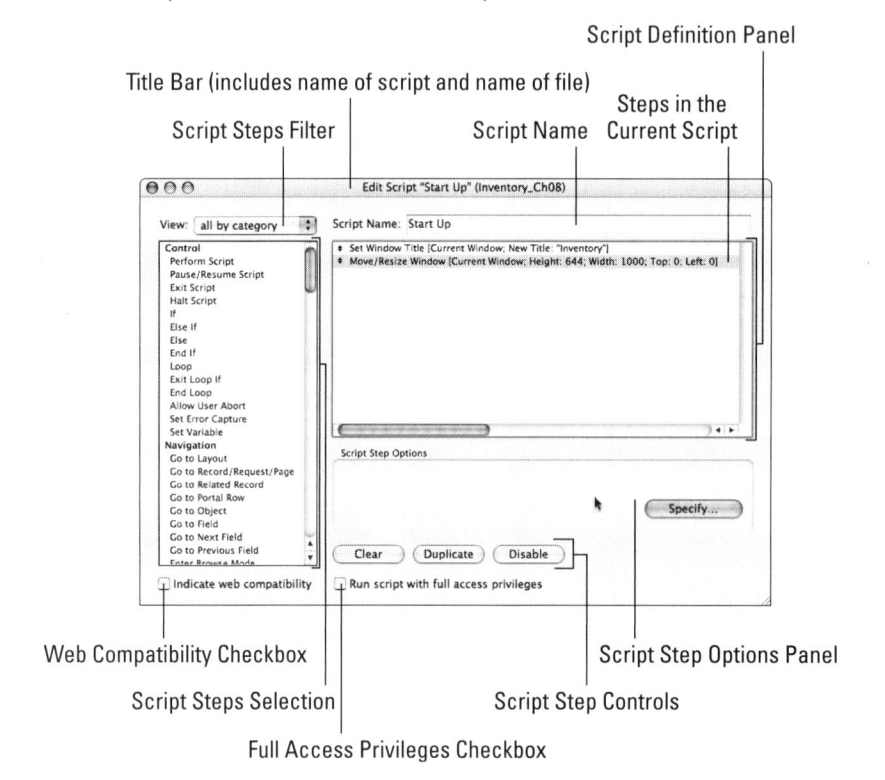

## The Processes: ScriptMaker 8

# Setting up a basic script

The process of creating a script to perform a common task requires that you first identify the component actions of the task. After you've done that, creating the script to put the actions into effect is relatively straightforward. For example, to create a script that prints a list of acquired items in the example Inventory database, follow these steps:

1. Choose File ⇨ Manage ⇨ Scripts. The Manage Scripts window appears.
2. Click New. A new script is created and an empty Edit Script window appears.
3. In the Script Name field, replace the default text for the script name with **Acquired Items Report**.
4. In the list of commands at the left (under the heading Navigation), locate the `Enter Browse Mode [ ]` command, and double-click it. An `Enter Browse Mode [ ]` step is added to the script definition panel.
5. Choose the Windows option in the View pop-up menu at the upper left of the Edit Script window; then, in the resulting list of commands, double-click the `Freeze Window` command.
6. Select the Navigation group of commands; then locate the `Go to Layout` command and double-click it.
7. With the `Go to Layout [ ]` command selected in the script definition panel, click the Specify: menu in the Script Step Options panel and choose the OrderLines layout.
8. Choose Found Sets in the filter menu that sits above the list of commands on the left in the Edit Script window; in the resulting list of commands, double-click the `Show All Records` command.
9. From the Found Sets group of commands, double-click the `Sort Records` command.
10. With the `Sort Records [ ]` command selected in the script definition panel, select the Perform without Dialog checkbox in the Script Step Options panel; then click the Specify Sort Order checkbox. The Sort Records dialog appears.
11. In the Sort Records dialog, locate the OrderLines table in the menu at the upper left and double-click the ItemID field. It appears in the Sort Order panel at the upper right.
12. Click OK to accept the Sort Records dialog settings
13. Choose Files in the filter menu at the top of the list of commands at the left of the Edit Script window and, in the resulting list of commands, double-click the `Print Setup` command.
14. With the `Print Setup [ ]` command selected in the script definition panel, select the Perform without Dialog checkbox in the Script Step Options panel and select the Specify Page Setup checkbox. The Page Setup dialog appears.
15. Choose page attributes for portrait orientation and either US Letter or A4 paper size (as appropriate to your region); then click OK.

## Part II  Introduction to Database Design

16. Double-click the `Print` command in the list at the left.

17. With the `Print [ ]` command selected in the script definition panel, select the Perform without Dialog checkbox in the Script Step Options panel and select the Specify Print Options checkbox. The Print Options dialog appears.

18. Choose an appropriate printer, a single copy, and — from the FileMaker Pro section of the dialog options — the Records Being Browsed radio button, and click Print (Mac) or OK (Windows).

19. In the Navigation group of commands, locate the `Go to Layout` command and double-click it. The content of the script is now complete, as shown in Figure 8.5.

20. Choose Scripts ➪ Save Script (⌘+S or Ctrl+S) to save your work.

21. Choose File ➪ Close (⌘+W or Ctrl+W) to close the Script Editor window.

22. In the Manage Scripts window, select the Acquired Items Report and the Include in Menu checkbox.

23. Choose File ➪ Close (⌘+W or Ctrl+W) to close the Manage Scripts window.

24. Test your new script (by choosing Scripts ➪ Acquired Items Report) to ensure that it produces a printed data sheet from the OrderLines table and returns you to the layout you were in when you chose the script from the Scripts menu.

> **NOTE** For reference purposes, a complete copy of the preceding script, with comments added, is included in the Inventory example file for this chapter. For the purpose of viewing the results of the script, we've also made some rudimentary changes to the InvoiceLines layout in this chapter's copy of the Inventory example, so the printout produced presents information in a list format.

**FIGURE 8.5**

The complete Acquired Items Report script definition as it is shown in the Edit Script window.

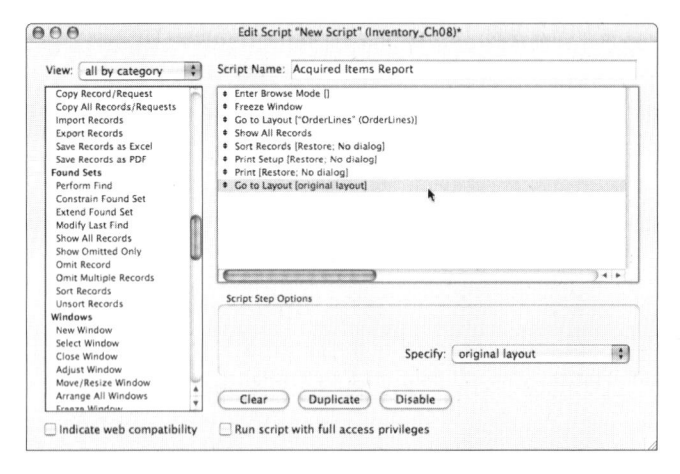

**CROSS-REF** In Chapters 9 and 10, we provide detailed instructions for formatting the InvoiceLines and OrderLines layouts to achieve more useful output.

After completion of this process, you've created a simple eight-step script that fully automates the process of creating a report from the OrderLines layout. The report can be generated by selecting the script from the Scripts menu from wherever you are in the solution. You will be returned to the screen you started from as soon as the report has been created.

## How script commands function

Script commands execute an action (or a group of actions) in real time as the script runs. Some commands, though, are more dependent on the interface than others. For example, commands such as Cut, Copy, Paste, Clear, and Insert work directly with fields in the user interface, placing the cursor into the field and acting on its contents. These commands are not only constrained by the current layout context, they are also dependent on the relevant field being present on the current layout (if you remove the field from the layout, these script commands will fail). Such commands can be described as *interface dependent*.

A second category of commands replicate the actions of menu commands throughout FileMaker. These include script commands such as New Record/Request, Show All Records, and Save Copy As. There are many commands of this kind, and they provide access to the broad range of activities that are routinely available to the user of a solution.

In addition, ScriptMaker provides a number of commands that directly leverage the underlying FileMaker engine. Commands such as `Set Field [ ]`, `Set Next Serial Value [ ]`, `Add Account [ ]`, and `Set Selection [ ]` exemplify this script step category. They allow your scripts to reach around behind the interface, directly manipulating components of the solution.

Finally, a significant number of commands provide control over the script itself, managing the flow of commands and altering their execution. The majority of these commands can be found in the Control group of commands — they include `If [ ]`/End If, Loop/End Loop, `Perform Script [ ]`, and numerous others.

A significant aspect of script commands is that they provide controls and options extending FileMaker's preset capabilities. You can achieve many actions via careful use of scripting that are not available via the standard user interface of FileMaker. A few of the many examples are `Execute SQL [ ]`, `Set Window Title [ ]`, `Dial Phone [ ]` and `OpenURL [ ]`. These commands and others like them extend FileMaker's functional capabilities, enabling you to use scripts to create a rich and varied experience for your solution's users.

## Changing the order of commands

When creating or editing scripts, you'll at least occasionally (in our experience, often) want to move a step to a different location within your script. One way to achieve this is via copy and paste. ScriptMaker also offers the capability to move a step using either the mouse or keyboard.

## Part II   Introduction to Database Design

> **NOTE** Unfortunately, there is no Cut command available when editing scripts — you need to first copy the step and then click Clear to simulate a Cut operation.

Using the mouse, you have the familiar FileMaker handle interface — the double-headed arrows to the left of each script step. Click the handle (the cursor turns into a pair of horizontal lines with arrows pointing up and down, as shown in Figure 8.6) and drag the step to the desired location in your script.

**FIGURE 8.6**

Drag the handle to move a script step to a new position.

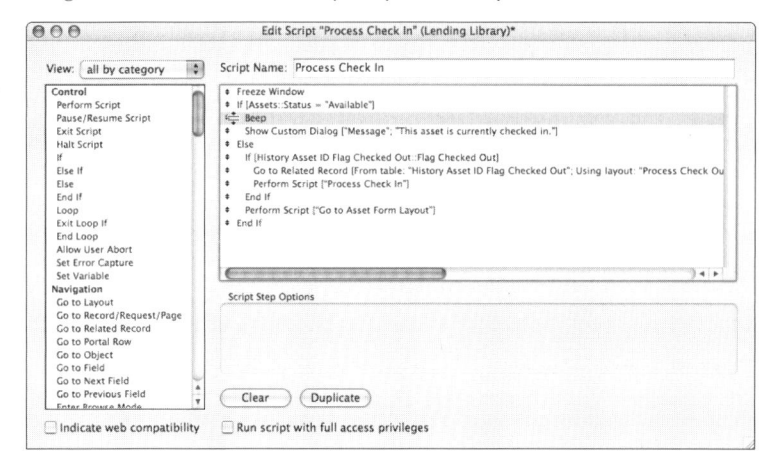

Alternatively, you can select the step and press ⌘+↑ or Ctrl+↑ to move the selected step up in the script and ⌘+↓ or Ctrl+↓ to move the step down in the script.

FileMaker does not provide direct support for moving a block of script steps all at once. There are two methods, however, that you'll find useful when you need to do this: the copy/clear/paste method and the inline duplication method.

Follow these steps to use the copy/clear/paste method:

1. Select the block of commands you want to move.
2. Choose Edit ➪ Copy (⌘+C or Ctrl+C).
3. Click the Clear button.
4. Select the script step immediately above the desired new location.
5. Choose Edit ➪ Paste (⌘+V or Ctrl+V).

Follow these steps to use the inline duplication method:

1. Select the block of commands you want to move.
2. Press ⌘+click or Ctrl+click to select a subsequent command immediately above the desired new location.

240

# The Processes: ScriptMaker

3. Click the Duplicate button.
4. Select the final line of the resulting (duplicated) block of commands.
5. Click the Clear button.
6. Reselect the original block of commands.
7. Click the Clear button.

Although the second method (inline duplication) is less versatile, it has the advantage of working in earlier versions of FileMaker and can be an effective method for some requirements in FileMaker 9.

In general, adding a script step (either by double-clicking it in the step list or selecting it in the step list and clicking Move) places that step at the end of your script. And, as described earlier, you can easily reposition the step to a different location. However, ScriptMaker lets you specify the step after which you want the new step to appear — just select the existing step in the Script Definition box and then add the new step to have it appear immediately following the previously selected step.

> **NOTE** Selecting a step in the step list deselects any selected steps in the Script Definition box, but have no fear — FileMaker remembers what you had selected. Also, if you want to add a step to the very top of your script, you'll need to move it to the top after adding it, because new steps get added after the last (or last selected) step.

We expand on these and other script editing techniques in the "Ease of Editing in ScriptMaker" section, later in this chapter.

## Assigning attributes to a command

Although some script steps are absolute, such as `Select All` or `Open Record/Request`, most accept (or require) configuration arguments specifying the target or scope of their action. For example, when creating a new window via the `New Window [ ]` script step, you can (optionally) specify a name, size, and position for the window being created. In this instance, if you don't supply one or more of the arguments, their values will instead be based on the currently selected window.

The Script Step Options area presents controls allowing you to configure a selected step, as shown in Figure 8.7. ScriptMaker keeps things clean for you by only offering controls pertinent to the selected step (so you don't have a cluttered display with a lot of inappropriate and disabled controls). The controls might be checkboxes, pop-up menus, or (very frequently) Specify buttons. Click the controls you want, and ScriptMaker fills in the step's argument list in the Script Definition box.

Clicking a Specify button presents a context-appropriate dialog, such as the Specify Field dialog, shown in Figure 8.8, which appears when you select the Specify Target Field checkbox (or its associated Specify button).

> **NOTE** Double-clicking a command in the Script Definition Panel — or selecting a command then pressing the Enter key — brings up the default dialog for commands that have one or more parameters configurable by dialog.

241

### FIGURE 8.7

Configure your script steps in the Script Step Options area.

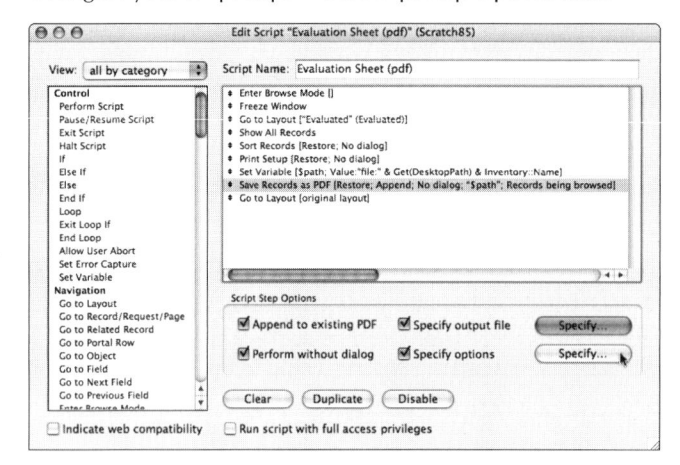

You can see examples of the process of setting parameters in the Acquired Items Report script described earlier in this chapter where you selected parameters for the `Go to Layout [ ]`, `Sort Records [ ]`, `Print Setup [ ]`, and `Print [ ]` script steps.

One of the most frequently used script steps, `Set Field [ ]` has two Specify options, as shown in Figure 8.8. One of the options determines the field to be set (the target field) via the Specify Field List dialog; the other determines the value to be set in the target field. When the `Set Field [ ]` command is selected in the Script Definition panel, you can access the Specify Field dialog by any of the following means:

- Clicking the first Specify button
- Pressing the space bar, the Return key, or the Enter key (Mac) or pressing Alt+S (Windows)
- Double-clicking the script step

Similarly, you can access the Specify Calculation dialog by any of the following means:

- Clicking the second Specify button
- Pressing the Ctl+Option+space bar (Mac) or pressing Alt+F (Windows)
- Option+double-clicking or Alt+double-clicking the script step

You can employ the same alternatives to access the Specify dialogs of most script commands that use the Specify Calculation dialog.

### FIGURE 8.8

Clicking a Specify button presents a corresponding dialog.

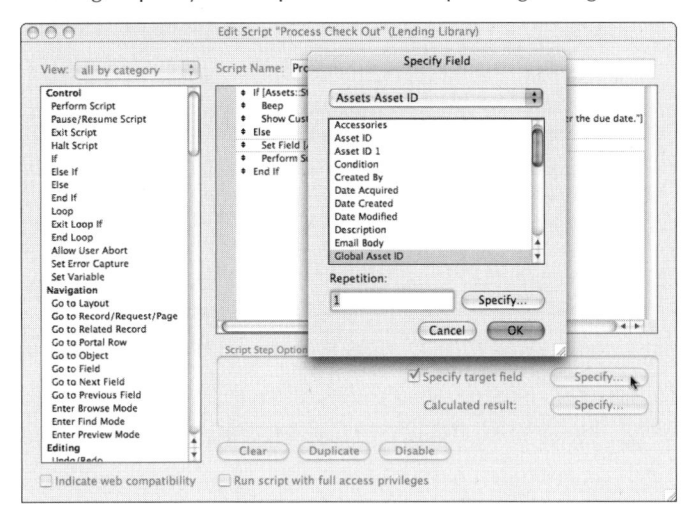

In many cases, you'll need to calculate a step's argument at runtime. For example, when setting a field's value via the Set Field script step, the value is likely to be dependent upon values in one or more other fields. Or, you may be creating a new window that you want to position relative to the user's screen size or resolution, so you calculate the parameters to New Window based upon the user's display. Once again, the Edit Calculation dialog presents a consistent interface, providing you with the Tables pop-up and the Fields list to retrieve values from database records and the Functions list (especially the panoply of Get functions) to obtain environmental information.

## Using the Script Menu

FileMaker enables you to display as many scripts as you want on the Scripts menu. Because menus provide a widely understood user interface paradigm, this is a way of immediately delivering the functionality of your scripts to your users.

If you want to provide a more complex menu interface incorporating your scripts (for example, distributing them among other menus), you can do this via the Custom menus feature of FileMaker Pro 9 Advanced.

**CROSS-REF** For a more detailed discussion of the creation and use of custom menus in FileMaker Pro 9 Advanced, refer to Chapter 18.

## Managing the Scripts menu

The order in which scripts appear in on the Scripts menu corresponds to the order of their arrangement in the Manage Scripts window. Thus resorting, rearranging, or grouping scripts in the Manage Scripts window directly affects the usability of the Scripts menu.

Only those scripts specifically enabled for menu access (via the checkboxes to the left of each script's name in the Manage Scripts window) appear in the Scripts menu — so the Scripts menu is typically a subset of a file's available scripts. Where a script's functions are specific to only one area of a file (for example, a group of layouts), you may prefer not to include it in the Scripts menu (which is accessible throughout your solution), instead making it available only from those layouts where it is appropriate.

When you add Groups to the Manage Scripts window and place scripts within groups, the groups will appear as submenus in the Scripts menu. When you add groups within groups, FileMaker creates corresponding cascading submenus in the Scripts menu.

**TIP** Don't go overboard with groups within groups. Users find traversing multiple layers of cascading submenus awkward, visually confusing, and frustrating. Although not cast in stone, two levels of submenus is a reasonable limit.

**CROSS-REF** Additional information is provided in the "Organizing Scripts" section, later in chapter.

## Other ways to trigger a script

FileMaker provides a number of alternative ways to call scripts in your solutions:

- Scripts called from the Scripts menu (or submenus of grouped scripts on the Scripts menu)
- Scripts designated to run automatically on file open and on file close via the File Options dialog (accessed by choosing File ⇨ File Options)
- Scripts launched from Buttons by using the `Perform Script [ ]` button command
- Scripts called from within other scripts by using the `Perform Script [ ]` script step
- Scripts called from other menu commands and interface widgets throughout the application, via the use of the FileMaker Pro 9 Advanced Custom Menus capability (see Chapter 18)
- Scripts called by plug-ins using the external function API (see Chapter 20)
- Scripts called by other applications or protocols (for example, AppleScript on the Mac or ActiveX on Windows).

## Using the single-threaded script engine

Scripts are sequential in nature — they execute one step at a time and one script at a time. Accordingly, script execution in the FileMaker client application is single-threaded. Only one script can be active at a time, and when a script is executing, the application is not available to the user.

# The Processes: ScriptMaker

To manage the execution of scripts, FileMaker keeps track of called scripts on a script stack. The script at the top of the stack is the active script. However, if a script calls another script, the calling script moves down the stack, waiting until the called script (often termed a *sub-script*) completes its run. Then the calling script moves up the stack and continues to execute. In this way, focus may move between a number of scripts during the completion of a single scripted procedure.

Because FileMaker is a multi-user application, it's important to note that each user has the ability to run his own separately executing script thread. Although this has certain advantages (users aren't delayed while other users run scripts), it does have implications for the way you structure your scripts — you need to consider that multiple instances of a script may be running (on different client workstations) simultaneously.

## Working with the script stack and paused scripts

When a script is indefinitely paused, it remains active. Meanwhile, the solution interface is made available to the user so that input can be provided or action taken. To facilitate this, the solution's functionality while in this state is limited — because the solution is waiting for input from the user, window switching and file closure are disabled, along with most other options and commands.

When a script is paused, the user can nevertheless run another script (or another instance of the same script). If you've used script pauses frequently in your solution, the user can encounter a situation where a number of scripts are paused and awaiting completion on the script stack. This situation is generally undesirable (because it's hard to predict the effects of part-scripts executing out of sequence) and should, therefore, be managed.

You can limit the likelihood of issues with multiple incomplete (paused) scripts by reducing users' access to scripts during periods when a script is paused, or by

- Appropriate use of the `Halt Script` command to terminate the current script and any other paused scripts.
- Employing the FileMaker controls for script stack management when launching scripts via buttons. An argument accepted by the `Perform Script [ ]` button command controls the fate of any currently running script when the new script begins, providing you with the option to halt, exit, resume, or pause the current script.

## Controlling Script Execution

ScriptMaker provides a meta-command framework — a series of script commands that give you control of the way other commands are executed. Using these process controls enables you to set up scripts to repeat a process (that is, looping and recursion) or to conditionally omit or insert sequences of commands within a process.

245

## Using conditional statements

In scripting, as in life, situations arise where you want to perform an action (or series of actions) only if a set of conditions are in effect. For example, in life you might want to shut down and unplug your computer if a lightning storm is approaching. Similarly, in a solution, you might want to generate an e-mail or form letter when a customer's bill is past due. Code reacting to the prevailing circumstances is called *conditional execution* and the programming constructs supporting it are *conditionals*. ScriptMaker provides If, Else If, Else, and End If script steps to implement conditionals.

> **NOTE** You've already encountered conditional evaluation in calculations (see Chapter 7) where, in addition to the If function, you also have the Case function. As you'll see in the next few pages, Case function alternatives and Else If steps are virtually identical in effect: both delimiting alternative results to return or steps to perform based upon a conditional evaluation.

The simplest conditional statement block consists of an If step, an action to be performed when the If statement's argument is true, and an End If step indicating the end of conditional evaluation and execution. For example, given a table with invoice date and payment status fields, you might employ the following condition script to determine whether a late notice should be sent:

```
If [(Payment_status ≠ "Paid") and (Get(CurrentDate) - InvoiceDate > 30)]
    Perform Script ["SendPastDueNotice"]
End If
```

> **NOTE** When you add an If step, ScriptMaker automatically adds the closing End If step, allowing you to add the remainder of your conditional logic between the two.

Frequently, when performing conditional tests, you encounter situations where you want to perform one sequence of actions when the condition is true and an alternative set when the condition is false. The Else step ends the commands executed when the It condition is true and introduces the commands to be executed when the If condition is false. For example, you might want to present a 20 percent off coupon to customers who spent more than $1,000 at your business on this visit and a 5 percent off coupon to the rest of your customers. One way to achieve this would be as follows:

```
If [ InvoiceTotal ≥ 1000 ]
    Perform Script [ "PrintCoupon [20 ]" ]
Else
    Perform Script [ "PrintCoupon [ 5 ]" ]
End If
```

Extending the previous example to allow for graduated discounts at a variety of points is a job the Else If step performs. For example:

```
If [ InvoiceTotal ≥ 1000 ]
    Perform Script [ "PrintCoupon [20 ]" ]
Else If [ InvoiceTotal ≥ 750 ]
    Perform Script [ "PrintCoupon [15 ]" ]
```

## The Processes: ScriptMaker

```
Else If [ InvoiceTotal ≥ 500 ]
    Perform Script [ "PrintCoupon [10 ]" ]
Else
    Perform Script [ "PrintCoupon [5 ]" ]
End If
```

> **NOTE** You can have as many `Else If` steps and their blocks of code as you want (or need) between the `If` block and the `End If` statement, but the optional `Else` block, if present, must be between the last `Else If` block and the `End If` statement.

## Using repetition

Repetition is boring, but it's sometimes necessary to achieve a goal. Many programming languages provide multiple constructs for repetition, such as C's `for` and `do while` statements or JavaScript's `For`, `While`, and `Until` statements. Only one construct is actually necessary, however, and that's what ScriptMaker offers, the one essential structure — `Loop`, with its compatriots `Exit Loop If` and `End Loop`.

To create a loop that is performed a fixed number of times, presenting a countdown dialog the user must dismiss each time, use the following:

```
Set Variable [$counter; Value:5]
Loop
Exit Loop If [$counter=0]
Show Custom Dialog ["Counter Dialog"; "Pass " & $counter]
Set Variable [$counter; Value:$counter-1]
End Loop
```

Similarly, you may want to perform a sequence of steps until a given condition is true. Although not exactly a real-world scenario, but illustrative of the technique, the following example increments a counter and informs the user how many times it has done so until the user clicks the informative dialog's Cancel button.

```
Set Variable [$counter; Value:0]
Loop
  Set Variable [$counter; Value:$counter + 1]
  Show Custom Dialog [ "Counter Dialog"; "Pass " & $counter & ¶ & "Click Cancel
    to end." ]
  Exit Loop If [Get(LastMessageChoice) = 2]
End Loop
Show Custom Dialog [ "Passes Dialog"; $counter & " passes until you got bored."]
```

> **TIP** The preceding example always executes the loop at least once, similar to Pascal's `Repeat` <statements> `Until` condition block or C's `do { `<statements>` }
while (`condition` )` block. If you test for the termination condition at the top of the loop, the loop statements don't execute at all if the termination condition is true on entry. One situation where you might desire this behavior is when you don't know what record will be current when your script executes and you want to display data from the first record (starting with the current record) where

247

your qualifying condition holds true. Something akin to the following could form the basis for your script:

```
Loop
   Exit Loop If [Inventory::Cost ≥ 2.00]
   Go to Record/Request/Page [Next; Exit after last]
End Loop
```

## Pausing for user input

Important aspects in controlling your scripts are your ability to pause scripts and to determine the timing of their execution.

When you want to pause a script to provide the user an opportunity to provide input, you have several options:

- Display a custom dialog allowing the user to make a button selection (in the dialog) or to enter information (into a dialog field).
- Select the Pause argument on a script step such as a mode change command (for example, Enter Browse Mode [Pause]).
- Add the Pause/Resume Script [Indefinitely] command.

In each case, the script will be placed on hold and partial control of the solution interface will be returned to the user, enabling the editing or entry of information, navigation in the current table, printing, launching of another script, or resumption of the current script.

FileMaker also provides you with the ability to pause a script for a defined period, placing the database into the same limited state, but automatically resuming the current script at the end of the allotted time. This is achieved by configuring the Pause/Resume Script [ ] command as shown in Figure 8.9.

**FIGURE 8.9**

The configuration dialog for the Pause/Resume Script [ ] command.

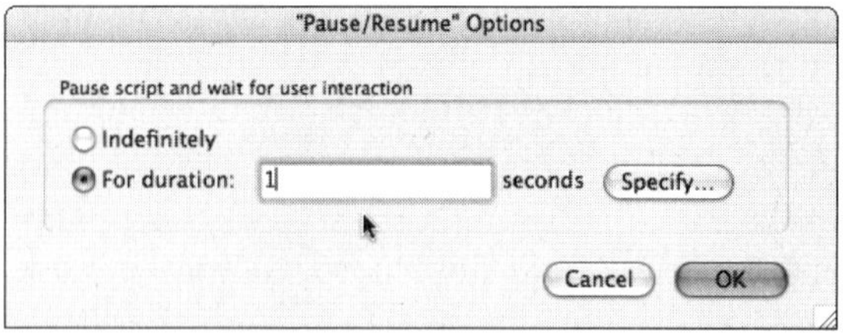

When defining a pause interval, you can enter a finite value in seconds, or use the calculation engine to determine a numeric value (also applied as seconds). Timed pauses are useful for creating processes that will run unattended.

**NOTE** FileMaker will accept sub-second pause durations; however, it does not apply them accurately, and the actual duration varies between platforms and hardware configurations.

## Some Notable Script Uses

Before you became familiar with the concept of scripting, you may have found it difficult to imagine how you would use it. After you've made a start, though, the possibilities seem limitless. Nevertheless, some processes are better suited to scripting than others, and it is important to identify the best candidates.

Scripting is essentially a process of automation. Any process that is performed in essentially the same way many times over may be a good candidate for automation — especially if it can be constructed to require minimal (or no) human intervention. However, the real test is

- Whether the amount of time saved (over a period of solution use) by scripting a process exceeds the time taken to create the script
- Whether the accuracy of the process will improve significantly if it is scripted (in which case, the reduction in errors may justify the investment of time in automating the process)

In short, spending five hours automating a process doesn't make sense if doing so saves the users five minutes a year. But five hours would certainly be worth spending if the result is a much more substantial saving or if doing so would reduce the scope for operator error.

### Navigation and view controls

Although you can provide basic navigation capabilities (such as layout switching and record browsing) using button commands, scripting such navigation may provide an opportunity to perform other functions, validations, or housekeeping operations, or to provide additional functionality along the way.

In the Inventory example, we had previously configured navigation buttons in the footer area, to take the user to other main layouts. However, if these buttons call scripts rather than being attached directly to the Go to Layout [ ] command, you can introduce additional functionality. To demonstrate this, we've created a script to find incomplete orders or invoices. We structured the script so that

- It finds either orders or invoices, depending on the script parameter it receives.
- It finds all orders or invoices unless the Shift key is depressed.
- If the Shift key is depressed when the script runs, it finds only those orders or invoices not marked as complete (that is, incomplete orders or invoices).

The definition of the script created for this purpose is shown in Figure 8.10. It is called Show Transactions [Type]. The bracketed suffix in the name serves as a reminder that the script requires a parameter to indicate what type of transactions are to be shown.

**FIGURE 8.10**

Definition of the Show Transactions [Type] script in the Inventory example file.

```
#PARAMETER: "Orders" or "Invoices"
#SHIFT KEY: isolates incomplete orders
If [Get(ScriptParameter) ≠ "Orders" and Get(ScriptParameter) ≠ "Invoices"]
    #Required parameter is not available.
    Beep
    Exit Script []
Else If [Abs(Get(ActiveModifierKeys) - 2) ≠ 1]
    #Locate all transactions of [type]
    Go to Layout [Get(ScriptParameter)]
    Show All Records
Else
    #Locate incomplete transactions of [type]
    Go to Layout [Get(ScriptParameter)]
    Enter Find Mode []
    Go to Object [Object Name: "Status"]
    Set Field [1]
    Omit Record
    Set Error Capture [On]
    Perform Find []
    If [Get(LastError) > 0]
        #Find failed - no incomplete transactions of the selected type are available for display.
        Go to Layout [original layout]
        Show Custom Dialog ["Selection Error:"; "No incomplete " & Get(ScriptParameter) & " were found."]
    End If
End If
#
```

After installing the `Show Transactions [Type]` script and configuring the navigation buttons to call the script (with an accompanying parameter of either Orders or Invoices, depending on the function of the particular button), it becomes possible to filter the displayed orders or invoices to include only incomplete transactions, by holding down the Shift key while clicking the corresponding button.

## Editing information via scripts

Scripts can be used to provide guidance for data entry or editing, and to perform associated checks and validations, providing the user with information and support and improving the quality of the data. Several ways of achieving this are:

- **Using dialogs and viewer windows for data entry:** Your scripts can present the user with a dialog (or a pop-up window controlled to behave in a way resembling a dialog) with fields for entry of required information. This can be advantageous as a prompt for required information, where the user cannot proceed until the relevant input is complete.

- **Scripts for batch processing of data updates:** Where a group of records periodically need to be updated (for example, to reflect the current date or to recalculate with respect to revised budget projections, and so on), a script can gather the necessary inputs, then work its way through a large number of records applying the required updates to each in turn.

- **Scripted find and data cleansing routines:** Scripts can be used very effectively for locating anomalous records and correcting known or anticipated issues. For example, if data imported into your solution frequently has undesirable characters such as tabs or trailing punctuation in the fields, you might create a script to search for records exhibiting these problems and cycle through them, checking and correcting them.

## Printing and managing files

As in the case of the example `Acquired Items Report` script you created earlier in this chapter, scripts provide an ideal mechanism for generating consistent reports, because they can apply the same criteria (find, sort, and so on) each time and produce printed copy using identical page and print settings. You can set up and refine all the details and settings for a report once (in the script) and then be confident of getting the correct output every time you use the script to create the same report.

Similarly, scripts can be used to greatly simplify and improve the repeatability of data import and export procedures, each of which can require painstaking configuration—with an attendant risk of error over repeated occurrences.

Finally, a simple script can be created (employing the `Save a Copy as [ ]` command) to automate the process of generating backup copies of a solution while it is used in stand-alone mode (or hosted using FileMaker Pro). An example of such a script is as follows:

```
If [Get(MultiUserState) < 2]
   Set Variable [$path; Value:
                "file:" & Get(DocumentsPath) & "BU_" & Year(Get(CurrentDate)) &
                Right("0" & Month(Get(CurrentDate)); 2) &
                Right("0" & Day(Get(CurrentDate)); 2) & "_" &
                Right("0" & Hour(Get(CurrentTime)); 2) &
                Right("0" & Minute(Get(CurrentTime)); 2) & ".fp7"]
   Save a Copy as ["$path"; compacted]
Else
   Beep
   Show Custom Dialog ["Backups must be performed on the host computer."]
End If
```

Whenever the preceding script is called, a fresh backup copy of the current database will be created in the current user's Documents folder with the filename including the backup's date and time (in a canonical format). This is a useful way to keep copies of a file as you're developing (enabling you to return to a previous version in case of a mishap).

**CROSS-REF** For a discussion of the process of setting filenames by calculation, as used in the previous script, turn to Chapter 13.

**ON the WEB** We've added the previous script to the Inventory example file for this chapter so you can refer to it if you want. Look for the script named Save Local Backup.

**NOTE** The preceding backup script can only be performed on the computer where the current database is located (that is, being hosted) and is, therefore, not suitable for solutions being accessed via FileMaker Server. FileMaker Server provides its own built-in backup scheduling options.

## Ease of Editing in ScriptMaker

FileMaker 9 enables you to open multiple Edit Script windows simultaneously. This has the obvious advantage of letting you compare scripts and copy and paste steps or groups of steps between scripts (from the same or different files). A less obvious advantage is that, in a hosted solution, multiple developers can work in ScriptMaker concurrently — while only one user can modify a specific script at a time, users can work on different scripts simultaneously.

> **TIP** When you open a script and make changes to it, an asterisk appears to the right of the script name in the window's title bar, indicating unsaved changes. Whenever the asterisk is present, you can choose Scripts ⇨ Revert Script to discard the changes and go back to the last saved version of the script.

## Selecting and duplicating multiple commands

Consistent with user interface behavior on both the Mac and Windows platforms, you can select contiguous blocks of steps by clicking the first step and Shift+clicking the last step. You can select noncontiguous steps by ⌘+clicking or Ctrl+clicking. Similarly you can deselect individual steps from an existing selection by ⌘+clicking or Ctrl+clicking the step(s) you want to exclude.

> **TIP** You can use the keyboard to extend a selection downward by pressing Shift+↓ or upward by pressing Shift+↑. After extending a selection, you can reduce it by using the Shift key with the opposite arrow (opposite to the direction in which you extended the selection).

When you select discontiguous blocks of script commands using the methods described here, you can clear, duplicate, or disable all the selected commands at once. When duplicating commands by this method, note that the duplicated commands will be placed together immediately after the last selected command.

An alternative method of duplicating script commands (or groups of commands) is to select them and copy and paste. Note that when you paste, the commands from the clipboard will be inserted after the current selection (or after the last command in the current selection, if multiple commands are selected).

## Copying and pasting scripts

In FileMaker Pro 9, you can copy and paste whole scripts in the Manage Scripts window (or between the Manage Scripts windows of different files). You can copy and paste multiple scripts as well as single scripts. The ability to open the Manage Scripts windows for multiple files simultaneously makes copying and pasting scripts easy to use.

In cases where you want to duplicate multiple scripts, copying and pasting them within the same Manage Scripts window is one option.

> **NOTE** The naming methodology FileMaker uses when pasting multiple copies of a script is different from the naming technique employed for duplicating scripts. For pasted multiples, FileMaker appends the number 2 (separated from the name by a space) and subsequent copies acquire an incremented number (3, 4, 5, and so on) — whereas, when using the Duplicate button, the first duplicate has Copy appended to the name (separated from the name by a space) and subsequent duplicates acquire an incrementing number (Copy2, Copy3, and so on).

Every script in a FileMaker file has a unique internal ID assigned. References to scripts (from buttons and scripts using the `Perform Script [ ]` command) are resolved using the assigned ID. This is useful because it means you can change the name of a script without affecting references to it.

When you paste a script, FileMaker assigns an internal ID to it. When a script you paste includes references to other scripts, FileMaker will try to resolve those references by name at the point of pasting. If the name does not match any existing script (or any script currently being pasted), the reference will be broken and will appear in the script as `<unknown>`. When this occurs, script references must be reassigned manually to correct the errors.

When copying and pasting scripts that include references to other scripts, you should do one of the following:

- Copy and paste all the scripts (referring to each other) at once.
- Copy and paste the scripts that are referenced first, and copy/paste the scripts that refer to them subsequently.

FileMaker resolves references to schema and other elements by name at the point when scripts are pasted into a file in the same way it resolves references to other scripts. If there is a reference in a script being pasted to a field called `Invoice::Serial#`, FileMaker will look for an `Invoice::Serial#` field in the file where you paste the script. If there is no exact match, FileMaker will not resolve the reference.

## Copying and pasting script steps

FileMaker supports copying and pasting of script steps between scripts — either between scripts in the same file or between scripts in different files. This capability is available in FileMaker Pro 9 as well as FileMaker Pro 9 Advanced.

Copying and pasting supports multiple (including discontiguous) script steps. The copied steps (or steps) will be added immediately after the current selection in the active Script Definition panel.

# Organizing Scripts

Scripts are defined within a FileMaker file, and their scope of action is limited to the file where they reside. Each file, therefore, has its own collection of scripts and a separate Manage Scripts window in which to access and organize them.

Scripts accept freeform text names of up to 100 characters on a single line (carriage returns are not permitted). Within these limits, you can name scripts as you choose; however, we recommend avoiding obscure character sets and keeping names brief and explanatory.

Although FileMaker permits duplicate script names, you should take care to avoid duplicates in cases where confusion may result. Moreover, some third-party products (such as plug-ins) reference scripts by name and may produce unintended results if script names are duplicated within a file.

## Creating list separators

Using scripts named with a single hyphen as separators in the Manage Scripts window is customary, and this is supported directly by FileMaker. In fact, the New Separator option on the New Item menu (near the lower left of the Manage Scripts window) automatically creates an empty script with a hyphen as its name, for precisely this purpose.

When you create list separators in the Manage Scripts window and set the Include in Menu option for them, they appear as menu separators in the Scripts menu. The use of a modest number of separators as a grouping or organizational cue can make the Scripts menu easier to use when there are more than a handful of scripts to display there.

You can use scripts, script groups (see the section "Creating script groups," later in this chapter), or a combination of both to introduce order into the presentation of scripts in your solution. This serves the dual purpose of improving script manageability during development and maintenance and improving the usability of the Scripts menu.

## Script commenting

We counsel you to document your work — we can't say it more directly than that. Unless you have a perfect memory, you'll benefit from a reminder in a few weeks, months, or years as to what a particular script does or how it does so when it comes time to update your solution or you need to fix a bug. Likewise, if someone other than you needs to modify your script, he'll likely find some pointers helpful.

Many schools of thought exist as to how much documentation is necessary, and large organizations (particularly governmental organizations) often mandate extremely rigorous and extensive templates for every function in a program. To our minds, most of these mandates are overkill and, indeed, are so onerous that the wheat gets lost in the chaff and programmers tend to supply only cursory information, defeating the intent. Extremely simple scripts, if appropriately named, might need no commentary at all, such as the Lending Library starter solution's Clear Sort Indicator script. Others, such as the Movie Library starter solution's Find script, might benefit from commentary describing why particular script steps are present. Finally, more complex scripts, such as those we present in the Inventory example as it develops, may warrant more extensive commentary.

As a general rule, you should avoid commenting the obvious. For example, when the New Record/Request script step appears, it does not require an adjacent comment stating that it creates a new record. Such comments may actually reduce the clarity of the code, because they add clutter without amplifying meaning. In such cases, comments may be used to good effect to label groups of steps to indicate their purpose.

## The Processes: ScriptMaker — 8

Conversely, obscure aspects of the logic of your scripts *should* be elucidated so they may be readily understood by those who follow. *Remember:* It isn't just the script that should be commented, but also its place in your solution—why is it there and what user action or other script might invoke it?

ScriptMaker's (Miscellaneous category) Comment function inserts a hash symbol (#) into your script. The comment step has only one option: a Specify button. Clicking the Specify button displays a really plain Specify dialog (see Figure 8.11) consisting of a text box into which you can type your commentary.

**FIGURE 8.11**
Enter your comment's text in the Specify dialog's text box.

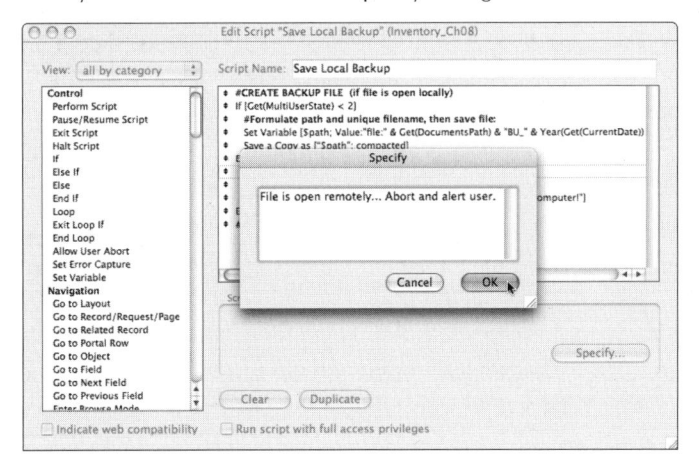

**NOTE**  You may also employ Comment steps with no text as white space, to visually separate blocks of steps.

## Creating script groups

FileMaker permits you to create groups, which serve as folders for organizing your scripts in the Manage Scripts window. Groups can contain scripts, separators, and other groups, enabling you to build ordered hierarchies of scripts.

When viewed in the Manage Scripts window, groups appear as a folder icon in the list of scripts, with an adjacent disclosure triangle to display or hide the contents of the group.

To add a script group, choose New Group from the New Items drop-down list at the lower left of the Manage Scripts window. An Edit Group dialog appears to prompt you to enter a name for the group. If a script is selected when you create a group, the group will be added immediately below the selected item; otherwise, the new group will appear at the end of the list of items in the Manage Scripts window.

255

## Part II  Introduction to Database Design

You can move scripts into and out of groups either with the mouse or the keyboard, as follows:

1. Open the script group by clicking its disclosure triangle with the mouse, or by selecting the group (using the keyboard arrow keys) and pressing →/{numeric keypad plus}.
2. Use the mouse or keyboard to position the desired script immediately below the open script group.
3. With the mouse, grab the desired script by its handle icon (a four-pointed arrow will appear, as shown in Figure 8.12), and drag the handle to the right, or press the ⌘+↑ or Ctrl+↑ key combination to add the script to the group.

### FIGURE 8.12

Using the four-pointed arrow cursor to move the Sold Items Report script into the Reports script group in the Manage Scripts window of the Inventory example file.

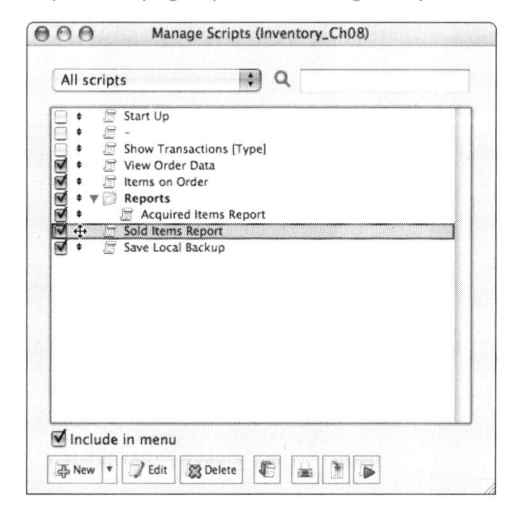

You can move scripts out of groups by dragging them with the mouse or moving them with the keyboard.

After you add scripts to a group, those set to appear in the Scripts menu will be presented in cascading submenus, as shown in Figure 8.13.

**NOTE** If items within a group are set to appear in the Scripts menu but the group itself is not, the items will appear on the Scripts menu at the previous level (that is, not in a submenu for their enclosing group). In this way, you can use script groups as an organizational tool in the Manage Scripts window without affecting the arrangement of Scripts menu items.

## The Processes: ScriptMaker 8

**FIGURE 8.13**

The Reports script group appears as a Reports submenu on the Scripts menu.

## Reordering and grouping scripts

Script groups can be dragged to new positions using their handles or using the keyboard commands, in the same way you can move scripts. Moreover, groups can be moved into or out of other groups using the procedures described in the preceding section. You can create multiple levels of script groups, although only 20 levels of cascading submenus are supported.

When you move a group (whether on its own or as part of a larger selection of items) to a new position in the Manage Scripts window, the groups contents are moved with it to the new location.

## Filtering scripts by group

When you create one or more script groups in the Manage Scripts window, you can filter your view of the Manage Scripts list by group. This is done by selecting the desired group from the group selection menu at the upper left of the Manage Scripts window, as shown in Figure 8.14.

257

**NOTE** If you name a group with a single hyphen, it will act as a separator in both the group selection menu and (if enabled for inclusion) the Scripts menu.

**CAUTION** If you use a script group as a separator, include it in the Scripts menu, and enclose scripts within it, the enclosed scripts will not be accessible on the Scripts menu, even if they're enabled to appear there. (The submenu that would otherwise contain them is inaccessible, being presented as a separator.)

**FIGURE 8.14**

Filtering the Manage Scripts item list to display the contents of a specific group.

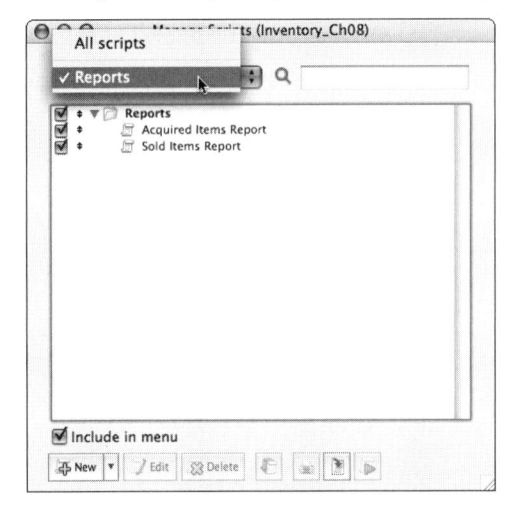

## Searching for scripts by name

If you have many scripts in your solution, FileMaker enables you to search for scripts by their names. To do this, enter one or more characters into the search field at the upper right of the Manage Scripts window. All character strings in a script name are targeted by the search.

Script groups containing scripts meeting the search criteria (or partial criteria as the search string is entered) will be pulled open (if they were previously closed) to reveal their contents. Only those scripts matching the entered criteria will be displayed while the search is active.

To disable a script search, delete the search string from the search field. All scripts will again be displayed in the script items list.

**NOTE** The search status of the Manage Scripts window has no effect on the contents of the Scripts menu.

# Some Examples to Start With

Earlier in this chapter, we refer to sample scripts implemented in the Inventory example file to illustrate techniques discussed here. In this section, we describe three straightforward scripts that automate actions common to most solutions.

## Performing a Find

If you need to view a list of items ordered but not received, you would navigate to the layout listing ordered items (the `OrderLines` layout), perform a search for items for which the order status is blank (that is, enter Find mode, select the Order Status checkbox, select the Status Area's Omit option, and then click Find). If any items are found, you may view or print the resulting list and return to where you came from.

If you (or your users) need to do this frequently, setting up a script automating the process makes sense. Before creating this script, perform the task manually, so that you're clear on the process. Doing so also sets up the Find criteria for the script you're about to create. When you're ready, create a script called `Items on Order` as follows:

```
Go to Layout ["OrderLines" (OrderLines)]
Set Error Capture [On]
Perform Find [Restore]
If [Get(LastError) ≠ 0]
  Go to Layout [original layout]
  Beep
  Show Custom Dialog ["Error:"; "No items were found."]
End If
```

## Printing a report

A frequent requirement in solutions of all kinds is to produce printed output of selected or summarized data in a predetermined fashion. In the "Setting up a basic script" section, earlier in the chapter, we give detailed instructions for the creation of an `Acquired Items Report` script. Along similar lines, we've created a `Sold Items Report` script in the inventory example for this chapter.

The script definition for the Sold Items Report is as follows:

```
Enter Browse Mode [ ]
Freeze Window
Go to Layout ["InvoiceLines" (InvoiceLines)]
Show All Records
Sort Records [Restore; No Dialog]
Print Setup [Restore; No Dialog]
Print [Restore; No Dialog]
Go to Layout [original layout]
```

## Acting on user input

You can improve the flexibility and versatility of your scripts by structuring them to receive input from the user. For example, when providing users with a script to display order data, you may want to give them a choice of formats. One way to achieve this is to display a custom dialog, then use the Get(LastMessageChoice) function to determine which selection the user has made.

For this example script, we configured the custom dialog with three buttons (corresponding to Get(LastMessageChoice) values 1, 2, and 3), as shown in Figure 8.15.

The script definition for the View Order Data script is as follows:

```
Show Custom Dialog ["Note:" Do you wish to view Orders or an Order Items List?"]
If [Get(LastMassageChoice) < 3]
  Go to Layout [If(Get(LastMessageChoice) = 1; "Orders"; "OrderLines")]
  Show All Records
End If
```

**ON the WEB** The example file containing the scripts and associated code discussed in this chapter is available among the download materials on the book's Web site.

**FIGURE 8.15**

Configuration of a custom dialog to prompt for user input.

# Part III

# Beyond the Basics

You have a working solution, but you want to make it better. You want your users to consider your solution easy and pleasant to use instead of an onerous chore they need to perform. You want to reach for insider tips and power user features to make FileMaker really work for you.

This part uses numerous examples to show you how to make your layouts aesthetically pleasing, your interface appear prescient, and your data presentation communicate clearly. Here, we harness the power of FileMaker as a developer platform.

## IN THIS PART

**Chapter 9**
The FileMaker Power User

**Chapter 10**
Building Advanced Interfaces

**Chapter 11**
Data Modeling in FileMaker

**Chapter 12**
Calculation Wizardry

**Chapter 13**
Scripting in Depth

# Chapter 9

# The FileMaker Power User

In the preceding chapters, you've employed the fundamental database creation techniques and used FileMaker's scripting, calculation, and interface tools. Along the way, you've glimpsed FileMaker's depth and power.

Because you've come this far, we figure you must be serious — and the fact that you're still reading means you've realized there is much more to learn. You're right — in fact, there is much more to know about FileMaker than we can cover in detail, even in a book of this size. Consequently we've chosen to encourage you to seek out additional details about the basics, in available resources such as the Users Guide, Help file, and online references. Going forward, we won't cover entire processes in great detail; instead, we'll focus on key insights and development strategies, to make best use of the available pages in this book.

So far, you've acquired the skills to set the core elements of a database in place — techniques that you'll use repeatedly. However, FileMaker is noted for, among other things, providing alternative ways of achieving any given outcome. It is the mark of the experienced user to be aware of the options and to make informed choices.

FileMaker is something of a chameleon insofar as it presents you with a friendly, easy interface for a range of basic tasks, yet possesses the sophistication to deal with more complex requirements when required. As a result, you'll encounter a steeper learning curve when transitioning to more demanding tasks. This is the transition between FileMaker's legendary ease of use and its hidden power.

In the following chapters, we introduce a range of techniques and capabilities that take you beyond the obvious and into the domain of the FileMaker power user.

### IN THIS CHAPTER

Working with Browse mode

Performing complex search operations

Sorting records

Formatting fields and text

Working with variables

Making sense of indexing

Discovering the table of dependencies

Seeing the benefit of caching

Working with global fields

## Part III  Beyond the Basics

# Making Browse Mode Work for You

When you open a database, a window appears enabling you to navigate between layouts and records — following the thread of your work processes. Although clear delineations between screens make sense structurally, work is apt to fall outside neat divisions. Interruptions and distractions often require that one task be paused so another can be performed.

Lucky for you, many more tools are at your disposal in the FileMaker Browse mode. You're not constrained by a single screen and its Status Area. Using a combination of advanced techniques, you can greatly increase the power and usability of your solutions.

## Using multiple windows and views

When you choose Window ➪ New Window — or use the equivalent button or script command — FileMaker leaves the current window in place and creates a new window in front of it. As you create a new window, FileMaker creates a separate workspace, allowing you to take actions in the new window without affecting the work you were doing in the previous window. This works in a way analogous to having two separate users logged in — each window can operate separately, but only one can edit a given record at any given time.

One of the immediate advantages of opening a new window is that each window has its own current layout, found set, and selected record. If you're viewing a found set and an interruption occurs requiring you to perform a search for a different group of records, you can do that in a new window without disturbing the found set, sort order, or active record in the window you're working in. You can open as many windows as you require, navigating between them by clicking them (if a portion is visible) or selecting them from the list appearing in the Window menu.

You can position windows in a variety of ways so that they overlay each other (the frontmost window obscuring the view of windows behind it), overlapping, or side by side. In the latter cases, users can still view a previous window after opening another, allowing them to see and compare information in different views. Thus, for instance, one window may display a summary list of available records while another window shows details of a selected record.

## Filtering portals and creating pick lists

Displaying small floating windows configured to operate like dialogs is one way to take advantage of the ability to show multiple windows, inviting the user to make a selection. After a selection is made, the smaller window is closed and the selection is applied to the original screen in the main (underlying) window. Allowing your users to select items from a list — especially for cases when the number of items on the list may be too long to be conveniently displayed in a radio button field, a list, or a menu — is one common application of this technique.

An example where you can use a selection window is specifying the customer to invoice in the Inventory example discussed in preceding chapters. Currently, the example provides a drop-down

## The FileMaker Power User

list displaying the contacts who are identified as buyers. However, as the number of customers becomes large, the list becomes unwieldy and an alternate selection method is desirable.

Implementing a pop-up selection window requires three separate components working in unison — a filtering relationship, a utility portal layout, and a control script. To set up the filtering relationship, open the Inventory file and follow these steps:

1. Choose File ➪ Manage ➪ Database. The Manage Database dialog appears.
2. Select the Tables tab and create a new table named Utility.
3. Double-click the new table's entry in the tables list to select it on the Fields tab.
4. Create a global text field named `gFilter_txt`.
5. Create a global calculation field named `cFilter_key` with a result type of text and enter the following formula:

   `If(IsEmpty(gFilter_txt); "0¶z"; gFilter_txt & ¶ & gFilter_txt & "zzz")`

6. Create a global text field named `gType_key`.
7. In the Relationships panel, select the Buyers TO and click the duplicate button at the lower left (third from the left with the double plus sign icon).
8. Double-click the duplicate TO and rename it ContactFilter.
9. Position the ContactFilter TO next to the Utility TO and drag a join between the Utility::gType_key field and the ContactFilter::ContactType field. Either resize the ContactFilter TO box or scroll its field list until its ContactType field is visible.
10. Drag a second join between the Utility::cFilter_key field and the ContactFilter::LastName field.
11. Double-click the box bisecting the relationship line joining the Utility TO to the ContactFilter TO. The Edit Relationship dialog appears.
12. In the panel in the middle area of the Edit Relationship dialog, select the `cFilter_key` – `LastName` join attribute line, choose the ≤ relationship symbol from the menu of operators between the field list boxes at the top of the dialog, and click the Change button.
13. Choose the ≥ relationship symbol from the menu of operators between the field list boxes, and click the Add button to create a third relationship predicate. The Edit relationship dialog now resembles the one shown in Figure 9.1.

> **TIP** Testing for both ≥ and ≤ against a pair of key field values (as in this case) is a technique to return just those values starting with a sequence of characters. Testing for equality returns only exact matches; however, the ≤ test eliminates any items starting with characters subsequent to those in the second of the pair of search strings, and the ≥ test removes all items starting with characters preceding those in the first of the search string pair.

14. Click OK to close the Edit Relationship dialog and again to close the Manage Database dialog.

265

## Part III  Beyond the Basics

**FIGURE 9.1**

The Edit Relationship dialog showing the completed relationship definition for the join between the Utility TO and the ContactFilter TO.

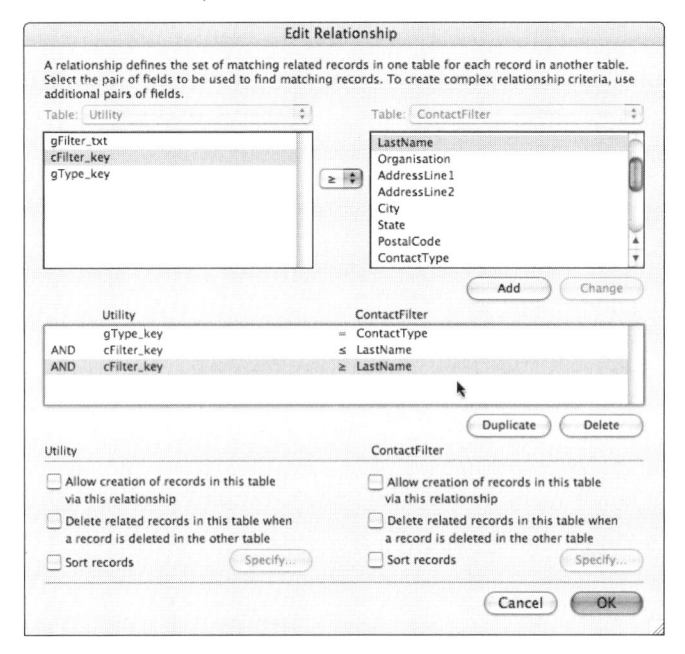

You now have a relationship in place using Utility table global fields to control a relationship with the Contacts table. By changing the global field values, the relationship retrieves only a selection of the available Contact records. You can use this mechanism to support selection functionality in a pop-up window.

When you create the Utility table as described earlier, FileMaker creates a default layout named Utility based on this table. Select the Utility layout and switch to Layout mode to prepare the layout for use as a selection window, by following these steps:

1. Drag the Header tab upward to the top of the layout to delete the Header part.
2. Drag the Footer tab up to the body part boundary to delete the Footer part.
3. Select the Body tab and choose a pale gray/mauve fill color.
4. Delete the cFilter_key and gType_key fields and their labels.
5. Select the gFilter_txt field box, apply the engraved effect, select lightest gray fill, and position it near the upper left of the layout.

## The FileMaker Power User

6. Edit the text label of the gFilter_txt field to read **Filter**:
7. Place a text object (10pt, plain style, centered) near the top of the layout and enter the instruction: Enter one or more characters in the filter field to filter the list by last name.
8. Select the Portal tool and drag across the left area of the layout beneath the Filter field to create a portal. Base the portal on the ContactFilter TO, specify a sort order by the LastName field, enable the vertical scroll bar, enter 12 as the number of rows, and choose an alternate background fill. The Portal Setup dialog with these settings is shown in Figure 9.2.

### FIGURE 9.2
The Portal Setup dialog for the filtered selection portal on the Utility layout.

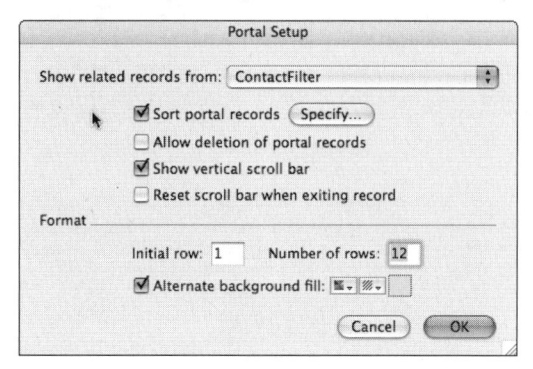

9. Click OK to accept the Portal Setup dialog settings. The Add Fields to Portal dialog appears.
10. Select the cFullName field, click the »Move« button to add it to the portal, and click OK to dismiss the dialog.
11. Create a button, attach it to the Close Window command, label it Cancel, and position it below the portal.
12. Create a button attached to the Go to Next Field command, label it Filter, and position it to the right of the gFilter_txt field.
13. Create a button attached to the Set Field command, set the target field as Utility::gFilter_txt, specify the calculated result as null (""), label the button Clear, and position it to the right of the Filter button. Your Utility layout should resemble the one shown in Figure 9.3.

## Part III  Beyond the Basics

**FIGURE 9.3**

The Utility layout configured to include the ContactFilter portal.

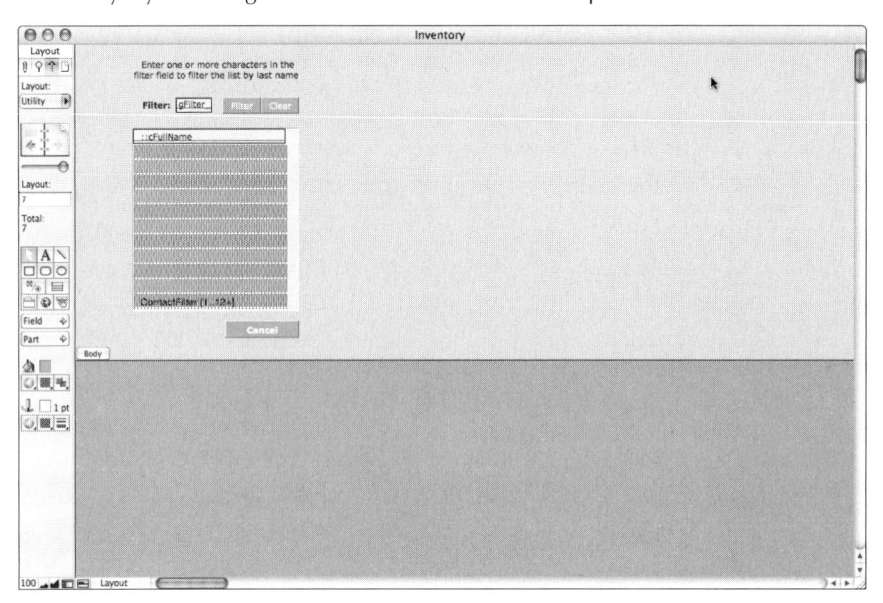

You now have your selection window's layout ready. The final preparations set a script in place to control the window's behavior. To create the required script, follow these steps:

1. Choose Scripts ➪ ScriptMaker. The Manage Scripts window appears.
2. Click New to create a new empty script. The Edit Script window appears.
3. In the Script Name field, enter **Select Contact [Type]**.
4. Using the command list at the left of the Edit Script window and, for each command, using the configuration buttons below the script panel, create the following script:

```
If [not IsEmpty(Get(ScriptParameter))]
    #Display Selection Filter Window...
    Set Field [Utility::gFilter_txt; "" ]
    Set Field [Utility::gType_key; Get(ScriptParameter) ]
    New Window [Name: "Select " & Get(ScriptParameter);
    Height: 400;
    Width: 340;
    Top: Get(WindowTop) + (Get(WindowHeight) – 400) / 2;
    Left: Get(WindowLeft) + (Get(WindowWidth) – 340) / 2 ]
    Show/Hide Status Area [Lock; Hide]
    Go to Layout ["Utility" (Utility)]
    Enter Browse Mode [ ]
    Go to Field [Utility::gFilter_txt]
Else
    #Select Contact record
```

## The FileMaker Power User 9

```
        Set Variable [$SelectID; Value:ContactFilter::ContactID]
        Close Window [Current Window ]
        Freeze Window
        Go to Object [Object Name: "ContactID"]
        Set Field [$SelectID ]
        Commit Records/Requests [Skip data entry validation; No
    dialog]
End If
```

5. Save the script, close the Edit Script window, and close the Manage Scripts window.
6. Select the cFullName field in the ContactFilter portal of the Utility layout.
7. Choose Format ➪ Field/Control ➪ Behavior. The Field Behavior for "cFullName" dialog appears.
8. Uncheck the options labeled In Browse mode and In Find mode at the top of the dialog, and then click OK to dismiss the dialog.
9. Choose Format ➪ Button Setup. The Button Setup dialog appears.
10. Choose the Perform Script command in the column at the left.
11. In the Current Script menu at in the panel at the right, choose Exit.
12. Click the Specify button in the panel at the right of the Button Setup dialog. The Specify Script Options dialog appears.
13. Choose the Select Contact [Type] script in the list of scripts, and click OK to dismiss the dialog.
14. Click OK to close the Button Setup dialog.

Your preparations are now complete. Now, it's time to add controls to the Invoices layout so that users can invoke the new selection window. To make the required adjustments, follow these steps:

1. Navigate to the Invoices layout and enter Layout mode.
2. Create a button to the right of the BuyerID field and attach the Perform Script command.
3. In the Current Script menu in the panel at the right, choose Exit.
4. Click the Specify button in the panel at the right of the Button Setup dialog. The Specify Script Options dialog appears.
5. Choose the Select Contact [Type] script in the list of scripts.
6. In the Optional Script Parameter box, near the bottom of the dialog, enter **Buyer**.
7. Click OK to dismiss the dialog.
8. Label the newly created button **Specify Buyer**.
9. Double-click the BuyerID field. The Field/Control Setup dialog appears.
10. In the Display As menu, select Edit Box, and click OK to dismiss the dialog.
11. If the Info palette is not currently displayed, choose View ➪ Object Info.
12. With the BuyerID field still selected, enter ContactID into the Object Name field.

Your Invoices layout should be similar in appearance to the one shown in Figure 9.4.

269

**Part III   Beyond the Basics**

**FIGURE 9.4**
The Invoices layout with the addition of the Specify Buyer control button.

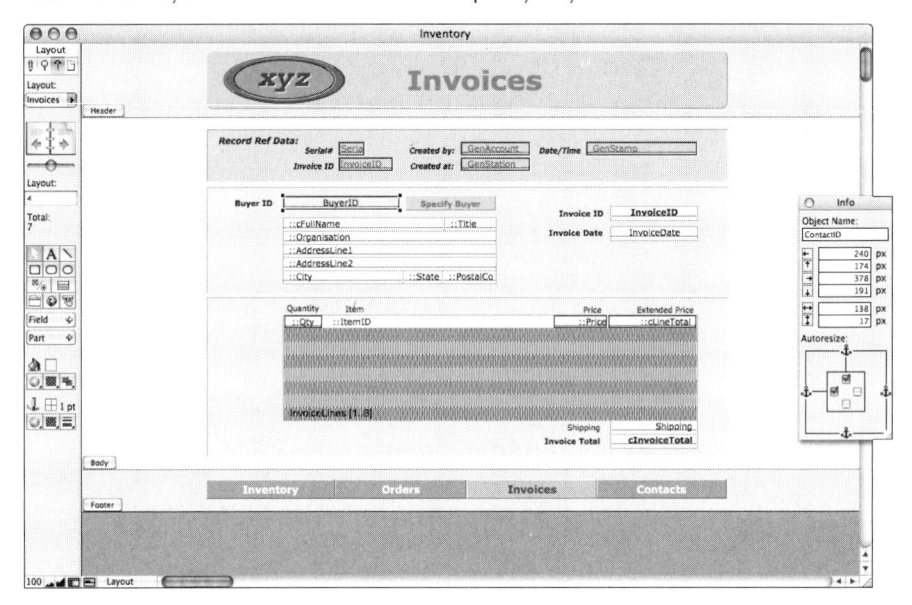

It's now time to test your modifications. To begin, enter Browse mode on the Invoices layout and click the Specify Buyer button. The Select Buyer window should appear centered over the Inventory window, as shown in Figure 9.5. The pop-up window displays the portal you created on the Utility layout. The portal lists all the Contacts who are flagged as buyers in the Contacts table. Entering one or more letters into the Filter field, and clicking the Filter button should reduce the list of names showing in the portal to include only those contacts whose last name begins with the letters you've typed.

Clicking a name in the portal should simultaneously close the window and enter the contact whose name you clicked as the buyer for the current invoice.

Although the number of buyers in the Contacts table remains small, the filtering capabilities of the new selection window are not needed. However, as the number of buyers extends to hundreds or even thousands, the filtered selection list provides users with a very efficient method to locate and select a specific customer for each invoice.

## Jump buttons: Shortcut navigation

In Chapter 3, we cover the use of shortcut navigation to enable the user to move efficiently between relevant views of data in your solutions. The Go to Related Record[ ] command, which you can use to automatically display associated data in an alternate layout, underpins shortcut navigation.

## The FileMaker Power User    9

**FIGURE 9.5**

Testing the Select Buyer pop-up window.

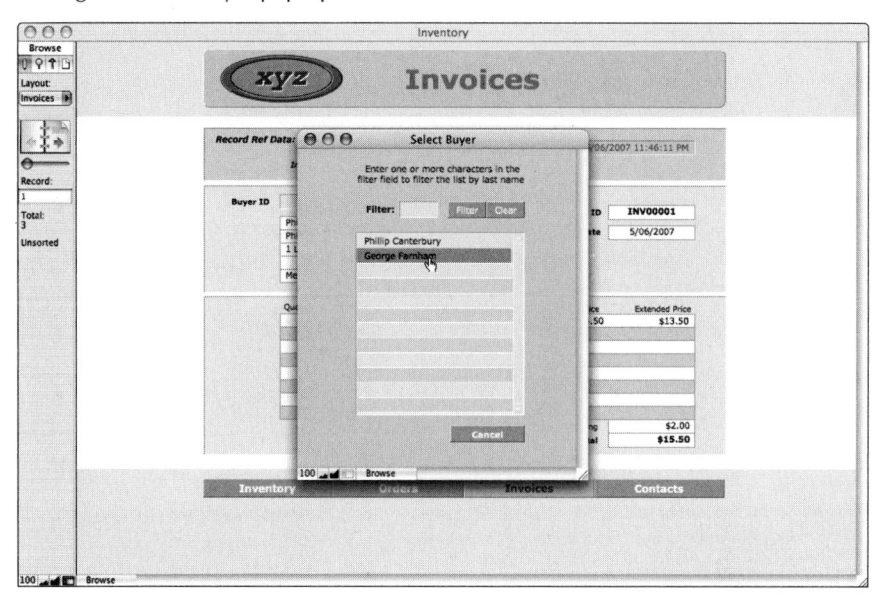

A useful `Go to Related Record[ ]` feature is the ability to simultaneously generate a new window to display the results. You can use this feature to show detail or summary data in a convenient pop-up window, without losing the context (found set, sort order, active record) in the window in which you're working.

Using the Inventory example file, if you change the Contacts layout to be based on the ItemSupplier TO, you can add a button to locate and display all the items available from the current supplier.

**NOTE**    To change a layout to a different TO, navigate to the layout, go to Layout mode, and choose Layouts ➪ Layout Setup, and then change the setting in the Show Records From menu.

After you've made this change, you also have to reassign any field objects on the layout so that they access the field via the appropriate TO. Double-click each field in turn to access the Field Control Setup dialog and use the menu above the list of fields in the dialog to select the TO identified as the current table.

After you've reassigned the Contacts layout, follow these steps to implement jump navigation to display supplier items in a pop-up window:

1. Navigate to the Inventory layout and choose Layouts ➪ Duplicate Layout.
2. Choose Layouts ➪ Layout Setup. The Layout Setup dialog appears.

271

## Part III  Beyond the Basics

3. Change the layout name to Inventory List and deselect the option to include it in the Layout menu.

4. Navigate to the Layout Setup dialog's Views panel, deselect the options for Form View and Table View, and click OK to dismiss the dialog.

5. Rearrange the elements on the layout as shown in Figure 9.6, deleting superfluous objects.

6. Navigate to the Contacts layout, create a button at the lower right of the Contact Details panel, and select the Go to Related Record command from the list at the left of the Button Setup dialog.

7. Click the Specify button in the panel at the upper right of the dialog. The Go to Related Record Options dialog appears.

8. Configure the Go to Related Record settings as shown in Figure 9.7.

9. When you select the Show in New Window checkbox, the New Window Options dialog appears. Configure the settings for the new window as shown in Figure 9.8.

> **NOTE** You can either type the formulas in the Window Name, Distance from Top, and Distance from Left text boxes or click the associated Specify buttons and create the formulas in the Specify Calculation dialogs that appear. The latter method reduces the potential for typographic errors.

### FIGURE 9.6

The arrangement of layout objects for the Inventory List layout.

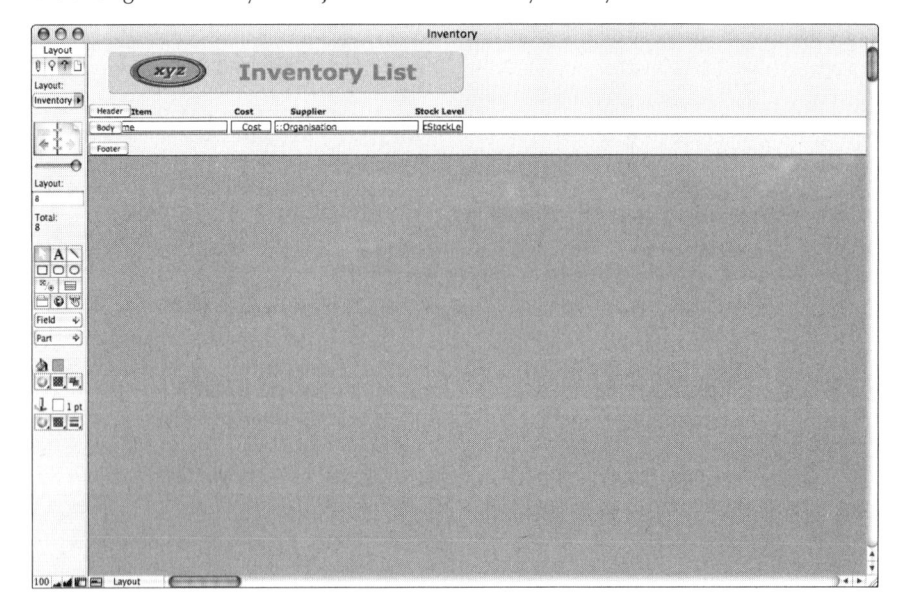

## The FileMaker Power User  9

**FIGURE 9.7**

Settings in the Go to Related Record Options dialog for the Available Items button.

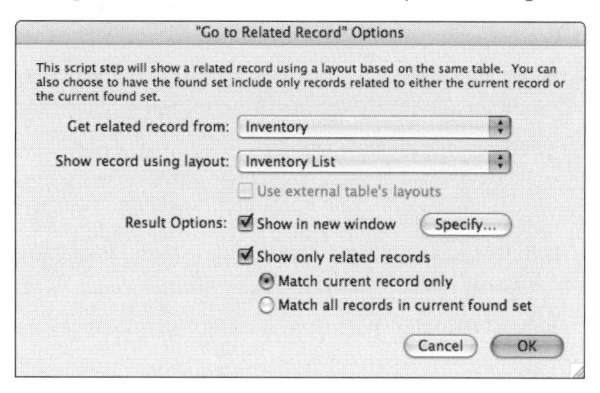

10. Click OK to accept the settings and dismiss each of the dialogs.
11. Label the new button Available Items, size and position it appropriately, and color it to match the Contacts layout's header panel.

**FIGURE 9.8**

The New Window Options configuration for the Go to Related Record command.

After completing these steps, return to Browse mode and locate a contact record with the Supplier option checked and entered as Preferred Supplier on some inventory items in your Inventory file.

Click your new Available Items button to invoke a pop-up window showing a summary list of items for the current supplier, as shown in Figure 9.9.

## Part III  Beyond the Basics

**FIGURE 9.9**

The pop-up Available Items window listing Inventory items supplied by the current contact.

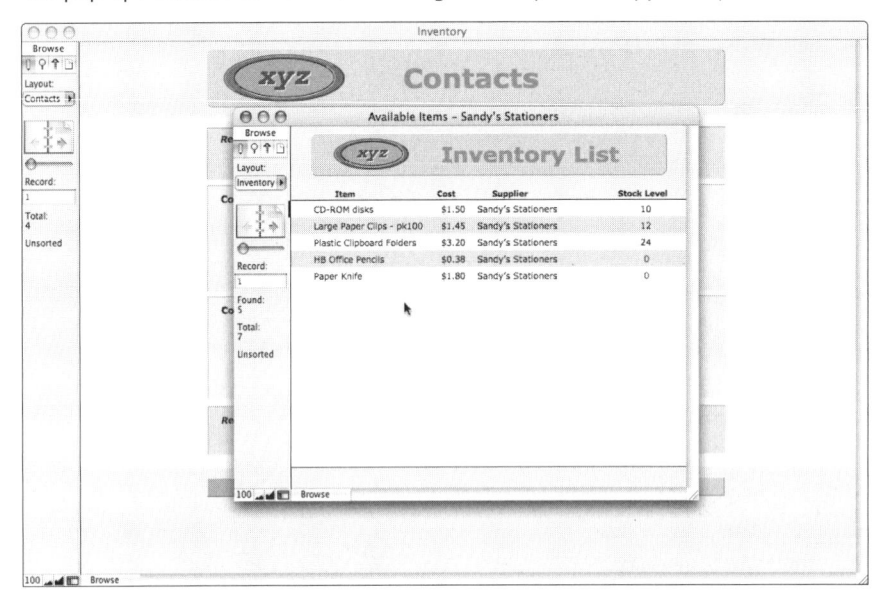

### Controlling one window from another

A further example of the flexibility that FileMaker's window management controls afford is the ability to display multiple windows and control their appearance and behavior from a single "main" window. To implement this functionality, you can create buttons and controls attached to scripts selecting the appropriate window, performing an action on it, and then returning the focus to the controller window.

Careful use of this technique enables you to provide one or more controller palettes allowing the user to navigate or manipulate images, text, or records in one or more windows displayed elsewhere on the screen. For example, such a technique can be used to provide controls for navigating a document preview where the controlling window is in Browse mode, as shown in Figure 9.10.

## FIGURE 9.10
Using controls in one window to modify the display in another window.

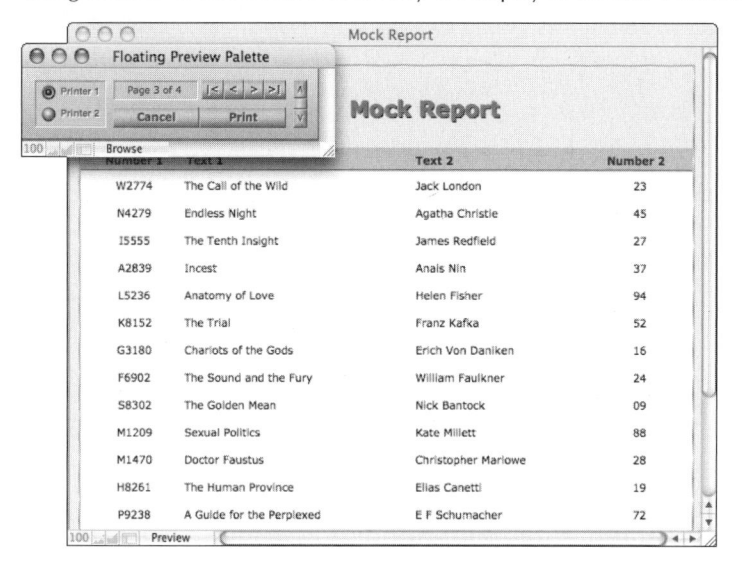

# Performing Complex Search Operations

The Find procedures discussed previously (see Chapters 3 and 5) allow you to search for partial word matches or whole word matches.

The special Find Symbols you can select from Find mode's Status Area extend the search capability, enabling you to search for ranges or employ wildcard operators. But there is much more, and we cover it in the following sections.

## Compound Find criteria: The AND Find

If your Finds are returning too many results, one option is to make your Find criteria more specific. FileMaker provides you with a straightforward way to approach this problem when constructing your initial Find criteria.

To extend the original Find criteria, you can enter additional detail into the search field (for example, entering **ja** instead of **j** returns Jackson but not Johnson). Alternatively, you can enter criteria into more than one field. For instance, entering **j** in the LastName field and **p** in the FirstName field tells FileMaker to return only those records satisfying both criteria (that is, those that have a last name starting with *j* and a first name starting with *p*). You can enter Find criteria into as many fields as necessary to locate the records you're looking for.

Additionally, FileMaker permits the use of multiple sequential Find requests, and the second or subsequent requests can be used to narrow the Find by omitting certain records from the found set. To achieve this, create a Find request (with appropriate initial criteria); then, while still in Find mode, choose Requests ➪ Add New Request. A second find request appears, ready to accept additional criteria. By selecting the Omit checkbox in the Status Area, you can instruct FileMaker to exclude from the found set those records returned by the first request meeting the second request's criteria.

**NOTE** When you use multiple Find requests, FileMaker processes them in the order in which you create them. When the Find is performed, the first request acts on all records in the current table, and subsequent requests add or omit records from the found set returned by preceding requests.

The processes outlined here provide ways to ensure that more than one criterion is applied in a Find, with additional criteria acting in sequence to make the search more specific.

## Stacking Find requests: The OR Find

You can create multiple simultaneous Find requests for Finds that return sets of records meeting any of the request criteria. That is, when multiple requests are created and do not have the Omit option (in the Find mode Status Area) selected, each request is independently evaluated and its results added to any preceding requests' results.

In this way, you can instruct FileMaker to search simultaneously according to different criteria, increasing the scope of the search. For example, if you create a Find request and enter **j** in the LastName field, then — before performing the Find — create a second request and enter **p** into the FirstName field, FileMaker returns all records that have an entry in the LastName field starting with j OR an entry in the FirstName field starting with p.

When creating multiple Find requests, specific requests can be set to omit records while others are not — the Omit option is specific to each request. Thus, you can assemble complex search operations involving multiple Find requests combining many details to locate records according to very specific requirements.

## Constraining and extending the found set

Find criteria assembled in the ways described in the previous sections are applied to all the records in the current table (as determined by the TO associated with the layout in the frontmost window). However, at times using the results of a previous Find as the starting point for your search is convenient. You can do this in either of two ways:

- **If you want to search only within the records already showing in a found set on the current layout,** go to Find mode, create your Find criteria, and choose Requests ➪ Constrain Found Set. FileMaker locates only records within the current found set meeting the criteria you supply.

- **If you want to preserve the current found set and *add* to it any records meeting your criteria,** go to Find mode, create your Find criteria, and choose Requests ➪ Extend

Found Set. When extending the found set, FileMaker applies the supplied criteria to currently omitted records (that is, those not in the current found set), adding the results to the preexisting found set.

In both instances, you're able to refine an existing found set, thereby progressively building the criteria until you've isolated the desired group of records.

## Saving Finds and found sets

In any solution where you're frequently performing complex Finds, you'll occasionally want to store Find criteria so that specific Finds can be efficiently and reliably repeated.

FileMaker provides for Find criteria to be stored within the properties of the `Perform Find[ ]` button or script command. When the command is first selected, you have the option to specify Find requests. On selecting this option, the Find properties automatically populate with the criteria of the last Find performed. Thus, one way to store a Find is to first perform it manually, and then create a button or script to execute the `Perform Find[ ]` command, reinstating (and storing) the criteria of the Find you just performed. Alternatively, the `Perform Find[ ]` command provides a Specify Find Requests dialog to receive the criteria for one or more Find requests.

Although the creation of scripts or buttons to automate Finds is a great feature, there are times when end users will perform complex Finds manually, and you'll want to be able to save a record of those Finds. Ideally, you'll want to be able to provide an easy way for users to reinstate saved Finds as well.

When discussing reinstating a Find, it's important to consider that the data may have changed since the Find was performed. Records that matched the criteria at the time of the Find may have been edited so they no longer match. Records that didn't match may have been edited so they do, and, of course, records may have been added or deleted. To reinstate a Find, you can either:

- **Locate the records that were located previously (if they still exist), whether or not they still match the original Find criteria.** This technique is useful when retrieving historical data.

- **Perform a new Find using the original Find criteria to locate the records (if any) matching those criteria now.** Use this technique to determine the current status.

Using FileMaker's scripting capabilities, you can configure your solutions to do either of the preceding — depending on the requirements of the solution and its users. In either case, you need a table (in the same file or another file) in which to store each Find and a script to build an array of information and store that information array in a Finds table record.

If you decide to store a record of the specific records located in a Find (rather than the criteria), the best way to accomplish this is by gathering the unique key values of records in the found set. Traditionally, developers have used a technique involving the use of the `Copy All Records/Requests[ ]` command on a special layout, then a `Paste` command to store the contents of the clipboard. We don't recommend this approach, because it modifies the clipboard and depends on the interface (special layouts with the correct fields present). Instead, we prefer to employ a script

277

## Part III  Beyond the Basics

looping through the found set, gathering unique key values into a variable, and then write the variable's contents into a text field in a new record in your Finds table.

> **NOTE** If you have access to FileMaker Pro 9 Advanced, another alternative for found sets of moderate size is to create a custom function to recursively retrieve unique keys for the found set via the use of the `GetNthRecord( )` function. See Chapter 18 for a further discussion of custom functions and recursion.

> **CAUTION** If found sets in your solution may be large (for example, tens of thousands of records or more), you should consider carefully whether an approach to gathering and storing unique keys is viable, because doing so involves significant storage and processing overhead.

The second approach to storing Finds entails the capture of the original Find criteria. It requires creating a script to run when a Find is performed, working through the fields on each request to gather the Find criteria into a text array for storage in your Finds table.

Because this approach is not as widely known as others, here's an example of the essentials of a script performing this task:

```
If [Get(WindowMode) ≠ 1]
    Beep
Else
    Commit Records/Requests[Skip data entry validation; No dialog]
    Go to Record/Request/Page [First]
    Go to Next Field
    Set Variable [$Layout; Value:Get(LayoutName)]
    Set Variable [$FirstField; Value:Get(ActiveFieldName)]
    Loop
      Loop
        If [not IsEmpty(Get(ActiveFieldContents))]
          Set Variable [$Criteria; Value:If(not IsEmpty($Criteria);
             $Criteria & ¶) & Get(RecordNumber) & "»" &
             Get(RequestOmitState) & "»" & Get(ActiveFieldName) &
             "»" & Get(ActiveFieldContents)]
        End If
        Go to Next Field
        Exit Loop If [Get(ActiveFieldName) = $FirstField]
      End Loop
      Go to Record/Request/Page [Next; Exit after last]
    End Loop
    Set Error Capture[On]
    Perform Find []
    If [Get(LastError) = 0]
      Freeze Window
      Go to Layout ["StoredFinds" (StoredFinds)]
      New Record/Request
      Set Field [StoredFinds::LayoutName; $Layout]
      Set Field [StoredFinds::Criteria_array; $Criteria]
      Go to Layout [$Layout]
    Else
```

## The FileMaker Power User

```
            Beep
            Show All Records
            Show Custom Dialog [Message: "No records were found."]
        End If
    End If
```

The preceding script requires that a StoredFinds table and layout be added to your solution and that it include text fields called LayoutName and Criteria_array. You probably would want to add other fields (such as a serial number, a date and/or time, a field to store the number of records found, the name of the user, and perhaps a brief description of the purpose of the Find). Whenever a Find is performed using a script such as this one, a record is created containing codified details of the complete criteria used for any and all requests in the Find in the StoredFinds table.

> **TIP** If you have access to FileMaker Pro 9 Advanced, we recommend that you use the custom menus feature to attach the preceding script to the Perform Find command so that it automatically runs whenever a Find is performed.

When you implement a process to store Find criteria sets, your users can browse or search through a complete Find history. You can also provide a simple process for users to automatically reinstate a Find (that is, to rerun the Find against the current data in the relevant table). The essentials of a script to reinstate a Find (stored in the form outlined earlier) are as follows:

```
            Set Variable [$Criteria; Value:StoredFinds::Criteria_array]
            Go to Layout [StoredFinds::LayoutName]
            Freeze Window
            Enter Find Mode [ ]
            Loop
                Set Variable [$RequestNo; Value:Leftwords($Criteria; 1)]
                Set Variable [$OmitState; Value:Let([
                  p1 = Position($Criteria; "»"; 1; 1);
                  p2 = Position($Criteria; "»"; 1; 2)];
                  Middle($Criteria; p1 + 1; p2−p1−1))]
                If [$OmitState]
                  Omit Record
                End If
                Loop
                  Set Variable [$FieldName; Value:Let([
                    p1 = Position($Criteria; "»"; 1; 2);
                    p2 = Position($Criteria; "»"; 1; 3)];
                    Middle($Criteria; p1 + 1; p2−p1−1))]
                  Go to Next Field
                  If [Get(ActiveFieldName) = $FieldName]
                    Set Field [Let([
                      p1 = Position($Criteria; "»"; 1; 3) + 1;
                      p2 = Position($Criteria & ¶; ¶; 1; 1)];
                      Middle($Criteria; p1; p2−p1))]
                    Set Variable[$Criteria; Value:RightValues(
                      $Criteria; ValueCount($Criteria) − 1)]
                  End If
                  Exit Loop If[IsEmpty($Criteria) or Left($Criteria;
```

279

## Part III  Beyond the Basics

```
            Position($Criteria; "»"; 1; 1)−1) > $RequestNo]
    End Loop
    Exit Loop If [IsEmpty($Criteria)]
    New Record/Request
End Loop
Perform Find [ ]
```

When you attach the preceding script to a button on the Stored Finds layout, users are able to click it to automatically view the results of a Find on the layout where the Find was originally performed. A complete history of Finds performed is available in the Stored Finds table. Figure 9.11 shows a Find Log, implemented in the updated Inventory example file for this chapter.

### FIGURE 9.11

An implementation of the Stored Find technique in the Inventory example file.

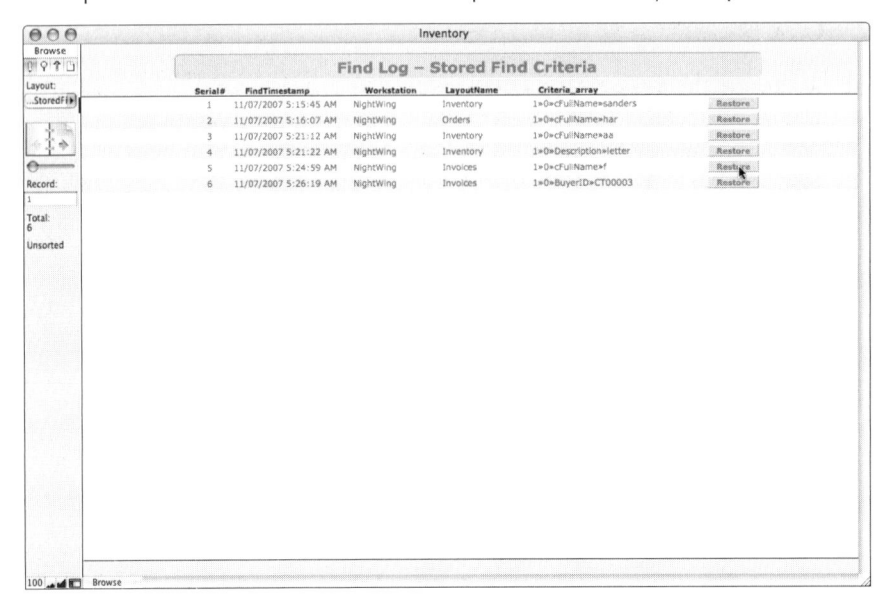

**ON the WEB** — In case you want to view the preceding scripts in action, or review them within the Script Editor in FileMaker, we've added them to the example inventory solution (see the file for this chapter among the Web resources).

## Sorting Records

A common misconception about sorting is that it depends upon (or is made more efficient by) field indexing. However, the truth is that sorting does not use field indexes at all. When operating on stored values (as opposed to unstored calculations), your sort operations are processed with the same efficiency irrespective of any field indexing.

Although sorting does not use indices, it does depend on data type and, for text fields, the indexing specification (that is, the selected language). For example, if you select Unicode as the default language for indexing and sorting text on a text field's Options for Field dialog's Storage panel, sorting on the field is case-sensitive (a, b, and c all come *after* X, Y, and Z).

When you choose a numeric data type (including date, time, and timestamp field types), FileMaker applies a different sorting principle. In conventional text sorting, aa comes before b. When this convention is applied to numerals, 11 comes before 2. Hence, a separate methodology is applied when sorting fields having a numeric value.

> **TIP** In cases where you need to store numeric values as text without losing the ability to sort according to numeric sequence, the solution is to pad the values with leading zeros (or spaces) so that they're of consistent length. Whereas a text sort places 11 before 2, 02 sorts before 11 (and 002 sorts before 011, and so on).

## Multiple sort keys

Sorting your data by multiple fields is a hierarchical process. FileMaker looks at the first field in the sort order first and applies it across the board. If there are two records with the same value in the first sort field, they're returned in default (creation) order unless there is a second field in the sort order — whereupon they're returned according to the sort order of the second field.

> **TIP** Only with very large or very constrained (that is, containing little variation in values regardless of the number of records) data sets are you likely to need to create sorts depending on more than one or two fields.

For relatively small or simple databases, FileMaker's Sort dialog is easy to use, and end users are able to achieve satisfactory results with it — as long as your field names are relatively short and intelligible to the user. However, when sorts must include data from multiple tables and the data model is complex, sorting can present some challenges for end users.

## Dynamic sort techniques

To provide a simple and efficient sorting interface for end users, a widely used technique is to store a series of predetermined sorts within a script and provide users with a simplified menu of sort options.

One variant of this technique involves creating a value list of sort options, a global field (where users select a sort option using a menu of values from the value list), and an adjacent button to run a script configured to apply the appropriate sort. For example, if the desired options are to sort by name, batch, or value, your value list requires values such as the following:

- Unsorted
- Name Order
- Batch Order
- By Value

## Part III  Beyond the Basics

When the value list is attached to a global text field (for example, called gSortSelecton), your sort script (attached to the button next to the sort selection field) can be constructed as follows:

```
If [Utilty:gSortSelection = "Name Order"]
    Sort Records [Restore; No Dialog]
Else If [Utilty:gSortSelection = "Batch Order"]
    Sort Records[Restore; No Dialog]
Else If [Utilty:gSortSelection = "By Value"]
    Sort Records [Restore; No Dialog]
Else
    Unsort Records
End If
```

**NOTE** In the preceding script, the sort order specified for each of the Sort Records[ ] commands must be set to correspond to the selection named in the preceding If[ ] or Else If[ ] command. For example, the first Sort Records[ ] command must be configured to sort by the Name field, the second by the Batch field, and so on.

Although this technique provides an adequate solution in some cases, occasionally the number of combinations makes it impractical (especially when sorts involving multiple fields are required). For such cases, we offer an alternative technique: To create an open-ended three-tier sorting system, follow these steps:

1. Create a value list of the names of fields you want to be available for sorting.
2. Create a value list called Switch with the value 1.
3. Create three global text fields (gSortField1, gSortField2, and gSortField3), place them on your layout, and configure them as menus, attaching the value list of fields to each of them.
4. Create three global number fields (gSortOrder1, gSortOrder2, and gSortOrder3), place them on your layout, configure them as checkbox fields, attach the Switch value list to them, size them to 12px by 12px, and position them beside the three global text fields.
5. Create an unstored text calculation called cSort1_asc and enter the formula:

```
Case(
gSortOrder1 = 1; "";
MiddleWords(FieldType(Get(FileName); gSortField1); 2; 1) =
    "text";
GetField(gSortField1);
Let([
nF = GetField(gSortField1);
nA = Abs(nF);
nS = nF > 0;
nT = Int(nA);
nM = Mod(nA; 1);
nX = If(nM; nM; ".0")];
Case(
```

## The FileMaker Power User

```
IsEmpty(nF; 0;
nS; "P" & Right("0000000000000000" & nT; 12) & nX;
"N" & (9999999999999999 - nA))
)
)
```

6. Create an unstored text calculation called cSort1_dsc and enter the formula:

```
Case(
gSortOrder1 ≠ 1; "";
MiddleWords(FieldType(Get(FileName); gSortField1); 2; 1) =
    "text";
GetField(gSortField1);
Let([
nF = GetField(gSortField1);
nA = Abs(nF);
nS = nF > 0;
nT = Int(nA);
nM = Mod(nA; 1);
nX = If(nM; nM; ".0")];
Case(
IsEmpty(nF; 0;
nS; "P" & Right("0000000000000000" & nT; 12) & nX;
"N" & (999999999999999 - nA))
)
)
```

**NOTE** The calculation formulas presented here are designed to dynamically retrieve the value of the selected sort field. They achieve this via the use of the `GetField( )` function. They then conditionally add leading zeros to ensure that numeric values will sort appropriately although the result is returned as text.

**CROSS-REF** The techniques used in these calculations and others like them are explored in greater detail in Chapter 12.

7. Create unstored text calculations called cSort2_asc and cSort2_dsc with the formula along the same lines as those in Step 6, except substitute references to gSortField1 and gSortOrder1 with gSortField2 and gSortOrder2.

8. Create unstored text calculations called cSort3_asc and cSort3_dsc with the formula along the same lines as those in Step 6, except substitute references to gSortField1 and gSortOrder1 with gSortField3 and gSortOrder3.

9. Go to Layout mode, create a button labeled Sort attached to the `Sort Records[ ]` command, configure the button setup to Perform without Dialog, and Specify the Sort Order configuration depicted in Figure 9.12.

Take particular note of the assignment of alternate ascending and descending sort order properties to the six calculation fields.

283

**FIGURE 9.12**

The Button Setup sort order settings for your dynamic Sort button.

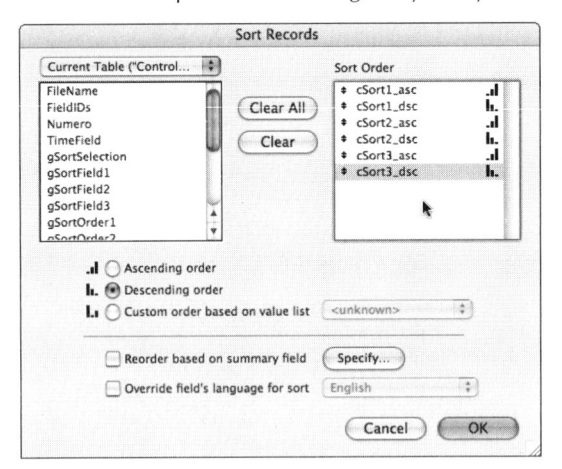

When you've completed these steps, return to Browse mode, select one or more field names in the gSortField fields, and click the Sort button to confirm that the sort settings are applied. Selecting the checkboxes in the gSortOrder fields reverses the direction of the sort for the corresponding sort field.

Using this technique, you can create entirely customized sorting control interfaces, providing your users with a clean and simple user experience that doesn't involve scrolling through lengthy lists of field names or negotiating a complex table structure. To illustrate the flexibility of such an arrangement, with lists of ten fields for users to select from, a three-tier sort interface of this kind permits users to select from well over 5,000 possible sort configurations.

Although we've described the process for creating an optional three-tier custom sort interface, the same principles can be applied to the creation of custom interfaces for fewer tiers or for additional tiers, according to the requirements of your solutions.

## Creating click-sort columns

The dynamic sorting technique described in the preceding section enables you to provide users with a custom sorting interface. The same approach can also be adapted to support a variety of other user interaction models. By way of example, a three-field sorting mechanism can be configured to provide column sorting where the user can click column headings to sort or, if already sorted, reverse the sort order of the corresponding column.

To implement this variant of the technique in the Inventory example file, follow these steps:

1. In the Utility table, create a global text field called gSortField.
2. In the Utility table, create a global number field called gSortOrder.

## The FileMaker Power User

3. In the OrderLines table, create a calculation field called cSort_asc with result type of text and enter the formula:

```
Case(
Utility::gSortOrder ≠ 1; "";
MiddleWords(FieldType(Get(FileName); Utility::gSortField); 2;
    1) = "text";
GetField(Utility::gSortField);
Let([
nF = GetField(Utility::gSortField);
nA = Abs(nF);
nS = nF > 0;
nT = Int(nA);
nM = Mod(nA; 1);
nX = If(nM; nM; ".0")];
Case(
IsEmpty(nF); 0;
nS; Right("000000000000" & nT; 12) & nX;
"000000000000" & (9999999999999 - nA))
)
)
```

4. In the OrderLines table, create a calculation field called cSort_dsc with result type of text and enter the formula:

```
Case(
Utility::gSortOrder = 1; "";
MiddleWords(FieldType(Get(FileName); Utility::gSortField); 2;
    1) = "text";
GetField(Utility::gSortField);
Let([
nF = GetField(Utility::gSortField);
nA = Abs(nF);
nS = nF > 0;
nT = Int(nA);
nM = Mod(nA; 1);
nX = If(nM; nM; ".0")];
Case(
IsEmpty(nF); 0;
nS; Right("000000000000" & nT; 12) & nX;
"000000000000" & (9999999999999 - nA))
)
)
```

5. Repeat Steps 3 and 4 to create identical calculation fields in the InvoiceLines table.

6. Create a new script called ColumnSort and define it as follows:

```
If[Get(ScriptParameter) = Utility::gSortField]
    Set Field[Utility::gSortOrder; Abs(Utility::gSortOrder –
    1)]
Else
```

## Part III  Beyond the Basics

```
    Set Field[Utility::gSortField; Get(ScriptParameter)]
    Set Field[Utility::gSortOrder;
  Abs(Get(ActiveModifierKeys)-2) = 1]
End If
Sort Records [Restore; No dialog]
```

*Note:* When defining the sort order properties for the final step of the script, select the four calculation fields created at Steps 3, 4, and 5, configuring them as shown in Figure 9.13.

7. Go to the OrderLines layout and enter Layout mode.

8. Delete the Serial#, _Gen, and _Mod field boxes from the layout and rearrange the remaining fields in a horizontal row at the top of the Body part, with their corresponding labels above them (at the bottom of the Header part).

9. Reduce the height of the Body part so it is just high enough to accommodate the fields.

10. Choose Layouts ➪ Layout Setup. The Layout Setup dialog appears.

11. Click the Views tab, disable the Form View and Table View checkboxes, and click OK to dismiss the dialog.

12. Click the tabs for the Header and Footer parts in turn, applying the lightest gray fill color to each.

13. Copy the header panel, label, and logo from the Orders layout, paste them into the OrderLines layout's header, reduce their size, and edit the label to read "Order Lines."

14. Choose File ➪ Manage ➪ Database (Shift+⌘+D or Ctrl+Shift+D), navigate to the Relationships panel, add a TO based on the Inventory table called OrderItems, and join it to the OrderLines TO matching the ItemID field in both TOs.

### FIGURE 9.13

Sort order properties for the final step of the ColumnSort script.

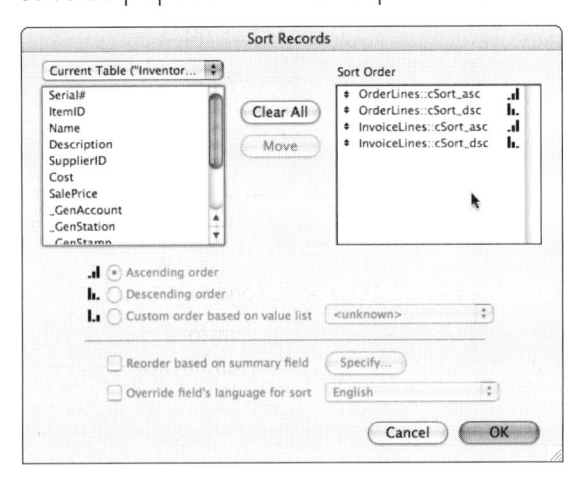

15. Repeat Step 14 to add an InvoiceItems TO joined to the InvoiceLines TO (again, matching the ItemID fields in both TOs).
16. Return to Layout mode and add the OrderItems::Name field to the OrderLines layout, positioning it beside the ItemID field.
17. Select the field labels, apply the embossing 3-D effect, and apply gray fill (a shade darker than the background fill of the Header part).
18. Select the OrdLineID label and choose Format ⇨ Button Setup. The Button Setup dialog appears.
19. Select the Perform Script command in the column at the left, choose Exit from the Current Script pop-up menu in the panel at the upper right, then click Specify. The Specify Script Options dialog appears.
20. Select the ColumnSort script in the list of scripts, then, in the Optional script parameter field near the bottom of the dialog, enter the formula:

    ```
    Get(LayoutTableName) & "::OrdLineID"
    ```
21. Click OK in the Specify Script Options and Button Setup dialogs to return to Layout mode.
22. With the OrdLineID label still selected, choose Format ⇨ Conditional. The Conditional Formatting for Selected Objects dialog appears.
23. Click the Add button and, in the Formula Is field, enter:

    ```
    Utility::gSortField = Get(LayoutTableName) & "::OrdLineID"
    ```
24. Select the Fill Color checkbox in the format area near the bottom of the dialog and, from the adjacent color palette, choose a medium-toned highlight color (for example, gray-blue ).
25. Click the Add button again and in the Formula Is field, enter:

    ```
    Utility::gSortOrder = 1 and
    Utility::gSortField = Get(LayoutTableName) & "::OrdLineID"
    ```
26. Select the Text Color checkbox in the format area of the dialog and, from the color palette, choose white.
27. Click OK to dismiss the Conditional Formatting dialog.
28. Select each of the remaining text labels in turn, choose Format ⇨ Conditional, and repeat Steps 23 through 27 to configure them, varying the formulas to correspond with the associated field.
29. Adjust the widths of the field labels to correspond to the widths of the fields below them.
30. Select the field boxes, choose Format ⇨ Field/Control ⇨ Borders, and apply light-gray side borders. Your OrderLines layout should resemble the one shown in Figure 9.14.

### FIGURE 9.14

The OrderLines layout reformatted as a list with dynamically sorting column headers.

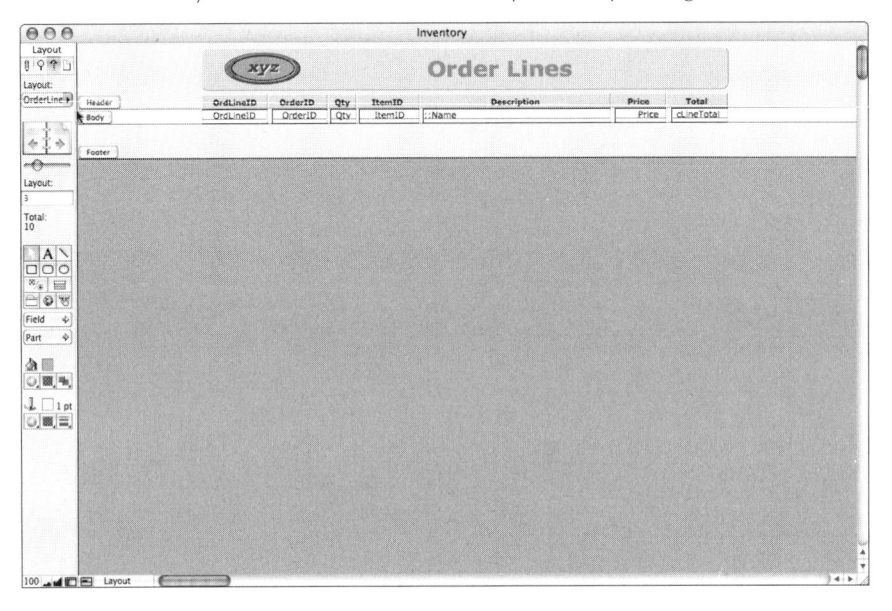

**31.** Repeat the layout formatting process to make comparable changes to the InvoiceLines layout.

Now, when you return to Browse mode on either layout, you can click the column headings to apply an ascending sort by the corresponding field. The first click on a heading sorts the column in ascending order and the column label highlights with a light blue shade, as shown in Figure 9.15. (You can see it in full color by opening the Inventory example database from the companion Web site.) A subsequent click on the same column heading toggles the sort order between ascending and descending and the highlight changes color accordingly. When you hold down the Shift key during your first click a column label, the initial sort order is reversed.

## Sorting related data

In the preceding section, you set up a sorting mechanism for a series of fields, including a field outside the table being sorted (for example, the OrderItems::Name field). When a related field is included in the sort order, FileMaker resolves the relationship and sorts the records according to the data it finds (for each record) in the related table.

## The FileMaker Power User

### FIGURE 9.15

The InvoiceLines layout sorted by clicking one column heading.

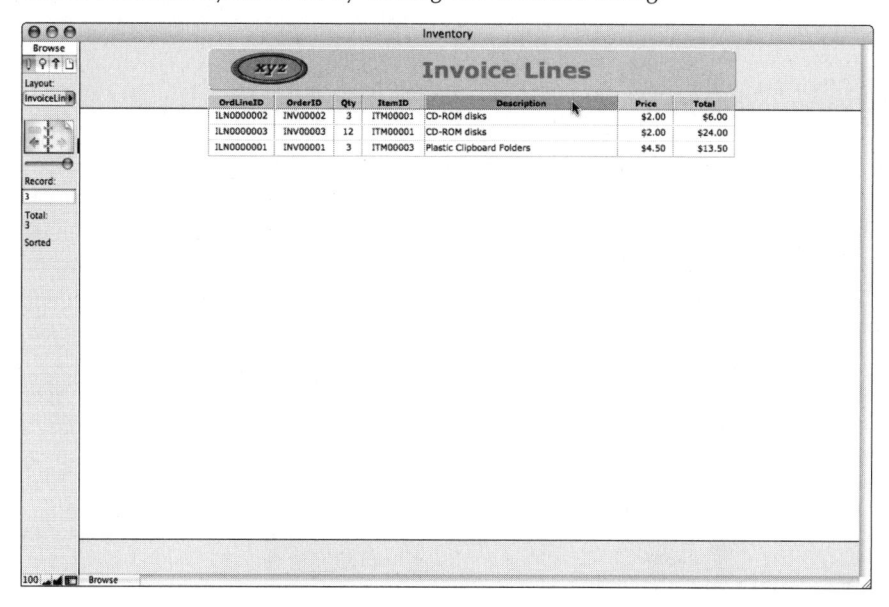

| OrdLineID | OrderID | Qty | ItemID | Description | Price | Total |
|---|---|---|---|---|---|---|
| ILN0000002 | INV00002 | 3 | ITM00001 | CD-ROM disks | $2.00 | $6.00 |
| ILN0000003 | INV00003 | 12 | ITM00001 | CD-ROM disks | $2.00 | $24.00 |
| ILN0000001 | INV00001 | 3 | ITM00003 | Plastic Clipboard Folders | $4.50 | $13.50 |

In addition to letting you sort the current table by related fields, FileMaker provides mechanisms for you to sort the related data so that when multiple records are related to the current record, they're presented in a specified order.

**NOTE** If related records are not explicitly sorted, then they're presented by default in the order of their creation.

When defining a relationship between any two TOs, you can specify the sort order for the relationship in either or both directions (that is, you can indicate the order in which records from either table should be presented to the other). You do this by selecting the Sort Records checkbox on the corresponding side of the Edit Relationship dialog, accessible from the Manage Database dialog's Relationships panel. You assign Sort properties using the same Sort dialog you see when sorting records in Browse mode, as shown in Figure 9.16.

**CAUTION** Bear in mind that sorting a relationship adds to the work that FileMaker has to do to return records for display in portals and found sets throughout your solution, especially when the number of records in the related table is large. Avoid redundant use or overuse of sorted relationships to avoid unnecessary slowdowns of your solutions.

**289**

## Part III  Beyond the Basics

**FIGURE 9.16**

Specifying the sort order for a relationship.

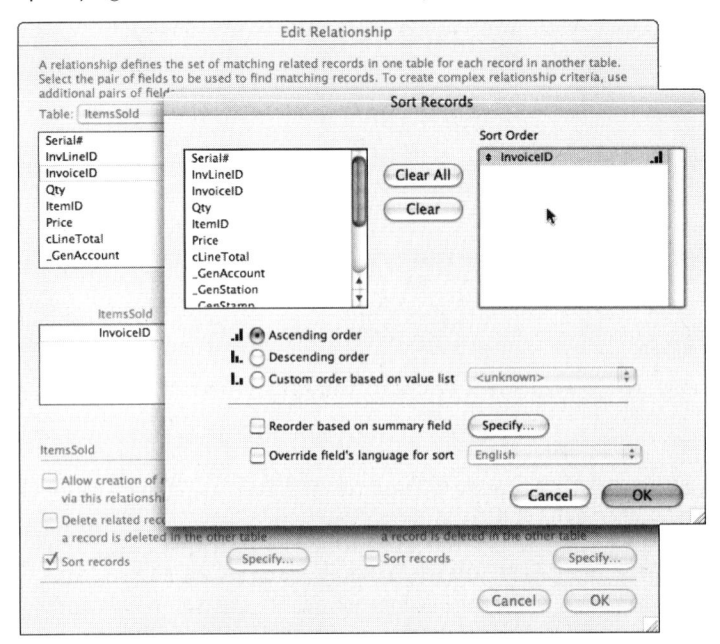

Regardless of a relationship's sort status, portals can be independently sorted. You can set up portal sorting by selecting the Portal Setup dialog's Sort Portal Records checkbox when adding or editing the portal. When alternate sorts of the same data sets may be required in different parts of your solution interface, leaving the relationship(s) unsorted and instead applying sorting to individual portals as required makes sense.

**NOTE** A variant of the dynamic sorting technique can be applied to portal data, to provide click-sort column functionality using portals.

**CROSS-REF** We discuss the use of portals, including interfaces for dynamic portal sorting, in Chapter 10.

# Understanding Formatting

FileMaker provides you with powerful mechanisms for applying and controlling text formatting; however, in order to make full use of these features, you need a thorough understanding of the way the different mechanisms interact. Format options include text style, text size, text font, text color, and a range of paragraph attributes such as indentation, margins, alignment, tab stops, and line spacing. Moreover, formatting can be applied at several different levels, with attributes at some levels overriding those at other levels.

## The FileMaker Power User 9

FileMaker includes support for formatting protocols shared between computer applications — so you can copy formatted content from a word processor, a Web browser, or another application and paste that content into FileMaker with its formatting intact. In fact, if you want to paste text without its original formatting, you need to use FileMaker's Paste Text Only option.

## The management of formatting: A three-tiered approach

FileMaker manages formatting at three distinct levels:

- Calculated formatting
- Embedded character and paragraph formatting
- Layout format filtering (including conditional formatting)

Each of these tiers of formatting takes precedence over the next. If calculated formats are in place, they override embedded or layout-based formatting. Embedded character/paragraph formatting overrides attributes applied at the layout level.

## Character-level formatting

Text within a FileMaker field can have formatting applied to it at the level of individual characters. You can select a single word or letter in a field and change its font, size, color, or style. When you do so, the attributes you apply remain in place wherever the text appears unless overridden explicitly by a calculation within the schema (or via a script). These formats are embedded.

In addition to applying formatting directly to selected text within a database field, you can paste data from other applications, preserving the formatting applied elsewhere. This is part of the same encoded character-level formatting stored with the data and displayed wherever the data appears.

**NOTE** Only formatting options available within FileMaker are preserved. For example, custom kerning or tracking from Adobe Illustrator and double-strikethrough from Microsoft Word would not be preserved.

To manually apply character-level formatting, click into a field box, select one or more characters, and use the commands on the Format menu to change the color, size, font, or style of the selected characters. When embedded formatting has been applied, it is retained by default even if the characters are copied and pasted to another field or combined with other data in a calculation (unless the calculation includes formatting commands to coerce the result into a specific format).

The process for pasting content (copied from other applications or from elsewhere within FileMaker) without including embedded formatting varies between operating systems. On the Mac, you can hold the Option key down while choosing Edit ⇨ Paste Text Only, or use the keyboard shortcut (Option+⌘+V). On Windows, you can choose Edit ⇨ Paste Special and use the resulting dialog to select the option for unformatted text, or use the keyboard shortcut (Ctrl+Shift+V).

**Part III** **Beyond the Basics**

**NEW FEATURE** When you paste formatted text into a field in FileMaker Pro 9, FileMaker treats this as performing two operations: pasting the text and then applying the formatting. Thus, choosing Edit ⇨ Undo (⌘+Z or Ctrl+Z) removes the formatting, leaving the unformatted text in the field. (A further Undo command is required to remove the pasted text altogether.)

## Paragraph-level formatting

Just as embedded character formatting can be applied to specific text stored within the database, embedded paragraph attributes (alignment, line spacing, and orientation) can also be applied and stored with the data. Paragraph formats apply to the text preceding a carriage return (or text in between two carriage returns, if there are multiple carriage returns in a field).

As with embedded font, size, color, and style attributes, embedded paragraph attributes can be applied directly to selected text in a field using Format menu commands or by interacting with the Text Ruler (accessible from the View menu in Browse mode).

As with character formatting, you can remove paragraph formatting when you paste text, by using the Paste [No style] script step or button command, or by choosing Paste Text Only (Mac) or Paste Unformatted Text (Windows).

Unlike character formatting, however, paragraph formatting cannot be overridden by calculation, because FileMaker does not provide calculation functions to control any of the paragraph format attributes.

## Layout format filters

When you place a field box onto a layout, it includes a full complement of attributes for both character and paragraph formatting. These layout object formats operate as defaults for the single instance they represent, applying only to characters and paragraphs that do not have embedded formatting for a given attribute.

Layout field boxes can be regarded as passive filters that apply their formats to any unformatted text viewed through them — but allowing formatted text to pass unmodified. The filtering effect applies to all aspects of the displayed text not governed by explicit (embedded) format attributes.

In addition to embedded formats, layout format filtering is also overridden by calculated character formatting.

Conditional formatting dynamically alters the filtering properties of layout objects, also operating as a default applied only to characters that do not carry embedded or calculated format attributes.

A significant feature of the operation of layout object formats is the "apply-if-different" rule. When you're applying formatting to content within the database via a specific field box, formatting instructions are interpreted by FileMaker with reference to the default formats specified for the particular field box. When you select format options matching the formats of the current field box, FileMaker removes embedded formatting, and when you select format options different from the field box defaults, they're stored as embedded formats.

For example, if you select the text in a 10pt field box and choose Format ➪ Size ➪ 10pt, no embedded character size formats are applied, because the selected format matches the field box default. However, if you switch to a different layout and select the same text in a 12pt field box and choose Format ➪ Size ➪ 10pt, embedded character size formatting is applied because the selected format differs from the field box default. Immediately, the selected text assumes 10pt size everywhere it appears, regardless of the default sizes specified for the field boxes where it's displayed.

## Precedence of number, date, and time formats

In addition to character and paragraph style and format defaults, layout objects associated with number, date, time, or timestamp fields accept formatting masks to control the way the relevant data is presented (to conform to various date, time, currency, and other numeric conventions). Unlike other layout-level format defaults, data masks take precedence over relevant formatting stored with the data.

Prior to FileMaker 9, data masks also suppressed character formatting in some cases. For example, number formatting, including the option to display negative numbers in a different color, overrode calculated text color. In FileMaker 9, however, the embedded or calculated formats of the first character are reflected throughout the entirety of a masked field.

**CAUTION** Although we applaud this behavior change, it may have implications for you if your solution is used in a mixed environment where some users access your files using earlier versions of FileMaker.

## Controlling formatting programmatically

FileMaker provides you with a suite of calculation functions to add and remove text font, size, style, and color settings. You can used these within calculation expressions along with other functions, enabling you to fully control the appearance of the text your calculations produce.

To supply a color value to the `TextColor( )` function, you can pass individual color values for red, green, and blue to the `RGB( )` function. The `RGB( )` function computes a composite number using the formula:

```
red * 256² + green * 256 + blue
```

Thus the entire RGB color spectrum is represented by the sequence of numbers between 0 (black) and 16,777,215 (white). In many cases, when you have determined a specific hue that you want FileMaker to return in certain conditions, it makes sense to calculate the RGB result number once and enter that directly into the calculation, instead of requiring FileMaker to compute it every time it is required. So for example:

```
TextColor("This is purple"; RGB(120; 40; 255))
```

can be reduced to:

```
TextColor("This is purple"; 7874815)
```

293

**TIP** Even better is defining a global variable with a suggestive name to hold this constant value (assign it once, when the solution opens). Seven- and eight-digit numeric literals don't tell you all that much when you come back to your solution in a few months to make enhancements or fix a bug.

By combining functions of this kind with logical and match operations, you can provide users with subtle cues to the significance of different elements of the data in your solutions.

**NEW FEATURE** A particularly useful technique is FileMaker's use of auto-enter calculations and their ability to self-reference. This has become even easier to set up using the new `Self` function in FileMaker 9. By defining an auto-enter calculation to replace itself with colored text, you can set up your database to respond dynamically (and colorfully) to data entry. For example, an auto-enter (replaces existing value) calc applied to a number field with the formula:

```
TextColor(Self; If(Self > 10; 11801640; 0))
```

automatically changes the color of any entered values greater than 10 to dark red.

## Creating style buttons

Because FileMaker provides fine-grained control over character formatting, you can build interface tools for your users that enable them to perform operations on text like those provided in a range of familiar text processing environments. You are also able to tailor the functionality to suit your solution's specific requirements.

For example, if you create a button attached to the `Set Field[ ]` command, with the target field left unassigned and the formula entered as:

```
Let([
text = Get(ActiveFieldContents);
start = Get(ActiveSelectionStart);
size = Get(ActiveSelectionSize)];
Left(text; start - 1) &
TextStyleAdd(Middle(text; start ; size ); bold) &
Right(text; Length(text) - start - size + 1)
)
```

clicking the button automatically applies bold character formatting to selected text in any field on the current layout.

**NOTE** A useful aspect of the `Set Field[ ]` command's behavior is that when you do not provide a target field parameter, it acts on the currently selected field (if any).

This example utilizes `Set Field[ ]` with `Get( )` functions to supply selection parameters, the `Left( )`, `Middle( )`, and `Right( )` functions for text parsing and the `TextStyleAdd( )` function to change the text appearance. When combined appropriately, these functions let you to automate the application of selective formatting.

Although this kind of button does its primary task of applying formatting, it has one significant shortcoming: After the formatting is applied, your text is no longer selected (the cursor is moved to the end of the field contents). If this is of concern, it can be remedied by incorporating the `Set Field[ ]` functionality into a short script as follows:

```
Set Variable [$size; Value:Get(ActiveSelectionSize)]
If [$size]
    Set Variable [$text; Value:Get(ActiveFieldContents)]
    Set Variable [$start; Value:Get(ActiveSelectionStart)]
    Set Field [Left($text; $start-1) &
      TextStyleAdd(Middle($text ; $start; $size); Bold) &
      Right($text; Length($text)-$start-$size + 1) ]
    Set Selection [Start Position: $start;
       End Position: $start + $size-1]
End If
```

You can attach the preceding script to your button using the Perform Script command so that when you click the button, the selected text acquires bold formatting. However now, the selection is remembered and reinstated, making the process self-contained and seamless.

Style buttons such as the one described earlier exploit the behavior of each of these elements (`Set Field[ ]`, `TextStyleAdd[ ]`, `Set Selection[ ]`, and so on) to provide users with useful and context-appropriate interface tools.

## Some Notes on Variables

FileMaker enables developers to store and manipulate information in temporary memory locations called *variables*. Variables have several advantages:

- Variables are very quick because they don't require FileMaker to reference the schema or read/write to disk.
- Variables aren't tied to the data structure, so you can reference them from a variety of contexts and modes regardless of the availability/accessibility of fields and relationships.

To be fair, variables also have a downside:

- They're difficult to keep track of in large and complex solutions.
- They're not particularly secure.
- They're specific to an individual file session.

Each of these issues simply requires some care and planning on your part as the developer.

Until the release of version 8, FileMaker did not provide native support for variables. Much of the work that you can now do using variables previously required the use of global fields. However, global fields retain some properties that ensure their continued usefulness, despite the many benefits of memory variables.

## The three kinds of variables

FileMaker provides three distinct kinds of variables, each working within a different scope:

- **Calculation variables:** This kind of variable is defined within the syntax of the Let ( ) function. You can use calculation variables to improve the efficiency and readability of calculations. Any variable you create in a calculation that is not named with a $ or $$ prefix is a calculation variable.
- **Local variables:** So-called local variables have a lifespan determined by an individual script thread in a single file on the current workstation (that is, they only exist while a given instance of the script they're associated with is running). Local variable names always commence with a single dollar sign ($).
- **Global variables:** Identified by names commencing with two dollar signs ($$), global variables persist throughout the file where they're defined, while it remains open on the current workstation.

Although these working definitions indicate the way variables are used, the boundaries are somewhat blurred. For example, you can declare local ($) or global ($$) variables within a Let ( ) calculation; then they have scope outside the calculation and can be retrieved by scripts or other calculations.

Similarly, you can declare local variables when no scripts are running — with the result that they're associated with a hypothetical "script zero" and available only when the script stack is empty.

Although variables are sometimes referred to a "script variables," we consider this something of a misnomer, because all three kinds of variables can be defined and referenced both inside and outside of scripts. A more apt description is the sometimes used *memory variables,* or simply *variables*.

## Variables and memory usage

In FileMaker, variables are created automatically when you assign a value to them — you don't need to specify or name them in advance. Values can be assigned to variables within any calculation expression (via the use of the Let ( ) function) or via the Set Variable[ ] script and button commands. The value you assign to a variable is held in memory at a fixed location, enabling you to retrieve the value within its scope of availability.

Because variables are stored in memory, they use a portion of the computer memory reserved for FileMaker. If you intend to create a large number of variables — or to store a large quantity of data in a variable, be aware that the amount of memory available for other operations is reduced, which may impact performance.

FileMaker does not differentiate between an empty (null) variable and a nonexistent variable. Thus, by setting a variable to null (" "), you can release the memory reserved for its contents and take it out of play.

## Instantiating and destroying variables

The creation of a variable is sometimes called *instantiation* (that is, creating an instance of the variable). Because variables can be created and destroyed at will, a number of instances of the same variable may exist over the course of an application session. A variable is created simply by assigning it a value, so the process of assigning a value to a variable is also frequently referred to as *declaring a variable*.

The most useful and flexible method of declaring variables is via a calculation expression. For example, you can create a variable named something by using the calculation expression:

```
Let(something = "107%"; "")
```

Because the name of the `something` variable doesn't include any leading $ characters, FileMaker scopes it to the calculation function where it is created (that is, it has meaning only within the enclosing parentheses of the `Let( )` function). However, if you add leading $ characters, FileMaker interprets the variable as having local or global scope and the accessibility and durability of the variable is set accordingly. You can define any mix of differently scoped variables within a single `Let( )` expression.

In addition, FileMaker provides button and script commands you can use to directly instantiate a local or global variable. Whether a variable you create using the `Set Variable[ ]` command is local (confined to the script where it's created) or global is determined solely by whether you prepend a single or a double dollar prefix to the name of the variable. Thus:

```
Set Variable [$something; Value:"107%"]
```

creates a local variable that persists only while the current script is at the top of the script stack; it is not accessible by other scripts that the declaring script might invoke via the `Perform Script[]` step.

Deleting the contents of a variable (setting the variable to null) is the only way you can destroy a FileMaker variable. Thus, you destroy variables using the same functions and commands that you use to create them. For example, you can destroy a global variable using the command:

```
Set Variable [$$name; Value:""]
```

Because calculation variables and local variables have narrowly defined scope and expire after the conclusion of the calculation or script in which they're defined, explicitly destroying them is rarely necessary. However, global variables persist throughout the current file session unless you destroy them — so when a global variable is no longer needed, we suggest you destroy it so that FileMaker can reclaim the memory it has occupied.

## Keeping track of variables

When you configure a script or calculation to declare or reference a variable, you choose a name for the variable. FileMaker has no mechanism to determine whether the name is correct (for example, that it won't overwrite an existing variable that is still needed). An ever-present danger when working with variables is that you lose sight of them, writing or referencing them with mismatched names, or inadvertently overwriting them.

When you work with calculation variables and local variables, because their scope is constrained, the task of managing them and ensuring you know what they are for and how they are named is finite. Global variables, however, present you with a significant challenge. For this reason, some developers prefer to avoid the use of global variables. Although we're not about to tell you not to use them, we recommend that you do so sparingly and with caution.

When you do use variables — and global variables in particular — you need a reliable way of keeping track of them. One way is to keep a register of variables in each solution, updating it each time you create or reference a variable. This is almost certainly preferable to tracking variables retroactively — after you've forgotten where they originated and what exactly they were for.

# Understanding Indexing

FileMaker does a great job of keeping the complexities hidden from the user and even the developer. Sometimes it does this a little too well, so that few people know how the program actually works or how best to use it. Field indexes in FileMaker have been the subject of myths of various kinds — in part because the interface obscures their status and role.

Indexes have two primary roles and a number of secondary roles. The two primary roles are

- To establish relationships
- To facilitate Finds

Both of these roles are important; however, although an index is essential for a relationship (it won't work without one), Finds can proceed (albeit more slowly) on unindexed fields.

## Text index types

Many FileMaker users are aware that indexes support both relationships and Finds, but fewer users understand that, for text fields, there are, in fact, two distinct types of index — one providing primary support for Finds and the other providing support for relationships.

### The word index

The index that FileMaker uses to support Finds on text fields is an index of words stored in a field. FileMaker treats most characters other than letters and numbers as word separators. So in addition to spaces, characters (such as &, ?, +, $, ~, and so on) are also used to delimit words.

**NOTE** The list characters used as word separators may vary on a field-by-field basis depending on the default language setting on the Options for Field dialog's Storage panel. For example, if Unicode is chosen as the default for a field, most characters other than a space, including those mentioned in the preceding paragraph, are indexed as part of words rather than treated as word separators.

The word index is created for a field the first time you perform a Find on the contents of the field, unless the default Automatically Create Indexes as Needed option has been disabled in the Storage panel for the field.

If indexing is enabled for a field, you can view its word index by placing the cursor in the field, choosing Insert ⇨ From Index, and, in the resulting dialog, selecting the Show Individual Words checkbox. As shown in Figure 9.17, FileMaker shows you each word as a separate entry in the index list.

## FIGURE 9.17

Viewing the contents of the word index for a text field.

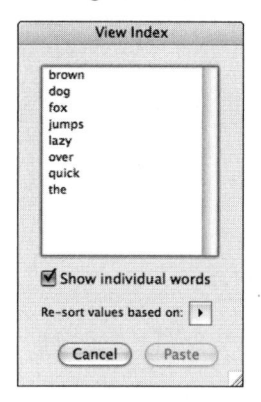

**CAUTION:** If a word index has not been created for a field, displaying the View Index dialog as described here causes FileMaker to create one, as long as the Automatically Create Indexes as Needed option is enabled for the selected field.

### The value index

To support relationship matching, as well as value lists and some special find operations (for example, a duplicate values search), FileMaker uses a value index. Value indexing is applied to numeric fields as well as text fields.

When FileMaker creates a value index for a text field, each line of text is treated as a single separate index entry. When a field contains no carriage returns, its contents are treated as a single value; however, when carriage returns are present, they serve as value separators.

**NOTE:** Although FileMaker indexes very long values, only approximately 110 characters are used when determining uniqueness or matching values (the precise number varies depending on the bit length of the characters involved). In other words, if the first 110 characters of two values are the same, FileMaker treats the values as a match regardless of what follows.

FileMaker creates value indexes when the Automatically Create Indexes as Needed option is enabled for a field, and a relationship or value list depending on the field index is used, or any other user action is taken (for example, insert from index) requiring the value index.

## Indexing myths exploded

Because we're talking about myths, we'll start off by reminding you that indexes aren't used for sorting, even though the default language selection in the indexing area of the Options for Field dialog does affect sort order. However, a field without an index sorts in exactly the same amount of time as a field with an index.

## Part III  Beyond the Basics

Another area of frequent confusion centers on the relationship between storage and indexing. Stored fields aren't necessarily indexed; however, unstored calculations cannot be indexed. The fact that a field is unstored means that it cannot be indexed; however, the fact that it is stored does not signify that it *has* an index.

Finally, you'll encounter a common belief that the index settings None, Minimal, and All in the storage tab of the Options for Field dialog equate to none, value index, and both value and word index. However the Minimal option refers to any case where only one of the indexes for a text field has been created. If you create a value list using values from an unindexed field with the Automatically Create Indexes as Needed option enabled, the Minimal setting appears selected. However, if you perform a Find on an unindexed field with the Automatically Create Indexes as Needed option enabled, the Minimal setting also appears selected. Thus, the minimal setting, as shown in Figure 9.18, indicates that only one index is present, but it doesn't indicate which one.

If you encounter a solution (perhaps developed by someone else) with the Minimal index indicator showing and the Automatically Create Indexes as Needed option disabled, how can you tell what kind of index the field has? One answer would be to try to use the field as the basis of a value list — if the field's index is a word index, an error dialog is displayed. Perhaps the simplest method is to choose Insert ➪ From Index to expose the View Index dialog. The Show Individual Words setting is inaccessible but nevertheless appears enabled (checked) if the field has a word index or disabled (unchecked) if the field has a value index.

**FIGURE 9.18**

The Minimal Indexing indicator in the Options for Field dialog.

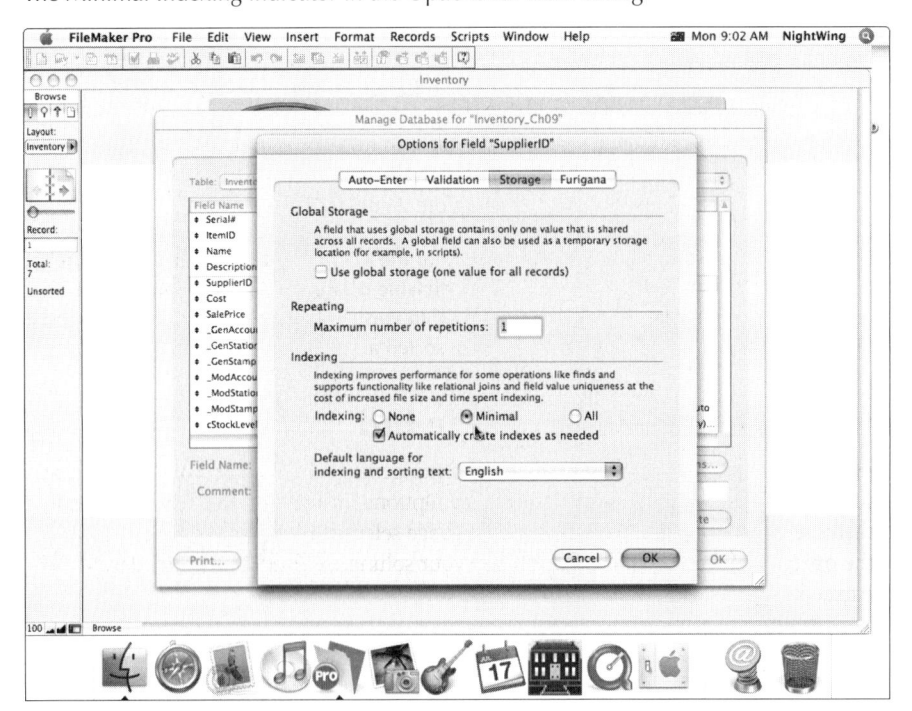

## Differences between numeric and text indexing

The most significant difference between the indexing of text and numeric fields is that text fields provide the option for two indexes that operate independently, as noted earlier. However, the sequence and behavior of a numeric index differs from a text index. As shown in Figure 9.19, if you view the index of a number field, the index entries appear as you would expect, arranged in ascending order according to their numeric value.

**FIGURE 9.19**

Index entries for a numeric field.

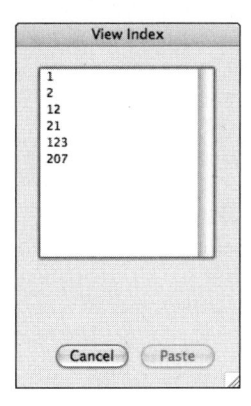

If a text field containing the same data as the field that produced the numeric index shown as Figure 9.19 is indexed, the presentation order follows a different convention.

The convention for sorting text data follows different rules, so numeric data stored in a text field is presented in a different format, as shown in Figure 9.20. In this circumstance, following the rules for alphabetic sorting, an ascending order places 12 before 2 and 207 before 21.

> **TIP** When you create relationships, make sure that the data types of the match fields are the same so that the indexing rules produce predictable results for all cases. Similarly, because the sorting conventions that FileMaker applies are adjusted to correspond to the data type, you should use numeric fields in cases where you expect to see data sorted according to ordinal values.

## Unicode and alternate language indexes

The way FileMaker treats a text field's character set is contingent on the Default language for indexing and the sorting text setting in the Storage tab of the Options for Field dialog. For most purposes, you'll achieve the desired results by using a language selection that corresponds to the language of the operating system in the region where your solution is used. However, there are some notable exceptions:

- If you specify Unicode as the language for indexing and sorting for a field, uppercase and lowercase characters are indexed, sorted, and searched separately, enabling you to set up case-sensitive relationship matching.

- If you choose the *Default* option for the Indexing and Sorting Language setting, then sorting, searching, and matching are not case-sensitive, but nevertheless, accented characters are differentiated from unaccented equivalents (for example, *é* does not match to *e*).

**FIGURE 9.20**

The index of a text field containing numeric data.

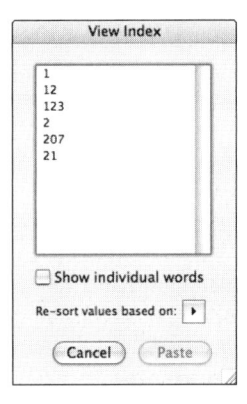

## Optimizing field index configurations

To support your solution design, some field indexes are essential. Relationships and field-based value lists, in particular, require that the field they address be indexed. In most other cases, indexes are optional.

When a field is used in a Find (especially if the record count is large), FileMaker can use the field index to significantly improve the Find's execution speed. This benefit comes at a cost, because FileMaker must do additional work to maintain the index as values in the database are added, deleted, and changed and the file's size increases to accommodate the indexes (impacting server and network performance in some cases).

It's a trade-off: The choice is faster Finds and slower overall performance, or faster overall performance, with some lengthy Finds on unindexed fields. In most cases, the best answer is to allow indexes to remain on frequently searched fields (as well as value indexes on fields used for relationships and value lists) and disable indexing on other fields. That may sound like a great theory; however, it only works well if you have reliable information about the fields where users frequently perform Finds. In large solutions with many users, this information may not be readily available.

Earlier in this chapter (in the "Saving Finds and found sets" section), we describe a technique for capturing and storing a complete history of Find criteria. One useful side benefit of implementing such a system is that it provides a comprehensive and reliable source of data about the frequency of

Finds on each field in the solution. With a little ingenuity and a small amount of additional code, you'll be able to capture other useful information about Finds performed by the users of your solutions — such as the execution times of Finds and the number of records found.

## The Table of Dependencies

The FileMaker Pro calculation engine is a thing of joy, with its combination of power and simplicity. A significant part of the reason you can "set and forget" with FileMaker calculations is because FileMaker does an excellent job of keeping track of things behind the scenes. In particular, calculations in FileMaker are supported by an internal table of dependencies. There is no direct user interface to the table of dependencies — it works almost entirely behind the scenes, keeping track of fields that reference other fields within a FileMaker table.

### Cascading calculation operations

As noted in Chapter 7, when you define a calculation referring to values in other fields in the record, you're creating a *dependency* — thus, creating a flow-on effect of the initial change. The plot thickens when you create calculations referencing other calculations. Then, FileMaker keeps track of dependencies extending through multiple stages (for example, when an input value changes, a calculation referencing it is targeted for re-evaluation). However, it isn't until FileMaker has computed and returned a new result for this first calculation that other calculations depending on that result can begin re-evaluation. Thus, complex dependencies can result in a cascade of operations.

> **CAUTION** Inexperienced developers sometimes create extensive chains of dependent calculations — every calculation is dependent on several others, which are dependent on still others, and so on. In this situation, FileMaker is given a great deal of work to do when a single input value is changed; moreover, it must work sequentially through the chain of logical dependencies until it has resolved them all. This type of poor solution design leads to performance issues in large or complex solutions.

### The limits of dependency

FileMaker manages calculation dependencies within the record structure of each table. In that sense, a record in a table is a discrete entity that's internally managed and resolved by the application. However, FileMaker does not track dependencies outside of the individual record.

You may be aware of several apparent exceptions to this rule. Lookups, for example, draw data from a field in another table, but their dependency is on the relationship key field residing in the same table, not on the related field. Similarly, unstored calculations may reference values in other tables, but they are re-evaluated when the screen is refreshed and not as a consequence of a change in any field outside the table where they reside.

The constraints on FileMaker's internal management of dependencies establish a discipline with which you must become familiar in order to anticipate the behavior of the application. Doing so helps you design solutions harnessing and exploiting FileMaker's strengths.

## Tiers of dependency

When calculations reference other calculations, FileMaker uses its table of dependencies to determine an appropriate order of evaluation. In this respect, *tiers* of dependency are created where directly dependent fields are re-evaluated before indirectly dependent fields. In many cases, you don't need to worry about this — it just happens!

In some cases, however, calculation logic does not resolve in a simple linear way. If Field C depends on Field B, which in turn depends on Field A, FileMaker can establish a clear chain of dependency, enabling it to perform evaluation A then B then C. However, in a more complex arrangement — for example, where C depends on both A and B, but B depends on both A and C — the logic does not resolve into a clear evaluation order. In a case such as this, fields B and C are evaluated in the order in which the fields were created.

# Caching Join Results

One of the challenges of relational data management is the way compound data accumulates. Via a one-to-many relationship, a single record may reference several. Each of these several may in turn reference several others. If the average number of related records is 10, as you reference data from more remote tables, 10 becomes 100, and 100 becomes 1,000 — an exponential burden, potentially requiring retrieval of large numbers of records to calculate and display a single screen of data.

## What caching does for you

FileMaker tackles the potentially exponential challenge of delivering related data by storing related data sets in a cache, thus reducing the number of disk reads and network calls required as you work. The object of caching is transparency — holding data until needed, yet refreshing data automatically as changes occur. FileMaker monitors the user to achieve this transparency, responding to actions impacting cached data and anticipating requirements for fresh data from the host.

In most cases, caching increases the responsiveness of the application without perceptible compromises. However, FileMaker can't anticipate every possible combination of elements, so occasionally situations arise when an update of cached data needs prompting. This occurs most commonly when an action occurring outside the frame of reference of the current window (for example, via a script) has implications for data on display.

## Solving caching problems

FileMaker provides a direct and disarmingly simple remedy to cache control issues arising as a consequence of scripted actions. The Refresh Window[ ] command includes options to flush

## The FileMaker Power User 9

cached join results and/or flush cached SQL data. By including an appropriately configured `Refresh` command at strategic positions in your scripts, you can correct most script-related caching issues.

In FileMaker Pro 9, a `Refresh` command is also available on the Records menu (Shift+⌘+R or Ctrl+Shift+R) as shown in Figure 9.21, as well as via a button command — so manual control of the cache is possible.

If you're confronted by a refresh issue not solved via these options, a further alternative that may be useful in some cases is to make use of dependencies in the current table (that is, the table the current layout is associated with). Any calculation dependency between a relationship key field and a modified field in the local table prompts a refresh of related data.

### FIGURE 9.21

The Records ➪ Refresh Window command — new in FileMaker 9!

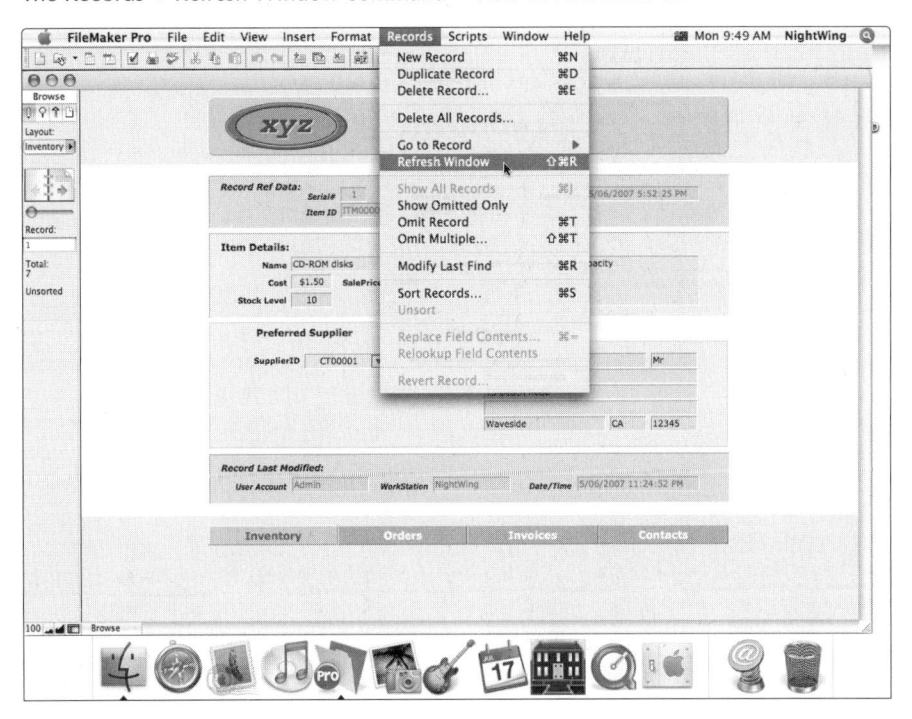

305

## Gaining control of the cache

Although we've suggested several ways you can ameliorate cache refresh problems should they arise, prevention is better than cure. If you approach your solution design with a view to minimizing complex dependencies on related data, issues are less likely to arise.

There are several strategies you can adopt to reduce the potential for refresh issues:

- By breaking down data views into focused groups of fewer elements and providing a modular series of screen displays, you reduce the reliance on caching and gain greater control over the data presentation sequence. Tab controls provide a useful interface mechanism supporting data modularization.

- Another technique that assists you to avoid potential caching issues is the use of a scripted solution interface. This approach is one where buttons and custom menu commands are provided for all the basic operations the user undertakes. Because all interface actions can be scripted, you can determine how and when displayed data is refreshed.

# Understanding Global Fields

It's all a matter of perspective, but we've been known to remark that global fields are not as global as their name suggests. One of the notable characteristics of global fields is that in a multi-user solution, each user sees his own separate set of values. When viewed in this way, the behavior of global fields seems decidedly parochial. So why are they called global?

A global field holds one value for all records within the table where it is defined. It's global specifically with respect to the table. However, another useful (and more recently acquired) characteristic of global fields is the fact that they're accessible from anywhere in a file without a relationship. That's a rather different sense in which they might be considered global.

From their inception well over a decade ago, global fields have provided repositories for constants, variables, and interface elements, as well as scratch fields and temporary storage. Several of these uses have diminished with the advent of memory variables, but other uses have arisen to make global fields indispensable.

## The behavior of global fields

You have to understand several aspects of global field behavior before you can use them to best advantage:

- They hold a single value (although that value might be a repetition) for all records and can be accessed without a relationship.
- They can be read and written even when there are no records in their table.

- Their value is saved only on the host computer (or when the file is edited in stand-alone mode). Each user sees the saved values from the host when the file first opens, but any changes the user makes are specific to that user's workstation.
- They're persistent in Find mode.

## Uses for global fields

Global fields provide input fields for custom dialogs, key fields for utility relationships, filter and option fields for interface controls, scriptable summary data fields for reports, portable accommodation for interface elements and corporate logos, and flexible containers for layout text, instructions, or labels.

In short, resourceful developers have thought of many ingenious global field uses, and they have become an essential ingredient in FileMaker's interface tool box.

## When to avoid global fields

There are several situations when the use of global fields is not desirable. Some of the most notable of these are

- When the persistency of values (between sessions) matters
- When data is to be shared among users in a multi-user solution
- When more expedient options are available

For many purposes, variables offer a good alternative to global fields — and they have certain advantages:

- Variables don't have to be defined within the schema — they can be created and destroyed as needed.
- Reading and writing to variables is more efficient than reading and writing to fields.

## Using global calculation fields

In the storage options dialog accessed from the Specify Calculation dialog, you can choose to define a calculation as globally stored. When you do so, the calculation takes on several of the key properties of all global fields, most notably one value for all records in the table, accessibility without a relationship, and persistence in Find mode.

Global calculations can be used to compute a result from values stored in global fields. However, global calculation fields also have some useful attributes when used to reference standard data fields. When used to reference standard data fields, they're re-evaluated with respect to the record where the referenced fields have been most recently edited on the current client workstation.

**CROSS-REF** For a more detailed discussion of the use of global fields, including an overview of the rules for re-evaluation of global calculations, refer to Chapter 12.

# Chapter 10

# Building Advanced Interfaces

Computer software may be powerful and innovative but, with few exceptions, software is only as useful as its interface allows. The user's ability to understand what his computer is telling him and effectively interact with it is an essential measure of a solution's effectiveness. Thus, your solutions' success is determined as much by your command of interface technique and design as any other single factor.

In Chapter 6, we introduced many of the essential concepts supporting FileMaker's interface building environment — Layout mode — showing you how to use essential interface building tools. We also introduced a number of design concepts, helping you make interface design choices that will enhance the ergonomics and intuitiveness of your solutions.

The goals of good interface design are clarity and consistency, as well as ease and efficiency of use. However, you also have to consider aesthetics. If you expect users to spend lots of time working with your solution, you have to keep in mind that your interface design choices will have a significant impact on user fatigue. Don't underestimate the solutions' cumulative impact on the user's mood and morale.

In the following pages we delve into a series of deeper challenges, providing specific techniques and recommendations, enabling you to address a variety of challenges, remedy shortcomings, and lend increased professionalism to your solution interfaces.

**IN THIS CHAPTER**

Developing for the cross-platform world

Changing layouts dynamically

Summarizing, reporting, and printing

Working with windows and views

Dealing with custom dialogs

Building enhanced layouts

Making use of I tab controls and portals

Exploring advanced Web viewer techniques

Delivering native charts and progress bars

Customizing the user experience

## Part III   Beyond the Basics

# Developing for Mac and Windows Users

One of several key benefits that FileMaker brings to the world of desktop databases is its cross-platform capability. Users have every expectation that they'll be able to choose freely among available operating systems and hardware platforms, without foregoing access to critical business applications. FileMaker's ability to run the same solutions on both Macintosh and Windows operating systems is a powerful plus.

Many businesses accommodate a mix of computer operating systems. And many of those that don't *currently* accommodate a mix of operating systems have done so at some time in the past. Staff members change, policies adapt, companies that resolutely embraced one technology for years sooner or later find themselves confronted with the unexpected need to support another.

> **TIP** We advise you not to lock yourself in with support for a single operating system, even if it seems unlikely at the outset that you'll need FileMaker's cross-platform capabilities.

In the following sections, we examine the key issues you must address to deliver solutions that work well and look good on both Mac and Windows computers.

## Selecting fonts

When you choose a display font for text in your solution, you may be surprised and disappointed to see the result when the solution is opened on another computer (even if the operating system is the same) where the chosen font is not installed. When the specified font is not available, operating systems use a process of font substitution to find an alternative — however, the sizing, spacing, and general appearance of characters may vary. On occasion, this leads to text being clipped or cropped and lines wrapping in unattractive ways — sometimes to the point where legibility is compromised. Even if it isn't that bad, your efforts in creating a polished appearance for your screens will be lost if the screens aren't rendered as intended.

For solution portability, carefully select fonts installed as standard with the operating system. That way, you have a high probability that, wherever the solution is viewed, the necessary fonts will be available. Ideally, the fonts you choose should also offer a high level of readability and intelligibility, consistency between operating systems, and a crisp and open appearance.

> **TIP** For best results, we recommend Verdana, Times New Roman, Trebuchet MS, Georgia, and Tahoma. For occasional touches, Impact, Arial Black, Comic Sans MS, Symbol, and Webdings are other alternatives. All these fonts are part of the standard installation on current and recent versions of both Mac OS and Windows.

Even with the most careful selection of fonts, differing font imaging technologies will result in the same fonts rendering in different sizes on different platforms, with variations according to the sizes and weights used. Frequently, plain styles render with slightly greater width on Windows, while italic styles generally render with a shallower slant on the Mac. Both of these effects are most evident at smaller font sizes (that is, below 12 points).

# Building Advanced Interfaces — 10

When working with small font sizes, leave an allowance to accommodate different rendering characteristics.

> **TIP** When designing layouts on the Mac, we recommend adding 2- to 3-pixel additional height (per line) on field boxes and text objects and approximately 10 percent extra length. This approach prevents overlapping and truncation of text when viewed on a Windows workstation.

## Paying attention to differences in screen rendering

To illustrate differences in font rendering between platforms, we created some text at three common sizes on a Mac. We took screenshots of the text (still on a Mac) and pasted them above the text objects. On opening the file in Windows, the text objects as rendered by the Windows operating system could be directly compared to the adjacent images of the appearance of the text on the Mac. We've enlarged the results and show them in Figure 10.1.

**FIGURE 10.1**

Enlargement of screen renderings of Verdana at three difference sizes on Mac OS and Windows showing differences in appearance and spacing.

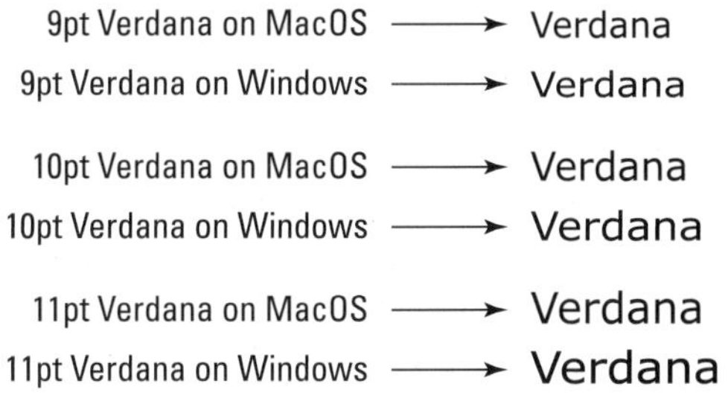

| 9pt Verdana on MacOS   | ⟶ | Verdana |
| 9pt Verdana on Windows | ⟶ | Verdana |
| 10pt Verdana on MacOS   | ⟶ | Verdana |
| 10pt Verdana on Windows | ⟶ | Verdana |
| 11pt Verdana on MacOS   | ⟶ | Verdana |
| 11pt Verdana on Windows | ⟶ | **Verdana** |

As Figure 10.1 shows, differences in rendering of screen fonts at moderate sizes occur on the Mac and Windows, for one commonplace cross-platform font in plain face. Comparable differences also exist for other fonts. If you don't allow for these differences when designing your layouts, they won't transition well between computers.

In addition to font rendering issues, several other factors affect the appearance of solutions on alternate platforms:

- **Color differences:** FileMaker uses the same color palette on both Windows and Macintosh. However, minor differences in operating system and hardware configurations (such as a different white point — 1.8 on Macs and 2.2 on Windows) generally result in perceptible differences in color rendering and overall color temperatures. Differences of this type may also be observed between computers of the same operating system, particularly where different color bit depths have been set in System Preferences (Mac) or the

311

Control Panel (Windows). You'll also often notice differences when using different monitors, particularly when comparing LCD with CRT implementations.

- **Screen layering:** FileMaker renders layouts progressively, building them in layers according to the layout objects' stacking order (working from back to front). This often results in some flickering or flashing, which is generally more noticeable on the Windows platform due to different graphics handling.

> **TIP** You can reduce or eliminate screen display artifacts such as flashing by avoiding the use of large and unoptimized images on layouts (these images load more slowly, generating flicker) and by applying opaque fill to as many layout objects (including graphics) as possible. You can further refine the appearance of screens as they're rendered by altering the stacking order of elements on the layout — particularly avoiding clusters of large graphical objects loading early (that is, at the back of the stacking order), thus delaying the load of other layout elements. Placing larger objects near the front of the stacking order generally results in a more pleasing rendering sequence.

- **Button click-shade highlighting:** Another notable difference between the appearance of your FileMaker solutions on Macintosh and Windows is the way buttons change appearance when you click them with the mouse. On Windows, the button changes to a color negative (inverted) image while the mouse button is depressed, whereas on Mac the button is shadowed (rendered several shades darker). This difference in visual effect is dramatic, especially when the buttons are large and/or rendered in bold tones. Check the appearance of the click-shade effect on both platforms before finalizing your button designs.

> **TIP** Very dark buttons lose most of the impact of the click shading effect on the Mac (they can't get much darker). Conversely, mid-gray buttons show little click-shading on Windows (their inverse is also mid-gray). Extremely light or dark buttons on Windows show such a marked Click Shade effect that they may be unappealing. Mid-toned and colored buttons give the most pleasing overall effect when viewed on either platform.

## Considering platform-specific window behavior

The most notable difference between the appearance and behavior of FileMaker on Macintosh and Windows is that on Windows, all database windows are contained within a single larger application window with the application's menu bar across the top of the application window. By contrast, database windows on the Mac appear separately, not enclosed by an application window, while the application's menus are fixed across the top of the screen.

The application window in Windows (see Figure 10.2) has its own discrete borders, title bar, and controls including the Application menus incorporated into the band immediately below the application window title bar.

A notable feature of the application window on the Windows operating system is that, by default, it includes a gray band along the bottom called the *status bar* (not to be confused with the Status Area, which is the control strip at the left of each database window). The application status bar displays brief annotations about the function of different commands as you use the application.

## Building Advanced Interfaces  10

However, the information it provides is of use only to novices and, even then, scarcely justifies the amount of precious screen real estate it consumes. There is no equivalent for the status bar on the Mac.

> **TIP** You can turn the status bar on the application window off or on by choosing View ⇨ Status Bar.

A less obvious — but no less important — consideration regarding the way FileMaker works on Macintosh and Windows is the way dialogs work. On Windows, the general convention places the Cancel dialog button at the lower right of dialogs and other buttons (for example, the OK button — usually the default) to the left. However, FileMaker custom dialogs use the rightmost button as the default. Unless you choose dialog and button text with care, Windows users may find this inconsistency confusing.

**FIGURE 10.2**

The application window contains all FileMaker database windows on the Microsoft Windows operating system.

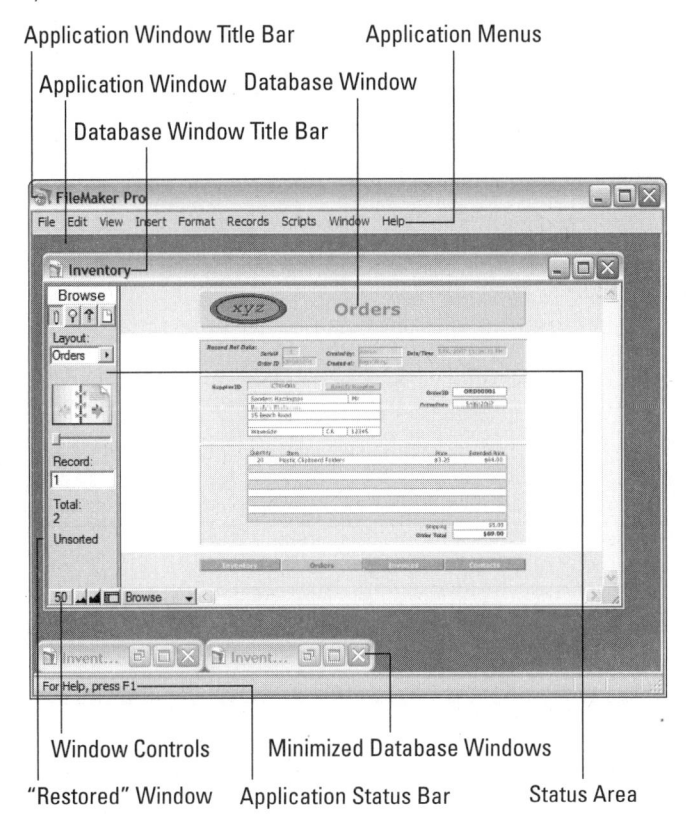

[Figure showing FileMaker Pro application window with labeled parts: Application Window Title Bar, Application Window, Database Window Title Bar, Application Menus, Database Window, Window Controls, "Restored" Window, Minimized Database Windows, Application Status Bar, Status Area]

313

# Using Dynamic Screen Elements

Computer users are accustomed to seeing interfaces change to reflect the currently available options or program state. Buttons light up when ready to be clicked or dim when not applicable. This is one way in which applications communicate their state to users. Even on the Web (commonly considered stateless), many sites devise ways to provide visual cues regarding state.

Because your solution's user experience is dependent on how well the interface communicates to the user, you need to provide visual cues about what's going on. How well you deliver an intuitive and appealing user experience depends on your command of dynamic interface techniques — ways of changing what users see to help them understand what's required or expected.

## Disappearing/reappearing objects

One key way to make your interfaces dynamic is to add or remove elements according to the current situation or context. For example, if your database only requires users to enter an e-mail address for contact records where the preferred communication method is e-mail, you may want to have the E-Mail field remain hidden except when E-Mail is selected in a `MethodOfContact` field.

There are a number of ways you can use FileMaker's interface tools to make things appear or disappear conditionally. In the following sections, we provide three examples.

### The portal invisibility trick

This technique has been around in a variety of forms for many years. It relies on the fact that, when a relationship is invalid (for example, if the key field on which it depends is empty), the contents of a portal depending on the relationship will not be displayed. If you apply transparent line and fill characteristics to the portal, neither it nor its contents will be visible until the relationship is established.

Using the example file from the previous chapter's Inventory layout, we can demonstrate the portal invisibility trick, displaying the Preferred Supplier tab's supplier details only when the user selects a valid value in the `SupplierID` field. To accomplish this, add a portal based on the `ItemSupplier` table, as shown in Figure 10.3.

Configure the portal to show a single row (Initial row: 1, Number of rows: 1). On the Preferred Supplier tab, size the portal just large enough to enclose the Supplier Details fields and label, position it behind the fields, and apply transparent line and fill.

When you return to Browse mode, you'll see that if you delete the value from the `SupplierID` field, the Supplier Details fields do not appear empty, as before. Instead, the fields and their label disappear completely, as shown in Figure 10.4.

# Building Advanced Interfaces 10

### FIGURE 10.3

Setting up a single-row portal on the Inventory layout.

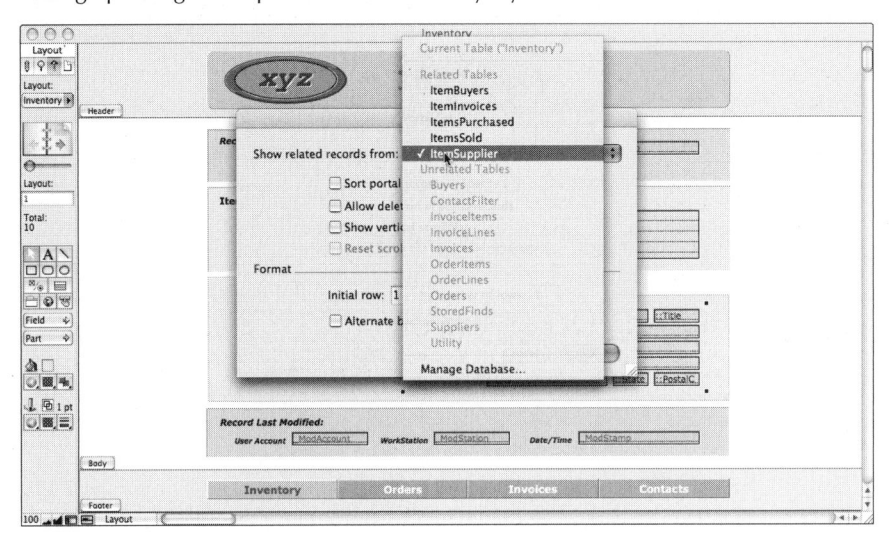

### FIGURE 10.4

Portal invisibility in action — hiding the Supplier Details fields until a SupplierID is entered.

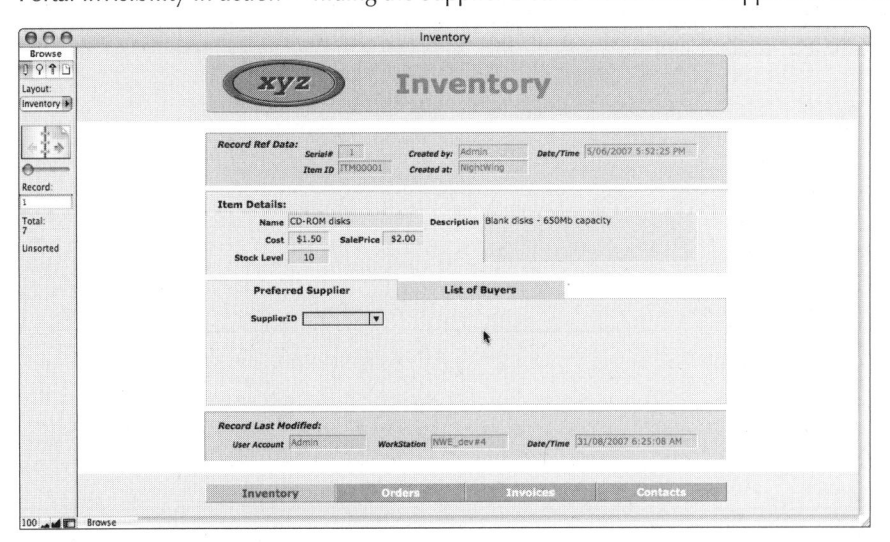

315

## Part III  Beyond the Basics

The portal trick described earlier has the advantage of being driven by the data — no separate action (by the user or by a script) is required to determine and apply the visibility state. Because it's possible to create a calculation field to use as the key field for a portal relationship to determine visibility, you can define calculation rules to determine the visibility of different layout objects

**CAUTION** Although the portal invisibility trick can be useful for occasional requirements, overuse can lead to undesirable clutter of additional calculation fields and relationships. The example described here has the advantage of leveraging an existing relationship and, therefore, has minimal impact on the solution.

### Concealed and remotely operated tab control

Another way you can control what appears when on your layouts is to provide a tab control that is remotely operated by scripts or buttons so that it changes to show (or hide) layout elements at will.

**NOTE** The visibility state created using a tab control object will only persist for the duration of the display of the current layout. When the user leaves the layout and returns, the layout will be presented in its default state. Moreover, the state of the tab control is not dependent on which record is displayed — if you require the state to change when the user navigates to a different record, a script will be required.

To implement this technique, follow these steps:

1. Add a tab control to your layout with two (or more) tab panels. Give the tabs brief names (such as numbers) to differentiate them and then click OK.

2. Select each of the tabs in turn and, via the Object Info palette (View ➪ Object Info), specify a unique object name. For example, if you're creating only two tabs, name them "invisible" and "visible," respectively.

3. Leave the first tab blank, but add the objects that you want to conditionally appear or disappear on the subsequent tab(s).

4. Apply a fill color to the tabs matching the layout background's fill color.

5. Select both tab panels, choose Format ➪ Size ➪ Custom, and enter a size of 1 point.

6. With the tab control selected, choose Format ➪ Tab Control Setup. The Tab Contol Setup dialog appears.

7. From the Tab Width pop-up menu at the lower right of the dialog, choose Fixed Width Of. In the field that appears below it, enter **0** and select Pixels from the adjacent measurement pop-up.

8. Still in the Tab Control Setup dialog, choose a default front tab from the pop-up menu at the upper right of the dialog, as shown in Figure 10.5. Select the tab you've assigned the "invisible" object name to if you want the tab contents to be invisible by default, otherwise select the other (another) tab as the default.

9. Click OK to accept the dialog settings.

10. Finalize the size and position of the tab control and its contents on the layout.

11. With the tab control selected, apply transparent line attributes and set the 3-D effects to None. After you make these changes, the tab will blend into the background.

# Building Advanced Interfaces   10

**FIGURE 10.5**

Setting up the tab control for tab width and default tab.

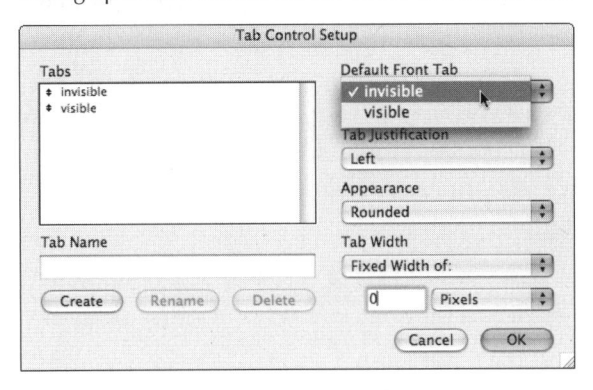

12. Create a script or button using the following command:

    `Go to Object [ "visible" ]`

    This displays the contents of the visible panel of the tab control.

13. Create a script or button using the command:

    `Go to Object [ "invisible" ]`

    This renders the contents of the tab panel invisible.

When these changes are complete, the scripts (and/or buttons) in your solution have control over the state of the tab control and will, therefore, display or hide its contents when appropriate.

One advantage this technique has over the portal-based technique is that, by using additional tabs, a number of alternate options can be invoked in the same area of the screen. Conversely, its chief disadvantage is that it requires scripted control to activate changes in the state of the tab control.

If you want to combine the flexibility of the tab control visibility approach with the comparatively automatic operation of the portal visibility technique, you may want to set up a script-triggering plug-in to allow you to define calculation rules that will call the script controlling your tab panels.

**CROSS-REF** For additional details about configuring and using plug-ins for script triggering and a range of other purposes, refer to Chapter 20.

## Using conditional formatting as a visibility control

In addition to the many possible variations of portal and tab control techniques for controlling object visibility, FileMaker 9 introduces a new set of options that, in some circumstances, provide an attractive alternative to the preceding techniques.

In the following section, we take a closer look at some of the ways you can use conditional formatting to achieve dynamic interface effects, including control of visibility.

317

## The hidden power of conditional formatting

FileMaker's conditional formatting options enable you to set up rules for applying formatting to text objects, including fields, buttons, and layout text. Using these options, you can configure FileMaker to make objects visible under specific conditions.

If you apply transparent line and fill characteristics to a text object, everything except the text it contains will be see-through. Similarly, if you set an object's font size to 1 point and choose a font color that matches the background, the object will disappear from view. When you subsequently apply conditional formatting to set the font color, font size, and/or fill color under specific conditions (determined via calculation), the object becomes visible according to the rules you've defined.

As an example of this technique, you may want to adapt the widely used Web form prompt of an asterisk next to required fields. Ideally, the asterisk should no longer appear after the field in question has a value. To achieve that using conditional formatting for the Inventory solution's SupplierID field, navigate to the Inventory layout and follow these steps:

1. Add a text object to the layout to the right of the SupplierID field and enter an asterisk (*).
2. Select the asterisk and choose Format ⇨ Size ⇨ 18 Point.
3. Choose Format ⇨ Conditional. The Conditional Formatting dialog appears.
4. Click the Add button and, in the Formula Is field, enter:
   IsEmpty(Inventory::SupplierID)
5. Select the Text Color checkbox and, from the adjacent color menu, choose a dark red, as shown in Figure 10.6.

### FIGURE 10.6
Applying conditional formatting attributes to an asterisk text object.

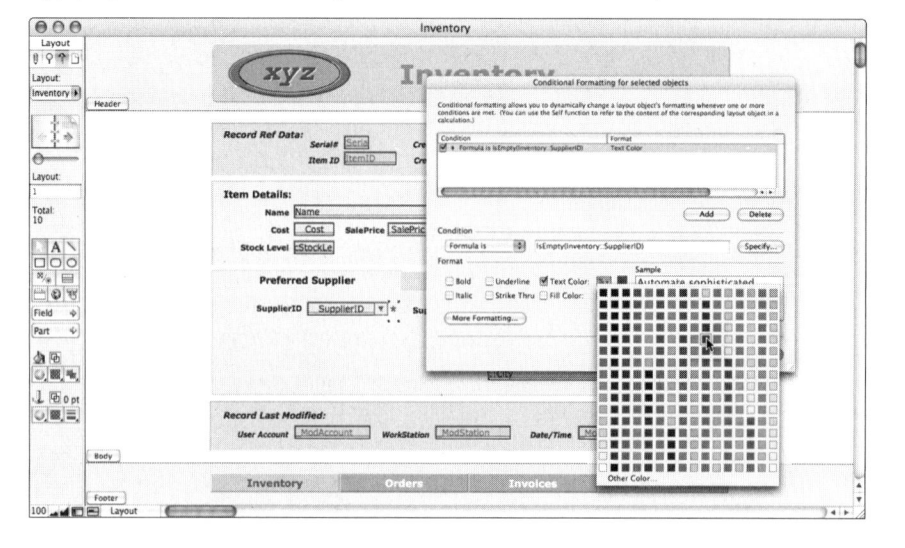

Building Advanced Interfaces | 10

6. Click the OK button to dismiss the Conditional Formatting dialog.
7. With the asterisk text object still selected, choose Format ➪ Text Color, and select a light gray to match the color of the tab panel behind the asterisk.

When these changes are complete, return to Browse mode and note that the asterisk appears when the SupplierID field is empty, disappearing when a value is entered or selected.

Using variations of this technique you can configure your solution's interface to direct the user's gaze to areas or elements on the screen requiring attention, post flags or messages, and/or highlight point(s) where the next data entry should occur. When you employ a thoughtful combination of measures of this kind, you achieve an interactive and adaptable visual interface, increasing the intuitive quality of the user experience.

## Multi-state buttons and objects

You can use variations of the technique outlined in the preceding section to create state-aware button objects that light up when the function they perform is available (and that otherwise dim). For example, a button that performs the Show All Records command after a Find has been performed will only be of use when a found set is in place. To have such a button light up when the user is viewing a found set and dim when all records are displayed, set default text and fill colors in pale gray with low contrast (for the dimmed state), and then specify conditional formatting to apply fill color and strong contrast (between text color and fill color), using the formula:

```
Get(FoundCount) < Get(TotalRecordCount)
```

With this condition in place, the button automatically lights up when one or more records are omitted, dimming again as soon as all records are returned to the display.

**NOTE** For an example of dynamically configured Show All buttons using the technique described here, refer to the lower-right corners of the OrderLines and InvoiceLines layouts in the copy of the Inventory example file for this chapter.

Similarly, you can use conditional formatting to change the appearance of background panels and dividers according to the current context. For example, a layout text object can readily be repurposed to provide a colored background panel in Find mode. This is a useful visual cue, reducing the likelihood that users will inadvertently attempt data entry in Find mode (and lose their work on returning to Browse mode).

A transparent text object placed at the back of the layout and formatted to apply colored fill with the conditional formatting formula creates a sharp visual delineation between Find and Browse modes:

```
Get(WindowMode) = 1
```

If, before applying transparent fill to the text object, you first apply a 3-D effect (such as engraving), the effect also becomes active when the fill color changes, further enhancing the drama of the effect.

319

# Working with Sub-Summary Parts and Part Controls

To enable you to group data and introduce summaries of the grouped data, FileMaker provides a special type of layout part called the Sub-summary part. Sub-summary parts only appear in Preview mode and only when the previewed data is sorted according to a particular field.

Using Sub-summary parts, you can instruct FileMaker to dice up a data set, presenting it grouped according to predetermined criteria — or even to dice your data multiple ways simultaneously (for example, to summarize by groups within groups in a hierarchical arrangement).

## Building adaptable screens

Clearly, not having to create a new layout for every version of a screen or report is preferable — and in many cases you don't have to do this. Two factors work in your favor, enabling you to create layouts that serve as both screen displays and versatile reports.

One of the keys to FileMaker's adaptability is its support for nonprinting objects. Select any layout object (or group of objects), choose Format ➪ Set Sliding/Printing, and, in the resulting dialog, enable the Do Not Print the Selected Objects checkbox, and you can determine what prints. This enables you to build a layout in layers, with the frontmost elements providing the screen view, yet disappearing in preview and print output to reveal the layer of items behind them.

This technique lets you provide graphically rich screens employing color and subtlety, yet produce clean and elegant grayscale printed output from the same layouts. Moreover, since Sub-summary parts operate dynamically to introduce summary data into the previewed and printed output, they add a further dimension of flexibility.

Sub-summary parts are associated with values in a sort sequence. When adding a sub-summary part to your layout, you're prompted to select a When Sorted By field, as shown in Figure 10.7. A leading Sub-summary part (one that's placed above the Body part) produces a heading above a group of records within the sort sequence with which it's associated, whereas a trailing Sub-summary part appears below each sorted group. You can have both a leading and trailing Sub-summary part associated with the same sort field.

## Stacking up multiple Sub-summary parts

FileMaker permits you to add multiple Sub-summary parts above and below the body part on your layouts. You may have two (one above and one below) for a given sort field, but you may add many additional Sub-summary parts associated with other sort fields. Each Sub-summary part remains dormant until the field with which it's associated is included in the sort order (and the layout is previewed or printed). Thus, by stacking up multiple Sub-summary parts, a single layout can be configured to provide a variety of alternate report formats dependent upon the current sort order.

# Building Advanced Interfaces    10

### FIGURE 10.7

Specifying the When Sorted By field for a Sub-summary part.

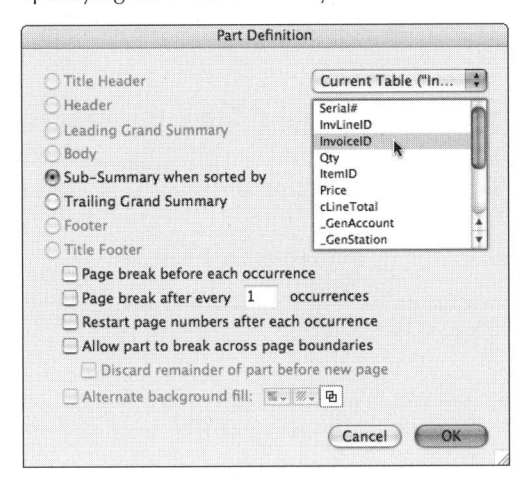

As an example, the Inventory database for this chapter has Sub-summary parts added to the OrderLines layout for both ItemID and OrderID sorts, as shown in Figure 10.8. In addition, the OrderLines layout has been reconfigured as described under the preceding heading, to print only some of the layout items, thus producing a clean and simple appearance when the layout is previewed or printed.

### FIGURE 10.8

Configuration of multiple Sub-summary parts on the OrderItems layout.

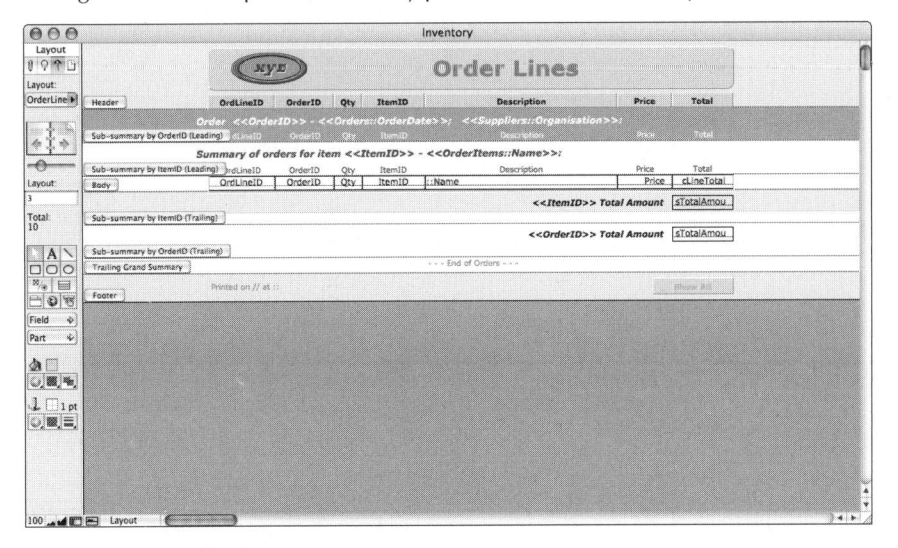

321

With the OrderItems layout so configured, the preview or print output can be broken out and summarized by either Orders or Items, simply by changing the sort order. You can see examples of layout previews showing the alternate options in Figures 10.9 and 10.10.

In the OrderLines layout, we chose to configure the appearance of the sub-summary parts for the two different sort configurations differently, so the reports previewed in Figure 10.9 and Figure 10.10 are distinct in appearance. However, you can choose to make the appearance of the Sub-summary parts identical if it suits the purposes of your solution.

**FIGURE 10.9**

A preview of the OrderItems layout sorted by ItemID.

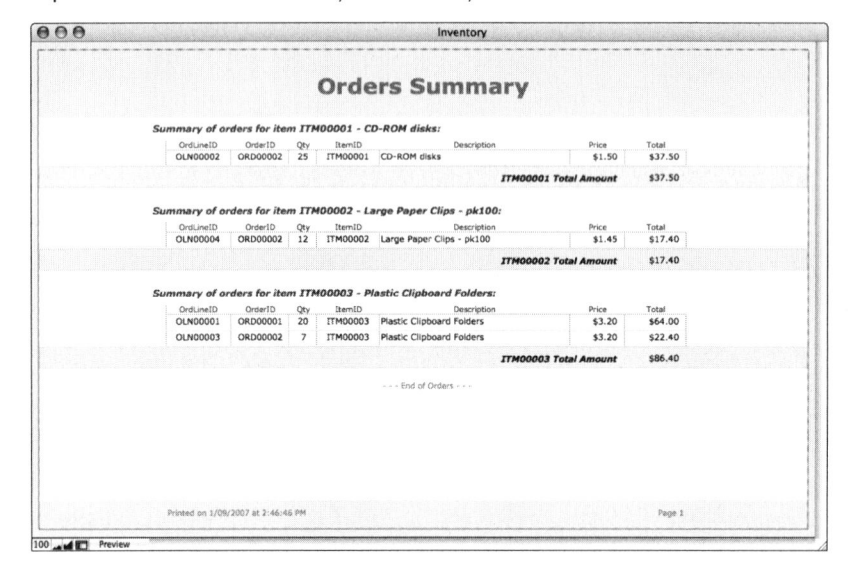

## Using multiple break fields

Sub-summary parts are included (in Preview mode and print output) whenever the field with which they're associated is included in the sort order. When you create sub-summary parts for multiple sort fields and then sort by multiple fields, FileMaker presents a hierarchical report break-out with group summaries nested within enclosing groups according to the order of precedence of the sort order.

# Building Advanced Interfaces

## FIGURE 10.10

A preview of the OrderItems layout sorted by OrderID.

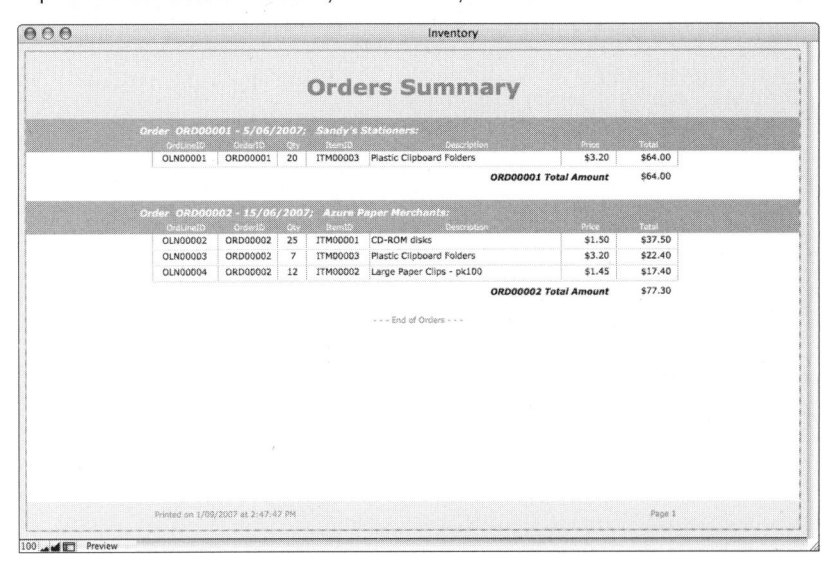

If, for example, you sort the OrderLines entries by ItemID and then OrderID, the result will be order summaries within each item summary. Conversely, by reversing the order of the sort fields, you can generate a tiered report that summarizes items separately within each order. Figure 10.11 shows the appearance of the OrderLines layout when sorted simultaneously by OrderID and ItemID (in that sequence).

As it happens, the dual-sort report in Figure 10.11 is not particularly useful — other than to illustrate a possibility. Rarely does an order have more than one line for the same item, so summarizing the items per order doesn't tell you anything. However, there are many other cases where it may be highly advantageous to produce a groups-within-groups summary report. For example, when a class of students has completed a series of assessment tasks each term, you'll want to be able to summarize each term's task results by student — and you may also want to summarize each student's task results by term.

Applying the logic of the preceding example, after creating sub-summary parts for term and student, the required reports would be achieved by sorting the data in the task results table by Term and then Student (for the first report) and by StudentID then Term for the second.

### FIGURE 10.11

A preview of the OrderItems layout sorted by OrderID and ItemID.

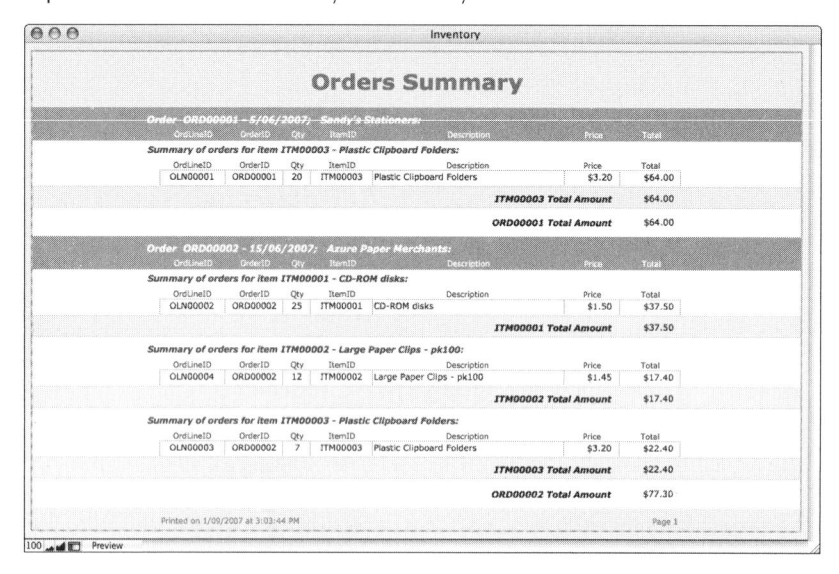

## Controlling pagination and page breaks

Using sub-summary parts in your layouts, in addition to controlling your reports' content and summary characteristics, also affords you a number of controls over where and how page breaks occur when your layout is prepared for preview and printing.

As shown in Figure 10.7, the part controls for pagination include

- Page break before each occurrence
- Page break after every *n* occurrences
- Restart page numbers after each occurrence
- Allow part to break across page boundaries
- Discard remainder of part before new page

The descriptions of these pagination controls are for the most part self-explanatory. However, keep in mind that these controls all relate to the position of page breaks with respect to parts — they don't give you control over the position of breaks relative to objects within parts. You need to make separate provisions to ensure that page breaks don't occur in the middle of a field or line of text.

When you specify a given report's or printout's paper size and orientation, adjust the size of the margin allocation and/or header and footer parts, so that the amount remaining for the body part (or other parts) is an exact multiple of the line height of the text you'll include on the layout. It may help to set the line height to a specific fixed value to ensure consistent behavior.

**Building Advanced Interfaces** | **10**

**TIP** To specify line height, select the relevant objects in Layout mode, and choose Format ⇨ Line Spacing ⇨ Custom. The Paragraph dialog will appear and, at its upper right, you'll find controls for line height. You can specify line height in lines, pixels, inches, or centimeters. When the height of all objects on the layout sums to a multiple of the line height you've determined, and the layout itself is also a multiple of the line height, you can be confident that page breaks will fall between lines.

**NOTE** The importance of designing complex print layouts to a height in multiples of the set line height forms a general rule for achieving clean/unbroken lines of text at page breaks. This "rule of multiples" becomes still more important when using sliding and reducing features, as described in the "Sliding objects and reducing parts" section, later in this chapter.

# Designing for Print

When preparing layouts for printing, consider the printed page as a cohesive whole, arranging elements on the page to direct the reader's eyes to the salient information. The factors making a printed report easy to read and understand are its simplicity, clean lines, use of white space separating distinct items, and the alignment and proximity of associated or related elements. FileMaker provides you with a number of techniques to assist you in creating clean and intelligible printed output, including the ability to determine which objects print (or are visible only onscreen), to control the size and placement of objects with sliding and reducing settings and techniques for merging data with static text.

## Non-printing objects

You can use FileMaker's setting for non-printing objects, a setting located in the Set Sliding/Printing dialog (Format ⇨ Set Sliding/Printing), shown in Figure 10.12, as part of the process of making adaptable layouts. For example, your screens may include various button objects for navigation or script control — objects that will serve only as a distraction on a printed report, so they should be set as non-printing.

**FIGURE 10.12**

Setting an object (or group of selected objects) as non-printing.

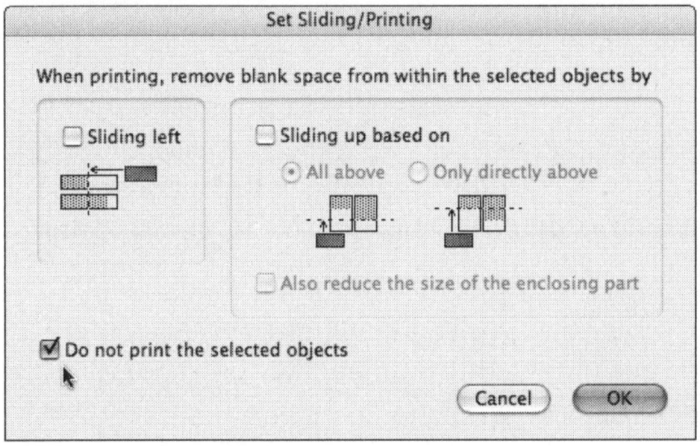

325

A further use of FileMaker's option for non-printing objects is to create alternate backgrounds for screen and print. Your screen designs will benefit from subdued, colored, or dark-toned backgrounds and may include graphical elements. By contrast, printed output generally serves best with light or white backgrounds and clear, open arrangement of elements.

> **TIP** To help you see at a glance which layout objects are set to print and which are not, choose View ⇨ Show ⇨ Non-Printing Objects. Objects set as non-printing will then be displayed with a screen border around them.

By creating layout objects to serve as screen backgrounds (for example, graphical rectangles) and setting them as non-printing, you can ensure your layouts show one background when viewed on screen but another when printed. Foreground objects set as non-printing are stripped away to reveal background elements more appropriate for print (especially monochrome print).

The header area of the layout pictured in Figures 10.8 and 10.9 is an example of this technique. The various items appearing in the screen display are eliminated from the print output to leave a clear and simple heading at the top of the page.

## Sliding objects and reducing parts

When setting out fields for screen display, it's customary to size them so they're large enough to show the largest amount of content likely to be entered. For example, if you'll be entering descriptions of up to four lines, you make the description fields four lines high so they show all the text. Although that works well for screen display, fields with fewer lines of text will leave the appearance of unwanted gaps when printed.

FileMaker enables you to configure fields to collapse, and the fields beneath (or to the right) to slide up (or across) to close unwanted gaps when the layout is previewed or printed. These settings are applied by selecting the relevant objects in Layout mode and choosing Format ⇨ Set Sliding/Printing. The resulting dialog (refer to Figure 10.12) includes separate controls for horizontal and vertical sliding.

> **TIP** As a reminder of which layout objects are set to collapse and slide, choose View ⇨ Show ⇨ Sliding Objects. Objects set to slide and remove white space will be identified with small black arrows on their right and/or bottom sides (according to the directions in which they're set to collapse and slide).

When objects are set to collapse and slide upward, an additional control labeled Also Reduce the Size of the Enclosing Part becomes available. Activating this option prevents blank pages from appearing at the end of a printout (or a section of a printout) where collapsing or sliding fields have been accommodated on a preceding page.

> **TIP** In order for a field or text object to collapse to the left, its contents must be left-aligned. Similarly, in order to collapse upward, an object's contents must be top-aligned. This applies to container fields as well as text objects.

# Building Advanced Interfaces    10

As an example, when printing a layout including names composed of a title, first name, and last name, you don't want the printed copy to include large gaps after each part of a name. Figure 10.13 shows a Browse mode view of fields arranged in columns with generous spacing—perfect for data entry, but less than ideal for a printed list (or an address on a letter and so on).

### FIGURE 10.13

Name fields in Browse mode—with ample room for long names.

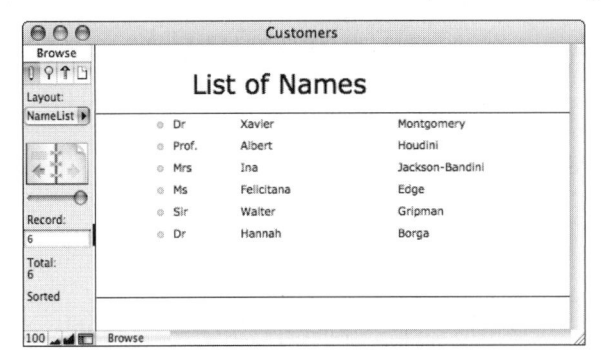

By selecting each of the fields in layout mode, choosing Format ⇨ Set Sliding/Printing, and setting the option to slide left, as shown in Figure 10.14, the fields can be configured to print their contents as a continuous line of text without gaps. Figure 10.15 shows the Preview mode appearance of the same layout, where you can see the effect of the sliding attributes.

### FIGURE 10.14

Name fields set to slide left to remove blank space.

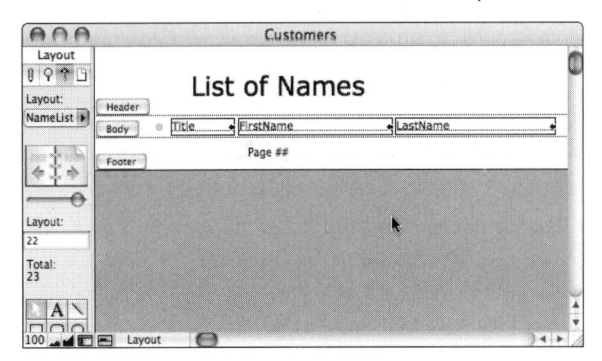

**FIGURE 10.15**

The result: Name fields sliding left to remove blank space.

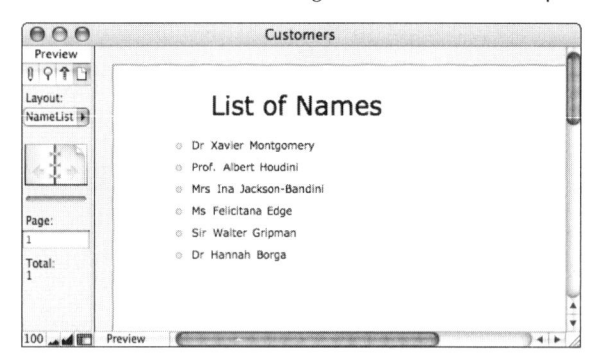

The careful application of sliding and reducing attributes helps you control field arrangement in printed output such as reports, labels, letters, invitation cards, and so on. However, although sliding deals with whole fields, it doesn't have the flexibility to combine blocks of text from multiple fields or text objects in a seamless way (for example, so that line wrapping will flow naturally throughout). For that, you require Merge fields (see the following section).

## Using Merge fields

Merge fields enable you to create layout text objects that include references to fields in the current record within the static text. Using this capability, standard text constructions can include dynamic elements such as names, amounts, addresses, dates, and so on.

To use Merge fields, first create a text object in layout mode, then choose Insert ➪ Merge Field (⌘+Option+M or Ctrl+M). The Specify Field dialog appears, prompting you to choose a field to insert into the current text object. After you select a field, it will be added at the cursor as a tagged reference enclosed in double angle brackets. The syntax for a merge field reference is:

    <<TableOccurrenceName::FieldName>>

**NOTE** The delimiters for a merge field are two successive left angle brackets, paired with two successive right angle brackets. Do not use the « and » single character quote marks — they aren't an acceptable substitute.

If the field you select is sourced from the table the current layout is based on, the field name is used for the Merge Field placeholder, but for all other cases the table occurrence name and the field name are required. Moreover, if you know the name of the table occurrence (if required) and the field, you can type the Merge field placeholder directly from the keyboard — you don't have to use the menu command for this purpose.

# Building Advanced Interfaces

**TIP** A Merge Field placeholder will be formatted according to the text formats (size, color, style, and so on) applied to the leading chevron bracket enclosing it (except where character formatting has been applied to the field contents of the referenced field—in which case the character formatting will take precedence).

In addition, FileMaker supports a number of generic text placeholders for system and contextual information, as follows:

// Resolves to the current date when the layout is displayed or printed

:: Resolves to the current time when the layout is displayed or printed

|| Resolves to the workstation user name when the layout is displayed or printed

## Resolves to the current page number when the layout is previewed or printed

@@ Resolves to the current record number (according to its current position in the found set or in the current portal display) when the layout is displayed or printed

**TIP** When a text object includes generic placeholders or Merge Fields including dates, times, timestamps, or numbers, you can control the format of the data when displayed by selecting the text object and choosing Format ⇨ Number, Format ⇨ Date, and/or Format ⇨ Time.

Merge fields and placeholders have a variety of uses; however, they have the limitation that they cannot be used to edit field data in Browse mode. Thus, they're suitable for displaying and printing data, but not as an editing interface. Consequently, merge fields are most frequently used on special-purpose layouts, such as generating form letters, certificates, or various formal documents.

## Creating a letter generator

Although merge fields provide a flexible way to create free-form letters using your database's data, they require a familiarity with Layout mode and high-level access privileges. As a developer or advanced user, you should have no hesitation creating or editing documents using layout text and merge fields. However, there are a few limitations:

- Solution users may not have the skills to make professional-looking letters in layout mode.
- If the data architecture of the solution is complex, users may have difficulty locating the appropriate fields and table occurrences to base merge fields on.
- Giving a large number of users access to creating or modifying your solution's layouts may be risky.
- If a lot of slightly different letters are required, over time the number of layouts required to accommodate them all may grow to unacceptable—or at least, unwieldy—levels.
- Layouts are not tied to specific records (only to a table occurrence), so they provide no indication which records were used to create which letters/documents or when.

If any of these issues are of concern, you require a different alternative — one that enables users to create letters dynamically without creating or editing layouts, meanwhile maintaining a record of the recipients of each letter. One way to achieve this aim is to set up a single letter layout where the text of the letter is supplied by a calculation field. You can then provide users with a letters table in which they can compose letters, using merge placeholders where they want to reference fields in your solution. Your calculation field (the one producing the letter text) can then perform a substitution to replace the merge placeholders with the appropriate field values for each record as the letters are printed.

When you structure your solution in this way, each letter will be stored in its own record in a letters table. Therefore, it is a simple matter to record in a separate table, such as, a join table, which contacts were sent which letters and on which date(s).

If your letters are stored in a field called MergeLetterText in a table named Letters — and if the text in MergeLetterText includes properly formatted field references in double angle brackets — you can use a calculation formula along the lines of the following to resolve the embedded placeholder tags, constructing the appropriate letter text for the current record in your Contacts table:

```
Evaluate("\"" & Substitute(Letters::MergeLetterText ; ["<<"; "\" & "]; [">>"; "
  & \""]) & "\"")
```

# Using Multiple Windows and Views

FileMaker enables you to display multiple windows showing the same or different views of a file's contents. Windows can be spawned manually by choosing Window⇨New Window or via button or script. In the latter case, your script can control the location and size of the displayed window, as well as selecting which layout to present to the user.

Given that you have a high degree of programmatic control over the scripted display of database windows, you can use them to perform the roles of pop-up information panels, graphs, auxiliary and drill-down displays of data, selection windows, detail windows, image viewers, and countless other related interface roles.

## Managing window placement and size

When you use the New Window[ ] script or button command to create a window, the options are available to set the window name, its height and width (in pixels), and its location. The location is also set in pixels, supplied as coordinates relative to the monitor's upper-left corner of the desktop area (Mac) or the Application window (Windows). You can enter each of these window parameters either as a literal value or as a calculation to be evaluated at runtime.

For example, if you specify the Distance from Top parameter using the following formula, the new window will be positioned 50 pixels farther from the top of the screen than the current active window:

```
Get(WindowTop) + 50
```

# Building Advanced Interfaces   10

Similarly, if you have specified the height and width of a window (for example, as 500 pixels wide by 300 pixels high) and want to locate the window in the center of the viewable desktop area of the user's monitor, you can do so using formulas for the Distance from Top and Distance from Left attributes as follows:

- Distance from top: `(Get(WindowDesktopHeight) - 300) / 2`
- Distance from left: `(Get(WindowDesktopWidth) - 500) / 2`

When these formulas are evaluated, they return the correct coordinates to center the 500 x 300 window on the user's monitor.

**CAUTION** When naming a window, bear in mind that window names are not required to be unique. However, if a window does not have a unique name, script commands will not be able to reliably select the window by name.

In addition to creating new windows at desired locations, you can move and resize existing windows, addressing them by their window names. This is achieved using the `Move/Resize[ ]` script or button command, using similar parameter options to those described for the `New Window[ ]` command. Similarly, the `Select Window[ ]` command brings a specified window (or the current window, if none is specified) to the front, making it active.

**NOTE** Parameters for size and location in both the `New Window[ ]` and `Move/Resize Window[ ]` commands are optional. If you don't specify a parameter, FileMaker makes no change to it. In the case of the `New Window[ ]` command, the result is that the window takes on attributes for size and/or location from the currently active window. However, where no window name is specified, the window name will be generated based on the active window name, but with a hyphen and incrementing number appended.

## Windows as pop-ups and drill-downs

FileMaker packs a lot of power and flexibility into the `Go To Related Record[ ]` command (GTRR), enabling you to locate related records, determine the Found Set, independently select a suitable layout, spawn a new window (or target the current window), and, if creating a new window, to set the name, position, and size of the new window and select it, all in one step. That's a lot of functionality in a tiny package.

Using the GTRR command, you can create simple layout buttons to move around your solution, including to spawn pop-up windows showing details or related data for content of a current screen, or drilling down into additional detail (showing the source data for an aggregate calculation and so on).

As a further example of the use of windows as pop-up "reveal' interaction elements, if you're storing images of products or people in your solution, it may be appropriate to display a thumbnail-sized image on the data-entry screen, configured so that clicking the thumbnail brings up a full-sized image in a window in the foreground of the user's monitor.

## Simulating modal window behavior

A common feature of computer interfaces is the *modal window* — a window or dialog that remains in front until the user takes an action to dismiss it. Most dialogs are modal, requiring a click on an OK or Cancel button before you can resume other activities. In some cases, you may want to have your database windows mimic modal behavior.

One of the ways developers achieve an effect similar to a modal window is by creating a new window in a script and terminating the script within a loop, so that the window will be held frontmost by the action of the script until the user cancels or takes some other action. The following script demonstrates the technique:

```
New Window [Name: "Select Item"; Height: 400; Width: 340; Top: 200; Left: 350]
Go to Layout ["Select Item" (Items)]
Show/Hide Status Area [Lock; Hide]
Loop
  Select Window [Name: "Select Item"; Current File]
  Pause/Resume Script [Indefinitely]
End Loop
```

With this script sequence in place, the new Select Item window is displayed and locked as the frontmost window until the user takes an action halting the script. You must, therefore, ensure that the displayed layout provides access to one or more buttons that will halt the looping script and restore control of the interface to the user.

**CAUTION** Although simulation of modal window behavior may provide a useful mechanism to guide the user, it should not be relied upon to enforce security. Various techniques (including the use of the Mac OS's Exposé feature) can be used to partially or fully circumvent a loop-locked window.

# Employing Custom Dialogs as an Interface Tool

Although harnessing database windows for a variety of dynamic interaction modeling techniques provides power and flexibility, simpler requirements can frequently be met by employing FileMaker's native custom dialogs. Custom dialogs can include a heading label, up to four lines of text, up to three buttons, and up to three input fields.

Providing standard and familiar interface techniques has a number of advantages — and users are familiar with the interaction models associated with dialogs. All computer users understand dialogs as alerts and as information entry prompts.

## Dialogs as a data-entry device

Using custom dialogs to accept input from the user requires using the input fields option. You configure these via the "Show Custom Dialog" Options dialog's Input Fields tab, as shown in Figure 10.16.

## Building Advanced Interfaces

### FIGURE 10.16

Configuring input fields via the "Show Custom Dialog" Options dialog.

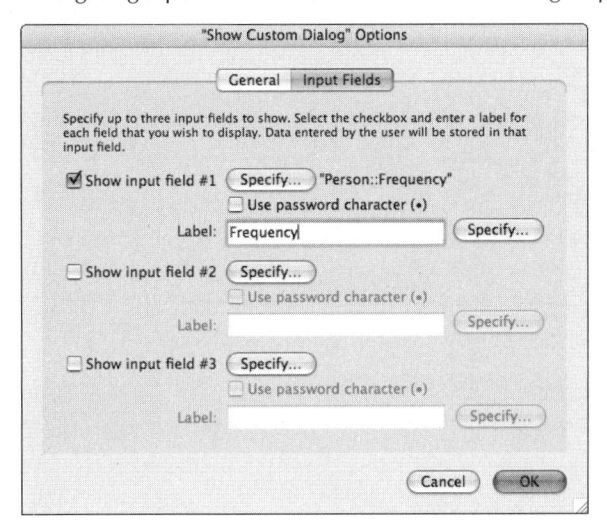

Custom dialog field input is always received as text, regardless of the data type of the fields selected to store the data. Moreover, standard data type error alerts will not be displayed when data is entered into fields via a custom dialog. When using dialogs, you must, therefore, perform your own checks for data type consistency.

Using global text fields to accept dialog input, and then performing data checks and conversions (if necessary) before writing the content into the appropriate fields in the current record, has some value. A single global text field with three repetitions (for example, located in a utility table in your solution) suffices for this purpose.

When using a script to present a dialog containing input fields, placing the dialog call within a loop with an exit loop condition based on a check for the presence of the required input is a common technique to confirm that data has been entered. A simple example of a script sequence achieving this is as follows:

```
If [IsEmpty(Person::Frequency)]
   Loop
      Show Custom Dialog ["Enter the contact frequency." Person::Frequency]
      Exit Loop If [not IsEmpty(Person::Frequency) or Get(LastMessageChoice) = 2]
   End Loop
End If
```

Note that the `Exit Loop If [ ]` condition includes the `Get(LastMessageChoice)` test to determine if the user has clicked Cancel.

**Part III**    **Beyond the Basics**

> **TIP** Data entered into a custom dialog's input field is discarded unless the user clicks the first button (the button appearing at the far right of the dialog) when accepting/dismissing the dialog.

### Dynamic dialog attributes

FileMaker's custom dialog's heading and message attributes can be determined by calculation. Thus, you can set them to reference fields in your solution, or to incorporate system variables such as time, account name, operating system, and so on.

To take advantage of the ability to set dialog attributes dynamically, click the Specify buttons in the General and Input Fields panels of the Show Custom Dialog Options dialog. A Specify Calculation dialog appears, and you can enter a formula to determine the text for use on the relevant dialog caption.

> **NOTE** Although heading, message, and field labels can be calculated, the fields themselves, plus the button text, must be specified in advance.

## Looking at Anchors and Resizable Layout Objects

Over the course of the past decade, computer users' experience with Web browsers and Internet content has increasingly influenced their expectations. Browsers are designed to reposition the content — and sometimes also resize it — according to the size of the browser window. The arrival of ever-larger-format monitors increases appreciation of this capability.

In some cases, resizing components of a database window makes sense (so a field accepting free-form text can be enlarged when there is a lot of text to read or enter/edit). Even when you think that there's no merit to resizing layout elements, you should consider setting window contents to maintain their position with respect to the center of the window.

### Objects that move according to window size

FileMaker provides a deceptively simple control mechanism for positioning and resizing layout objects, in the form of a set of four anchor checkboxes. These controls appear on the lower section of the Object Info palette (View ➪ Object Info). When you select an object in Layout mode (with the Info palette in display), its anchor settings are shown and can be modified.

By default, all layout objects are anchored to the top left. That means when you select an object and view its settings in the object Info palette, the default state is top and left anchors on, right and bottom anchors off, as shown in Figure 10.17.

334

## Building Advanced Interfaces   10

**FIGURE 10.17**

The default anchor state for all layout objects — anchored to the top and left.

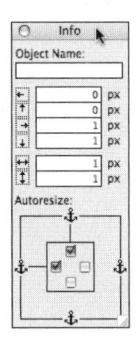

When you disable one or both of the default anchors, the selected object is free to move away from the edge of the layout to which it was anchored. This means that if the window is enlarged above the original layout size, the object moves in order to maintain an equal distance from the center (horizontal) or middle (vertical) of the layout area.

> **NOTE** The original size of the layout (used as the reference size to determine object moving and scaling) is based vertically on the combined height of the layout parts and, horizontally, on the distance from the left side of the layout to the right border of the rightmost layout object.

A layout's moving and resizing behavior in Browse and Find modes depends on the view format of the layout. When you set a layout to List view (View ➪ View as List), vertical resizing is disabled (enlarging the window exposes additional records instead of increasing the vertical size of records). When you set a layout to Table view (View ➪ View as Table), both vertical and horizontal resizing are disabled. Only in Form view (View ➪ View as Form) are both vertical and horizontal resizing (and repositioning) attributes activated.

> **NOTE** Vertical repositioning and resizing is applied to objects in all layout parts. However, if a layout part contains no objects set to reposition or resize vertically, that part will not resize. Layout parts containing objects set to reposition or resize are scaled proportionally in Browse and Find modes when the vertical height of the window is enlarged to a size greater than the combined height of all layout parts.

It's common to leave some "breathing room" at the left and right sides of your layouts. In other words, fields or labels are not positioned flush against the edges of the layout. When using repositioning and resizing (as when using the `Adjust Window [Resize to Fit]` command), you need a way to ensure that FileMaker respects the surrounding space at the right side of your layouts. One way to achieve this is to include an invisible object (for example, a graphical rectangle) at the right edge of the layout area you're using. This establishes a boundary that FileMaker respects when resizing windows and the objects they contain.

335

**TIP** We suggest that you use an empty text object to establish the right boundary. You can then format it to acquire the same fill color as the background except when in Layout mode (the conditional formatting formula to achieve this is `Get(WindowMode)` ≠ 4). This means that the boundary object will always be visible in Layout mode (so you can keep track of it) but not in other modes or in printed output.

## Objects that grow and shrink

When an object is simultaneously anchored to opposing edges of the layout (both top and bottom, or both left and right), it will increase in size as the size of the window exceeds the size required to accommodate the contents of the layout.

If your layout is area is configured to be 500 pixels wide (that is, the right edge of the rightmost object is 500 pixels from the left edge of the layout), the width of a window sized to exactly accommodate the layout (with the Status Area visible) will be 584 pixels on the Mac and 597 pixels (in a restored database window) on Windows. The difference of 13 pixels is due to the added size of the scroll bars and window borders on Windows.

When an object is anchored to both the left and right of the layout, its size will be increased in Browse and Find modes, when the window width exceeds the minimum width required to accommodate the layout. Given a layout width of 500 pixels, as described in the preceding paragraph, if the window size on the Mac is set to 600 pixels, an object anchored at both left and right will be increased in width by 16 pixels (600 − 584 = 16).

**CAUTION** Because the size increase of resizing objects is equal (rather than proportional) to the size increase of the window, adjacent objects anchored to opposing sides will overlap as the window size increases.

## Managing complex layout resizing

Multiple objects set to resize in the same direction, within the same area of the screen, will collide and overlap as the window size is increased. This may be ugly or disconcerting—but regardless, it compromises usability in most cases. It's incumbent on you to ensure that this sort of unintended side effect is avoided when resizing.

We recommend a "zoning" approach to the management of resizing—zones being arbitrary horizontal or vertical segments of your layout parts. Identify only one object to resize vertically within a given vertical zone and horizontally within a horizontal zone (you can choose to work with multiple notional zones if you want). To illustrate this approach, Figure 10.18 shows a layout comprising nine fields, in which, by using the zoning method, you should identify one column for horizontal resizing and one row to resize vertically.

When determining how to gracefully apply resizing properties to the fields in the example layout shown here, we first visualized the layout as comprising three horizontal zones and determined that one field within each zone would expand horizontally. We chose to set Field02, Field04, and Field09 as the horizontally expanding fields. In addition, we visualized the layout as comprised of three vertical zones and chose to apply vertical resizing to Field07, Field08, and Field09.

## Building Advanced Interfaces    10

**FIGURE 10.18**

An example layout of nine fields, at the minimum (default) layout size.

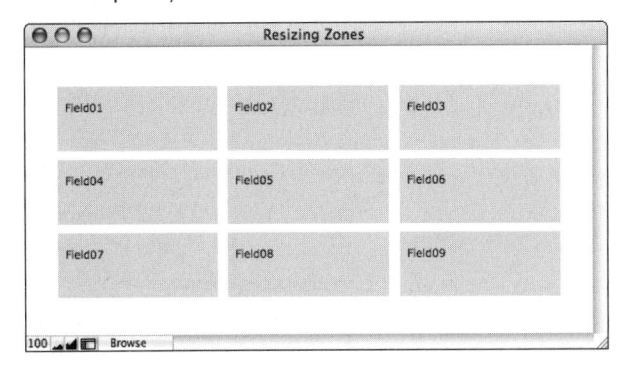

**NOTE**
When you've anchored an object to both left and right, all objects to the right of it should be anchored to the right and not anchored at the left; likewise, all objects to the left of it should be anchored to the left and not the right. This ensures that as the dual-anchored object increases in size, objects to the right of it will move across to accommodate it. Similarly, when an object is anchored at both the top and bottom, other objects below it in the same layout part should be anchored at the bottom and not at the top; likewise, all objects above it should be anchored to the top and not the bottom.

With the appropriate anchor properties applied, the fields resize as the window is enlarged, without colliding with one another, as shown in Figure 10.19.

**FIGURE 10.19**

Resizing according to the zone method to avoid overlapping objects.

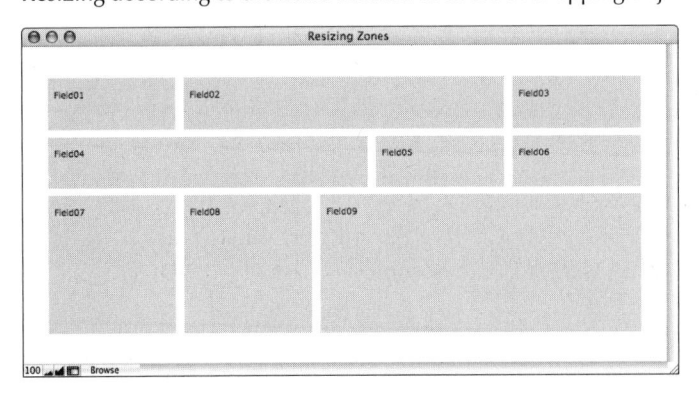

Although the zoning method allows you to design layouts that work within the resizing limits of FileMaker Pro 9, sometimes you may want to be able to resize all fields proportionally. Proportional horizontal resizing is not supported in FileMaker 9.

**337**

## Part III   Beyond the Basics

There is, however, a technique you can use for proportionally resizing fields vertically in a Form view screen layout. Because sub-summary parts are displayed in form view, different "zones" can be assigned to sub-summary parts. A modified version of the file used as the example for this section is pictured in Figure 10.20, showing the application of this technique to provide proportional vertical resizing to all nine fields.

> **CAUTION** The proportional vertical resizing technique described here is best suited for layouts that will not be used for printing, because further work would be required to ensure that layout parts used to control resizing appear in printed output (and in a desired sequence).

**FIGURE 10.20**

A workaround to achieve proportional vertical resizing for a screen-only layout.

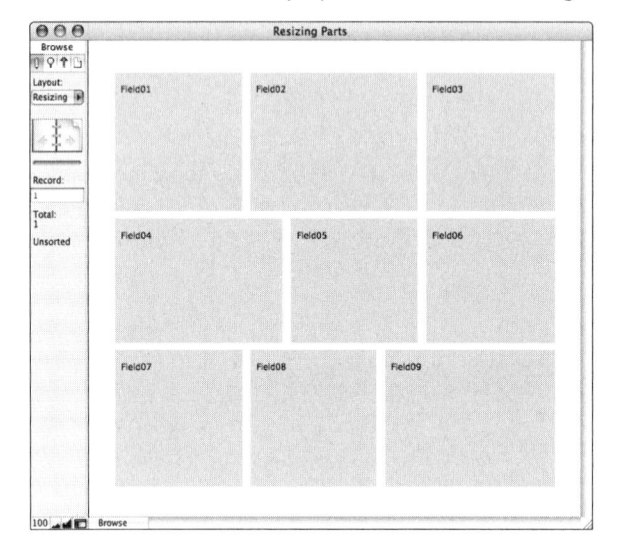

## Resizing behavior of enclosing objects

Unlike other layout objects, tab controls and portals influence the behavior of the objects they enclose. The first thing to note is that when an object is placed within a portal or a tab control object, its anchor settings no longer refer to the edges of the layout. The object is, instead, anchored to the boundaries of the enclosing object. Thus, objects within an enclosing object inherit (or are limited by) the anchor properties of the enclosing object.

Additionally, portals exhibit different vertical resizing behavior depending on the anchor properties of the objects within them. If all the objects within a portal are anchored to the top (but not to the bottom) and the portal is anchored to top and bottom, when the portal height increases it will display additional rows. However, if any items within the portal are anchored to the bottom and/or not anchored to the top (that is, set to move or resize vertically) the portal rows will increase in height rather than number: The number of rows will remain constant and their sizes will increase proportionally as the portal is enlarged.

# Building Advanced Interfaces | 10

## Centering objects within the viewable area

By disabling the anchors on opposing sides, an object is treated by FileMaker as being anchored to the center of the viewable area of the layout (or, vertically, to the layout part). For example, this setting allows you to ensure that a heading remains in the center of the header part when increasing the window size.

Similarly, if an object in the body part has all its anchors disabled, it will float free and remain equidistant from the center (both vertically and horizontally) of the body part as the window is enlarged above the size required to accommodate the layout.

Although this technique does not increase the usability of individual layout objects in the way that resizing may, it can contribute to the sense of balance, aesthetic appeal, and/or dynamism of your solutions. This is clearly evident if you open an old solution designed for a small format (for example, 800 x 600) monitor and set to maximize on startup. On a modern, large-format monitor, the blank area at the right and bottom of the layout dwarfs the small usable area at the upper left. Centering objects in the usable area of the window allows your solutions to transition between screens of different sizes more gracefully.

**NOTE** For examples of object centering, repositioning, and resizing, see the layout header and footer objects in the Inventory example for this chapter. If your monitor is not large enough to increase the window above the layout size, you'll be able to view the effect by zooming the layout to 75 percent or 50 percent.

# Implementing Shortcut Navigation

A well-configured relational database manages the connections between all the components of your data. Items having relationships to other items are intrinsically connected to them via the solution's structures.

Why not exploit the structure of the relationships in your solution to provide navigational pathways from one place to other related places? Instead of requiring the user to laboriously exit from an invoicing screen, then navigate into the products module and search for a product to view its record, why not allow the user to jump directly to any product that appears on any invoice? If you set your solutions up appropriately, the schema can serve as a network of "rabbit holes" for the user to jump through.

## The power of the Go to Related Record command

In Chapter 9, we describe in detail the implementation of jump buttons for shortcut navigation using the Go to Related Record [ ] command (GTRR), and earlier in this chapter (in the "Windows as pop-ups and drill-downs" section) we looked at some other applications of the same command.

Instead of providing isolated and idiosyncratic navigation options, well thought out use of the GTRR command can provide a central and essential framework for navigation of your solution. Each instance of a GTRR saves users multiple steps versus conventional navigation methods.

## Part III   Beyond the Basics

An important option that GTRR provides is its ability to isolate a group of records within a found set on a layout associated with the related table (that is, the table where the related records are stored). The resulting found set can be presented to the user in the current window, in a new window, or in another file (if the related table is stored elsewhere). This effectively enables you to "find" a group of records without using Find mode.

Equally important is the ability of the GTRR command to transfer found sets between layouts based on the same underlying table (but on different table occurrences). If you've performed a find to locate a subset of records on the current layout, you can use any other layout associated with a TO that (in turn) is associated with the same base table, to view the found set, by using GTRR to navigate to the desired layout.

## One interface, many paths

Sophisticated computer users are aware that there are multiple ways to access many computer features. Menus, buttons, keyboard shortcuts, and so on all provide access to the same commands. Similarly, in your solutions, alternative mechanisms should be available to move from one point to another. In the interest of both utility and ergonomics. you should provide your solutions' users with alternatives suitable to different work processes and styles.

When your solution navigation is designed ergonomically and paths through layouts and records are intuitive and follow work processes and business rules, users will rely less upon FileMaker's Status Area tools and will use Find mode less frequently.

**CROSS-REF** For further discussion of the design and implementation of navigation and menu structures for your solutions, refer to the "Using Interface Elements" section, later in this chapter.

## Building Back button functionality

Something all users of the Internet rapidly learn is the value of being able to go back. Providing similar functionality in FileMaker, however, may require that your solution keep a log of where the user has been in relation to both layouts and records.

One relatively straightforward way to achieve an automatically updating log of where the user has been is to set up an unstored calculation to capture the current context and append it to a global variable. This can be done with a calculation along the following lines (where CurrentTable::Serial# is a reference to the primary key in the current table):

```
Let([
Sn = CurrentTable::Serial#;
Bn = ValueCount($$trace);
Vc = GetValue($$trace; Bn);
Sc = RightWords(Vc; 1);
Lc = LeftWords(Vc; WordCount(Vc) - 1);
La = Get(LayoutName);
$$trace = $$trace & If(Sn ≠ Sc or La ≠ Lc; Left(¶; Bn) & La & " " & Sn)];
"")
```

## Building Advanced Interfaces

Such a calculation would be required in every table on which a user-accessible layout is based—and although empty, the field would be required to be present on each layout (it may, however be both invisible and inaccessible). This method is seamless in operation, automatically capturing a history of navigation steps between both records and layouts, regardless of the method(s) the user uses to move around your solution.

> **TIP** If your solution includes fields that calculate values for display (for example, navigation text or the current user/account name, and so on), the `$$trace` calculation could readily be combined with an existing calculation.

When a mechanism is in place to capture user navigation, a single script, structured as follows, can be used to return through the list of previous locations in your solution:

```
If [ValueCount($$trace) < 2]
 Beep
Else
 Set Variable [$PrevCtxt; Value:GetValue($$trace; ValueCount($$trace) - 1)]
 Set Variable [$LastLayout; Value:LeftWords($PrevCtxt; WordCount($PrevCtxt)-1)]
 Set Field [Utility::gTrace_key; RightWords($PrevCtxt; 1)]
 Freeze Window
 Go to Layout ["-" (Utility)]
 If [$LastLayout = "Inventory"]
  Go to Related Record [From Table:"Inventory_trace"; Using layout:$LastLayout]
 Else If [$LastLayout = "Orders"]
  Go to Related Record [... ]
  # etc
 End If
 Set Variable [$$trace; Value:Let(Nt = LeftValues($$trace; ValueCount($$trace) -
   1); Left(Nt; Length(Nt) - 1))]
End If
```

The technique as presented here requires a utility relationship for each base table in the solution and a single corresponding GTRR command in the script to invoke the relevant relationship.

> **NOTE** A working example of Back button functionality has been implemented in the accompanying Inventory example file for this chapter.

## Building Depth and Dimensionality

A long time ago, humans discovered that the world is not flat. But even before that discovery, people's minds were wired for three dimensions. Humans are geared for spatial concepts and understand the world in terms of three-dimensional space.

When you use a computer, your understanding and experience aid the interpretation of what the monitor presents to you. Thus, the best computer interfaces are those you perceive as metaphors for tangible objects and mechanisms you've encountered in the world around you.

341

## Using embossing and engraving effects

The embossing effect (available in an elementary form on FileMaker's 3-D effects pop-up menu in Layout mode) provides a simple but effective illusion of depth, creating the appearance of a foreground and background, introducing the semblance of spatial and even tactile qualities to the screen image. As embossing raises, engraving recesses — and stacked (nested) 3-D objects increase the perceived layers of depth.

Although the effect is a simple visual illusion, things that appear raised (with embossing) have the illusion of inviting you to press on them — like buttons — or intruding upon you like neon signs or placards. Conversely, engraved objects carry the illusion of depth, inviting you to enter or suggesting interior or enclosed spaces. Moreover, engraved objects enclosed inside other engraved objects appear to take you additional layers inwards, suggestive of hierarchical structures.

For added impact, you may also want to create an embossed or engraved effect for key text elements in your interfaces. Although FileMaker does not directly support embossing and engraving effects for text objects, you can produce such effects using native layout text objects by duplicating the object, stacking the duplicate atop the original, shifting it 1 pixel left and 1 pixel up, and changing its hue (darker for engraving, lighter for embossing). Alternatively, you can add text effects in a third-party program and import the results.

**CAUTION** We recommend that imported graphics be optimized and used sparingly, to avoid unduly enlarging file sizes or impacting solution performance. This is a significant consideration for solutions that will be remotely hosted.

## Spatial cues for added meaning

The illusion of depth enhances your perception of a screen layout in several ways. The simplest of these is the way in which it tricks the eye — the illusion helps reduce the fatigue associated with long periods viewing flat objects at close range. Equally important, it taps into spatial associations, assisting you to visualize the relationships between groups of objects — it invokes spatial metaphors and, thus, makes screen arrangements easier to view and easier to interpret.

Careful and consistent use of protruding objects and receding or enclosing spaces creates a much stronger sense of separation and spatial relationships than any flat lines and borders could. This can aid the comprehension of information being presented. Understanding how these tools work is the first step to using them effectively when designing interfaces for your solutions.

## Delineation of element groups

Engraved areas of the screen create catchments within which you naturally understand elements to be grouped in a relationship. An additional level, or tier, of engraving can enhance this effect; however, employing more than two levels begins to lose impact and risks complicating rather than simplifying the visual order being imparted.

Similarly, one or (at most) two levels of embossing can enhance the perceived order and separation of elements in a layout. Moreover, embossed elements, seeming closer to the user, take on a more present, urgent, or immediate quality.

## Color

Bright colors grab attention and impress themselves vividly upon your eyes. Thus bright colors are best reserved for those screen elements the user should see first, the ones that are most urgent or important.

Overuse of strong or bright colors creates an impression of conflict and competition and is visually fatiguing. An overly bright (or overly strong colored) screen may seem loud and/or angry. Conversely, softer tones are less fatiguing but also leave a fainter impression. Ideally, a screen should contain a few splashes of color (used to draw the user's eye to key elements) among ordered and more subdued elements.

The use of clean subtle lines throughout your interface provides maximum scope for emphasis of key elements and alerts, while serving to gently guide the user. After you have the user's attention, you don't need to keep shouting (and it's better if you don't). We recommend the use of coordinated themes of subtle tones and backgrounds, with one or two brighter colors for emphasis and contrast.

## Transparency and translucency

Although FileMaker's native graphic elements are basic, imported graphics are supported in a range of formats. These include support for translucent and transparent effects in formats such as PNG (Portable Network Graphics, an Internet graphic standard). Judicious use of graphics and visual effects created in third-party graphics environments can significantly extend and enhance the visual appeal of your FileMaker interfaces.

> **TIP** To preserve the integrity of translucent and transparent images in supported formats, choose Insert ⇨ Picture in Layout mode. Images pasted from the clipboard will not retain these properties.

Including graphical elements can also increase the tactile and dimensional quality of your screens, introducing subtle shadows and light effects. This sort of subtle touch lends a strengthened illusion of depth and space, reinforcing the spatial metaphors throughout your interface.

However, avoid excessive use of graphical elements in the interest of maintaining performance, particularly over busy network connections. For best performance, optimize your graphics for smallest size, and after inserting once, duplicate the graphic within FileMaker, pasting copies to other locations. FileMaker stores a single library copy of the graphic and references it elsewhere, thus reducing the resources required to download and display interface images.

The example Inventory database for this chapter includes several imported graphical elements (in PNG format) to add shadow, light, and enhanced depth and dimensionality to the screens.

# Working with Tab Controls

In addition to designing your screens to form data into logical groups and present the user with a natural sequence of information, it's important to avoid presenting too much information at once. Clutter is problematic because the user's focus becomes lost.

**Part III**  Beyond the Basics

One solution to the problem of clutter is to spread information out over a larger number of screens. However, this introduces a different problem—fragmentation. An alternative solution that avoids either problem is to nest data within a single screen, keeping data out of sight until it's needed. Tab controls provide an elegant way to achieve that aim.

## Organizers and space savers

FileMaker's tab controls can be as large as the layout or as small as a postage stamp. They can work side-by-side in multiple arrays. Tab control panels can contain any combination of other objects including fields, Web viewers, portals, or other tab controls. If you place tab controls inside other tab controls, your layouts will be capable of holding large amounts of data in an ordered hierarchy, while presenting the user with a clean and simple interface design.

The hierarchical principle introduced by tab controls is a familiar way of creating order, and your users will instinctively understand. Just as buildings have levels that contain apartments that contain rooms that contain cupboards that contain drawers, your solutions can organize information into multiple levels of order. As long as the allocation of data to each place in a hierarchy makes simple and logical sense, your users will have no difficulty grasping the principle and locating the data they need.

## Tab navigation via keyboard

By default, tab controls are mouse-driven. However, you can include a tab control into the layout tab order, so that users can select it using the keyboard tab key, just as they can move between fields on your layouts (see Figure 10.21).

When a tab control has been added to the layout tab order:

- The first (or default) tab becomes selected when the user tabs to the tab control.
- The right arrow and left arrow keys will select alternate tabs across the top of the selected tab control.
- The Return key or the space bar will bring the currently selected tab to the front.

## Scripting tab operations

Alternatively, you can provide scripted navigation to take users directly to a specific tab on a given layout. To do this, you must first select the tab panel in layout mode (the tab area of the panel will become outlined in black when it's selected), and assign an object name via the Object Info palette. After you've named the panel, you'll be able to script the selection of a specific tab with a sequence such as:

```
Go to Layout ["YourLayout"]
Go to Object ["YourTabPanel"]
```

Similarly, you can build custom menus including menu commands (using FileMaker Pro Advanced) to take the user to specific tabs. To achieve this, a script such as the preceding one should be assigned to a menu selection.

## Building Advanced Interfaces | 10

**FIGURE 10.21**

Assigning a tab control to the layout tab order so it can be selected via the keyboard.

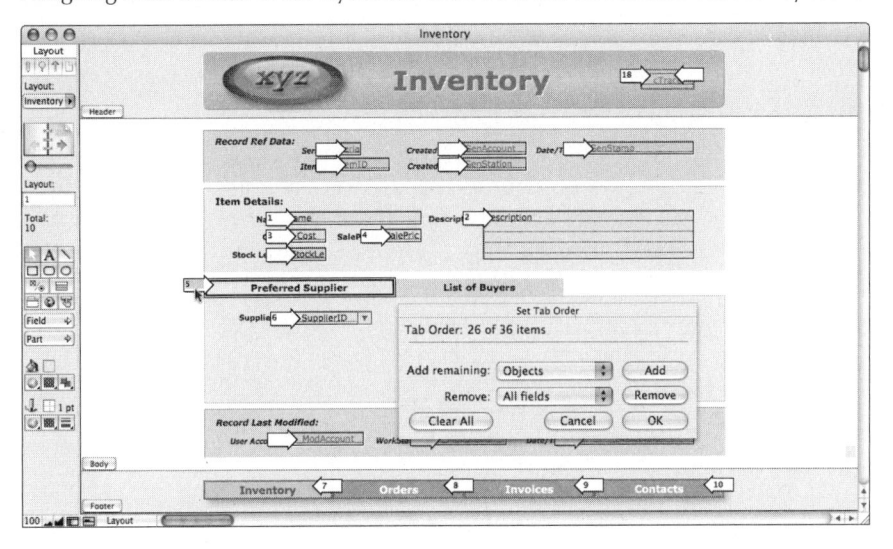

**CROSS-REF** For additional information about the use of FileMaker Pro Advanced features such as custom menus, refer to Chapter 18.

# Recognizing the Flexibility of Portals

FileMaker's portal object is a powerful tool — providing you with the ability to create windows into alternate spaces in your solutions, using them to combine data from multiple tables within a single layout. Portals are also adaptable, enabling you to implement them in a variety of different ways according to the needs of your solution.

## Lists in many guises

By default, FileMaker portals present a range of records from a related table, appearing in a continuous list. However, you can specify a commencing row for a portal (other than the first related record), thus creating portal editions and displaying noncontiguous record sets.

Portals can include a scroll bar, configurable to snap back to the first related record (or first record for the current portal) when the record is exited, or to remain at the scrolled position. When the scroll bar option is disabled, a portal presents a fixed list of a predetermined number of related records.

By using multiple portals in conjunction with a tab panel, portal displays can be paginated. For example, the first 20 records can be shown on one tab, records 21 to 49 on a second tab, and so on. This can provide a more convenient interface for addressing related records in defined ranges.

345

## Portals as a navigation device

A portal row can contain a button so that clicking the row (or a button at the edge of the row) executes a GTRR command, navigating to the relevant record on another layout. This navigation technique is useful for moving the user between related locations in your solution. By providing a portal based on the current table (for example, via a self-join relationship), a portal can provide an efficient navigation tool for the current table.

When displaying records from the current table in a portal, you should consider how to treat the portal display of the current record. One option is to configure the portal to display all records except the current record. Another option is to display all records and highlight the current record in the portal.

To omit the current record from a self-join portal, you should structure the relationship as a *Cartesian product* (one where all records in the first table are matched with all records in the second table, regardless of the value in the match fields), with an added predicate for a nonequal join matching the primary key to itself. This compound join criterion will be expressed in the relationship definition as the following (where `TableID` is the primary key for the current table):

```
          TableID      ×     TableID
   AND    TableID      ≠     TableID
```

Alternatively, to highlight the current record in a self-join portal, you first need a method to capture and declare the ID of the current (displayed) record. One such method is to include an expression declaring a global variable (setting it to the primary key of the current record) and including the expression within an object set to evaluate as the layout (displaying the current record) is drawn onscreen. The calculation can be included in an unstored calculation field displayed on the layout, in a Web viewer, or in a conditional formatting argument. The form of the expression declaring the variable will be:

```
Let ($$ActiveRecord = YourTable::TableID; "")
```

After the mechanism for capturing the ID of the active record is in place, you can set a conditional formatted object to highlight the portal row with the following formula:

```
$$ActiveRecord = PortalTO::TableID
```

**NOTE** The layout object being used to capture the ID of the current record should be set at the back of the layout's stacking order so that it's drawn first, ensuring that its calculation expression is evaluated (and the `@@ActiveRecord` variable instantiated) prior to evaluating the conditionally formatted object highlighting the portal row.

## Dynamically sorted portals

A variety of methods are available for setting up dynamic portal sorting. One of the easiest to configure involves the use of a tab control and a series of portals, each configured with a different sorting criterion.

By setting the tab control's tabs to match the columns and column widths of the portal, the tabs can serve as portal heading labels. Multiple copies of the portal can then be positioned within each panel of the tab control and adjusted to present the related records in the appropriate order. The result is an efficient portal sorting mechanism that's implemented in a matter of minutes.

## Innovative portal implementations

Occasionally, a conventional list of related records is a less-than-ideal way to view or interact with related data. For example, calendars are customarily viewed in grids with one week occupying each block in sequential rows of data.

Displays of data requiring grids or matrices call for a little extra ingenuity (and some additional work) in implementing portals on your layouts. To create the effect or a horizontal portal or grid, you can add a series of single-row portals each starting with a different related row. Thus each separate portal shows one row — a different row — of the data in the related table. These separate "cells" of related data can then be arranged in whatever configuration you choose — according to the seating plan of a theater, according to a calendar of the lunar cycles, according to the grid positions of a football team. . . . All these things and more are possible.

# Using Advanced Web Viewer Techniques

In Chapter 6, we introduce the concept of using Web viewers as a way to extend your solution's scope, providing a window into related online information from a company's own Web site or from other online resources. The Web viewer has a number of other potential uses.

Because FileMaker's Web viewer taps directly into the same operating system resources as Web browsers, it provides access to the range of Web-compliant technologies including HTML, JavaScript, CSS, Flash, and others. If you have skills in these or other related areas, the Web viewer allows you to exploit them, and even if you don't, the Web viewer still lets you tap into the vast collections of Internet resources made available by others. We don't propose to go into these fathomless possibilities in great detail — that's not the focus of this book (and there are boundless resources available if you need to explore Web technologies). However, we would like to outline the scope of this FileMaker feature.

## Access to advanced functionality

The FileMaker Web viewer can load and display Web-compliant code objects and widgets created using Flash, JavaScript, or other technologies, without needing to load them from a remote site — they can be stored locally. The most obvious way to achieve this is to reference objects as resources stored on a local hard disk. Moreover, FileMaker 9 enables you to store resources as data and output them at startup to the `Temp` directory on the current computer. To script this process, you can use the following code (where `gSWFresource` is a global container field holding a resource file — in this case, a Flash file — that you want to export with the filename, `Resource.swf`, into the Temp directory):

```
Set Variable [$path; Value:"file:" & Get(TemporaryPath) & "Resource.swf"]
Export Field Contents [Utility::gSWFresource; "$path" ]
```

You can use this technique to make a variety of resources available, including images, to be referenced via Web viewers in your solutions.

After you've created the required resources locally, they can be referenced directly (for example, in a Web viewer) by dynamically inserting path references as URLs, using a calculation construction such as:

```
"file:/" & Get(TemporaryPath) & "FileName.xtn"
```

Using these supporting techniques, you can configure a Web viewer to address local resources as well as remote URLs. The ability to so configure a Web viewer becomes much more useful and powerful when you embed references to local or remote resources into source content that your solution generates on demand.

## Rendering internally calculated content

When you load a URL into a FileMaker Web viewer, the content of the file at the specified location is retrieved, interpreted, and rendered in the Web Viewer. However, FileMaker 9 makes it possible for you to generate content within FileMaker and pass it directly to the Web viewer. For example, you could store the text content of a page of HTML in a text field and have the Web viewer display it.

To pass content directly to the Web viewer (rather than a URL pointing to the location of some content), you need to employ the data URL protocol. Assuming you've placed the text of a fully formed HTML page in a field called Content in a table in your solution called ViewerData, you're able to load the page into a Web viewer by specifying Web viewer address as follows:

```
"data:text/html," & ViewerData::Content
```

Because you're calling upon FileMaker's calculation engine to form the syntax of the content to be displayed, however, you can manipulate the HTML source via calculation, or combine elements from a number of fields for the definition of the page to be displayed. For example, to produce a fully formed HTML report based on a tagged report template stored in a global field in your solution, you can use a calculation such as the following:

```
"data:text/html," &
Substitute(SystemData::gReportTemplate;
["«Heading»"; SystemData::CompanyName & " Report"];
["«ReportYear»"; Year(Get(CurrentDate))];
["«Preamble»"; ReportData::Notes]
["«QuarterSum»"; ReportData::QuarterlyRevenue]
["«YTD»"; Sum(Income::AmountReceived)]
["«Projected»"; Sum(Budget::Income)]
)
```

This approach takes a basic, premade page layout (complete with hypertext formatting, links, images, and other content), inserts relevant data from your solution, and passes the result to be displayed in your Web viewer. Moreover, the content of the Web viewer is then linked live to your data via the calculation engine — so in the preceding example, if a staff member on the next floor processes an additional payment, you'll see the Year to Date amount on your dynamic report change to include the additional amount.

Although this example is relatively simple, you can apply the same principles to dynamically modify almost every aspect of the content of a page to be displayed in a Web viewer. You can use variations on this approach to create and display live graphs of your data, dynamic summaries, diaries, calendars — essentially any formatted representation of information in your solution.

## Scraping data from Web pages

In addition to enabling you to create displays and render data by sending information directly to the Web viewer, FileMaker provides tools you can use to retrieve data from the Web viewer and store it in fields in your solution. This is the process commonly known as *Web scraping*.

Before attempting to retrieve data from a Web page on a remote Web site, you must first provide the URL of the page you want to "scrape" and ensure it has fully loaded into a Web viewer in your solution. To start the process, begin a script with a command to load the required Web address, such as the following:

```
Set Web Viewer [Object Name: "YourViewer"; URL: "http://www.RemoteSite.com"]
```

If you attempt to retrieve the content of the Web viewer before the page has fully loaded, you may either get nothing or get only part of the page source. To ensure that the page has fully loaded, pause and check for the presence of the closing body tag (`</body>`) before proceeding. In case the Internet connection fails or the remote site is not available, you'll require a timeout. Here's an example of a script sequence implementing the required pause and check:

```
Set Variable [$start; Value:Get(CurrentTimeStamp)]
Loop
   Pause/Resume Script [Duration (seconds): .1]
   Set Variable [$html; Value:GetLayoutObjectAttribute("YourViewer"; "content")]
   Set Variable [$elapsed; Value:Get(CurrentTimeStamp) - $start]
   Exit Loop If [PatternCount($html; "</body>") or $elapsed > 9)]
End Loop
If [PatternCount($html; "</body>") < 1]
   Show Custom Dialog ["Timeout Error: Remote site not responding."]
Else
   # $html has been retrieved for processing:
   # etc...
End If
```

When this process runs, as long as the remote site responds within the allotted timeout (in this case, approximately 10 seconds), the source of the targeted page will be returned as text via the variable named `$html`. It can then be parsed for use in your solution.

**CAUTION** If a process such as this—which may entail a processing delay—will run while users are accessing your solution, it's important to provide ongoing feedback to ensure they're aware the process is under way. This reduces frustration and avoids situations where users force-quit under the impression that the solution has stopped responding. (In the "Progress Bars and Native Charting Techniques" section, later in this chapter, we suggest some of the ways you might address this requirement.)

To successfully complete the process of retrieving data from a remote site, you need to extract the relevant information from the HTML source returned by the previous script sequence. To do that successfully, first examine the HTML content to locate elements that identify the location of the information you require.

If, for example, your script is automatically retrieving a list of movies shown at a local chapter clubhouse, as posted on its Web site, it's likely that the information you require will routinely follow the segment of text Now Showing:<big><b> and will always immediately be followed by </b></big><br>. In that case, the required calculation expression to retrieve the name of the currently showing movie will be:

```
Let([
p1 = Position($html; "Now Showing:<big><b>"; 1; 1) + 20;
p2 = Position($html; "</b></big><br>"; p1; 1)];
Middle($html; p1; p2 - p1)
)
```

By adding a Set Field [ ] command configured to write the result of the preceding calculation into a field in your solution, you'll complete the process so that each time the script runs, the name of the current movie feature will be retrieved and stored in your solution.

While the example used here involves a single piece of information (which you could look up and copy/paste into your solution without a great deal more time or trouble) the same procedure can be used to automate complex processes where hundreds of items are retrieved at intervals throughout the day or night, saving a great deal of labor and bringing significant benefits to your users. Alternatively, you could be extracting image source (IMG SRC) hyperlink references to retrieve a graphic associated with the data, such as a book cover thumbnail from Amazon or a product image from an online catalog.

# Progress Bars and Native Charting Techniques

User feedback is always a good idea, but when your solution runs a process that takes more than a few seconds, it's essential. Without it, the user is left hanging, wondering what's going on and worrying that the solution is nonresponsive. At best, users will become frustrated; at worst, they'll force-quit or restart, interrupting the process partway and risking damage to the solution files.

There are many ways to provide user feedback, and some of them are very simple to implement. For example, you can post a dialog before a lengthy process begins, saying "This may take a

# Building Advanced Interfaces

while — please come back after your coffee break." However, contriving a form of feedback that stays in place while the process is ongoing, providing a clear indication that the process is active, and that gives some indication of the state of the process and how much longer it has to run, is even better.

## Creating script progress monitors

One of the simplest ways to display a dynamic progress indicator is to show a window, such as the one shown in Figure 10.22, with a percentage-complete updating as the task progresses.

**FIGURE 10.22**

A simple numeric progress indicator in a floating FileMaker window.

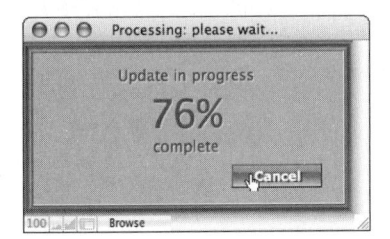

To update a percentage-complete progress indicator, first you need to estimate the size of the task being undertaken and then update the display at intervals to indicate how much has been completed. Many intensive and time-consuming scripting tasks involve repetitive processing (for example, when looping through a series of records). The following is an example of a looping script used to control a progress display while summing the values in the found set:

```
Set Variable [$task; Value:Get(FoundCount)]
Set Field [System::gProgressPercent; 0]
New Window [Name: "Processing: please wait..."; Height: 200; Width: 370; Top:
   Get(WindowTop) + 120; Left: Get(WindowLeft) + 350]
Go to Layout ["ProgressIndicator" (Meetings)]
Set Zoom Level [Lock; 100%]
Show/Hide Status Area [Lock; Hide]
Adjust Window [Resize to Fit]
Freeze Window
Loop
  Set Variable [$summary; Value:$summary + Meetings::Attendees -
   Count(Apologies::Serial#)]
  Set Variable [$completed; Value:Int(Get(RecordNumber) / $task * 100)]
  If [$completed > System::gProgressPercent]
    Set Field [System::gProgressPercent; $completed]
    Refresh Window
  End If
  Go to Record/Request/Page [Next; Exit after last]
End Loop
Set Field [Person::Frequency; $summary]
Close Window [Name: "Processing: please wait..."; Current file]
```

With a few added steps, the preceding script maintains a record of its progress in a global number field (`System::gProgressPercent`), with the result displayed onscreen as an incrementing percentage complete. Although this technique is not difficult to implement, with very little additional effort, a variety of other attractive progress indicators are possible.

For solutions that will be deployed in a mixed environment, a graphical progress indicator can be created relatively simply. For example, to create a text-based progress bar, you can create a global calculation field with a formula such as:

```
Substitute(10^System::gProgressPercent - 1; "9"; "|")
```

The preceding formula will return a row of pipe characters (|) representing the percentage completion of the process task (as per the incrementing number in the `System::gProgressPercent` field). By stacking several copies of the field (offset by 1 pixel), applying transparent fill, and using bold condensed text format, the appearance of a solid bar can be produced, as shown in Figure 10.23.

**FIGURE 10.23**

A text-based progress bar in a floating FileMaker window.

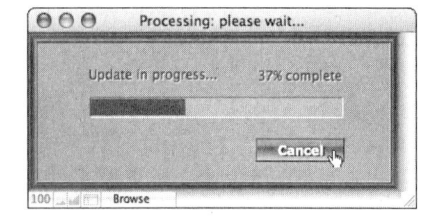

If your solution will be accessed only using FileMaker 9, several additional possibilities are available for the creation of graphical progress indicators, using either conditional formatting or a Web viewer.

## Native indicators and graphical displays

The FileMaker 9 Web Viewer alternative for creating progress indicators provides an excellent example of the ease with which data can be displayed visually using Web technologies. The progress indicator shown in Figure 10.24 uses a small rectangular Web viewer in place of the text field used in the previous example.

To create the progressive movement of the indicator, the relative widths of two cells in an HTML table are varied according to the value in the `System::gProgressPercent` global field. The table cells can have graphic backgrounds (using standard HTML tags), including animated GIFs if desired. The result is aesthetically pleasing, while having a very light footprint. The essence of the calculation code used to implement this (enclosed within a standard HTML table with a single row) is:

```
"<td height=\"17\" width=\"" & System::gProgressPercent * 2 & "\"> </td>
 <td height=\"17\" width=\"" & 200 - System::gProgressPercent * 2 & "\"> </td>"
```

### FIGURE 10.24

A Web viewer progress bar in a floating FileMaker window.

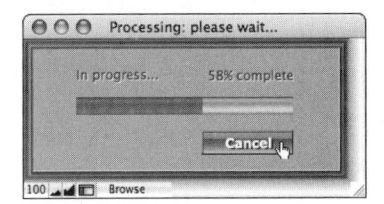

A further advantage of the Web viewer progress-bar technique is that the same viewer can be used to display other kinds of indicators — such as a barber's pole indicator for processes of indeterminate duration, or a variety of other animations, using Web-based image manipulations.

A wide variety of other graphical renderings of FileMaker data can easily be created using variations and alternate applications of this technique. As discussed earlier in this chapter, graphs and live data visualizations can be achieved by making use of the data URL capabilities of the Web Viewer object.

## Using Interface Elements

Being different and challenging prevailing wisdom is fashionable, but it isn't always wise. Computer users have become accustomed to a number of ways of interacting with computer applications, and collectively, these familiar patterns form a language. You, as a solution developer, use this language to communicate with your users, and they communicate (impart information) in response. Users do not want or need to learn a new interface vocabulary for every new computer application.

A number of widely understood user interface elements are common to most modern applications. Because they're familiar in function and (often) in operation, standard interface techniques can provide guideposts, focusing the users' attention on the tasks they are supposed to perform.

### Splash screens

The splash screen provides a first point of reference, often appearing as an application is first launched. The splash screen performs a welcoming and orienting function — letting the user know he is entering your solution, and providing the context for what is to follow. As a first impression, the splash screen sets the standard for your solution.

It is of most help to the user if your splash screen is distinctive in appearance and contains brief essentials about version, authorship, and support of your application. Including ownership, copyright, and/or brief acknowledgments on the splash screen is customary; however, avoid clutter and stick to essentials.

Users should be able to return to the splash screen at any time if they want to check the information set out there (for example, the solution version). After doing so, users should be returned to the place (screen or menu) they left.

## Main menus

In all but the simplest of solutions, there are too many functions for users to remember all at once. Ideally, users should be presented with no more than five or six choices at any one time. Any more than that and users have to work much harder to keep track of what the options do.

You can make it easier for users to find their way around your solution by grouping controls into broad logical categories. When you've done that, you'll have the essence of a main menu. How you present that to users is a matter of style; users will rapidly adapt to your style provided it has clear logical underpinnings and you're consistent in its usage.

We recommend that all your decisions about the grouping of functions and controls in your interfaces be based on the way users do their work. The system should follow the natural workflow, minimizing the frequency with which users must switch between sections/modules during a work session. You may find it helpful to consider your interface as a series of interconnected role-based modules.

As a general principle, users should always be able to return to familiar territory with a single click of the mouse, and they should always be able to tell where they are.

## About and version info

Although we've mentioned that splash screens often incorporate vendor, copyright, and version information, providing this information separately can make sense. A simple menu command can be invoked (for example, returning a custom dialog) to set out authorship, version, and support information. Doing so leaves the splash screen less cluttered and creates a more positive impression. If you want, a link or button on the splash screen could invoke the version information.

## Online Help for your users

We encourage you to consider providing built-in documentation for your solutions. In many cases, the extent of documentation required to get users started and answer basic questions is not great, and, if the system design conforms to intuitive principles, users may only infrequently have to call to check the documentation. Providing answers to the top 10 or 20 questions that a user may ask goes a long way toward building confidence in your solution and your work.

Ideally, because FileMaker is so good at managing data, your support documentation should be made available as a searchable database within your solution. This has the advantage that it can be readily updated and can provide a facility for users to make notes and additions or ask questions. However, the documentation should also be available in a printed format or PDF and, preferably, generated fresh from your solution's Help database on request.

A further option to consider is providing Help content via a Web viewer, where the source documentation is hosted remotely. This approach can have a number of advantages, allowing the developer to update and extend the documentation as questions are asked, problems are solved, or changes are made to the solution.

# Handling User Preferences

The best solutions are those that directly respond to the needs of the user, providing a tool to accelerate productivity. However, unless you create solutions for only one user, you have the dilemma of reconciling competing users' needs and preferences.

The ideal answer to many competing requests and concerns is to accommodate a variety of system behaviors by enabling users to control how some features work. When you do this, be sure to structure your solution so it keeps track of the selections made by each user, reinstating them automatically when the user returns.

## A user-centric development philosophy

One of the essential purposes of most solutions (including, but not limited to, FileMaker solutions) is to free users from a variety of mundane and repetitive actions or tasks. Many solutions, however, bring with them a host of new mundane and repetitive tasks, specifically because the developer does not understand how the users want to get from point A to point B.

One answer is to have the developer watch users to determine repetitive sequences of tasks and build the solution around the emerging patterns. Another approach is to build flexibility into the interface and permit users to select how the solution will operate.

## Capturing state by user

To capture information about users' preferences and their use of your solution, we recommend you include a users table, with a record automatically created for each login account. The users table provides a place to store preference settings for each user, so that when the user logs in again (whether from the same or a different workstation), your login script can locate the user record, retrieve the user's preference settings, and configure the solution accordingly.

A convenient way to manage this process is to:

1. Load the user's account name (after login credentials have been accepted) into a global key field.
2. Use a GTRR to isolate the corresponding record in the user table.
3. Load the preference settings into global fields. Because global fields can be accessed without a relationship, the user preferences will be available for read and write from anywhere in your solution throughout the user's login session.
4. Restore the state (selected layout and record) where the user last left the solution. In most solutions, this step should be optional — the user should be able to select whether he wants his logout state restored on next login — and this should be stored as one of the user preference settings.

At the conclusion of the user's session (either logout or file close) your scripts should capture the current state and return to the user table to write the current contents of the preference and state global fields back to the appropriate record in the user table.

## Example — a multi-lingual solution interface

One of the most profound kinds of user preferences is language. Many solutions are used by people who speak different languages and who require (or desire) an interface that speaks their language. Although we've seen a number of methods used to create multi-lingual interfaces, most of them require many additional relationships; some stop working when the user enters Find mode and may make working in Layout mode a chore. Here is a method that avoids these problems.

The technique we recommend entails some extra work during development, but after it's in place, providing support for additional languages requires only an additional record in the language resource table. The technique adds two tables to your solution, but they don't have to be related to anything else (just to each other), and no other relationships are required. Moreover, field labels remain reasonably compact and intelligible in Layout mode.

To implement a multi-lingual interface, follow these steps:

1. Gather a list of the fields, headings, labels, tooltips, dialog messages, window titles, and other text elements required throughout your solution.

2. Create a table called LanguageResources with a primary key (LanguageID), a LanguageName field, and a flag field (container type), plus one text field for every entry in your list from Step 1. Name each field with the logical name (in your own native language) of the element to which it corresponds.

3. Create two or more records in the LanguageResources table, entering the appropriate translations of the element names and text into their respective fields.

4. Create a table named **I**. The uppercase I stands for Interface but is abbreviated for compactness.

5. In the I table, create a global field called gLanguageID, of the same data type as the LanguageID field in the LanguageResources table.

6. Create a relationship from I::gLanguageID to LanguageResources::LanguageID.

7. For every field in the LanguageResources table, create a corresponding field in the I table, making the I field a global calculation field with the following formula (where the field in question is I::FirstName):

    `Evaluate("LanguageResources::FirstName"; gLanguageID)`

8. Create a value list called InterfaceLanguages and define it to use values from a field. Configure the value list to draw values from the LanguageResources::LanguageID and LanguageResources::LanguageName fields and to show values only from the second field, as illustrated in Figure 10.25.

9. On your user preference screens (and elsewhere as appropriate), place the I::gLanguageID field and attach the InterfaceLanguages value list.

# Building Advanced Interfaces

**FIGURE 10.25**

Configuration for the InterfaceLanguages value list.

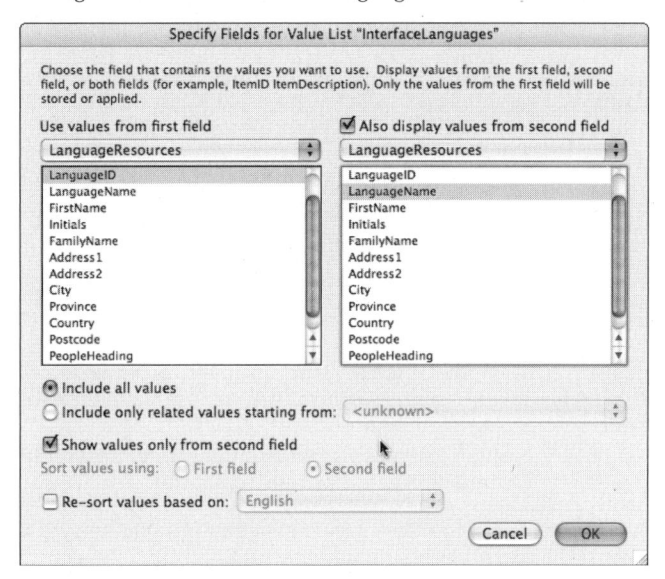

10. Adjacent to the I::LanguageID field, place the I::LanguageFlag field so that the selected language will be identified with a corresponding national flag (for the benefit of those not familiar with the language names).

11. Configure the layouts throughout your solution with labels next to them in the form `<<I::FirstName>>` where the field in question is called FirstName (as shown in Figure 10.26).

12. For all window titles and dialog messages, reference the relevant field in the I table.

13. Create a field in your user table for preferred language.

14. Script a prompt for preferred language the first time each user logs in.

15. Set your login script to write the ID of the user's preferred language into the I::gLanguageID field.

16. Set your logout and file close scripts to write the current value of the I::gLanguageID field into the LanguagePreference field of the current user's table. If the user changes interface language preference during the session, the change will be remembered.

Whenever the user makes a new selection in the I::gLanguageID field, all the text on the layouts throughout your solution's interface of your solution's layouts changes to the new language selection.

### FIGURE 10.26
The format for field labels and headings in Layout mode.

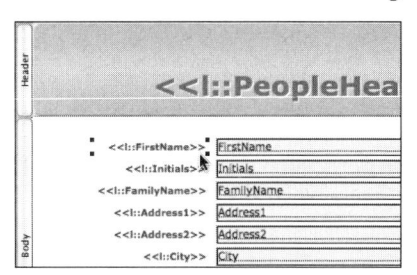

> **TIP**
> If you require the window title to change when a new language selection is made, you have to script the language change procedure and reset the window title according to the user's new language selection.

The field labels, headings, and so on will be present in both Find and Browse modes. In Layout mode, however, you can readily read and work with the labels, and adding more languages only requires an additional record in the LanguageResources table.

> **NOTE**
> Although the language selection will control layout and custom dialog text, FileMaker's native dialogs will continue to display text in the language chosen at the operating system level. For a full language makeover, system preferences must be updated as well.

For international vertical market, runtime, or shrink-wrapped solutions, consider verifying the current operating system language using `Get(SystemLanguage)` during your solution's on-open script, and making a corresponding language selection as the commencing (default) language for your solution.

# Chapter 11

# Data Modeling in FileMaker

FileMaker is as much a problem-solving tool as it is a development platform. As such, it provides you with the means to achieve a wide variety of ends (and in the process, solve many problems). How you use the tools FileMaker makes available is less important than the functionality your solutions are able to deliver. Nevertheless, considering the underpinnings of a well-formed relational data model is helpful — not so much so that you will be bound to adhere rigidly to it, but so that you'll be able to make informed choices about how and when to depart from it.

Regardless how you choose to work in FileMaker, you need a clear plan for the storage of data, including the main connections and interactions between different data types. This over-arching plan is your data model. It doesn't matter where it exists — it could be in your solution itself, on a whiteboard in your office, on a diagram in your diary, or a vision in your imagination — but without it, little will work well, and your solutions will quickly become mired in confusion and complexity.

A data model's purpose is to establish clarity and simplicity, enabling you to see — from any vantage point — what belongs where, and how to bring together the available elements to achieve required outcomes.

## Background in Relational Theory

Modern database applications — including FileMaker — take a set of ideas based on the theoretical work of Edgar F. Codd (first made public in 1970, while Codd was working at IBM) as a starting point for implementation of a relational data management model. Databases implementing Codd's central ideas are commonly referred to as *Relational Database Management Systems*

### IN THIS CHAPTER

Understanding relational theory

Recognizing the FileMaker Relationships Graph symbols

Using relationship operators

Exploring different relationship techniques

Working with data sets and arrays

Managing your Relationships Graphs

Documenting the structure of your database

Working with layers in your solution

Understanding the differences between file architecture and data structure

Using separation and external SQL sources

Implementing separation retroactively

Considering deployment

(RDMS). Although relational principles are now widely used, no commercially available RDBMS fully implements the detailed model articulated by Codd and his colleagues.

An essential tenet of data theories (including relational theory) is that data form part of a model of the universe. Each datum describes (accurately or otherwise) something in the universe. Thus, an organized data collection represents a model of the universe (and this is true, whether or not the organizers of the data recognize it).

The shortcomings, such as they are, of computer implementations of relational data management concepts are due in part to pragmatism. In other words, rather than exhaustively modeling all the intricacies of the universe, real-world system designers introduce compromises for various reasons. Some of the reasons for compromise (economy, expediency, and business imperatives) are more admirable than others (ignorance or carelessness).

Despite Codd's efforts — publishing dozens of papers on the relational model between 1968 and 1988 — myths and misconceptions about its central tenets abound.

## Set Theory in the management of data

When you collect and manage data (by whatever means), you're collecting many facts to describe the properties of an entity or class of entities. In the simplest analysis, you have sets of facts about sets of things, which gives rise to the forms of tables where rows and columns organize things and the facts about them, respectively.

An essential problem when the information you require pertains to more than one kind of thing is that you then have multiple sets of data comprising part of a whole. For example, an organized group of facts about people and an organized group of facts about houses can be considered a unified fact set when it becomes clear that people live in houses. At this point, 19th-century posits regarding Set Theory (first proposed by Georg Cantor) provide a way to resolve seeming conflicts in the organization of complex data.

By using an organizing principle where facts about things (attributes of entities) are organized into tables (one table per entity) and the relationships between those entities are expressed or managed mathematically (which people live in which houses), you can model relationships in the real world. This insight is at the heart of Codd's genius.

Giving form to this concept are the applications of ratio principles to describe relations as one-to-one (1:1), one-to-many (1:n), many to one (n:1), or many to many (m:n), and the concept of join types such as the equi-join (=) and others describing the kinds of relationships between entities within different tables (sets and subsets). These abstract concepts rapidly acquire concrete meaning and usefulness within applications, such as FileMaker, where they enable you to solve problems organizing your data.

## Modeling the real world

To model the world (or, at any rate, a part of it) using relational principles, you first need to be clear about the entities each group of facts pertains to. Using the example of people and houses, you may have a number of facts about each person, such as an address. In this simple scenario, you have two entities (each requiring a table) and a relationship between them (based on people's residency). Because more than one person may live at a house, the relationship from houses to people may be one-to-many. By breaking information down into entities and defining relationships between them, you establish a relational model of the real-world "things" your database describes.

A relational solution's data organization centers around using tables to hold information about each class of item (object, thing, or entity). Each row in the table holds all the information about a particular instance of the kind of item, and each column holds a particular fact about the thing. For example, if you have a people table, each person has a single row in the table, and each column holds a different kind of fact, such as eye color, date of birth, sex, and so on. A separate table about vehicle models may have columns for engine capacity, number of seats, manufacturer, paint color, and so on.

### Think about clarity of organization

When applying the concept of relational modeling to your data, the first step is to separate different kinds of entities and to group fundamentally similar entities. The purpose of this exercise is to gain clarity about what belongs where — confusion at this first stage leads to conflicts in the data model. An *entity* is a "thing in the modeled universe," so people, vehicles, houses, and jobs are all entities of different kinds.

**CAUTION** Don't describe different kinds of entities within the same table. Vehicles don't belong in the people table, for example. Similarly, you should avoid describing different attributes in the same column within a table — for example, in a people table, eye color doesn't belong in the date of birth column, and vice versa. In addition, don't separate fundamentally similar entities into different tables. You don't need to put sports cars in one table and sedans in another — rather, they're all vehicles, and chassis type is one of their attributes, so it is properly represented as a column in the vehicle table. Similarly, you don't require a separate table for people with brown eyes, as eye color is clearly one of the attributes of a person and should be represented as data in a column of a People table.

### Keep the big picture in view

Although in simple examples the choices may appear obvious, other times the decision isn't so clear or easy. For example, if you're designing a college database, you may think it's reasonable to have separate tables for staff and students — and there are many such implementations in existence. However, all of them produce anomalies when a staff member enrolls in a class or a student is offered employment at the college. (The "solution" then involves creating a duplicate record for that person and then manually keeping the two records in sync by entering everything twice.) This situation is one example of how a departure from one of the central principles of relational design can lead to confusion and burden you with extra work.

In the college database example, an alternative data model, in keeping with relational principles, is to create three tables, not two. Instead of having two marginally different people tables for staff and students, you could create tables for people, enrollments, and job roles, which then allows you to have a single table for all people, with associated records in either or both of the related tables. By the time a college expands its data requirements to keep track of donors, alumni, governors, and visiting fellows (at which point some individuals may require six separate entries if each type of person is in a separate table), it becomes clear that storing each of these associated characteristics as an attribute of a single record in the People table — with an associated table for accompanying details or donations, visits, enrollments, and so on — is preferable.

Data structures are a way of describing reality. If, in reality, one person may be associated with several different kinds of roles, a data model in which a single person's record is associated with role records in a number of related tables more accurately reflects reality.

> **NOTE** Any discussion of relational data modeling principles can rapidly descend into a minefield of purist ideologies, conflicting interpretations, debates about "normal forms," and deeper esoterica. However, our interest here is to provide guiding insights and practical advice. A wealth of specialist resources exists for those who want to explore the intricacies of relational theory.

## Remembering some guiding principles

You need to be clear about the reasons for modeling data in a particular way. The central purposes of relational modeling are clarity, simplicity, accuracy, and efficiency in managing the data (and, incidentally, in representing the reality the data seeks to describe).

One essential way a good relational model achieves these aims is by storing each piece of information only once (while providing access to it as needed, via data relationships). If your solution has multiple people tables, then almost inevitably you'll end up having multiple records for some people. As soon as this event happens, the following occur:

- **Efficiency** is compromised because data must be updated in two different places every time a change occurs.
- **Accuracy** suffers because of the risk that data will be updated in some places but not others. In other words, the potential for data integrity problems is increased.
- **Clarity** is reduced because it's no longer obvious where to go to locate a particular piece of information — and because when the information in alternate parts of the system differs, it's not clear which is correct.
- **Simplicity** is eroded as increasing numbers of duplicate records move the data farther away from a representation of reality and system users are burdened with additional work, such as the need to search in multiple tables to find data about a person, to collate multiple reports to summarize all information about one person, or to aggregate information about all persons. In such cases, working with the system involves negotiating burgeoning lists of exceptions.

There are good reasons for investing your time and effort in clarifying data relationships early in the solution design process. Of course, one solution isn't necessarily right for all cases, and you must make your own judgments about how and when to apply the principles we outline in the following sections.

### Separate entities by type

Relational principles are best served by creating separate tables for each basic kind of entity, with fields (columns) only for the attributes reasonably expected to apply to all the table's entities. Similarly, information about essentially similar entities should be consolidated in one table.

**CAUTION** Although you may be tempted to view the methodology described here as absolute, form your decisions with due consideration of the importance and purpose of each kind of entity in relation to the business at hand.

For example, in a sales system, you may want to treat everything being sold as the same kind of entity, storing it in the Products table. In a social club database, however, cars may belong in a Vehicles table, whereas trampolines belong in a Facilities table. In yet another kind of solution, both cars and trampolines may belong in an Assets table. You should consider an entity's basic nature, as well as its purpose, in context.

### Delineate fields clearly

Each field in a table should hold a specific kind of fact, such as a date, color, or measurement, about the entity described in the table. Try to minimize fields with general names like Appearance or Facts, which are so nonspecific that they could be used to hold all sorts of different kinds of information. Try to minimize reliance on Notes, Comments or Other fields in each table.

**TIP** Your users may insist on including a Notes or Comments field and, if so, we encourage you to consider doing so. If you have modeled the users' data requirements effectively, however, such ancillary fields will prove superfluous (take it as a measure of your success when such fields are largely or entirely unused.

### Place multiples in a separate table

Frequently, multiple instances of an attribute for a particular entity is an indication that the attribute should instead be classed as an associated entity and should be in a table of its own (with a relationship to the current table). For example, where students may enroll in a variety of classes, it's clear that enrollments aren't a student attribute; instead, they belong in a separate table.

As part of separating multiples, it's often desirable to store abstract objects, such as ownership or association, in separate tables. For example, if you have a table of people and a table of car models, you may find that one person can own multiple vehicles (at once, or over time), in which case you may want to create a separate table where the multiple cars for each individual are recorded (one record for each). This kind of table is sometimes referred to as a *join table* or an *association table*. An enrollment table is a good example because it joins a student with courses or classes.

**CROSS-REF** We discuss techniques for implementing join tables — along with other methods of managing multiple related values — in the section "Alternative Relationship Techniques," later in this chapter.

### Store everything once only

An objective of successful relational data modeling is that it allows you to store each piece of information only once, yet refer to it from multiple locations within the solution. One benefit of achieving this goal is that when information is updated via one part of your solution interface, the modified information then appears everywhere else the information is referenced.

A successful data model, therefore, is one where you can store each piece of information only once, where it is clear where the information should reside, and where the single instance of each piece of information can nevertheless be accessed wherever required throughout your solution.

### Identify the major players

In addition to the practical steps outlined in the preceding sections, we encourage you to discover the centers around which your solution's processes or workflow revolve. Most solutions have several centers, while a few have only one. While it's likely you'll identify a number of entities requiring tables in your solution, knowing which tables are the main focus points for the activities your solution supports greatly aids the clarity of your model.

### Put it into practice

A key to successful data design — in FileMaker or any other application — is establishing a clear understanding about the nature of the information to be stored and accessed and the relationships between its elements. By applying the broad guidelines outlined in the preceding sections, you arrive at a map of the data your solution must support. At this preliminary stage, your outline is necessarily somewhat abstract. In the ensuing sections, you give concrete form to a data framework supporting your data model, using the relational toolset provided by FileMaker.

## FileMaker Relationships Graph Symbols

The FileMaker Relationships Graph — as a spatial and visual metaphor for the data structure — provides you with an environment where you can give form to your solution's data architecture. Nevertheless, given the practical and procedural implications for your solution's operation, the graph is more an implementation tool than a visual model. Moreover, as your solution becomes more complex, essentials of the data model are obscured (on the graph) as it becomes increasingly crowded with components serving functional, rather than structural, purposes.

To make best use of the graph and the tools it provides for creating and managing data relationships, you need a deep understanding of the way each of its components fit together.

### Visual cues and clues

The graph presents a collection of miniaturized table icons commonly called *Table Occurrences* (TOs) that are aliases or pointers to tables, not the actual tables. This is an essential distinction. Several TOs can point to the same base table, and TO names need not relate in any way to the names you've assigned to the underlying tables.

> **TIP** Because TOs aren't tables, as such, the Tables panel in the Manage Database dialog provides more direct insight into the data structure. However, bear in mind that in a multi-file solution, some or all of the tables may be defined in other files.

The lines connecting TOs on the graph represent relationships and are drawn between the operative key fields in the tables represented by the TOs they join. However, FileMaker displays different line endings according to the status of the field at each end of the relationship.

Figure 11.1 shows four relationships between a Main table and a Related table, where a different Main field is used as the key field for each relation. Note that the lines all end in the "crows foot" terminator where they connect to the Related~ TOs. This terminator signifies that the connection to Related is valid and capable of supporting a ~to-many (1:n or m:n) join to records in the Related table. The two determinants of this status are

1. The match field in Related ("Key") is indexed (or indexable), thus supporting the retrieval of record data from the Related table via this relationship.
2. There is no constraint or mechanism for uniqueness of the match field's values.

### FIGURE 11.1
Alternative relationship line representations.

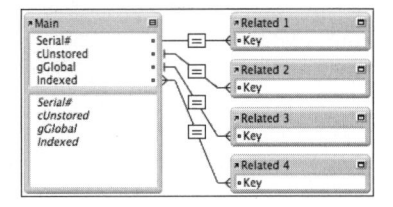

In the Main TO, however, the line terminators show as:

- A straight line connecting to the Serial# field, because the field is set to auto-generate unique numbers
- A terminal line connecting to cUnstored because the field is an unstored calculation and therefore can't be indexed (so retrieval of record data from Main via this connection isn't supported)
- A terminal line connecting to gGlobal because, as a global field, it also can't be indexed and doesn't support retrieval of record data from Main
- A crows-foot line connecting to Main::Indexed because it's an indexable and (potentially) non-unique data field supporting retrieval of record data from Main

These line terminators provide visual clues to the operative abilities of each of the relationships, according to the definitions of the fields they connect. The crows-foot symbol doesn't signify that a relationship *is* used to support a ~to-many join, but merely that it *may* be.

Bisecting each relationship line on the graph is a small, white box displaying a join symbol describing the kind of relationship. By default, the join symbol is an equal sign (=), as exemplified in Figure 11.1.

> **NOTE** The relationship operators and their uses are explained in the upcoming section "Relationship Operators."

## The TO as a pointer

Because TOs aren't actually tables but pointers to tables, you can refer to the same table in multiple ways or in multiple places on the graph. By using separate TOs for multiple references to a table, you avoid circular references so that there is never more than one relationship path between any two TOs on the graph, thus avoiding referential ambiguity.

Because you can have multiple instances of the same table on the graph, you can establish multiple views of the content of the same table. For example, by setting up a relationship based on a field holding the current date, you can display all of today's transactions in a portal. At the same time, a relationship to the Transactions table on status will give you a portal display of outstanding payments. Meanwhile, in the Customer table, you may require a filtered view of transactions for each customer. By creating three separate TOs, each a pointer to the Customer table, you're able to connect in different ways (and from different places on your graph) to the same underlying table.

Similarly, the ability to add multiple occurrences of a table enables you to connect a table to itself. For example, you may want to show fellow team members in a portal on a staff member's record. Joining two TOs of the relevant table (for example, matching TeamID in both TOs) achieves this goal.

## Understanding the graph metaphor

The FileMaker Relationships Graph may contain elements of your data model, but it must also contain a variety of functional and procedural elements supporting interface requirements and process logic in and around those parts supporting the data model. If you try to use the graph as the locus of your data design, you risk becoming mired in a mass of extraneous information.

**NOTE** A more extensive discussion of alternative graph modeling techniques appears in the section "Graph Techniques — Spiders, Squids, and Anchor Buoy," later in this chapter.

Two alternative ways to consider the Relationships Graph are

- As a map of data flows and data controls
- As a context diagram linking interface to data structure

In either case, choose a TO as the current TO, and the graph becomes instructional for data availability, access to records and tables, and related options possibilities and constraints from the current layout's vantage point.

# Relationship Operators

FileMaker creates relationships displaying an = symbol by default. The symbol is referred to as the relationship operator and indicates the type of join. The = symbol signifies a type of join referred to as an *equi-join*, where the relationship is based on matching values on opposing sides of the join. Only records with the same value in the fields in both tables used for the relationship will be related.

**NOTE** The fields used in relationships are commonly referred to as *match fields* or *key fields*. The unique ID field used to identify the records in a table is often referred to as the *Primary Key* in that table. A Primary Key from another table may be referred to as a *foreign key*.

## Data Modeling in FileMaker

The equi-join is one of seven relationship operators supported in FileMaker. To change the default "=" operator to one of the other alternatives, you must edit the relationship. For an existing relationship, double-click the symbol box bisecting the relationship line to view the Edit Relationship dialog. As shown in Figure 11.2, a drop-down list in the upper center of the dialog (between the two field lists for the connected TOs) gives you access to the alternative operators.

### FIGURE 11.2

Accessing alternative relationship operators in the Edit Relationship dialog.

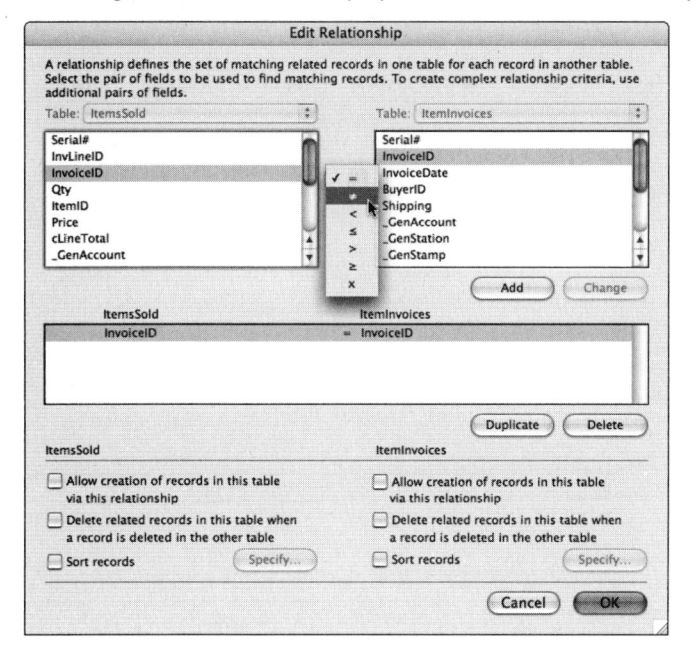

Each relationship operator engenders different relationship behavior, giving you the capability to filter and connect data to serve a variety of purposes, as detailed in the following sections.

## Equi-joins and non-equal joins

Most relationships are based on exactly matching values in the connected fields in both tables and therefore use the equi-join (=) operator. FileMaker looks up the value in the current record of the current table in the index of values for the matching field in the related table and returns records having a matching index entry.

Because the matching process uses the field index of the related table, the indexing method chosen for the field(s) used in the relationship affects the way matching occurs. Thus, the data type, such as whether it's text or number, is significant, because numbers and text are indexed differently.

To achieve expected results, the key fields on both sides of a relationship should be of the same data type.

If you're using text fields for a relationship, alternative indexing protocols are available (via the Options for Field dialog's Storage tab). For example, if you choose English language indexing, relationship matches aren't case sensitive (although punctuation and spaces are still observed when matching), whereas if you choose Unicode as the indexing protocol, full-case sensitivity is observed in relationship matching. Conversely, if you choose Default text indexing, accented characters are differentiated from unaccented equivalents, but matching is not case sensitive.

**TIP** The text index protocol for the key field in the related table determines the method of matching.

For many purposes, you'll require relationships matching key values (for example, to link invoice items to an invoice or courses to a study program). In most cases, text matches based on the native language of your solution (for example, English) will suffice. However, note that indexing in external SQL tables is generally case-sensitive by default.

**CROSS-REF** For an in-depth discussion of indexing and its implications, refer to Chapter 9.

FileMaker also provides an inverse of the equi-join, in the form of the not-equal join operator (≠), also known as the anti-join. This operator makes a join for all records in the related table key field values (including an empty value) that *don't* match the key field value in the current record. On the other hand, an empty key field value in the current record will not match any related records, even though the empty value in the current record does not match non-empty values in the related key field.

## Comparative operators (theta joins)

FileMaker provides four comparative operators (commonly referred to as *theta joins*), represented by the less-than (<), greater-than (>), less-or-equal (≤), and greater-or-equal (≥) symbols, enabling you to establish relationships based on a range of values.

### Note regarding theta joins in relational algebra

In relational algebra, the category of joins known as *theta joins* also includes the equi-join and anti-join. In common parlance, however, the term is frequently reserved for those members of the join set other than equi- and anti-joins.

Using the available comparative operators, you can make use of range-based joins with text, number, date, time, and timestamp data types, creating relationships for uses such as the following:

- Identifying records with a due date prior to the current date (in other words, overdue)
- Listing records with a family name in the range m to z
- Displaying records of customers with more than $200 outstanding

## Cartesian joins

The last of the seven relationship operators is the Cartesian product operator (×), which provides a join where all records in one table are matched to all records in the other, regardless of the values (or lack of values) in the match fields. For this type of relationship, the selection of key fields is immaterial, as their contents are ignored.

Cartesian product relationships (also referred to as a cross-join) are useful for relationships used to aggregate whole-of-table data (for example, returning the `Max()` and `Min()` values for a related table), for portal navigation where users will select from all available records, and a variety of purposes, such as reference tables or logs, where access to a continuous data display is desired.

## Multi-predicate relationships

FileMaker supports *multi-predicate* (sometimes also called *multi-criteria*) relationships where you select more than one pair of key fields to define the join. The effect of multiple predicates is cumulative — all the matches must be satisfied for the join to be valid, meaning that only AND predicate operators are permitted.

Multi-predicate relationships are created in the Edit Relationship dialog by selecting additional pairs of match fields (and an associated operator) and clicking the Add button, as shown in Figure 11.3.

**FIGURE 11.3**

Defining a multi-predicate relationship in the Edit Relationship dialog.

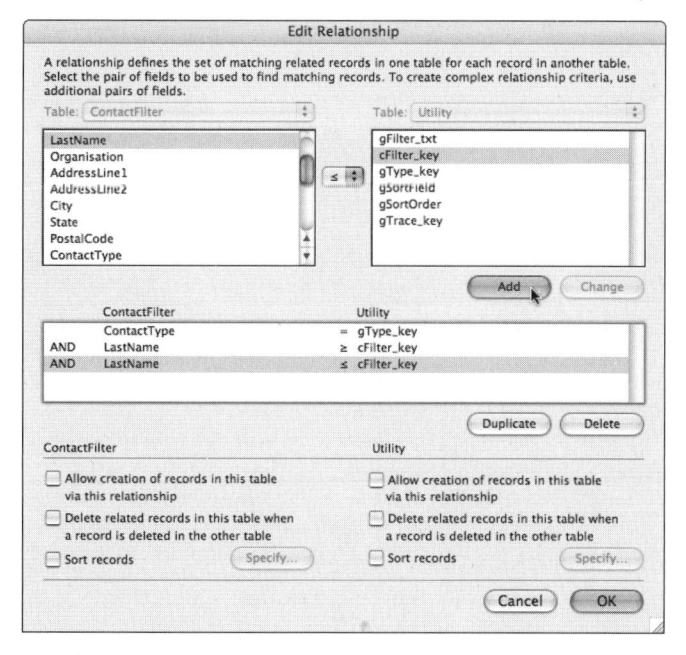

## Part III  Beyond the Basics

The relationship definition shown in Figure 11.3 is the one used for filtering a portal of contacts by name and contact type in the Inventory example file, as discussed in Chapter 9. However, there are many other uses for multi-predicate relationships. For example, you can use a relationship definition to locate records with dates falling between two dates:

```
         ItemDate   >   StartDate
AND      ItemDate   <   EndDate
```

Multi-predicate relationships employing a mix of different operators are represented in the Relationships Graph by the generic dyadic operator, as shown in Figure 11.4.

### FIGURE 11.4
The dyadic operator representing a mixed-operator, multi-predicate join.

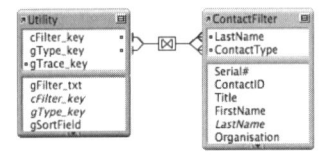

## Alternative Relationship Techniques

Frequently, FileMaker offers you a variety of methods to achieve similar outcomes. That's certainly the case when working with relationships, where you can use other means to produce many of the effects you can achieve with different relationship operators and multi-predicate joins.

In the interests of an expanded toolkit of relationship management techniques, here is a brief survey of alternative techniques.

### Multi-key fields

When you enter more than one line of text into a text field (separated by carriage returns), FileMaker treats each line as a separate value. Related records that match either value (in accordance with the relationship operator) are deemed valid. Key fields holding more than one value are termed *multi-key fields*.

Because any value in a list of values (in a relationship key field) will provide a match, multi-key fields provide one mechanism to support one-to-many or many-to-many joins. Moreover, because multiple value matches occur simultaneously, multi-key techniques enable you to relax relationship constraints, introducing OR logic into relationship definitions (whereas multi-predicate relationships permit only AND logic).

## Data Modeling in FileMaker

Among the many uses of the multi-key techniques in FileMaker are calculation of exploded keys to support partial match filtering. For example, if the target key in the related table is a calculation rendering the value of a field in the related table as an exploded array in the form

```
e
ex
exp
expl
explo
explod
explode
exploded
```

then incomplete matches from a related table (via an equi-join relationship) become possible. As a result, users can start typing part of a word or name and then select from a portal list of possible matches. While this technique is useful in some situations, it imposes a penalty of increased storage and indexing requirements in the related table.

An alternative application of a multi-key technique achieving similar functionality in some circumstances is the use of a calculation in the parent table, generating two values to represent the lower and upper limits of a text range. For example, set up a field for user-entered data (say, a global text field called gSearch) and an unstored calculation called cSearch (of result type text) in the same table defined as:

```
gSearch & ¶ & gSearch & "zzz"
```

Set up a relationship based on the calculation field defined along the following lines:

```
        cSearch     ≤ RelatedKey
AND     cSearch     ≥ RelatedKey
```

With the preceding calculation and relationship in place, when the user enters **ez** into the gSearch field, the cSearch field will produce a multi-key value array containing two values:

```
ex
exzzz
```

Because multi-key matches are evaluated simultaneously on all values (as an OR sequence), values in RelatedKey that are both greater than and less than the two values in cSearch are those falling between `ex` and `exzzz` in alphabetical sequence. This method is suitable for a variety of range matching, filtering, and partial completion relationships.

**CROSS-REF** See Chapter 9 for implementation notes for a filter relationship using the essentials of this technique.

## Compound keys

Compound keys (usually calculation fields) concatenate the several values into a single value (or group of values) for matching purposes. Keys of this type are frequently encountered in solutions migrated from earlier versions of FileMaker (for example, solutions created in FileMaker 6 or earlier), because multi-predicate relationships were not directly supported prior to Version 7.

An example of the former use of concatenated keys is a relationship based on a concatenation of last name and date of birth in both tables. When compound keys are matched in this way, only records with the same value in both last name and date of birth will match — so the relationship is functionally equivalent to a multi-predicate relationship referencing both fields. For this reason, most uses of compound keys in current solutions serve other purposes.

A useful contemporary technique using compound keys is the creation of *multi-purpose relationships* (relationships you can switch between different purposes at will). For example, if you have three key fields in Table1 (keyA, keyB, and keyC) and three corresponding key fields in Table2 and you need at various times to relate Table1 and Table2 according to different pairs of keys, you can achieve this with a single relationship by creating a compound key in Table2 (as a stored text calc named cMasterKey) defined as:

```
"keyA" & Table2::keyA & "¶keyB" & Table2::keyB & "¶keyC" & Table2::keyC
```

In Table1, create a global text field called gKeySelection and an unstored calculation field called cDynamicKey with the formula:

```
gKeySelection & GetField(gKeySelection)
```

With the preceding fields in place, define a single relationship between Table1 and Table2 as:

```
Table1::cDynamicKey       = Table2::cMasterKey
```

With such a relationship in place, you can modify the relationship between Table1 and Table2 to match any pair of the three original (Table2) key fields by putting the name of the desired key field for the relationship into Table1::gKeySelection.

## One-way relationships

In most cases, FileMaker relationships work in both directions. So for example, an InvoiceLines layout can display data from the Invoices table sourced via the same relationship you use to display InvoiceLines data on the Invoices layouts.

Relationships that are dependent on an unstored calculation work in one direction only, however, because the matching of records utilizes the index of the key field(s) in the related table — and unstored fields can be indexed. Although you can use such relationships to retrieve data from other tables, data won't flow in the other direction.

Similarly, global fields cannot be indexed, so relationships where the destination key field is a global field do not return matching records. Instead, they act as Cartesian joins (when retrieving records from the table where the global key field is located), returning all records, regardless of the value (or lack of value) in the global field.

> **NOTE** Due to a bug in the initial release of FileMaker 9, the Cartesian product behavior of a relationship to a global field did not work if the opposing key field was empty. This issue has been corrected with the release of the 9.0v2 update available from www.filemaker.com.

Despite their limitations, one-way relationships prove useful in a variety of situations because they have other helpful behaviors. In many cases, a utility relationship from a global field to a related table is useful for addressing individual records in the related table. Similarly, relationships where one of the keys is an unstored calculation field exhibit more dynamic behavior than their stored-key counterparts.

## Join tables

While you can use multi-key fields to support various forms of one-to-many and many-to-many relationships, in many cases storing associations between entities in an intermediary table is preferable. Tables used in this way are commonly known as *join tables*.

The use of join tables is particularly advantageous in any situation where:

- You need to store or process data connected with each join event.
- You need to track the joins and report on join activity.

For example, when associating people with clubs, you can create a memberships table to manage the connections. Each person would then have a record in the memberships table for each club they were a member of. In such a case, you need to store data connected with the join (such as the person's membership expiration date, their status, and perhaps the fee paid). You also need to be able to track memberships — for example, producing membership pattern reports by year for each club — which is much easier to do when you can search, sort, and summarize the records in the memberships table.

## Naturally occurring joins

Like the preceding memberships example, there are many types of data that are a familiar part of life that, in database terms, are a join table. For example, a college Enrollments table is, in fact, a join table connecting People and Courses. An Employees table is a join tables between People and Companies. The Tickets register in an airlines database is a join table between Passengers and Flights.

The preceding examples are so familiar that you're likely to think of them as entities in their own right. However, in each case (and there are many other examples), the joins have no independent existence — they're not tangible entities in the way that, say, people and companies are.

For the efficient management of data relationships involving ~to-many joins, facilitation of organizational clarity and ease of reporting/summarizing available information often warrants creating one or more join tables.

373

**Part III**    **Beyond the Basics**

# Working with Data Arrays

In any work you do with structured data, arrays make an appearance (whether you're aware of it nor not). An *array* is a group of data elements you can access via an index (value number). It can be as simple as a numbered list or as complex as a compilation of keys and associated values from a set of related records.

Any time you store a list of record IDs in a field, you have, in effect, an array — you can reference the record IDs by their position in the list, using functions such as `GetValue()`. Similarly, value lists, delimited text, and name/value pairs may all be considered array types.

## Repeating fields as an array handler

FileMaker provides a built-in method of storing multiple discrete values in a single field and referencing them according to a value's index (position) within the set of values assigned to the field. FileMaker calls this feature a Repeating Field. Moreover, FileMaker also supports repeating variables, so arrays can be stored and accessed efficiently in memory (and therefore outside your solutions' data structures).

Most programmers know that arrays can be really useful, yet repeating fields gets a bad rap among old hands in the FileMaker developer community for two reasons:

- Historically (prior to the release of FileMaker Pro v3 in 1995), FileMaker provided only rudimentary relationship support, so repeating fields provided a surrogate (albeit an inadequate one). When relational structures became available, this type of use of repeating fields was deprecated.

- Inexperienced users without grounding in relational theory have been known to tie themselves in knots trying to use repeating fields for purposes far better served by related tables.

Although these concerns have a legitimate basis, a variety of valid and appropriate uses of repeating fields as array-handling mechanisms exist. In particular, using global repeating fields as index references or repositories for system resources, such as text and graphics for use in your solution interface, aids efficiency and clarity.

## Collapsing and expanding arrays

FileMaker provides a number of alternative forms for lists and arrays. On occasion, you may consider using arrays to extend your data structure — for example, storage of anything from test measurement sets in research databases to binomial indices in quantum plotters to rolling transaction logs in audit systems.

In some cases, such as when a *static array* (one fixed in size) is appropriate to your needs, repeating fields may be adequate. However, in many cases, you may not know in advance how many

# Data Modeling in FileMaker

elements need to be accommodated. In those cases, you should consider using text arrays (managed using FileMaker's ~Values ( ) functions) for stored arrays or variables for temporary arrays. In both cases, you can achieve dynamic array functionality, where the array size may be extended at will, within the limits of available memory or FileMaker's text field size limit of 1 billion characters.

> **TIP** Arrays are a great way to pass more than one parameter to a script — or returning more than one result. Name/Value pair syntax is one of the formats many developers find ideal for this purpose.

## Relationship-based techniques for managing data

One of the choices you make as soon as you start building a solution is what values to use as the keys for relationship match fields. For each table in a relational database, it's a good idea to have a unique ID field to use as the primary key (and for all other purposes, to identify the record).

> **CROSS-REF** For a discussion of the selection requirements for key field values (especially primary keys), refer to Chapter 7.

When you have relationships in place, a variety of useful options become available to you. For example, you can use relationships in place of Finds to locate groups of records instantly (by using the Go to Related Record [ ] command), and it becomes possible to automatically generate *dynamic* (data-driven) value lists filtered via relationships.

From a single vantage point (layout or base table) within your solutions, your users (and the scripts you provide them) can access related data and create, update, or delete related records. A brief overview of techniques available for these purposes appears in the following sections.

### Allowing creation via relationship

When you define a relationship, you can choose for either (or both) TOs of the relationship to Allow Creation of Related Records in This Table via This Relationship. You make this specification via a pair of settings in the lower panel of the Edit Relationship dialog, shown in Figure 11.5.

> **NOTE** The Allow Creation of Related Records option requires that key fields in either or both tables be writable so that FileMaker can automatically synchronize key field values when establishing the relationship to a new record. Moreover, the relationship definition may only include the =, ≥, and ≤ operators. (Otherwise, FileMaker is unable to determine an appropriate corresponding key value to establish a relationship match.)

When this setting is enabled, portals based on the TO in question acquire an empty last line into which data can be entered to automatically create a new record. Thus, with a portal based on such a relationship present on the current layout, a script sequence along the following lines will generate a new related record:

```
Go to Portal Row [Last]
Set Field [RelatedTable::AnyWritableField; AnyValue]
```

### FIGURE 11.5

Setting the Allow Creation option to enable creation of new records in the OrderLines TO from layouts based on the Orders TO.

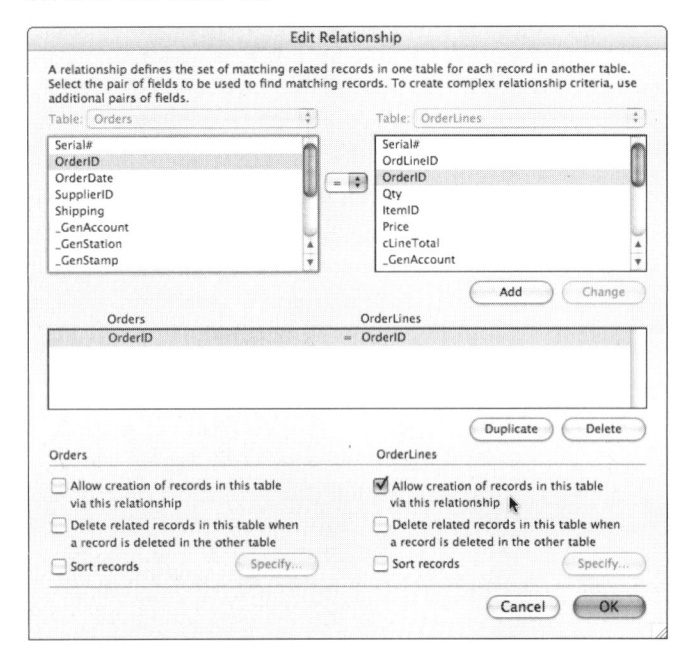

**NOTE** In the absence of a portal, related records can still be created via a relationship set up as noted; however, a new related record is created only when no related records exist for the current match key value(s). Nevertheless, you can use a utility relationship to generate new related records (see "The isolating relationship" section, later in this chapter).

## Using self joins

The self-join relationship is an important technique in creating sophisticated solutions. Self-joins require two TOs of the same base table for the purpose of connecting them. The primary purpose of self-join relationships is to permit records to read from and/or write to other records in the same table.

Self-join relationships serve a variety of different needs, including joins on the primary key to isolate the current record (by using a GTRR to present it alone in a found set), joins on foreign keys, or other attributes grouping or summarizing records on common characteristics (to see other person records listing the same profession, other employee records in the same work group, other invoices for the same customer, and so on). Self-joins are also frequently used for navigation, filtering, selection summarization, and new record creation.

## The isolating relationship

You can employ utility relationships to create a temporary one-to-one relationship to any record in a table so that its data can be retrieved or updated. Such relationships generally match a global field in the current table to the primary key field in a TO based on the same or a different table. By writing the ID (of any related record) into the global field, you can establish a temporary relationship isolating the related record, without changing layouts or modifying the found set.

By this means, you can create a script to work its way through a group of related records (without using a portal), updating each in turn. Alternatively, with a relationship configured to allow creation of related records, you can clear the global field and generate a corresponding related record by writing a value into a field in the related table via the relationship. FileMaker will generate a new auto-entered ID in the related table and will automatically add it to the global field to complete the relationship.

**CROSS-REF** For a detailed description of scripted processes using an isolating relationship to address groups of related records, refer to Chapter 13.

# Graph Techniques — Spiders, Squids, and Anchor-Buoy

When FileMaker first introduced the Relationships Graph (FileMaker Pro 7), many users assumed it was primarily a data modeling tool and tried to build ERD-like structures. However, the required supporting relationships for interface and process added complexity, and the original concept was almost invariably lost. With a certain amount of irony, some developers have described the relationships graphs from their early efforts as *spider graphs*, meaning that the clusters of TOs amid myriad relationship lines resembled spiders in webs.

Over time, developers confronted with the need to manage the relationship structures of complex solutions came up with alternative strategies for organizing the graph's elements and increasing its manageability. One of the first — and perhaps least useful — methods to emerge (though it can be argued that it has helped some developers make the transition to the fp7 format) is an approach that in its variants is sometimes referred to as either *squid* or *anchor-buoy*. These graph management models introduce an orthodoxy in which a specific TO of each table is reserved for layouts, and each reserved TO becomes the anchor (or squid-head) for a discrete group of TOs built entirely and independently to support the needs of layouts based on the anchor TO. These methods make no use of two-way relationships, introduce high levels of redundancy, and trap the developer in a confined (though predictable) paradigm of relationship management closely analogous to the constraints operating in FileMaker 6 and earlier.

Meanwhile, among developers dissatisfied with the limits of these approaches, several other useful graph management models have emerged. Although we don't propose to exhaustively explore the possible techniques in the following sections, we'd nevertheless like to indicate some directions for you to consider.

## Constellations and modular centers

A useful emerging technique for managing the Relationships Graph in complex solutions is to group graph activity into modules around several functional centers that form a natural focus of activity in the solution. Many solutions support several overlapping areas of activity and readily lend themselves to being conceptualized in this way.

## Part III  Beyond the Basics

This *modular-centric approach* enables you to begin by building several independent ERD-like graph structures from the foundation tables of each modular center. These structures remain separate, while you extend them by adding supporting TOs (drawn in some cases from base tables represented in the cores of other modular centers) to serve the range of process, interface, and reporting requirements within each module.

While the Relationships Graph example shown in Figure 11.6 supports a solution of moderate complexity, where five interactive functionality centers are used as the basis of organizing the supporting relationship structures, it is clear that each of the TO groupings is of manageable size and complexity. In this solution, the ratio of TOs to tables is approximately 4:1, so there is moderate redundancy, and the solution is efficient in operation and relatively straightforward to maintain. We compared this solution to one of equivalent size and functionality developed using an *anchor-buoy approach*, requiring over 500 TOs (ratio approx 15:1) and presenting a significant challenge to development.

Some solutions lend themselves more readily to a modular graph management approach than others. This implementation style works best when each center has relatively few supporting tables (in the case of our example, an average of seven tables per operational group) and where not all tables from other groups are required to be accessed throughout the solution.

### FIGURE 11.6

An implementation of Graph Modeling based on the modular-centric approach, in a 35-table solution.

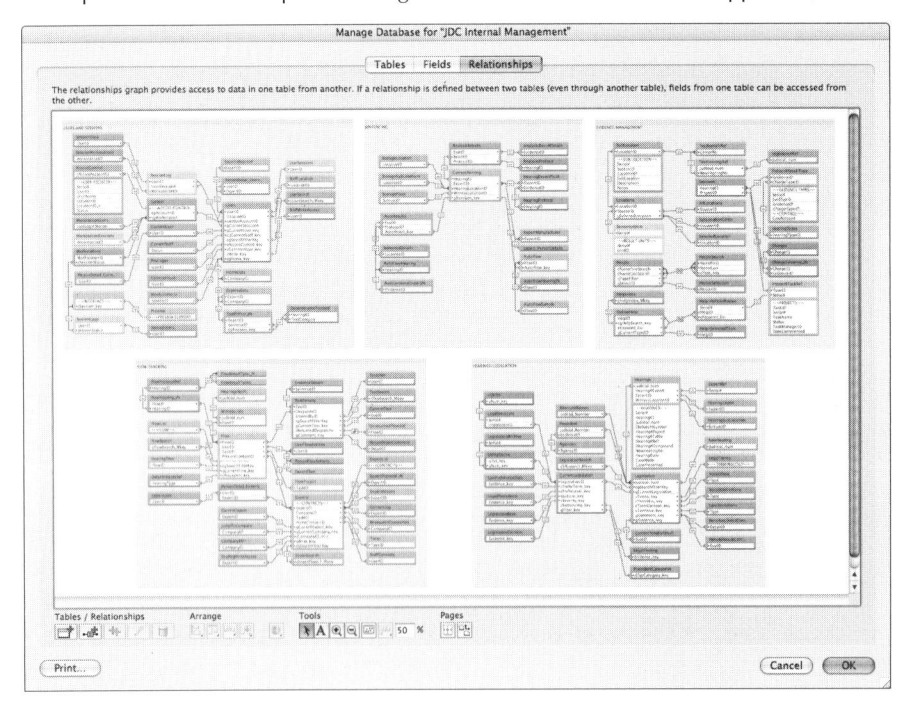

## A satellite-based graph solution

When modularization of the graph begins to reach burdensome levels of redundancy, you have other alternatives. For example, you can draw together the essential elements of the data model into a simplified cluster at the heart of your graph design. For all operational requirements not catered to within the simplified central group of TOs, you can add separate utility structures that control specific functions, reports, and processes.

The Relationships Graph displayed in Figure 11.7 represents the final result of a process commencing with solution design around an anchor-buoy graph model requiring over 350 TOs. When the original developer sought a more streamlined design, a modular approach was first considered; however, due to the nature of the solution, a modularized graph would still have required around 180 TOs.

By stripping the graph model back to bare essentials and defining a limited number of two-directional reusable satellite structures, you can deliver the same functionality using only 73 TOs, as shown in Figure 11.7.

Although alternative approaches to graph modeling, as illustrated by the preceding examples, can result in more manageable and efficient data designs and graph structures, the more radical reductions, such as the satellite-based approach, have implications for the solution's logic. To use such a model, the solution is heavily dependent on scripted processes transferring the action to appropriate layouts to access graph element utility clusters. So the solution is more tightly scripted than would be required for some other data designs—and requires a significant number of ancillary layouts to support the scripted processes.

The use of a satellite graph model, therefore, becomes a trade-off between competing concerns. A reduction of complexity in one area of your solution may be counterbalanced by constraints or complications elsewhere. When determining an appropriate graph model, consider the balance of requirements for your particular solution to identify a harmonious mix of elements.

## Segmentation on functional lines

The foregoing examples of Relationships Graph models are best suited for solutions of moderate size and complexity. To varying degrees, they take a task focus rather than an entity relationship model as their alternative organizing principle. While these techniques are scalable within reason, if you use this type of structure, you'll encounter problems supporting solutions with hundreds of base tables.

You need to think about the overhead any complex Relationships Graph imposes on FileMaker's cache management processes. To support a data-on-demand usage model, FileMaker maintains an internal map of joins with respect to the layout (and its associated TO) of each window. When the user (or a script) takes action impacting the joins, FileMaker must work its way through each affected join, discarding outdated cache and (subsequently, when required) rebuilding it. A layout that reaches out through hundreds of relationship joins therefore imposes a greater burden than one with a more moderate graph overhead.

To ease concerns about interactions between large numbers of tables, you could consider separating the graph between two or more files. Even though all the base tables may reside in a single file, placing some components of the graph functionality into alternate files (to support various script and interface requirements) can yield noticeable benefits in both manageability and solution performance.

## Part III  Beyond the Basics

### FIGURE 11.7
A graph implementation based on a cluster and satellite approach in a 23-table solution.

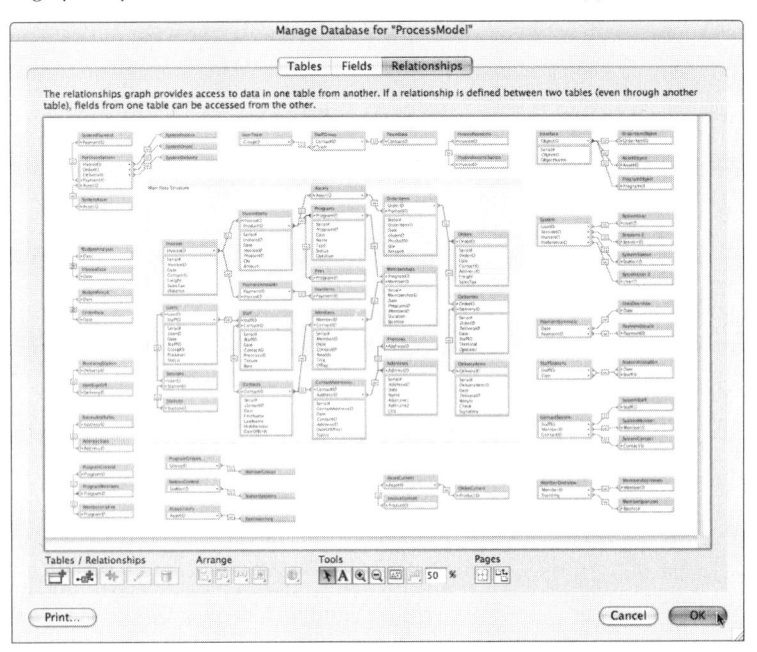

One of the candidates for segmentation is reporting. A large solution can benefit from separating and modularizing reporting requirements, enabling them to be served by separate graph structures that come into play only when the reporting functionality is required. Thus, data entry and business process support can proceed without the added cache management associated with reporting relationship structures. Conversely, reporting can operate unencumbered in a graph environment of its own when required.

**NOTE**  A deeper exploration of the separation of solutions into elements — including the separation of data and interface — is provided in the section "Implementing Separation in an Existing Solution," later in this chapter.

## Documenting the Database Structure

In every area of every solution, the value of documentation increases as the mix of elements and structure becomes more complex, as time passes and memory fades, or as the number of people working on a system increases or changes.

## Data Modeling in FileMaker

In a solution of less than a hundred lines of code, even if you've never seen it before, you can probably comprehend its entire scope and purpose in the space of an afternoon. A solution of a thousand (or 10,000) lines of code, however, is a different proposition. At this point, some well-placed sign posts may be the only thing preventing you from becoming hopelessly lost.

A problem, however, arises when you put off documenting your solutions — at first because they're small (everything starts small, after all), and then because you're onto the next thing (and, besides, you can remember where you've been). But soon, a solution grows to the point where retrospectively documenting it is a major undertaking. When it comes to documentation, "Don't wait, or it will be too late" is an excellent motto.

## Graph annotations

The FileMaker Relationships Graph provides a text tool for adding notes to the graph. Conveniently, the notes always sit behind TOs and relationship lines, so the essentials aren't obscured. You can add text notes as sticky labels, headings, explanatory notes, or frames and bounding boxes for groups of TOs. Figure 11.8 shows a selection of styles and uses of graph notes objects created with the Text tool.

The upper-right corner of the graph text object (see Figure 11.8) provides a disclosure button. Clicking the button collapses the note into a heading; subsequent clicks toggle the display of the body area of the note. You can use this feature to add information and then tuck it out of sight until it's needed.

You can also apply color to notes, note text, and TOs on the graph. By using color systematically to identify TOs (either by the base table they point to or according to their function), you can make the graph considerably more comprehensible.

**FIGURE 11.8**

You can create a variety of text notes to provide supporting information on the Relationships Graph.

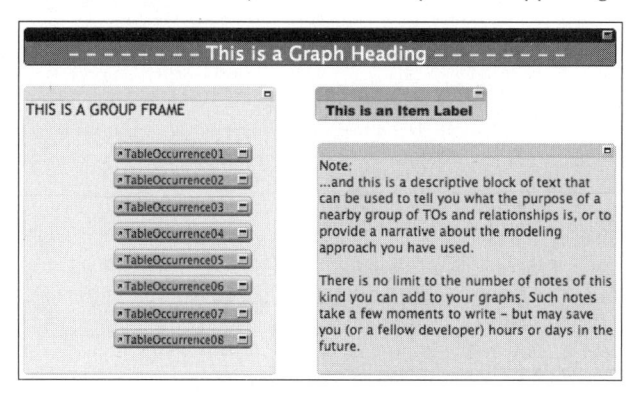

381

## Naming conventions

A significant aspect of the trail you leave behind for yourself or others to follow is the way you name the components of your solutions. Nowhere is naming more important than for tables, table occurrences, and fields.

**NOTE** FileMaker accepts free-form text names for most elements in the schema — you can use spaces, alphanumeric characters, plus a variety of other characters or punctuation marks. However, integration with other systems and technologies can be problematic if your naming is nonstandard. For compatibility, we recommend that you use only alphanumeric characters, underscore, and hash characters

We're not about to instruct you to follow standards. The problem with standards is that they're all different. Numerous public documents recommend various possible approaches to naming in FileMaker. Most recently, in November 2005, FileMaker Inc., published a Development Conventions paper documenting the practices and recommendations of a number of developers. Although it contained some useful advice, along with a broad range of suggestions, it has gained no more widespread acceptance than various other proposed standards that preceded it.

While we don't insist on a specific standard, we strongly recommend that you take care to be consistent — and to strive for simplicity, logic, and readability. We recommend the use of Hungarian notation (in other words, a prefixed c or g) to identify calculation fields and global fields, along with the use of CamelCase (often called *intercapping*) to delineate words in a compact way without spaces.

While some developers recommend suffixes such as _pk for primary keys and _fk for foreign keys, we think the inclusion of ID in the name of a key field is sufficient for clarity in most cases. It's already obvious that an InvoiceID field is the unique identifier and serves as the primary key in an Invoices table — and it's equally obvious when it appears in another table that it is a foreign key. In both cases, suffixes would clutter without clarifying.

As a part of a common-sense and minimalist approach to naming, we do recommend care in ensuring that your names are clear and descriptive. Try to avoid similarly named fields with different purposes — and differently named fields with similar purposes. Aim for clarity.

## Field commenting

In complex solutions, the importance of brevity in field names limits the amount of meaning or explanation you can reasonably hope to pack into field and TO names. While FileMaker permits names of up to 100 characters, long names are problematic and counterproductive. For example, the long field name shown in Figure 11.9 is only 48 characters long — but only the first 27 characters

# Data Modeling in FileMaker 11

show in the default column width in the Fields panel of the Manage Database dialog. Moreover, other dialogs, such as the Sort dialog, show even fewer characters of the field name and can't be enlarged.

### FIGURE 11.9

Long field names are truncated in many dialogs, including the Field Name list on the Fields tab of the Manage Database dialog.

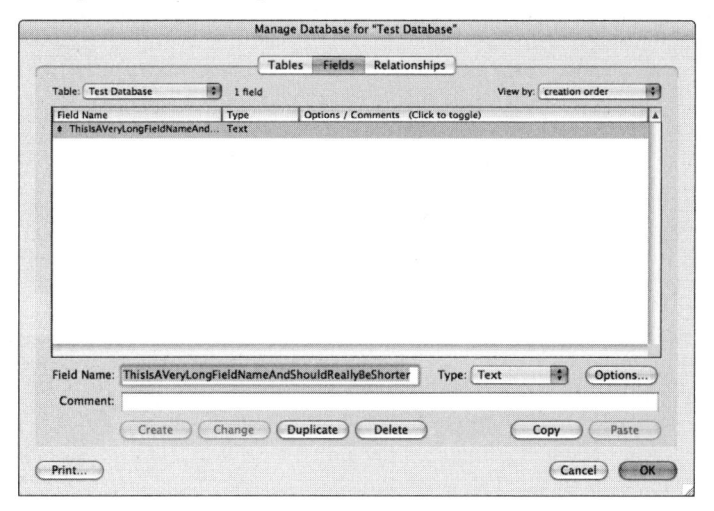

In fact, if you choose the same starting characters for several fields, differentiating them only by the characters at the end of the name, such as

> Companies_Select_update_ALL
>
> Companies_Select_update_CURRENT
>
> Companies_Select_update_NEXT_c
>
> Companies_Select_update_NEXT_g

you'll encounter a usability issue when the field names are truncated in dialogs throughout the application. Figure 11.10 displays fields that are indistinguishable from others because they all start with the same characters.

383

**FIGURE 11.10**

Long field truncated in the Sort Records dialog—presenting a usability issue for both developer and end users.

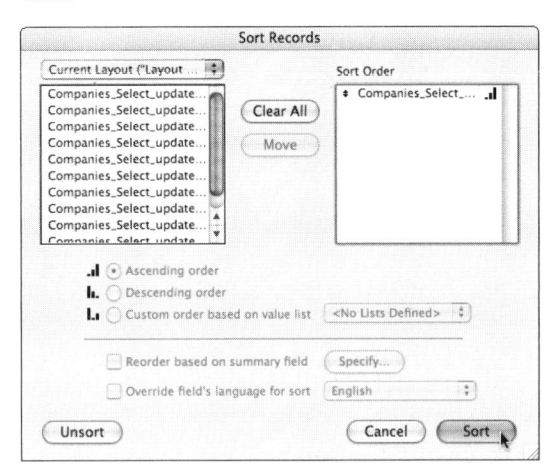

**NOTE** You can resize some FileMaker dialogs to enlarge the viewing area, but it doesn't solve the problem in cases where only the right-hand column is resizable.

We recommend field names of 25 characters or less. If you want to include more information than fits comfortably within these constraints, use the field commenting facility to add an explanatory note. As shown in Figure 11.11, you can enter field comments directly below the field name and, if desired, view these in the main field list in the Manage Database dialog by clicking the column heading labeled Options/Comments.

**CROSS-REF** In addition to field comments and graph notes, FileMaker supports the use of C and C++ style commenting within calculation expressions. Refer to Chapter 12 for additional details about the use of commenting in calculation expressions.

## Ancillary notes and documentation

You can also leave additional notes within the database itself. For example, you might consider adding a table called DeveloperNotes where you can store design concepts and annotations regarding aspects of the structure and code so that you can have ready access to your notes about things you need to remember.

In addition, accumulating programming notes during the course of solution development can provide various forms of input information as you begin to assemble user documentation and help text for your solution. Users generally need slightly different information—and may need it expressed in different terms. However, both kinds of documentation should often cover many of the same broad issues.

### Data Modeling in FileMaker

**FIGURE 11.11**

Adding and viewing field comments via the Manage Database dialog.

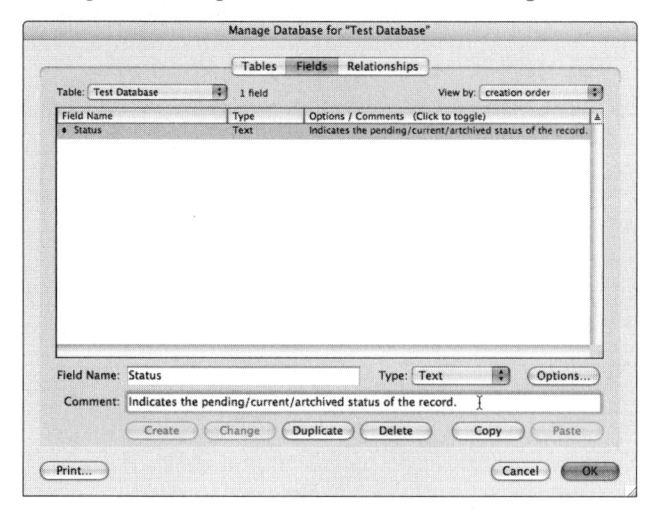

## The Concept of Layers

Database systems are frequently comprised of a collection of elements working together to provide data storage, logical processing, and user interaction. Thus, it can be helpful to think about solution design in terms of the data layer, the logic layer, and the interface layer. FileMaker's unified file structure incorporates some elements of all three layers in every file — and permits you to deliver your entire solution in one file, if you want.

FileMaker is nothing if not flexible, however, and if you choose to do so, you can divide your solution to some degree, delineating the purpose of different files according to layers of functionality — or other criteria as dictated by the needs of your solution and its users.

Some developers believe that a benefit of considering the layers of your solution independently (whether or not you choose to use a single file or multiple files) is that it gives you an opportunity to think through the data structure and get it right before worrying about the logic or interface aspects. We're not persuaded by this viewpoint because in FileMaker the requirements of logic and interface are substantially imposed on the graph model (and vice versa); thinking about any one layer in isolation may lead to decisions that are ultimately detrimental.

### "Back end" and "front end"

Another concept familiar to many database developers is the back end or data end of a solution. Although FileMaker has layouts in the same files as tables, you enter a different environment (the

**385**

Manage Database dialog) to create or change the data structure, so it is not difficult to recognize that the data end requires somewhat different skills and has its own rules.

Because FileMaker enables you to set up references to external data — in other FileMaker files or in SQL data sources — you have the option to create some degree of distinction between the data storage function and the logic and interface functions in your solutions. For example, you can choose to use a specific file primarily to store data and little else (giving it only the most rudimentary interface and few scripts) and then create one or more files to use the data in the first file as the basis of layouts and scripts to make a presentation layer for your solution. Arrangements of this kind form the basis of what has become known as the *separation model* of FileMaker development.

The separation model is important to understand — not merely because it provides you with additional architectural options for your solutions, but also because understanding it is essential to grasping the elements of the structural model FileMaker provides.

FileMaker ties code to data to the extent that a *back-en*d file must always have more than just data in it. For example, calculations or lookups require some supporting relationships in the file where they're defined. Moreover, FileMaker's security model is file-based; to protect the data, you need to build appropriate security in the data file. With this security in place, some scripts will be necessary to let users log in appropriately in the data file so that they can access the information it contains. In all these respects and others, it becomes clear that a purist approach to the separation of data from the remaining frameworks of a solution is neither feasible nor desirable when working with FileMaker. Nevertheless, you may choose to create one or more files primarily as data files and others primarily as interface files.

Just as a FileMaker data file will never be purely or exclusively data, a FileMaker interface file will necessarily include the logic (security and scripting) and probably also at least some data (if only user preferences, global filter attributes, and the like).

## The business or procedural layer

In some database development environments, the process or logic layer of a solution subsists in a collection of stored procedures. FileMaker, on the other hand, distributes your solutions' logic layers throughout a number of places.

The first and perhaps most important logical and procedural control FileMaker affords you is its calculation capabilities. When you define a calculation, you are in effect setting up a process that automatically responds to certain inputs and follows the rules you specify to produce corresponding outputs. This is true of calculations residing in the tables of your solution, but it's also true of calculations in scripts, on buttons, in conditional formatting, or anywhere else in your solution. Calculations are one expression of rules governing how your solution should work and what should happen when the user acts in a certain way.

FileMaker's scripting capability is the second focus of logic and process in your solutions. In many respects, scripts more closely resemble the procedure methods available in other environments and their implementation provides self-contained process logic.

**CROSS-REF** For a more detailed discussion of the FileMaker scripting engine's logical capabilities, refer to Chapter 13.

## FileMaker as an integrated environment

One reason to consider a solution structure separating data and interface is the ability to modify one part without affecting the other. Because FileMaker is designed as an integrated database tool, using it to create solutions comprising separate data and logic interface components can be viewed either as perverse or ingenious — your choice. You may not choose to adopt such an approach for all cases, but it is important to be aware that separation is available for occasions when it may be desirable or even necessary.

When a solution created in a version of FileMaker prior to Version 7 is migrated to the current file format (identified by the file suffix .fp7), it acquires a structure that reflects the constraints of the legacy environment. Prior to the release of FileMaker 7, solutions were constrained to a single table per file, so all relationships were between files (even self-join relationships were defined as a link from a file to itself). Migrated solutions, therefore, typically start out with tables distributed across multiple files and with the interface elements related to a particular table residing in the same table as the file.

Other reasons to depart from the obvious (single-file) architecture for your FileMaker solution include

- **Network performance considerations:** You can keep your dependence on a slow network connection to a minimum if you separate a solution into two components and place the shared data component on a remote server and the static reference data, archival data, and graphics-intensive interface files on the user's local workstation.

- **Divergent user requirements:** If your solution serves different groups of users with different preferences or different needs (but common data requirements), you can provide access to a single data source via multiple interfaces representing the different groups' requirements.

FileMaker has the power to leverage a range of different structural models to deliver a variety of user experiences — all underpinned by a seamless application delivering a holistic database environment.

## Separation anxiety

No matter how you're considering separating your solution on data and interface lines, on modular lines, or in some other way, you need to be aware of several issues and weigh the potential benefits against possible concerns:

- When you choose a multiple-file structure, you need to duplicate some components of code, content, and/or structure. For example, if you create a two-file solution, some scripts may be required in both files (and some processes may require that a script in one file call a script in the other and vice versa). Moreover, you need to configure appropriate security settings in each file. These requirements add complexity and, therefore, may increase development time.

- When you deploy a multi-file solution, you need to decide what goes where and (when you have a choice) what combination or distribution of elements best serves the needs of the users and the requirements of the solution. For example, you don't want to have users perform some actions, such as logging in, twice just because you have two files.

- You also need to be aware of what works where, such as how environment variables are evaluated when a calculation is being performed in a different file. You must also understand the scope of action of all the elements in play (variables, security, scripts, and so on).

# File Architecture versus Data Structure

There is a long history of confusion between file architecture and data architecture. Since the inception of the .fp7 file format, FileMaker has supported multiple tables per file up to 1 million, according to the technical specifications published by FileMaker, Inc. (We'll leave it to you to test that assertion!)

A database system's file architecture, however, doesn't determine the relational structure — FileMaker Pro has supported relational data architectures since the release of Version 3. Prior to the release of Version 7, each file was constrained to contain only a single table, so a multi-table relational solution required multiple files. Solutions converted to the .fp7 format from earlier versions retain their multi-file architecture initially — and, in fact, you can create new solutions in FileMaker 9 that work this way, if you choose.

Remember that although the file structure has implications for how you work and how your solution appears to users, it's entirely independent of the data structure. You get to choose where to store and access each data table your solution uses.

## Multi-file solutions

In a few situations, it's advantageous to have every table in a separate file, but it's frequently useful (or necessary) to build a solution around data residing in more than one file. Occasionally, a multi-file solution architecture is required so you can incorporate or reference data in a pre-existing system (either a separate FileMaker solution or an external SQL database). Even when there is no imperative to use multiple files for your solution, you may choose to do so for a variety of reasons:

- To improve network performance by storing static data or interface components on users' local workstation
- To make installing an update of the interface or process components of a solution easier (without the need to import current data into each new version)
- To give different users different views of the data or different functionality according to their needs or preferences
- To reduce the complexity and overhead associated with each "module" in a complex system where, for example, a single Relationships Graph supporting the entire solution would be unduly complex

Your objectives dictate whether you seek to gather all data into a single file while providing one or more other files to access it, present your interface in a single file with data being sourced from multiple locations, or some combination of both. In other words, you may choose to create

- A single file comprising both data and interface
- A single data file and a single (separate) interface file
- Multiple data files supporting one interface file
- Multiple interface files accessing a single data file

- Multiple interface files sourcing data from multiple files
- A mixed-model solution incorporating multiple files, which may have both interface and data elements within them

## The modular approach

If you can readily divide your solution's functionality into discrete (though perhaps overlapping) areas of functionality, a mixed model or multiple interface approach may provide several benefits. For example, you may choose to provide separate modules to support sales, inventory, and accounts, even though the data for all three subsystems is stored in a single file.

With a modular approach, each department in an organization can have immediate access to the results of the work being done elsewhere (using other system "modules"), yet each works within a system specifically designed to support the needs, preferences, and business processes at hand. For example, the screens, scripts, reports, and menus seen by Accounts personnel need bear no resemblance to those used in the warehouse or on the shop floor, even though the supporting tables and relational structure of the back-end data file are common to all.

Other uses of a modular approach may involve separation of functionality along process lines. For example, you can create a single file or pair of files (interface and data) to support data entry and general solution functionality but provide a separate file for reporting. One advantage is that end users may be given considerably broader access to make changes in the reporting file, while the scripts and interface of the main files remain tightly secured.

While a modular approach can serve a number of needs, the advantages must be counterbalanced against the additional file infrastructure requirements, version control, and complexity introduced. There is, nevertheless, often a payoff from using a modular approach to solution architecture.

## Interface files

Whenever you have a FileMaker file containing data and interface, you can create an interface file by establishing an External Data Source reference from a new file to the existing file. For example, in a new file, if you choose File ➪ Manage ➪ External Data Sources and then click the New button in the lower left of the Manage Data Sources dialog (to expose the Edit Data Source dialog), you can create a link to a copy of the Inventory example file, as illustrated in Figure 11.12.

**NOTE** When you're working on the Relationships Graph (in the Manage Database dialog), you can also access the Manage External Data Sources dialog from the Data Sources menu in the Specify Table dialog.

With a named reference to an external database in place, you can then begin to add TOs to the interface file's graph (by clicking the "+" tool button in the lower left of the dialog, as described in Chapter 5) referring to tables located in the external file, as shown in Figure 11.13. Once TOs are in place, you are able to work with the interface, developing scripts and layouts in the same ways as if the tables were defined and stored within the file; however, all changes to the definitions of tables and fields — and associated access privileges — must still be made directly in the file housing the tables.

### FIGURE 11.12

Creating a link between two files.

The most significant difference when you develop in a separated solution where the interface is in one file and the data in another is the need to maintain an awareness of the location of different elements and the scope of each component of the solution. For example:

- The Run Script with Full Access Privileges setting only influences the access privileges in the file where the script resides—so a script in your interface file won't gain full access to data in the external data file when this option is selected. To achieve full access to the data, you must either call a script (with appropriate privilege settings) in the data file, run a re-login process to temporarily change the level of privileges in the data file, or otherwise modify settings affecting the privilege status of the data file.

- Variables are scoped to the file where they are declared—so calculations in the data file will not be able to "see" variables declared in the interface file and vice versa. To pass values between files, your solutions will have to write the values to a field (for example, a global field) or pass them as a script parameter or script result so that they can be accessed externally.

- You should be mindful that environment data returned by Get( ) functions in the interface file won't always be applicable in the data file and vice versa. For example, if a script in the data file evaluates the function Get(ActiveSelectionStart), it returns a result with respect to whatever is (or is not) selected in the data file. Even if the user's cursor is in a data-file field in the current active window of the interface file, the function being evaluated in the data file will not recognize it. To achieve the desired result, you need to structure the scripted sequence to pass the relevant value(s) from the interface to the data file via a script parameter or script result.

## Data Modeling in FileMaker

**FIGURE 11.13**

Choosing an external file when adding a TO to the Relationships Graph in an interface file.

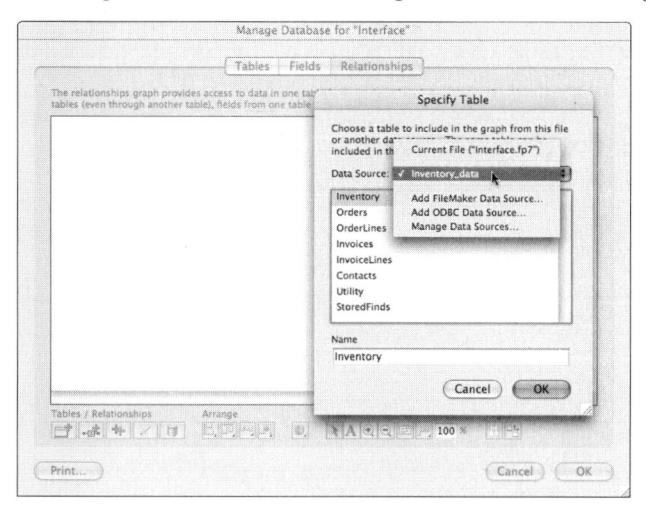

These concerns, and other examples like them, introduce some constraints and stringencies to multi-file development. However, taken as a whole, FileMaker's support for external data sources is broad and effective, with most features operating the same way regardless of the file architecture.

One of the most challenging issues in a multi-file solution is the management of security, because you need to script processes — such as login, logout, account creation, and password change — to occur simultaneously in all files. That way, the user is not prompted for credentials multiple times and the appropriate access privileges are in place in all files throughout a work session.

## Approaches to separation of data

Some developers take the view that to achieve separation of data and interface, the data file should ideally contain nothing but data, and that one should aim to get as close to this ideal as possible. Doing so, however, presents some challenges when working with FileMaker, preventing you from using some of FileMaker's features to the best advantage. For example, FileMaker's calculation fields and the schema to support them can be viewed as part of the logic of the solution rather than strictly part of the data and therefore a strict separation would exclude their use.

Such an approach may enhance the ability to perform updates to a solution without a need to import data to a new file by reducing the likelihood that updates will require modifications to the data file. In extreme cases, however, this convenience is achieved at a considerable cost in foregone functionality and produces inconvenience in other areas. We take the view that the more extreme approaches to separation cost more than they gain in a majority of cases, and you should carefully weigh the trade-offs before going to lengths to achieve "pure" separation.

A more conservative approach to separation, however — where schema, scripts, and calculations are present in the data file, but kept to moderate levels and the majority of code and configuration resides in the interface file — is highly tenable and provides a viable option for many solutions.

In this latter method, some redundancy occurs because the data file requires the essentials of a data model for the solution, much of which may also be required in the interface file. Moreover, in addition to login and security management scripts, some supporting sub-scripts (able to be called from scripts in the interface file) may also be present in the data file, especially where actions beyond the user's access privileges are required.

Although the essential calculation requirements of a solution may be performed in the original data file in a separation model solution, if you want to minimize changes to the data files after deployment, you can structure your solution to script the calculation and storage of derived values for all calculation requirements not covered in the original implementation. Similarly, the addition of reserved (unused) fields in tables in the data file can enable you to anticipate changes and make adjustments to the implementation without modifying the data file.

## Costs and benefits of separation

Data separation introduces a well-understood architecture common to many other data systems with clarity regarding the independence of the interface and logic layers from the data layer of your solution. This clarity is poised in counterbalance against the minor penalties and added complexities noted in the preceding sections, making the decision to opt for a separated solution difficult to justify in the absence of other considerations.

One of the most frequently repeated arguments in favor of the separation of data and interface is the added ease and efficiency of updates after deployment. In some cases this contention is more valid than others. For example, when a solution is in use around the clock and holds millions of records, you want to avoid the inconvenience of taking the system offline to transfer records to an updated database file, if possible. In such cases, if you're able to construct the solution so as to minimize the impact of updates, it makes sense to do so.

Conversely, if your solution is of moderate size or doesn't need 24/7 availability, offline updates involving migration of the data to a new master copy of the updated file are feasible and often desirable because they

- Allow updates to the data structure, including calculations, additional fields, and data relationship definitions to support changed or extended functionality.
- Enable you to refresh the file at each update with a pristine master copy of the development file, thus minimizing the risk of corruption or data loss.

In the latter case, we recommend creating a migration utility to automate the transfer of data between versions of the file. This utility increases the efficiency of an offline update so that it can be performed routinely as required. You can view the creation and maintenance of an update utility as a cost of working with an integrated (single file) solution, avoided by opting to separate the data and interface between two or more files.

## Data Modeling in FileMaker 11

In addition to the considerations regarding updates, potential benefits for network optimization and added deployment flexibility make various forms of separation and multi-file solution architectures attractive in a number of cases.

# Separation and External SQL Sources

As part of the repertoire of options for accessing external data, FileMaker 9 provides support for live access to data in supported external SQL databases. Because SQL systems can't contain any FileMaker script or calculation code, an instance of the use of live SQL data requires you to adopt strategies for dealing with separation of data and interface, as outlined in the preceding section ("File Architecture versus Data Structure"). In such a solution, you can rely entirely on one or more SQL data sources for the data content of a solution, while using FileMaker to provide the interface and business process logic.

The use of SQL data with FileMaker has several potential advantages, chiefly being the capability to integrate seamlessly with other systems supporting SQL standards and the relative ease with which supported SQL databases can accommodate very large data sets, making them available simultaneously to thousands of users.

## Understanding the rules

You may be tempted to consider FileMaker a candidate for duties as a front end for SQL databases. However, bear in mind that FileMaker doesn't provide some capabilities normally found in SQL front ends, including the ability to modify schema in the SQL back end and the ability to incorporate SQL syntax in its normal interactions with the data source.

> **NOTE** FileMaker includes an Execute SQL command you can use for scripted queries against an ODBC data source. However, normal Find operations on SQL tables in FileMaker use the native FileMaker Find interface, which is translated internally into SQL syntax for transmission to the host database.

You should also be aware that FileMaker's ability to deal with very large data sets (such as when performing finds, sorts, or other data-management tasks) is constrained by its internal architecture and may not be optimal when dealing with extremely large numbers of records. The performance limits you encounter when working with data stored in a SQL database will not necessarily be significantly different from those you deal with in native FileMaker deployments.

Also consider the absence of stored calculation capabilities in SQL databases. If you're used to defining calculations for a variety of purposes in FileMaker tables, you'll have to adopt alternate strategies when working with SQL data, which reduces some of the data modeling flexibility characteristic of an all-FileMaker implementation.

## Working within constraints

To work efficiently with SQL data sources, consider adopting some different solution design approaches to compensate for the reduced data model flexibility. For example, one option is to provide an editing interface where the data is presented in holding fields (for example, global fields in the FileMaker interface file) and written back to the SQL database via script at the conclusion of user editing. Such a model where all changes to the remote data are made via script allows you to add calculations and perform operations on the data prior to storage.

If you're working with SQL databases holding very large sets of data, consider defining your links to the SQL data via views rather than direct to the SQL tables, as views can present more manageable subsets of the data in large tables. Figure 11.14 shows the configuration at the lower-right corner of the Edit Data Source dialog where you can specify the form of SQL data to be presented to FileMaker.

> **NOTE** SQL data views don't necessarily have predefined primary key values. If you choose to access such a view in FileMaker, you're required to identify a suitable key value for use as a unique key.

## Supporting the user

Delivering solutions combining data from a variety of environments — even connecting simultaneously to multiple remote host systems — is challenging as well as exciting. The effort required to resolve differences in the way different technologies are implemented is worthwhile because it gives you the ability to provide enhanced support to the users of your solutions.

**FIGURE 11.14**

Configuring the settings for an external ODBC data source to present views instead of tables.

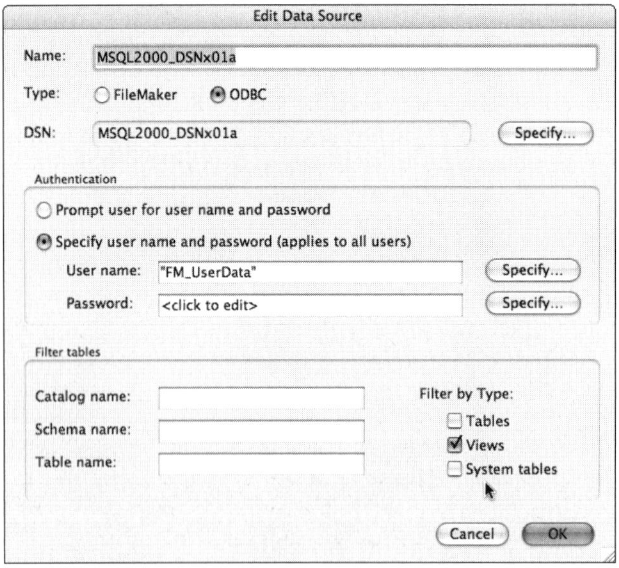

With user requirements in play, it's important to set aside theoretical models and examine the practical realities. The functional requirements and the best interests of the solution's owners and users dictate the decision to build a separated solution, an integrated solution, or a part FileMaker and part SQL solution.

The starting point for any solution modeling exercise should be a user requirements audit. When developers listen, it's been our experience that users are more than ready to talk.

# Implementing Separation in an Existing Solution

When you create a single-file solution in FileMaker Pro 9, all the elements of the file — tables, layouts, scripts, accounts and privileges, and so on — connect directly within FileMaker's integrated file format. Even after a solution is in an advanced stage of development, however, you can redeploy with an alternative solution architecture, introducing layers of separation.

The simplest method for adding multi-file functionality to an existing solution is to create an additional file with links to the tables in the main file and configure the new file to provide specific additional functions (for example, a search interface, an Instant Web Publishing interface, a reporting interface, and so on). However, converting the file into a completely separate data/interface architecture is a more challenging task.

## Establishing data source(s)

To begin the process of converting a solution from a single-file architecture to a separated architecture, you should first store a backup copy of the file in a secure place, then create a duplicate of the file, and name it appropriately for the data file of the solution. You now have two copies of the file, both containing the existing interface and the existing data. Here's how you convert a solution:

1. Add the data file as an external data source in the interface file.
2. Reassign the TOs in the interface file to point to the corresponding tables in the data file.
3. Remove data tables (and their contents) from the interface file.
4. Test to restore any functionality affected by the change.
5. Remove or disable interface elements in the data file.
6. Add scripts to manage security (login and logout) as required across the two files.

Figure 11.12 shows the method of adding a data file as an external data source by choosing File ➪ Manage ➪ External Data Sources. After adding the path to the data source to the interface file, it appears as an available option on the Data Sources menu when selecting or assigning a TO to a data table in the Manage Database dialog.

**Part III**  Beyond the Basics

## Re-pointing table occurrences

The second step in implementing separation is to select each of the TOs in the Relationships Graph and reassign it to the corresponding table in the external data file, as shown in Figure 11.15. Here's how to do so, making sure that you keep the same TO names:

1. Note the table the TO is attached to.
2. Copy the TO name.
3. Select the external data source.
4. Reattach it to the corresponding table in the external file.
5. Paste the original TO name into the name field.
6. Repeat Steps 1–5 for each TO.

After you've changed each TO, its name in the header band appears in italics to indicate that the table it references is in an external file. After completing this process, visit the Manage Database dialog's Tables panel in the interface file. As shown in Figure 11.16, you now see nothing in the Occurrences In graph column of the tables list. (If you do see some, then you missed one and should go back to the Relationships tab to reassign it to the external data file.)

After you've confirmed that all the tables in the interface file are unreferenced, you can delete them from the file. The solution now uses data exclusively from the data file.

**FIGURE 11.15**

Reconnecting a TO to the corresponding table in an external data source.

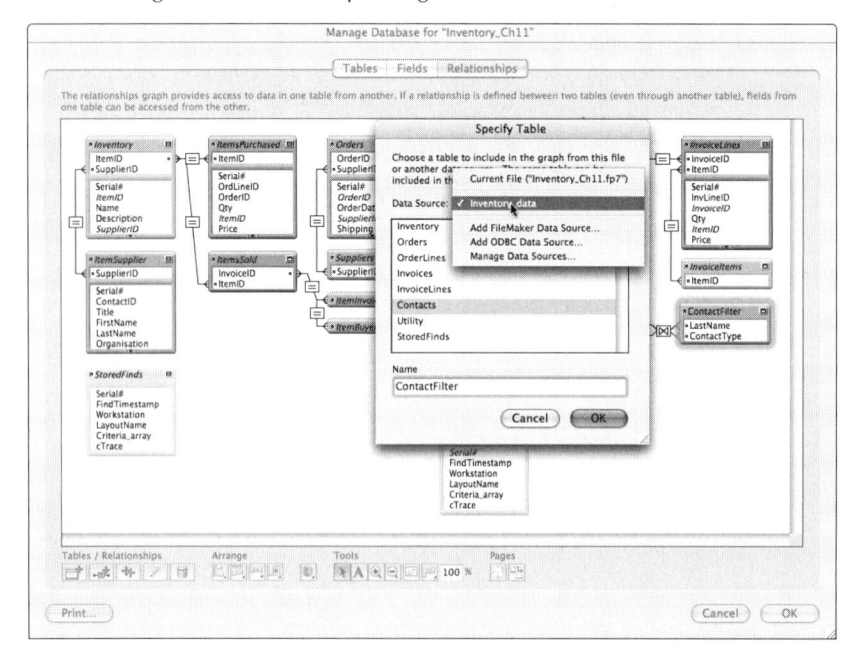

## FIGURE 11.16
No graph occurrences of tables appear in the Interface file.

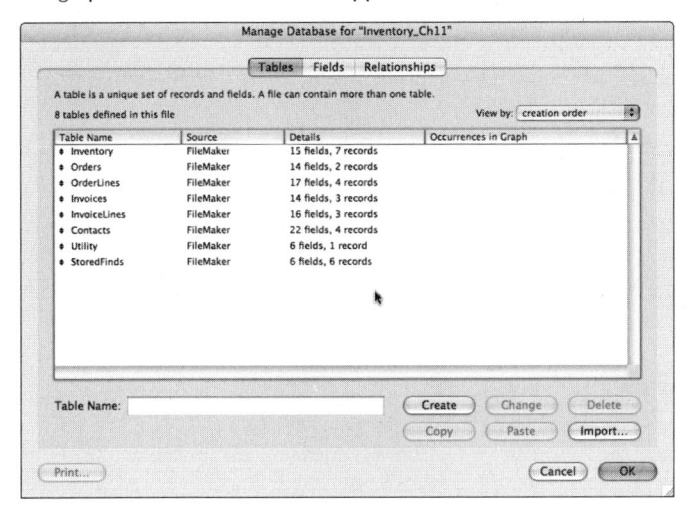

As an important part of the redeployment procedure, you should conduct tests to confirm that the solution's functionality is intact, making any required modifications to restore the intended behavior. In the case of the example inventory solution, our testing revealed that the Back button functionality required modifications because it depended on a $$trace variable declared within the cTrace calculations in schema. The value of a variable declared in the data file where the schema now resides is no longer available to the Go Back script in the interface file. This example is typical of the kind of issue that arises when you change to a separation architecture, as noted in the section "File Architecture versus Data Structure," earlier in this chapter.

We addressed this issue in the example files for this chapter by placing a variant of the cTrace calculation expression into the conditional formatting calculation of replacement Back buttons in the interface file. After this change, we deleted the cTrace fields from the tables in the data file.

Additionally, we made minor changes to the Go Back script to address a refresh issue arising from cached external data in the Utility relationship used by the script. With these changes, we restored the example solution to its former functionality, yet in a separated architecture.

## Creating separate graphs

Once data sources for all TOs have been reassigned according to plan, rationalization of the two identical Relationships Graphs can begin.

The first step toward tailoring each file for its new role is removing extraneous process and interface support elements from the data file's Relationships Graph. In the example Inventory Solution, we identified that 12 of the 24 TOs on the original graph were required for script or interface support, but they were nonessential to the schema in the data file. Consequently, we were able to halve the number of TOs in the data file. Similarly, we removed scripts and layouts from the data file.

When making changes to both files at this stage in redeployment, multiple test cycles are a good precautionary measure. Extra testing ensures that adjusting graph and/or other elements in either of the files allows preservation (or restoration, if necessary) of required functionality.

After making the preceding changes, the Inventory example reached the desired redeployment aim: a more flexible architecture without sacrificing features or usability. The programming style adjustments required to accommodate the structural change are minimal, and we could efficiently make the required modifications at this stage of development.

The more complex a solution is at the time a change of deployment strategy is indicated, the greater the risks involved and the greater the work and testing required to ensure that the solution will not be adversely affected by the change. However, while determining an appropriate architecture for your solutions at the outset is desirable, change can be achieved.

# Deployment Considerations

The option to separate elements of a solution makes a number of innovative deployment models viable, including modularization, separation of data, and interface and integration of external SQL data. However, we encourage you to carefully weigh the options to determine a mix that best serves your solution.

The conventional deployment mode — where one or more FileMaker database files (comprising both data and interface) reside on a network server and are accessed over a high-speed internal network — is giving way to other innovative solution topographies.

## Your remotest dreams

Employing solution separation architectures enables some elements of your solutions to reside on network hosts (including multiple or remote/WAN hosts) while others are stored and accessed locally from the end user's workstation. Deployment models of this type permit new levels of flexibility and performance for distributed systems.

Systems drawing agency data for supporting databases in branch offices at considerable distances can now achieve satisfactory performance with appropriate optimizations — and a single server can be used as the conduit for data from any mix of FileMaker and supported SQL data systems.

## The model of adaptability

The introduction of FileMaker's fp7 file format in 2004 signaled a shift in focus only fully realized with the release of the FileMaker 9 suite of products. FileMaker has evolved and, with the introduction of support for external SQL data sources, the evolutionary leap is evident.

With FileMaker 9 as your tool of choice, a robust and ambitious feature set is available to you. FileMaker delivers its own flexible relational database management system — and puts it, along with a plethora of alternative (and even competing) technologies, into your hands. Access to these capabilities enables you to combine technologies in new ways and to solve new problems by doing so. It is up to you to devise data models and solution architectures to take advantage of FileMaker's new horizons.

# Chapter 12

# Calculation Wizardry

In Chapter 7, we introduce you to the Specify Calculation dialog and demonstrate a few aspects of its utility and capability. However, if you have the impression that calculation is mainly about numbers, we have some surprises in store for you. Calculating in FileMaker is about getting the computer to work things out, but not necessarily just with numbers. In fact, calculations are great for people who aren't all that impressed with numbers. A bit of clear thinking will go a very long way, and the computer can do the rest!

Like scripting, calculations are integral to structuring and automating your solution. You can use calculations to determine access, control displays, and implement a variety of other features in your solution, as demonstrated in this chapter.

With FileMaker, a little work upfront can save you a lot of work later on. Calculations are one of the most extreme examples of this principle. Set one up, and it will keep chugging away producing results for thousands or even millions of records—enough to wear the buttons off a whole storeroom full of portable calculators.

You can employ the 243 built-in calculation functions FileMaker 9 offers, each of which is designed to do something very particular. However, what calculation functions can do on their own isn't the subject of this chapter, but how you can combine them together to achieve everything from clever tricks to downright astonishing feats is.

> **NOTE** A full alphabetical list of the calculation functions in FileMaker 9, including links to descriptions and basic examples, is available online at www.filemaker.com/help/func-alp.html. And you

## IN THIS CHAPTER

**Building compound calculation expressions**

**Understanding order of operations and Boolean constructs**

**Using variables in different contexts**

**Processing, parsing, and formatting text**

**Calculating with dates and times**

**Working with summaries and arrays**

**Layers of Abstraction**

**Working with different kinds of calculations**

**Employing global calculations**

**Making use of environment and meta-data**

**Extending your code with Custom Functions**

**Keeping track of what you've done**

**Part III**     **Beyond the Basics**

can download a comprehensive FileMaker Pro 9 Functions Reference (248 pages in PDF format) at `www.filemaker.com/downloads/pdf/fmp9_functions_ref.pdf`.

Because these materials are so readily available, we don't repeat their content in this book, reserving the space instead for usage recommendations and examples. We recommend that you download the PDF reference and refer to it as a supplement to this book.

## Compound Calculation Expressions

A *formula* is the statement of your calculation, and an *expression* is something that can be evaluated. Thus, a formula is an expression, but not all expressions are necessarily formulas. Therefore, when we say formula, we mean the entirety of what appears in the Specify Calculation dialog's formula box, and that formula will consist of one or more expressions.

A *function* is a named expression that, when provided with zero or more arguments (frequently called *parameters*), returns a value. FileMaker Pro 9 provides a collection of precisely 243 calculation functions for you to employ in your formulas; however, they are *black boxes* in that you don't get to see the code that implements them.

Symbols such as +, -, *, /, ^, and also and, or, xor, and not are termed operators and instruct FileMaker how to treat adjacent parts of your calculation expressions. The adjacent parts acted upon by operators are often termed *operands*. In the calculation 2 + 3, for example, the 2 and the 3 are operands and the + is the operator.

**CROSS-REF**    You can supplement FileMaker's built-in functions by creating your own custom functions using FileMaker Pro 9 Advanced, as described in Chapter 18.

In the simplest of formulas, a function receives appropriate input parameters and returns a result. For example, the expression `Rightwords("The Jean Genie"; 1)` returns `Genie`, extracting one word from the right of the supplied phrase. However, each parameter you supply to a function such as `RightWords()` can be a literal value (as in the preceding example), a field (in which case the function acts on the field's value for the current record, or an expression combining one or more functions, constants, and/or operands.

Because one function's result can be passed as the input to another function, you can assemble complex structures according to simple rules, using functions and expressions like the words and phrases of a magical language that does the things it says.

If you begin with a simple function such as `Get(CurrentDate)` (which returns the current date as per the current computer's system clock) and enclose it within the `Month()` function as in `Month(Get(CurrentDate))`, FileMaker returns the number of the current month (for example, 3 for March, 7 for July, and so on). Similarly, enclosing `Get(CurrentDate)` within the `Year()` function returns the number of current year (for example, 2008).

# Calculation Wizardry

All these numbers are moderately useful in themselves, but they're more useful if you use them in turn to supply arguments to the Date function:

```
Date( Month(Get(CurrentDate)) + 1; 1; Year(Get(CurrentDate)) )
```

In this formula, 1 is added to the month number, and it's passed as the month parameter to the `Date()` function. The day is specified as the constant value 1, and the current year is provided as the year parameter. Thus, the entire expression returns the date of the first day of the following month.

An important thing to understand about the foregoing Date trick is that it will still work even when the current month number is 12. FileMaker is smart enough to accept the resulting month parameter of 13, convert the month to 1 (January), and increment the year so that a valid date is returned for all cases. This sleight of hand is typical of the FileMaker box of tricks.

> **NOTE** The `Date( )` function also resolves zero and negative parameter values. So, for example, if zero (0) is passed as the second parameter (day number) in the preceding function, the result will be the last day of the current month, regardless of how many days are in the current month.

## The language of logic

In the example,

```
Date( Month(Get(CurrentDate)) + 1; 1; Year(Get(CurrentDate)) )
```

you're instructing FileMaker to tell you the date where the month is the current month plus 1, the day is the first of the month, and the year is the current year. The form—also called *syntax*—that FileMaker requires you to use when asking it for a date is

```
Date(Month, Day, Year)
```

This form imposes a structure like any other language. First, you must say what you want to do and then (in parentheses afterward) you must say how, when, or where (as the case may be). FileMaker's calc syntax is based on the English language, presented in a simplified and codified form. After you get used to the structured language, it becomes easier to scan, write, and understand.

The calculation language's rules are consistent and straightforward, and the vocabulary (function names, operators, constants and some reserved words, plus the table and field names in your solution) isn't too challenging. Most of the rules simplify things; prepositions and conjunctions are omitted, and parentheses, semicolons, or operators are used in their place, as appropriate.

FileMaker's native function set defines not only the core of the vocabulary of calculations, but also the form and syntax. Each function in the vocabulary has simple rules for the inputs it requires and the outputs it returns, all of which are defined in the FileMaker 9 Function Reference. (To access this reference, go to www.filemaker.com/downloads/pdf/fmp9_functions_ref.pdf.)

**401**

## Part III  Beyond the Basics

Almost all native FileMaker calculation functions require parameters. The only five exceptions are

- `DatabaseNames`
- `Pi`
- `Random`
- `Self`
- `WindowNames`

Each of the first four functions stands alone, returning its appropriate value without qualification, whenever you use it. The last, `WindowNames`, can stand alone or can accept an optional parameter specifying the name of the file for which it is to return the names of current windows. All other functions, however, require one or more parameters, either to control the way they work or to provide input.

When parameters are required, they're always enclosed in parentheses immediately after the name of the function they're associated with. Multiple parameters are separated by semicolons. A few functions (20 in total, including `WindowNames`) include optional parameters. Whereas `WindowNames` has only one parameter, however, all other functions with optional parameters have one or more required parameters. An example of a function with an optional parameter is the `If( )` function:

```
If(test; resultIfTrue {; resultIfFalse})
```

The `If( )` function can accept either two or three parameters — the first two are required, and the third is optional. The first parameter is the test to determine the result the function returns. The second parameter supplies the result if the test succeeds (is evaluated as true). The final, optional parameter supplies a result to be returned if the test fails (proves false). A simple expression using `If( )` can therefore be written as

```
If(DateOfBirth = Get(CurrentDate); "Happy Birthday, " & FirstName)
```

This formula returns a message such as "Happy Birthday, Jan" when the value in the `FirstName` field is "Jan" and the value in the `DateOfBirth` field is the same as the current date on your computer's system clock. However, if you want the function to return a result on days other than Jan's birthday, you can use the optional third parameter:

```
If(DateOfBirth = Get(CurrentDate); "Happy Birthday, "; "Welcome, ") & FirstName
```

In this example, whenever it is not Jan's birthday, the optional second result is returned, so the text will simply read "Welcome, Jan". One day per year, the text returned will be Happy Birthday, Jan".

## Functions and schema references

You can supply parameters to your functions in one of three ways:

- **As text or numbers entered directly into the calculation:** Parameters supplied in this way are usually referred to as a *constant* or a *literal* value. Commonly, constant refers to numeric values and literal to text values, but the names are applied somewhat interchangeably.

- **As a reference (by name) to a field or a variable in your solution:** In this case, FileMaker retrieves the current value of the field or variable at the time it evaluates the calculation, using it as input to the function.
- **As an expression:** This expression can be made up of one or more functions, operators, and other elements combined in such a way as to produce a result that will provide the required parameter.

When you enter text literals into a calculation, they must be enclosed within quotes (" "). Numeric literal values don't require quotes. When you enter more than one item, an operator is required in between them (and which operator you choose controls how they're interpreted). For example, the + operator tells FileMaker to add the numeric values of the supplied values, whereas the & operator tells FileMaker to append them as text. So the expression 23 + 4 will return 27, whereas the expression 23 & 4 will return 234.

**CROSS-REF** For a detailed discussion of the mechanics of defining calculations in the Specify Calculation dialog, refer to Chapter 7.

When you want FileMaker to retrieve the value from a field in your database, you must generally supply the name of the field, preceded by the name of the relevant TO, in the form

```
TableOccurrenceName::FieldName
```

The only exception is when you define the calculation within the schema, and the field is returned from the current record — in which case the TO name is optional.

Adding the TO name enables FileMaker to determine the relationship path to use when retrieving a value from the field. Resolving the path requires both a start point and an end point. The TO name you supply with the referenced field name defines the end point. The start point is set via the Evaluate This Calculation From The Context Of menu at the top of the Specify Calculation dialog, as shown in Figure 12.1.

Because FileMaker requires that only one relationship path be between any two TOs on the Relationships Graph, supplying the starting and ending TOs for a field reference is sufficient to indicate exactly from which instance of the field to retrieve a value.

**NOTE** When a relationship you use to reference a field in the current record points to multiple related records, FileMaker returns the first related record (according to the sort order for the relationship, if specified, or otherwise according to the creation order of records in the related table). To reference a field in a record (other than the first related record), enclose the field reference within the `GetNthRecord( )` function, supplying (as the second parameter) the number of the record you want to reference.

**Part III**    **Beyond the Basics**

**FIGURE 12.1**

Setting the context for evaluation of a calculation via the Specify Calculation dialog.

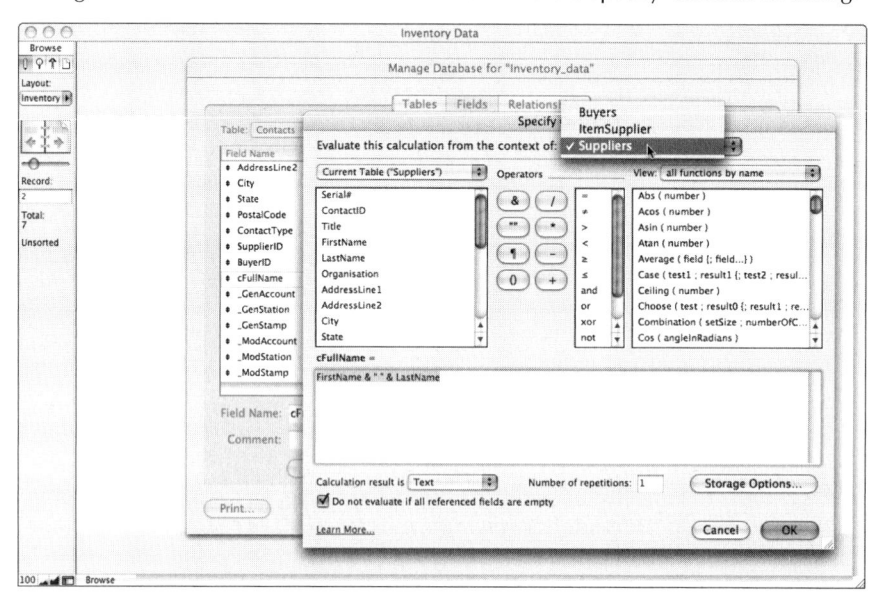

## Structured syntax and nesting

Although we recommend that you obtain a copy of the FileMaker 9 Functions Reference and use it as a supplementary resource, you don't need to refer to it to remember the syntax required for each calculation function. FileMaker lists all its available functions in the panel at the upper right of the Specify Calculation dialog, along with a key to the syntax requirements of each function. The listed functions may be filtered by category (in 16 predefined categories) to make it easier to find what you're looking for.

Two of the 16 categories of functions — `Get` functions and `External` functions — are included only as a single reference each in the list of all functions by name. To see the available options in each of these groups, you must choose the respective function category.

> **NOTE**    Functions in the Specify Calculation dialog list are categorized by data type according to the kind of input value they're expected to receive, rather than the kind of output they generate. For example, `GetAsTimestamp( )` is listed as a text function because it receives a text input, even though it returns its result as a timestamp value.
>
> Similarly, the `Length( )` function is listed among text functions because it treats the input value as a text string, even though the result it returns will be a number (representing the length of the supplied string).

When you select a function from the Specify Calculation dialog functions list, it's inserted into the calculation panel at the current cursor position, along with the prompt for its syntax, such as parentheses, semicolons, and names of the required parameters. For example, if you select the `Upper ( )` function, it is inserted into your calculation as `Upper ( text )` with the parameter name (`text`) selected, ready for you to overwrite it with an appropriate value. You can supply the parameter as a literal value (within quote marks):

```
Upper("Strawberry Fields Forever")
```

or as a reference to a field or variable:

```
Upper(Songs::SongName)
```

```
Upper($$CurrentSongName)
```

or as an expression, incorporating any combination of literal values, field or variable references, and/or functions:

```
Upper("Song Title: " & Songs::SongName)
```

In each case, FileMaker first resolves any expressions within the enclosing parentheses then converts the result to uppercase text.

## Putting it all together

To connect components of a calculation together, FileMaker provides six basic types of operators:

- **Arithmetic operators:** +, -, /, * (, ), and ^.
- **Comparison operators:** <, >, ≥, ≤, =, and ≠.
- **Logical operators:** and, or, not, and xor.
- **Text operators:** &, " ", \, and ¶.
- **Comment operators:** /* */ and //.
- **Reserved Name operator:** ${ }.

**NOTE** If you prefer, you can use the combinations <> in place of ≠, >= in place of ≥, and <= in place of ≤.

Frequently, your calculations will involve a decision, taking action or applying logic accordingly. For this purpose, the comparative and logical operators are indispensable. When two or more values are compared, FileMaker returns a true or false (Boolean) result that you can use to determine the outcome of the calculation. For example, if you're inviting interested parties to a house inspection on a different date depending on where in the alphabet their name falls (for example, A to M on date 1 and N to Z on date 2), you might use a simple logic calculation along the following lines:

```
If(Visitors::LastName < "N"; VisitDates::Day1; VisitDates::Day2)
```

In this example, the logic hinges on the test `Visitors::LastName ≤ "N"` returning either of the two possible dates from the `VisitDates` table contingent on the test outcome. However, if you also want to ensure that anyone who has made telephone contact is also invited on the first available date, you need a more complex logic. Your calculation now appears as

```
If(Visitors::LastName  ≤"N" or Visitors::PhoneContact = "Yes";
   VisitDates::Day1; VisitDates::Day2)
```

Again, the formula includes an expression and two alternative results; however, this time the test brings together two comparisons (using the comparative operators < and = respectively) with the logical operator or to accommodate the additional requirement. Note that the meaning of the calculation is clear, and it reads almost like a narrative.

# Order of Operations

When you place parentheses around part of a calculation, FileMaker resolves that part first. Therefore, adding parentheses makes the order of evaluation explicit. Consider the classic example of a simple arithmetic calculation:

```
24 - 2 * 3
```

The rules of math require that multiplication and division take place before addition and subtraction, so the correct answer is 18 (24 minus 6). However, if parentheses are used to re-order the calculation

```
(24 - 2) * 3
```

the parentheses change the normal order of computation so that the subtraction must be performed first—making the correct answer now 66 (22 times 3). Similarly, all FileMaker's operators have a natural or default order of operations for all cases except where you specify the order by including one or more sets of parentheses. In fact, parentheses themselves are an operator acting on the calculation to determine the outcome.

Although some operators take precedence over others, some are of equal weight (for example, addition and subtraction). When these equal operators are combined in a calculation, the evaluation proceeds from left to right (again, unless parentheses are included).

Each kind of operator serves a different purpose and produces a different kind of result. Arithmetic operators perform sums and produce numeric results, whereas comparative operators perform tests and return a Boolean result. Logical operators combine multiple tests to determine a composite test result, and so on. Each has a clear role and operates according to basic (and largely intuitive) principles.

FileMaker 9 applies the following default order of operations:

1. Comment operators take precedence over all else.
2. Reserved name operators and Quotation marks are evaluated second, with whichever occurs first or outside the other taking precedence.

## Calculation Wizardry

3. Expressions in parentheses are evaluated next.
4. The `not` operator is evaluated before all remaining operators.
5. ^ is evaluated before any other arithmetic operator, * and / are evaluated before + and –.
6. With the exception of the third operation in this list, arithmetic operators are evaluated before text operators.
7. Arithmetic and text operators are evaluated before comparison operators.
8. With the exception of the `not` operator, comparison operators evaluate before logical operators.
9. The `and` operator is evaluated before `or` or `xor`.

This order of operations determines how your expressions are evaluated, except where you use parentheses to determine the order of evaluation. Where no parentheses are included and operators are at the same level in the preceding hierarchy, evaluation takes place from left to right.

Although the order of operations we provide here may appear daunting at first glance, in most cases the order supports natural flow and readability in your calculation expressions. In many cases, beyond the rules of simple arithmetic, you don't need to pay any special attention to evaluation order because the default order determined by FileMaker is the correct order for a significant number of cases.

Take, for example, the test in the `If( )` function cited in the preceding section:

```
Visitors::LastName < "N" or Visitors::PhoneContact = "Yes"
```

Because comparative operators take precedence over logical operators, both comparisons take place first and are then joined by the evaluation of the `or` operator and no parentheses are required to deliver the expected and desired outcome. In many such cases, FileMaker makes the same sense of your code as you would make reading it — making your task simple.

You can combine elements to produce a desired result in many ways, and many calculations can be achieved using alternative approaches. Some methods may be easier to read, while other methods may be more compact. Still others may be more efficient in operation. You get to decide which is best for your purposes.

Because the parameters for a function can be supplied by a combination of calculation elements (including functions), you can nest calculation functions within themselves. For example, you can use the `Replace( )` function with a size parameter of zero, to insert a phrase into a block of text:

```
Replace("The fox jumps over the dog."; 5; 0; "quick ")
```

This syntax returns "The quick fox jumps over the dog." However by passing the preceding expression as the input parameter to a further `Replace( )` function, you can insert a text string at a second point in a single operation:

```
Replace(Replace("The fox jumps over the dog."; 5; 0; "quick "); 30; 0; "lazy ")
```

407

This expression returns "The quick fox dumps over the lazy dog." Although the preceding expression is a conventional example of nesting, extending the scope of the original operation, you can also place one function within another to perform complementary operations. For example, you can make sure that a number never goes below 1 with the following expression:

```
Max(1; YourNumber)
```

The `Max( )` function returns the highest number from those supplied to it as parameters, so if the value in the field called `YourNumber` is greater than 1, it will be returned, but if it is lower, 1 will be returned instead. Similarly, the `Min( )` function can be used to determine an upper limit:

```
Min(10; YourNumber)
```

Here, the result will never exceed 10 because FileMaker will return the lesser of the two values supplied. You can nest one expression within the other to ensure that `YourNumber` always falls within the range from 1 to 10:

```
Max(1; Min(10; YourNumber))
```

With this expression in place (using a technique such as an *auto-enter calculation/replaces existing value*, on the YourNumber field), you have set both upper and lower bounds for YourNumber, using a single formula.

# Boolean Operations

Many tasks you perform in a database implement decisions. If a student has achieved a certain score, he may be admitted to the next grade. If the full amount of an invoice has been paid, its status may be changed to Closed. These decisions are simple logical determinations you can build into your database via calculations.

When you write a formula to compare values and determine a result, you use comparison operators. Comparison operators return a true/false result in numeric format where 1 is true and 0 is false. This true/false result is called a *Boolean result*—meaning that the result is always either true or false, and no other possibilities exist.

## Zero, empty, and everything else

FileMaker interprets numbers (in fields, variables, and literal values) as Boolean according to the rule that zero and empty values are false and other numbers (whether positive or negative, integer or decimal fraction) are true. Text strings (containing no numerals), because they have no numeric value, are treated as empty for the purposes of a Boolean test. However, text values that contain a number (such as "Julie has 3 socks") are interpreted as having a true Boolean value.

Date, time, and timestamp fields, because they also stored numeric values, are interpreted as true when they hold a non-empty, non-zero value. Otherwise, they're interpreted as false. Container fields do not hold numeric data, but FileMaker interprets them as true if they're not empty and false if empty.

## Calculation Wizardry    12

If you set up a number field to display a value list with only a single value of 1, checking or unchecking the checkbox will change the value of the field from null (empty) to 1 and back. Because FileMaker interprets null values as false and other values (such as 1) as true, such a field can be used as a logical switch to control other calculations.

## Implicit Boolean coding

Alternately, if you reference the `AmountPaid` field within an operation calling for a Boolean result, FileMaker registers it as true if it contains an amount or false if it contains zero or is empty. This coding is an implicit conversion of the field value to a true/false status. You might use this, for example, to set a Paid flag on the invoice.

Although FileMaker handles this conversion for you, it is generally preferable to code your solution explicitly rather than relying on FileMaker to interpret it for you. (That way, when you or another developer looks at your code, you'll have no doubt as to what you intended.)

## Explicit Boolean coding

You can make Boolean behavior explicit in several ways. Perhaps the clearest and simplest is to enclose the reference within FileMaker's `GetAsBoolean( )` function. So, for example,

```
GetAsBoolean(Invoice::AmountPaid)
```

always returns either zero (false) or one (true). Not only is this simple and direct, but it plainly states the purpose of the expression.

Another way to make a reference to a field explicitly Boolean is to use it in a comparative operation:

```
Invoice::AmountPaid > 0
```

Because comparative operations always return a Boolean result, this expression is an acceptable alternative way to make a field reference in your solution explicitly Boolean. However, in the case of this example, you may want to avoid situations where a part payment will set the payment flag, so comparing the `AmountPaid` value to the `TotalPayable` value for the invoice is preferable, rather than merely confirming that it is a nonzero amount. So the formula for your paid flag field may best be

```
If(Invoice::AmountPaid ≥ Invoice::TotalPayable; "PAID IN FULL")
```

When written in this way, your Boolean code is clear and unequivocal, leaving you in no doubt as to its intent — and leaving FileMaker no room for alternative interpretations of your code.

> **NOTE** FileMaker's interpretation of null values is also affected by the setting labeled Do Not Evaluate When All Referenced Fields Are Empty. If this checkbox is enabled in the Specify Calculation dialog, the calculation will return no result if the referenced fields are null.

409

# Part III   Beyond the Basics

# Variables — Calculation, Script, and Global

*Memory variables* — values such as calculation results or data held temporarily in application memory — are both convenient and efficient (much faster than referencing a field, for example) as ways to pass information between calculations or between expressions within a calculation.

FileMaker supports three essential kinds of memory variables for use in your solution:

- **Calculation variables:** Calculation scoped variables are those that have names that don't begin with a $ character.
- **Local variables:** This category includes all variables that have names commencing with single $ character.
- **Global variables:** Global variables have names commencing with a pair of dollar sign characters ($$).

The variable types differ in their scope and/or persistence and are therefore useful in different ways. However, their usages aren't immediately obvious from the names appearing in official documentation and common use. In particular, the use of the term *script variables* is misleading.

Significantly, all three kinds of variables can be defined in a calculation anywhere in your solution, via the use of the Let ( ) function. Moreover, although calculation variables can't be defined or referenced outside a calculation, the calculation in which they're defined can occur within a script or anywhere else in your code — for example, in schema, in a calculation defined as part of a button command, in a formula evaluated as part of conditional formatting, and so on.

## Declaring calculation variables — the Let( ) function

Calculation variables exist only within the confines of a Let ( ) statement within a single calculation expression. Such variables are defined singly or in a list at the beginning of the Let ( ) function and persist only through to the closing parenthesis of the function they're defined in (unless explicitly cleared or redefined earlier in the function syntax). For example, the expression

```
Let(x = 10; 70 / x)
```

returns 7 because for the duration of the expression (between the enclosing parentheses of the Let ( ) function), the variable x has been declared as having a value of 10. When the expression 70 / x is evaluated, x resolves to its declared value, and the formula is treated as 70 / 10. Similarly,

```
Let([x = 10; y = 70]; y / x)
```

also returns 7 because both the operative values x and y have been declared with their respective values in the list expression (between the square brackets). Moreover, once a variable has been declared, you can use it as part of the argument in the declaration of subsequent variables:

```
Let([x = 10; y = x * 7]; y / x)
```

In this way, each named variable acquires a declared value for the purposes of the enclosed expression. If a variable name is reused in the list of variables in a single Let ( ) statement, the later declared values supercede earlier ones. If Let ( ) statements are nested, the value of variables declared in the enclosing statement can be accessed within enclosed statements, but not vice versa. In other words, enclosed statement variables aren't accessible outside the specific instance of the Let ( ) function where they're declared.

## Understanding variables' scope

Variables with names not starting with dollar symbols are operable only within the confines of the function where you define them. Thus, their scope is tightly constrained, they expire instantly, and they can't be referenced, even while evaluation is in process, anywhere else in the solution.

When a Let ( ) statement variable's name commences with a single dollar sign (for example, $x), you can access the variable outside the calculation where you define it, but only while the current instance of the currently running script is *active* (in other words, at the top of the script stack).

**CROSS-REF** For a detailed discussion of FileMaker's script-threading and the operation of the Script Stack, refer to Chapter 8.

Such variables are termed *local* because, though accessible throughout the current file, they persist only for the duration of the current script. They may also be considered *script variables* because in addition to being declared in a Let ( ) statement within a calculation expression, they can be created independently by the use of the Set Variable[ ] script step or button command.

**TIP** When no scripts are running, FileMaker deems a hypothetical Script Zero to be at the top of the script stack. Therefore, if a local variable is declared while no scripts are active (that is, in a calculation expression), it retains its value throughout the file whenever the script stack is empty, for the remainder of the current file session.

When you declare a variable with a name commencing with two (or more) dollar signs, FileMaker makes its value available throughout the current file regardless of the status of the script stack. Variables of this type are called *global* variables because of their wider scope; however, they're not persistent — in other words, they're constrained to the current file session. If you want a value to persist between FileMaker sessions, you should store it in a standard (non-global) field and then set your solution's start-up script to retrieve and reinstate the value in a subsequent file session. Global fields, like global variables, are session specific in a hosted solution.

**NOTE** A file session is the period between when a file is opened and subsequently closed on a particular workstation. If a file is closed and reopened, a new file session begins, and any $$ variable values associated with the previous file session are lost.

Within their respective scope, each type of variable persists until explicitly destroyed. A variable is destroyed in FileMaker by setting its value to null (" "), at which point the memory it has occupied is released.

## Benefiting from variables in a calculation

The use of the `Let( )` function to declare variables in calculation syntax has several potential advantages, especially in compound or complex expressions. Foremost among these advantages are

- The capability to calculate a component value once and use it multiple places in the calc expression, thus reducing redundancy and minimizing the processor cycles required to evaluate the expression
- The capability to break logic of a compound statement down into its elements and improve readability, simplicity, and clarity

As an example of the elimination of redundancy, consider the following simple expression:

```
Item::Qty * Item::Price +
If(Item::Qty * Item::Price < 100; Item::Shipping)
```

The logic of this expression is straightforward: Customers aren't charged shipping on orders over $100. To resolve the logic, however, FileMaker must retrieve the `Item::Qty` and `Item::Price` values from their respective fields twice and perform the multiplication twice, consuming slightly more resources (processor cycles, memory, network bandwidth, and so on) in the process and taking slightly longer.

Instead, the components of the preceding calculation can be reworked as

```
Let(
Amt = Item::Qty * Item::Price;
Amt + If(Amt < 100; Item::Shipping)
)
```

In this reworking, you calculate the product of quantity and price only once, significantly reducing the work involved in evaluating such a calculation — it's almost halved. In more complex functions where the time taken to calculate a component of the expression is significant, and especially where one or more components may recur multiple times, the reduction in evaluation time is greater and may make a significant difference to your solution usability.

**CROSS-REF** For a further discussion of elimination of redundancy and efficient coding practices in your solutions, refer to Chapter 19.

# Text Processing and Parsing Functions

One useful capability in FileMaker's calculation repertoire is the ability to modify text in your databases in a wide variety of ways, including correcting errors; updating entries; organizing; sorting; merging; separating words, lines, and sentences; and more.

When your database contains e-mail addresses such as `mary@greatgizmos.com`, you'll likely need to convert them into a corresponding URL, such as one for the GreatGizmos Web site. Or perhaps you need to extract all the part numbers from a file full of correspondence with a major

## Calculation Wizardry

client. These tasks and many others are trivial when you're familiar with the use of FileMaker's text processing functions.

## Substitute, Replace, and Trim

One of FileMaker's most versatile functions is `Substitute()`. You can use this function to swap all occurrences of any character or sequence of characters in a field or text string for text you specify. For example, if you have a list of values (one on each line) that you'd prefer were presented with a comma and space between each, you can achieve that elegantly with a calculation expression, such as

```
Substitute(YourList; ¶; ", ")
```

If the items on your list are preceded by bullet characters that have no place in your new comma separated presentation, you can remove them as part of the same function call by using the list syntax:

```
Substitute(YourList; [¶; ", "]; ["• "; ""])
```

> **TIP** Wherever parameter lists are supported in FileMaker calculations, each list item, as in the preceding example, is enclosed within square brackets, and successive items are separated by a semicolon.

The ability to perform multiple substitutions in a single function call makes your calculations both powerful and efficient. Because the `Substitute()` function is case sensitive, if you need to replace a word or phrase regardless of case, you may need to list all likely permutations. For example, to ensure that the name of your database software is correctly capitalized wherever it occurs in a text field, you could use

```
Substitute(YourTO::YourTextField;
    ["filemaker; "FileMaker"];
    ["Filemaker; "FileMaker"];
    ["FILEMAKER; "FileMaker"];
    ["FIleMaker; "FileMaker"];
)
```

When you need to replace a specific sequence of characters without regard to what they are, you'll be better served by the `Replace()` function. Unlike `Substitute()`, `Replace()` enables you to specify the text to be modified by its position in the target string, rather than by matching it to a string you supply.

Suppose that the value in a field always begins with a letter of the alphabet, followed by a punctuation mark (but not always the same punctuation mark), a space or tab, and then some subsequent text, and your objective is to make all of the second and third characters consistent. In such a situation, `Substitute()` is less useful—not only because the combination of characters to be replaced may be different each time, but also because you don't want to change other punctuation later in the field. (You're concerned only with the second and third characters in each field.) You can achieve an update with surgical precision using a formula such as

```
Replace(YourTO::YourTextField; 2; 2; ". ")
```

413

which tells FileMaker to start at the second character and replace two characters with the string you're providing (a period followed by a space).

> **TIP**
> If you supply a zero as the third parameter for the `Replace()` function, it doesn't remove any text. Instead, it inserts text at the point determined by the second parameter. For example, you can use this feature to add a space between the third and fourth characters of a telephone number.

Before long, when editing or cleaning up text in your solutions, you face the challenge of superfluous spaces at the start or (particularly) the end of a field value or text string. Spaces at the end of a field can go unnoticed until you compare text or combine text together, such as when you're adding names to the top of a letter. As soon as you do, the extra spaces can create problems and produce unwanted results.

FileMaker provides the `Trim()` function to enable you to efficiently discard leading and trailing spaces without disturbing the spaces between words). So

    Trim("     The Hendersons will all be there...     ")

returns "The Hendersons will all be there..." without all the extra space before and after. Similarly:

    TrimAll("  For    the   benefit   of  Mr    Kite...   "; 1; 1)

returns "For the benefit of Mr Kite..." with just a single space between each word, as well as the superfluous leading and trailing spaces removed.

> **NOTE**
> The `TrimAll()` function also has uses controlling full- and half-width spaces when working with non-Roman characters and words. Consult the online help entry on this function for full details of all its configuration options.

## Left, Right, and Middle

When you get down to working with text, you frequently need to extract part of the text from a larger block. For example, if names have been imported into your solution in a single field, but you require them to be separated into Title, FirstName, and LastName fields, you're facing a minor challenge known as *parsing*.

The `Left()`, `Middle()`, and `Right()` functions provide you with the means to extract a specific number of characters from either end, or anywhere within a string of text. For example, if your `ClientDetails` field contains the name Mr Fandangle Pranderghast, the following three expressions return the three separate text strings Mr, Fandangle, and Pranderghast, respectively:

    Left(Contacts::ClientDetails; 2)

    Middle(Contacts::ClientDetails; 3; 9)

    Right(Contacts::ClientDetails; 12)

## Calculation Wizardry

These functions are powerful and precise—provided that you're able to accurately supply them with the correct coordinates (more on that in the following section, "Position and PatternCount").

Another example of using these great functions is the elimination of unwanted characters at the start or end of a text string. For example, if you want to remove the punctuation from the end of a sentence in a field, you can use

```
Left(YourSolution::YourTextField; Length(YourSolution::YourTextField) - 1)
```

Whatever is in the text field when this expression is evaluated will be returned with one character removed from the right.

Similarly, when you have fields containing To Do list items in the form

    A: *Don't forget your lunch!*

and you want to discard the first three characters and the trailing punctuation mark, you can accomplish that in a single stroke with the expression

```
Middle(ThingsToDo::Reminder; 4; Length(ThingsToDo::Reminder) - 4)
```

By starting at character 4, it leaves off the first three characters, and by running for the length of the string minus 4, it stops short of the last character, giving as its result "Don't forget your lunch".

## Position and PatternCount

The text processing operations' capability increases greatly when you can instruct FileMaker to look for particular characters or text strings and return their position or the number of them encountered. FileMaker provides the `Position( )` and `PatternCount( )` functions for this purpose, and they add flexibility and precision to the text-handling arsenal.

For example, in the following example, FileMaker is extracting text from the middle of a string commencing at the fourth character:

```
Middle(ThingsToDo::Reminder; 4; Length(ThingsToDo::Reminder) - 4)
```

However, this syntax only produces the desired result if all the strings you apply the procedure to are structured the same. If any of them has an additional (leading) character or missing initial character, the fixed start parameter results in an inappropriate result. In other words, the first character of the required text may sometimes be 5 or 3 rather than 4.

Because `Position( )` returns the exact location of a specified character or starting location of a string, it can be incorporated to lend greater accuracy to the text extraction:

```
Position(ThingsToDo::Reminder; ": "; 1; 1)
```

This expression returns the location (in characters starting from the left) of the first occurrence of a colon and space. By using the result of the `Position( )` expression as a reference point (adding

## Part III  Beyond the Basics

two to it to determine the start of the extract string), you can make your `Middle( )` operation responsive to changes in the format of the Reminder text.

In the form shown in the preceding example, the `Position( )` function is set (via its last two parameters) to locate the first occurrence of the search string (": ") starting from the first character of the content of the `ThingsToDo::Reminder` field. However, you can structure the function to operate differently by supplying different values for these parameters:

```
Position(ThingsToDo::Reminder; ": "; Length(ThingsToDo::Reminder); -1)
```

The preceding syntax instructs FileMaker to begin its search at the end of the field (`Length(ThingsToDo::Reminder)`) content and to search backwards(`-1`). Thus, with this variant of the expression, the last occurrence of the search string's location is returned, rather than the first.

**NOTE**  If the search string is not present in the supplied text (or field value), the Position( ) function returns a zero.

In some cases, however, you'll want to confirm the presence or frequency of occurrence of the search string before proceeding to act on it. For example, when you need to locate the middle occurrence of an item in a continuous text sequence (where each item is prefaced by a label and colon, as in the previous example), you can determine the number of items using the following syntax:

```
PatternCount(ThingsToDo::Reminder; ": ")
```

Thus, to calculate the middle occurrence, you should divide by two and enclose the result in the `Ceiling( )` function:

```
Ceiling(PatternCount(ThingsToDo::Reminder; ": ") / 2)
```

To ascertain the location of the middle occurrence of the search string, you can use a compound formula, where the preceding expression is supplied as the *occurrence* parameter for the `Position( )` function:

```
Position(ThingsToDo::Reminder; ": "; 1;
    Ceiling(PatternCount(ThingsToDo::Reminder; ": ") / 2))
```

This result, in turn can supply the *start* parameter to the `Middle( )` function, when you are seeking to extract text from the middle To Do list item in a text block. By using a comparable technique to determine the location of the end of the middle item (and subtracting the end from the start to determine the size of the middle item), you're able to neatly extract (parse) the middle item from a block of text containing multiple items. For example, when the text in the `ThingsToDo::Reminder` field is as follows

> *A: Don't forget your lunch! B: Deliver term papers to office. C: Collect bus pass! D: Pay electricity bill. E: Photocopy timetable.*

# Calculation Wizardry

you can use a compound construction along the following lines to extract the middle item (Collect bus pass!) from the field:

```
Let([
    ItemNo   = Ceiling(PatternCount(ThingsToDo::Reminder; ": ") / 2);
    StartPos = Position(ThingsToDo::Reminder; ": "; 1; ItemNo) + 2;
    EndPos   = Position(ThingsToDo::Reminder; ": "; StartPos; 1) - 3];
Middle(ThingsToDo::Reminder; StartPos; EndPos - StartPos)
)
```

**NOTE** In the preceding example, we employed the `Let( )` function to separately calculate the expression's components, declaring each as variables, and then combined those variables in the final line. Determining parameters dynamically increases the clarity and efficiency of a compound expression used to parse elements dynamically from a text string.

While combinations of `Position( )` and `PatternCount( )`, along with the `Left( )`, `Middle( )`, `Right( )` functions, are sufficient to isolate and extract a word or phrase from a longer text string, doing so can be challenging. FileMaker makes it easier by giving you a variety of other options, including the ability to extract text in whole words rather than individual characters.

## The xWords suite

The `LeftWords( )`, `MiddleWords( )`, `RightWords( )`, and `WordCount( )` functions streamline many text operations, giving you a direct and simplified method of performing many language and narrative related manipulations and analyses. Working in whole words takes much of the drudgery out of parsing and assembling text.

When parsing text by whole words, FileMaker uses separator characters to recognize the start and end of each word. The most obvious example of a word separator is the space, but FileMaker also treats many common punctuation marks and glyphs as word separators. For example, in addition to spaces, the following characters are treated as word separators:

- < > ? / ; " { } [ ] | \ ~ ` ! @ # $ % ^ & ¶ • * ( ) _ + =

Additionally:

- A period is treated as a word separator if the characters on either side of it are a letter and numeral, but not if both characters are of the same type, such as both letters or both numerals.
- A forward slash, colon, comma, and hyphen are treated as word separators except when the characters on both sides of them are numerals (useful for selecting dates, times, and numbers as single words).
- An apostrophe is treated as a word separator except when the characters on both sides of it are letters.
- Both a tab character and a carriage return, as well as a literal pilcrow (¶) character, are treated as word separators for all cases.

417

## Part III  Beyond the Basics

By applying these rules, FileMaker offers a relatively automatic method of text manipulation. Using this capability, text in the form

> A:  *Don't forget your lunch!*

can be more easily reduced to "Don't forget your lunch" with the expression:

```
RightWords(ThingsToDo::Reminder; 4)
```

Because an artifact of the `xWords` functions is that they omit leading and trailing word separator characters from the returned (or counted) string, they're often exploited as a way to strip unwanted characters, including spaces, carriage returns, and punctuation, from the ends of a text string. For example, the expression

```
LeftWords(" •  Endless rain into a paper cup??!  ¶ "; 9999)
```

returns "Endless rain into a paper cup", cleanly excising the bullet, tab, punctuation, carriage return, and associated spaces from both ends of the text string—rather like a `Trim( )` function on steroids!

## Parsing in practice

The logic of parsing operations (location and extraction of text within a field or other string or value) conforms to a common set of principles whether you're using functions such as `Left( )`, `Middle( )`, and `Right( )`, or the powerful yet simple `xWords` functions. Either way, you must locate a start point and an end point and then pass these parameters to the appropriate function to grab everything in between.

Sometimes, however, what you leave out, not what you include, makes the difference. Consider a situation where you want to omit a particular text string that occurs in several thousand records. For example, in a tournament database, each match will be entered in the following form:

> Peter Van Elking - challenging - Jerry Glover
> Janice Thorn - rematch - Jenny-Lee Shackles
> Gemma P. Harding - face-off - Susan Marchent

However, you may be asked to produce a program where the names are listed with a simple comma between the opponents' names instead. One way to do this is to use the `Position( )` function to locate the "–" characters and use that to reassemble the strings as follows:

```
Left(Game::Set; Position(Game::Set; " - "; 1; 1) - 1) & ", " &
Right(Game::Set; Length(Game::Set) - Position(Game::Set; " - "; 1; 2) - 2)
```

When this expression is applied to each line (that is, each Game::Set field value) in turn, the names are returned with a comma in place of the intermediary dashes and words.

In this expression, the location of each of the en dashes is determined by the `Position( )` functions and passed respectively to the `Left( )` and `Right( )` functions to extract the name from either end of each string, despite the fact that the length of the intervening text is not consistent. The two names are then joined in a new string using the concatenation operator (&), along with a separating comma and space supplied as a text literal (and therefore enclosed within quote marks).

# Text Formatting Operations

FileMaker's suite of text formatting calculation functions enables you to control character level (embedded) formats applied to text within fields in your database, including applying and removing custom text style, color, size, and font attributes.

You can display text you've formatted via calculation in calculation fields, set it into conventional data fields via script, or apply (or remove) formatting using auto-enter calculations, depending on the content of the field (or other fields in the record).

## Applying text formatting

You can use any combination of the `TextFont( )`, `TextColor( )`, `TextSize( )`, and `TextStyleAdd( )` functions to apply formatting. Formatting you apply with any one of these commands is added to the specified text's existing character formatting (if any).

To apply more than one style at once, you can list multiple style parameters within a single instance of the `TextStyleAdd( )` function:

```
TextStyleAdd("Mad World"; bold + italic + underline)
```

The preceding expression results in the text **_Mad World_**.

Similarly, you can apply multiple formats simultaneously by nesting two or more format functions. For example, to simultaneously change the font of a text string to Verdana and the size to 11 point, you can use

```
TextSize(TextFont("I Saw Her Standing There"; "Verdana"); 11)
```

Formatting applied in this way overrides field formats applied to the field object on a layout (and also conditional formats applied to the layout field object).

**CROSS-REF** For a detailed discussion of formatting and the different ways it's applied and managed in FileMaker Pro, refer to Chapter 9.

## Removing text formatting

You can remove text formatting either selectively or indiscriminately. To remove all fonts, styles, font size, and font color attributes from a text string, use the formula

```
TextFormatRemove(YourTable::YourTextString)
```

This calculation returns the text in the `YourTable::YourTextString` field as plain text that is stripped of all character styles and paragraph formatting

However, if you prefer to remove some aspects of the custom formatting while retaining others, you can do so with precision by using the `TextFontRemove( )`, `TextColorRemove( )`, `TextSizeRemove( )`, and `TextStyleRemove( )` functions. You can remove a single format with each of these functions by supplying an associated format parameter. Or you can remove all formats of the relevant type by supplying a text string and no format (size, color, style, or font) parameter. For example, to remove bold character styling while leaving other styles (italic, underline, and so on) in place, use an expression such as:

```
TextStyleRemove(YourTable::YourTextString; Bold)
```

As when adding formatting, you can nest multiple functions (if desired) to remove a number of specific format attributes simultaneously (while leaving others in place).

## Applying selective formatting

You can combine logic and formatting functions to apply to text (or parts of the text, such as individual words) according to the data in your solution. For example, to display part of a sentence in italics depending on the data available, you can use the following formula:

```
"This issue is " &
TextStyleAdd(Issues::Status; If(Issues::Status = "Urgent"; Italic; Plain))
```

Alternatively, to spotlight all occurrences of a search term in a block of text using bold formatting, you can use

```
Substitute(Issues::Description; Issues::gSearchTerm;
   TextStyleAdd(Issues::gSearchTerm; Bold))
```

This formula locates all occurrences of the value in the `gSearchTerm` field within the content of the `Description` field, changing each to bold formatted text. Because formatting functions can be nested, the preceding example can be extended to apply color as well as style attributes, by enclosing the final part of the expression within an additional function:

```
Substitute(Issues::Description; Issues::gSearchTerm;
   TextColor(TextStyleAdd(Issues::gSearchTerm; Bold); RGB(0; 0; 255)))
```

**TIP** The `TextColor( )` function accepts, as its second parameter, a color number in the range from 0 (black) to 16777215 (white), where the 8-bit color value of red, green, and blue (each in the range from 0 to 255) is combined using the following formula:

```
Red * 256^2 + Green * 256 + Blue
```

For convenience, FileMaker provides the RGB( ) function for computing this value from the individual values for red, green, and blue. However, if you know or can precalculate the number for a desired color, you can enter the number directly into the TextColor( ) function.

## Creating a Format button

If you routinely need to mark words or passages in a text field, you can easily create a button that applies the marking to the selected text. For example, to underline text, follow these steps:

1. Attach the `Insert Calculated Result[ ]` button command to your button.
2. Disable the Select Entire Contents checkbox.

3. Leave the Go To Target Field checkbox unchecked and specify the calculation as
   ```
   Insert Calculated Result[
   TextStyleAdd(Middle(Get(ActiveFieldContents);
      Get(ActiveSelectionStart); Get(ActiveSelectionSize));
      Underline)
   ]
   ```
4. Close the Button Setup dialog and name the button (for example, with the U symbol).

You can then click the button to apply character formatting to selected text in any accessible field.

**NOTE** Because the button described here works on the basis of insertion (overwriting the current selection with a formatted copy of itself), the selection will be lost, and the cursor will appear at the end of the selected text after the formatting is applied. If you don't want this to happen, consider attaching a script to the button and configure the script so that it captures and stores the selection (in a local variable), inserts the formatted text, and reinstates the selection of the formatted text.

In this case, the button applies but doesn't remove the formatting. If you need to also simplify the process of removing formatting, you can provide a second button using the essentials of the same procedure while employing the `TextStyleRemove( )` function. Alternatively, you can use a more complex calculation to determine whether the selected text is underlined and either remove or apply underlining accordingly. This enables a single button to toggle the underline formatting.

To determine within a calculation whether text is underlined, you can retrieve the selected text as CSS using FileMaker's `GetAsCSS( )` function, search it for the presence of the `text-decoration:underline;` tag, and modify the result accordingly. You can incorporate such an expression into a scripted process to provide buttons that add or remove formats dynamically.

**CROSS-REF** The appendixes include references to online resources where you will find examples of techniques for creating scripted style buttons for FileMaker 9.

# Dates, Times, and Timestamps

As part of almost every solution we've seen, storing and tracking dates or times is needed, whether to record the creation date of records, the acquisition date of assets, the start time of a recording session, the expiration date of perishable goods, or myriad other temporal factors. In many cases, you can significantly increase a solution's utility by performing checks and calculations using date and time values.

FileMaker uses a robust method of storing and manipulating date, time, and timestamp values, and when you comprehend the basics, many operations become simple to understand and execute.

## How FileMaker manages dates

FileMaker stores all dates internally as a numeric value representing the number of days since 1/1/0001 inclusive. For example, 2 January 0001 is stored as 2, whereas 1/1/2008 is stored internally as the number 733042. You don't normally see this value because FileMaker receives and displays accepted date formats (according to the current file or system regional settings) — but you don't need to take our word for it. Enter the calculation:

```
GetAsNumber(Date(1; 1; 2008))
```

FileMaker returns the number 733042.

What is great about this storage format is that you can add and subtract using dates, and FileMaker will resolve the calculation appropriately. For example, the expression

```
GetAsNumber(Date(3; 1; 2008)) - GetAsNumber(Date(2; 1; 2008))
```

returns 29, because there are 29 days between February 1 and March 1, 2008 (it's a leap year).

Although the examples here cite explicit dates for the sake of clarity, the calculations work the same way when the values involved are references to date fields, variables containing date values, or functions or expressions returning dates, such as `Get(CurrentDate)`.

## Plotting time

FileMaker stores all times internally as a numeric value representing the number of seconds since midnight. For example, when you enter 9:25 a.m. into a time field, it's stored internally as the number 33900 but displayed as 9:25:00. Enter the following calculation expression:

```
GetAsNumber(Time(9; 25; 00))
```

It returns the number 33900.

Storing values in this form enables you to perform calculations comparing times (to get the difference between them in seconds). So, for example, the following expression returns 180 — the number of seconds in three minutes:

```
GetAsNumber(Time(9; 28; 00) - Time(9; 25; 00))
```

However, if you remove the enclosing `GetAsNumber( )` function, FileMaker returns the difference as a time value in the form 0:03:00.

Using these temporal arithmetic capabilities in your solutions could not be easier. For example, when you have a start and stop time for any activity, you can determine the duration of the activity with an expression such as:

```
Meeting::ConcludeTime - Meeting::StartTime
```

Similarly, you can calculate the appropriate end time of a scheduled 90-minute meeting that starts at, say, 10:42:16 a.m., by entering the start time into a time field in FileMaker and using the following calculation expression:

```
Meeting::StartTime + 90 * 60
```

## Calculation Wizardry

Such calculations enable you to deal with time calculations falling within a given day with ease. However, when you encounter the need to calculate time periods spanning several days, the Timestamp data format is better suited to the task.

### The number of seconds in 2007 years

FileMaker stores timestamps internally as a numeric value representing the number of seconds since midnight preceding 1/1/001. In this way, a timestamp value combines both date and time into a single reference value. Thus, the timestamp value for 9:25 a.m. on 1/1/2008 is stored internally as 63334776300 — a fact that you can readily demonstrate by having FileMaker resolve the expression:

```
GetAsNumber(Timestamp(Date(1; 1; 2008); Time(9; 25; 00)))
```

Working with timestamp data, you combine the benefits of both date and time calculations, enabling you to compare times many days apart to easily determine the amount of time elapsed between them. For example, the expression

```
Timestamp(Date(1; 1; 2008); Time(9; 25; 00)) -
Timestamp(Date(1; 1; 2007); Time(9; 25; 00))
```

returns 8760:00:00, which is the number of hours in 365 days (365 × 24 = 8760).

Even if you have chosen to store date and time values in their own respective formats, you can still take advantage of timestamp capabilities when resolving calculations spanning days or weeks. For example:

```
Timestamp(Trip::EndDate; Trip::EndTime) -
Timestamp(Trip::StartDate; Trip::StartTime)
```

is one of the more straightforward ways to calculate a trip of several days' duration's total length.

### Juggling days, months, and years

When you're working with either date or timestamp values, being able to perform simple math operations on the component values can prove invaluable. For example, just as subtracting one date from another works to give a duration, you can also add or subtract numbers from date values. For example:

```
Get(CurrentDate) + 7
```

returns the date of the corresponding day of the following week. Similarly,

```
Timestamp(Get(CurrentDate) + 7; Time(9; 0; 0))
```

returns 9:00am on the corresponding day of the following week.

**Part III**  Beyond the Basics

By combining other options from among FileMaker's date and time functions, you can calculate many other useful intervals and dates. For example:

```
Get(CurrentDate) - DayOfWeek(Get(CurrentDate)) + 6
```

always returns the date of the current week's Friday. Moreover, using the same principle, but with a little additional sleight of hand, you can use an expression such as

```
DateValue + Choose(Mod(DayofWeek(DateValue), 7), -1, 1)
```

to return the date of the nearest week day. In other words, if the date falls on a Saturday, the date returned is the preceding Friday; if the date falls on a Sunday, the date returned is the following Monday; but if the date is a week day, it is returned without change.

By extending these techniques, you can calculate the date of the corresponding day of the next month with the expression

```
Date(Month(Get(CurrentDate)) + 1; Day(Get(CurrentDate)); Year(Get(CurrentDate)))
```

or the date of the last day of the preceding month (even when the current month is January) using

```
Date(Month(Get(CurrentDate)); 0; Year(Get(CurrentDate)))
```

or the date of someone's birthday in the current year, using

```
Date(Month(Person::DateOfBirth); Day(Person::DateOfBirth);
   Year(Get(CurrentDate)))
```

Moreover, you can combine the preceding elements to accurately calculate a person's current age in whole years using a relatively simple expression such as

```
Year(Get(CurrentDate)) - Year(Person::DateOfBirth) -
GetAsBoolean((Month(Get(CurrentDate)) + Day(Get(CurrentDate)) / 100) <
(Month(Person::DateOfBirth) + Day(Person::DateOfBirth) / 100))
```

Many other examples are possible, using different combinations of FileMaker Pro 9's available date and time functions. With a little logic and ingenuity, you have all the resources you need to gain mastery over a wide range of date and time calculation requirements.

# Summary Data

FileMaker's summary field options (Total, Average, Count, Minimum, Maximum, Standard Deviation, and Fraction of Total) accommodate a variety of basic requirements for analyzing and reporting on your data. However, you can greatly extend these capabilities' scope by bringing FileMaker's calculation capabilities into play.

To complement summary fields, FileMaker provides you with a comparable range of calculation functions to aggregate data in various ways, producing calculated summary data.

## Using aggregate functions

You can use aggregate functions in three essentially different ways:

- To summarize values in a supplied array or in multiple designated fields on the current record
- To summarize values in nonempty instances of a repeating field
- To summarize values in a field across all related records

FileMaker does not support combinations of the first two methods. If you supply a list of fields to an aggregate function such as Sum( ), the returned result ignores values in the second or subsequent repetitions of those fields. (In other words, only values in the first repetition of each referenced field are summed.) Only where a single field is referenced do the aggregating functions address values in field repetitions.

Similarly, you can't combine the first and last methods. If you include a reference to a related field in an array of fields being passed to a summary function, FileMaker ignores values in the second or subsequent related records, summarizing the values on the current record along with the first related record only.

You can, however, combine the last two methods. When you reference a related repeating field in an aggregate function, FileMaker summarizes the values in all repetitions of all related records.

When you reference fields in the current TO within an aggregating calculation as in

```
Average(Score1; Score2; Score3)
```

FileMaker determines an average with respect to values in the Score1, Score2, and Score3 fields in the current record only, without regard to other records in the found set. Similarly, if you reference a repeating field, such as

```
Average(Score)
```

in a record where the Score field has three repetitions, FileMaker determines an average of the non-blank repetition values in the current record only. Meanwhile, if you reference a related field within an aggregating function, such as

```
Average(Games::Score)
```

where Games is a related TO, FileMaker returns the average of values in nonempty instances of the Score field on all Games records related to the current record.

When supplying an array of values to an aggregate function, you can include any mix of constant values, field references, variables, and expressions. For example, if you enter the following expression into a calculation in an InvoiceLines table:

```
Min(100; InvoiceLines::Value; InvoiceLines::Qty * InvoiceLines::Price; $$var)
```

FileMaker returns a result representing the lowest of the four values:

- 100
- value (if any) in the `InvoiceLines::Value` field
- product of Qty * Price on the current `InvoiceLines` record
- numeric value (if any) of the `$$var` variable at the time the calculation is evaluated

**NOTE** Should any of the supplied references or expressions in an array of values passed to an aggregate function evaluate to null, they're excluded from the calculation.

## The ballad of Max and Min

Among the aggregating functions, `Max( )` and `Min( )` are particularly useful for the ways they work together when you define limits or ranges.

In the example in the preceding section, given that the number 100 appeared as one of the values in the array being passed to the `Min( )` function, the number returned by the expression will never be higher than 100. Thus, the `Min( )` function is being used to set a maximum value for the field to which it is applied. At first glance, this setup may seem counterintuitive, but its logic is sound (so much for intuition!).

Similarly, by applying `Max(N; YourValue)` to a value in your solution, you can establish a minimum — the resulting value will never be lower than N. You can combine the two functions into a single expression to set both an upper and lower limit, containing a value within a fixed or variable domain.

**CROSS-REF** For additional details on the use of the `Max( )` and `Min( )` functions, refer to the example of their use with `Evaluate( )` in the section titled "The value of Evaluate( )", later in this chapter.

## Referencing summary fields

An essential difference between the ways summary fields and aggregate calculations behave lies in the fact that summary fields always calculate with respect to the found set, whereas aggregate functions act on the current record or the related record set, without regard to the found set. Moreover, summary fields depend upon the sort order to tabulate and break the data into Sub-summaries when previewing or printing.

You can, however, combine calculation capabilities with the behavior of summary fields in various ways, by including references to summary fields within calculations. For example, in a table containing scheduled examinations for a college semester, summary fields defined to return the Minimum of the `ExamDate` field and the Maximum of the `ExamDate` field will dynamically return the start and end of the exam period for the semester. Additionally, when a Find is done to locate the exams for a particular course or a particular student, the summary fields update to show the start and end of the exam period for that course or individual.

# Calculation Wizardry    12

In this example, when you need to determine the length of the exam period — either overall or for a particular found set of exams — you can do so by defining a calculation field referencing the summary fields:

```
1 + sLastExam - sFirstExam
```

`sLastExam` and `sFirstExam` are the summary fields providing the maximum and minimum of `ExamDate`, respectively. This example produces a valid result across the found set in the exams table as a whole, but will not produce separate Sub-summary results for each student or course when the data in the examinations table are included in a report. To have the calculation return separate Sub-summary results for each group of records when the found set is sorted, you should enclose the references to the summary fields within the `GetSummary( )` function, as follows:

```
1 + GetSummary(sLastExam; cSortBy) - GetSummary(sFirstExam; cSortBy)
```

In this example, `cSortBy` is the field used to sort the examination table records by course or student according to the report required. The calculation result returned now correctly reflects the Sub-summary values of the `sLastExam` and `sFirstExam` summary fields for grouped data.

**CROSS-REF** For a further discussion of techniques for calculating a multiple-use sort field for retrieval of summary data according to two or more break fields (as per the `cSortBy` field in the preceding example) refer to the section "Layers of Abstraction," later in this chapter.

## Lists and Arrays

In solutions of all kinds, you frequently require ways to retrieve and manage sets of values — often as lists or arrays. The essential techniques are much the same whether you're retrieving a list of the most common symptoms of an illness, a list of the top three students in each class, a list of low-stock items to be reordered, or a list of tasks to be performed before next Monday's meeting.

A *list* is any sequence of data elements (generally of the same or similar type), and an *array* is the mechanism use to store or handle such data. The simplest structure for an array is a delimited list, where each list item is separated from the next by a known (reserved) character or sequence of characters — and the most ubiquitous form of such arrays is the carriage-return (CR) delimited list where each list value is on a separate line. In this context, the character used as a delimiter is reserved arbitrarily by the user or developer rather than by FileMaker (though FileMaker does provide support for external file formats using a variety of common delimiter characters, such as tabs and commas).

### Retrieving values as a list

FileMaker provides several powerful features for the retrieval of lists of values, each applicable to different requirements and operating according to its own rules.

The first and longest-standing method is the creation of value lists (either custom lists, or lists dependent on field indices), and the retrieval of their contents via the `ValueListItems( )`

function. This method requires the separate configuration of the list (via the Manage ➪ Value Lists command and associated dialogs) and a reference to it by name from within the preceding calculation function. Values are returned as a CR-separated list in an order determined by the value list referenced — in other words, where values are sourced from a database field, listed values are sorted in ascending order according to the data type assigned to the referenced field.

A second method of retrieval of CR-separated values is via the List( ) function. As an aggregating function, you can use List( ) to return a list from an array of supplied elements including any combination of constant values, referenced fields, expressions, and variables:

```
List(100; InvoiceLines::Value; InvoiceLines::Qty * InvoiceLines::Price; $$var)
```

As is the case for other aggregating functions, null values are ignored (and do not appear as empty lines in the resulting list of values).

Similarly, you can use List( ) to return all nonblank values from a repeating field on the current record, or from a related field (in which case values from all related records will be returned).

In addition, you can use the GetNthRecord( ) function, alone, in a compound expression, or in a custom function to assemble a custom list of values, either from field values among records in the found set, or from field values among related records.

**CROSS-REF** For additional information regarding custom functions and their uses, refer to Chapter 18.

Similarly, if you're working with repeating fields or repeating variables, you can use standard array notation, such as YourField[7] or $YourVariable[8], to build a custom CR-separated list of values for further manipulation. In the case of repeating fields, you can also use the GetRepetition( ) function to reference the values in specific repetitions (cells).

## Managing lists — the xValues functions

Extending the parsing functions detailed in the section titled "Text Processing and Parsing Functions" earlier in this chapter, FileMaker provides you with a suite of functions purpose-built for managing values in lists: LeftValues( ), RightValues( ), MiddleValues( ), and ValueCount( ). In combination, these functions enable you to combine lists, separate lists, and add and remove list values.

**CAUTION** Although the LeftValues( ), RightValues( ), and MiddleValues( ) functions are in many respects equivalent in operation to the Left( ), Right( ), and Middle( ) functions, dealing with whole lines of text rather than individual characters, an important difference is that the **xValues** functions always include a trailing carriage return on the result, even in cases where no trailing carriage return was present in the original string being interrogated. For example:

```
LeftValues("Line One."; 1)
```

returns "Line one.¶" In other words, it adds a trailing carriage return not present in the original string.

# Calculation Wizardry

**NOTE** Carriage return characters are always represented in calculation code by the pilcrow (¶) character.

The `PatternCount( )` function lets you measure a text string's contents. This useful test helps you confirm that a string contains what you're looking for, before your calculation proceeds to extract it, and also helps to determine the contents of a string without examining it exhaustively. Why not let FileMaker do the work for you?

One of the many invaluable uses of `PatternCount( )` is determining the number of times an entry appears in a list. For example, if you have a list of late returns to your school Library, you may want to check how many times the name of a certain student appears on the list. Although `PatternCount( )` can do this search for you, there is a trick to making it work reliably.

If you simply have FileMaker search the list for a name—say, "Mary"—you risk also inadvertently counting entries for **Mary**anne or perhaps Rose**mary**, or some other name of which Mary is a substring. (Note: `PatternCount( )` is not case-sensitive.) To address this problem, we recommend that you enclose the search item within word or list delimiter characters. For example, with a carriage-return delimited list, place a carriage return at either end of the search string to ensure that only complete-value matches are counted. For this search to work, you must also ensure that the list itself is enclosed within leading and trailing carriage returns; otherwise, the first and last list values will not qualify to be counted because they won't match to a search value having a carriage return on either side. The resulting expression is

    PatternCount(¶ & Library::LateReturnsList & ¶; "¶Mary¶")

The preceding expression returns 3 if Mary's name appears three times in the `LateReturnsList` field.

## Extracting one value from a list

As is often the case, FileMaker provides multiple ways to solve a given problem. And the extraction of a specific value from a list is no different. One of several ways to extract, say, the third value from a list is to use the `MiddleValues( )` function, with a "start" parameter of 3 and "size" parameter of 1:

    MiddleValues(Library::LateReturnsList; 3; 1)

While the preceding method works and is straightforward to implement, it returns the text of the third list entry with a trailing carriage return. If the purpose of your calculation is assembly of a new list and you're adding the extracted item to it, the trailing carriage return is of benefit because you won't have to add a carriage return before appending a subsequent item. However, for most other purposes, the trailing carriage return is either redundant or problematic.

For cases where you want to extract a single list value without a trailing carriage return, FileMaker provides the `GetValue( )` function. Thus, the expression

    GetValue(Library::LateReturnsList; 3)

performs the task with simplicity and efficiency, returning the referenced value (in this case, the third) without a trailing return.

## Adding or inserting a list value

Adding an item to the end of a list is straightforward if you know whether the list already has a trailing carriage return. If it does, and assuming that the list is in a field called Roster in a table called Library and the new value to be added is in a global field called gNewValue in a Utility table, you can use

```
Library::Roster & Utility::gNewValue
```

If the same list doesn't have a trailing return, you should use

```
Library::Roster & ¶ & Utility::gNewValue
```

The preceding example appends the required return as well as the new value. However, both these approaches are fragile and may produce undesired results if the field is not in the state you expect. A far more robust approach is to have your calculation check for the presence of a trailing carriage return, adding one only if necessary:

```
Library::Roster & If(Right(Library::Roster; 1) ≠ ¶; ¶) & Utility::gNewValue
```

The preceding technique is a robust way of adding a value to the end of your list, but if you want to insert the new value into the midst of the list, you require a different approach. For example, if you want to insert a value after the fourth value in a lengthy list, you could split and recombine the list (inserting the new value between the parts) using an expression such as

```
LeftValues(Library::Roster; 4) &
Utility::gNewValue & ¶ &
RightValues(Library::Roster; ValueCount(Library::Roster) - 4)
```

By altering the number in the first and last lines of the formula, you can vary the position in the list where the new value will be inserted. In the example, the new item becomes the fifth item in the list. However, when you change both 4s to 7s, the new item is inserted as the eighth list item.

Although you can insert a value in other ways, such as by using the `Replace( )` function, the preceding method has the advantage that it gracefully handles a situation where the list contains fewer items than the position specified in the formula. For example, if the list in the `Library::Roster` field contains only two items, the preceding expression simply appends the contents of `Utility::gNewValue` to the end of the list.

## Removing a value from a list

You can approach the task of removing a value from a list in different ways, depending on the nature of the list and the information you have about the item to be removed. For example, if you are confident that the items on the list are unique, you can remove the value by substitution, using an expression such as

```
Middle(
Substitute(¶ & Library::Roster & ¶; ¶ & Utility::gValueToRemove & ¶; ¶)
; 2; Length(Library::Roster) - 1 - Length(Utility::gValueToRemove) *
PatternCount(¶ & Library::Roster & ¶; ¶ & Utility::gValueToRemove & ¶)
)
```

Note that both the list and the value to be removed are first enclosed in carriage returns to ensure that partial matches do not occur, and the `Substitute( )` function is enclosed within a `Middle( )` expression (with a starting parameter of 2) to remove the leading and trailing carriage returns that would otherwise be appended.

This method is unsuitable if the list may include duplicate values, because multiple non-adjacent occurrences of the target value will be removed. However, by first identifying the list position of the value to be removed, you can cleanly excise it using a variation of the split list technique. For example, to remove the fourth item from the list, you could use the following expression:

```
LeftValues(Library::Roster; 3) &
RightValues(Library::Roster; ValueCount(Library::Roster) - 4)
```

This technique is clean and simple, but requires that you know — or can first determine — the list position of the item to be removed. Assuming that you know the item but not its list position, you can calculate the list position of the item's first occurrence by using an expression such as

```
ValueCount(Left(Library::Roster;
Position(¶ & Library::Roster & ¶; ¶ & Utility::gValueToRemove & ¶; 1; 1)))
```

By incorporating the logic of this process into a composite expression with the preceding calculation, you can remove an item's first occurrence in your list as follows:

```
Let([
p1 = Position(¶ & Library::Roster & ¶; ¶ & Utility::gValueToRemove & ¶; 1; 1);
n1 = ValueCount(Left(Library::Roster; p1));
v1 = LeftValues(Library::Roster; n1 - 1);
v2 = RightValues(Library::Roster; ValueCount(Library::Roster) - v1)];
v1 & Left(v2; Length(v2) - 1)
)
```

**NOTE** For simplicity and brevity, we have used algebraic naming for the variables in the `Let( )` function. However, you're at liberty to employ more descriptive names if you prefer.

## Layers of Abstraction

The previous calculation formula introduces a form of abstraction in that you don't have to know which list item is to be removed; the calculation determines where the item is in the list and then uses that information to complete the process of item removal. Although this is a simple and relatively minor form of abstraction, FileMaker's calculation engine supports a number of more profoundly abstract techniques, letting you structure your solution so that different outcomes occur depending on the state of the data your calculations encounter.

The essential principle of code abstraction is the use of FileMaker to calculate what should be calculated. A simple and direct example of this is the `GetField( )` function.

## Building blocks with GetField( )

The `GetField( )` function returns the value in the field named in its parameter, enabling you to calculate the name of the field from which a value is to be retrieved, at the time the calculation is evaluated.

At the conclusion of the "Summary Data" section earlier in this chapter, we proposed employing a calculation field named `cSortBy` as the `GetSummary( )` function's break field parameter in a case where it might be used to return exam period data either by course or by student. To achieve this task, you can create a reference field (a global field in a Utility table) and store a value there determining which field (`CourseID` or `StudentID`) the `cSortBy` calculation should reference. A simple logical expression to achieve this would be

```
Case(
Utility::gSortField = "StudentID"; StudentID;
Utility::gSortField = "CourseID"; CourseID
)
```

Although this approach is adequate when you have only two options that can be defined in advance, an alternative and more flexible way to achieve the same result is with the expression

```
GetField(Utility::gSortField)
```

This expression returns the contents of whichever field (if any) is named in the `Utility::gSortField` field. It has the advantage of simplicity and directness, but more importantly, it is open-ended and can accommodate a variety of other sort fields of the same data type (requiring only that they be named in the `Utility::gSortField` global field).

The `GetField( )` function's various uses enable you to build calculation code that can source input values from different fields in your solution according to need or context, enabling you to build a single calculation with multiple uses.

## The value of Evaluate( )

While your solutions can operate more flexibly with judicious use of the `GetField( )` function, a range of considerably more powerful options is provided by the `Evaluate( )` function, enabling you to determine part or all of the syntax of a calculation expression within the calculation itself.

As usual, FileMaker's online help gives a number of basic examples. Using the `Evaluate( )` function, however, opens a range of new possibilities and provides alternate ways to solve problems. Consider for a moment that you can use the `Max( )` function to ascertain the highest value in a related field, but there is no obvious way to find the second-highest value, should you need to.

One way to solve such a problem is to

1. Retrieve all the related values using the `List( )` function.
2. Determine the maximum related value using the `Max( )` function.

3. Use the list management techniques described in the section titled "Lists and Arrays" earlier in this chapter, to remove the first occurrence of the maximum related value from the list of related values.

4. Present the list of remaining values as an array formatted appropriately for the syntax required by FileMaker's aggregate functions.

5. Pass the resulting string, enclosed within `Max()` function syntax, to the `Evaluate()` function.

In this way, you use text and list manipulation functions to modify the inputs to the calculation, eliminating the highest related value. Rather than acting on the raw related data, `Evaluate()` is used to apply the `Max()` function to the modified text string.

The following composite calculation expression uses `Evaluate()` to determine the second-highest related value in the `Entries::Points` field:

```
Let([
Lv = List(Entries::Points);
Lc = ValueCount(Lv);
Mv = Max(Entries::Points);
p1 = Position(¶ & Lv & ¶; ¶ & Mv & ¶; 1; 1);
v1 = ValueCount(Left(Lv; p1));
Lr = LeftValues(Lv; v1 - 1) & RightValues(Lv; Lc - v1);
Mf = "Max(" & LeftWords(Substitute(Lr; ¶; "; "); Lc - 1) & ")"];
Evaluate(Mf)
)
```

When seven related records contain values in the points field of 77, 65, 83, 22, 91, 58, and 63, the function retrieves all the values as a list (Lv), identifies the maximum of 91 (Mv), eliminates 91 from the list (Lr), and then substitutes semicolon characters for carriage returns in the resulting list, placing it in the text format of the `Max()` function (Mf). The value of the Mf variable is therefore resolved to the following text string:

```
"Max(77; 65; 83; 22; 58; 63)"
```

When the text string Mf is passed to the `Evaluate()` function on the final line of the calculation, the calculation is resolved, and the second-highest related value — 83 — is returned. By using a calculation to determine what is to be calculated, this procedure is able to produce a result outside the primary scope of native FileMaker calculation functions (there is no native function to return the second-highest related value).

Although this example is somewhat arbitrary (albeit a useful technique in solutions where you need to calculate penalties or handicaps or plot top scores), we offer it as an indication of the extended scope of calculation capabilities made possible by creative uses of calculation abstraction.

# Unstored Calculations

FileMaker manages dependencies within each record of each table so that if a field is updated, other fields (stored within the same record) referencing it are re-evaluated. However, FileMaker provides an option for calculation fields to be unstored, in which case they're evaluated whenever referenced or displayed. Moreover, calculations directly referencing fields outside the current record (global fields or related fields) are required to be unstored. (FileMaker converts them to unstored data automatically when accepting the formula.)

> **NOTE** Unstored fields are commonly confused with unindexed fields, but they're not the same thing. There is a connection between storage and indexing insofar as a field must be stored to be indexed. However, although all unstored fields are always necessarily unindexed, stored fields my also be unindexed.

Unstored fields have both advantages and disadvantages. They have some capabilities and useful properties that other fields don't, but they also have several notable limitations.

## Why and when calculations are unstored

An unstored calculation comes into being for one of several possible reasons:

- The calculation directly references one or more global fields, and FileMaker has automatically converted it to unstored storage.
- The calculation directly references one or more related fields, and FileMaker has automatically converted it to unstored storage.
- The calculation directly references one or more unstored fields, and FileMaker has automatically converted it to unstored storage.
- The unstored option has been manually enabled in the Storage Options dialog for the field.

The first three reasons are required by FileMaker, because they introduce dependencies outside the record and not tracked by FileMaker's internal dependencies table. The fourth is optional; you may decide to make a field unstored to save on storage space, to improve the performance of certain tasks, or to enable the field to update to reflect the current state of system variables such as those returned by FileMaker's `Get ( )` functions. For example, a calculation defined with the expression

```
Get(CurrentTimestamp)
```

has no dependencies on fields or objects in your solution — it derives its value from your computer's system clock. If the calculation is stored, it records the date and time at its evaluation (when you leave the Manage Database dialog after defining the calculation). If your intent is to simply display the current date and time (when a layout is displayed) you should make the calculation unstored. Note, however, that unstored calculations are re-evaluated only when the screen is re-drawn, so the value shown on screen will not always be current.

Similarly, calculations created to display navigation details, such as the number of the current record in the found set, login details, or a variety of other system or environment variables, will only refresh if you define them as unstored.

## Understanding the benefits and trade-offs of unstored calculations

Unstored calculations have several benefits. When a calculation is unstored, the file size is reduced because the results of the calculation are not written to disk. Some operations, such as the update of dependent field values or import of records, may proceed with greater efficiency given that they don't require re-evaluating the calculation. Moreover, changing data in unstored calculations is refreshed frequently; for example, every time a layout containing an unstored calc is refreshed, the calculation is re-evaluated.

Conversely, unstored calculations use many processor cycles over time because they're evaluated whenever needed and, therefore, may be evaluated many times in the course of a work session rather than being evaluated once and stored. The re-evaluation of unstored calculations can lead to a processing burden that affects your solution's speed of operation if the number of unstored calculations is large, and particularly if unstored calculations are implicated in actions repeated across large record sets. If you're sorting records by an unstored calculation field, for example, the sort duration may be noticeably slower if the record set's size is larger than a few thousand — especially on older, slower hardware.

**CAUTION** In cases where unstored calculations reference other unstored calculations, FileMaker must resolve each in turn before a result can be displayed. If you create multiple cascading dependencies of this kind, serious performance degradation often results because you're requiring FileMaker to resolve an extensive chain of dependencies at every turn.

Design flaws of this kind can result in an unresponsive and inefficient solution and should be avoided.

## Discovering the hidden secrets of unstored calcs

Because an unstored calculation placed on a layout is re-evaluated each time it is referenced, you can use it to track user activity, increment values in your solution, or, with the aid of a third-party plug-in, perform other operations automatically as users navigate your solution.

For example, when you define an unstored calculation to increment or update a local or global variable, the variable is re-created each time a user performs an action resulting in screen re-draw. A practical example of one of the many uses of this capability is in Chapter 10 with the example of adding "back-button" functionality to the Inventory sample file.

Similarly, you can use a calculation defined to declare the current record ID to a variable each time the user navigates to a new record or layout as the basis of a conditional row-highlight in a portal. In other words, where the portal displays the results of a self-join relationship, you can highlight the current record's row in the portal. Here's how:

1. Create a stored calculation field called RecordID in the current table defined with the formula
   
   `Get(RecordID)`

2. Define (or modify) an unstored calculation displaying on the current layout to commence with the expression
   
   `Let($$CurrentRecord = Get(RecordID); ...`

3. Add a text object containing only a space to the layout to provide the portal row's background and apply conditional formatting to invoke a custom fill color with the formula

   ```
   $$CurrentRecord = PortalTO::RecordID
   ```

   where PortalTO is the name of the table occurrence your portal is based on.

4. Apply transparent fill to the text object, size it to fit in the portal row, and set it behind other objects in the portal.

5. Adjust the stacking order on the layout so that the unstored calculation field in Step 2 is further back in the object order than the portal. To do so, select the portal and all its contents and then choose Arrange ➪ Bring To Front.

On records where the portal display includes the current record, after you complete these steps the portal row showing the current record is highlighted with the fill color you selected in Step 3.

Because other kinds of calculations, such as tooltip calculations, conditional formatting calculations, Web viewer calculations, and so on, are also evaluated when the screen refreshes or when users interact with your solution, you can exploit several alternatives to invoke functionality depending on evaluation of calculations embedded in layout objects.

# Calculation Fields versus Auto-Enter Calculations

A FileMaker calculation field acquires a value according to the formula specified for it, updating when local fields it references are edited. The same is true of an auto-enter calculation, when the option labeled Do Not Replace Existing Value Of Field (If Any) is disabled, as shown in Figure 12.2. Consequently, some commentators have suggested that the calculation field is redundant, and auto-enter capabilities suffice.

The functionality of conventional FileMaker calculation fields and auto-enter calculation fields overlap. However, both kinds of calculations are useful in their own right, making them both highly desirable in different circumstances.

## The user over-ride capability

FileMaker calculation fields do not accept user input under any circumstances; their result is always determined by the calculation expression defining them. Users can enter a calculation field if you make it accessible on a layout, but although they can select and copy the contents, they can't overwrite them. Any attempt immediately results in the error dialog shown in Figure 12.3.

## Calculation Wizardry

**FIGURE 12.2**

De-selecting the Do Not Replace Existing Value of Field (If Any) option for an auto-enter calculation.

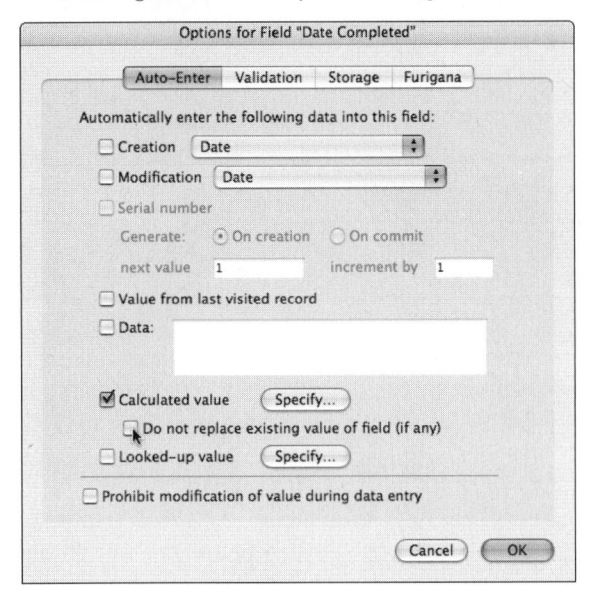

Auto-enter calculation fields can partially mimic the behavior of conventional calculations when you select the Prohibit Modification of Value During Data Entry option in the Options for Field dialog. However, you can override this option using a variety of methods, including disabling the Perform Auto-Enter Options While Importing option or by using a `Set Field[ ]` command on either a button or a script.

In most cases, however, the user can freely overwrite auto-enter calculations. This feature is valuable for occasions when your users need to manually over-ride a value, such as to mark down the price of a damaged stock item or waive a fee for a needy student. Whenever business rules call for the exercise of discretionary powers, mechanisms to depart from calculated norms are called for.

**FIGURE 12.3**

Users can't modify conventional calculation fields.

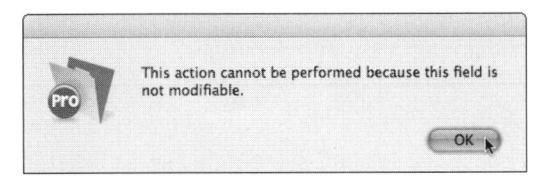

Just as auto-enter calculations offer the user the capability to over-ride the calculation result, so, too, can they be configured to respond to data input, overwriting the data entered by the user with the result of the calculation expression. This feature is useful for automatically applying or removing formatting or cleaning up sloppy data entry. For example, an auto-enter calculation with the formula

```
TextFormatRemove(Trim(Self))
```

accepts user input but immediately and automatically (as the user leaves the field) removes leading and trailing spaces and formatting. Similarly, a phone number field (defined as a text field, with an auto-enter/replaces existing value calculation) automatically updates to apply a standard telephone number presentation format (mask), regardless of the way the data is entered, thanks to the following formula:

```
Replace(Replace(Filter(PhoneNo; "0123456789"); 4; 0; "-"); 8; 0; "-")
```

With this formula and configuration, entering any of the following

0123456789
012.345.6789
012 345  6789

results in the field displaying and storing the value 012-345-6789.

**NOTE** The phone format formula is a simple and single example that indicates a way to solve this genre of problem. You may need to vary this formula to match the requirements of phone numbers in your area or to support multiple formats if your solution will contain contact details from different provinces or countries.

## Auto-enter calculations and storage

Auto-enter calculation options apply only to stored fields, so they don't share the capability of conventional calculations to be unstored and therefore to refresh "spontaneously" on screen re-draw. The capability to define unstored calculations has a number of specific uses and benefits. (See the section "Understanding the benefits and trade-offs of unstored calcs," earlier in this chapter.) These advantages are therefore unattainable with auto-enter calculations.

Conversely, in some cases, you can use auto-enter calculations to address shortcomings of unstored calculations. Because an auto-enter calc can never be unstored, even if it references global fields or related fields, the result of its calculation will be stored in the current record. In cases where the related data will not change — or where changes will not be relevant to the current record, such as where the data are part of a historical transaction record — incorporating related data into a stored auto-enter calc result has the advantage that the field can then be indexed and used for optimized searches, relational filtering and matching, and/or as a source of data for field-based value lists.

**CAUTION** Because calculation dependencies do not extend beyond the current record, an auto-enter calculation field referencing related data will not automatically update when the related fields it references are changed. Therefore, you should reference the data in place in the related table or use an unstored calculation whenever current data is required.

## Calculation Wizardry

### The Do Not Replace option

Figure 12.2 shows the Options for Field dialog, containing the Do Not Replace Existing Value of Field (If Any) setting. The way this option is named is perverse insofar as it results in a double negative when you deselect it — by turning it off, you are instructing FileMaker to "*Do Not Do Not Replace...*" — all very sensible if you're the kind of person who drives to work in reverse; for the rest of us, it can be downright confusing.

Notwithstanding the convolutions of its naming, this option is a powerful and essential feature in its own right, enabling you to configure auto-enter calculations to dynamically determine a default value for a field and then remain in the background allowing free-form data entry thereafter.

When the Do Not Replace checkbox is selected, auto-enter calculations support the user unobtrusively, leaving the user entirely in control of the data and the process of updating/maintaining it. When the option is turned off, the auto-enter calculations more closely mimic the behavior of conventional calculations, overwriting their current contents whenever local fields they reference are edited.

## Global Calculations

A rather underrated (and perhaps, poorly understood) feature of FileMaker is the global calculation field.

To define a calculation field as global, go to the Storage Options dialog by clicking Storage Options in the lower right of the Specify Calculation dialog and, as shown in Figure 12.4, select the checkbox labeled Use Global Storage (One Value for All Records).

**FIGURE 12.4**

Defining global storage for a conventional calculation field.

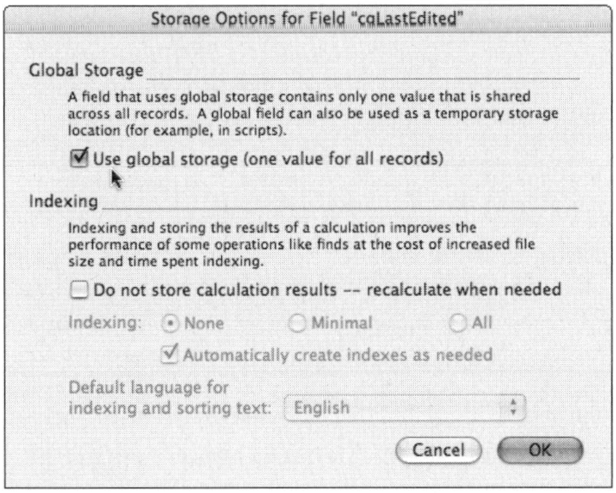

A calculation field defined to use global storage acquires the same essential (and valuable) characteristics as other types of global fields, to wit:

- As indicated in the Storage options dialog, it returns a single value for all records in the current table.
- It is accessible throughout your solution without requiring a relationship between the current context and the TO where it is defined.
- Its value (if changed during a user session in a multi-user solution) is specific to the current user and session.
- Its value does not depend on any records being present (or being present in the found set) of the table where it resides.
- Its value is persistent in Find mode.

These advantages are surely powerful, providing reason enough to make use of global calculations. However, global calculations exhibit some additional characteristics, making them especially useful for a range of requirements.

## The moon follows you everywhere

Like a full moon in the late afternoon sky, global calculations shadow your movements, recalculating always with respect to the current user's current context. Like all other calculation fields, their dependencies are restricted to fields in the current table. However, they update according to changes in the current record — whichever record that may be from the context of the current user.

Global calculations also have a unique role in relation to other kinds of global fields. Normally, a calculation based on a global field value must be unstored. However, if the calculation is global, it will respond to global fields as a regular calculation field responds to data fields within the record — updating according to internally managed dependencies.

These two important behavioral attributes of global calculations give them considerable power. Unfortunately, their unique combination of behavioral attributes has resulted in some confusion about how they interact with other field types and when they will and won't update. To assist you in coming to grips with the behavior of global calculations and to understand and predict their behavior, we've assembled a brief description of their characteristics.

## Managing global dependencies

If you're uncertain about the way global calculations behave with respect to changes in fields they reference, the following 12 observations provide you with guidance. These characteristics of global calculations apply to all versions of FileMaker supporting the .fp7 file format:

- A global calculation updates automatically if it references a global field that is located in the same table and that field is edited by the current user.
- A global calculation updates automatically if it references a regular field that is located in the same table (and referenced directly) when that field is edited on any record by the

current user. In this instance, the value of the global calculation depends on the value of the referenced field in the record in which that field has most recently been edited.

- When a global calculation references multiple regular fields, its value depends on the values in the instances of all those fields located on the particular record where the most recently edited (by the current user) of any of those fields resides.
- A global calculation does *not* update if it references a global field that is located in another table, if that field is edited by the current user.
- A global calculation does *not* update if it references a global field (in the same table and referenced directly, or in another table) that is edited by different user. (Users see their own separate global values.)
- A global calculation does *not* update automatically if it references a regular field that is located in the same table (and referenced directly) when that field is edited on any record by another user.
- A global calculation does *not* update automatically if it references a regular field that is located in a related table (even if a self-relation) if that field is edited on any record by the current user or by another user.
- If a global calculation references one or more related fields and *also* directly references a local field, either global or regular, the value of the global calc depends on the related values that are current (for the current user) at the time when the local (to the table in which the global calc resides) value(s) are edited.
- The value of a global calculation when a solution is opened remotely is the value that it had on the host when last closed. (Sound familiar?)
- The values of global calculations in a hosted solution can be prompted to update at login by changing a local field which they reference. For example, if you have several dozen global calculations with formulas constructed along the lines of

```
If(not IsEmpty(GlobalsTable::RegularTriggerField);
   RelatedTable::DataField)
```

they all update to reflect the current (related) values at start-up when the start-up script includes the command

```
Set Field [GlobalsTable::RegularTriggerField; "1"]
```

- Changes made to referenced regular fields on another workstation do not appear in global calculation results until a refresh event has occurred on the current workstation — such as the next time the start-up script runs. If no triggering mechanism occurs, then remote changes do not appear at all until the solution is taken offline, updated in a client session, closed, and reopened on the server, as is the case with noncalculating globals.
- When a global calculation field references regular fields located in the same table, it retrieves values from the record in that table that is the current record at the time the calculation is evaluated. If no current record exists at the time of such an update (for example, the active layout is not based on the table containing the global calculation field and there is no relationship from the current layout's TO to the TO containing the field), the current record is imputed to be "record zero" and the values of regular fields will be read as null.

Within these constraints and guidelines, the behavior of global calculations is entirely consistent and predictable. After you're familiar with their behavior, they're an invaluable addition to your technical repertoire.

## The freedom and efficiency of global calculations

In addition to their useful characteristics as global fields — they're session specific, accessible without a relationship, and so on — global calculation fields also share several key behaviors common to regular calculations:

- They're automatic triggered by dependencies according to specific rules as set out in the preceding section titled "Managing global dependencies."
- Their values are determined and cannot be overwritten, deliberately or inadvertently, as a result of either user error or script error.

Taken as a whole, these attributes make global fields indispensable for a variety of purposes related to handling of user, state, and reference data, as well as process support and interface elements in your solutions.

**CROSS-REF** As an illustration of the use of global calculation fields to support extended solution functionality, refer to the multilingual solution interface example in Chapter 10.

# Environment and Metadata

Enabling your solutions to interact sensitively and dynamically with the environments where they operate, FileMaker includes a significant number of functions allowing you to retrieve information about the solution and the state of the hardware and operating system.

## The Get( ) functions

An essential part of the calculation process, FileMaker provides Get( ) functions to return information about process, context, and environment. FileMaker 9 has 90 Get( ) functions, and we urge you to familiarize yourself with each of them. The online Help files are a great place to start for brief descriptions of each function.

As a simple illustrative example, the Get(ApplicationVersion) function returns a text string identifying both the kind of access the current user has to the solution and the specific version and revision number if applicable. Obtaining the application version number can be useful in several ways. For example, the expression

```
GetAsNumber(Get(ApplicationVersion))
```

returns 9.02 when the solution is currently being accessed by FileMaker Pro 9.0v2, FileMaker Pro Advanced 9.0v2, or a runtime created using FileMaker Pro Advanced 9.0v2. If your solution has been created using features introduced in FileMaker 9, such as conditional formatting, data URLs, or External SQL Data Sources, it won't work as intended if opened using an earlier version of FileMaker. You should consider including a test, like the following, in the On Open script of your solution, configured to alert the user to the required version and close the file if it evaluates as false:

```
GetAsNumber(Get(ApplicationVersion)) ≥ 9
```

Alternatively, when your solution is accessible by a variety of means, you will find it useful to calculate script branching (or otherwise tailor the functionality of your solution) using the following expressions:

```
If(PatternCount(Get(ApplicationVersion); "Web"); ...
```

and

```
If(PatternCount(Get(ApplicationVersion); "Pro"); ...
```

These calculation expressions enable you to determine whether the current user is accessing your solution via Instant Web Publishing or one of the FileMaker client application versions (Pro or ProAdvanced). With the information the calculations provide, you can set up calculation or script functionality to branch according to version.

Similarly, when your solution may be accessed on a variety of computers, you should routinely test for the computer platform and operating system version using `Get(SystemPlatform)`, `Get(SystemVersion)`, and/or `Get(SystemLanguage)`, enabling your solution to respond differently according to the requirements of different computing environments.

The many available `Get( )` functions in FileMaker 9 offer you a rich source of information about many aspects of your solution, its use, and the environment in which it is operating, each offering enhanced control over the results your calculations return and the ways your solution operates.

**CROSS-REF** Refer to the appendixes for references and additional resources regarding abundant collection of `Get( )` functions in FileMaker 9.

## Design functions

Like the `Get( )` functions, design functions in FileMaker are principally concerned with the retrieval of metadata and environmental information. Functions such as `DatabaseNames`, which returns a list of the filenames of FileMaker databases open on the current workstation, or `FieldType( )`, which indicates the data storage type (number text, date, etc.) of a named field, enable you to code your solution to adapt to present conditions.

Design functions also serve many more central purposes in your solution design. For example, if you build code in your solution to refer to a specific layout by its layout number, the code may cease working correctly if the layouts are reordered. However, if you refer to the layout by name instead, you risk the code failing if the layout is renamed in the future. Instead, you can use design functions to refer to a layout by its layout ID, which can never change. For example, to determine the internal ID of a specific layout, you can first use a calculation expression such as

```
Let ([
Ln = LayoutNames(Get(FileName));
ID = LayoutIDs(Get(FileName));
p1 = Position(¶ & Ln & ¶; ¶ & "Name of Layout" & ¶; 1; 1);
n1 = Left(Ln; p1);
p2 = ValueCount(n1)];
If(p1; GetValue( ID; p2 ))
)
```

Having ascertained FileMaker's internal ID number for a specific layout, you can then code your solution to determine the current name of the layout at any time, based on its ID, by passing the ID to a calculation reversing the process:

```
Let ([
ID = LayoutIDs(Get(FileName));
Ln = LayoutNames(Get(FileName));
p1 = Position(¶ & ID & ¶; ¶ & "ID of Layout" & ¶; 1; 1);
n1 = Left(ID; p1);
p2 = ValueCount(n1)];
If(p1; GetValue( Ln; p2 ))
)
```

**NOTE** You can adapt these techniques to enable you to refer to a variety of other solution elements by ID, including fields, table occurrences, scripts, and value lists.

Although this example shows you one way you can use design functions to improve the robustness and adaptability of your solutions, you have many other options. FileMaker 9 offers 21 design functions to provide dynamic information about the essentials of your solutions.

## Calculations Using Custom Functions

FileMaker Pro includes a category of functions available in calculation dialogs for custom functions. You can see the functions listed in the menu of function types appearing at the top right of the Specify Calculation dialog, as shown in Figure 12.5.

In a new database file created in FileMaker Pro, the Custom Functions category is empty. You must create and install custom functions into a file using FileMaker Pro Advanced. However, this capability alone is well worth the cost difference between FileMaker Pro 9 and FileMaker Pro 9 Advanced, and we encourage you to consider the benefits of designing additional calculation functions to serve the needs of your solutions.

Once a custom function has been created and installed, you can select and use custom functions in calculations in the same way that you use other kinds of functions, assuming that your account does not have restricted access.

# Calculation Wizardry

**FIGURE 12.5**

Selecting the Custom Functions category from the menu of function types in the Specify Calculation dialog.

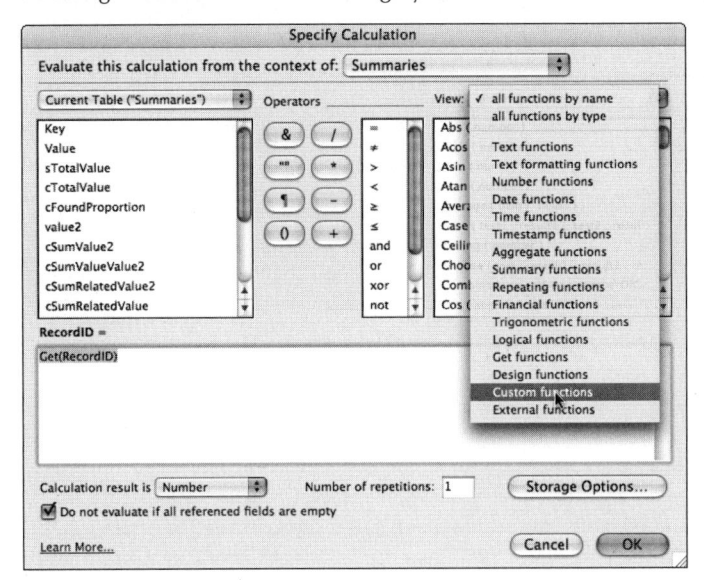

Here are three chief reasons why custom functions can significantly enhance the calculation code of your solutions:

- You can use custom functions to simplify calculation syntax and improve legibility and convenience in calculation code.

    For example, when your solution contains a custom function called Platform Is MacOS defined as:

    `Abs(Get(SystemPlatform)) = 1`

    you can check which platform your solution is presently running on with plain English readable code, such as

    `If [Platform Is MacOS]`

    This and many other examples like it can streamline development and add clarity to your code.

- Custom functions can encapsulate complex, but frequently used, code in a compact and convenient form, enabling you to reference the code with a single function call. Incorporating complex code within a custom function is not merely a simplifying move; it also enables you to maintain the block of code in one place (the custom function definition) knowing that any change to the stored function definition will propagate everywhere the function is called throughout your solution.

**NOTE** When you change a Custom function definition, previously stored values created using the function will not automatically change, but any new values will be calculated using the revised function definition. If you want to update previous values, you'll have to prompt reevaluation of stored calculations using the Custom function.

For example, in the preceding section, we provide a sample function to retrieve the current name of a layout based on its ID number. If you plan to use such a function frequently, it may be preferable to place the code within a custom function with the syntax

```
GetLayoutName ( LayoutID )
```

where the function definition is

```
Let([
ID = LayoutIDs(Get(FileName));
Ln = LayoutNames(Get(FileName));
p1 = Position(¶ & ID & ¶; ¶ & LayoutID & ¶; 1; 1);
n1 = Left(ID; p1);
p2 = ValueCount(n1)];
If(p1; GetValue( Ln; p2 ))
)
```

With a `GetLayoutName ( )` custom function installed in your file, you can incorporate it in your code whenever you want instead of repeating the more unwieldy expression it represents.

- You can configure custom functions to perform feats not available to ordinary calculations. In particular, you can design custom functions to use *recursion,* a process where a function repeatedly calls itself until predetermined conditions are met.

As an arbitrary example of a recursive process, consider the elementary example of a custom function defined with the syntax `ShuffleString(text)` and with the definition

```
Let([
a = Length(text);
b = Int(Random * a) + 1];
If(a; Middle(text; b; 1) &
ShuffleString(Left(text; b - 1) & Right(text; a - b)))
)
```

This simple recursive function is designed to receive a text string and return the supplied characters in random order. The following example expression returns a result such as BLFVWNAQUMOIRTGPYCSDJKHXEZ:

```
ShuffleString("ABCDEFGHIJKLMNOPQRSTUVWXYZ")
```

Because the recursive process repeats its work until complete, the function can process input strings of variable length. In doing so, it achieves a result that cannot readily be matched using a conventional calculation expression. There are many kinds of problems—both common and obscure—that you can solve elegantly using an appropriately constructed recursive function.

A comprehensive tutorial on the creation and use of custom functions is beyond this chapter's scope. Nevertheless, the calculation capabilities in FileMaker are powerful and extensible, well beyond the limits of the 243 built-in calculation functions in FileMaker Pro 9.

**CROSS-REF** For further discussion about the creation and use of custom functions using FileMaker Pro Advanced, refer to Chapter 18.

## Your Code's Documentation

As you work with the calculation expressions in FileMaker, their syntax becomes increasingly familiar, and you find them intelligible. To a degree, therefore, calculation code in FileMaker is self-documenting. With only the most basic familiarity with the calculation engine, the following expression can be accurately interpreted:

```
If(IsEmpty(Invoices::TimeField); Get(CurrentTime))
```

So much so that including an explanation along the lines of "if the invoice time field is empty, get the current time" adds bulk without aiding clarity.

The use of descriptive field, table, and variable names aids the readability of your calculations.

In some cases, however, your calculation code's meaning or purpose is difficult to discern without additional information — particularly when calculation expressions are long or complex, or where they form a small part of the logic distributed between a number of solution components. In such cases, the judicious use of code formatting and code commenting can improve intelligibility.

### Code formatting

A variety of styles for the formatting of code are available, including use of line breaks and indenting to delineate enclosing elements and map out the logic of compound expressions.

Although simple one-line expressions rarely require formatting, longer expressions do benefit from some attention to the arrangement of elements for readability. For example, the definition of the `GetLayoutName( )` custom function in the previous section titled "Calculations Using Custom Functions" would have been considerably more difficult to interpret if presented as follows:

```
Let([ID=LayoutIDs(Get(FileName));Ln=LayoutNames(Get(FileName));p1=Position(¶&ID&
    ¶;¶&LayoutID&¶;1;1);n1=Left(ID;
    p1);p2=ValueCount(n1)];If(p1;GetValue(Ln;p2)))
```

## Part III  Beyond the Basics

As the expression is of moderate complexity, we chose to include line breaks to delineate the components of the code. For more convoluted expressions, indenting may also help to clarify meaning. For example, a fully formatted rendering of the same function definition is

```
Let(
    [
        ID = LayoutIDs( Get( FileName ) );
        Ln = LayoutNames( Get( FileName ) );
        p1 = Position( ¶ & ID & ¶; ¶ & LayoutID & ¶; 1; 1 );
        n1 = Left( ID; p1 );
        p2 = ValueCount( n1 )
    ];
    If( p1; GetValue( Ln; p2 ) )
)
```

Here, like elements and enclosing braces are aligned to give the syntax maximum form and structure.

## Code commenting

Another aid to comprehending complex code is the judicious use of commenting. FileMaker supports the inclusion of either C or C++ style commenting (or any mix thereof) within calculation expressions. In general, C++ comment syntax is best suited to labeling and brief annotations, whereas if you need to include extensive explanatory notes, C syntax will be preferable.

To add comments in C++ syntax, precede each comment with a pair of slashes and terminate it with a line break:

```
//this is a C++ comment
//you can include multiple lines
//but each line must commence with a new pair of slashes.
```

Alternatively, you can provide more discursive multi-line comments by adopting the C syntax, where a comment is preceded by a slash and asterisk (/*) and terminated with an asterisk and slash (*/):

```
/* This is a C style comment, running across multiple lines
and enclosed at either end with the appropriate terminators.*/
```

As a general rule, commenting should highlight important or obscure points, providing signposts and pointers to aid understanding. However, it should remain unobtrusive, contributing as little as possible to code bloating.

# Chapter 13

# Scripting in Depth

Chapter 8 describes what ScriptMaker does and how to use it — we provide various practical examples of scripts automating a number of frequently performed database tasks. The examples we show you in Chapter 8, however, barely exercise the FileMaker scripting engine's power. In this chapter, we provide that deeper insight into a number of ScriptMaker's central concepts.

The FileMaker Pro 9 scripting engine evolved through previous versions and has grown into a powerful coding environment. Originally, FileMaker scripting offered a way to automate repetitive or tedious user actions. Consequently, many scripts and script commands work with and through the solution interface, performing actions and accomplishing work in the same ways the user does. However, scripts can go far beyond mimicking the user and provide an environment of power and extended functionality.

Scripts in FileMaker Pro 9 have the ability to act directly on data and file elements and interact with other applications and services. Nevertheless, the scripting framework retains some of its original focus on the interface as the primary way of interacting with a solution. In this chapter, we explore a number of essential techniques to increase the depth of your command of FileMaker scripting.

## IN THIS CHAPTER

Controlling interface objects via script

Trapping for errors

Scripting around access privilege issues

Automating the automation

Using parameters, results, and variables in your scripts

Utilizing dynamic and indirect controls in ScriptMaker

Nonlinear logic

Working with modular script code

Managing database windows via script

Scripting data import and export

Pivoting data between tables

# Scripting the Control of Objects and Interface

Consider for a moment the ways your FileMaker solutions interact with users. A FileMaker solution's user interface is comprised of a series of layouts containing a variety of objects, some of which are static, but many of which have embedded attributes linking them to the solution's data and code.

The variety of FileMaker layout objects include static objects (text labels, graphical lines and shapes, plus inserted images) augmenting the visual appearance of your solution but without an active or interactive role. Other layout object types are designed as controls or devices with which the user can access and interact with the solution's code and data. These include:

- Field boxes
- Buttons
- Portals
- Tab controls
- Web viewers

In FileMaker Pro 9, you can assign names to both layouts and layout objects. The object names that you assign provide a basis for scripts to target and interact with specific objects. In fact, each of these kinds of objects can be explicitly named and then have scripts specify an object by name when the script needs to interact with the object.

**TIP** You can assign or edit layout names while in Layout mode by choosing Layouts ⇨ Layout Setup and entering a name in the name field in the upper part of the Layout Setup dialog.

Object names are assigned when you enter them into the Object Name field in the Info palette after selecting the object in Layout mode. Choose View ⇨ Object Info command to display the Info palette.

## Addressing objects by name

After you create an object and place it on a layout in Layout mode (and after you save the changes to the layout) it immediately becomes visible and available to users viewing the layout in Browse or Find modes. Additionally, the object becomes accessible to scripts running in either of those modes. When you assign a name to an object, scripts are able to select the object using its name. Selected objects (by the user or via script) are said to be *active* or to *have focus*. Similarly, only one layout — the layout showing in the frontmost window — is active at a time.

When interacting with objects, your scripts are constrained to those objects present on the current (active) layout. Moreover, FileMaker's current mode determines the possible forms of interaction with each kind of object. Consequently, to ensure that your script can perform the intended action, you should commence your script code with a command explicitly establishing the required mode and then add commands navigating to the appropriate layout and (if appropriate) the desired record.

## Scripting in Depth

For example, to have your script place the focus on the `FirstName` data field (with an object name of `"Contact first name"`) on the Contact Details layout in Browse mode in the most recently added record of the Contacts table, commence it with the following six script steps:

```
Enter Browse Mode [ ]
Go to Layout ["Contact Details"]
Show All Records
Unsort Records
Go to Record/Request/Page [Last]
Go to Object [Object Name: "Contact first name"]
```

The preceding sequence of commands sets the focus where you want it — on the FirstName field. However, it only succeeds if a number of conditions are satisfied. In this case, the script requires that the "Contact Details" layout exists, that there are (one or more) records in the `Contacts` table, and that an instance of the `FirstName` field on the Contact Details layout has been assigned the object name `Contact first name`. Should any of these conditions not be met, the script fails.

> **TIP** Each object type mentioned at the start of this section can have focus. Consequently, you can use the `Go to Object[ ]` script command in a sequence such as the one shown here, to direct the focus toward named objects of any of the kinds listed.

The names you assign to objects must be unique within a given layout. FileMaker will not accept an object name if it is already used on the current layout. Therefore, you can employ a single instance of the `Go to Object[ ]` command to address an object even if it is enclosed inside other objects on the layout. For example, suppose a named field object is located inside a named portal that, in turn, is located inside a named tab control panel. You can place the focus on the field and both its enclosing objects simply by addressing the named object's unique name. This is sufficient for the relevant tab and portal to also automatically acquire focus. You can use this behavior to address a layout's objects in a straightforward manner.

You should bear in mind that while object names must be unique within a layout, objects with the same names may appear on other layouts. The process of directing focus to a named object with the `Go to Object[ ]` command is valid only when the correct layout is active. Avoid using the `Go to Object[ ]` command unless your script has previously established or confirmed the layout context. In this and many other respects, context is crucial.

In fact, the concept of context, as outlined in Part I, governs every action that your scripts take. The methods outlined in this section provide a key part of the strategy you can use to ensure that your scripts manage context throughout their execution by placing the focus where required for each scripted action.

> **TIP** We suggest that you first ascertain and store the user's current context (mode and record or request) so that the script can reinstate context at its conclusion and return control of the database to the user in the same state as when it started.

## Locking down the interface

When you configure your script to establish focus on a specific field, your purpose might be to have the script prompt the user to enter a name for the most recent client contact record. If so, to achieve its aim, your script relies on the user to provide necessary input.

To ensure that such a scripted procedure is completed successfully, you must ensure that the user is unable to leave the selected layout until the required information is entered. In this case — and other similar situations — it makes sense to prevent the normal use of navigation controls until the matter at hand has been addressed. In this manner, you can configure your scripts to guide and constrain users. Doing so establishes and enforces procedures and business rules in keeping with the solution's objectives.

Frequently, hiding and locking (disabling) the FileMaker Status Area suffices to constrain navigation. However, you may also want to set the layout size and magnification (zoom) level (to ensure that the field is in view) and to ensure the layout is being viewed as a form rather than a list or table (so that the user cannot scroll to other records). You can implement these restrictions by configuring the following four additional script commands:

```
Show/Hide Status Area [Lock; Hide]
Set Zoom Level [100%]
View As [View As Form]
Adjust Window [Resize to Fit]
```

Although a sequence of commands such as this adds to the length of our script, it enhances the script's ability to meet its objectives, so its inclusion is justified.

> **TIP** When the Status Area is hidden and locked, not only are the navigation controls (the layout menu, rolodex, slider, and so on) inaccessible to the user, the scroll wheel, standard keyboard navigation shortcuts, and menu commands for navigating between layouts and records are also disabled.

## Managing user interaction

In the previous sections, we describe a script that takes the user to a particular layout and record, locks the interface, adjusts the window, and places focus on the `FirstName` field. However, you cannot be certain that the user will know what to do next. Users are apt to have minds of their own. Moreover, no process has been implemented for returning the users to their starting point after they complete the required task.

In addition to setting the conditions for the task and hand — and doing all the heavy lifting — your scripts should inform users what is required of them. One way your script might achieve this is to post a dialog prompting the user to enter a name in the name field. The `Show Custom Dialog[ ]` script command can be found in the Miscellaneous group of commands near the bottom of the Edit Script window's script step list, as shown in Figure 13.1.

After adding and configuring the dialog command (to display a prompt along the lines of `"Enter the contact's first name, then press enter"`), you need a way to maintain scripted

## Scripting in Depth 13

control of the process. One way to do so is by having the script pause (for user input) and then return the user to their previous location or context.

If using the pause-for-input approach, you should add a pause command after the Show Custom Dialog[ ] command, followed by a further pair of commands that return the user to their previous layout and reinstate the Status Area. The whole script now looks like this:

```
Enter Browse Mode [ ]
Go to Layout ["Contact Details"]
Show All Records
Unsort Records
Show/Hide Status Area [Lock; Hide]
Set Zoom Level [100%]
View As [View As Form]
Adjust Window [Resize to Fit]
Go to Record/Request/Page [Last]
Show Custom Dialog ["Enter the customer's name, then press Enter."]
Go to Object [Object Name: "Contact first name"]
Pause/Resume Script [Indefinitely]
Go to Layout [original layout]
Show/Hide Status Area [Show]
```

**FIGURE 13.1**
You can select Show Custom Dialog from the Miscellaneous group of commands in the Edit Script window.

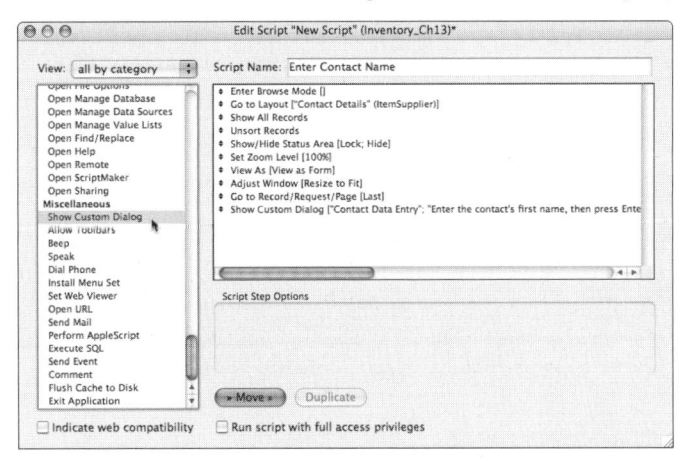

With the script paused, as indicated at the third-last line of the script as set out here, pressing the Enter key causes the script to resume from its paused state, at which point the subsequent command takes the user back to whichever layout was active when the script was triggered. However, if the user presses Enter without first typing a name in the FirstName field, the script will proceed without the requested input.

453

So far, so good — the sequence of steps now appears workable. However, the process is more heavy-handed than necessary, in part because it is modeled on the series of actions a user would take to perform the same task manually. While this is not a bad starting place, you can use other options to achieve similar results in a more streamlined fashion.

In this case, rather than taking the user on a whirlwind tour to the customer table and back, an alternative is to use the custom dialog to collect the required information in one step (before even changing layouts) and then perform the remaining action(s) efficiently behind the scenes without the user's knowledge or intervention. This process makes use of the custom dialog's ability to include input fields.

To achieve more graceful execution, try using alternative sequencing of essentially the same script, such as the following:

```
Show Custom Dialog ["Enter the customer's name, then press Enter.";
   Contacts::gTempText]
Freeze Window
Enter Browse Mode [ ]
Go to Layout ["Contact Details"]
Show All Records
Unsort Records
Go to Record/Request/Page [Last]
Set Field [Contacts::FirstName; Contacts::gTempText]
Go to Layout [original layout]
```

This modification improves the script in several respects. The script accomplishes the same task with fewer steps but, more importantly, it accomplishes its work with less interruption and visual discontinuity for the user. The dialog appears and, after it is closed, the window is frozen momentarily while the rest of the work is done unseen.

> **NOTE** To collect the user input up front using a dialog requires a temporary place to store the data until it can be used. A global text field is suitable for this purpose.

## Trapping for Errors

A clean and simple user experience is certainly an improvement, but truly graceful execution also requires that your script detect problems and handle them efficiently.

The previous script is vulnerable to a number of possible problems that you can anticipate. Think about the following:

- The user might dismiss the dialog without entering anything into it.
- The Contact Details layout may have been deleted.
- While the user was entering a name in the dialog, another user, elsewhere on the network, may have deleted all the records in the contacts table.

- Another user may have added a new record to the customer table, so that the last record is no longer the one that the current user's value should be entered against.
- Another user may presently be editing the last record in the Customer table, so it may be temporarily locked, and the script is consequently unable to apply the change.

These and other similar conditions could cause one or more of the script commands to fail, in which case the script may not complete or may complete with unintended results. At worst, the script may write its data into the wrong record, perhaps overwriting data already stored there. Such occurrences threaten a solution's data integrity and are more common than many people suppose.

There are two ways to achieve a more robust script:

- Introduce additional code into the script to detect errors and respond appropriately.
- Further modify the design of the script so that it is less vulnerable to error.

Both of these techniques are possible. For example, FileMaker Pro 9 provides error management capabilities within scripts. As a script is executed, step by step, it returns a succession of error codes (each of which refers to a specific error class or condition). The calculation function Get(LastError) provides a means to determine whether an error was encountered and if so, of what type.

## Retrieving error codes appropriately

At any point in time, only one error code is available — the code relating to the most recently executed script command. If another command executes (aside from the exceptions noted below), its error code replaces the previously stored result. In other words, FileMaker does not maintain a history or log of errors. It is up to you to retrieve the error codes and then act on them or store them as you see fit when designing and implementing a script.

**NOTE** In all cases, when no error has occurred (including when no script steps have yet been executed), the Get(LastError) function returns zero.

Not all script commands return an error code. Most notably, #comment script lines are not evaluated or executed in FileMaker Pro 9, so they return no code. Similarly, the Halt Script and Exit Script [ ] commands are ignored by the error handler (the error result from the preceding command will continue to be available). Additionally, various commands — including most of those in the Control group, such as Allow User Abort [ ], Beep, Pause/Resume Script [ ], among others — are not vulnerable to failure and routinely return a zero error result.

The error code relating to the most recent script's last action remains available even after the script has concluded, so you may evaluate the Get(LastError) function at any time to discover the error result of the most recent script's last command. Moreover, error result codes are specific to the FileMaker application session but not to the file, so even if the most recently run script was in Solution A, its closing error result will remain available even after switching to Solution B — until another script is executed (in either solution) or until you quit from FileMaker.

## What the error codes mean

FileMaker Pro 9 provides a total 135 script commands. However, more than 200 error codes are available, each relating to a particular problem (or category of problem) preventing a command or process from executing successfully. A complete list of the codes, with a brief explanation of each, can be found under the heading FileMaker Pro error codes in FileMaker Pro 9 online help.

In some circumstances, an error code is returned even though the script command may be regarded as having succeeded. For example, a Go To Related Records[ ] command with the Match All Records in Found Set option enabled will return error code 101 (Record is missing) if the current record had no related records, even though other records in the found set had related records and they have been located and displayed. If there were no related records for any of the records in the found set, FileMaker returns error code 401 (No records match the request) and the command fails.

Not all of the error conditions represented in the list of error codes are relevant to any one script command. For example, error code 400 is defined as Find Criteria are empty. This error code is clearly applicable only to those few script commands that can be used to execute a find and that may therefore fail if no find criteria have been provided. Similarly, error code 209 is defined as: New password must be different from existing one, which is applicable only to the Change Password[ ] script command.

However, other results (such as error code 1, User canceled action or error code 9, Insufficient privileges) can arise in a variety of situations and may be associated with many of the available script commands. Although you may be able to anticipate specific error conditions when using particular script steps, accounting for the possibility that other errors may also arise is prudent.

## Why bother with error handling?

In most cases when an error is returned, something is amiss and there are likely to be consequences. FileMaker, as an application, is relatively tolerant of errors (that is, it rarely crashes or hangs) but if a sequence of commands fail, the following scenarios may result:

- The user will be confused.
- Data will be inappropriately written or overwritten.
- Data which should be written won't be.
- The wrong records will be deleted or duplicated.
- The user will be left stranded on the wrong layout.
- Any of a range of other unexpected events will occur.

The purpose of a script is generally to improve the efficiency, accuracy, and usability of your solution. It is somewhat self-defeating if the script itself becomes the cause of errors or usability problems.

Scripts are executed sequentially from the first step to the last, so when a command partway through a script cannot be performed, it may be problematic if the script proceeds. Conversely, if the script stops partway through its run, the procedure it was intended to implement may be left in

# Scripting in Depth 13

an incomplete or otherwise unacceptable state (for example, an address that is partially updated may be rendered meaningless).

In general, users are likely to embrace your solution if it supports their work, increases their efficiency, or makes life easier, but not if it produces unpredictable results and leaves them confused. To address this, you should selectively add code to trap errors as they occur during the execution of your scripts.

## Handling errors

FileMaker Pro 9 applies default error handling to many processes, which is what we see when an error occurs while we are operating the database manually. For example, if you go to Find mode and then try to execute the Find without having entered any criteria, FileMaker posts a standard alert dialog, as shown in Figure 13.2.

When a comparable error is encountered as a result of a script's execution, FileMaker (by default) posts an essentially similar dialog, with the addition of a button allowing the user to continue the script regardless. In this case, the Cancel button not only cancels the current action but also terminates the script. Figure 13.3 shows the variation of the dialog that appears by default when the same error is encountered as a result of a failed Perform Find [ ] script command.

**FIGURE 13.2**

The native FileMaker error dialog for the empty Find criteria condition.

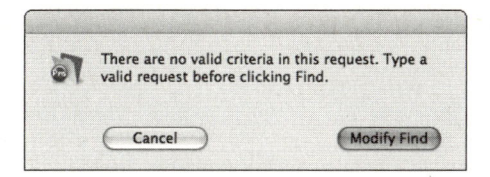

**FIGURE 13.3**

The default script error dialog for the empty Find criteria condition.

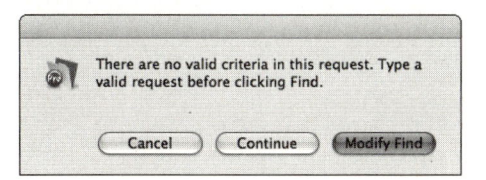

When comparing the dialogs shown in Figures 13.2 and 13.3, notice that apart from the addition of a Continue button, the dialogs are identical. However, while the default dialog in Figure 13.2 is generally adequate for a situation when the user initiates a Find without first providing criteria, the dialog appearing when a script throws the same error is less helpful — especially because the user,

457

not being closely acquainted with your script code, may be unable to discern the cause or consequences of the error.

> **NOTE** When a scripted Find procedure is preceded by the Allow User Abort [Off] command, a variant of the dialog shown in Figure 13.3 appears, with the Cancel button omitted.

The default error dialog is unable to tell the user what role the failed command had within the script or why it has failed on this occasion. Similarly, it does not explain the consequences of canceling or continuing, or what criteria it would be appropriate to enter if choosing the Modify Find option. The user is placed into a position of uncertainty, if not confusion, and the choices he makes to resolve this dilemma may only compound the problem. This is an inherent limitation with reliance on default error handling within the context of a scripted procedure.

The first thing to do when implementing appropriate error handling within a script is to turn off the default error messages within the script. You do this by adding the script command Set Error Capture [On].

> **NOTE** After error capture is turned on, all default error handling is disabled until the script concludes or error capture is explicitly turned off.

A script's error capture state is also "inherited" by any and all sub-scripts that the script may call. Changes to the error capture state occurring within sub-scripts will subsequently be inherited by the calling script (when it resumes execution).

When you include the Set Error Capture [On] command at the start of a script, it is important to ensure that you provide adequate error handling within the ensuing script sequence, because no default error messages will be displayed. Otherwise, when the script encounters an error while error capture is on, it will continue regardless.

> **TIP** You can use the Set Error Capture [ ] command to turn error capture on and off at will during the course of a script (or script thread involving calls to sub-scripts).

If you determine that native error trapping will be adequate for some portion of a script you may want to turn on error trapping for only those passages that require custom error handling.

Whenever you enable error capture, you should add an error-check sequence after each command that you might reasonably expect to fail under some conditions. We recommend that you trap for less likely errors as well as highly probable ones.

Here is a practical example of a simple two-step script to which error trapping might be added:

```
Go to Layout ["Invoices" (Invoices)]
Perform Find [Specified Find Requests: Find Records;
   Criteria: Invoices::Status: "Open"]
```

The preceding script is designed to locate and display open invoices, if there are any. Of course, if there are no open invoices in the Invoices table at the time of script execution, the second line

## Scripting in Depth  13

produces an error and the user is left stranded. Below is a revised copy of the same script, including error handling:

```
Set Error Capture [On]
Go to Layout ["Invoices" (Invoices)]
If [Get(LastError) ≠ 0]
    Beep
    Show Custom Dialog [Title: "Find Open Invoices: Error Alert";
            Message: "The Invoice Layout required for this process could not
            be accessed.¶¶Please report this problem to the developer.";
            Buttons: "OK"]
    Exit Script [ ]
End If
Perform Find [Restore; Specified Find Requests: Find Records;
    Criteria: Invoices::Status: "Open"]
Set Variable [$LastError; Value:Get(LastError)]
If [$LastError ≠ 0]
    Beep
    Show Custom Dialog [Title: "Find Open Invoices: Error Alert";
      Message: Case(
            $LastError = 401; "There are no open invoices at present.";
            $LastError = 9; "Your privileges do not permit this action.";
            "An unexpected error occurred [ref#" & $LastError & "].¶¶Please
      report this problem to the developer."
            ); Buttons: "OK"]
    Go to Layout[original layout]
End If
```

The original two-step script is now expanded to 14 steps, with the inclusion of the Set Error Capture [ ] command and an If [ ]/End If sequence after each of the substantive steps.

> **NOTE** The example shown here illustrates two different approaches to error trapping. The first (which follows the Go to Layout [ ] command) is generic and responds without regard to the cause of the error, while the second approach stores the error code so as to be able to respond in a way that is specific to the nature of the error.

At first glance, the implementation of error handling may seem unduly onerous. Consider the following before you throw your arms up in despair:

- In practice, the work required can be greatly reduced by placing the repetitive error trapping code into a sub-script. (Examples are provided later in this chapter.)

- When the script is executed, if no errors are detected, the steps within the enclosing If/End If commands will be bypassed, so the revised script does not take significantly longer to run.

- Adding error handling is a significant enhancement that greatly improves the user experience. In many cases, the quality of the data and reliability of the solution also improves substantially.

459

# Scripts and Access Privileges

FileMaker scripts assume control of your solution for the duration of the tasks they perform, working with your solution's code and interface like a powerful (and extremely efficient) user. By default, therefore, your scripts inherit the current user's login account access privileges and constraints.

**CROSS-REF** For a detailed discussion of security configuration and user accounts and privileges, refer to Chapter 14.

You can take three approaches when dealing with access privileges within your scripts. You can:

- Design your scripts to work within the limits of the current user's account privileges, working on the basis that if, for example, the user does not have record creation privileges, then scripts running while the user is logged in should be similarly limited.

- Designate your scripts as super-users, granting them access to everything in the file regardless of the privileges of the current user.

- Configure your scripts to re-login under an account of their own, changing the applicable access restrictions one or more times during the course of execution (perhaps requiring the user to re-authenticate at their conclusion).

Needless to say, you may mix and match — take one approach for some scripts and another for others. Whichever approach you take, however, must be reflected in the way your script tests for and handles privilege-related error conditions.

When you take the first approach indicated, your scripts will encounter different permissions depending on the current user's login account. Moreover, user access privileges may change over the solution's life, so you should assume that access restrictions may arise subsequently, even if they are not a consideration when your script is first created.

To take the second listed approach, you should enable the checkbox option at the lower edge of the Script Editor window labeled Run Script with Full Access Privileges, as shown in Figure 13.4.

When your script is set to run with full privileges, access restrictions of the privilege set assigned to the current user's account are overridden for the duration of the script.

**CAUTION** If a script set to run with full access privileges script calls other scripts via the Perform Script[ ] command, the called scripts do not inherit the full privileges setting (unless they are also set to run with full access privileges, they are constrained by the privilege set assigned to the current user's account).

If you decide to have your script log in with a different account to perform certain operations, be aware that the user's login session will be terminated. If you intend that users continue to use the database by using their own login accounts after the script completes its task, you need to request (or otherwise supply) the user's password to re-login with the user's account.

## Scripting in Depth  13

### FIGURE 13.4

Select the full access privileges option for a specific script by using the checkbox at the bottom center of the Script Editor window.

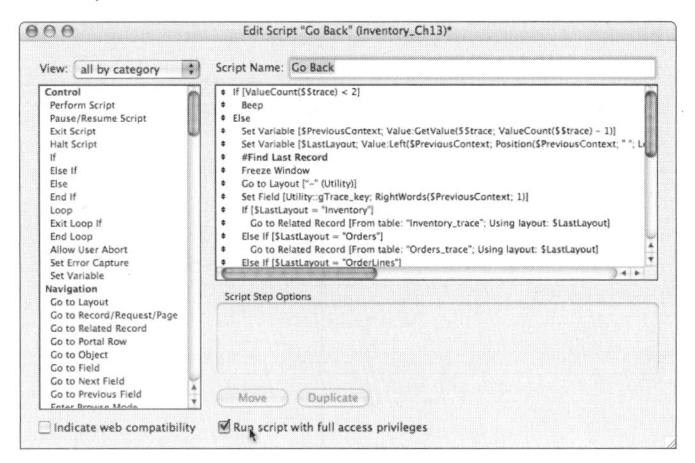

### Privilege-based errors

When a script action fails due to privilege restrictions, the error code returned is not necessarily directly related to privileges. For example, if the Contacts::FirstName field is configured as "no access" for the Privilege Set assigned to the current user's login account, the following script command will return `error 102, Field is missing`:

```
Go to Field [Contacts::FirstName ]
```

FileMaker returns this same error code if the field targeted by the `Go to Field[ ]` script command is not present on the current layout. In this, and other examples like it, the error returned may arise from a number of causes, of which privilege restrictions are only one.

In light of this, we recommend that you trap for a variety of errors in addition to the Insufficient privileges error, when dealing with processes subject to access restrictions.

### Run script with full access privileges

As indicated in Figure 13.4, individual scripts can be set to run with full access privileges. When this option is enabled, your script behaves in all respects as though the current user is logged in with an account assigned to the file's default `[Full Access]` privilege set. As part of this, the `Get(PrivilegeSetName)` function will return `"[Full Access]"` if evaluated while the script is active — however, the `Get(AccountName)` function will continue to return the name of the current user's account.

Be aware that the Run with Full Access Privileges option affects access only within the file where the script is defined. If your users are accessing data, scripts, or other elements stored in other

461

files (either FileMaker files or external SQL data sources), privilege restrictions in those files remain unchanged. When working with data or other content distributed between multiple files, the options for overriding privilege restrictions within your scripts are consequently limited.

> **TIP** If your script needs to act on an external FileMaker file's content and may encounter privilege restrictions in the source file, one possible solution is creating a script within the external file to perform the required operations, set that external script to run with full access privileges, and use the `Perform Script[ ]` command in your original script to call the external script.

## Determining the substantive privileges

If you have created a script to perform actions outside the privilege restrictions of the current user (and have enabled the Run Script with Full Access Privileges option for the script), you may want to set the script up to function differently according to the user's assigned privileges. To achieve this, your script will require access to the name of the current (substantive) user's privilege set; however, as noted earlier, the `Get(PrivilegeSetName)` function does not return the substantive privilege set during the execution of such a script. Here are two alternative options allowing your script to nevertheless ascertain the current user's assigned privilege set:

- Ensure the script is always called via a method that supports script parameters (for example, a button or a custom menu command) and specify the script parameter using the `Get(PrivilegeSetName)` function.

  Because the parameter expression is evaluated prior to the script's commencement, it is not affected by the Run Script with Full Access Privileges setting, and your script can retrieve the name of the substantive privilege set by using the `Get(ScriptParameter)` function.

- Create a single step script (without the Run Script with Full Access Privileges option enabled) containing the command:

  `Exit Script [Result: Get(PrivilegeSetName)]`

  Then call the script from within your original script, afterwards retrieving the name of the user's substantive privilege set by using the `Get(ScriptResult)` function. Note that the same one-step script can serve this purpose for all the scripts in a solution file set to run with full access privileges.

> **CROSS-REF** For additional details about defining custom menus using FileMaker Pro 9 Advanced, see Chapter 18.

## Automating the Automation

Every solution has processes that can benefit from automation — so the question is not whether to make use of ScriptMaker's ample capabilities, but which tasks to automate first and how to design the automation so that it requires as little user input or intervention as possible.

## Scripting in Depth

Most scripts — even the most self-contained and robust — require user initiative to launch them. In Chapter 8, we detail seven methods of calling scripts, most of which depend on an explicit action from the user (a button click or a menu selection). However, several script triggering methods offer less direct ways to set scripted procedures in motion.

We encourage you to consider all options for setting your scripts in motion at the appropriate times — both in the interests of saving work for your users and also to improve the reliability and integrity of the processes your scripts encapsulate. The most elegantly conceived script is only useful if it is used!

## Defining a script to run on file open

Foremost among the *indirect* methods of launching a script are the "when opening" and "when closing" perform script options accessible in the Open/Close tab panel of the File Options dialog (File ➪ File Options), as shown in Figure 13.5.

When you specify a script to run on file open, it is automatically triggered every time the file is opened, the first time a window from the file is displayed. When a file is opened in a hidden state — such as when FileMaker opens it via a relationship or script call — the start-up script is not invoked. However, if the file is selected for display, the start-up script will then be activated.

Specifying a script to run when opening your solution files is as simple as selecting a checkbox and choosing the script from a list of scripts defined in your file. However, determining what to include in your opening script is a challenge of a different order.

**FIGURE 13.5**

Setting the options to perform a script when opening or closing a file, via the File Options dialog.

463

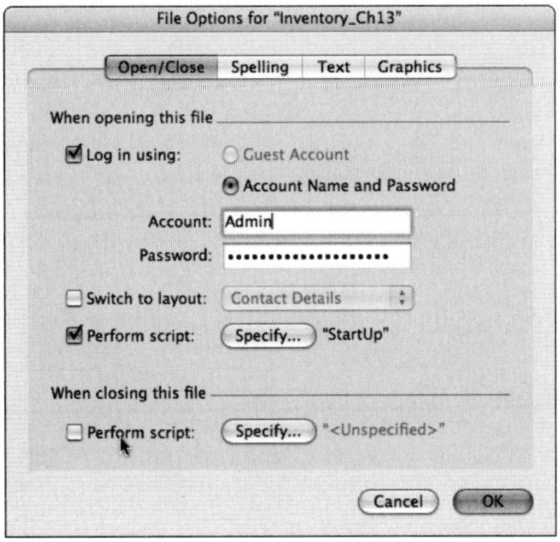

## Housekeeping practices for start-up scripts

The processes you include in your start-up scripts vary according to the needs of your solution, but a range of operations common to many solutions' start-up scripts are worth considering.

You should also keep in mind that a start-up script is considerably more useful if you can be confident it has launched and completed its run on every occasion your solution is accessed. One part of ensuring this is to include the command:

```
Allow User Abort [Off]
```

Placing this command at or near the commencement of the script reduces the likelihood that the user will (intentionally or inadvertently) interrupt your script before it executes fully (for example, by pressing the Escape key).

**CAUTION** Don't assume that the Allow User Abort option is an absolute guarantee of uninterrupted passage for your start-up script — or any other script, for that matter. A knowledgeable user can contrive a number of ways to halt a running script. However, it is a reasonable first-line safeguard.

**CROSS-REF** For a further discussion of start-up scripts and security considerations, refer to Chapter 14.

Consider including the following when configuring your start-up scripts:

- **Application verification:** When your solution has been developed to take advantage of the features of a recent version of FileMaker, it may be prudent to have your start-up script confirm that it is being opened with the required version (or later).

- **Security and login procedures:** Unless your solution is configured to prompt the user for credentials prior to opening, your start-up script is an opportunity to present a scripted login procedure.

- **Window placement and management:** Positioning and sizing of the window (or windows) required for your solution's optimal use should not be the first task for your solution's users.

- **Setting user preferences:** When you've configured your solution to store a range of settings, preferences, state variables, or other user-specific or computer-specific usage information, the start-up script is a convenient place to restore the appropriate configuration for the current user or workstation. The configurations sequence in your start-up scripts may also include loading custom menu sets and ensuring your solution and/or its interface options conform to the current computer's language and regional settings.

- **Usage logging:** For diagnostic and planning purposes, have your solution maintain a record of the history of its use, including opening and closure on different computers. This, too, may be a job for the start-up script.

- **Initialization of third-party plug-ins:** If your solution's functionality depends on plug-ins, start-up is a good time to verify the availability of compatible versions of plug-ins and to pass any registration or enabling codes to them for the current session.

- **Refreshing any external resources required by your solution:** For example, if you have configured Web viewers to display Flash files, images, and so on, the start-up script provides an opportunity to install or update the required resources on the current workstation.

- **Uploading or updating online content:** When your solution depends on current information from remote servers or Web sites, the start-up script can check the current online information, downloading fresh data when necessary.

- **Restoring global values and declaring variables:** The start-up script is a good place to establish the default state of any values and variables on which your solution depends. Moreover, the practice of establishing solution-wide reference values in the start-up script is a good discipline (and a point of reference for the existence and operational state of any/all such values required by your solution).

- **Providing the user with solution version confirmation, basic usage statistics (last used, last back-up, file size, number of records, and so on), and/or support resources and contact information:** A splash layout displayed for the duration of the starting script may be a good way to achieve this.

There are a variety of other tasks you might also consider assigning to a start-up script in your solutions. The previous list includes only some of the more common usages. However, as you can see, there is no shortage of work in store for you as you prepare your solution for an encounter with its users.

## Scripts that run on file close

Just as a start-up script can perform a wide variety of useful operations, a script set to run on file closure can take care of numerous important checks, updates, and other housekeeping. Because the user can choose to terminate the application (or file) session at any time, a first concern to be addressed by the closing script is whether the data is in a valid state (for example, your closing script might prompt the user to provide data to finalize a partially complete record, or to either correct an invalid entry or discard the record containing it).

Like the start-up script, your closing script should restore the solution to its default state by:

- Capturing and storing any preference or state data for the current user (for example, so the user's session can be restored on next login)
- Updating any solution logs to indicate closure of the client session
- Ensuring any ancillary or supporting files are gracefully closed
- Presenting the user with any relevant statistics or exit system messages or data

You should also consider that in the event of a system or hardware failure (power outage or force-quit, for example) it is possible your closing script will not run or will not execute completely. An additional subroutine in the start-up script that verifies that the previous session was terminated appropriately and, if not, undertakes whatever checks and other remedial steps are appropriate (updating logs, for example) may be necessary.

# Harnessing the Power of Parameters, Results, and Variables

In Chapter 8, we mention that a script parameter can be passed to a script and referenced within the script as a way of controlling the script's behavior; however the concept is not pursued in depth in the examples we provide. In the example cited earlier in this chapter, we suggest you use a single line script to declare the name of the substantive privilege set as a script result, for retrieval by a *parent* script, where the Run Script with Full Access Privileges option is enabled. There are, however, many other benefits to the ability to pass data directly to and retrieve data from your scripts.

## Getting data into a script

FileMaker provides you the option to specify a script parameter—data to be passed as input to the script—either literal text or the result of a calculation expression evaluated as the script is queued when a script is triggered by the following methods:

- Using the Perform Script [ ] button command
- Being called as a sub-script from the current script
- Selecting an item in a Custom menu
- Using an external function (using FileMaker's plug-in API with an appropriate third-party plug-in installed)

For example, when configuring the Perform Script [ ] button command, the Specify Script Options dialog, as shown in Figure 13.6, includes a field for an optional script parameter below the list of available scripts.

In the example shown in Figure 13.6, the script parameter has been specified as literal text (enclosed in quotes); however, the Edit button to the right of the parameter field provides access to the Specify Calculation dialog in which you can define a calculation to determine the content of the parameter based on the state of your solution at runtime (for example, when the button is clicked).

**NOTE** An expression determining the parameter to be passed to a script is evaluated before the script commences—which determines the state of local variables in play, the scope of any local variables declared in the expression itself, the status of privileges with respect to the "Run with full access privileges" setting, and the value returned by the Get (ScriptName) function. In all these respects, the context of evaluation of the script parameter expression reflects the state of play immediately before commencement of the script.

### FIGURE 13.6
Specifying a script parameter when defining a button on the Specify Script Options dialog.

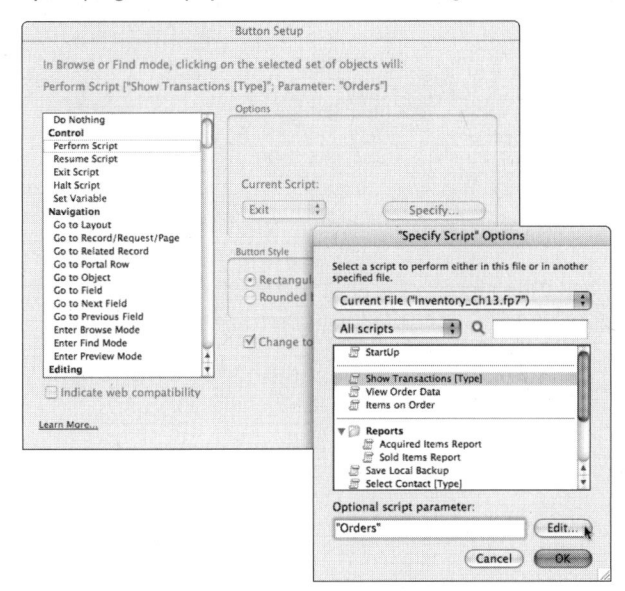

## Branching according to state

Your solution's state when a script is triggered is largely beyond your control. By restricting the means of triggering your script to a specific layout button (or to a set of custom menus assigned to particular layouts) you can constrain users' options a little — for example, you can be confident that they are on an appropriate layout when launching the script. However, you cannot predict what mode the user will be in, what record (or request) will be active, what the found set will be, what other windows will be open, or what processes are running.

By capturing data about your solution's state either at the commencement of the script or by passing the data as a script parameter (evaluated immediately prior to the script's commencement), you can ensure your script has crucial information about the environment it is to act upon. Additionally, you have the option to call the same script from different buttons, passing a different parameter from each to determine alternate script behavior. For example, you may choose to use the same script for two buttons, requiring different behavior for Browse and Find modes, thereby producing four alternate script sequences.

One way to implement a branching of process and functionality within your script is to create a control structure for your script by using FileMaker script control commands (those grouped in the Control category of commands in the Edit Script window). For example:

```
If [Get(WindowMode) = 0]
  #Solution is in Browse mode
  If [Get(ScriptParameter) = "Button 1"]
    >>> {insert script sequence 1 here}
  Else If [Get(ScriptParameter) = "Button 2"]
    >>> {insert script sequence 2 here}
  End If
Else If [Get(WindowMode) = 1]
  #Solution is in Find mode
  If [Get(ScriptParameter) = "Button 1"]
    >>> {insert script sequence 3 here}
  Else If [Get(ScriptParameter) = "Button 2"]
    >>> {insert script sequence 4 here}
  End If
End If
```

A simple control framework such as the one shown in this example lets you apply process differentiation to part or all of your script, contingent on mode and the trigger button selected. However, although simple to design and implement, such a structure may lead to redundancy or repetition in your scripting model.

**CROSS-REF** For alternative approaches to branching and alternate script functionality according to state or context, refer to the discussion of dynamic and indirect controls later in this chapter.

By first mapping out an appropriate control structure for your scripts, you can accommodate varying (though related) functional requirements within a single script, enabling one script to serve for diverse situations and contexts.

Two concerns you must address when structuring scripts for dynamic execution are the frequent need to pass more than a single datum to the script as parameter and the desirability of establishing a consistent framework of context indicators for the duration of the script. For example, the simple control framework described earlier directly tests for window mode during its execution. However, in a more complex script where branching may occur at intervals throughout its execution, mode may change during the course of the script. Thus, it's necessary to capture and store context at the commencement of the script to provide a consistent point of reference throughout.

## Declaring variables

We recommend that you declare relevant information in local ($var) variables during the commencing steps of your script so that you can capture context at the start of a script (or at key points throughout its execution) and maintain the data for reference during the script. For example, the control framework discussed in the previous section can be restructured as follows:

```
#Declare state variables:
Set Variable [$Mode; Value:Choose(Get(WindowMode); "Browse"; "Find")]
Set Variable [$Button; Value:GetAsNumber(Get(ScriptParameter))]
#Process control:
If [$Mode = "Browse"]
  If [$Button = 1]
    >>> {insert script sequence 1 here}
  Else If [$Button = 2]
    >>> {insert script sequence 2 here}
  End If
Else If [$Mode = "Find"]
  If [$Button = 1]
    >>> {insert script sequence 3 here}
  Else If [$Button = 2]
    >>> {insert script sequence 4 here}
  End If
End If
```

In this rudimentary example, with only two state variables in play and a basic branching structure, you can notice an improvement in readability, because intelligible variable names replace function calls and potentially convoluted expressions throughout the script's body. The work of retrieving parameter and environment data is performed once at the script's commencement, and the variables are then available throughout the course of the script. Overall, structuring your scripts in this way offers the following potential improvements:

- **Efficiency:** Functions and calculations determining state need be evaluated only once and thereafter variables are available to be referenced. Variables are held in memory; referencing uses minimal resources.

- **Reliability:** Given values are determined once and remain in memory throughout, so if a script action changes the state of your solution, the execution of the script's logic is not impacted.

- **Readability:** Variable names and values can be chosen to aid clarity and transparency of the ensuing logic throughout the main body of the script.

- **Maintainability:** An adjustment to the calculation used to retrieve and declare a mode variable requires a change in only one place (otherwise the change would be required to be repeated throughout logical expressions distributed through the script).

Although a series of `Set Variable[ ]` commands at the top of your script is moderately compact, yet accessible and readable, an alternative approach is to use a single command containing a `Let( )` calculation declaring multiple variables within its syntax. Some developers prefer this approach because it increases compactness of the code, tucking the variable definitions out of the way until needed. We regard this as largely a matter of style or personal preference, and we acknowledge that the desirability of having all the variables laid out may vary according to the solution's nature and complexity. If you prefer to use the hidden-until-needed approach, the first three lines of the example cited previously would become:

```
Set Variable [$All State Variables; Value:Let([
    $Mode = Choose(Get(WindowMode); "Browse"; "Find")
    $Button = Value:GetAsNumber(Get(ScriptParameter))]; "")]
```

Because the bulk of the code in this construction is contained within the parameter of a single `Set Variable[ ]` command, only one line of the script is used, and it stays out of sight until you select and open the step for viewing.

Either of the methods outlined in this section provides the means to pass data efficiently into appropriately named local variables to serve the needs of your script. The usefulness of these techniques remains limited, however, until you find a way to pass more than a single parameter value to your scripts.

## Passing and retrieving multiple parameters

Although FileMaker accommodates a single text parameter when calling a script, you need not regard this as a limitation. You can contrive to pass multiple parameter values several ways.

One of the most straightforward techniques for passing multiple parameter values is to place each value on a separate line in a predetermined order, and then write your script to retrieve each line of the parameter separately — such as by using the `GetValue( )` function to selectively appropriate the individual values from the composite string passed as the original parameter. For example, when you have a script designed to write a new value into a given field for a specific contact record, you require the ability to pass three values to the script: ContactID, FieldName, and NewValue.

When a script you define requires parameters, we recommend that you append their names to the name you give the script (preferably listed at the end in square brackets), thus:

Update Contact Record [ContactID, FieldName, NewValue]

Having determined the order that you will pass the parameter values, you can then specify the script parameter using an expression such as:

```
Contacts::ContactID & "¶AddressLine1¶" & Utility::gUpdateValue
```

This expression passes to the script a carriage-return separated list of values such as:

CT00004
AddressLine1
17 Coventry Road

## Scripting in Depth — 13

Within the opening lines of your script, you can then efficiently retrieve the separate elements of the parameter, declaring them as separate named variables, with the following commencing steps:

```
Set Variable [$ContactID; Value:GetValue(Get(ScriptParameter); 1)]
Set Variable [$FieldName ; Value:GetValue(Get(ScriptParameter); 2)]
Set Variable [$NewValue; Value:GetValue(Get(ScriptParameter); 3)]
```

This procedure is easy to implement for small numbers of values and, providing the values will not contain carriage returns, gives satisfactory results. However, such a procedure is vulnerable to error if you are not careful about the order you provide the variables. The risk of error and intelligibility of the parameter and code rapidly diminish if you have more than two or three values to pass to your script.

To address these shortcomings — and especially to serve more demanding requirements — we recommend an approach where each component value is passed together with its name. The resulting array format is what is commonly termed name/value pairs. The most frequently encountered format for name/value pairs is the FileMaker internal display of command parameters (in the script definition panel of the Edit Script window, for example). The value name is supplied, followed by a colon, and then the value followed by a semicolon. For example, the three parameters in our preceding example could be represented as name/value pairs as follows:

ContactID: "CT00004"; FieldName: "AddressLine1"; NewValue: "17 Coventry Road"

A set of parameter values passed in this format has several advantages. It is extensible; you can include additional values at will. Each value is clearly identifiable regardless of how many there are. The order of the values is immaterial, because each value will be located according to its name. The downside is that retrieving the values requires a more complex calculation. For example, to retrieve the individual values from the preceding parameter string, you could use a parsing expression (such as those introduced in Chapter 12), such as:

```
Let([
Vn = "FieldName";
Ln = Length(Vn);
Sp = Get(ScriptParameter);
p1 = Position(Sp; Vn & ": \""; 1; 1) + Ln + 2;
p2 = Position(Sp & "; "; "\"; "; p1; 1)];
Middle(Sp; p1; p2 - p1)
)
```

This expression returns `AddressLine1`, but if you change the value of the `Vn` calculation variable to `"ContactID"` it returns `CT00004`, and if you change `Vn` to `"NewValue"` it returns `17 Coventry Road`.

In this technique, you have the rudiments of an extensible system, but in the form described here the unwieldy calculation is a drawback. Either creating a sub-script to perform the task or defining a custom function (using FileMaker Pro 9 Advanced) to encapsulate the required code obviates needing to repeat an exacting expression to parse individual parameter values.

## Part III  Beyond the Basics

In fact, if you have access to FileMaker Pro 9 Advanced, we recommend taking this process a step further using the capabilities of custom functions. A self-contained custom function can be designed to parse an unlimited number of name/value pairs and declare them as local variables in a single call. With such a function in place, a parameter string, whether containing one or several dozen name/value pairs, can be declared as local variables in a single opening script command.

One custom function definition example with these capabilities follows:

```
//Custom Function Syntax:  DeclareVariables ( ParameterString )
Case(
  not IsEmpty( ParameterString );
  Let(
    [
      p1 = Position( ParameterString; ": "; 1; 1 ) + 2;
      q1 = Middle( ParameterString; p1; 1 );
      s1 = (q1 = "\"");
      t2 = Choose(s1; "; "; "\"; ");
      q2 = Left("\""; 1 - s1);
      p2 = Position(ParameterString & t2; t2; 1; 1);
      n1 = Left(ParameterString; p1 - 3);
      c1 = Middle(ParameterString; p1; p2 - p1 + s1);
      v1 = Evaluate("Let( $ " & n1 & " = " & q2 & c1 & q2 & "; \"\")" );
      r1 = Right(ParameterString; Length( ParameterString ) - p2 - 1 - s1)
    ];
    DeclareVariables( Trim( r1 ) )
  )
)
```

**NOTE** Custom functions must be defined in your file using FileMaker Pro Advanced but once installed can be used and deployed in FileMaker Pro.

**CROSS-REF** For more information about the creation and use of custom functions, see Chapter 18.

The preceding custom function is structured so that the enclosing quotation marks on the values in your name/value pairs are optional, being required only when semicolons are present in a particular value. With this custom function in place, a script parameter such as the following, including eight name/value pairs

> date: 8/12/2005; address: 33 Drury Lane; city: Gemmaville; state: Louisiana; amount: $343.00; process: recursive; title: FileMaker Pro 9 Bible; url: http://www.wiley.com/

can be converted to eight separate local variables (with names corresponding to those supplied in the parameter string) by using the following single line of script code:

```
Set Variable [$x; Value: DeclareVariables ( Get(ScriptParameter) )]
```

**NOTE** The Inventory example file for this chapter includes the `DeclareVariables( )` custom function and employs the function to declare name/value pairs in the supplied parameter for the Show Transactions [type; filter] script.

# Specifying and retrieving a script result

Script results are specific to the situation where you program one script to call another using the `Perform Script[ ]` command. In such situations, the calling script (sometimes called the parent script) may need to receive a confirmation or error message back from the sub-script, after the sub-script concludes and the parent resumes.

When one script calls another, a parameter can be passed to the sub-script. A script result can be viewed as the inverse functionality, allowing the sub-script to pass a value back to the calling script. Like a script parameter, the script result value is available only to the specific script to which the sub-script passes it. To declare a script result, the sub-script must conclude with the `Exit Script[ ]` command, with the result value declared as its parameter. For example, a sub-script that creates a record in a related table can be structured as follows:

```
#Create child record:
Set Variable [$layout; Value:GetValue(Get(ScriptParameter); 1)]
Set Variable [$parentID; Value:GetValue(Get(ScriptParameter); 2)]
Freeze Window
Go to Layout [$layout]
Set Variable [$ErrorLog; Value:Get(LastError)]
If [GetAsBoolean($ErrorLog)]
   Exit Script ["ResultLog: " & $ErrorLog]
End If
New Record/Request
Set Variable [$ErrorLog; Value:$ErrorLog & ¶ & Get(LastError)]
If [GetAsBoolean($ErrorLog)]
   Go to Layout [original layout]
   Exit Script ["ResultLog: " & $ErrorLog]
Else
   Set Variable [$NewID; GetField(Get(LayoutTableName) & "::ID")]
End If
Go to Object[Object Name: "ParentID"]
Set Variable [$ErrorLog; Value:$ErrorLog & ¶ & Get(LastError)]
If [not GetAsBoolean($ErrorLog)]
   Set Field [$parentID]
   Set Variable [$ResultLog; Value:$ErrorLog & ¶ & Get(LastError)]
End If
Go to Layout [original layout]
Exit Script ["ResultLog: " & $ErrorLog & "; NewID: " & $NewID]
```

This example sub-script has several important features. It does the following:

- Receives direction as to the layout of the child table and the ID of the intended parent record
- Traps (cumulatively) for errors throughout, storing them in a local variable
- Declares a script result at each point of exit, including a complete log of error values returned by the four error-sensitive commands in the sequence
- Returns (if successful) the ID of the newly created child record

## Part III  Beyond the Basics

The example provided here is structured so that (subject to layout, field, and object naming) it can be reused to create related records in any table in a solution, returning a result in name/value pair format to the calling script.

> **TIP**
> Whatever method you use for passing and parsing multiple parameters can also be used to declare and retrieve multiple values through the FileMaker script result mechanism.

With a utility script in place in your solution and assuming that your solution has implemented the `DeclareVariables ( )` custom function described under the previous sub-heading, a controlling script can create a child record for the current record using a sequence along the lines of:

```
#Create child record in Invoices table:
Perform Script ["Create child record"; Parameter: "Invoices¶" & Products:ID]
Set Variable [$x; Value: DeclareVariables ( Get(ScriptResult) )]
If[GetAsBoolean($ResultLog)]
   Beep
   Set Field [SystemLog::Errors; $ResultLog]
   Show Custom Dialog ["An error occurred - child record not created!"]
   Exit Script
End If
Set Field [Products::gNewInvoice; $NewID]
#New child record successfully created...
```

> **NOTE**
> The preceding code is a fragment of a larger script. For brevity and clarity, we have shown here only the segment of the parent script calling the sub-script and receiving/handling the result.

The foregoing process provides you with a framework for handling errors progressively throughout a multi-script sequence, enabling two-way communication between your scripts.

## Storing and accumulating data as you go

A significant feature in the `Create child record` sub-script's error-trapping process is the use of a local variable ($ErrorLog) to store a cumulative log of error codes returned by key steps in the process. Because variables are passed directly to and from memory, they are stored and retrieved with little or no overhead (delay or processor cycles). This method is far more efficient than writing to or referencing fields in your solution's database schema.

You can use variations of the logging technique exemplified in the previous example to perform a range of tasks requiring the accumulation of data. For example, if you need an on the spot summary to show you the proportion of radio airtime devoted to local talent in the current days' broadcast program, you could set up a script as follows:

```
#Local talent airtime:
Go to Layout ["Air Schedule" (Prog)]
Enter Find Mode [ ]
Set Field [Program::AiredDate; Get(CurrentDate)]
Perform Find [ ]
```

```
If [Get(LastError) = 0]
  Go to Record/Request/Page [First]
  Loop
    Set Variable [$all; Value:$all + Prog::Duration]
    Set Variable [$local; Value:$local + If(Prog::Local = 1; Prog::Duration)]
    Go to Record/Request/Page [Next; Exit after last]
  End Loop
  Show Custom Dialog ["Local talent: " & Round($local / $all * 100; 1) & "%"]
Else
  Beep
  Show Custom Dialog ["Sorry - nothing has been scheduled for today yet!"]
End If
Go to Layout [original layout]
```

This is another of many examples of scripted data accumulation using variables. Although this example is by no means the only way (nor necessarily the best way) to calculate quick summary data, it may be an ideal method in cases where:

- You don't want to (or can't afford to) clutter schema with additional fields (such as summary fields) for the purposes of performing such a check.
- The summary or calculation you require is not readily supported by the FileMaker built-in summary and aggregation operations.
- You need to spot-check a host of different things at different times (in which case your script can be repurposed—for example via script parameters—to perform a variety of calculations at will).
- The information to be extracted is solely as input to a subsequent script operation.

If one or more of these conditions applies, scripted data aggregation should be among the options you consider. There are many instances when the aggregation of information available during the course of a script is both opportune and practical—with variables providing the ideal mechanism for all such operations.

# Dynamic and Indirect Controls in ScriptMaker

You can configure many FileMaker scripting commands to explicitly target a specific layout, field, or object in your solution, and when you do, your scripts are clear, direct, and simple but not very flexible.

For example, when you create a script with the Go to Layout [ ] command and you assign a specific layout as the command's target, your script is easy to read and interpret, but it can only be used for operations to be performed on that one layout.

## Part III   Beyond the Basics

## Example – Go to Layout by name or number

In the case of the Go to Layout [ ] command—as with many other script and button commands—FileMaker provides options for the destination object (in this case, layout) to be determined by calculation. This has two profound implications:

- The target layout will be determined as the command is evaluated, based on the result of the calculation (and, therefore, on the inputs available at the time).

- The script or button can be configured to serve different purposes in different circumstances, making the code more flexible and dynamic and allowing it to be repurposed.

As shown in Figure 13.7, the Go to Layout [ ] command offers two By Calculation options. It can be configured to select a target layout by either its name or its number. When choosing either option, make sure that the calculation expression you supply will return a valid result in all cases.

**NOTE** In the context of the Go to Layout [ ] command, "by number" means according to the numeric position of the layout in the layout order of the file (including any layouts used as separators or not set to appear in the layouts menu).

**FIGURE 13.7**

Configuring the Go to Layout command to determine the target layout at runtime using a calculation.

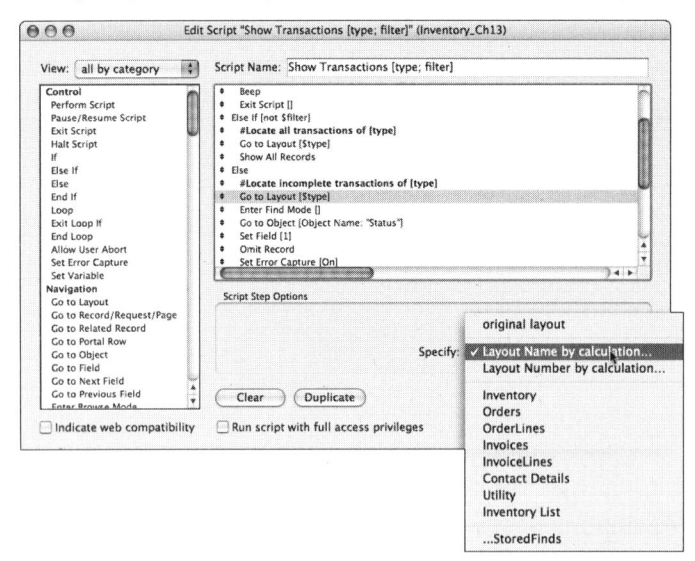

**CAUTION** If you choose to target a layout by name and the layout names are subsequently edited, or to target a layout by number and the layouts are subsequently reordered, the command may either fail or select the incorrect layout.

## Scripting in Depth 13

If you are concerned about the possibility of changes in the future impacting the accuracy or applicability of calculated results used to control commands dynamically, it is possible to devise a more robust method by using FileMaker design functions to determine an object's name or number from its internal ID.

**CROSS-REF** A method for calculating a layout's internal ID from its name (and vice versa) to enable you to increase the robustness of references to objects in your code is provided in Chapter 12.

## Dynamic file paths using variables

In most cases, the option to determine a target object by calculation appears in the FileMaker script and button command interface — at least when you know where to look, as in the case illustrated in Figure 13.7. However, one of the less obvious examples is the ability to provide the filename and/or file path for import and export of files (including the creation of PDF and Excel files using the `Save Records as PDF[ ]` and `Save Records as Excel[ ]` commands).

FileMaker accepts a variable as the specification (path and filename) of a file in the Specify File dialog you use to set the target file for all import and output file operations. Figure 13.8 shows a variable named $ReportPath being entered into the Specify Output File dialog in this chapter's Inventory example file's Acquired Items Report script (in the `Save Records as PDF[ ]` command).

**FIGURE 13.8**

Supplying a predefined variable to provide the path and filename to create a file on the current workstation.

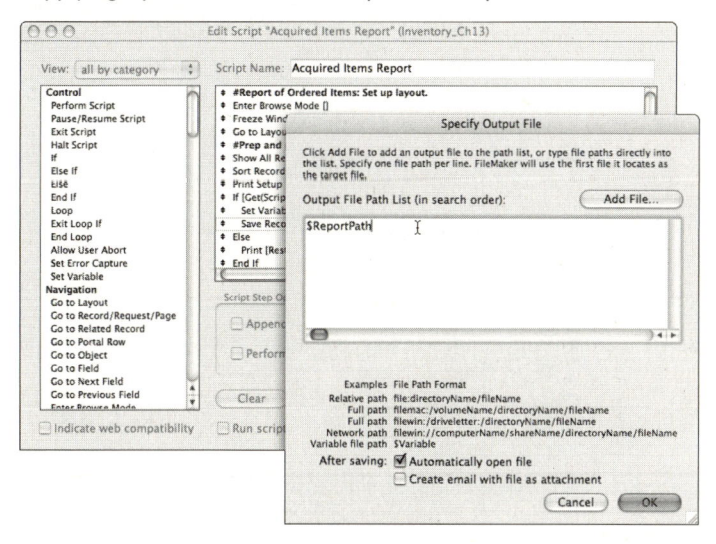

477

## Part III  Beyond the Basics

For a file operation to complete successfully when the file has been specified using a variable, the variable must have a value resolving to a valid file path and filename for the current computer when the command is executed. Therefore, a preceding step in your script must declare the variable, giving it a value in the appropriate format (the accepted syntax for paths and files of various types is indicated in the lower portion of the Specify File dialogs for each operation).

To assist in the creation of appropriate paths for the configuration of the current computer, you have recourse to a number of useful functions including:

```
Get(DesktopPath)
Get(DocumentsPath)
Get(FilemakerPath)
Get(FilePath)
Get(PreferencesPath)
Get(TemporaryPath)
```

Moreover, the `Get(SystemPlatform)` function will enable you to ensure your calculation expression returns a path and filename in keeping with the requirements of the current computer's operating system.

### Dynamically building Find criteria

Although many script and button commands provide for indirect or dynamic targeting, several are lacking in this capability. For example, although you can configure the `Perform Find[ ]` command to apply specific search criteria, there is no provision for the criteria themselves to be determined by calculation. There is, nevertheless, a reasonably straightforward way to achieve dynamic search capability.

If you followed Chapter 8 closely, you already encountered a simple example of a dynamically scripted Find procedure in the `Show Transactions [Type]` script section. The script is designed to find incomplete records in either of two tables and therefore places criteria into a different field in each case (though the criteria placed into the field is always "1"). The technique for scripting a dynamic Find is, essentially, to build the find step-by-step using a series of discrete script steps, rather than using the "Restore" option to pre-populate Find criteria within the `Perform Find[ ]` step.

**NOTE** Because performing a dynamic Find requires multiple commands in sequence, it cannot be performed directly by a single button command — it requires a script (however, your button can call the script to achieve the desired effect).

The essence of a dynamic Find is a script sequence in which you enter Find mode, specify criteria, and then perform the Find — thus, at a minimum, three lines of script code are required. For example, when you need a script to locate all agenda submissions entered within the past 28 days, you can set it up as follows:

```
Enter Find Mode [ ]
Set Field [Submissions::Date; "≥" & (Get(CurrentDate) - 28)]
Perform Find [ ]
```

## Scripting in Depth

In this case, a single Find request is used (FileMaker creates a request automatically when entering Find mode), with a single criterion entered into the `Submissions::Date` field; however, the criterion is calculated with respect to the current day's date, as a calculation using the `Set Field[ ]` command.

By extension, the same technique can be used to build more complex Finds. For example, when scripting a Find similar to the one described, to locate all `"topic"` submissions since the start of the current month but excluding those marked as `"deferred"`, you can build a two-request dynamic Find script as follows:

```
Enter Find Mode [ ]
Set Variable [$now; Value:Get(CurrentDate)]
Set Field [Submissions::Date; "≥" & Date(Month($now); 1; Year($now))]
Set Field [Submissions::Type; "Topic"]
New Record/Request
Set Field [Submissions::Status; "Deferred"]
Omit Record
Perform Find [ ]
```

**NOTE** When used in Find mode, the `Omit Record` command toggles the state of the Omit checkbox option appearing in Find Mode's Status Area.

In this more complex example, two Find requests are created — the first with compound criteria in the Date and Type fields and the second configured to omit records matching a criterion in the Status field. Since the parameter of the `Enter Find Mode[ ]` command is empty, the sequence is executed without pausing and as the parameter of the `Perform Find [ ]` command is empty, the extant criteria, such as that created by the preceding steps, are used for the Find.

**CAUTION** For the sake of clarity and compactness, we have omitted additional error trapping commands from the foregoing script code. This may be acceptable where a script concludes with the `Perform Find[ ]` command, but in most cases, as discussed earlier in the chapter, error trapping steps would be appropriate in addition to those shown here.

## Editing field data on the fly (indirection)

A further area of frequently desired (and often required) dynamic functionality is the ability to determine at runtime the field to be set (got example by the `Set Field[ ]` command) or selected, for example, by the `Go to Field[ ]` command). In either case, the functionality is only indirectly achievable in FileMaker Pro 9.

One of the more elegant methods for having your script target a field without predetermining which field (determining which field via runtime calculation) is employing the `Go to Object[ ]` command to select a named field on the current layout. This technique requires that:

- An instance of each of the fields to be targeted be present on the current layout when the `Go to Object[ ]` command executes.
- Each field to be targeted is assigned an object name on the current layout.
- Your calculation for the `Go to Object[ ]` command returns the appropriate field's object name, rather than its logical (schema) name.

## Part III  Beyond the Basics

Thus, to reliably replicate the behavior of the `Go to Field[ ]` command with or without its Select/Perform parameter enabled, but with the target field being determined by calculation, you require (in addition to the earlier conditions set out) two lines of script code, as follows:

```
Go to Object [If(Submissions::Status = "Pending"; "Reason"; "Action")]
Select All
```

to choose the field and select its contents, or

```
Go to Object [If(Submissions::Status = "Pending"; "Reason"; "Action")]
Set Selection [Start Position: Length(Get(ActiveFieldContents)) + 1]
```

to place the cursor at the end of the selected field's current content.

**CAUTION** These field selection methods are applicable to field types other than containers. The Select All command does not prompt the commencement of multimedia program content in a container field.

In cases where you need to dynamically target a field for the purposes of having your script update its value, the `Go to Object[ ]` command can also be pressed into service for the first part of the task. Rather than using a subsequent selection command, however, you can use a `Set Field[ ]` command with no target field specified (when the cursor is in a field and a `Set Field[ ]` command with no target is executed, the result of the `Set Field[ ]` calculation replaces the contents of the current field).

Thus, to set a field without specifying which field in advance, you can use a two-step sequence such as:

```
Go to Object [If(Submissions::Status = "Pending"; "Reason"; "Action")]
Set Field ["Prep for next meeting"]
```

A similar approach can be applied to achieve the effect of indirection using other editing and inserting commands, such as `Cut`, `Copy`, `Paste`, `Clear`, `Insert`, and so on.

## Using Nonlinear Logic

Although the basic structure of the FileMaker scripting processes is linear, several of the control options let you construct script sequences that execute in a nonlinear way. These can result in repeated sequences, alternate or parallel logical paths, and a variety of conditional code options.

Throughout the execution of all script processes, however convoluted, FileMaker nevertheless remains single-threaded — only one command is executed at any point in time, and the process remains sequential in nature (each command completes its task before the next begins).

## Nested and sequential If/Else conditions

A mainstay of scripting control is provided by the logical controls `If[ ]`, `Else If[ ]`, `Else` and `End If` sequence of commands. You can use them to introduce dynamic elements to your code to satisfy a wide range of requirements. They're not as compact or dynamic as the indirection methods discussed under the previous heading, but they're nonetheless invaluable for their breadth of application and their explicit control of any sequence of steps in your scripts.

In some cases, a sequence of `If[ ]` and `Else If[ ]` conditions can be used where indirection capabilities are not provided by FileMaker. For example, to call a different sub-script according to which TO the current layout is based on you might define the following sequence:

```
If [Get(LayoutTableName) = "Contacts"]
   Perform Script ["Add Contact Address Record"; Parameter: Contacts::ContactID]
Else If [Get(LayoutTableName) = "Invoices"]
   Perform Script ["Create InvoiceLines Record"; Parameter: Invoices::InvoiceID]
Else If [Get(LayoutTableName) = "Orders"]
   Perform Script ["Create InvoiceLines Record"; Parameter: Invoices::InvoiceID]
Else If [Get(LayoutTableName) = "Invoices"]
   Perform Script ["Create InvoiceLines Record"; Parameter: Invoices::InvoiceID]
End If
```

Although this code is entirely explicit regarding what should happen and when, it is nonetheless extensible. And although we include provision for only four conditions, much longer conditional statements are possible.

When FileMaker evaluates a conditional sequence such as the one shown here, it works down from the top evaluating the `If[ ]` and `Else If[ ]` expressions until it finds one that returns true (a non-empty and non-zero value). It then performs the enclosed commands and jumps to the following `End If` command.

For logical purposes, therefore, the order of the conditions is significant. For example, if more than one condition could evaluate as true, the one coming first will gain focus and the subsequent one(s) will be bypassed. However, if the conditions you supply are mutually exclusive, it is preferable to order the conditions from the most probable (or frequently occurring) to the least probable, because doing so reduces the number of evaluations performed (and therefore execution time) for a majority of cases.

**CROSS-REF** For further discussion of techniques for optimizing your script and calculation code, see Chapter 19.

## Looping constructs

FileMaker includes control commands you can use to create recursive script sequences. Direct support for this functionality is provided in the form of the `Loop`, `Exit Loop If[ ]`, and `End Loop` group of script steps (refer to Chapter 8).

In Chapter 9, we present a method of saving and restoring Finds using a pair of loops; however, we do not discuss in detail the mechanism used to support this. The relevant steps from the first example script we do include (the script appears in the Inventory example as "...Perform/Store Find") are as follows:

```
Go to Record/Request/Page [First]
Go to Next Field
Set Variable [$FirstField; Value:Get(ActiveFieldName)]
Loop
  Loop
    If [not IsEmpty(Get(ActiveFieldContents))]
      Set Variable [$Criteria; Value:If(not IsEmpty($Criteria);
        $Criteria & ¶) & Get(RecordNumber) & "»" &
        Get(RequestOmitState) & "»" & Get(ActiveFieldName) &
        "»" & Get(ActiveFieldContents)]
    End If
    Go to Next Field
    Exit Loop If [Get(ActiveFieldName) = $FirstField]
  End Loop
  Go to Record/Request/Page [Next; Exit after last]
End Loop
```

As you can see from the two adjacent Loop steps, the construction of this sequence sets up a loop within a loop. The outer loop contains only two elements — the inner loop, plus the Go to Record/Request/Page[Next; Exit after last] command. Therefore, the outer loop serves to *walk* the current requests starting from the first and exiting after the last.

While the first (outer) loop is working its way through the current set of Find requests, the inner loop executes multiple times on each record, working its way through all the fields in the current layout and assembling details of the Find criteria (if any) in each field.

The number of times each loop executes depends on the circumstances when the script is executed. In the case under discussion, when there are three Find requests, the outer loop will execute three times — and when there are 12 fields on the current layout, the inner loop will execute 12 times on each pass of the outer loop for a total of 36 passes.

## Specifying exit conditions

Whether you use an incrementing or decrementing counter, as we describe in Chapter 8, or an exit condition such as those employed in the loops in the preceding example, the essentials of the technique are the same — the loop iterates though the enclosed steps until the exit condition is satisfied.

In some cases, the use of a loop with an enclosed pause (set for a specific time interval) can be used to confirm completion of a task before proceeding. For example, when your script issues the Set Web Viewer[ ] command to load a page from a remote site, you can use a loop and pause technique to wait until the page has completely loaded before proceeding. One way of doing this is

## Scripting in Depth    13

to check the `html` source of the loading Web viewer to confirm if the closing body tag has been received. For example:

```
Set Variable[$counter; Value: 0]
Loop
   Set Variable[$counter; Value: $counter + 1]
   Set Variable [$source; Value:GetLayoutObjectAttribute("Viewer"; "content"]
   Exit Loop If [PatternCount($source; "</body>") or $counter > 100]
   Pause/Resume Script [Duration (seconds): .1]
End Loop
If [not PatternCount($source; "</body>")]
   Show Custom Dialog ["Web Connection time-out"]
   Exit Script [ ]
End If
```

In this code example, note that we've included a counter in addition to the check for the presence of the closing body tag, so that in the event the network is unavailable, the script will not be indefinitely locked within its loop.

One occasion when your loop will not require an exit condition is when the loop's purpose is to force a pause (for example, holding the active window in frontmost position) until the user clicks a button. In this case, the button the user clicks may be defined to halt or exit the current script — as shown in Figure 13.9.

### FIGURE 13.9

Defining a button to halt or exit the current running script to terminate a paused looping sequence.

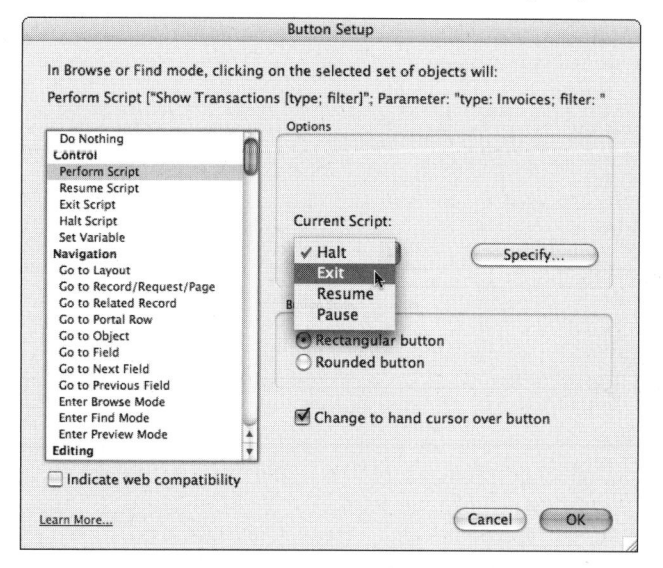

483

## Part III  Beyond the Basics

> **NOTE** The Current Script option is available only on buttons you attach to the `Perform Script [ ]` command, though you can separately define a button to halt or exit the current script (by attaching the separate `Halt Script` or `Exit Script` commands).

> **TIP** By default, when you define a button to execute the `Perform Script [ ]` command, the Current Script control is set to the Pause option; however, this is rarely the most appropriate choice, so it is a good practice to consider the circumstances where a button will be used and select accordingly.

In most cases, looping conditions aside, it's been our experience that the most appropriate Current Script setting for a `Perform Script [ ]` button is either Exit or Resume, with Pause or Halt rarely giving the most acceptable or desirable behavior.

# Modular Script Code

When your scripts are long and complex, you may want to consider breaking them up into self-contained smaller blocks of code that can be called in sequence to complete longer tasks. However, we counsel against doing this for its own sake. A lengthy scripted procedure does not necessarily become more manageable when its contents are split between several scripts and, in fact, the reverse can be true. Keeping track of a scripted sequence when it ducks and weaves between multiple scripts can be a considerable challenge.

So when should you divide a scripted process into multiple scripts? Here are some things to consider:

- Is a section of your script code repeated at intervals during the process (in which case a single sub-script might be called at each of those points)?
- Could part of the process of your script be shared with one or more other scripted processes in your solution? (Again, if there is common code, separating it into a self-contained module may have benefits.)
- Does part of your script require a different level of access than the rest (for example, should one part run with the Run Script with Fill Access Privileges option enabled, while the remainder does not)?
- Is it desirable or necessary that part of your scripted process reside in one file while another part resides in another of your solution's files?

Unless you answered a resounding "yes" to one or more of the preceding questions, you're unlikely to benefit from introducing component logic into your script. In fact, it's likely that the added complexity and overhead (more scripts to manage, more convolutions, and dependencies to keep in view) will outweigh any advantages.

## Using sub-scripts

When you design a script so that it can serve a particular kind of need in a number of contexts in your solution, ideally it becomes a self-contained parcel of code available to you whenever you need it when creating other scripts. Earlier we cited the example of a script designed to create child records from various locations in your solution.

**Scripting in Depth** 13

Another example would be a script designed to display a progress bar while other processes are under way. The code to manage either of these processes might best be located in one place for your whole solution—so that when you need to update it, you know exactly where to find it and a single change will be reflected throughout the solution (for example, wherever the sub-script is used).

A further area that is frequently a good candidate for separation into a sub-script is error trapping. Many steps in many scripts require similar checks and error-handling mechanisms. If you centralize all your error handlers into one script designed to receive the error code as a parameter, you can then provide error handling throughout all your other scripts by adding the following line of code:

```
Perform Script ["Error Handler"; Parameter: Get(LastError)]
```

You can add it after each script step where an error condition is possible. Such a script should, as its opening line, exit if the parameter is equal to zero (no error), so the parent script can continue.

An advantage of using a sub-script for error trapping is that it enables you to apply much more exhaustive interpretation and response to various error types (and logging of errors) than would be feasible if you are required to repeat the error-handling code in every script throughout your solution. When you have created an appropriate error-handling script, it becomes a simple matter to reuse it wherever there is potential for error.

## Script recursion

Intentionally or otherwise, the use of sub-scripts creates the possibility of circular logic and, therefore, infinite loops. This is one of many ways FileMaker gives you enough rope to hang yourself. Whenever you create a call from one script to another script, it is wise to confirm that the script you are calling does not itself call the current script. If it does—and you haven't added an intercept or exit condition—calling either script will bring your workstation to its knees.

While you should be mindful of the risks, the possibility of script recursion may be useful in some situations. Provided you enclose a script's call to itself (or its call to another script that, in turn, calls it) within an `If [ ]/End If` condition with an appropriate expression to terminate the cycle when the desired aim is achieved, such a code model is viable.

In general, we recommend the use of `Loop/End Loop` structures in situations where recursive functionality is required within your scripts. It is clear and readable, while providing support for a variety of code architectures. We've yet to encounter anything achievable with circular script calls that couldn't be done elegantly (and perhaps more manageably) with loops.

## Scripted Window Management

Among the 14 script commands appearing under the Windows group of commands in the list at the left of the Edit Script window, there are 7 commands you can use to control the appearance of the content display in the current window, and 7—highlighted in Figure 13.10—acting on the window itself.

485

**Part III**  Beyond the Basics

**FIGURE 13.10**

Seven of the available Windows script commands act on windows themselves rather than the current window's contents.

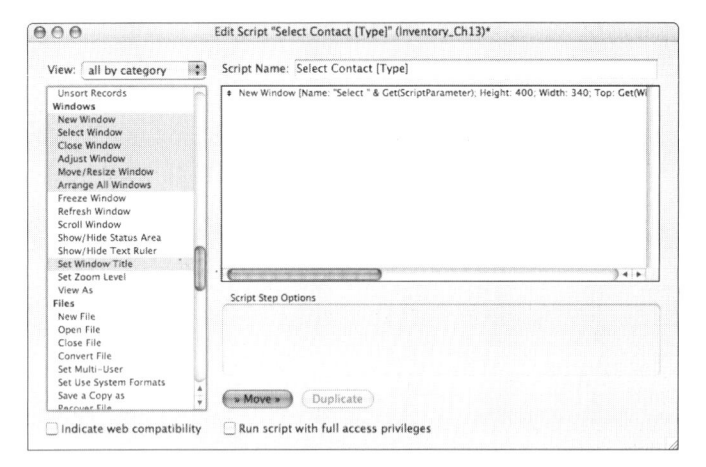

## Addressing windows by name (title)

We'd love to have been able to provide a less equivocal subheading here, but the fact is that the text appearing across the top of windows is referred to as the window name in some places in FileMaker Pro 9, while in others it's called the window title. But rest assured that they are both referring to the same thing—for example, when you execute the command Set Window Title ["xyz"] then subsequently evaluate the Get(WindowName) command, it returns "xyz".

Nowhere is this quirk more evident than in the "Set Window Title" Options dialog (shown in Figure 13.11) where the dialog itself is labeled "Title" but the fields within the dialog prompt you for "Window Name."

**FIGURE 13.11**

Filling in the Window Name fields in the "Set Window Title" Options dialog.

486

## Scripting in Depth

When you first open a solution file, FileMaker sets the window name to the file's name. When you create a new window using the `New Window[ ]` script or button command, FileMaker allows you the option of specifying the new window's name. If you don't provide a window name at this point, however, FileMaker uses a default naming convention where the new window is assigned a name based on the current window name (with a trailing hyphen and number appended — such as "Inventory – 2"). If you create a window manually by choosing Window ➪ New Window, FileMaker applies the same default naming procedure to determine the name (or should that be title?) of the new window.

Whatever it's called and however it got there, the label across the top of the window is useful for a variety of purposes:

- It gives you a way to let your users know which window is which and what each window is for.

- It lets you differentiate between windows in calculations throughout your solutions (for example, by using the `WindowNames( )` and `Get(WindowName)` functions to apply window-specific highlighting or other attributes in your solution).

- It provides scripts with a mechanism to control the behavior of one window from a script running elsewhere (even from a script in another file).

For all these reasons, we encourage you to supply unique and descriptive names to the windows in your solutions and keep window naming in mind when managing windows through your scripts. As part of this, you can issue custom (calculated) names to all new windows created by using the `New Window[ ]` command, as shown in Figure 13.12.

### FIGURE 13.12

Specifying a name by calculation when scripting the creation of a new window.

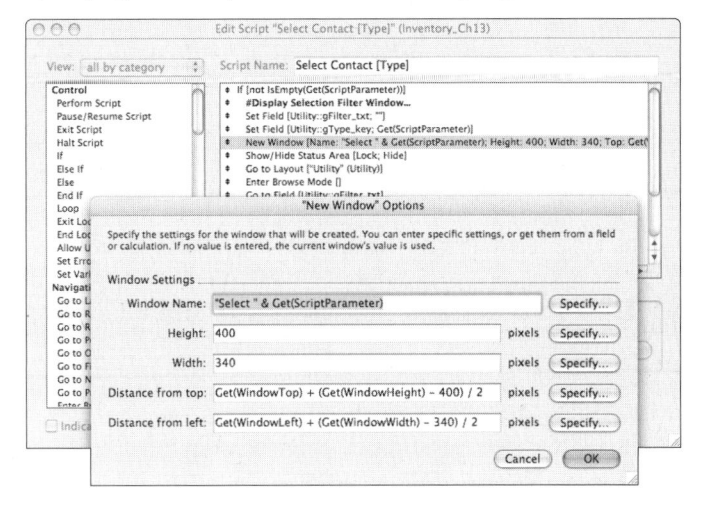

### Part III  Beyond the Basics

When you name a window, its name remains in place until it is closed unless your scripts or button commands explicitly change it. Thus, care in window naming provides you with a way to be explicit when subsequently selecting, moving, resizing, hiding, or closing a window.

## Moving and resizing windows

When you script the creation of a window, the New Window Options dialog, shown in Figure 13.12, provides the option to specify the size (height and width in pixels) and location coordinates (distance from top and left of the main monitor in pixels).

Whether or not you've chosen to make use of the options to set a window's initial dimensions and location when creating a new window by script, you can subsequently modify the window's position or proportions by using the Move/Resize Window[ ] command. Like the New Window Options dialog, the Move/Resize Window Options dialog accepts values for height and width in pixels, and for top and left in pixels from the upper-left corner of the main monitor.

### Determining window dimensions

Because the values for all four Move/Resize values can be determined by calculation, you can size and position the window with respect to other windows on the screen. For example, if you are setting your window to a width of 340 pixels and your monitor size is 1024 × 768 pixels, the unused horizontal space on either size of your window will be 768 _ 340 = 684 pixels. Thus to position a window with a width of 340 pixels in the center of a 1024 pixel monitor, the "Distance from left" coordinate should be supplied as 342 (half of 648).

In cases when your solution may be opened on a number of monitors of different sizes, you can set your window placement calculations to determine the correct placement of your window by using the appropriate Get() functions. For example, to center a 340-pixel window horizontally on a monitor of any size, you can specify the distance from left coordinate as:

    (Get(ScreenWidth) - 340) / 2

Similarly the vertical location (for a 400-pixel-high window) can be set to find the middle of the monitor according to its height with:

    (Get(ScreenHeight) - 400) / 2

**NOTE** When determining sizes and locations of windows on the Windows operating system, remember that they will be contained within the Application window frame. It is preferable to calculate your window coordinates with respect to the application window dimensions rather than the screen size. This can be achieved by using the Get(WindowDesktopHeight) and Get(WindowDesktopWidth) functions. On Mac OS, Get(WindowDesktopHeight) returns the main monitor height minus the height of the menu bar.

Alternatively, if you prefer to center a new (say, 400 × 340) window with respect to an existing window (for example, the foremost window), it is easiest to use the Get(WindowHeight) and Get(WindowWidth) functions to pass the current window's coordinates to the expressions

## Scripting in Depth

specifying the new window's location when creating the new window. As shown in Figure 13.12, this can be achieved with the following expressions:

```
Distance from top:  Get(WindowTop) + (Get(WindowHeight) - 400) / 2
Distance from left: Get(WindowLeft) + (Get(WindowWidth) - 340) / 2
```

### Creating windows off-screen

Extending the ability to control the placement and size of windows, you can create windows off-screen and therefore (potentially) invisible to the user. This is a documented feature of FileMaker Pro 9 and is useful for cases where you require a scripted procedure to undertake actions in another window so as to leave the user's environment undisturbed, while avoiding the visual discontinuity of a new window appearing and disappearing onscreen during the process.

**NOTE** FileMaker keeps track of found sets and relationship caching — along with other environment and state characteristics such as current layout, active record, commit state, and so on — separately for each window. Therefore, if your script changes some of these attributes (especially the found sets, which may be onerous to reinstate), creating a separate window to give your script its own separate contextual environment in which to operate (and closing the window upon script completion) is advantageous.

Using this technique, you might, for example, activate a message in the user's current window (or a floating window positioned above it) saying "processing — please wait..." perhaps accompanied by a progress indicator (especially if your script procedure may take more than a few seconds). Bear in mind that the visual effects of this technique vary between platforms, and window placement requires restored window states on the Windows operating system.

**CROSS-REF** For a detailed discussion of various approaches to the implementation of progress indicators, refer to Chapter 10.

After user feedback is in place, your script can create a window out of view and undertake its processing in a discreet contextual environment without impacting the user's selections and environment. From its point of focus in the off-screen window, your script can update a global variable value controlling the progress indicator onscreen, to provide up-to-date user feedback throughout the process.

**CAUTION** If the user's computer is equipped with multiple monitors, a window created a short distance off-screen may simply appear on a different monitor (this applies particularly to Mac OS where the visibility of windows is not constrained by the limits of an Application Window). We recommend using coordinates above 10,000 pixels to place your script's window well out of the user's visual range (values up to 32,766 in all directions are supported on all platforms — higher values are supported in some cases, but we don't recommend their use for reasons of cross-platform compatibility).

### Freezing and refreshing the screen

In some circumstances creating off-screen windows will not suit your requirements — for example, if your approach is maximizing your solution's windows on the Windows platform, creation of windows of specified dimensions and placement causes FileMaker to revert to the restored window state. Moreover, creation of off-screen windows on Windows OS causes the application window to acquire scroll bars indicating the presence of objects outside the user's field of view.

For these and other reasons, in certain circumstances, you may prefer to maintain the focus on the current window while your script is in progress, yet don't want to expose a screen display of the script's actions. In such cases, issuing the `Freeze Window` script command prior to script steps that would otherwise change the display in the current window is an alternative. The `Freeze Window` command frees your script to proceed without updating the screen.

A common misconception is that when your script freezes the window, it should subsequently refresh the window using the `Refresh Window[ ]` command; however, this is not the case. The `Freeze Window` command carries an implicit window refresh after the freeze is released (such as when the script pauses or concludes). Therefore, adding a `Refresh Window[ ]` command is not only superfluous but may cause screen flicker as the screen is refreshed twice in quick succession.

We recommend that you only use the `Refresh Window[ ]` command at the conclusion of a script sequence if either:

- You have not used the `Freeze Window` command throughout the course of the script.
- You need to explicitly flush cached join results or cached SQL data (both of which are options of the `Refresh Window[ ]` command).

**CAUTION** Over-use of the Freeze and Refresh commands may add to rather than ameliorate screen flickering. We recommend that you use them sparingly and only when needed. However, lengthy scripts — such as those looping through the found set — generally benefit from including a Freeze command before commencing the loop.

## Scripting Data Import and Export

One of many strengths of FileMaker is its ability to import data from and export data to a wide variety of formats. This ability makes it a good player in medium to large organizational environments where a number of tools and technologies are in use. These capabilities become considerably more powerful when you're able to control them within your solution's scripts.

**CROSS-REF** Our description of the technique for specifying dynamic file paths using variables earlier in this chapter is pertinent to the following examples. You can use a calculation to determine the filename and file path for any of the file creation and import operations discussed here.

### Exporting field contents

With very few exceptions, anything that is stored in a FileMaker field can be exported to a file on your computer, and the process can be scripted. The exceptions are limited to container images not in a supported external graphical format (such as layout vector objects pasted directly into container fields). All other data — including text, movies, sounds, images, and files — can be used as

## Scripting in Depth

the basis of creation of a file or files on the current computer or any volume (such as network file server) accessible to it.

The `Export Field Contents[ ]` command requires only that you select a target field and specify an output file. For example, if your solution includes a text field called `Description` in a `Library TO`, you can use the following two lines of script code:

```
Set Variable [$FilePath; Value "File:Description.txt"]
Export Field Contents [Library::Description; "$FilePath"]
```

Doing so results in the creation of a text file called `Description.txt`, containing the text in the targeted field.

> **TIP** The suffix of the filename you specify for an output file must be one your computer's operating system recognizes as valid for the kind of data you are exporting. If the suffix does not conform to system requirements the export may return an error. Or, if the file is successfully created, it may be associated with an inappropriate application (and therefore not recognized when a user attempts to open it).

### Exporting table data

When you choose to export structured data from your solution, by default FileMaker exports from the table associated with the current layout and includes only the records in the current found set. The same applies when your export is scripted — the export is conducted from the current context at the time the `Export Records[ ]` command executes.

To script a successful export, you must therefore structure your script to first:

- Select an appropriate layout (providing table context, including relationships to other tables if you are including data from related fields in the exported data set, including calculations in your primary TO referencing related table data).
- Establish an appropriate found set for the records you want to export.
- (Optionally) Set a path and filename for the file to be created.

In addition to the preceding preparatory steps, you must configure the `Export Records[ ]` step to include the selection of fields to be exported (and the order they are to appear in the export file), the output file path and the file format for the export (csv, tab separated text, XML, Excel, and so on), as shown in Figure 13.13.

The rudiments of a script exporting the contents of all Meetings table records in your solution in ASCII text in a CSV (comma separated values) format, into a file called `"AllMeetings.csv"` on the desktop of the current computer, are as follows:

```
Go to Layout ["Meetings" (Meetings)]
Show All Records
Set Variable [$FilePath; Value "file:" & Get(DesktopPath) & "AllMeetings.csv"]
Export Records [No Dialog; "$FilePath"; ASCII(DOS)]
Go to Layout [original layout]
```

491

## Part III  Beyond the Basics

This script (with the addition of appropriate error handling) executes efficiently, creating a file ready for transfer into another system or for a variety of other purposes.

> **TIP** If your objective is to move records from one table to another in your solution or to move them to another FileMaker file, rather than exporting, you can perform a direct import into the other table or file.

**FIGURE 13.13**
Specifying the file type in the Specify Output File dialog for the Export Records[ ] command.

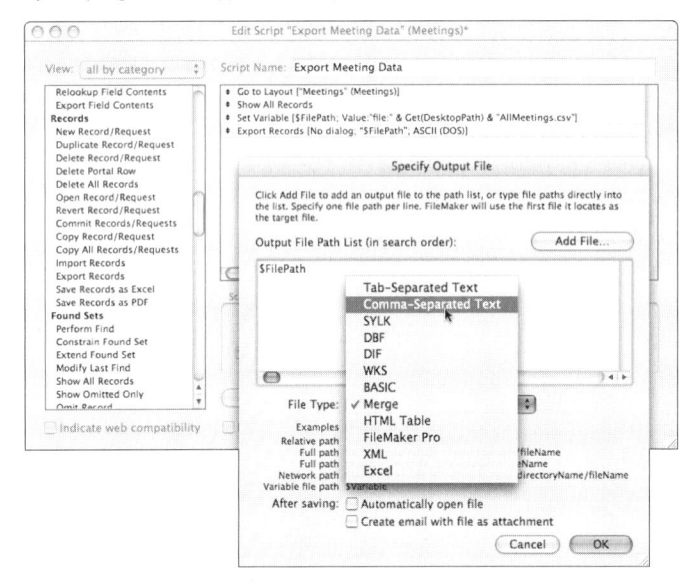

## Selecting fields for export

When setting up an export, the fields to be included in the export and the order in which the fields appear are determined by the settings you create in the Specify Field Order for Export dialog, as shown in Figure 13.14.

Using the Field Order dialog, you can choose the source table for each field from the pop-up menu at the upper left, and then select fields from the list at the left and use the buttons in the center to move them to the Field Export Order or Group by list boxes at the right.

> **NOTE** The checkbox option at the lower left of the Specify Field Order for Export dialog refers to the data format (such as number, date, and time presentation formats) rather than to character styles and formats applied to text.

## Scripting in Depth | 13

> **TIP** Most export file options are suited for plain text only, so you cannot include container field data, and any embedded text styles (including colors, fonts, and font sizes) will be lost. An exception is when you are exporting to a FileMaker file — both container data and embedded character styles are retained.

After you have added fields to the Field Export Order list, you can change their order by selecting them and then using the ⌘+↑ or Ctrl+↑ and ⌘+↓ or Ctrl+↓ to move them up and down, or by dragging them with the handle icon to the left of each field, as shown in Figure 13.14.

**FIGURE 13.14**

Specifying the fields and field order for export from the Meetings table.

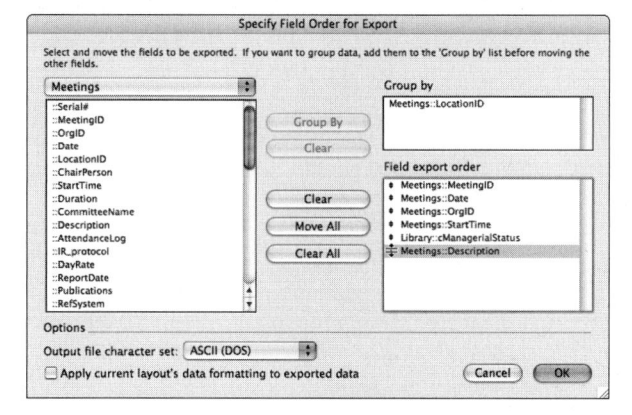

## Import options

When scripting a data import process into your solution, several steps of the process mirror the export procedure described earlier. In particular, specifying a source file from which the data is to be imported and choosing an appropriate file type are achieved in the same way using a variant of the Specify File dialog, as shown in Figure 13.15.

The choice of file type you make when specifying the file for import determines how FileMaker interprets the data and parses the values in the file you select (for example, FileMaker breaks fields using the appropriate delimiter for the chosen file format).

## FIGURE 13.15

Specifying the file path and type for import of data into your solution.

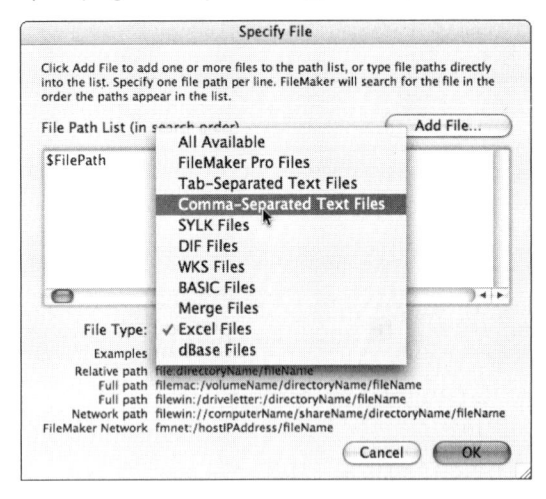

## Data matching for import

The configuration of options to match fields from the incoming data (or database) file to the field structure of a table in your solution requires that you select a destination table in your solution, and then designate fields or values in the external file to align with some or all of the fields in the selected table, as shown in Figure 13.16.

Individual fields in the Target Fields column at the right of the Import Field Mapping dialog can be moved up and down to correspond to incoming data by selecting them and using the ⌘+↑ or Ctrl+↑ and ⌘+↓ or Ctrl+↓ to move them up and down, or by dragging them with the handle icon to the left of each field. Moreover, you can click the arrow in the center column adjacent to any field to enable or disable import into a specific field.

### Synchronizing and updating data

You can import data into only one table at a time. However, you can choose a variety of import, matching, and synchronization options, enabling you to add new data, update existing data (to match the corresponding records in the external file or table), or a mix of both. The controls for these options are found at the lower left of the Import Field Mapping dialog, as shown in Figure 13.16.

**TIP** If you Shift+click or ⌘+click or Ctrl+click to select multiple contiguous or discontiguous fields in the Import Field Mapping dialog, as shown in Figure 13.16, you can enable or disable them all as a group by clicking the symbol in the center column.

## Scripting in Depth | 13

**FIGURE 13.16**

Aligning incoming data to fields in your solution by using the Import Field Mapping dialog.

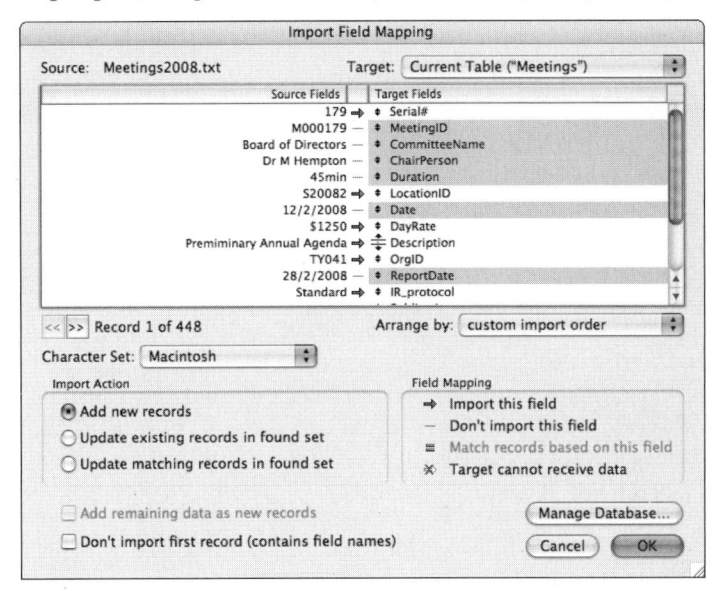

Additionally, you can choose from the Arrange By pop-up menu (below the field list at the right), one of six field presentation orders for the fields in your solution, as follows:

- Matching names
- Last order
- Creation order
- Field names
- Field types
- Custom import order

**CAUTION** If new fields are created in the destination table (in your solution) after you have defined a scripted import, they will be automatically added to the end of the import order. If you do not want new fields included in subsequent imports (or you want them in a different place in the import map) you should revise all script import maps targeting the table after adding fields.

### Other import options

In addition to the import of raw data as described previously, FileMaker provides options to import from an XML source. If the source data is formatted using the FMPXMLRESULT encoding format, you can import it directly; otherwise, you need an appropriately formed XSLT style sheet to enable

FileMaker to interpret and transform the XML data. Many data sources are available for which style sheets already exist or can readily be adapted.

After you have specified an XML source and (if necessary) an XSLT document to interpret it, FileMaker lets you configure an import field map to import the XML data as described earlier.

Additionally, FileMaker supports import from Open Database Connectivity (ODBC) data sources. To take advantage of this option, you first need to install an appropriate ODBC driver and employ it to define a Data Source Name (DSN).

**CROSS-REF** For full details of the process of installing and configuring an ODBC driver and defining a DSN, refer to Chapter 7.

When your driver and DSN are configured, you are prompted to authenticate for the remote data source and then passed to the SQL Query Builder for the remote data source, letting you select fields from the ODBC data to be included in the import mapping process in FileMaker.

## Loading and unloading container objects

Although container data are not supported in import and export formats, you can batch import text or multimedia (picture or movie) files by using the Folder Import option. This option has a number of advantages, including the ability to simultaneously import (into different fields in your table) the Text Content, File Name, and File Path (for text file folder imports), or the Image, File Name, File Path, and Image Thumbnail (for image or movie imports).

Alternatively, you can readily script a process by using FileMaker's scripting commands to Insert Picture[ ], Insert QuickTime[ ], Insert File[ ], and/or Export Field Contents[ ] to loop through a group of records inserting or exporting container field contents to or from a predetermined directory (using filenames calculated and passed to the relevant commands via the attendant Specify File dialog, as noted earlier in this section). So, for example, to export student photos from the Students Table to a pix folder in the current solution directory on your computer, using the StudentID as the filename, you could use a script structured in essentials along the lines of the following:

```
Enter Browse Mode [ ]
Freeze Window
Go to Layout ["Students" (Students)]
Show All Records
Go to Record/Request/Page [First]
Loop
  Set Variable [$ImagePath; Value "file:pix/" & Students::StudentID & ".jpg"]
  Export Field Contents [Students::StudentPhoto; "$ImagePath"]
  Go to Record/Request/Page [Next; Exit after last]
End Loop
Go to Layout [original layout]
```

By using a similarly structured script with the `Go to Field[ ]` and `Insert Picture[ ]` commands in place of the `Export Field Contents[ ]` command, the reverse procedure can be accomplished and appropriately named files can be uploaded from the pix directory. The variant of the script to achieve this is as follows:

```
Enter Browse Mode [ ]
Freeze Window
Go to Layout ["Students" (Students)]
Show All Records
Go to Record/Request/Page [First]
Loop
  Set Variable [$ImagePath; Value "image:pix/" & Students::StudentID & ".jpg"]
  Go to Field [Students::StudentPhoto]
  Insert Picture ["$ImagePath"]
  Go to Record/Request/Page [Next; Exit after last]
End Loop
Go to Layout [original layout]
```

**CAUTION** Both scripts described in this section require the addition of error handling as discussed earlier in this chapter, particularly to deal with the situation where, in the second script, no image is available to match a given record in the `Students` table.

## Pivoting Data between Tables

While import and export provide a number of essential methods for moving your data around in a number of circumstances, you will require more control over the process — for example, when modifying or massaging data into the appropriate form and structure for the table it is to occupy.

When you are working with data stored according to a different data model (such as FirstName and LastName in the same field — something you're most unlikely to have done in your own solutions, having read Chapters 7 and 11 of this book!), you'll require what is sometimes referred to as an Extraction, Transformation, and Loading (ETL) process between your data and the destination data structure.

### Using utility relationships

One of the most powerful methods of data transfer and transformation in FileMaker is via a scripted update using a utility relationship. Such a relationship is based on a global field in the table from which the data is to be sourced, and relates either to the primary key of the destination table, or to an intermediary table you will use for final data vetting before export or before importing to the destination table.

The relationship between the tables should be set to Allow Creation of Related Records, as described in Chapter 11. By populating the global key field in your source table with each of the primary keys for the remote table in turn, you are able to write to or create corresponding records using the data in your primary source table and any tables related to it, within the structure of your solution.

## Managing related data (walking through related records)

Using your utility relationship to isolate individual records to be created or updated in the target table, you can build a transformation script in your solution along the following lines:

```
Enter Browse Mode [ ]
Freeze Window
Go to Layout ["SourceData" (Source)]
#Locate records to be loaded to external system via ETL
Perform Find [Restore]
Go to Record/Request/Page [First]
Loop
   #Load external system key to activate utility relationship
   Set Field [gETL_key; Source::LegacySystemID]
   Set Variable [$ETL; $ETL + 1]
   #perform required transformations for each external data field
   Set Field [External::Name; Source::FirstName & " " & Source::LastName]
   Set Field [External::Chk; Choose(Source::Status; "pending"; "complete")]
   Set Field [External::Date; Day(Billed::Date) & "." & Month(Billed::Date)]
   Set Field [External::NetCost; Billed::Amount - Source::Discount]
   #etc - to complete full set of required data transformations
   Go to Record/Request/Page [Next; Exit after last]
End Loop
Go to Layout [original layout]
Show Custom Dialog ["Extract/Transform/Load of " & $ETL & " records completed"]
```

This process outlined in its essential form pivots data through the utility relationship from the Source TO to the External TO, drawing on data from the Source and Billing TOs (and others as required) to modify and transform the data into the appropriate form and content for upload to the external system.

**TIP** An ETL process along the lines set out in the previous script can be used effectively to pass data between external data sources and FileMaker data tables to facilitate reporting on ESS data, archiving or warehousing of FileMaker data, or the interchange of data between complementary systems.

# Going over Some Practical Examples

Throughout this chapter, we've delved into a selection of the essentials of scripting, providing you with guidance, tips, and examples designed to help you solve problems and elevate your solution's scripts to new levels of power and efficiency. To add to the wealth of examples included in this chapter, here are two useful techniques to round out your repertoire.

## Locating unique records

A common problem encountered in all database systems is identifying unique examples of an entity or attribute when duplicates exist. For example, if your parking register has a field for the car model of each client and you need to produce a list of car models (including each only once), you can use the following script:

```
Enter Browse Mode
Show All Records
Sort Records [Restore; No dialog {by Clients::CarModel}]
Go to Record/Request/Page [First]
Freeze Window
View As [View as Form]
Loop
  Set Variable [$prevNo; Value: Get(RecordNumber) - 1]
  Set Variable [$prevValue; Value: GetNthRecord(Clients::CarModel; $prevNo)]
  If [$prevValue = Clients::CarModel]
    Omit Record
  Else
    Go to Record/Request/Page [Next; Exit after last]
  End If
End Loop
Unsort Records
View As [View as List]
Go to Record/Request/Page [First]
```

In this disarmingly simple procedure, your script sorts the records in the Clients table (by the field where you want to isolate unique values) and then walks the records, comparing each with the preceding record to selectively omit those already represented in the found set.

## Building a multi-part PDF report

FileMaker Pro 9 introduces the ability to combine several reports or report components into a single, composite PDF document. For example, you can generate a polished presentation document with a cover page, data pages, and a concluding summary page within a single document.

Generating a composite report of this kind first requires three layouts: one providing the summary page, one formatted as a list layout providing the report document's body, and one containing header, footer, and sub-summary parts only to generate an overview of grouped data. With the required report layouts in place, you can then set in place a script along the following lines:

```
Set Variable [$ReportPath; Value:"file:PurchasesReport.pdf"]
Go to Layout ["ReportCover" (InvoiceLines)]
Save Records as PDF [Restore; No Dialog; "$ReportPath"; Current record]
Go to Layout [ "PurchaseReport" (InvoiceLines) ]
Show All Records
Sort Records [Restore; No dialog ]
Save Records as PDF [Restore; Append; No Dialog; "$ReportPath"; Records being
    browsed]
Go to Layout ["BuyerSummary" (InvoiceLines)]
Sort Records [Restore; No dialog ]
Save Records as PDF [Restore; Append; No Dialog; "$ReportPath"; Automatically
    open; Records being browsed]
Go to Layout [original layout]
```

With this script in place, a multi-page PDF report will be created representing current data and then opened on your computer.

**NOTE** This script is implemented in the Inventory example file for this chapter and is available among the download materials on the book's Web site.

# Part IV

# Integrity and Security

This part helps you broaden and stratify your user base. Not all users have the need to know all aspects of your operation — for example, customers checking availability don't need to see your cost of goods. As users unfamiliar with your solution access it, you discover what's called "monkey mode" by some — the apparently random wanderings, keystrokes, and mouse-clicks.

The chapters in this part use numerous examples and incisive insights to introduce account management, guard against nonsensical data and careless operation, and maintain a recovery system and an archival system to improve your solution's data consistency and resistance to corruption.

## IN THIS PART

**Chapter 14**
In Control with FileMaker Security

**Chapter 15**
Maintaining Referential Integrity

**Chapter 16**
Making FileMaker Systems Fail-Safe

**Chapter 17**
Maintaining and Restoring Data

# Chapter 14

# In Control with FileMaker Security

If data doesn't matter to you, you're unlikely to store it at all, much less build a database solution to accommodate it — so the fact that you've done so is as good an indication as any that the data matters. Because it matters, it should be protected — from unauthorized access or sabotage or simply from mishap or loss. Security takes a number of forms and helps protect your data in a variety of ways.

FileMaker provides a robust database environment with a multifaceted security architecture that you can configure to meet various needs — from a simple single-user database to a diverse multi-user system with dozens or even hundreds of users. FileMaker conforms to industry standards in its security framework implementation and supports a range of best practices for secure handling of sensitive data.

Technology, however, is only effective when used skillfully and appropriately, and an arsenal of security capabilities is of no use whatsoever if it remains unused. Security should form part of your solution's design from the outset and should be built into the fabric of your code. Too often security is added as an afterthought.

## IN THIS CHAPTER

Exploring security concepts

Understanding privilege sets

Working with granular security

Dealing with user authentication

Managing accounts via script

Creating a custom logout option

Deciding how much security you need

Recognizing the importance of physical file security

Implementing secure deployments with FileMaker server

## Concepts of Security

In the broadest sense, security represents a collection of safeguards against potential risks, threats, and problems. An important first step toward creating an appropriate security strategy is planning, which involves assessing the possible risks, understanding their impact, and considering the probability of the various risks.

# Part IV: Integrity and Security

There is no one way to address all aspects of security, so we encourage you to think and act broadly and to implement a mix of strategies addressing your solution's needs. Security can't be considered in isolation; it is an essential and core part of every aspect of your solutions' creation and use.

## Balance and perspective

Among life's copious ironies are a collection of sad stories about misplaced effort, including backup files that can't be opened, passwords on sticky notes along the tops of computer monitors, and heavily secured buildings with open access Wi-Fi networks. It's a long and sorry tale.

Keeping things in perspective is important when considering solution security. It's too easy to focus your attention on one area of concern while largely overlooking others. For example, a beautifully implemented login system won't protect your data from the hazards of disk failure or human error — each presenting a real risk of potentially equal magnitude. You need different kinds of security to address different risks.

### Identifying threats

Taking time to identify the various risks, threats, and contingencies impacting your solutions makes sense. These risks include the possibility of malicious acts, unauthorized access to your data or your solution's code, and careless modification or deletion of data, not to mention hardware failure or errors within your solution's code.

We suggest a measured approach to security. Address the various hazards and potential issues by responding to them in proportion to their relevance (the probability of each type of issue arising in your particular situation) and make sure the level of security you implement is in line with your solution's value.

### Assessing value

Your solution has value in several ways, the most readily identifiable being the expenditure (of both time and money) to develop, implement, and maintain it. In many cases, however, the value of your solution is best measured by the amount of work it does for you, your business, or your employer — and the costs that would be incurred or the amount of income foregone if your system failed or were unavailable.

Against this background, even the simplest of solutions has a value sufficient to warrant some thought, time, and resources devoted to identifying its vulnerabilities and setting strategies in place to manage those vulnerabilities.

## Protecting your investment

Before deciding on a security strategy for your solutions, take a moment to consider what's at stake. Security is a way of protecting your investment, and the level of your investment may be greater than you first think. You invest in your database solutions in several ways:

- The solution is almost certainly an investment in time and ingenuity. It may well be worth more than the software or computers it runs on.

- Your solutions, by nature, contain the essentials of many of your business rules, operating procedures, and work preferences. (A solution is in fact a way of codifying your way of working.) A solution may also incorporate your "mental map" of ways to solve a host of problems.

- The accumulation of work collecting, processing, refining, and organizing information in your solution has a value. Whether you enter information yourself, pay others to do so, or acquire information in a variety of other ways, it nevertheless has a value.

- When information is sensitive or privileged it must be protected—as required by law as well as common sense. Whether the reasons are positive (competitive advantage) or negative (breach of privacy), they amount to a compelling need for controlling the flow of information.

Each way your solution has value presents a range of different issues and security concerns. Maintaining data confidentiality is of little use if the data itself has become subject to corruption or is generously peppered with user errors. Conversely, protecting your solution from a malicious attack won't help if your scripts malfunction and delete the wrong records.

Although there are some cases where risks are low or the security is not a paramount concern, nonetheless, there is an investment (both in the data and in the solution itself) to consider. Even for solutions operating in a secure environment or including no private or sensitive data, the levels of risk are needlessly high if security is left to chance.

## Interface vulnerabilities

There are several ways your solution interface can challenge or threaten security. The simplest of these are the impact of clutter and confusion. Confusion leads to errors, misplaced data, incomplete processes, and the diminishing returns arising from user frustration and incomprehension.

### Taking things at interface value

Care and attention to interface design can lend clarity and simplicity to your solutions, resulting in great improvements in data integrity and worker productivity. Rather than bolting your interface down, adding layers of code to prevent users from doing the wrong things, and still more layers to detect and correct errors after they are made with some changes to the interface, many problems evaporate.

Along with your solution's interface layer, you should also consider the interaction model. If your solution has a natural flow to it and users find that it mirrors their work processes, they will be engaged and energetic in maintaining the solution, because they understand and appreciate its value. Conversely, when you introduce onerous login processes and complex or convoluted requirements, the easy flow turns to a struggle, with users working in opposition to the system.

### More than a semblance of security

An entirely different way your solution's interface can get you into trouble is by providing the appearance of security in place of real security. You may be tempted to consider fields not in view as being inaccessible, or to suppose users will be constrained to follow the processes laid out in your scripts.

Don't allow your interface and script designs to lull you into a false sense of security. They are the front door to your solution, and it's certainly important that they guide the user and present only the appropriate information in layouts and reports. Be aware, however, that many alternate ways exist for a solution to be accessed by a resourceful or mischievous user — so the fact that a field doesn't appear on any layouts does not mean that it is secure. Similarly, having your scripts impose a certain sequence of events does not guarantee that users cannot contrive other passages through your solution.

FileMaker supports links to external files, so solutions can be structured to include data from other files. Unless you have given careful thought to security, a user can create a file with a reference to your solution and use it to view and edit data in every corner of your solution, regardless of the interface you have set in place.

**CAUTION** Unless you have set safeguards in place — in the form or through robust security measures assigning appropriate privileges to each user — every field can be accessed and edited by anyone with a mind to do so.

### File-based security

To provide you with the tools to control access to key components of your solution (including layouts, scripts, and value lists as well as field data), FileMaker provides a security architecture centered on assigned user privileges in each file. Therefore, if a user is accessing the contents of your file from another file, the constraints and privileges in place will be those (if any) you have defined in your file, not those they define in the external file being used to gain access.

The file-centered security model has numerous advantages — allowing you to offset a variety of security concerns — but also presents some challenges, especially when your solution is comprised of multiple files. In such cases it is incumbent on you to build appropriate security into each file, while ensuring that the solution files can nevertheless interact and provide a seamless user experience.

**CROSS-REF** The implications of file-based security for aspects of the design and use of your solutions are explored in Chapters 11 and 13.

## The Privilege Set

At the heart of the FileMaker security model is the concept of the privilege set, a named collection of specifications for access levels and restrictions throughout the file where it's defined.

By default, all FileMaker files contain the following three privilege sets:

- [Full Access]
- [Data Entry Only]
- [Read-Only Access]

## In Control with FileMaker Security | 14

**NOTE** The enclosing square brackets around FileMaker's default privilege set names enable you to easily differentiate them from other privilege sets in your solution files. When creating your own privilege sets, you can enclose their names in square brackets. However, we recommend against doing so, to preserve the distinction between default privilege sets and those created specifically for the solution.

The default [Full Access] account provides the level of access required for solution development and is an essential component of any file under development or maintenance.

By choosing File ➪ ManageAccounts & Privileges and navigating to the Privilege Sets panel, as shown in Figure 14.1, you can view the current privilege sets in each solution file, as well as creating and configuring new ones.

**FIGURE 14.1**

Default privilege sets showing in the Manage Accounts & Privileges dialog.

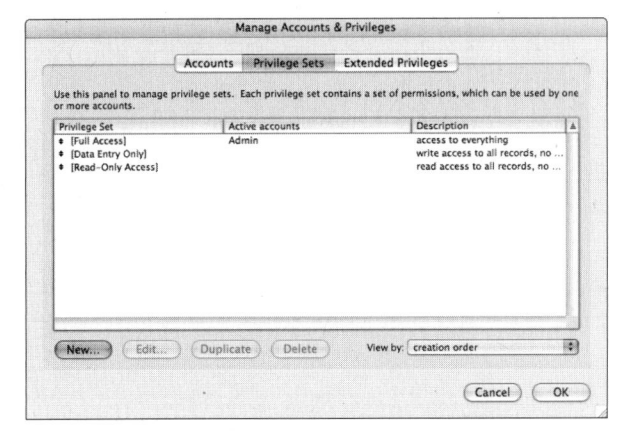

Before your solution's initial deployment and preferably early in its development, you should begin building appropriate privilege structures to support and enhance your solution's operations and to define the scope and limits of use.

## Concepts of role-based security

A privilege set comprises a comprehensive definition of field, layout, value list, and script access permissions, as well as a number of broad functional capability permissions (such as printing and exporting). Collectively these permissions are assembled to meet the requirements of a particular user or (better still) a group of users.

When you define a privilege set to meet the needs of a group of users, you tailor the permissions according to the role or roles to be performed by the users. If a different group of users performs different roles, you create another privilege set. Thus, a collection of privilege sets is modeled on

507

the various roles performed by users of the solution. Organizing privileges in this way provides a framework of clarity that helps you determine appropriate access for each group and enables efficient management of privileges. For example, a single change to the privileges assigned to a particular privilege set affects a change for all users assigned to that set.

Each user logs in with personal credentials (account name and password), but each account is assigned to a privilege set that determines the access levels the account enjoys. By assigning multiple accounts (requiring similar access privileges, according to the users' roles) to each privilege set, you simplify the setup and management of access for multiple users. The grouping of accounts with similar requirements against appropriate privilege sets is the essential principle of role-based security management.

## Defining and constraining access

To create and configure privilege sets for your solution's users, click the New button (lower left of the Privilege Sets panel of the Manage Accounts & Privileges dialog) to open the Edit Privilege Set dialog, and then enter a name for the privilege set in the field at the top left. You can also enter an optional description in the adjacent field as a reminder of the privilege set's purpose.

The Edit Privilege Set dialog is divided into three sections, as shown in Figure 14.2. The Data Access and Design section lets you specify access controls for records and fields in the file's data structure (data stored in tables within the file, for example), as well as access levels to layouts, value lists, and scripts.

**FIGURE 14.2**

Configuring a new privilege set in the Edit Privilege Set dialog.

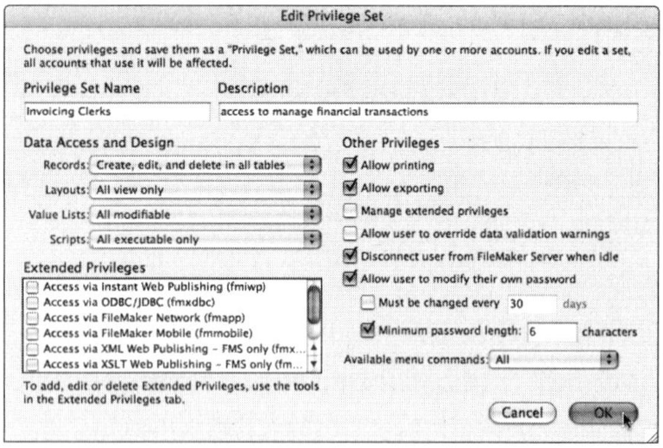

The Extended Privileges section lets you enable or disable each of a list of access modes or options. By default, FileMaker includes seven extended privilege options associated with different modes of access to your data. You can add to or modify the list. Each extended privilege optionally associates a keyword with the privilege set. You can see the keywords listed in parentheses to the right of each entry in the Extended Privileges list box at the lower left of the dialog, as shown in Figure 14.2.

# In Control with FileMaker Security

Finally, the Other Privileges section (on the right) gives you access to a series of general controls over the current solution file's behavior for users whose logins are associated with the privilege set. Among the most significant of the privilege settings in the Other Privileges section are the controls for ability to print or export data.

> **CAUTION** Be aware that disallowing printing or exporting of data will not stop determined users from taking screen captures, copying and pasting data from your solution into other applications on their workstation, or using other methods of access to circumvent your file-based security measures. These controls determine only the range of functionality available within the file where they are defined.

## Schema privilege controls

At the centre of the FileMaker security model is the ability to control users' access to the elements of schema — the fields and tables throughout your solution's data structure — as part of Data Access and Design privilege controls. In the Edit Privilege Set dialog's Data Access and Design section, the pop-up menus provide several categories of access, each offering several predetermined access levels including:

- All Modifiable
- All View Only
- All No Access

The first pop-up menu, labeled Records, differs from the others because the All Modifiable option is further subdivided, as shown in Figure 14.3, supporting editing capabilities either with or without the ability to delete records. As the wording in these options indicates, when you make a selection at this level it applies equally to all tables within the file.

**FIGURE 14.3**

Access options in the Data Access and Design privileges pop-up menus.

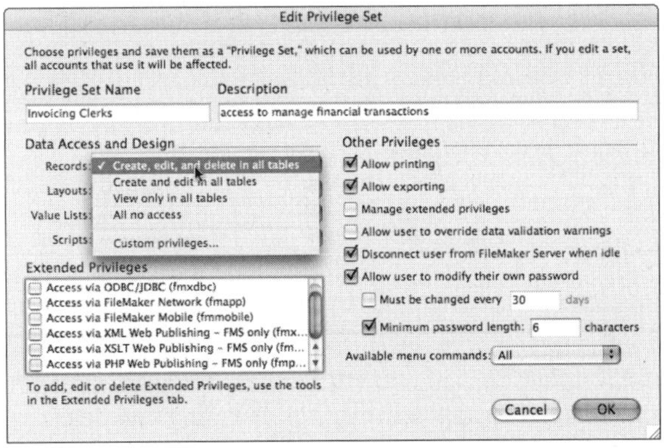

509

## Part IV   Integrity and Security

The generic access options suit your requirements in many cases. If you need more fine-grained control, you can choose a Custom Privileges option. These options appear below a separator at the bottom of each pop-up menu.

# Granular Security

On each of the pop-up menus, the Custom Privileges options give you access to dialogs listing the corresponding elements in the current file (tables, lists, scripts, and layouts), letting you specify a range of access attributes separately against each item.

The range of access controls operates at a number of levels from the most broad categories (for example granting or denying access to a whole table) down to the most finely granular (controlling access for the individual record or field). In this section, we describe the processes for configuring granular access appropriate for the needs of your solution.

## Access to value lists and scripts

The Custom Privileges options open list dialogs that allow you to select items and choose the desired access levels. For example, the Custom Script Privileges dialog, shown in Figure 14.4, offers radio button settings for Modifiable, Executable Only, or No Access on a script-by-script basis.

**FIGURE 14.4**

Specifying access levels for individual scripts.

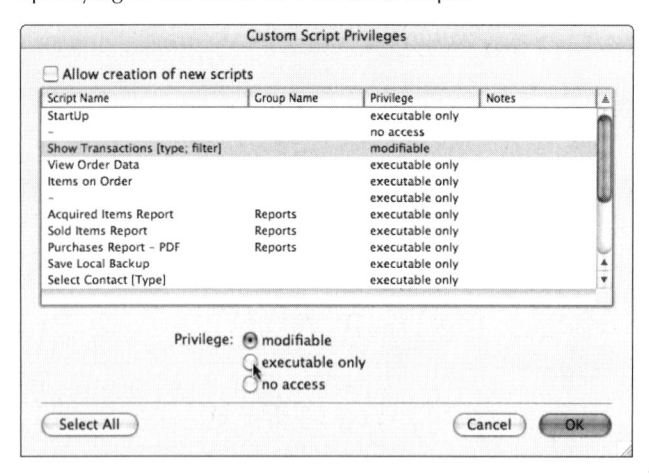

The Custom Value List Privileges dialog is similar to the dialog shown in Figure 14.4, offering options for Modifiable, View Only, or No Access for each value list in the current file.

## The two dimensions of layout access

The Custom Layout Privileges dialog provides dual controls for each layout — one for the layout (to allow or deny layout design changes or layout viewing, for example) and another to control access to records when viewed using each layout.

Figure 14.5 shows that you can independently select the options provided by the dual controls when configuring layout privileges.

**FIGURE 14.5**

Setting access for both layouts and records via layouts in the Custom Layout Privileges dialog.

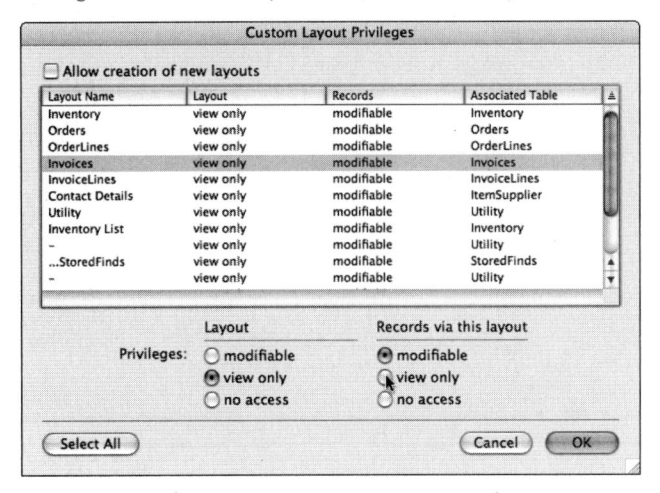

## Privileges for table, record, and field access

The Custom Record Privileges dialog differs from the three custom privileges dialogs described earlier. This dialog provides multiple access controls for records in each table and governs View, Edit, Create, and Delete permissions, as shown in Figure 14.6. The pop-up menus for View, Edit, and Delete include an option labeled Limited. Selecting this option opens a Specify Calculation dialog where you can define an expression that determines on a record-by-record basis the level of access to individual records users assigned to the current privilege set enjoy. For example, in the Inventory example file for this chapter, if you select the Orders table, choose Limited from the Edit pop-up menu and then enter the expression:

```
Status ≠ 1
```

Users logging in against the privilege set so defined are prevented from editing records flagged as complete in the Orders::Status field (that is, only incomplete records may be edited). In this example, it would be appropriate to apply a similar control to the Delete option so that only incomplete orders can be deleted.

511

## Part IV   Integrity and Security

### FIGURE 14.6

Specifying record level access permissions by table in the Custom Record Privileges dialog.

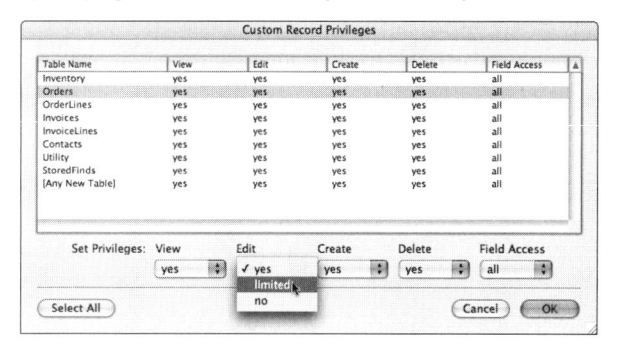

Using the Field Access menu option (lower right of the Custom Record Privileges dialog) you gain access to a further layer of granular control over users' access to individual fields in the selected table. As shown in Figure 14.7, you can independently designate each field in the table as No Access, View Only, or Modifiable for the current privilege set.

### FIGURE 14.7

Specifying field-level access privileges for the selected table.

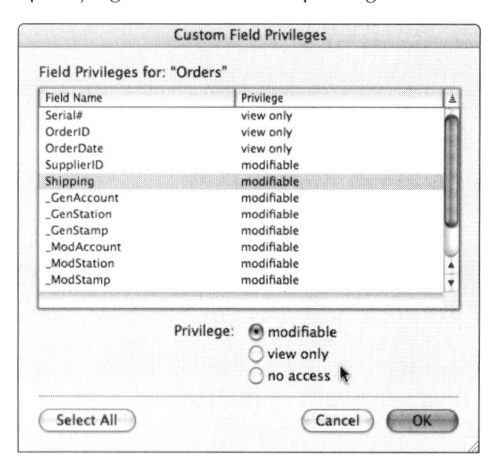

Using these controls as described, you can configure explicit and dynamic access privileges for individual elements throughout the current file, ensuring access at all levels as appropriate to users assigned to the selected privilege set.

Additionally, each Custom Privileges dialog includes an option to set the default access level applicable to new elements added to the file. For example, in Figure 14.6, the last line specifies access for [Any New Table]. Similarly, the Custom Privileges dialogs for Layouts, Value Lists, and Scripts include a checkbox option at the top left allowing users to create new items — for example, at the upper left of Figure 14.5 the Allow Creation of New Layouts option is shown.

> **NOTE** At the bottom of each custom privileges list is a line that allows you to set default access privileges for new (subsequently created) entities. For example, Figure 14.6 shows the entry for [Any New Table] at the bottom of the Custom Record Privileges list.

In the case of the Custom Layout Privileges dialog shown in Figure 14.5, there is an interplay between the Allow Creation of New Layouts option and the default [Any New Layout] privilege setting. When you grant users the privilege to create new layouts using the checkbox setting, you can also determine the level of access they will have to those new layouts using the [Any New Layout] privilege setting.

## Using and managing extended privileges

FileMaker Pro and FileMaker Server use the seven default extended privileges keywords to control a range of network and remote access capabilities. You can enable or disable each of these keywords independently for each privilege set, giving you precise control over the means of interaction with the solution available to each role-based group of users.

FileMaker provides a number of default extended privileges in each new file, including the fmapp extended privilege to control access to the file when hosted (for example, using FileMaker Server). The default extended privileges also various forms of web access, mobile and external connectivity (ODBC/JDBC) access.

You can also create keywords of your own and associate each with one or more privilege sets, as a means of establishing granular and customized access control over your solution's elements (such as calculations and scripts). For example, when you have a script — say, a reports script — that should include monthly totals for some groups of users (but not others), you can create an extended privilege keyword to manage this for monthly reports. To do so, follow these steps:

1. Navigate to the Extended Privileges panel of the Manage Accounts and Privileges dialog.
2. Click the New button at the lower left. The Edit Extended Privileges dialog appears.
3. Enter a brief keyword (such as MthRep) and a description of the purpose of the privilege, as shown in Figure 14.8.
4. Select one or more privilege sets for access to the extended privilege you've created.

After an extended privilege, as outlined, is in place, you can code your calculations and scripts to refer to it. In this example, you can set up a script to include the additional (month report summary) functionality, conditional on the current user's login having the MthRep privilege assigned, by adding script code, such as:

```
If [PatternCount(¶ & Get(ExtendedPrivileges) & ¶; "¶MthRep¶")]
    Go to Layout ["Month Summary Report" (Orders)]
    Sort Records [Restore; No dialog]
End If
```

# Part IV  Integrity and Security

With this additional code in your report script, users whose login account is assigned the MthRep extended privilege will see an alternate report based on the Month Summary layout, whereas other users will not.

> **NOTE** You can assign the Manage Extended Privileges option to one or more privilege sets, enabling some users (managers and team leaders, for example) to edit and reassign extended privileges to existing privilege sets. Extended privileges, like all privilege set characteristics, are only available to scripts and calculations in the file where you define them. For a multiple file solution you may need to define extended privileges in more than one file.

**FIGURE 14.8**
Entering details for a new Extended Privilege in the Edit Extended Privilege dialog.

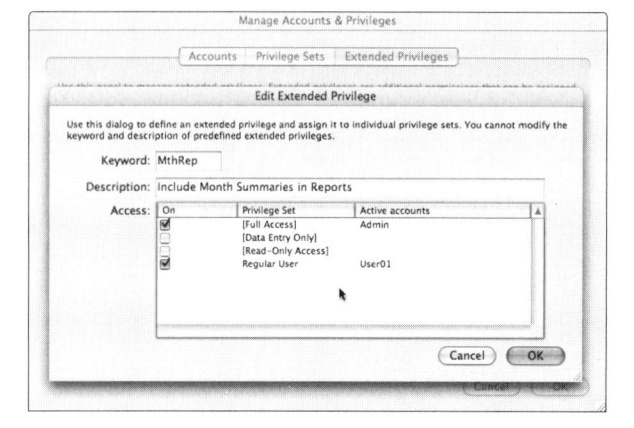

## User Authentication

You can create privilege sets for groups of users according to their role within the solution, and create multiple accounts in each solution file. Each account can be assigned to an existing privilege set in the file to facilitate assigning appropriate privileges without having to individually specify and manage each user account's permissions.

Each user of your solution should therefore be assigned an account, giving them personal credentials (account name and password) to log into your solution.

> **NOTE** An essential principle underpinning security and solution access management is that accounts and credentials are never shared. Each user has their own login account name and a password they are expected to keep secret.

# In Control with FileMaker Security    14

## Creating user accounts

User accounts provide you with a basis to control the access of individual users to a solution file. You should therefore add a separate account for every person who will access the solution (and to each file within the solution). To add accounts in your solution files, follow these steps:

1. Choose FileManageAccounts & Privileges. The Manage Accounts & Privileges dialog appears with the Accounts panel selected as the default.

2. In the Accounts panel of the Manage Accounts & Privileges dialog, click the New button at the lower left. The Edit Account dialog appears, as shown in Figure 14.9.

**FIGURE 14.9**

Creating a new account using the Edit Account dialog.

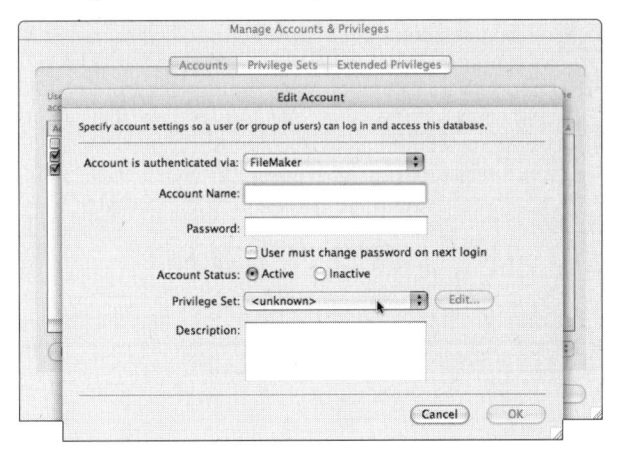

3. Enter an account name, a password, and select a privilege set from the pop-up menu in the lower part of the dialog. Optionally, add a description elucidating the purpose of the account.

4. Click OK to accept the settings and close the Edit Account dialog.

> **TIP** We recommend that you assign intelligible and recognizable account names — so that when data about the current user is returned (by the `Get(AccountName)` function, for example), the user's identity will be evident. Straightforward naming conventions such as first name and last initial (JulietteB, GeoffreyR, and so on) or first initial and last name (RFiennes, CBlanchett, for example) are compact, yet readily recognizable.

515

## Internal and external authentication

By default, FileMaker accounts are set to authenticate with a password you supply, as shown in Figure 14.9. However, when you choose the external authentication option from the pop-up menu near the top of the Edit Account dialog (Figure 14.10), user credentials are retrieved from the domain server when the file is hosted using FileMaker Server, within a network managed by an Open Directory (Mac OS) or Active Directory (Windows) domain controller.

**FIGURE 14.10**

Specifying field-level access privileges for the selected table.

Rather than supplying an account name and password, when you choose external authentication you need only supply the name of a group corresponding to a group assigned to users in the domain authentication server.

**NOTE** The authenticating computer for an external authentication configuration may be the same computer where FileMaker Server is installed — though in most cases a separate domain controller will already be performing this function.

When a user logs in at the domain level and then accesses a FileMaker file, FileMaker compares the groups associated with the user's network login with groups assigned to externally authenticated accounts in the file. The file is opened with the first externally authenticated account with a name matching one of the group names for the current user's network login (working downwards from the top of the accounts in FileMaker, when viewed in authentication order). A Windows-based domain configuring external authentication as described here provides users with single sign-on functionality.

On Mac OS the user is still presented with the familiar login dialog to access the file (or server, if so configured). However, a similar level of functionality is available via the use of the Mac Keychain to manage credentials for the user, enabling the user to bypass the FileMaker authentication dialog and providing a convenience proximate to single sign-on.

**TIP** You can change the authentication order of accounts in the Manage Accounts & Privileges dialog by dragging the accounts up or down in the list on the Accounts pane.

When you create accounts configured for external authentication, the FileMaker external server account operates as a connection between existing network credentials and a defined privilege set within your FileMaker files. All the work of verifying the user's credentials takes place outside of FileMaker. (This step happens at the designated authentication server, as configured in FileMaker Server settings.)

One significant benefit of using external authentication is that the accounts and passwords are managed centrally for multiple FileMaker files. So, for example, when users change their password, you do not need to provide a mechanism to apply the change separately to each FileMaker file — the credentials for such accounts are not stored within your solution.

**CAUTION** We advise against assigning any externally authenticated accounts to the [Full Access] privilege set, as this presents a potential vulnerability if users can gain access to the physical files.

## Scripted Account Management

For the purpose of setting up the initial security configuration for the database files in your solution, you must use the controls in the Manage Accounts & Passwords dialog's panels, as we describe in the previous sections — no alternative exists. After your solution's security infrastructure is in place, FileMaker lets you automate a number of the key maintenance and usage operations associated with logging in and manipulating accounts. These and other tasks may be managed by using scripts.

### Provision for automation of database security

As shown in Figure 14.11, ScriptMaker provides you with six essential commands for controlling security in your files, including adding and deleting accounts, resetting or changing passwords, activating or deactivating accounts, and account login and re-login.

**NOTE** Contrary to expectation, the Enable Account command is not used to enable an account. Instead, its function is either to activate or deactivate a designated account (in fact the latter option seems directly contrary to the function suggested by its name). Despite this oddity, the function efficiently performs its activation and deactivation tasks.

FileMaker also provides three calculation functions you can use to determine the current security status of the solution, as follows:

```
Get(AccountName)
Get(ExtendedPrivileges)
Get(PrivilegeSetName)
```

**Part IV** Integrity and Security

**CROSS-REF** As noted in Chapter 13, the `Get(PrivilegeSetName)` returns `[Full Access]` when evaluated during the course of a script set to Run with Full Access Privileges. A method of determining the name of the user's substantive privilege set in this situation is detailed in Chapter 13.

**FIGURE 14.11**

FileMaker's suite of Account and Security Management Script commands.

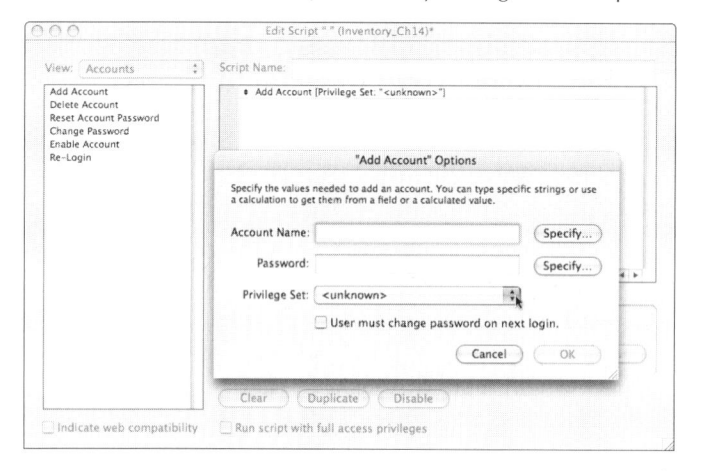

[Figure: Screenshot of Edit Script dialog showing "Add Account" Options with Account Name, Password, and Privilege Set fields]

Moreover, although you can't directly change the privilege set to which an account is assigned, you can delete an account and recreate it. And when you recreate an account, it can be assigned to any privilege set in the file.

**CAUTION** Avoid having your scripts deactivate or delete the account of the current login session (lest the script and the current user be orphaned without access to the file). Instead, if you need to modify the current user's account, have your script log into a different account first, modify the user's account, and then log back into the modified account.

## Working with multi-file solutions

If your solution contains more than one file, having a synchronized security configuration is helpful. In particular, you should ensure that the same accounts are present in each file (and with comparable privileges).

If you are using external authentication, you should ensure that accounts exist in the same authentication order for all the same groups in all files in your solution, so when a user's credentials are accepted, their access is simultaneously granted to all required components of your solution.

If you are using the FileMaker internal password authentication and if the account names and passwords in each file match, opening one solution file (where the user is prompted to login before the file opens) will generally pass the user's credentials to other files. However, if your solution provides an option for users to re-login during a file session, it will fall to your scripts to coordinate synchronous re-logins in all the required files, to keep the security status in alignment across all the solution files.

Similarly, if users are allowed to change passwords in your solution, in order to ensure the passwords remain in sync across multiple solution files, we recommend that you provide a scripted password change procedure. The procedure should prompt the user for old and new passwords, authenticate them, and then apply the change automatically in each file. For this purpose, the initial script can collect the required password (or passwords) from the user, and then transmit them (for example, as script parameters) to scripts in the other solution file (or files) configured to apply the same authentication update (login, password change, and so on) in those files.

## Safe scripting implementations

A potential security risk arises when you have your script collect a password from the user and then transmit it as data. The concern is that while the password is being held and transmitted as data it might be intercepted or otherwise revealed to an unauthorized party. Configuring your scripts to avoid these types of risks is very important. To achieve this, we recommend that your controlling script is implemented as follows:

1. Turns off the Allow User Abort[ ] capability, presents the user with a layout devoid of any buttons that could halt the script, and then hides and locks the Status Area.
2. Displays a custom dialog requesting the user's password (and new password, in the case of a password change procedure).
3. Retrieves the password(s) supplied by the user immediately (storing them as variables) and deletes them from the global fields used for the custom dialog, before proceeding.

**NOTE** For all processes involving user password entry, you should configure the custom dialogs your scripts display to use the bullet character to conceal the actual password entry. This option is available in the Input Fields panel of the Show Custom Dialog Options dialog.

When your scripts follow these steps, the period of time when the password is held as data is constrained to the time from when the user accepts the dialog until the global fields are cleared immediately afterwards. The vulnerability is limited to the user's computer, because global field values are specific to the client workstation—and the client workstation is in use with its interface and abort options locked during the millisecond or so while the password is held as data. This minimizes any risk of a password being intercepted as data.

After your scripts retrieve passwords the user enters (clearing the global fields used for this purpose), the passwords exist in memory but not in data. With unauthorized access to the workstation at this juncture, a third party might contrive to pause the script and retrieve the contents of variables. However, because the process follows immediately from the user dismissing the dialog, such an intervention is unlikely in practice. However, if you're concerned about this potential threat, then you might consider encoding or encrypting passwords when declaring them as variables and/or transmitting them as parameters to other files.

**Part IV** Integrity and Security

> **TIP** You can use text processing functions or custom functions (created using FileMaker Pro Advanced) to modify the format of passwords for added security — provided you create calculations in the scripts in the receiving files to reverse the process and extract the original password text.

## Creating a Custom Logout Option

The way the FileMaker security system works, you log into a file when first opening it and remain logged in until you either close the file or use a script or button command to re-login (using the Re-login[ ] command). As long as a file is open, a user (or at least, an account) is logged in. For best security, however, it can be advantageous for users to be able to secure your solution while they are away from their desk, without the tedium of closing the solution files and reopening them on their return.

In such cases, you can create a process analogous to a logout where your solution remains open but is in a secured state — requiring that the user enter their account name and password to regain operational access and resume working with the solution. Because responding to a password prompt may be considerably quicker and less onerous than reopening the solution files from the host, users appreciate and are likely to use this convenience.

### The locked-down database

A first step toward securing your solution's files for a logged out state is to create a layout with limited options, attached to a utility table. Typically, such a layout should include your solution's name, version, support or admin contact information, a button to exit the solution (close all solution files), and a button to login (to run a login script requesting the user's credentials).

The second step completes the securing of your solution, giving you a lock-down state. The three additional features of a secured solution required for this step are

- The Status Area is hidden and locked (using the Show/Hide Status Area[ ] command). This has the effect of also disabling the menu commands for Go to Layout and Go to Record (and also the corresponding keyboard commands, including the mouse scroll wheel), to restrict users' navigation options.

- The menus are restricted so the user cannot use them to perform any significant actions or to navigate away from the current record or layout. This can be achieved using the custom menus capability of FileMaker Pro Advanced (if available), or by using a restricted Privilege Set as described in the following topic.

- The access privileges are constrained by logging into the solution with an account assigned to a special privilege set having minimal capabilities.

> **CROSS-REF** For additional information about using FileMaker Pro Advanced to create and deploy custom menus, turn to Chapter 18.

**In Control with FileMaker Security** | 14

## Structuring a solution for logging out

Strange though it may sound, the third step in securing your solution, as we discuss in the previous section, involves logging in with a "logged out" account.

The procedure required to complete custom log-out functionality is for you to create a special restricted lockdown privilege set where the user has no record creation, deletion, or editing capabilities, where the only accessible layout is your login layout, and the only executable scripts are the start-up script, your exit script (if any), and a login script attached to the corresponding button on your "logged out" layout.

> **TIP** If your login script will use a custom dialog to have the user enter an account name and password, you must provide fields in your solution to temporarily accommodate the values entered into the dialog (global fields in a utility table will suffice). These must be accessible while the login script is running, either because they are assigned as writable fields under the lockdown privilege set or because you have set the login script to run with full access privileges.

As Figure 14.12 shows, your lockdown privilege set should constrain the user, including applying the Minimum setting for the Available Menu Commands option.

**FIGURE 14.12**
Setting up a lockdown privilege set with constrained access and minimum available menu commands.

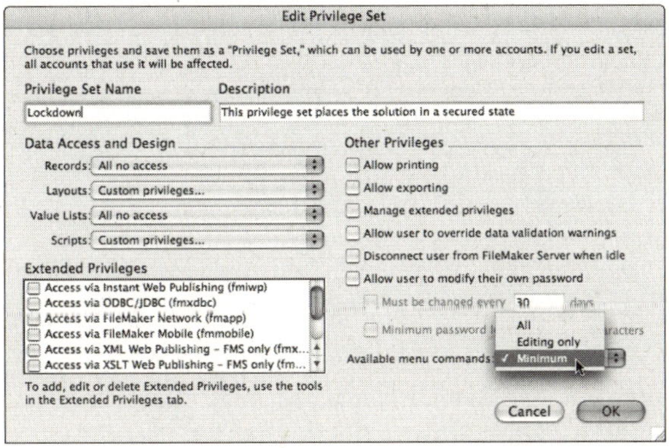

With the lockdown privilege set, you can create a lockdown account assigned to this privilege set, for use as the default account for your solution files and for occasions when users want to temporarily log out of the solution without closing it.

> **TIP** When your solution has multiple files, you should create a lockdown privilege set and associated lockdown account in each file, so that your logout script can call a sub-script in each file, placing it into a secured state as part of a single-user action.

To complete the securing of your solution, we recommend that you specify your lockdown account as the default account for each solution file, as shown in Figure 14.13.

521

Additionally, you should configure your solution's start-up script (or scripts) to take the user to the login layout and hide and lock the Status Area, ensuring that the user must provide valid credentials before proceeding.

**FIGURE 14.13**

Defining the lockdown account as the default account for when each solution file is opened.

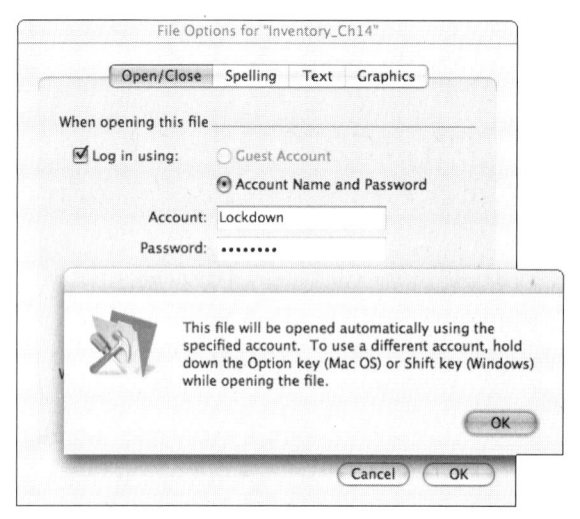

As an added security measure, you can set your login scripts to automatically activate the requested account prior to login and deactivate it again on logout. This can reduce the solution's vulnerability in the event the solution files fall into the wrong hands.

**CROSS-REF** Security can be further strengthened by using the Developer Utilities in FileMaker Pro Advanced to remove full access accounts from all production copies (or published copies) of your solution files, as outlined in Chapter 18.

We've updated this chapter's Inventory solution example file to include a basic security architecture along the lines described here, including a dual-file custom logout system and a master script to manage the login and logout procedures. Passwords for the two accounts in the file are provided via a button labeled "get passwords" appearing at the lower right of the main panel on the login screen.

**ON the WEB** The Inventory example files may be downloaded from the book's Web site, as detailed in Appendix A.

## Security logging

As a further aid to security, we recommend you include a script process that tracks user activity. The tracking process should capture login and logout times and associated workstation and network locations. To do so, you need to add a user sessions table to your solution, plus a few extra steps in your login/logout script(s) to create and update a record for each user login session.

A security log serves a number of purposes, including enabling users to see an up-to-date register of who is logged in and from which workstations, at any time during their use of the system. Moreover, a security log can provide important diagnostic information in the event of data anomalies or malfunctions of any kind. (You can match record creation and modification times to the details in the sessions table.)

In addition, a security log is a useful monitor of access and login attempts, providing you with an overview of system activity and alerting you to potential flaws, vulnerabilities, or irregularities in the solution's security or related to its usage patterns.

# How Much Security Is Enough?

Realistically, all security measures (in FileMaker or anywhere else) can be defeated, given unlimited time and resources. However, potential thieves or saboteurs do not have infinite time or money to devote to the task of getting around your security — so your job is to ensure that your solution's security exceeds any reasonable expectation of threat. Additionally, some security threats, such as spyware (keystroke loggers, for example), are system-wide and are therefore beyond the purview of an application or solution developer.

## Ways to evaluate risk

When evaluating risk, begin by determining the incentives for a range of possible attacks on your system. For example, perverse human actions may be motivated by greed or spite, but whatever the motive, you can reasonably assess the value their perpetrators may place on success. If your solution supports a business with an annual turnover of $10 million in a highly competitive market, an unscrupulous competitor may be prepared to spend millions mounting corporate espionage or sabotage. The value you and others may place on (or derive from) the solution or the data it contains is the first and best indication of the extent of security warranted.

When considering possible threats, think about positive and negative value as well as indirect value. For example, the privacy of client records may not be a salable commodity as such, but nevertheless is highly valued by the clients to whom it belongs. A breach of client or customer privacy may expose you to legal challenges, but its indirect implications may be still more serious. The flow-on effects of a compromise of privacy may result in indirect consequences such as a loss of confidence in the business or the business practices your solution supports. Although you may not regard client details as saleable, identity thieves and Internet marketers may take a different view.

In all these respects, the nature of your solution, the data it contains, and the investment it represents form the basis of your assessment of its value. In simple terms, your job is to ensure the cost and inconvenience of any effort to circumvent your solution's security exceeds any perceived gain.

## A balanced view of threats

When you deadbolt your front door, the adjacent open window becomes the most likely vulnerability to your home's security. When the window is bolted and shuttered, the point of least resistance moves elsewhere. To achieve reasonable levels of security, you must pay adequate attention to all potential vulnerabilities, raising area of vulnerability above the threshold of incentive for those who might pose a threat.

Also, be mindful of the many ways your solution may be compromised that don't involve any malicious intent. User error, hardware failure, or a variety of other mishaps may present as great a risk as any other and should be kept in view when considering how to safeguard your solution.

Additionally, make sure that the ways you address potential risks don't create new risks. For example, if your password security implementation is cumbersome for users, they will be reluctant to use it and may (actively or inadvertently) undermine it. A classic example of this is the organization so concerned about security that they implement multiple levels of password screening for various different functions or procedures — with the direct consequence being that users who cannot remember all the passwords end up writing them on notes stuck to their monitors. The net effect of this ill-conceived strategy is a diminution rather than an enhancement of security.

### A strategic model for response

After pondering the range of possible vulnerabilities for your solution and the data it accommodates, considering the relative impact of potential mishaps of different kinds, and assessing the value of your solution and its contents to various contenders, you have the model for strategic risk management.

Using your appraisal of the potential threats, we encourage you to map out priorities for solution safeguard measures, paying heed to each identified risk in accordance not only with the perceived likelihood of mishap, but also with the consequences (direct and indirect) should a mishap occur. By doing so, you achieve a balanced strategy providing a reasoned response to a broad view of hazards and susceptibilities. Error correction, audit systems, data backup, and login security can all work together to address risks and provide recovery options when a problem is encountered.

## The Importance of Physical File Security

In any situation in which third parties can gain direct physical access to copies of your solution files, a number of avenues of attack are open and your files are vulnerable. Would-be hackers can attempt to use software other than FileMaker to try to read, interpret, or even change the content of your files — or they may use other tools to try to break past your login security systems.

Whenever external authentication is used, the importance of the physical security of your solution's files is further increased. Someone obtaining copies of the database files may seek unauthorized access by configuring a bogus domain (with groups named according to the group names in the legitimate server environment).

### Layers of protection

As we mention in the last section, you want to consider ways to maximize the physical security of your solution. If the only (or primary) means of access to your solution will be through a network (if your solution resides on a server) the location and accessibility of the server is an important consideration. If possible, the server should be located in a secure environment (such as a locked room) where it cannot be accessed or removed by unauthorized persons.

Similarly, restricting access to the network where your solution operates, and to the workstations commonly used to access your solution, helps to ensure your security's integrity. Be aware that keystroke logging software (spyware) and other malware finding its way onto client computers may compromise the security of your data, despite your best efforts in other areas.

**NOTE** It's worth noting that FileMaker files do not store user passwords internally. Instead, a hash (a complex checksum) is computed and stored — in a form that can't be used to reconstruct the original password. This makes some forms of attack more difficult, but it does not stop third-party tools from overwriting the relevant sections of the file with bogus password hashes to break your file's security, replacing the legitimate passwords with impostors. This is one of several ways someone who has physical access to your files may wreak havoc, potentially compromising the integrity and security of the files and their contents.

## Alternative forms of protection

In cases where you cannot safeguard the physical security of your files — for example, when your solution is to be distributed to end users to run on their own computers, rather than being accessed from a server — we recommend that you use the FileMaker Pro Advanced capability to permanently remove [Full Access] accounts from all copies of your solution files distributed to others or used in production.

The removal of [Full Access] accounts provides good protection against direct access to your solution's code (file structure, calculations, scripts, and so on) within your database files. Additionally, it provides some protection against various methods that might be used to gain indirect access to the code. However, the removal of [Full Access] accounts may not prevent a skilled user from using third-party tools to tamper with the remaining accounts or to directly read or modify your solution's files.

**CROSS-REF** For additional details regarding the removal of [Full Access] accounts using FileMaker Pro Advanced, see Chapter 10.

## A multi-faceted approach

Using a variety of methods to guard against potential hazards and threats is the best approach to take for your solution's security. If your solution's start-up script and File Options configuration place the files into a secured state and direct the user to use your login scripts to present credentials and gain authorized access to your solution, it is important to ensure that your scripts will be used — and that other avenues to the use of your solution will not be viable.

One way to constrain users to operate within the limits of your scripts is to have the start-up script and login script generate dynamic token values and place them in fields in your solution (such as global fields created for the purpose). You can then configure other key scripts and calculations throughout your solution to check for the presence of valid tokens before proceeding (or calculating). By doing this, you can effectively disable your solution unless the current user has logged in using the scripts you have provided.

**Part IV** Integrity and Security

Another part of your approach — to guard against tampering with your solution's security structure — is to build in a second lockdown account, and then have your start-up script perform a re-login (into the second lockdown account) by using a fixed password. If the password verification data stored in the file have been tampered with, the scripted re-login will fail and your start-up script (detecting the failure of this procedure via the Get(LastError) function) can lock and close the solution.

In addition to the approaches we mention earlier, consider using various third-party products including:

- Data encryption systems (either native or plug-in based)
- External dongles, hardware keys, and locking devices
- Identification card readers and biometric scanner systems
- Online authorization and activation services

Using the range of available techniques and tools, your solution can be configured to provide efficient and convenient, yet effective measures to guard against a broad range of potential problems and hazards.

**CROSS-REF** For additional information about plug-ins and third-party resources, see Chapter 20, and for details of some sources of information and tools, see Appendix B.

# Security in Deployment: FileMaker Server

In several respects, the deployment of your solutions through the use of FileMaker Server software running on an appropriately configured and secured machine is advantageous from a security perspective (as well as in various other respects). One of the advantages, as noted in the "User Authentication" section, earlier in this chapter, is the support for external authentication enabling your FileMaker Server deployments to conform to domain or external credential checks, providing, in effect, single sign-on capabilities for one or more solutions on a local network.

There are several additional options FileMaker Server provides that are worth taking a few moments to consider (and to configure).

## Filtered display of files

FileMaker Server gives you an option to filter the display of files to users accessing the list of available databases (by using FileOpen Remote in the FileMaker Pro client application) based on a user's account name and password.

By enabling this option, you can prevent unauthorized individuals from seeing or presenting credentials to any database files other than those they are approved to access.

## Secure Socket Layer encryption

FileMaker Server 9 provides an option to encrypt data in transit between the server and client workstations using industry standard SSL (Secure Socket Layer) encryption.

Network encryption can be activated simply by selecting it as an option in configuring your server deployment (then restarting the server). We have seen no performance penalty resulting from the use of SSL encryption for data transfers with FileMaker Server—and we recommend its use as a further means of protection for your hosted solutions.

## Server checks and logs

As a standard part of its operation, FileMaker Server 9 provides automatic logging and optional e-mail notifications for a variety of events and potential problems. This includes commencement and conclusion of client sessions (remote connections, not user account logins), automated backups, and consistency checks.

The availability of server event and error logs is an important additional step toward ensuring the health and security of your solution, giving you insight into its use as well as alerting you to problems and issues arising as your solution is accessed.

In addition to its performance capabilities, the added safeguards and security of FileMaker Server represent a significant benefit over peer-to-peer hosting options (for example, hosting files with FileMaker Pro). Of course, the increased expense of a dedicated server and the FileMaker Pro Server license is an element in your security cost-benefit analysis.

> **NOTE** Remember that the added safeguards require some experienced and trusted user or IT professional's time to administer the server and software, as well.

# Chapter 15

# Maintaining Referential Integrity

Referential integrity, an essential concept, lies at the very heart of relational database development. Ideally, the end users of your solutions take referential integrity for granted — and you, as developer, place it before many other considerations. We think it's important enough to devote an entire chapter to the topic because we know that without referential integrity, all your beautifully built solutions will crumble and come to nothing.

## Pinpointing Common Causes of Referential Integrity Problems

Referential integrity has many dimensions, the problem of orphaned records foremost among them. Consider, for a moment, an invoicing system where you have an invoice table and a line items table storing the items for each invoice; however, an invoice has been deleted without the corresponding line item records being deleted. Now, when you perform a search, you get a different result searching in the Invoices table than when you search in the Line Items table. The difference arises because the deleted invoice's items remain in the Line Items table, so they appear there, but no related record exists in the Invoices table, so they don't appear when you search there.

When you get different results searching in different places, you no longer know what is correct, and you have a lot of work to do to determine the

### IN THIS CHAPTER

Surveying threats to referential integrity

Understanding the importance of relational keys

Working with keys and data types

Bringing data into line with optimal relational design

Automating the removal of redundant data

Considering data integrity in wider contexts

Managing a solution's data dependencies

discrepancy's cause. This example is one of several common problems affecting referential integrity. Three of the most common causes of referential integrity problems are

- Deleting records without deleting related or dependent records or values
- Modifying key field values without modifying the corresponding foreign key values in related tables, so match field values no longer match
- Non-unique (duplicate) primary key values

## The potential impact on your solution

On rare occasions, these problems may go undetected, and the consequences may be minimal. However, even a single instance of one of these problems means that your data is no longer in sync — the data in one table no longer agrees and fully conforms with data elsewhere in your solution. Such issues can rapidly erode confidence in a solution and may have profoundly negative consequences when business decisions are based on compromised data.

If your data ever falls out of sync, you'll understand why we say that prevention is better than cure. Vetting and correcting anomalies in a large data set can be an enormously time-consuming task.

## Costs and benefits

You have a great deal to gain from using relational data structures in your solutions. Key information is stored once and is instantly available elsewhere — wherever it is needed. An update in one part of the system is propagated instantly throughout the solution. These significant benefits depend on taking the time to understand and implement robust and reliable links throughout your solution, to support its relational data architecture.

In Chapters 7 and 11, we address many of the concepts that underpin the design and implementation of relational structures in FileMaker Pro. Although we comment on some relational integrity issues in those chapters, we do not spell out exactly why it matters or how best to avoid the potential pitfalls when working with complex data interdependencies. Several strategies are essential to successful management of complex related data sets, as outlined in the following sections.

# Using Unique Keys

Should the keys for a relationship in your solution be edited, deleted, or duplicated, relationships depending on them will break. Re-establishing relationship connections after such a mishap is, at best, an unenviable task. A first checkpoint when assessing the relational integrity of your solution is, therefore, the appropriateness of selected keys and methods of handling them.

Consider using ways to generate key values automatically (for example using auto-enter serial numbers, calculations, or scripts) to ensure their integrity. On occasions when keys are not generated automatically, you need to implement some safeguards to ensure the key values are appropriate, as described in the following section.

# Maintaining Referential Integrity  15

## Key safeguards

The validation options in FileMaker let you require that a field has a value ("Not empty") and that it is unique, as shown in Figure 15.1. If your solution requires user entry of primary key values, such as when records originate within another system, using both these validation checks can help minimize errors.

**FIGURE 15.1**

Setting Unique, Not Empty validation for a PrimaryID field.

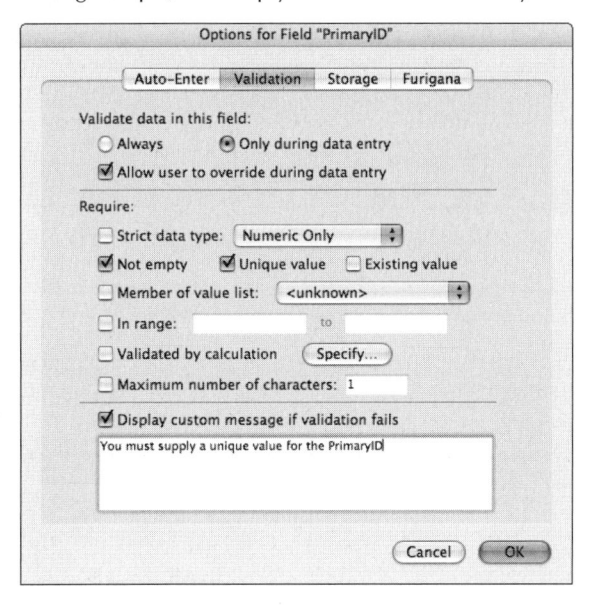

**CAUTION** Any situation where users directly enter or edit key values is risky, even if you have existence and uniqueness validations in place, because any unique value will be accepted and then used for relationship matching (and the creation of related records). Any errors the user subsequently corrects will post a risk for relational joins involving the record in question.

Few values originating outside your solution can be relied upon to be unique — or to exist for all cases. Even purportedly unique values, such as a Social Security Number (SSN), have been known to be duplicated on occasion — and you can't assume that they will always be available. Input data types that can be relied upon as suitable for use as a key value in all cases are the exception rather than the rule.

531

## Keys and meaning (existence, persistence, uniqueness)

Relational keys should be unique, persistent, and non-empty, and these requirements are frequently best met by assigning special values for the purpose. There is no absolute rule about this. Classical relational theory proposes that key values be derived from data, if suitable. However, if you do so, you introduce risks and should proceed carefully. In general, we counsel against using keys based on or derived from data, as data is subject to data-entry errors, the correction of which may compromise the persistence of key values. Instead, we recommend that your key values be generated automatically (via auto-entry options) and protected by selecting the Prohibit Modification of Value During Data Entry option in the Auto-Enter tab of the Options for Field dialog.

One case where key values are frequently legitimately derived from data is within the context of an association table (also known as a join table), it the primary key is commonly formed from the conjoining of two or more foreign keys. This is an example of a situation where the data provides a basis for suitable keys.

In situations where an ID value, such as an SSN, bank account number, or vehicle registration number, is required to be entered, you can also generate a separate unique value to use as the record's primary key. When you do so, even if the entered value changes (or is entered inaccurately and subsequently corrected), referential integrity is maintained.

> **NOTE** For most purposes, you don't need to display key values to the user; in fact, doing so may complicate matters needlessly. However, where you can't rely on any of the data values to be unique, a serial number or other unique value can be useful to users.

In a student database, for example, where several students are named Peter John Smith, a student ID may be a convenient way for users to identify to which Peter Smith a given piece of information refers.

# Generating Keys

A majority of database solutions are designed to operate as single or separate instances — in other words, only one copy of the solution is deployed at a time. Or, if there are multiples, data from them will never be combined. In most cases an efficient way to generate suitable key values is to produce record serial numbers in each table. The auto-entry serial option is an ideal way to address this need. Even so, it has several possible variations, described in the following sections.

## Serial numbers

The option to auto-enter serial numbers is the cleanest and simplest way to generate key values for single-instance solutions. Although the concept and name suggest that values created via this mechanism will be numeric, you can store the values in either text or number fields. If the values are stored as text, they may include alphabetic prefixes. For example, as shown in Figure 15.2, you can configure serial values to include leading zeros or other characters.

## Maintaining Referential Integrity    15

FileMaker also provides you with the option to have serial values assigned either on creation of a new record or when the record is first committed. You can use the radio buttons shown in Figure 15.2 to specify which option you want. In situations where consecutive serial numbers are desired, using the On Commit option avoids serial number incrementation in a case where users change their mind and revert the new record. In this situation, however, be aware that relationships or other operations depending on the presence of the serial value will not be available until after the record is committed.

To assist you in managing serial numbers, FileMaker provides the `GetNextSerialValue( )` and `SerialIncrement( )` calculation functions and the `Set Next Serial Value[ ]` script command. Thus, in a script designed to import records into your solution, you can sort the records and reset the serial number for the table so that serial numbers assigned to subsequently created records will not overlap those among the imported data. For example, you can structure the relevant portion of such a script along the following lines:

```
Import Records [No dialog; "OldFile.fp7"; Add; Windows ANSI]
#Re-set next serial value:
Show All Records
Sort Records [Restore; No dialog]
Go to Record/Request/Page [Last]
Set Next Serial Value [Data::Serial#; SerialIncrement(Data::Serial#; 1)]
Unsort Records
```

**FIGURE 15.2**

Defining an alphanumeric serial value with an alphabetic prefix.

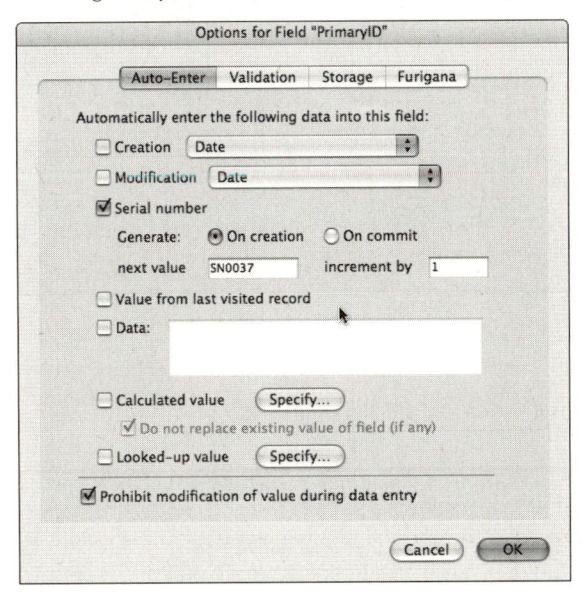

533

**Part IV** Integrity and Security

> **NOTE** This script sequence's correct operation requires that the `Sort Records[ ]` command be configured to sort the records in ascending order by the `Data::Serial#` field and on the data type and content of the `Data::Serial#` field.

Additionally, FileMaker can reassign serial numbers to a field, at the same time resetting the auto-entry options to follow sequentially from the last assigned number, using the Records ⇨ Replace Field Contents menu command or the corresponding script or button commands. As shown in Figure 15.3, if the selected field is defined to auto-enter a serial number, the procedure can simultaneously update the serial number (the next value) in Entry Options.

> **CAUTION** Replacing a key field's contents will compromise any relationships already depending on existing key field values. You can't revert or undo changes made using this command.

You should also avoid using a Replace Field Contents procedure while your solution is hosted because locked records, if any, are skipped. In the case of serialization, skipping locked records can lead to duplications, where the skipped records may hold the same value as some of the values assigned elsewhere during the process.

If the Prohibit Modification Of Value During Data Entry option is in force for the selected field, the Replace Field Contents menu command isn't available. However, scripts or buttons calling the corresponding command can still succeed. Therefore, you should consider the implications for relational integrity and the potential for error (especially if the solution is hosted) before using this procedure on a primary key field.

**FIGURE 15.3**

Generating a new serial number sequence and resetting the next serial value in auto-entry options via the Replace Field Contents dialog.

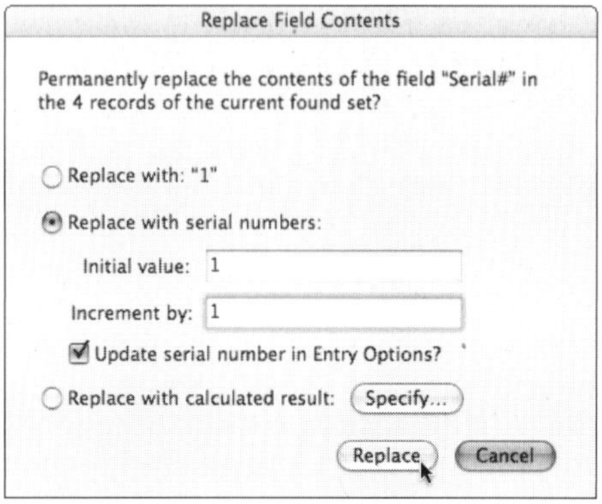

## Record IDs

In addition to serial numbers, FileMaker assigns a sequential record ID to each record in every instance of a file. Record IDs are a numeric value starting from 1 in each table. You can retrieve this internal value for the current record by using the `Get(RecordID) calculation function`.

## Maintaining Referential Integrity

Although the record ID value is useful in some circumstances, it isn't well suited as a key value's sole basis because

- The record ID sequence is particular to a specific copy of the file. If records are imported into another copy of the file, they will be assigned new record IDs in the receiving file.
- All record IDs are reset (and therefore commence again from 1) when a file is cloned.

For these reasons, if you use record IDs as keys you can't prevent the assignment of duplicate values in all situations. However, it has the advantage of not being vulnerable to being reset inappropriately (for example, via the Replace Field Contents command) or not being reset when it should, such as when records are imported. It can, however, contribute to a solution in cases where records will be combined from multiple files into a single set (and where it is desirable to avoid key field duplications in the combined record set).

## Unique identification (UID) values

The concept of a universally unique ID value, commonly known as a UID, is known and used in a variety of computing contexts; however, FileMaker does not support it directly. This kind of value is called for in distributed solutions where multiple sets of new records will be created separately and later combined (and where it is essential to avoid duplication of ID values when the record sets are merged or synchronized).

One way to meet this requirement is by allocating reserved serial ranges, where each instance of the solution files assigns IDs within its own separate range. Whereas the allocation of reserved ranges is feasible in limited cases, it requires careful management, and its success depends on accurately configuring every instance for an appropriate range. As a result, the scope for error becomes greater if more than a few instances of the solution are in operation.

In cases where you can't reliably predict the number of copies of the database that will be in use, or where managing the assignment of serial ranges is difficult, one solution is to assemble a unique identifier. You do this by combining the identity of the current computer, the assigned ID of the current record, and the timestamp of the second when the record is created. FileMaker provides the means to assemble a UID in several ways:

- You can determine the identity of the computer by retrieving its unique network address — the ID of the hardware Network Interface Card (NIC) installed in the computer — using the Get(SystemNICAddress) function. Because a computer may be equipped with more than one network interface device, you can obtain a sufficient identifying value by retrieving the address of the first available device, using the calculation expression

    `GetValue(Get(SystemNICAddress); 1)`

- You can access the sequential number of the current record within the current copy of the file via the Get(RecordID) function.

- You can generate the current time (in the form of a number representing the seconds elapsed since midnight on 1st January 0001) using the calculation expression

    `GetAsNumber(Get(CurrentHostTimestamp))`

535

By concatenating the three values — NIC address, record ID, and timestamp — you can produce a key value that will be unique regardless of the circumstances of its creation. The chief drawback of this approach is that the resulting string will be lengthy. We recommend ameliorating this concern by converting the values first to base 10 (the NIC address is supplied as a hexadecimal value) and then to base 36 for compactness. Using this approach, a record created with the record ID 123,456,789 on a computer with an NIC address of 00:14:51:65:4d:6a and generated at 5:47:37 pm on October 21st 2007 is allocated the UID NI1PM Z3J50 JG9ZH 6HI2H.

The base conversions required to transmute the source data into the compact base36 format require some mathematical manipulation of the original values that is best performed via a custom function.

**CROSS-REF** An example of a custom function you can use to create UIDs along these lines is included among the materials referenced in Appendix C.

# Exploring Keys and Data Type

Because serial numbers and record IDs may be numeric, defining ID fields as number fields is tempting. However, you'll frequently have occasion to use multi-key relationship capabilities (for example to filter a portal or to use the `Go to Related Record[ ]` command to isolate a group of records in a found set). In a multi-key relationship, multiple values in a key field are simultaneously matched to values in the related table. If you have used number fields as the key fields in either table, however, matching won't work as desired because number fields aren't designed to hold multiple values. You must use text fields to take advantage of multi-keyed relations. For maximum flexibility, we recommend using text fields as keys.

Using text fields as keys presents a different kind of problem. If you have conventional numeric sequences stored as text, they will not be sorted appropriately — for example, 3 will be sorted after 12. You can address this problem in two ways:

- Pad the numbers with leading zeros so that they're all the same length. They then will sort correctly in a text field.
- Use a number field to generate the serial values (and for sorting) but use a text calculation referencing the number field as the key field.

For maximum flexibility, we suggest that you consider using both these strategies simultaneously. You then have both a numeric and text field you can use for relationships, for sorting, and for other purposes, as appropriate.

An added benefit of using text values as relational keys is that you can prefix them with one or more letters identifying their table of origin. For example, INV0001 is recognizable as an invoice number and ORD0001 as an order number. Although this classification may be of little consequence in the table of origin, when data containing a primary key and several foreign key values is exported or imported, the prefixes greatly reduce the likelihood that the keys will be imported into the wrong fields (or, if they are, the problem will be considerably easier to detect and correct).

## Maintaining Referential Integrity — 15

Consider, for example, an import procedure where the import mapping dialog presents you with the following:

| Source Fields | | Target Fields |
|---|---|---|
| 21 Jan 2008 | → | TransactionDate |
| 1217 | → | ReceiptID |
| 1921 | → | ClientID |
| 921 | → | AccountID |
| 3119 | → | InvoiceID |
| 2174 | → | StaffID |
| 3550 | → | Amount |

In this example, importing a data set from a delimited file is error prone, because the source values other than the transaction date are not differentiated. If, however, text key values are used with the appropriate prefixes, you can more readily see that the correct import order in this case is as follows:

| Source Fields | | Target Fields |
|---|---|---|
| 21 Jan 2008 | → | TransactionDate |
| 1217 | → | Amount |
| R00001921 | → | ReceiptID |
| CL00921 | → | ClientID |
| AC03119 | → | AccountID |
| ST02174 | → | StaffID |
| INV003550 | → | InvoiceID |

Whereas the use of redundant (text and numeric) serials and padded keys adds slightly to the amount of data your solution must store, the improved flexibility, reliability, and diagnostic transparency offered usually outweighs the penalty.

**NOTE** The ID fields throughout the inventory example file created in previous chapters of this book provide an example of a structure incorporating a numeric serial and a prefixed text ID value, along the lines we recommend.

## Retrofitting Keys

When you encounter a situation where the key fields in use are unsuitable and their format is presenting a threat to referential integrity, you may need to retroactively add key fields to existing tables. For example, suppose that you have inherited a solution where the client table's `LastName` field has been used as a key field to associate invoices with clients, but it's come to your attention that two more families named Johnson have moved into the neighborhood and will soon be added to the clients table along with the Johnson client you already have.

537

## Part IV   Integrity and Security

Rather than loading the new clients as Johnson2 and Johnson3 — a kludge at best — you can correct the structure by adding appropriate key fields to the solution and reconstructing the relationship between Clients and Invoices tables to use them. To retrofit appropriate keys to the solution in this example, proceed as follows:

1. Take the database offline if it is hosted. You can't make a change such as this one reliably while other users are accessing the solution.
2. Create a text field called `ClientID` in the Clients table. In field options, configure the ClientID field to auto-enter a serial number.
3. Place the `Clients::ClientID` field on a layout based on the Clients TO.
4. In Browse mode, choose Records ➪ Show All Records.
5. Place the cursor into the `ClientID` field and choose Records ➪ Replace Field Contents. The Replace Field Contents dialog appears.
6. Select the Replace with Serial Numbers option, enter **CL00001** in the Initial Value field and **1** in the Increment By field, and then click the Replace button.
7. Choose File ➪ Manage ➪ Database, navigate to the Clients table on the Fields tab, and double-click the ClientID field. In the Auto-Enter tab of the Options for Field dialog, select the Prohibit Modification of Value During Data Entry option and click OK to accept the change.
8. Select the Invoices table on the Fields tab of the Manage Database dialog and create a text field called `ClientID`. Click OK to close the Manage Database dialog.
9. Navigate to a layout based on the Invoices TO and add the `Invoices::ClientID` field to the layout.
10. In Browse mode, still on the Invoices layout, choose Records ➪ Show All Records.
11. Place the cursor in the `Invoices::ClientID` field and choose Records ➪ Replace Field Contents. The Replace Field Contents dialog appears.
12. Select the Replace with Calculated Result option; in the resulting Specify Calculation dialog, enter `Clients::ClientID`.
13. Choose File ➪ Manage ➪ Database, navigate to the Relationships tab, and double-click the box bisecting the relationship line connecting the Clients and Invoices TOs. The Edit Relationship dialog appears.
14. Select the `ClientID` field in the Clients TO's field list, select the `ClientID` field in the Invoices TO's field list, and click the button labeled Change in the middle right of the dialog.
15. Click OK to dismiss the Edit Relationship dialog and again to dismiss the Manage Database dialog.
16. Choose File ➪ Manage ➪ Value Lists. If an existing value list of clients was used to select a related client for each invoice, select it and click Edit; otherwise, click New.
17. Configure the value list to use values from a field, choosing the `Clients::ClientID` field as the first field. Select the Also Display Values from the Second Field option, and

then choose the `Clients::LastName` field in the second field list. Click the OK button to save the value list and then dismiss the Manage Value List dialog.

18. In Layout mode on the Invoices layout, configure the `Invoices::ClientID` field to use the Clients value list (the one edited or created in Step 17) and position the field in place of the `ClientName` field previously used as the key field.

After completing these steps, your solution is updated to use the new `ClientID` field as the basis of the relationship between Clients and Invoices. After testing the solution to confirm that the update has been successful (and assuming that no relationships, calculations, or scripts depend on it), you can delete the `Invoices::Client` field and instead use a related field (`Clients::LastName`) to display the name of the client on the Invoice.

If other relationships depend on the `Clients::LastName` field, you should repeat the process from Step 8 onward to update each of the related tables to include `ClientID` as a foreign key field. Once the change is complete, the relationship architecture of the solution is significantly improved.

# Deleting Redundant Records

The usefulness of your data is proportional to its accuracy. The harvest from a garden of weeds is not sustaining. As well as taking the trouble to add the data you need, you must take the time to excise erroneous, obsolete, irrelevant, or duplicated data. If you don't, you can't rely on the results of any find, calculation, or report as encompassing only current or accurate content.

In a relational database, data is distributed among tables according to its type. Data about cars is in the Vehicles table, and data about their owners is in the People table. To ensure that your database does not become a repository for accumulations of redundant and obsolete information — not merely a dead weight but a compromise of data integrity — you should configure your solution to manage group deletion of related records, wherever appropriate.

## The use of cascading deletion

To assist you in maintaining referential integrity, FileMaker provides an option to automatically delete related records when deleting a record in any table in your solution. You can enable this option by accessing the Edit Relationship dialog for the join between the two table occurrences in question and selecting the checkbox option labeled Delete Related Records In This Table When A Record Is Deleted In The Other Table. This capability is commonly known as *cascading deletion* because it can be configured for a series of relationships such that deletion of a record in one table can result in follow-on deletion of records in a number of related tables.

Figure 15.4 shows the Edit Relationship dialog for the join between the Orders and OrderLines TOs in the current chapter's Inventory example. As you can see, the Delete Related Records option is enabled on the OrderLines side of the relationship; if an Order is deleted, the associated item records will automatically also be deleted.

The cascading deletion option imposes an essential referential integrity constraint ensuring that the dependency between associated entities is preserved. Without it, the integrity of your data will be compromised.

**FIGURE 15.4**

Enabling cascading deletion for the Orders-to-OrderLines relationship.

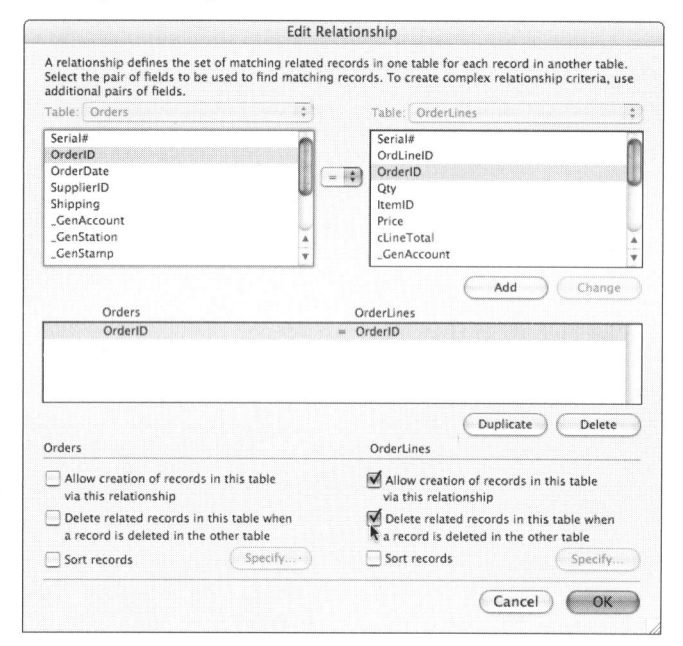

## Configuring relationships for referential integrity

When setting up your data model, take care to enable cascading deletion only where an entity's existence is fully contingent on the associated "parent" entity. Moreover, consider the flow-on effects of cascading deletion, lest their scope exceed your intent. To avoid unintentional consequences of the use of integrity constraints, we recommend

- No more than one TO for each base table be configured with the Delete Related Records option
- The TO targeted by the Delete Related Records option be named to match the underlying table
- The Delete Related Records option be enabled only in the file where the corresponding base table is defined

In addition (and especially should you have occasion to depart from any of these recommendations), you may want to consider making a separate record or annotation regarding the cascading deletion configuration in each file. A text note on the Relationships tab of the Manage Database dialog in the data file is often appropriate.

**CAUTION** Although FileMaker permits you to activate the Delete Related Records option on both sides of a relationship, it's generally not appropriate to do so. In fact, activating this option, depending on the nature of the relationships and data, may set up a ricochet effect as deletion calls pass back and forth between the two tables, with the result that deleting a single record in one table may decimate the contents of both tables.

## Privilege requirements for cascade delete

Users must have sufficient privileges to delete all the dependent records in order to be able to delete a record in the current table when referential integrity constraints (via cascading deletion) are configured. For example, if the user is viewing a record from table A and a constraint has been applied that requires that records in table B be deleted if a record is deleted in table A, the user will be able to delete the current record in table A only if

- The Privilege Set assigned to the user's login account permits deletion of records in both table A and table B.
- No records in table B relate to the current record in table A (and the user's privileges allow deletion of records in table A).

In the event that there are records in table B and the user's account doesn't include privileges to delete records in the related table, deletion of the current record in table A will fail, and FileMaker will post an error dialog, as shown in Figure 15.5.

**FIGURE 15.5**

FileMaker posts an error if the user doesn't have sufficient privileges for cascading deletion to occur, even if the user's privileges permit deletion of records in the current table.

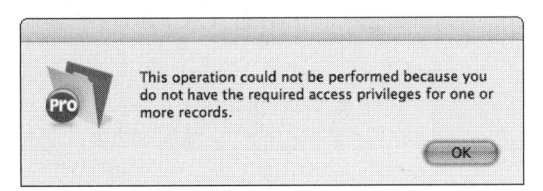

If the deletion command is issued via script with error capture enabled, no error dialog will appear, but the deletion will nevertheless fail, and FileMaker will return error code 200 (defined as Record Access Is Denied).

**TIP** If record deletion is undertaken by script and you enable the Run Script With Full Access Privileges option, the deletion will succeed regardless of the privileges assigned to the current user's account, and all cascading deletions will succeed.

## Controlled cascading deletes at runtime

Configuring your files to delete records automatically can save your users a lot of work and/or a lot of headaches when configured appropriately. However, in some situations, cascading deletes may result in problems. For example, if your solution requires that data in one of the tables be refreshed from an external source, such as via selective deletion and re-import of updated records from a reference file, the presence of cascading deletes may interfere with the desired process, requiring that related record sets also be refreshed/imported (because they'll be deleted as a result of referential integrity constraints, when the parent records are deleted).

You can respond to such a requirement so that cascading deletion does not prevent you from delivering the required functionality in several ways:

- Avoid the necessity to delete and re-import parent records by restructuring the process around synchronization or conditional update of the existing records. In some cases, you can do so by using the Update Existing import option. In others, it may warrant importing the reference data into a holding area, such as a utility table, and provide a scripted reconciliation process.

- Script the process to delete the values from the primary key fields in the parent table (the key field used for the relationship defined to delete related records) before deleting the parent records. Alternatively, if this step introduces an unacceptable delay to the procedure, set up the cascading delete to operate via a secondary (utility) relationship where the parent key is an unstored calculation depending on a global field. For example, use a calculation formula for the key field along the lines of:

    ```
    If(ParentTable::gRI_Switch = 1; ParentTable::PrimaryID)
    ```

    Clearing the `gRI_Switch` global field can disable the relationships depending on the unstored calculation throughout the table at a single stroke; you can re-enable them by setting a 1 into the global field. With this mechanism in place, your scripts can turn cascading delete functionality on and off by controlling the value in the `gRI_Switch` field.

- Build a separate file containing a reference to your solution data file(s) and build a graph in the separate file containing your referential integrity constraints, such as all Delete Related Records options. Then script your solution to open the file (as in open hidden) when you require the constraints and close it when you want to switch off the constraints.

    We recommend this last technique for cases in which cascading deletion will not be part of normal operation but is to be invoked for specific procedures.

By using these techniques (and other variations and permutations), you can control your solution's functionality, ensuring that cascading deletion serves its intended purpose, yet avoiding circumstances where it interferes with the required functionality.

# Considering Other Integrity Issues

One essential of efficient data management is a solution designed to store each piece of information only once — displaying it whenever and wherever it's needed. The fact that you can update the data once and expect the change to flow throughout your solution is an efficiency advantage. However, the integrity advantages are greater still.

When you store the same information twice, you risk that one instance will be edited so that it no longer agrees with others, and then you no longer know which instance is the correct one. Any time you duplicate data, you're compromising solution integrity as well as solution efficiency.

## Lookups and when to use them

FileMaker supports auto-entry lookups where a field is set to automatically copy the contents of a related field. The `OrderLines::Price` field in the Inventory example demonstrates the use of this functionality, as shown in Figure 15.6.

**FIGURE 15.6**

The use of a data lookup for the `OrderLines::Price` field.

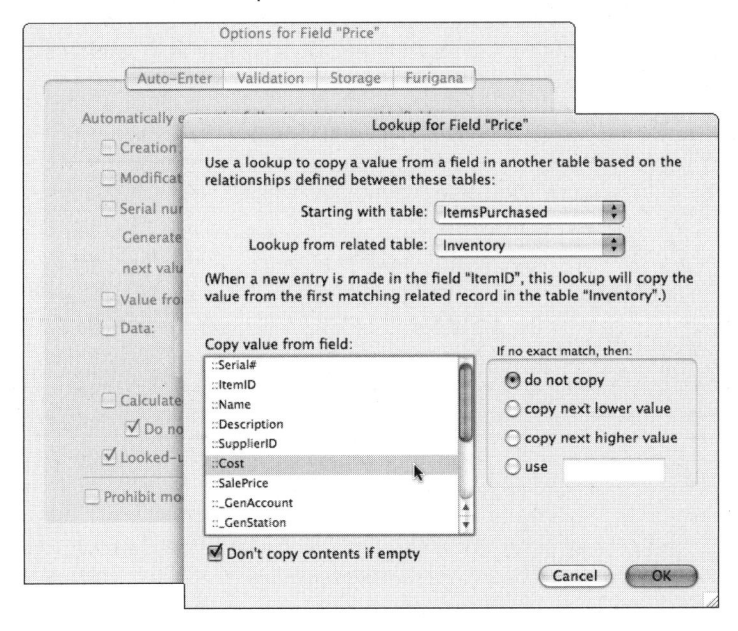

When is it appropriate to use a lookup, and when is it preferable to reference the data in place in its source table? The straightforward answer is that Data should be referenced in place if its meaning is undifferentiated.

## Auto-entry lookups and references

In the case of the price field discussed in the preceding example, the Inventory table's cost field represents the current purchase price of the item. When the item is ordered, the price against the individual order line takes on a different meaning because it represents the price at the date of the order. If a price change occurs in the future, the price in the `Inventory::Cost` field may change, but the change won't apply automatically to the history of previous orders. Only subsequent orders will be affected. Moreover, a discount or bulk order price may be negotiated for a specific purchase, but it will not be reflected in the list price for the item. Thus, the ongoing reference price is a different piece of information from the specific price for any one instance of a purchase of the item, so it makes sense to store each instance independently. They may in fact all be different.

By contrast, you can't expect other details about an item to change or differ from one transaction to another. The name of an item and its description are immutable facts about the item. If you were to set lookups to create copies of each of these item attributes for every order, referential integrity and solution efficiency would be compromised by data duplication.

## Data design issues

The principle of making data storage decisions according to differentiation of meaning is broadly applicable to a range of design decisions you make when determining your solution's data model. In addition to lookups, it applies to auto-entry calculations, relationships, and even regular calculations. Unless an element has a distinct role and meaning, it is redundant and should not be included in your solution's data model.

Throughout your solution, avoid duplicating data, structure, and code. This general maxim is part of a larger framework considered part of the DRY (Don't Repeat Yourself) programming principle.

**CROSS-REF** Issues relating to the elimination of redundancy and the application of the DRY principle are discussed in depth in Chapter 19.

# Managing Dependencies

The handling of data about the design elements of your solution (fields, tables, scripts, layouts, and so on) in FileMaker operates in a framework where, when you change an element's name, the new name is reflected in all references to the element throughout your solution. For example, if you rename a field referenced in scripts and calculations, the next time you open the calculation to review its definition, or open the script in the Edit Script window, you see the updated name.

## Maintaining Referential Integrity

FileMaker uses internal IDs to track references to solution elements, looking up their current names as required. The process is analogous to your use of relational data structures to store your data only once (yet make it available throughout multiple contexts).

### Literal text references

A notable exception to automatic handling and updating references to solution elements in FileMaker arises when you incorporate references to elements as literal text within your calculations. For example, if you supply a layout name by calculation when defining a Go to Layout [ ] script or button command, FileMaker does not change the literal text values (the text within the quotes) if the names of your layouts are subsequently changed:

```
Go to Layout [If(User::Preference = "Tips"; "Instructions"; "Report Listing")]
```

Where you've used literal references to layouts, files, fields, scripts, layout objects, or any other elements of your solution, you must keep track of them and update them manually if you change the name of the object to which they refer.

### Indirect object/element references

Given that FileMaker doesn't automatically update literal text references to elements and objects for you, you may prefer to minimize your use of them. However, including literal references in your code is occasionally advantageous because doing so enables you to construct dynamic code referring to different elements according to the current context. Thus, you have a trade-off between richer and more flexible code and maintenance convenience.

Ironically, you can produce compact and reusable code by incorporating calculated references to solution elements and objects. Literal references to objects by name, like those used in the Go to Layout example shown in the preceding section, are easier to troubleshoot and maintain in most other respects (in particular, because the technique allows you to greatly reduce repetition and duplication in your code). You must strike a balance.

### Filename references

One area in which the use of literal references can compromise referential integrity is in the use of the FileMaker Design functions, many of which require you to supply the name of the file containing the required information. For example, you can retrieve the contents of a value list using the following function syntax:

```
ValueListItems ( FileName; ValueListName )
```

You can supply both parameters required by the ValueListItems() function as text literals, so the resulting expression may be incorporated into your solution along the lines of

```
ValueListItems ( "Inventory.fp7"; "Suppliers" )
```

Declaring calculation arguments as text literals, as in this example, is high maintenance because if the filename or value list name ever changes, you will have to manually edit the names in quotation marks to restore the intended functionality. You can solve this problem in several ways. In relation to the filename:

- When the reference is to the current file, you can structure your syntax to retrieve the name of the file using the `Get(FileName)` function. This function continues to work without any adjustment in the event the file is renamed.

- In a multi-file solution, including a reference table containing details such as the names of the solution files may be advantageous. If all functions referring to a particular file reference its name in the relevant data field (rather than as a text literal), you only have to update the file's name in the reference table if it changes, rather than separately locating and updating each function referring to it.

**CROSS-REF** A method of making references to field, layout, value list, script, and table occurrence names impervious to name changes (referring to them by their internal ID rather than by their current name) is detailed in Chapter 12.

## Structural anomalies

On occasions when you have included literal text references to an object or element (or where others may have done so) and you need to change that object's (or element's) name, you'll need a reliable way of locating the literal references so that you can update them.

One option is to select all tables (in the Manage Database dialog's Tables tab) and all scripts (in the Manage Scripts window) and print them, sending the output not to a printer but to a PDF or text file. Then you can search the file for the text string to locate all occurrences of text references to the object or element you are renaming.

**CROSS-REF** Third-party diagnostic tools (such as BaseElements from Goya or Inspector from FM::Nexus) in conjunction with FileMaker Pro Advanced, can also provide invaluable help when tracing dependencies. For additional details about the uses of FileMaker Pro Advanced with these and other third-party diagnostic tools, refer to Chapters 18 and 19.

# Chapter 16

# Making FileMaker Systems Fail-Safe

## IN THIS CHAPTER

Being prepared for problems

Taking care of error trapping

Opening databases remotely

Working with temporary edit interfaces

Screening errors with masks and filters

Building audit trails and script logs

Offering undo and roll-back functionality

Considering logging alternatives

---

Database solutions serve many purposes, including supporting essential, even critical processes. Whether the consequences of data errors or problems are dire — or merely inconvenient — designing your solutions to be as robust as possible is beneficial. In many cases, additional cost or effort to make your solution resistant to failure and improve the ability to recover from a variety of errors is more than justified.

Fortunately, there are many steps you can take to safeguard your solution's data, improve user accountability, avert mishap, and recover from calamity. In the following pages, we gather together a number of techniques and options you can use to strengthen your solution's defenses against a variety of potential hazards.

## Expecting the Unexpected

Systems fail for any number of reasons — usually, they're the reasons you didn't consider, because otherwise you'd have taken preventive measures. The circumstances that cause your system most harm, therefore, will be the problems you didn't anticipate.

Although you can't anticipate every possible error or mishap, you can be confident that sooner or later something will crop up. Luckily, you can take steps to ensure that when a difficulty arises, you have some options available to minimize its impact and recover with a minimum of fuss.

# Successful backup strategies

Foremost among survival strategies for any computer system—and especially any database solution—is a backup regime. A reliable backup routine can get you out of trouble almost regardless of the cause. Accidentally deleted records, power failure, disk corruption, bugs in your code—all these things can be alleviated if you have previous copies of your database to which you can revert.

Several questions arise when you're considering your approach to solution backup, and the way you resolve them determines your backup strategy's viability. The key questions are:

- How often should you back up?
- How long should you retain each backup?
- How will you be sure that your backup copies are sound?
- How and where should your backups be stored?
- Which components of your solution should you back up?

## Backup frequency

Backing up too infrequently reduces protection against mishap and leaves you exposed to the possibility of greater loss of data. In the event of a catastrophic system failure, you may lose all the data entered or edited since the last backup. If you backed up less than an hour ago, you are therefore in a much better position than if your last backup was a week or a month ago.

Frequent backups, however, consume time and resources. If your solution is large, they may begin to impact the solution's performance. Often, the ideal backup regimen is one that sets the frequency of backups just below the level where their impact on performance would begin to affect productivity. The level that adversely affects productivity varies depending on the size of you system, the deployment configuration and the number of users. However, you should aim to avoid any significant slowing or interruption or work due to backup cycles (if sufficiently frequent backups present a performance problem, consider upgrading server hardware).

You also need to consider the relative costs of data loss. If the labor costs of repeating a day's work are significant, then you should consider running backups more frequently than once a day. Determine how much time and data you (and your solution's owners and users) can afford to lose.

## An appropriate backup cycle

If you overwrite each backup with the next one, at any point you only have one backup copy. This situation is risky for several reasons, including the possibility that an error or problem may not be immediately detected. If several hundred records were erroneously deleted some time in the last week, but you are only keeping backups from the last day or hour, backups will not enable you to recover the lost data.

If storage capacity is limited, we recommend that you keep backups for two weeks. However, in any situation in which the preservation of data is critical, consider archiving backups to cheap long-term storage media ( such as DVD-ROM).

# Making FileMaker Systems Fail-Safe

As part of your short-term backup strategy, we recommend setting up an external process. For example, you might consider deploying a third-party back up application or operating system script (AppleScript or VBScript or Shell script) to transfer the backup files to a remote volume (for example, a network share or ftp directory) after the creation of each backup file set is completed.

### The integrity of backups

All too frequently, it is not until *after* a system failure — when they attempt to restore from a backup — that people discover that all their backups are empty, corrupt, or otherwise useless. Backup failure can occur for a variety of reasons, including simple hardware failures (such as write errors) on the media where the backups are being stored.

To be certain, therefore, you need a procedure in place that confirms the integrity of the backup files. If your solution is hosted using FileMaker Server 9, you can configure it to perform both the scheduled backups and their verification automatically. Otherwise, you will need a manual process to regularly verify that backup copies of your files are accessible and usable. In fact, even where Server verification is enabled, periodic manual checks are good practice, helping to place focus on the restore process, which is where backup strategies most frequently fail.

### The location of backups

It may seem obvious, but if your backups are stored on the same disk drive (and on the same workstation) that the solution itself resides on, failure of that drive will cause your backups to be lost — along with the deployed copy of your solution.

Ideally, your backups should be stored not just on a different system, but at a different location. In the event of a fire, flood, earthquake, or other physical calamity, multiple computers in the same room, building or wider area may be affected simultaneously. Ideally, you should store frequent copies of backups at a secure remote location, such as on an ftp server accessed over the Internet.

### Back up the code, not just the data

Keep in mind that the investment in your solution's structure, logic, and interface may be at least as valuable as the data it contains. Thus, you should back up not only while your solution is deployed, but also while it is under development. We recommend that you keep a pristine (never deployed, never improperly closed) reference copy of your solution from each stage of its development. In the event your file's code or structure is compromised, the existence of a reference master will prove invaluable.

## The hazards of copying open files

Some ways to create backup files are right — and some are wrong.. One of the most risky actions you can take is to use external applications (third-party backup utilities or your computer's operating system) to make copies of your solution files while they are in use.

**CAUTION** Copying database files while they are being accessed by users can result in corruption, not only of the copies but also of the original files. Avoid doing this under any circumstance.

## Part IV  Integrity and Security

Copying database files while they're open is a bad idea for two reasons:

- FileMaker (and FileMaker Server) read substantial amounts of an open file into cache, maintaining the data there, writing parts of it back to disk only when necessary or during idle time. Therefore, the valid structure and content of the file is an amalgam of what is on disk and what is in memory — with neither, alone, representing a valid or complete file. If you attempt to copy the file while it is in this state, you are at best copying only the disk component of the file, which will be neither current nor complete.

- FileMaker (and FileMaker Server) requires exclusive access to a file it is hosting so that data can be read and written with maximum efficiency and integrity. External applications copying files frequently place successive locks on sectors of the disk while reading data from them. If FileMaker needs to flush data from its cache while part of the current file is locked by a third-party application, the consequences can include data loss and/or file corruption.

Of similar concern are ancillary programs, such as indexing and anti-virus applications, which may interfere with the connection between FileMaker Server and the files it is hosting. Any external process that accesses database files while they're being hosted presents a threat to file integrity.

> **TIP** Always use FileMaker or FileMaker Server to create a separate backup copy of open files. Only use the operating system or third-party procedures to subsequently copy the backup files, not the deployed files. This way you can securely transfer copies of the backup files to remote storage locations.

## Backing up local files

If you are hosting a solution using FileMaker Pro, or FileMaker Pro Advanced (rather than FileMaker Server), you must create backups by using the File ➪ Save a Copy As command, or by closing the solution files and then using your computer's operating system (or a third-party application) to make copies.

You can, however, simplify the process of making solution backups in a stand-alone solution (or a solution hosted using FileMaker Pro) by creating a script along the following lines:

```
If [Get(MultiUserState) < 2]
  #Set Backup reference time
  Set Variable [$time; Value: Year(Get(CurrentHostTimeStamp)) &
       Right("00" & Month(Get(CurrentHostTimeStamp)); 2) &
       Right("00" & Day(Get(CurrentHostTimeStamp)); 2) & "_" &
       Right("00" & Hour(Get(CurrentHostTimeStamp)); 2) &
       Right("00" & Minute(Get(CurrentHostTimeStamp)); 2)
  #Set Backup path
  Set Variable [$path; Value: "file:" & Get(FileName) & "_BU" & $time & ".fp7"]
  #Create backup of current file:
  Save a Copy as ["$path"; compacted;
Else
  Beep
  Show Custom Dialog ["Backups can only be run on the host computer"]
End If
```

Where your solution has multiple files, we recommend that you create a backup script in each file, and then from the main file (the interface file) add steps to the backup script to call the backup scripts in each of the other files.

> **ON the WEB** Example backup scripts similar to the one provided here have been added to the Inventory example files for Chapter 16 on this book's Web page.

Such a script is only useful if you remember to run it on the host computer at regular intervals. Relying on someone remembering to run backups at regular intervals may be adequate for a small or single-user solution; for all other cases, we recommend the use of FileMaker Server, where automatic backup scheduling is built in.

### Backing up hosted files

If your solution files are hosted (multi-user), backup copies can only be generated on the computer on which the files reside. The script shown under the previous topic includes a check to confirm that the file is hosted on the current computer before it creates a backup copy. If your solution is hosted using FileMaker Pro, you need to ensure that the backup procedure is completed at regular intervals.

As noted previously, if you are using FileMaker Server to host your solution, you can use the option (recommended) to create automatic backup schedules. FileMaker Server 9 also provides the means to automatically verify the integrity of each backup file after it is created and to generate an e-mail notification confirming task completion.

Regardless of the way your solution is hosted, a separate procedure to transfer the backup files to an appropriate secure location is required. FileMaker Server includes the ability to schedule OS-level scripts. If you create an appropriate script on the host computer to archive and/or transfer backups to a secure location, you will be able to schedule it to run after each backup has been created.

> **CAUTION** When scheduling a file transfer procedure to copy backup files to a remote storage location, ensure that the copy procedure does not commence before FileMaker Server has had time to complete the creation of the backup files.

> **CROSS-REF** See the resources listed in Appendix B for sources of information about the creation of external scripts for archiving backup files.

## A Comprehensive Approach to Error Trapping

While anticipating problems and setting in place appropriate backup procedures is an essential first step toward protecting your solution, undoubtedly prevention is better than a cure. Adopting a broad-based approach to error handling when designing your solution's code can help you avoid a significant class of possible problems before damage occurs.

FileMaker, Inc., provides documentation listing more than two hundred error codes FileMaker may return, so trapping independently for all of them at every step would be an onerous task. Fortunately, you don't need to do that, because many errors are particular to specific circumstances. For example, error 508 (Invalid value entered in Find mode) is specific to actions in which field contents are updated while the database is in Find mode — so unless both these conditions apply, error 508 will not be returned. Similarly, error 100 (File is missing) is specific to an action involving a reference to an external file (and that file is unavailable).

**CROSS-REF** Full details of all FileMaker Pro error codes and their definitions appear in the online help and are listed in resources referenced in Appendix B of this book.

Bearing in mind the context of a given script and script action, you can narrow the range of possible script commands considerably, and then test explicitly for those errors you deem most likely to occur in context. When you do this, we suggest that you ensure the final lines of your error-handling code test for any other errors and handle them generically.

**NOTE** Not all error codes indicate that the preceding command has failed (or failed inappropriately). For example, error 1 is defined as User cancelled action. This error can only occur in a situation where the user has been presented with an option (for example on an application dialog) that includes a Cancel button, and has clicked it. Because this is a valid option for the user in such a situation, your scripts should handle it, but it need not be considered an error.

Similarly, a `Go to Related Records[ ]` command with the Match All Records in Current =Found Set option enabled will return error 101 (Record is missing) if the current record had no related records, even though other records in the found set did and they have been successfully displayed.

In such cases, the error code FileMaker returns provides information about the result of the previous action but need not be considered an indication of an error as such.

In all cases, when implementing error trapping, we recommend that you also maintain a log of errors within your solution. Have your scripts create an entry in an error table indicating what error was encountered, at what point in what script, on what record in which layout, and which user was logged in, and so on. Doing this greatly aids system maintenance and problem diagnosis if errors should occur.

## Dealing with record locking

When your solution is hosted on a busy network, one of the most frequent errors your scripts may encounter is 301 (Record is in use by another user). However, this error can be produced even if your database is not hosted, when the record currently being edited is already being edited in another window on the current user's workstation. In this situation, FileMaker produces the error dialog shown in Figure 16.1 (if error capture is not enabled).

With multiple users working simultaneously on a hosted solution, error 301 is apt to occur more whenever users or scripts simultaneously attempt to open or edit the same record.

**NOTE** Records can be viewed while another user is editing them, and the cursor can be placed into a field. FileMaker returns an error only when an attempt is made to change the contents of a field while the record is being edited by another user.

# Making FileMaker Systems Fail-Safe 16

**FIGURE 16.1**

The error dialog associated with an attempt to edit a record already being modified (in a different window) on the current user's computer.

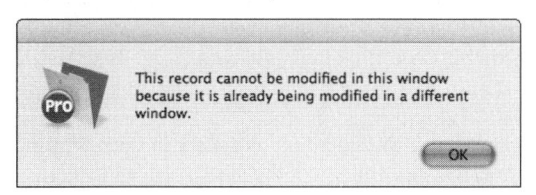

> This record cannot be modified in this window because it is already being modified in a different window.
>
> [ OK ]

When another user, elsewhere on the network, causes the record lock, FileMaker displays an error dialog (if error capture is off) indicating the identity (workstation "user name" and login account name) of the user currently modifying the record and provides an option to display a message to the user encountering the error, as shown in Figure 16.2.

**FIGURE 16.2**

The error dialog associated with an attempt to edit a record already being modified by another user on the network.

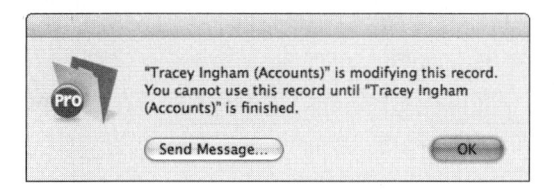

> "Tracey Ingham (Accounts)" is modifying this record. You cannot use this record until "Tracey Ingham (Accounts)" is finished.
>
> [ Send Message... ]   [ OK ]

Although the error dialogs FileMaker displays when encountering these two distinct error conditions are different, (refer to Figures 16.1 and 16.2) the error code returned in both cases is the same (301), so you need to construct your error handling to deal appropriately with both issues.

We recommend that you build window management procedures into your scripts to handle situations where the user may have several windows open, closing those not required and ensuring the state of those remaining open do not impede subsequent scripted edits. If you build appropriate context management (including window management) procedures into your scripts as a matter of course, you can minimize or eliminate situations where error 301 results from the current record being edited in another window.

Regarding occurrences of error 301 resulting from the activities of other users, your error handling code should do the following:

1. Pause and try again several times. If the other workstation edit is brief, such as when it results from another user's computer performing a scripted update, the record can be expected to be released quickly and your script can then continue.

553

2. Timeout after several attempts and store the unique ID of the record where the error occurred.
3. If the script has significant processing to do on other records, consider structuring it so that it returns to records skipped because of error 301 and tries again after concluding its work on other records. Frequently, the locked records will have been released in the interim.
4. Notwithstanding Step 3, if the record(s) remain locked through timeout and after the conclusion of the script, have your script either report the error to the user (with the IDs of records not updated) and/or log the errors (including the IDs of the records where errors occurred and the details of the update that failed on those records) to an error log for later attention.
5. Consider having your script's error-handling sequence automatically generate and send an e-mail to the solution administrator with details of the error.

Although this mix of steps may vary according to the nature of the update your script is applying, following such a process provides the best protection against data anomalies arising when records in a set being updated are unavailable due to record locking in a hosted solution. The way of dealing with record locking described here addresses one of the most common causes of data integrity issues arising from inadequate code and error handling.

## Techniques to avoid in multi-user or multi-window environments

Several development techniques you can effectively employ in single-user solutions present risks or have adverse consequences when used in a multi-user solution — either because they cause errors or because their use cannot be adequately protected by error-handling procedures. Several deserve special mention here.

### Replace Field Contents

Although the scripted update of a batch of records (such as via a script looping through the found set and updating each record in turn) is vulnerable to record locking in a multi-user solution, appropriate error handling, as described in the previous section, can mitigate the associated risks. However, if your solution (or its users) use the Replace Field Contents [ ] script step in a button, script, or menu command, error data regarding locked records (if any) will be available during or after the update. In other words, if records were locked they are skipped and while a generic error code (201, defined as Field Cannot Be Modified) is returned, the identities of the locked records remain unknown.

For this reason, you should avoid using the Replace Field Contents [ ] command in a multi-user solution. Because it doesn't lend itself to error handling, it poses an unacceptable risk when used in a hosted database.

## Record marking and flagging techniques

Inexperienced developers sometimes build procedures depending on setting flag values on or marking certain records so they can be summarized, found again, or included in a process being performed by the current user. If the number of records involved is moderate, these techniques can provide an acceptable method in a single-user solution. However, as soon as the solution is made available to multiple simultaneous users, problems arise because the marks applied or removed by one user's workstation are overridden by another's.

We've encountered solutions in which one user's order items routinely end up on another user's invoices or where records marked by one user for archiving are instead duplicated by another user's script. These errors, and others like them, arise from the use of flagging and marking techniques that are inappropriate for multi-use deployments.

> **NOTE** The use of flags to indicate the status of a record with the purpose of enabling other users to see the record's status is multi-user friendly and falls outside the caution mentioned here.

An example of the legitimate use of a flagging technique to manage custom record locking is discussed in the "Temporary Edit Interface Techniques" section later in this chapter.

## Uses of global fields

One further technique you should avoid when developing solutions that may at some point form part of a hosted data system is the use of global fields to store persistent data.

When a solution is accessed in stand-alone mode, the contents of global fields are saved when the solution files are closed and are therefore available again when the file is subsequently reopened. In this situation, global field values persist between sessions. However, in a multi-user database, changes made to global field values during each client session are seen only on the workstation where they're made (every user "sees" their own set of global field values) and are discarded at the conclusion of the client session.

Once understood, global field behavior in a hosted solution is valuable and even essential. However, procedures predicated on the behavior of global fields in stand-alone mode fail spectacularly — and without returning any error codes — when hosted.

# Opening Remote Files

The method you use to access database files has a bearing on their performance and their vulnerability to corruption.

Database applications, especially for hosted databases, are I/O (input/output) intensive. A lot of data is read and written to disk, sometimes in short periods of time, so FileMaker (or FileMaker Server) performs a lot of two-way communication with the disk on which your database files are stored. The speed and reliability of the connection between the CPU where the host application is running and the volume where the files are stored are therefore critical determining factors in the response times and reliability of the application.

**Part IV** **Integrity and Security**

> **TIP** Database files should always be opened and/or hosted from the computer where they are stored. Opening files from a remote (network) volume is both risky and suboptimal. We acknowledge that technology advances rapidly and new storage protocols are emerging, including new mass storage opportunities in high bandwidth networked environments. While each case must be considered on its merits, we presently consider local hardware connected storage to be the safest and (in most cases) best performing option.

For additional information about the reasons for this caution, refer to the sections "File sharing risks" and "Network spaghetti," later in this chapter.

## Peer-to-peer hosting

FileMaker Pro 9 can be used to host a solution for up to ten concurrent users (nine client connections, plus the host itself), so you can start sharing files straight away over a local network, directly from your desktop computer. To do this, you should follow these steps:

1. Make sure that your computer is connected to a TCP/IP network and that other computers on the network have copies of FileMaker Pro 9 (or FileMaker Pro 9 Advanced) installed.

2. Open the solution you want to install (including all solution files, if your solution comprises more than one file) from a disk drive directly connected to the current computer (either an internal hard drive or an external drive attached through high-speed USB, FireWire, SCSI, or SATA connections).

3. Choose File ➪ Sharing ➪ FileMaker Network. The FileMaker Network Settings dialog, shown in Figure 16.3, is displayed.

**FIGURE 16.3**

Enabling Network File Sharing from the FileMaker Pro client application.

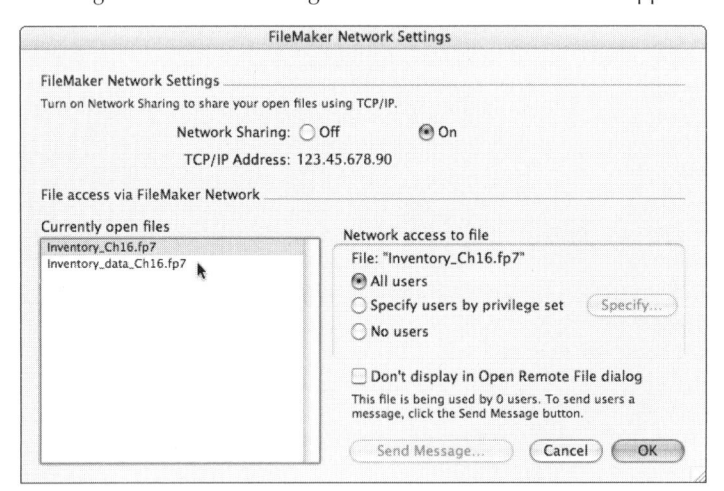

## Making FileMaker Systems Fail-Safe

4. Select the Network Sharing On radio button in the upper section of the dialog.

5. Select each of your solution's database files in the Currently open files lists (lower left of the dialog) and enable network access to the file in the panel at the lower right — either for all users or users by privilege set.

> **TIP** If your solution has a main file and one or more ancillary files, consider enabling the checkbox labeled "Don't display in Open Remote File Dialog" for the ancillary file(s), so remote users will be guided to open your main file first.

6. Click OK to accept the settings and close the FileMaker Network Settings dialog.

After following the preceding preparatory steps, elsewhere on your network, other workstations running FileMaker Pro are now able to open the solution files remotely. To confirm this, go to another computer on the network, launch FileMaker Pro, and choose File ⇨ Open Remote. The Open Remote File dialog appears, as shown in Figure 16.4.

### FIGURE 16.4
Select a file to open in the Open Remote File dialog.

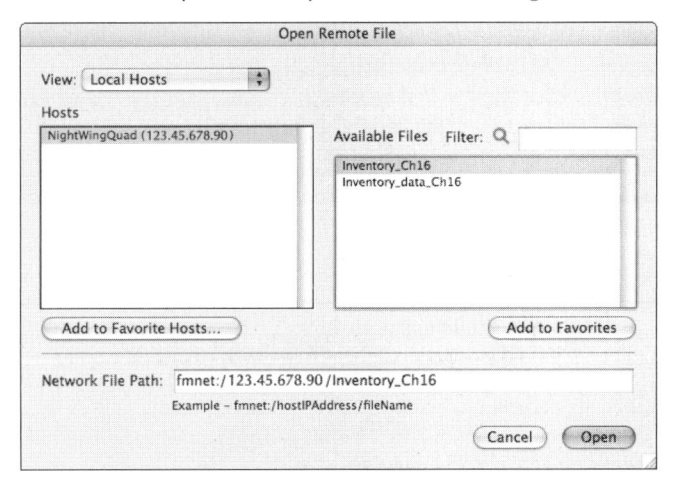

The list of available hosts in the Open Remote File dialog, when Local Hosts is selected in the View pop-up menu at the top left, shows computers on the local network configured for FileMaker sharing. When you select the workstation where your solution is hosted, the files enabled for network sharing appear in the Available Files list at the right of the dialog. When you select your solution's main file and click OK, the solution opens remotely on the current workstation.

**Part IV** | **Integrity and Security**

## File sharing risks

FileMaker network sharing provides you with a built-in data sharing protocol available with minimal setup, right within FileMaker Pro on your computer. There is an important distinction between this capability and conventional file sharing, where users open a file directly from a disk on another computer. The key difference is that with FileMaker Network sharing, multiple users can open the solution simultaneously, whereas file sharing permits only one user at a time to have write access to a file.

When you enable your solution for FileMaker Network Sharing, we recommend that you avoid having the same computer available for conventional file sharing on the network. There are several reasons for this, but foremost among them is that doing so provides two alternative ways users can open the solution — one via FileMaker Network sharing and the other by opening the files directly with file sharing. Should users open your files directly (as host) via file sharing rather than through FileMaker's Open Remote dialog, your files are placed at risk (for example, if a network drop-out occurs) and performance is severely compromised.

A further significant risk presenting itself whenever database files are stored on a volume enabled for file sharing is that multiple copies of the files will be available (users may make their own copies). After this occurs, users are highly likely to inadvertently open the "wrong" copy of the database for a given work session. Then, when next they log in (to the correct copy of your solution) all the work from their previous work session is absent. Even if users realize immediately what has occurred and where all their work from the previous day is located, reconciling the data between the two copies of your solution may present significant challenges (particularly if some users have been updating one version while others were updating another).

You can avoid all the aforementioned problems and potential pitfalls by ensuring that File Sharing is never enabled for volumes where copies of your database files are stored and, particularly, for the computer (or computers) you are using to host databases via FileMaker Network Sharing.

## Network spaghetti

Risks of file corruption, data loss, and general confusion aside, a further set of issues arises when database files are accessed via file sharing. Every element of data to be displayed, edited, or entered when a database is opened via file sharing must be passed to and fro between the computer accessing or hosting the databases and the network volume where they are stored. Moreover, the computer's access to the storage media is impeded not only by network traffic and inherent network latency but by other tasks being serviced simultaneously by the file share.

When users connect remotely to a database file open on a computer, if that computer has in turn opened the files via file sharing from elsewhere on the network, all remote calls for data must travel to the host computer, then to the file sharing computer, then back to the host — and then on to the client workstation. Data entered or edited must negotiate the same obstacle course in reverse. By the time you have several client workstations connected, network traffic becomes convoluted and multiple bottlenecks can arise.

## Making FileMaker Systems Fail-Safe | 16

In a busy office or production environment, the last thing you need is an overburdened and sluggish network configuration — notwithstanding the risks to file integrity should the connection between host and file server/file share ever be interrupted.

## Opener files

One way of simplifying the remote connection procedure for users of your solution is to provide a file to be stored on the user's desktop as a gateway to your solution. Such files are commonly termed *opener* files.

The basic principle of an opener file is a simple one. It opens the solution file(s) from a remote network address (the computer configured as host) and then closes itself. In the process, it gives the user an icon on the desktop that simultaneously launches FileMaker Pro and opens the remote database, saving the user a number of intermediary steps. For users who access your database infrequently — and who may be relatively unfamiliar with FileMaker Pro — an opener file provides a direct and easily remembered way to access your solution.

Within your opener file, you create a link to your solution as an external data source, so the opener can find your solution on the network. The syntax for the data source should be entered in the following form:

```
fmnet:/hostIPAddress/FileName
```

If your solution may be hosted in one of several alternate locations, you can list them, each on a separate line (FileMaker opens the solution from the first location where it finds it, working down from the top of the list). The start-up script in your opener file can be set up along the following lines:

```
Set Error Capture [On]
Open File ["Inventory_Ch16"]
Set Variable [$result; Value: Get(LastError)]
#Create opener log entry
New Record/Request
Set Field [OpenerLog::CurrentIP; Get(SystemIPAddress)]
Set Field [OpenerLog::DateTime; Get(CurrentTimestamp)]
Set Field [OpenerLog::ConnectionStatus; $result]
If[Result ≠ 0]
   Show Custom Dialog ["The solution is not currently available"]
End If
Close File [CurrentFile]
```

You can define a script such as this one to run automatically on file open (via the Open/Close tab panel of the File Options dialog). When you configure it in this way, the opener file automatically launches your solution remotely, logs the event, and then closes. If an error is encountered (if the solution is not available on the network, for example) the opener file posts a dialog stating this before closing.

559

**Part IV**  Integrity and Security

> **NOTE**  We have added several lines to the suggested opener script to log the result of its use in a table within the opener file itself. This means that if a user is reporting problems or as part of routine maintenance, you can verify the exact times and details of any failed connections, including the specific error code FileMaker returned on each occasion.

## Sending an e-mail link

New in FileMaker 9 is the ability to send an e-mail link to a hosted database. This capability is a useful alternative to an opener file in cases where those accessing your solution may change frequently or be spread far and wide. An e-mail link doesn't require that any files be added to the user's desktop, and the e-mail bearing the link can be distributed to large numbers of users speedily and efficiently.

To create an e-mail containing an embedded link (URL), users can click to access a hosted solution and then choose File ⇨ Send Link, as shown in Figure 16.5.

The Send Link command creates an unaddressed e-mail containing a URL for the current host and solution file, in the form:

```
fmp7://123.45.678.90/Inventory_Ch16.fp7
```

The IP address of the host computer on the network in this example is 123.45.678.90, and Inventory_Ch16.fp7 is the name of the hosted file. The text of the automatically generated e-mail also includes a summary of the conditions that are required when clicking the link.

In order to connect to the database using this link:

- The client must have FileMaker installed on their computer.
- The database file must be open on the host machine.
- Any firewalls between the client and server must allow FileMaker sharing.
- The client must have a valid account and password.
- The client and the host must be on the same local area network.

E-mail links may be sent from FileMaker 9 databases hosted either peer-to-peer or by using FileMaker Server 9.

> **TIP**  Users receiving an e-mail link may save the e-mail or add the link to bookmarks in their Web browser. The link works whenever the solution file is open on the host computer indicated in the URL.

## Making FileMaker Systems Fail-Safe | 16

**FIGURE 16.5**

You can send an e-mail link for the current (hosted) FileMaker database file to a prospective user.

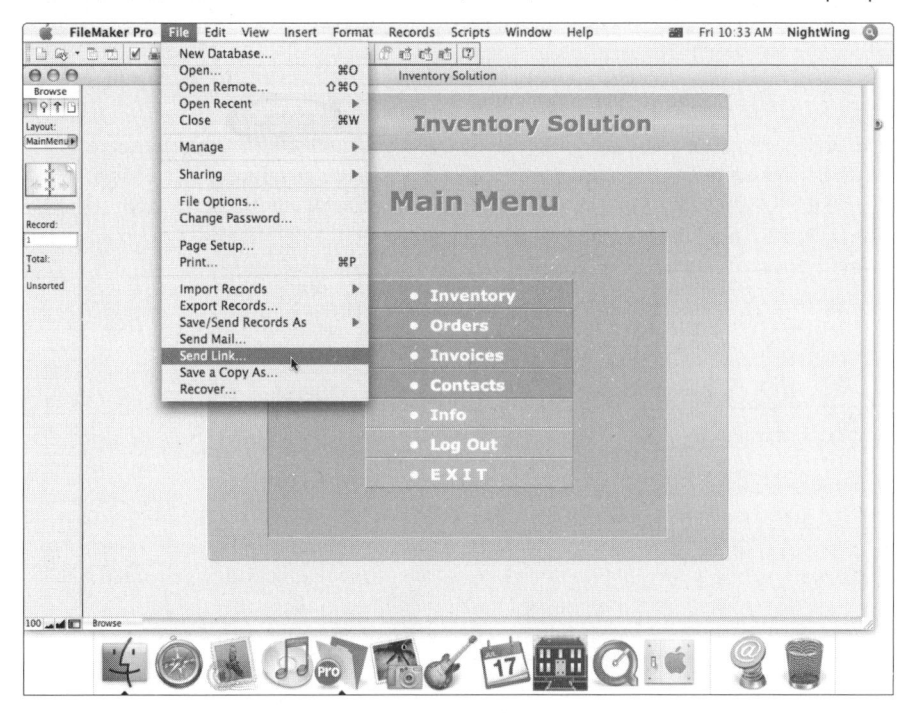

## Temporary Edit Interface Techniques

When you exit a field or record (click in an inactive area of the layout outside of FileMaker's fields, buttons, and so on.) the record is automatically committed, validation rules are evaluated, and the data (if validation succeeds) is written to the record. After a record is committed, the Records ⇨ Revert Record and Edit ⇨ Undo commands are no longer available, and the changes become permanent.

In cases where the accuracy of data entry and editing is of paramount importance, you're likely to require greater control over what goes into the database and how it gets there. To achieve this, you can create a holding area where data entry can occur and be subject to more rigorous checks or screening before being stored in your solution's main data tables.

561

## The data viewer concept

You can create a separate data viewer interface so that users can edit in an offline area where you control how and when the data is saved to the database. You can create a FileMaker data viewer interface by following these steps:

1. Set user access privileges to View Only for the table(s) in question.
2. Create global fields (for example, in a utility or temporary data table) corresponding to each of the user-editable fields in your table.
3. Make a copy of the main form layout for the data to be edited via a viewer screen and re-point the fields on the copy to the temporary global fields created in Step 2.
4. Create an Edit script that
   a. Opens the current record (if necessary looping until it is available).
   b. Checks a lock flag on the current record and, if it is not set, sets it (but if it is set, exits the record and posts an error alert telling the user the record is locked).
   c. Writes the values from each field in the current record to the corresponding global field (as per Step 2).
   d. Switches to the layout showing the global fields
   e. Locks down the interface (so the user cannot navigate using menus or the Status Area).
5. Attach the Edit script to a button on the original layout.
6. Create a Save script that:
   a. Checks all the values in the global fields, performs all required validations (alerting the user and exiting whenever a problem is found).
   b. On successful completion of all checks, opens the current record (if necessary looping until it is available).
   c. Writes the values from the global fields back to the current record.
   d. Clears the lock flag on the current record.
7. Attach the Save script to a button on the copy of the layout with the global fields.

**TIP** Because the user's privilege set does not have write access to the main data table, both the Edit and Save scripts must be set to run with full access privileges.

With this configuration in place you have a custom record editing procedure, one in which changes to the record cannot be committed until the Save button is clicked — and then only in accordance with requirements built into your Save script. No data can be entered or updated in the live solution table until (and unless) all your validation requirements are met.

One advantage of this approach is that it enables you to perform multiple validation tests on each field, returning a custom error message for each, indicating the exact nature of the problem encountered and what to do to resolve it. (The FileMaker built-in validation system provides only a single custom message regardless of the validation rule breached.)

## The legitimate purpose of record locking

You may have encountered cases where a data-viewer concept somewhat like the one described under the preceding topic has been proposed (or even implemented) as a palliative for issues arising from record locking. Such an approach resembles the one described in the preceding section but omits the custom record locking (the lock flag) procedure. We strongly caution against disabling record locking without providing a viable alternative.

Record locking serves an essential purpose in a multi-user database. It prevents one user's changes from being overwritten by another's and, perhaps more importantly, prevents data integrity from being threatened by the merging together of data of different origins. For example, without a record lock procedure, two users can select the same record for editing more or less simultaneously. If one user replaces a contact address while another user corrects the spelling of the suburb of the existing address, there is a risk that when both users confirm their changes, the result will be the new address but with the old suburb — an address that doesn't exist and therefore corrupt data. Each user independently did the right thing, but a flawed solution design crunched their data together inappropriately.

To prevent this, you should either use record locking (either FileMaker's native record locking, or a custom alternative as described in the preceding topic) or:

- Ensure that all fields are overwritten with new data when the edited record is saved (so data from two separate user edits can never be blindly combined).
- Store the modification time when a record is opened for editing and check it has not changed before writing changes back to the record.
- If the record has been modified since the user began editing, post an error dialog and either discard the changes or require that the user review changes made by the other user to decide which value to keep for each field (and subject the combined result to a further round of validations).

With these additional measures, your edit interface provides a viable alternative method of dealing with potential editing conflicts. This resembles the "optimistic" locking model FileMaker itself uses when dealing with data in *ESS* (External SQL Source) tables.

## Creating double-blind entry systems

You can extend temporary edit interface techniques to provide support for *double-blind data entry* — where each record or edit must be processed independently and identically by two operators before being accepted into your solution's data. Double-blind entry is a requirement in some data processing environments and is considered desirable in others to safeguard against error and fraud.

Implementing a double-blind entry system requires all the essentials of the data viewer outlined in the preceding pages, with the addition of a holding table. Moreover, data to be entered requires a unique ID number prior to entry (for example, from serialized stationery). The Save script then performs an additional procedure as follows:

1. After completing data validations on the entered/edited data (refer to Step 6 in the procedure to create a data viewer earlier in this chapter), the script checks for the presence of a corresponding record (by unique form ID) in the holding table. Then one of the following happens:

   - If no corresponding record is found in the holding table, the data is transferred to a new record in the holding table.
   - If one (or more) corresponding record is found in the holding table, the values in each field of the entered or edited data are compared with the values in the holding record.
   - If there is an exact match between the entered/edited data and any holding record, the corresponding holding record (or records) is deleted, and the entered edited data is saved to the main table
   - If the entered or edited data does not match any of the holding records, the data is transferred to a new record in the holding table.

2. Return the user to the main viewing layout.

With this additional procedure in place, data cannot become part of the main system unless entered identically by at least two operators. In such an implementation it is normal practice to record the user IDs of both operators (those creating each of the matching entries) either with the updated record or in a separate log table. Some businesses require that records from the holding table be transferred to an archive rather than deleted, when an entry or edit is transferred to the main table. Doing so provides a comprehensive audit trail of additions and modifications to the data. The presence of errors is greatly reduced, while user accountability is enhanced.

Since double-blind entry systems require a more complex solution design — and twice as much staff time for data entry — their use is restricted to solutions where the accuracy of data (and accountability of staff) is of critical importance. Nevertheless, the double-blind technique provides an added option in the design of a fail-safe system.

**CROSS-REF** Methods of creating audit trails without requiring double-blind entry or separate edit interfaces are discussed in detail in the later sections of this chapter.

# Field Masking, Filtering, and Error Rejection

When your data is required in a standard format and you want to avoid variations or rogue characters accumulating amidst your data, validations are only one of the options — and not necessarily the best option — for achieving your objective.

## Making FileMaker Systems Fail-Safe

An alternative approach is to intercept data at the point of entry and modify it to conform to your requirements. In FileMaker Pro, you can do this via the use of auto-entry calculations that reference the current field (and with the Do Not Replace Existing Value of Field option disabled). A field with auto-entry options configured by using this option automatically replaces the contents of an entry into it with the result of the calculation expression.

> **TIP** Data modification at entry is generally best suited for use with text fields, because they are designed to accept data in a variety of presentation styles and configurations.

### Applying standard data formations

A frequent requirement when setting up database fields is to store telephone numbers according to a common convention — for example, the 123-456-7890 format is common in some parts of the world.

If you require all values entered into your Contacts::PhoneNo field converted onto a standardized 3-3-4 format, you'll require an auto-enter (replaces existing) calculation to remove characters other than numerals and to insert hyphens at the appropriate places. The following is an example of a calculation formula that achieves this:

```
Let(
Dgts = Filter(Contacts::PhoneNo; "0123456789");
If(not IsEmpty(Dgts);
Left(Dgts ; 3) & "-" & Middle(Dgts; 4; 3) & "-" & Middle(Dgts; 7; 4)
)
)
```

When this calculation expression is entered as an auto-enter calculation definition and the Do Not Replace option is disabled, entries such as the following are automatically converted:

(12) 345 678 90

1-2345-678 #9

123 456 7890

and 1234567890

Each of these input values is converted and stored as:

123-456-7890

> **CAUTION** Before enabling strict filter formatting, consider the possibility that users may need to enter international or out-of-state numbers according to a different convention. If so, an override option (using a modifier or a global field checkbox, for example) may be appropriate.

The following is an example of a variation of the formula configured to provide an override (accepting data in whatever fashion it is presented) if the Shift key is depressed while leaving the field after entering or editing a value:

```
Let(
Dgts = Filter(Contacts::PhoneNo; "0123456789");
Case(
Abs(Get(ActiveModifierKeys) - 2) = 1; Contacts::PhoneNo;
not IsEmpty(Dgts); Left(Dgts ; 3) & "-" & Middle(Dgts; 4; 3) & "-" &
   Middle(Dgts; 7; 4)
)
)
```

## Dealing with trailing spaces and carriage returns

Using variations of the masking technique discussed in the preceding topic, you can configure a field to reject trailing spaces or carriage returns automatically as the user leaves the field. For example, to remove leading and trailing spaces from entered values in the Contacts::Address field, select the auto-entry by calculation option, deselect the Do Not Replace checkbox, and enter the formula:

```
Trim(Contacts::Address)
```

Alternatively, to remove trailing carriage returns from values entered into the same field, specify the auto-enter calculation expression as:

```
Let([
Rchar = Right(Substitute(Contacts::Address; ¶; ""); 1);
Pchar = Position(Contacts::Address; Rchar; Length(Contacts::Address); -1)];
Left(Contacts::Address; Pchar)
)
```

**NOTE** The previous formula removes carriage returns only if they occur at the end of the text string entered into the field. If carriage returns are included elsewhere in the entered string, they are left in place.

Building on the previous two examples, if you want to simultaneously remove trailing carriage returns and leading and trailing spaces, you can accomplish that using a calculation expression such as the following:

```
Let([
Rchar = Right(Substitute(Contacts::Address; [¶; ""]; [" "; ""]); 1);
Pchar = Position(Contacts::Address; Rchar; Length(Contacts::Address); -1)];
Trim(Left(Contacts::Address; Pchar))
)
```

**TIP** You can combine the logic of these expressions with other filtering requirements by nesting additional code within the example expressions.

## Rejecting out-of-scope characters

FileMaker's auto-entry calculation technique, in combination with the `Filter()` function, lets you cleanly eliminate inappropriate characters, defining the character set to be retained and stored in a field.

For example, to ensure that the Contacts::Address field contains only letters, numbers, and spaces, you can use a formula such as the following:

```
Let(
Charset = "ABCDEFGHIJKLMNOPQRSTUVWXYZabcdefghijklmnopqrstuvwxyz 0123456789";
Filter(Contacts::Address; Charset)
)
```

With this expression applied as an auto-entry (replaces existing) calculation, all punctuation, carriage returns, and other extraneous characters are stripped from the text string entered by the user.

## Handling styled source text

If users paste data into fields in your solution (after copying text from a word processor or Web browser, for example), the text may include embedded character formatting—text colors, text styles, fonts, or nonstandard font size attributes. These styles can wreak havoc on the data legibility in your solution's screens and printed output. Stripping them out at data-entry time can be accomplished cleanly and simply with an auto-enter (replaces existing) calculation employing a formula such as:

```
TextFormatRemove(Contacts::Address)
```

With this auto-enter calculation configured, users can paste styled text into the field, but as soon as they leave the field, all styles and character format attributes are removed.

> **TIP** If desired, the techniques described in this section can also be used to conditionally apply text styles and character formats to data at the point of entry.

# Built-In Logging Capabilities

Your data's safety depends on your solution being able to detect errors and, when errors are detected, acting to correct them and prevent their recurrence. To achieve that goal, you need information about the data and the sources of errors. FileMaker provides several ways to capture additional information that can be of assistance in tracing and troubleshooting errors.

## Making use of auto-enter options

As a first line of defense, you should add a standard set of metadata fields to each table users will edit directly.

In Chapter 5, we describe adding fields to capture creation account, creation workstation, creation timestamp, modification account, modification workstation, and modification timestamp for every record in each table.

We commend this practice to you as a standard procedure for data-entry tables. Although standard metadata fields provide a first port of call when checking the origins of your data, there are a number of more useful options to be explored.

## Capturing and extending standard metadata

In addition to the basic set of metadata fields provided among FileMaker's standard auto-entry options, you can capture a number of additional pieces of information regarding the circumstances of each record's creation and modification. These include:

- The user's IP Address and/or network hardware address — such as their computer's MAC address (Media Access Control, not an Apple computer)
- The version of FileMaker being used to make the change
- The operating system version and platform of the user's workstation
- The layout the user is using the make the edit
- The name of the script (if any) running when the record is committed
- The name of the account the user uses to login to their computer (not the database)

Each of these (except the last) can be achieved with a text field that is set to auto-enter based on a reference to the record modification time field and then using one of FileMaker's native Get( ) functions. For example, an auto-enter text calculation field can capture the IP address of the computer used to make the most recent modification to the current record, with the following calculation expression:

```
If(_ModStamp; Get(SystemIPAddress))
```

To obtain the name of the user's login account on the current computer, you can extract it from the result returned by FileMaker's Get(DesktopPath) function using the following calculation expression:

```
Let([
Dp = Get(DesktopPath);
Ln = Length(Dp);
p1 = Position(Dp; "/"; Ln; -3) + 1;
p2 = Position(Dp; "/"; Ln; -2)];
Middle(Dp; p1; p2 - p1)
)
```

**TIP** If you require extensive data about this information, rather than adding a large number of fields to every table, we recommend that you create a session table and have your login script add a record to it each time a user logs in or out.

With all the required information stored in the session table, you will be able to reference it as required based on the user's account name and the creation or modification timestamp value.

A significant limitation of the metadata capture process is that it contains information only about the most recent modification. If the record has been modified multiple times, information about the previous modifications is overwritten. However, you can readily build a variation that captures the account names and dates/times of all changes or recent changes to each record. For example, if you want to capture a rolling log of the date, time, and associated login account of the last six modifications of the current record, you can do so by defining an auto-enter text calculation (replaces existing) called _ModHistory, with the calculation expression:

```
LeftValues(
If(_ModStamp; GetAsText(Get(CurrentHostTimeStamp)) & " - " & Get(AccountName)) &
If(not IsEmpty(_ModHistory); ¶ & _ModHistory)
; 6)
```

**NOTE** As an example, a _ModHistory field using this formula has been added to this chapter's Inventory example's Inventory table. We used FileMaker Pro Advanced to add a tooltip displaying the recent modification history, as captured by the _ModHist field to the "Record Last Modified" panel near the bottom of the Inventory layout.

**CROSS-REF** For additional information about defining tooltips using FileMaker Pro Advanced, see Chapter 18.

## Script Logging

An important part of the reference information about the access, performance, and data history of your solutions is the timing, context, and results of script execution. If things go awry, in either a small or a significant way, your ability to determine what has been occurring and why depends on the quality of information available — including information about what happens when each of your scripts executes.

For any solution where performance, reliability, and data integrity are crucial, we recommend that you consider incorporating a script logging procedure to capture details about script activity as your solution is used.

### Infrastructure for script logging

To keep track of script activity in your solution, create a ScriptLog table with a single table occurrence, no relationships, and one layout (the layout may remain blank, because only the script accesses the table). In your StartUp script, create a window called ScriptLog, either off-screen or hidden.

In the ScriptLog table, create the fields as set out in Table 16.1

**TABLE 16.1**

## ScriptLog Table

| Name | Type | Options |
|---|---|---|
| ScriptLog# | Number | Auto-entry serial number, Can't Modify Auto |
| Script | Text | Auto-entry Calc with formula `Get(ScriptName)` |
| Parameter | Timestamp | Auto-entry Calc with formula `Get(ScriptParameter)` |
| Start | Timestamp | Auto-entry Calc with formula `Get(CurrentHostTimestamp)` |
| Account | Text | Auto-entry Calc with formula `Get(AccountName)` |
| Workstation | Text | Auto-entry Calc with formula `Get(UserName)` |
| Layout | Text | Auto-entry Calc with formula `$layout` |
| Mode | Number | Auto-entry Calc with formula `$mode` |
| RecordNo | Number | Auto-entry Calc with formula `$record` |
| Window | Text | Auto-entry Calc with formula `$window` |
| Conclude | Timestamp | |
| ResultArray | Text | |

## Tracking script execution

With the script log table in place, commence each significant script with a sequence along the lines of the following:

```
#Capture Context and Log Script Start
Set Variable [$x; Value:Let([
   $window = Get(WindowName);
   $record = Get(RecordNumber);
   $mode = Get(WindowMode);
   $layout = Get(LayoutName)]; "")]
Select Window [Name: "ScriptLog"; Current file]
If(Get(LastError)]
  New Window [Name: "ScriptLog"; Top: -5000; Left: -5000]
  Go to Layout ["ScriptLOG" (SCRIPTLOG)]
End If
New Record/Request
Select Window [Name: $window; Current file]
```

After each significant or error-vulnerable step, include the step:

```
Set Variable [$result; Value: $result & "|" & Get(LastError)]
```

## Making FileMaker Systems Fail-Safe

At the conclusion of the script, include the following:

```
Select Window [Name: "ScriptLog"; Current file]
Set Field [ScriptLog::Conclude; Get(CurrentHostTimestamp)]
Set Field [ScriptLog::ResultArray; $result]
Select Window [Name: $window; Current file]
```

> **NOTE** When using the error logging method to build an array in the $result local variable, the expression `RightWords($result; 1)` retrieves the error code of the most recently logged script command (as the script progresses).

### Script-specific context variables

As part of the opening lines of the script described in the preceding topic, the starting context of the script (window, record number, layout, and mode) are captured, and these values are subsequently logged, along with several others.

An added benefit of this procedure is that where appropriate, you are able to use the same values at the conclusion of the script to return the user to the context as it was when the script began. There are exceptions to this depending on the nature and purpose of the script.

### Script diagnostics

With a script logging procedure in place, you will be able to export the accumulating history of solution use into a separate developer database in which you can analyze script usage patterns, identify performance bottlenecks, and locate errors indicating where revisions of your solution's code are appropriate.

In some solutions, you may conclude that only a few of the scripts warrant logging; in complex solutions, it may be appropriate to include logging on all scripts. When you include script logging in your solution from the outset, you'll discover its value immediately during the build and beta testing phases of development.

## Capturing User Edits in Detail

In the earlier section "Built-In Logging Capabilities," we provide you with techniques for capturing data about who has modified each record and when. To provide a true audit trail, however, you need to know which fields were edited and what their values were before and after the change.

A number of methods exist enabling you to build an audit trail capability into your solutions. As noted earlier, if you are using a temporary edit interface technique, your "Save" script can store a record of the changes. However, if your users edit data directly in layouts attached to the main solution tables, you need to create a calculation field to automatically capture field changes.

> **NOTE** When your scripts change data in your solution, it is a simple matter to have them also record the change to a record of edits — so scripts can be self-logging. However, capturing edits made by users presents a challenge of a different order. The following techniques focus on methods of capturing a reliable history of user-initiated changes.

**Part IV**    Integrity and Security

## Trapping edits, field-by-field

If you want to capture a history of values in a single field, you can efficiently achieve that goal via a slight extension to the auto-entry method we describe earlier in this chapter. For example, to add a field audit log to capture the history of values in the Contacts::Organization field in the Inventory example database, proceed as follows:

1. In the Inventory Data file, choose File ➪ Manage ➪ Database. The Manage Database dialog appears.
2. Navigate to the Fields tab panel and select the Contacts table from the pop-up menu at the upper left of the dialog.
3. Create a text field called _DataLog.
4. In Field Options for the _DataLog field, navigate to the Auto-Enter tab panel and select the checkbox labeled Calculated value. The Specify Calculation dialog appears.
5. Enter the following calculation formula:
   ```
   Let([
   p1 = Position(_DataLog; "-»"; 1; 1) + 3;
   p2 = Position(_DataLog; ¶; 1; 1);
   Prv = If(p1 < 4; "[---]"; Middle(_DataLog; p1; p2 - p1));
   Crt = If(IsEmpty(Organization); "[null]";
      Substitute(Organization; ¶; "‡"))];
   Get(AccountName) & "" &
   GetAsText(Get(CurrentHostTimeStamp)) & "" &
   Prv & "      -» " & Crt & ¶ & _DataLog
   )
   ```
6. Click OK to accept the Specify Calculation dialog.
7. Disable the checkbox option labeled Do Not Replace Existing Value of Field (If Any).
8. Select the checkbox option labeled Prohibit Modification of Value During Data Entry.
9. Click OK to close the Options for Field dialog, and again to close the Manage Database dialog.

With this method in place, the _DataLog field accumulates a history of edits for the Organizations field, as shown in Figure 16.6. The history includes the account name of the person performing the edit, the data and time the edit occurred, the previous value (if any) of the field, and the value it was changed to.

**NOTE**    We have made these modifications (shown in Figure 16.6) in the copy of the Inventory example files for this chapter. You can view the field modification history for the current record by holding the mouse over the Organization field on the Contacts screen to display its tooltip. (See Chapter 18 for additional information about tooltips.)

## FIGURE 16.6

A tooltip in the Contacts layout of the Inventory example for this chapter shows the history of edits of the Contacts::Organization field on the current record.

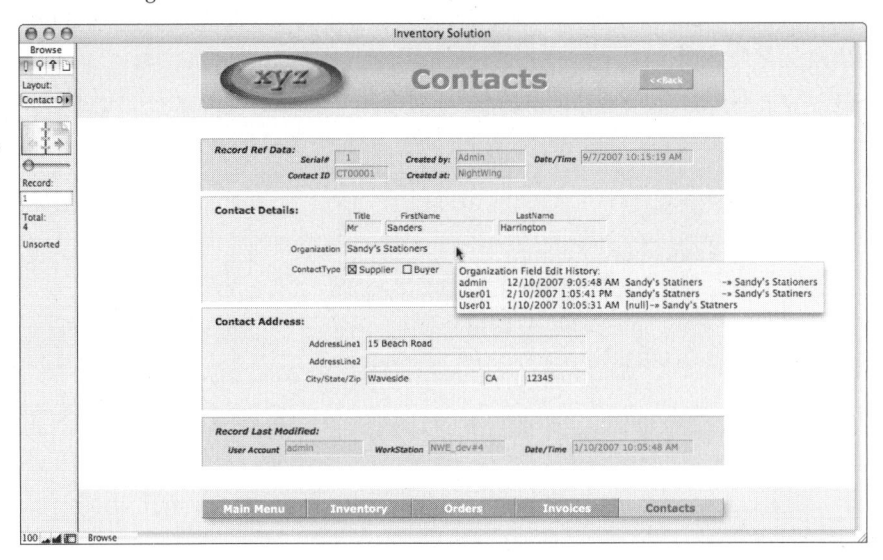

## Incorporating ancillary data

The method we describe in the previous section can be used to log any text or number field. And with minor adjustments, it can also log date, time, and timestamp values. However, if using this approach, you need an additional field in each table for every field you need to audit. Instead, a more complex formula can log user edits of multiple data-entry fields within a single (log) text field.

The following example is a formula to capture edits from multiple fields (including any mix of text, number, date, time, or timestamp fields, and including repeating fields) within a single text field.

```
Let ([
Trg = Field1 & Field1[2] & Field2 & Field3 & Field4;
Lval = Length(AuditTrail);
Scpt = Get(ScriptName);
Rpt = Get(ActiveRepetitionNumber);
Rflg = If(Rpt > 1; "[" & Rpt & "]") ;
Fnm = Get(ActiveFieldName) & Rflg;
Pref = Position(AuditTrail; "        " & Fnm & "        "; 1; 1);
Pst = Position(AuditTrail; "       -»         "; Pref; 1) + 4;
Pnd = Position(AuditTrail & ¶; ¶; Pref; 1);
Pval = If(Pref; Middle(AuditTrail; Pst; Pnd - Pst); "[---]");
Tval = Get(CurrentHostTimeStamp);
Fval = GetField(Fnm);
```

573

```
Sval = Substitute(Fval; ¶; "‡");
Nval = If(Length(Fval); Sval; "[null]")];
If(Length(Fnm) and Length(Scpt) = 0;
GetAsDate(Tval) & "" &
GetAsTime(Tval) & "" &
Get(AccountName) & "          " &
Fnm & "     " & Pval & "          -»          " &
Nval & Left(¶; Lval) & AuditTrail; AuditTrail)
)
```

In this formula, the fields listed on the second line (Field1 & Field1[2] & Field2 & Field3 & Field4) are the fields to be logged, and the name of the log field itself appearing throughout the formula is AuditTrail.

Because this formula is unwieldy, we recommend that you use a custom function to incorporate its logic. Doing so allows you to use it with a single function call and two parameters. A custom function that provides logging capabilities along the lines of this example was the basis of the FileMaker SuperLog demo (a free online download example file) published by NightWing Enterprises in 2006.

The calculation expression shown previously (and the SuperLog( ) custom function, on which it is based) produces a composite (multi-field) audit trail for the current record, in the form shown in Figure 16.7.

**FIGURE 16.7**

The audit trail text for a record, as shown in the SuperLog example file.

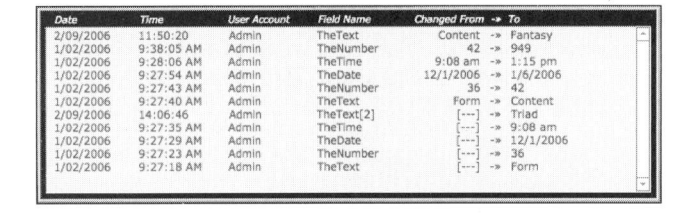

| Date | Time | User Account | Field Name | Changed From | -» | To |
|---|---|---|---|---|---|---|
| 2/09/2006 | 11:50:20 | Admin | TheText | Content | -» | Fantasy |
| 1/02/2006 | 9:38:05 AM | Admin | TheNumber | 42 | -» | 949 |
| 1/02/2006 | 9:28:06 AM | Admin | TheTime | 9:08 am | -» | 1:15 pm |
| 1/02/2006 | 9:27:54 AM | Admin | TheDate | 12/1/2006 | -» | 1/6/2006 |
| 1/02/2006 | 9:27:43 AM | Admin | TheNumber | 36 | -» | 42 |
| 1/02/2006 | 9:27:40 AM | Admin | TheText | Form | -» | Content |
| 2/09/2006 | 14:06:46 | Admin | TheText[2] | [---] | -» | Triad |
| 1/02/2006 | 9:27:35 AM | Admin | TheTime | [---] | -» | 9:08 am |
| 1/02/2006 | 9:27:29 AM | Admin | TheDate | [---] | -» | 12/1/2006 |
| 1/02/2006 | 9:27:23 AM | Admin | TheNumber | [---] | -» | 36 |
| 1/02/2006 | 9:27:18 AM | Admin | TheText | [---] | -» | Form |

**CROSS-REF** You can find a link to the NightWing Enterprises SuperLog example file among the resources included in Appendix B.

Implementing an audit trail mechanism throughout your solution by using a technique such as the one described earlier requires an AuditTrail field in each table, alongside other metadata fields. Field modification data is then captured automatically as users work.

## Logging record deletions

Although the processes described in the preceding sections provide mechanisms for tracking user edits, the method is such that if a record is deleted, its recent log entries are deleted with it.

One way to address this shortcoming is to provide (and require the use of) a script for deletion of records, and to have the script first transfer details of the record being deleted (including all its data) to a log table. This way, you can keep track of which records have been deleted by whom as well as having the basis to restore lost information, if necessary.

## Managing the Accumulation of Log Data

A potential disadvantage when you set up a field in each table to capture user edits is that in solutions where data changes frequently, the history of edits and previous field values can accumulate, adding significantly to the size of the file and thereby impacting performance. In fact, the volume of data associated with logging each record's history is necessarily larger than the current data in the solution. In addition, while audit data is stored in a single text block within each record, it cannot readily be searched or sorted.

Both these shortcomings can be mitigated by periodically archiving audit data to a separate table and/or file for reference.

### Archiving options

Audit log data is more useful when you store it in a separate data table, where a separate record holds the details of each field edit in your main solution tables. When stored separately in this way, log data can be searched and analyzed, as well as being accessed and updated independently of the main database. Separate data storage provides a more convenient format for audit log data when it is archived. When you allocate a separate record per field edit, each column of data from the originating log field array can be stored in a separate field in your log table. A script that loops through the lines of each record's audit log and parses each to the fields of a separate record in an audit utility table provides the first step toward consolidating audit data in a convenient indexed and searchable format.

**CROSS-REF** For details of techniques for looping through data and parsing elements from data arrays, refer to Chapters 12 and 13.

With your audit data stored in its own table, you can search for all changes made by a specific user or containing a particular value. Your ability to pinpoint errors and to discern patterns in the evolution of your solution's data is increased exponentially.

### Generating secondary output

Depending on the volume of data edits taking place in your solution, you may consider running a maintenance script that transfers log data to an audit table nightly (after close of business), weekly (over the weekend), or on some other convenient cycle. If you need to review up-to-date audit summaries, more frequent consolidations may be desirable.

Your secondary repository of audit data is generally most useful if it spans a recent period (for example, ranging from a quarter to a year), rather than being an accumulation of edits for all time.

**Part IV**    **Integrity and Security**

In most cases, periodically transferring aged transaction logs to external storage (either an archive database or delimited text files) is appropriate. Once exported, these data can be deleted from secondary storage.

# Implementing Roll-Back Capabilities

A key benefit of implementing logging procedures — both for user edits and for record deletions — is the opportunity it affords to detect errors and reverse them. At its simplest, this means going back through the logs to locate an entry made in error and manually re-entering (or copying and pasting) the original value back into the relevant field and record.

A much more useful and powerful feature is the automated roll-back of log entries. In effect, this feature provides multiple undo capabilities at the record level.

## Chronological roll-back

By using a record-based text field log as described in the preceding pages, you can create a relatively straightforward script to reverse the most recent edit on the current record. By running such a script multiple times, you can step a record back through its previous states in reverse chronological order.

As an example, the following script applies record-specific roll-back, one edit at a time, based on a log field in the format shown in Figure 16.7.

```
Set Variable [$LogEntry; Value:LeftValues(Data::AuditTrail; 1)]
Set Variable [$field; Value:Let([
   p1 = Position($LogEntry; " "; 1; 3) + 1;
   p2 = Position($LogEntry; " "; 1; 4) - p1;
   f1 = Middle($LogEntry; p1; p2);
   Ln = Position(f1 & "["; "["; 1; 1) - 1];
   Left(f1; Ln)
   )]
Set Variable [$repetition; Value:Let([
   p1 = Position($LogEntry; " "; 1; 3) + 1;
   p2 = Position($LogEntry; " "; 1; 4) - p1;
   f1 = Middle($LogEntry; p1; p2)];
   If(PatternCount(f1; "[") = 0; 1; RightWords(f1; 1))
   )]
Set Variable [$value; Value:Let([
   p1 = Position($LogEntry; " "; 1; 4) + 1;
   p2 = Position($LogEntry; " "; 1; 5) - p1];
   Middle($LogEntry; p1; p2)
   )]
If [$value = "[--]" ]
   Beep
```

# Making FileMaker Systems Fail-Safe

```
Else
    Go to Object [Object Name: $field; Repetition: $repetition ]
    Set Field [If($value ≠ "[null]"; $value) ]
    Set Field [Data::AuditTrail; RightValues(Data::AuditTrail;
    ValueCount(Data::AuditTrail) - 1)]
    Commit Records/Requests [Skip data entry validation; No dialog]
End If
```

**NOTE** The preceding script requires that the fields being logged have object names matching their field names assigned on the current layout, so that the `Go to Object[ ]` command can locate each field by its name.

Although the previous script implements a roll-back procedure that is chronological with respect to a specific record in isolation, it allows you to roll back one record without affecting others edited during the same time period. A possible shortcoming of this roll-back procedure is that, because it deals with a single record in isolation, associated changes to child records (if any) aren't automatically rolled back as part of the same action, potentially leaving related data sets in an erroneous state unless comparable roll-back procedures are performed in each related record.

## Alternative undo and roll-back capabilities

By using the principle that provides the basis for the chronological roll-back discussed under the previous heading, you can implement a roll-back option for audit log records in a consolidated log table.

Because records in a consolidated log table can be searched and sorted in various ways, selective roll-back is possible. The scope of selective roll-back can be adjusted to include all references to a particular event, all edits made by a particular user, all edits made to a particular field — or any other criterion you choose to apply to the edit history.

To implement selective roll-back capabilities, first create a script that reverses a single edit by following these steps:

1. Have your script transfer the name of the edited field, the before-edit value, the location, and the ID of the edited record into variables.

2. Your script should then navigate to the appropriate record and place the before-edit value into the edited field.

3. Your script should return to the log table and update the status of the current log record to indicate it has been reverted.

With the script described here in place, selective rollback of a group of edits can be achieved by performing a find in the log table to locate the edits that are to be reverted and then calling a master script that loops through the found set applying the revert script to each.

577

**CAUTION** If you roll back edits to a particular field and record out of chronological sequence (for example, reinstating a value other than the second-last value of the field), the remaining log records may not have continuity.

We recommend that if you are rolling back log table entries, rather than deleting the entries you have reversed, you mark them as rolled back. Using a log status field to indicate which log records have been reverted has the added advantage that you can provide a counterpart procedure to roll forward.

### Using logs to roll forward

If you have implemented comprehensive audit logging capabilities in your solution, a further option providing additional fail-safe security is a generic roll-forward script. Again, such a script operates on the same principle as the roll-back example provided in this chapter.

Rolling forward enables you to do the following:

- Reverse a roll-back. If you have rolled back too far, or where you wished to roll the database back to the state it was in on a previous date to run a report or summary of the data as at that date, then roll the database forward to the present.

- In the event of file corruption, providing your consolidated logs are intact, roll-forward enables you to apply the logged edits to a backup copy of the database, bringing the backup forward to the state the solution was in at the most recent consolidation.

If you provide a mechanism for the reversal of roll-back, we recommend inclusion of a status check to ensure that each log entry to be rolled forward has previously been rolled back. (Log entries not marked as rolled back should be skipped.) This requirement should be waived when applying a roll-forward through consolidated edit logs to a back-up copy of your solution.

## Alternative Logging Approaches

Although we have explored several facets of audit logging in the closing pages of this chapter, a variety of other approaches are possible, and with a little research you can find examples of other methods suited to a number of different requirements.

In particular, logging methods depending on third-party tools can provide additional flexibility and improved protection against unforeseen events. These potential benefits must be weighed against the additional costs and deployment considerations for such products.

**CROSS-REF** Additional information about extending FileMaker capabilities with third-party tools is provided in Chapter 19.

## Logs as Data

The accumulation of audit logs and journals as additional data in your solution has advantages for searching, sorting, summarizing, and reporting based on log data. However, it also presents a risk. If your solution encounters a problem that could be rectified by referring to the logs, it is possible that the logs also will be affected by the same event.

If, for example, your server crashes, you have the prospect of being able to rebuild the current state of the data if your logs are intact. For this reason, we suggest recording your log data on a server in a different location and outputting your logs to a different format. (For example, a text file format on a remote file server.) According to the needs of your solution, you must balance convenience and flexibility of data logs against the additional safeguards of remote or external log formats.

## Scripted and triggered logging

When your audit trail of user edits is captured within the record by using the FileMaker calculation engine, compiling consolidated logs is necessarily a two-step process, with log data being stored first in the calculation used to capture it and subsequently transferred to a separate table or file.

By using a fully scripted approach to audit logging, you can avoid the necessity for a two-step approach, instead writing details of each change directly to a consolidated log table. This approach requires either of the following:

- The use of a scripted edit interface where changes are always committed and written to the main data tables via a script. As noted earlier, in this situation, you can include log maintenance procedures within the Save scripts when you use this approach to editing your solution data.

- The use of a third-party tool to trigger a script or external event when an edit occurs (or when the record is committed). A variety of products (such as plug-ins) can be used in conjunction with FileMaker Pro 9 to support script-driven or event-driven logging functionality.

# Chapter 17

# Maintaining and Restoring Data

When handled appropriately, FileMaker Pro solutions give years of faithful and trouble-free service — and, in fact, they've been known to survive a variety of forms of abuse. Nevertheless, problems can and do arise, and you need to know what to do — and what not to do — when responding to them.

As is frequently the case in many areas of computing, fiction and misinformation abound. In this chapter, we set out the facts for you so that you're able to address any potential problems with confidence and dependable strategies.

For more techniques to increase your solutions' fault tolerance and robustness, see the previous chapter. Here, we provide you with techniques to manage your solution's data.

## IN THIS CHAPTER

Understanding file recovery

Working with data export and import

Cleansing your data

Setting up data synchronization

Managing stored files and embedded images

Transforming text and text formats

## Some Notes on File Recovery

The Recover command (File ➪ Recover) is arguably one of the most universally misunderstood features in FileMaker Pro. Despite many theories about what it does and how and when you should use it, much of the original confusion persists.

The uncertainty surrounding the Recover command stems in part from the fact that its name is misleading. *Recover* simultaneously suggests regaining full health and regaining something lost or misappropriated. Neither sense aptly conveys what the recover command in FileMaker Pro actually does, a task that may be better characterized as a "partial salvage" in a brutal jaws-of-life kind of fashion

## Debunking common myths and misconceptions

The first and most egregious misconception you'll encounter regarding the Recover procedure is that it's a good maintenance health check, and it's okay to run it routinely on your files — whether they have exhibited problems or not. If you're the kind of person to clean your new Porsche with a crowbar or steel wool, then go right ahead — but otherwise, please think again.

A second widely circulated fallacy is that a database file, if it survives the Recovery procedure, is whole, intact, clean, and safe to use or develop further. You may be able to drive your car — after a fashion — following a nasty crash and an encounter with hydraulic salvage machinery. The stereo may even work; however, the safety of such an undertaking is in serious doubt.

A further myth, arising all too frequently, is that the Recover procedure *not* being a reliable repair utility — a machine for restoring files to pristine condition — is itself a myth and that no one has ever experienced severe problems with recovered files. This myth seems to be a curious extension of "it will never happen to me" thinking.

## The Recover process

Before deciding when and how to use file recovery in FileMaker Pro, you should know that this feature's mandate is to do whatever it takes to get a file in a state such that its *data* can be extracted. Consider, for a moment, the process Recover follows:

1. The Recover command produces a copy of your original file.
2. As the copy of the original file is created, each piece of the original file is examined by using an algorithm designed to swiftly identify possible corruption.
3. When a component of the original file's code or structure is identified (accurately or otherwise) as potentially problematic, a pessimistic approach is taken, and the element containing the suspect code is omitted from the recovered version of the file. Recovery, therefore, is an aggressive process placing priority on getting your data out of a severely compromised file — and it will sacrifice code, interface, or the essential logic of your solution in service of this aim.
4. On completion of the 16-step recovery operation, a dialog appears with the briefest of reports regarding the edited highlights of its journey of recovery, as exemplified by Figure 17.1.

It is important to note that although recovery passes through 16 multi-part stages, working through layouts, tables, indexes, relationships, scripts, dependencies, and more, the confirmation dialog mentions none of these steps (even in summary). In other words, most of what occurs (including most of the checks resulting in file components being included or skipped) during recovery is not mentioned in the confirmation dialog. The dialog's focus is almost exclusively on your data (Records, fields, field definitions).

# Maintaining and Restoring Data    17

Based on considerable experience, both good and bad, with this feature (including previous and current versions of FileMaker), we can confirm that the Recover process:

- Typically (but not invariably) omits items preventing a file from opening

**FIGURE 17.1**

The overview dialog appearing on completion of a recovery cycle.

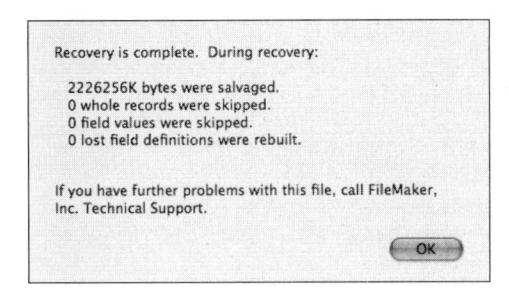

> Recovery is complete. During recovery:
>
> 2226256K bytes were salvaged.
> 0 whole records were skipped.
> 0 field values were skipped.
> 0 lost field definitions were rebuilt.
>
> If you have further problems with this file, call FileMaker, Inc. Technical Support.
>
> OK

- May omit items (scripts, layout objects, and so on) not among the elements mentioned in the concluding dialog summary
- May remove logical components of a file (layout, layout element, script step, et. al.) suspected to be corrupt, even though they were causing no apparent problems
- May skip damaged or corrupt content, leaving it in the recovered file if the presence of that content does not prevent the file from opening

Damaged files usually open after recovery and may even appear to operate normally. However, you should not assume (regardless of what the confirmation dialog stated or omitted to state) that your recovered file is complete and contains all the code and logic of the original — nor that it will work as intended in all respects.

**WARNING** In rare cases, recovered files have been known to contain duplicates of some records or to reinstate deleted records. Our observation has been that the Recover procedure uses as its guiding principle "When in doubt, exclude it" regarding file structure and code content, while using "When in doubt, include it" with respect to your data.

Occasionally, damaged files may continue to exhibit problems after recovery. Furthermore, we have seen cases where otherwise normal and fully operational files are missing essential components and therefore malfunction after recovery.

## Salvaging data

File recovery provides you with a fallback option if you encounter difficulties resulting from a system crash, hardware failure, and so on. However, the process is imperfect and is not exhaustive (see preceding section), so don't assume that your file is complete or will function as you intended after recovery.

583

Rather than take the risk of running the Recover process, the preferable options, in priority order, are

1. Revert to a recent backup of your file — one predating any problems leading to your file becoming inaccessible — and then re-enter data or otherwise modify the backup to bring it up to date. If you have been making frequent backups, this path may be the least onerous or inconvenient to take, particularly if you've employed transaction logging as described in Chapter 16.

2. Locate a clean and uncompromised (never crashed or improperly closed) copy of your solution file(s), make a clone, and then import data from a recovered copy of your solution into the clean clone(s).

**NOTE** Because the data in a recovered file may not exactly match the data in the original file (damaged records may have been omitted, deleted records reinstated, or duplicates included), if you opt for making a clone, you should expect to comprehensively check the resulting data set's completeness and accuracy. Unless your most recent backup is well out of date, the combined effort to recover, re-import, and verify your data will likely be greater than the work of re-entering information to bring a backup up to date.

Consider deploying a recovered file only if neither of the preceding options are available (for example, your file has crashed, and you have no suitable backups or clean clones of the current file structure). Before doing so, be prepared to undertake a thorough check of both the data and the code (including all layouts, layout objects, scripts and script steps, and calculation definitions) to confirm the solution is in a deployable state. If your solution is of any size and complexity, an adequate check of the deployment-worthiness of a recovered file is likely to be more onerous than preferred options 1 and 2 combined.

## Understanding file corruption

You can define *file corruption* in several ways, with the broadest definition perhaps being "anything that is not as you intended." FileMaker, however, cannot know what you intended and must therefore use a considerably less ambitious definition. For this purpose, rules of well-formed data are applied; FileMaker looks for block integrity throughout a file, seeking to restore lost pointers when file architecture contiguity is compromised.

FileMaker manages its own (internal) file structure, independent of the block structure of the storage device and, in doing so, depends on internal pointers to establish the status and order of each segment. When the integrity of the pointers is compromised or FileMaker is unable to resolve and interpret the contents of one or more segments of your file, FileMaker determines the file to be corrupt and posts an alert dialog such as the one shown in Figure 17.2.

## FIGURE 17.2

The warning FileMaker provides when file integrity problems have arisen.

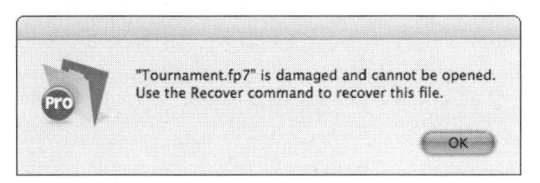

The most common problems affecting FileMaker files arise from improper closure, and FileMaker is able to correct these anomalies in most instances, with nothing more onerous than a consistency check when the file is next opened. More serious problems can result if data was partially written to disk at the time of a crash, power outage, or hardware failure — in which case one or more segments of your file's data may be incomplete and/or damaged. File corruption may result from a variety of other causes, such as power spikes, faulty device drivers, operating system errors, malicious software, or plain-old bugs. Fortunately, file damage from these various causes is rare.

The kind of damage your files may sustain when impacted by one of the events we mention may vary, from a single overwritten bit to whole sections of the file missing. For the most part, damage is random and therefore unpredictable. Occasionally, damaged data resembles valid data, and occasionally it is valid data (written into the wrong place), whereas on other occasions damaged bits are simply unintelligible. Faced with almost infinite possibilities in the forms corruption may take, the Recover procedure in FileMaker balances efficiency and efficacy by checking for the most commonly encountered and problematic issues.

## Exporting and Importing Data

An important consideration when deploying any database is your ability to get data into and out of it in bulk, in formats appropriate for a variety of requirements. FileMaker Pro helps you out by supporting a broad range of data formats for both import and export.

In addition to general utility and exchange of data with other applications (for example, drawing in data from legacy systems, sharing data with others, and using information from your solution for word processing or publishing tasks), data exchange enables you to take advantage of the summarizing, reporting, or data analysis capabilities of other desktop applications or to share data with external accounts or financial management suites.

A further purpose of data export and import is archiving data from your system, to move data between versions of your solution, or to process, filter, or validate your data externally as part of maintenance and/or restoration procedures in the event of solution integrity problems.

**CROSS-REF** Refer also to details about importing and exporting procedures and automating data transfers provided in Chapters 3 and 13.

## File format considerations

One of the essential issues when you're considering moving data between formats is supported functionality. While your data remains in FileMaker, you benefit from a variety of automatic calculation, summary, and data presentation options. Because other applications don't support many of these options, you may face compromises when preparing to export to an alternative format. As a result, you may want to perform calculation, filtering, sorting, or summarizing in FileMaker prior to export.

When transferring data, it is usually preferable to deal with each table separately. However, where data relationships are central to your solution, but cannot be replicated in the destination application, you can accumulate data from multiple tables into a single (flat) file export. Figure 17.3 shows a simple example where the `cFullName` field from the suppliers table occurrence is included in an export of data from the Orders table.

**FIGURE 17.3**

Inclusion of related fields in the Field Export order.

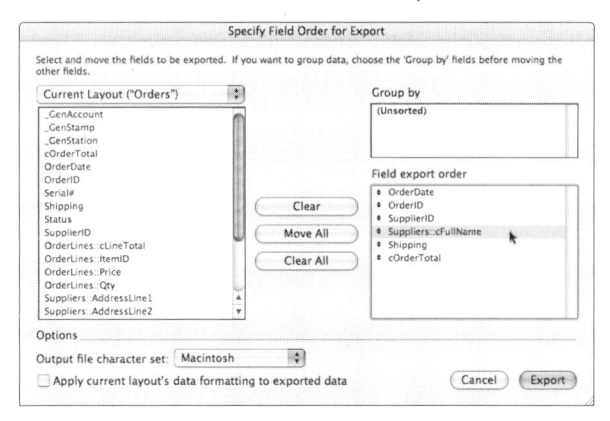

Along with relational and data presentation limitations in many of the available export file formats, most formats don't support inclusion of container data, such as files, images, sounds, or movies. Unless you choose FileMaker Pro as the export file format, FileMaker posts an alert dialog and prevents you from adding container fields to the field export order, as shown in Figure 17.4.

**FIGURE 17.4**

FileMaker displays an error alert if you choose a container field for export.

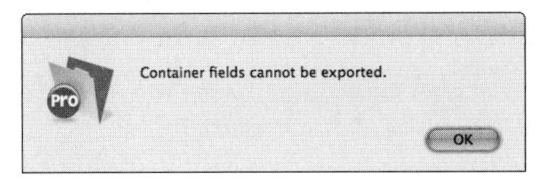

Even though you can't include container data in most data exports, you can output container fields' contents into a folder, from which you can later import them (if desired).

## Exporting to and importing from a folder

In most cases, you can export container field contents individually (one field and one record at a time) by choosing Edit ➪ Export Field Contents command. In situations where you need to export a batch of container field contents — for example, from a found set of records or a whole table — you should create a script to automate the process, including assigning an appropriate (and unique) filename to each exported file.

**NOTE** In one particular case, you can't export container contents directly to a file using the Export Field Contents command: when container data has been pasted from the clipboard and is not in a supported file format.

In this case, you can copy and paste the contents into a graphics application where you are able to select a suitable file format to save it, or, if you prefer, you can use a third-party plug-in in conjunction with FileMaker to automate the process.

Chapter 13 describes methods for scripting export or selective import of container field data, including details of scripts for accomplishing each of these tasks and also briefly covers the ability to import an entire folder of files. To commence this process, choose File ➪ Import ➪ Folder. You select the options for folder import, including text files, pictures, or movie files, from the Folder of Files Import Options dialog shown in Figure 17.5.

After you select an appropriate folder (one that contains files of the selected type), you're then prompted to select up to four values for import. As shown in Figure 17.6, you can simultaneously import the file (into a container field), the filename and file path (into a text field), and a thumbnail image (also into a container). When importing text files, only the first three of these options are available.

## Part IV  Integrity and Security

**FIGURE 17.5**

Selection options for a folder import.

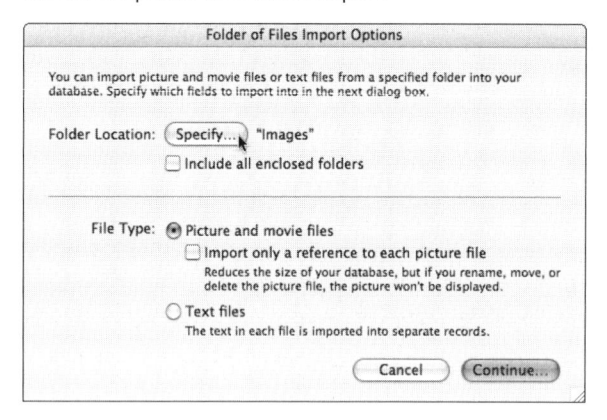

When your data includes both text and files, you may require separate processes to bring both types of data into FileMaker from other data formats. However, you can script both processes, if desired, even managing them sequentially within a single script.

**FIGURE 17.6**

Setting the import field map to upload a folder of picture files into FileMaker.

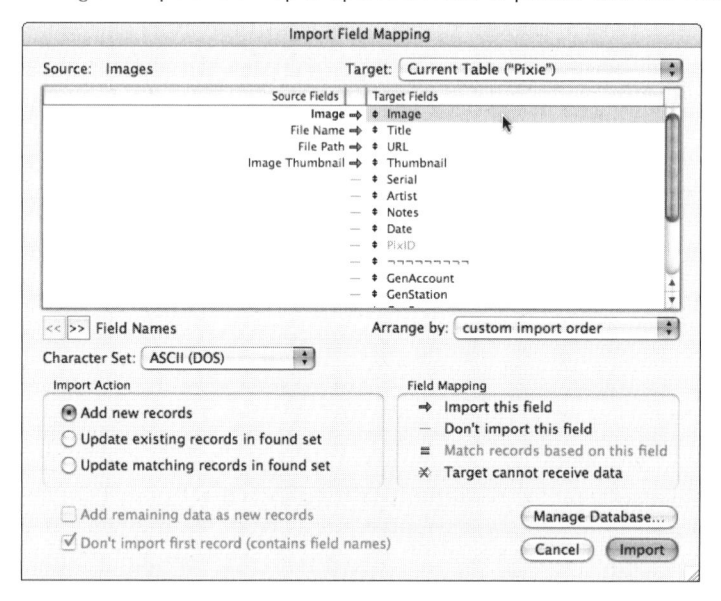

## Delimiters and EOL markers

Most data formats represent each record as a separate line or paragraph of text, containing one or multiple field values. The field values within each line are separated by a character or sequence of characters, referred to as *delimiters*. For example, a tab delimited file has tab characters separating field values within each record and carriage returns marking each End-Of-Line (EOL), which separates each record from the next.

So what happens when carriage returns or tab characters appear in a field in your FileMaker data? FileMaker solves this dilemma for you:

- Carriage returns within fields are converted to vertical tab characters (ASCII character number 11) in the exported data. This conversion takes place automatically when you use the Export Records command in FileMaker.

- Tab characters within fields are converted to standard spaces (ASCII character number 32) when you choose the tab-delimited text export format. When you choose other formats where tabs are not treated as delimiters, such as in comma-separated values (CSV), the tab characters are preserved in your export output.

You should consider your data content when choosing your export formats. In other words, if your data includes tab characters, the tab-separated export format is less suitable than others because your tab characters are translated to spaces during the import. Fortunately, FileMaker provides a dozen different export file formats, letting you find a suitable way of preserving your data in most cases.

**CROSS-REF** Import and export options and procedures are addressed in detail in Chapters 3 and 13.

# Data Cleansing Operations

Exporting and importing data is a relatively straightforward task if the data is clean and well formed, and you are either transferring data between two systems using identical data structures or have control over both the applications (so that you can make changes to facilitate data transfer).

In situations where the data has integrity issues or isn't compatible with the required format or structure, you face an additional challenge: You have to transform the data as part of the data transfer procedure.

## Extract, transform, and load

The process of modifying data to correct formation and structural issues or mismatches is called an *Extract, Transform, and Load* (ETL) cycle and is especially important when migrating data between different kinds of systems. For example, when you need to load data into a data-warehousing or external-reporting tool, you invariably require a modified organizational format and possibly require individual values in a data format specific to the destination system. Similarly, migrating

589

data between a legacy database system and a new solution environment necessitates converting data to the structure and format required by the new system.

You may also require an ETL cycle if your data has been subject to abuse or system malfunction and must be retrieved from a damaged solution file (such as a recovered file). After extraction from a damaged file, you should perform checks and cleansing procedures on the data prior to loading it into a clean reference copy (clone) of your solution.

Depending on the nature of transformation and/or data cleansing required, you may want to build a rapid FileMaker transformation tool. To do so, first drag the extracted file onto the FileMaker application icon to create a temporary database file containing the migratory data. Within the temporary file, you can then build scripts and calculations to correct issues with the data, combine groups of data together, separate concatenated values, remove unwanted characters, and eliminate unneeded duplicates. Your FileMaker calculation and scripting skills will get a thorough workout!

## Data format considerations

Data organization, data presentation, and data domain are three aspects of data formation you should consider separately during the transformation process — each requiring a different set of skills and strategies to successfully update your data.

### Data organization

First and foremost, your data must be aligned with the receiving application's data model. This alignment includes an appropriate delineation of data elements to conform to the entity/table definitions and the data model used in your data's new home. Moreover, within grouped records, you may require a different distribution of attributes. For example, when migrating data from a legacy database, you may find the extracted data has a single field for address, whereas the destination data model may require street address, city, state, and postal code each in a separate field. The legacy system's address data must be parsed during the transformation stage — using appropriate calculation techniques — to separate the original single address value into the required four (or more) values to match the requirements of the receiving system.

Other aspects of the data organization challenge may include

- Eliminating redundant or duplicated data
- Allocating appropriate unique key values
- Establishing metadata or summary data if required
- Setting a suitable sort order for the records in each data subset

As part of the data organization procedure, you should also prepare a basic inventory of available data so that you can confirm the transfer's success. This may be as simple as the number of data subsets (tables), the number of fields in each subset, and the record count of each subset. If the data will include null values, a count of nulls per subset (including null rows, null columns, and individual null values per table) is also a useful check.

# Maintaining and Restoring Data   17

## Data presentation

The foremost data presentation issue relates to the receiving system's data type requirements. If your data currently includes alphabetic characters in attribute data required to be numeric, you need to either eliminate or substitute values to meet the presentation requirements. Similarly, you should pay attention to the strings used to express date and/or time values. For example, if your legacy system has produced date columns in dd/mm/yy presentation format and the destination solution is configured to receive mm/dd/yyyy dates, your transformation stage must modify all the dates to conform to the latter requirement. You can make such a change in a FileMaker transformation tool by running a `Replace Field Contents [ ]` on the data as text, using a formula such as

```
Let([
txt = Substitute(TransformationTool::LegacyDate_ddmmyy; "/"; " ");
mm = MiddleWords(txt; 2; 1);
dd = LeftWords(txt; 1);
yy = RightWords(txt; 1);
yyyy = (19 + (GetAsNumber(yy) <= 50)) & yy];
mm & "/" & dd & "/" & yyyy
)
```

**CAUTION**   This calculation deals with conversion of the two-digit years to four-digit years by placing all years less than 50 (00 through 50) into the 21st century and dates with year values above 50 into the 20th century. This conversion is likely to be appropriate for transaction dates or budget projection dates, but may be inappropriate for dates of birth or other historical data (which may include dates prior to 1951, but will not include dates in the future).

An alternative form of the date text transformation calculation suitable for dates including only past values (such as date-of-birth data) is

```
Let([
txt = Substitute(TransformationTool::LegacyDate_ddmmyy; "/"; " ");
mm = MiddleWords(txt; 2; 1);
dd = LeftWords(txt; 1);
yy = RightWords(txt; 1);
yyyy = (19 + ((2000 + yy) <= Year(Get(CurrentDate)))) & yy];
mm & "/" & dd & "/" & yyyy
)
```

By varying your approach according to the needs of each data element, you can automate the transformation of large sets of data to efficiently address each data presentation issue.

A further dimension of data presentation relates to the data format itself — the delimiter and end-of-line characters determined by the export and import formats. In cases where you need to prepare data for upload into a system not supporting any of the standard export formats provided by FileMaker, you may need to use text calculation operations to generate data using different delimiters, such as pipe characters or square brackets. Again, you can accomplish this task with relative ease by using text calculations in a temporary transformation tool.

### Data domain

Data transformation considerations also encompass confirming your data falls within acceptable ranges, both with respect to the characters occurring within the data, and the range of values occurring across all instances of fields, cells, or attributes within each data set or subset. This transformation involves addressing several specific requirements:

- Establishing that the range of values in each field is within the range of values supported for the field in the destination solution — for example, within the permissible numeric or date range, or for text, within the character limit (if any) of the destination field

- Ensuring the data is appropriately current — in other words, if the data includes records due for archiving due to a long period of inactivity, they should be segregated during transformation

- Eliminating redundant or inappropriate characters from data, including leading or trailing spaces or carriage returns, superfluous punctuation, or characters outside the required or approved character set (such as low or high ASCII characters not forming part of the language of the data)

> **TIP** Although it is possible to perform a variety of transformation operations within FileMaker, if you have extensive requirements, consider using a special-purpose external data cleansing application.

The transformation stages do have some overlap, and some data problems may relate to more than one stage. For example, extraneous characters included in a date or number field are a data presentation problem, because the affected field values do not conform to data type requirements of the destination system. However, these cases should also be regarded as data domain problems, as the characters are also out of range and redundant.

You ensure that key data integrity, structure, and content issues are not overlooked by considering and addressing each of the transformation stages.

## Filtering capabilities in FileMaker

FileMaker is very forgiving regarding what is stored in the fields of your database. Field validation and data type constraints aside, you can store any string of characters from the vast compendium of the Unicode character set. However, in practice, you likely require a considerably narrower scope, and in many solutions, you can define the permissible character set to include no more than a few hundred characters.

The presence of out-of-range characters may present several problems for your solution. Most fundamentally, it compromises your data's meaning and may lead to calculations producing unexpected results. In particular, low-range characters (generally referred to as *control characters* — those in the range from 0 to 31) are frequently invisible, and their presence leads to confusion at the very least. For example, take a calculation including the following expression:

```
If(Deliveries::DestinationState = "Utah"; Amount * TaxRate; Amount)
```

# Maintaining and Restoring Data

Your users will be concerned if they can see "Utah" in the `DestinationState` field, but the State tax has not been included. However, the presence of an invisible control character (an ASCII #011, a.k.a. DC1) on one end of the value in the field prevents it from matching the literal comparison value in the calculation expression.

The concept of invisible characters seems contradictory. Although you may not be familiar with all the control characters supported in the ASCII and Unicode character sets, you have probably encountered programs, such as word processors, that include the ability to *show invisible characters*. Invisible characters include tabs, carriage returns, line feeds, and numerous other characters serving as instructions or placemarkers. While tabs and carriage returns are standard fare, most control characters have no place in your solution's data, yet the fact that they're invisible can make them difficult to detect and remove.

> **TIP** Rarely are invisible characters entered from the keyboard, but users may paste them in inadvertently, having copied text from another application or (more commonly) from a Web site. Out-of-range characters can also be imported into your solution if data has not undergone appropriate cleansing transformations prior to import.

Provided you can determine an "approved" character set for use in your solution, the most straightforward way to reject undesired characters is via the use of the `Filter( )` function. For example, to constrain a field to contain only characters suitable for numeric values (integers and decimal fractions), you can use a calculation with the expression

```
Filter(YourTable::YourField; "0123456789,.")
```

> **TIP** If the values you're filtering may include negative numbers or numbers in scientific notation, you should include both the characters e and – within your filter string.

> **NOTE** This filter only removes invalid characters from the field and does nothing to validate that the resulting string is a valid numeric representation. For example, it doesn't verify that only one decimal point is present or that the comma separators are appropriately placed.

If you apply such a formula as an auto-entry calculation (replaces existing), the field automatically rejects out-of-range characters. Similarly, to constrain a text field to include only alphanumeric characters, spaces, and hyphens, you can use the calculation formula:

```
Filter(YourTable::YourTextField;
   "0123456789ABCDEFGHIJKLMNOPQRSTUVWXYZabcdefghijklmnopqrstuvwxyz -")
```

When you use calculation expressions such as the preceding ones as an argument within the Replace Field Contents [ ] command, you can efficiently constrain the character set across significant numbers of records. The use of filters (along with selective substitution in cases where the permitted character set is too large to be readily defined or included in a Filter calculation) forms an essential part of data cleansing and transformation processes.

> **NOTE** Alphanumeric value filtering using the 64 characters shown in the preceding example is suitable only for limited cases. In many circumstances, you'll want to include a considerably larger range of characters (including punctuation, accented characters, glyphs, and so on).

593

# Synchronizing Data Sets

As part of the process of managing data in your solutions, you may have call to synchronize disparate data sets in separate copies of the same solution (or in comparable solutions). For example, when your main database resides on the server at your office, and you go on offline field visits, taking a copy on your laptop (modifying records and adding new records as you go), a problem of synchronization of the two record sets (the server database and the laptop database) arises. On your return, you need to load the added and edited work from your laptop into the main solution file, but without deleting new records added by your colleagues while you were gone.

An important feature of the import and export functionality in FileMaker is that it acts on the found set of records in the frontmost window showing a layout based on the table occurrence from which you are importing. To import only the new records you added while on your field trip:

1. Copy the file from your laptop onto a client machine logged into the main copy of your solution.
2. Open the field copy and perform a Find to locate the records you added while on your trip. One way to locate the added records is to perform your search on the record creation timestamp field in your table.
3. With the found set of new records still showing in the window of the field copy, switch to the main solution.
4. Perform an import in the main copy of the solution, importing records from the field copy.
5. Only the new records (those in the current found set in the field copy of the file) are added to the main solution.

**CAUTION** When consolidating records from different copies of a solution file, take care to ensure that you're not introducing duplicate primary key values (for example, serial numbers).

To avoid duplication of key values, consider allocating separate ranges of serial numbers to each copy of the file or try generating unique IDs using a combination of timestamp, NIC address, and recordID values.

**CROSS-REF** Chapter 15 covers methods of generating robust unique IDs (UIDs).

Assuming that your work while traveling offline with your laptop also involved editing some of the pre-existing records originating in the main solution, you will need to use a different process to upload modified records as well as new additions. Import matching allows you to merge records from the original and secondary copies of the file into a single data set.

**NOTE** When merging data sets as described here, the incoming data is given preference, overwriting corresponding data (if any) in the receiving file. If you require a more finely tuned synchronization process (such as one that retains the most recently modified version of each record), you need to build an intermediary transformation process to compare the data in both sets and selectively update either or both files.

## Import matching

To match records while importing, select the file for import via the normal import process (choose File ➪ Import Records ➪ File) and proceed to the Import Field Mapping dialog. As well as ensuring that the fields shown in the current table at the upper-right align appropriately with the data in the column at the upper-left area, select the Update Matching Records in Found Set option in the panel at the lower left, as shown in Figure 17.7.

**NOTE** Assuming that the source and destination are both FileMaker files and the source and destination table structures are the same, you should select the Matching Names option from the Arrange By pop-up list in the Import Field Mapping dialog.

For synchronization during import, FileMaker provides you with two options, as represented by the Update Existing Records in Found Set and Update Matching Records in Found Set options appearing in the lower left area of the dialog, as shown in Figure 17.7.

When you choose the Update Existing Records in Found Set option, the selected fields in records in the found set are overwritten with values from corresponding (according to sort order) records in the source table. Alternatively, when you select the Update Matching Records in Found Set option, you can identify one or more match fields to synchronize existing records in the current table with corresponding records in the source. With this option selected, you choose the match ("=") symbol adjacent to the relevant fields in the import order list, as shown beside the `ItemID` field (the selected field) in Figure 17.7.

**CAUTION** When determining match fields for an Update Matching Records in Found Set import, take care to ensure that the field (or combination of fields) you choose will be unique. If more than one match is found, the subsequent matches will overwrite data imported from previous matches, resulting in the last match in the source file determining the final value for a record in the current file.

When performing an update import process, you can select the checkbox option to add remaining data as new records. Note, however, that if you're updating the values in a subset of fields in the current table (as determined by your configuration of the import field map), only the selected values (and match values, if any) are imported into the resulting new records.

**NOTE** If you require additional fields uploaded for the records added in an Update import, you should isolate the new records in a reduced found set after the import completes and then run a second import using the Update Matching Records in Found Set option to populate the remaining fields in the new records.

### FIGURE 17.7

Setting the import field map to update modified records.

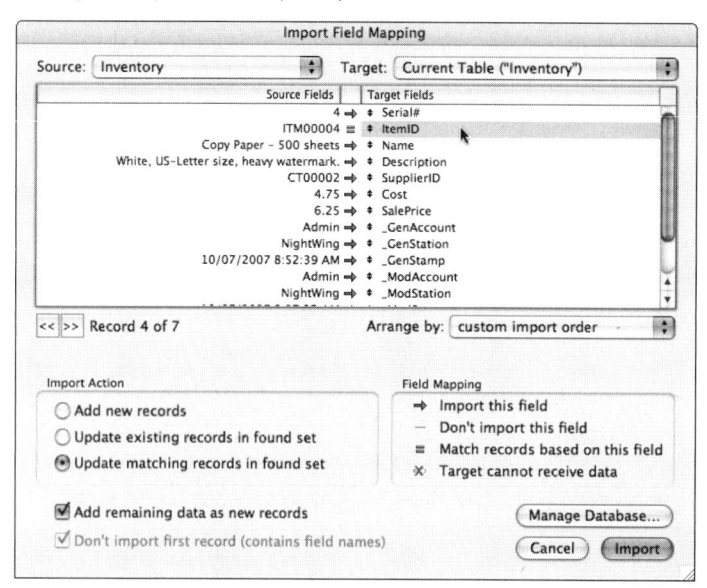

| Source Fields | | Target Fields |
|---|---|---|
| 4 → | ‡ | Serial# |
| ITM00004 = | ‡ | ItemID |
| Copy Paper - 500 sheets → | ‡ | Name |
| White, US-Letter size, heavy watermark. → | ‡ | Description |
| CT00002 → | ‡ | SupplierID |
| 4.75 → | ‡ | Cost |
| 6.25 → | ‡ | SalePrice |
| Admin → | ‡ | _GenAccount |
| NightWing → | ‡ | _GenStation |
| 10/07/2007 8:52:39 AM → | ‡ | _GenStamp |
| Admin → | ‡ | _ModAccount |
| NightWing → | ‡ | _ModStation |

Import Action:
- Add new records
- Update existing records in found set
- ● Update matching records in found set

Field Mapping:
- → Import this field
- − Don't import this field
- = Match records based on this field
- ✕ Target cannot receive data

☑ Add remaining data as new records
☑ Don't import first record (contains field names)

## Importing selectively

To import selectively, one option is to open both the source and target files and perform a find in either or both files and then run an Update Records in Found Set import. Providing the file containing the source table is open and is showing the required found set in its frontmost window, only the found records are included in the import. (Otherwise, all records in the source table are imported.)

In cases where data synchronization requires the application of more complex criteria than can be addressed by performing a find in either or both files prior to import, such as where you need to compare the values in corresponding records in both data sets to determine whether to import values from a given record, you will require a custom synchronization process. Custom synchronization requires one of the following:

- One file be defined as an external data source for the other so that a relationship between the source and target tables can be established (and a script can then loop through records comparing them and selectively transferring values in either direction).
- A utility table be created in one of the files as a temporary holding place for data from the source file. Selected records can then be imported into the utility table, and a

post-processing script can perform the required comparisons and selective transfers prior to deleting the records from the utility table.

- An external control file be created with the source and target files defined as external data sources and containing the logic for comparison and selective transfer of data between one or more tables in the two original files.

The use of a control process, as described in the first and last options, is powerful and flexible, giving you the option to

- Selectively transfer data in both directions, achieving two-way synchronization of data between tables in two files
- Efficiently synchronize data between systems with different data structures, where some data transformation and/or cleansing is required as part of the procedure
- Selectively transfer records from tables in other supported database environments, such as external SQL data sources

The utility table method described in the second option introduces additional processing time, because external data must first be imported and then separately reconciled. However, the absence of calculations, auto-entry actions, or validations (and minimization of the use of indexes) in the utility table enables the initial import to proceed efficiently. Moreover, this method's added flexibility lets you build synchronization procedures for data extracted or exported from a wide variety of sources, including unsupported mobile databases, spreadsheets, online sources, and third-party data systems.

# Handling Embedded Images and Stored Files

The container fields in FileMaker Pro can store a wide variety of files containing text, images, or other media content. If your solution will store a significant number of files of this kind, however, they will add to the bulk of your solution file(s), impacting performance, making backups and other procedures slower, and complicating some data transfer procedures. (Keep in mind that container fields cannot be exported directly, as noted in the "Exporting and Importing Data" section, earlier in this chapter.)

One option to consider if your solution is carrying a significant quantity of container data is to place container fields into tables in separate files, defining those files as external data sources and creating 1:1 relationships from your existing tables to the tables housing container data. This approach enables you to back up your data more efficiently by setting a different backup schedule for the file(s) containing large quantities of container content.

Another option FileMaker provides is external storage of container objects, where you instruct FileMaker to store only a reference to the file (for example, the path to the file's location on your computer or an accessible volume such as a file server). For example, when inserting a picture into a container field in Browse Mode by choosing Insert ➪ Picture, the resulting dialog, as shown at the lower left of the dialog in Figure 17.8, includes a checkbox option to Store Only a Reference to the File. This option is also available when using script or button commands to insert a file into a container.

**FIGURE 17.8**

Setting the import field map to upload a folder of picture files into FileMaker.

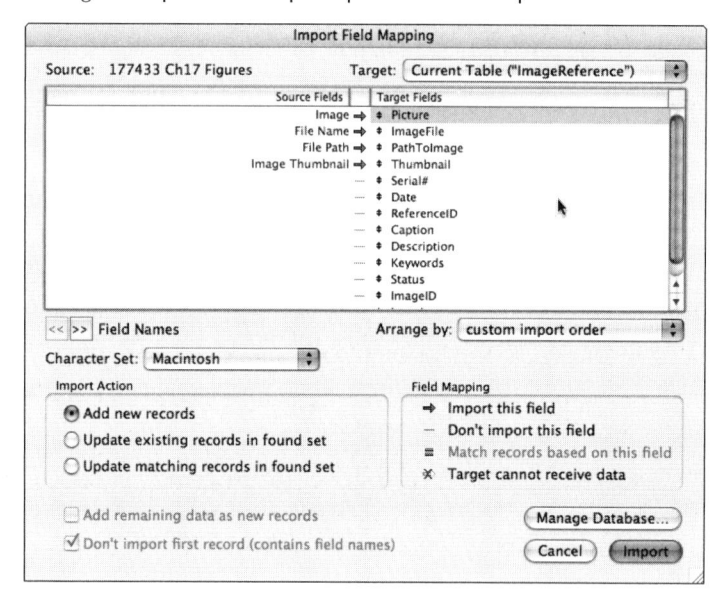

Storing a reference to a file, rather than storing the file itself, has both advantages and disadvantages. Among the advantages:

- You can access or update the files independently of FileMaker.
- The references don't cause your database files to bloat with their extra content.
- You can back up the files separately from your database backups.

Among the disadvantages:

- The path to the files must be the same from all client workstations if the files are to be accessible by multiple users when your solution is hosted.
- Your solution may break (or its content may no longer make sense or be complete) if the files are moved, renamed, or deleted.

# Maintaining and Restoring Data

You are, however, able to choose the most convenient method of storage depending on your priorities and the deployment considerations for your solution. Among other things, the ability to choose the storage mode can lead to

- Some containers being stored in the database and others stored only as a reference
- Changes of circumstance wherein you need container contents stored via the alternate method

Fortunately, the decisions you make aren't final; the means are available to convert container fields (individually, or as a batch) between the two modes of storage.

## Assigning and retrieving paths

When a file has been stored (embedded) in a container field using the Insert menu commands (or an equivalent script or button command), you can ascertain the file's name by passing the container field's name to the `GetAsText()` function. Similarly, if a file is stored as a reference in a container field, you can retrieve the path to the file (along with other information about the file, if available) by the same method.

When you script the insertion of a file into a container field, you can use a variable to supply the path, as described in Chapter 13. Additionally, when you set a valid path to a file (as text) into a container field, FileMaker stores the reference and displays the file (or its icon) in the container.

By exploiting the capabilities of the `GetAsText()` function and the `Set Variable[ ]` command, you can build scripts to control the storage state of container fields.

## Scripted field updates

A script along the following lines toggles the storage state of a container field used to store image files between embedded images and store-as-reference images:

```
If [IsEmpty(Products::Image)]
   Beep
Else If [PatternCount(GetAsText(Products::Image); "image:")]
   #Container is stored as path. Embed image:
   Set Variable [$Path; Value:Let([
                           pf = GetAsText(Products::Image);
                           p1 = Position(pf; "image:"; 1; 1);
                           p2 = Position(pf & ¶; ¶; p1; 1)-p1];
                           Middle(pf; p1; p2)
                           )]
   Go to Field [Products::ProductImage]
   Insert Picture ["$Path"]
Else
   #Image is embedded: Store as path
   Set Variable [$Path; Value:"file:images/" & GetAsText(Products::Image)]
   Export Field Contents [Products::Image; "$Path"]
   Set Field [Products::Image; "image" & Right($Path; Length($Path)-4) ]
End If
```

> **TIP** You can readily adapt the scripting techniques used in the preceding script to produce a script that loops through the found set — or all records in the current table — converting the contents of a container field between embedded and stored-as-reference storage modes.

## Text-Handling Considerations

In this chapter, we provide you with strategies and techniques for dealing with a broad range of data migration, transformation, and synchronization challenges. However, another issue deserves special mention. When presenting data in a range of export formats, FileMaker uses the standard convention of including a carriage-return character (ASCII character 13) as the delimiter between successive records in the exported data. Consequently, carriage returns appearing within fields in your data are substituted with alternate characters (ASCII character 11) in the exported data. This substitution presents a challenge when situations arise requiring that exported data include the original carriage-return characters.

### Export field contents

One way to solve the problem of ensuring carriage returns will be preserved in text output from your database is to gather content for export, such as data from multiple records, into a single text field, including carriage returns as required. You can then output the text field's complete contents — with carriage returns in place — using the Export Field Contents[ ] script command.

You can employ this technique to script a custom export process to build a text report document containing lines of text and carriage returns in configurations outside the normal constraints of the FileMaker export formats. For example, if you're required to export the contents of a series of Description fields in a Products table as continuous text, including any carriage returns residing within the text in the field, you do so by creating a global text field (for example, Products::gExportText) and a script along the following lines:

```
Set Error Capture [On]
Perform Find [Restore]
If [Get(LastError) ≠ 0]
  Beep
  Exit Script []
End If
Go to Record/Request/Page [First]
Set Field [Products::gExportText; ""]
Loop
  Set Field [Products::gExportText; Products::gExportText & If(not
    IsEmpty(Products::Description); ¶ & Products::Description)]
  Go to Record/Request/Page [Next; Exit after last]
End Loop
If [not IsEmpty(Products::gExportText)]
  Set Variable [$path; Value:"Products_" & Year(Get(CurrentDate)) & Right("0" &
    Month(Get(CurrentDate)); 2) & Right("0" & Day(Get(CurrentDate)); 2) & ".txt"]
  Export Field Contents [Products::gExportText; "$path"; Automatically open]
  Set Field [Products::gExportText; ""]
End If
```

After running this script, you have a text file containing the description field entries with their carriage returns preserved, providing there are records meeting the criteria you specified for the `Perform Find [Restore]` command, and the `Products::Description` has text in it on one or more of the found records.

## Designing a custom export process

The process of passing data first into a global text field and exporting from there provides you with, in effect, a customized export where you gain increased control over the resulting file's form and content. By extension, you can use this process to build export files employing custom delimiters and to perform a variety of other procedures on the data — substitutions, character filtering, and so on — before exporting to the external file.

If you need still greater control over the export process, we recommend that you create a transformation utility within your solution. To create this utility, create a Transformations table where your scripts can create records (for example, via a relationship from the source table for the export, set to Allow Creation of Related Records). In this way, you can create Transformations table records for export in whatever form is required, applying calculations to the content to combine or separate data, or to address data presentation or domain requirements.

Once the transformation process is complete, your script can either export the transformed data directly from the Transformations table or perform further processing by compiling output content in a global field as described under the "Export field contents" section, earlier in this chapter. By combining these techniques, you can attain a high degree of control over the resulting data export, generating data in whatever form circumstances may require.

# Part V

# Raising the Bar

Your solution is solid. Your command of FileMaker Pro features is building, and you're implementing top-notch solutions for your customer or client. But, what if you want to add polish, professionalism, or power or to customize your databases, to tailor your solutions to specific customers, or to meet the exacting standards of a commercial product?

This part walks you through the additional capabilities that the FileMaker Pro 9 Advanced product offers, including diagnostic tools, custom interface, navigation and calculation capabilities, runtime versions, and kiosk mode. We delve into the art of making solutions, scalable and robust, and extending FileMaker's reach with external scripting calls, plug-ins, and a variety of Web-related options. We also point you to a sampling of some third-party tools that can help you with your FileMaker development efforts.

## IN THIS PART

**Chapter 18**
FileMaker Advanced Features

**Chapter 19**
Efficient Code, Efficient Solutions

**Chapter 20**
Extending FileMaker's Capabilities

# Chapter 18

# FileMaker Pro Advanced Features

If you're reading this chapter, we figure the fact you are here means you're serious, right? When the going gets tough, FileMaker developers' reach for FileMaker Pro Advanced, an extended version that does everything FileMaker Pro can do, with a host of powerful additions.

FileMaker Pro Advanced makes things easier, giving you professional tools to debug and document your code. By itself, this benefit may be reason enough to pawn your second computer and buy a copy, but FileMaker Pro Advanced offers you several other powerful features.

In this chapter, we walk you through what we consider the key features of this leading-edge FileMaker Pro version, giving you insights into where your development can take you when you become an Advanced developer.

## Script Debugger

Scripts run at blinding speed, doing their thing; when they work, it's a bit magical, but when your scripts don't do what you expect them to do, figuring out the cause can be quite a challenge. To help, FileMaker Advanced provides a Script Debugger that lets you step through your script one line at a time, watching what happens, and checking for errors.

Choosing Tools ⇨ Script Debugger prior to running a script activates the Script Debugger. While the Script Debugger is active, its window "floats" over your solution's windows and, when you run a script, the text of the script appears in the Debugger window, as shown in Figure 18.1.

### IN THIS CHAPTER

Employing the Script Debugger

Making use of the Data Viewer

Documenting solutions with the Database Design Report

Demystifying file maintenance

Adding tooltips to your solutions

Building and controlling custom menus

Working with custom functions

Understanding custom functions and recursion

Distributing solutions as runtime applications

Considering kiosk mode

## Watching code in action

Along the top of the Script Debugger window are ten buttons and immediately below them the definition of the current script appears, with the current step highlighted. Below the script pane, the Last Error code is displayed. Most of the time when using the Debugger, you will be stepping through a script using one of the two buttons nearest the left along the top of the Script Debugger window (Step and Step Into), while checking the effect on your solution and noting the error code at each step.

Even if your script isn't malfunctioning, stepping through it with the Script Debugger activated enables you to better understand how ScriptMaker works and how to improve your script's code and make it more fault tolerant.

**FIGURE 18.1**

Viewing the Show Transaction script (from the Inventory example file) in the Script Debugger.

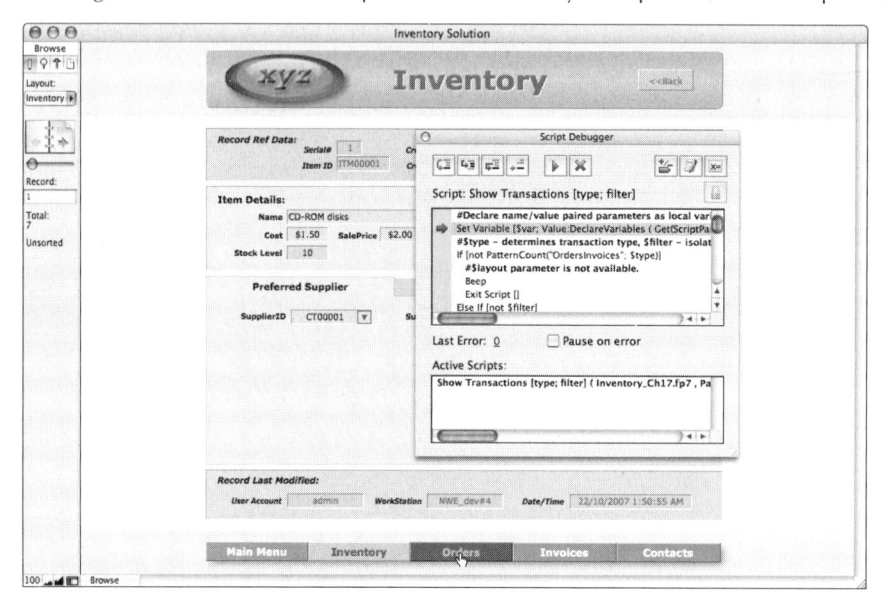

When your script calls other scripts (via the Perform Script [ ] command), the Script Debugger displays the stack of active scripts in the pane at the bottom, allowing you to select and review any script in the stack.

**TIP** You can double-click any script listed in the Active Scripts pane to open it for editing in a corresponding Edit Script window.

# FileMaker Pro Advanced Features

## Debugging restricted privilege scripts

**NEW FEATURE** An important FileMaker Pro 9 Advanced addition to the Script Debugger's capabilities is the ability to separately authenticate the Debugger so that you can view and debug a script while logged in with a privilege set that doesn't have edit access to the script.

To authenticate the Debugger for debugging while in restricted privilege access accounts, click the button at the right above the script pane and enter a full access account and password. When you do, the access account and privileges for your current database session are unchanged, but the Script Debugger nevertheless admits you "behind the scenes" to see what is going on.

**NOTE** Authentication applies to the Data Viewer (see next topic) as well as the Script Debugger. If you authenticate in one, the authentication provides coverage of the other, as well.

## Getting used to the Debugger controls

The buttons along the top of the Script Debugger (see Figure 18.2) take a little getting used to, mainly because they're adorned by rather obscure icons and aren't labeled. They do, however, have tooltips you can view by holding the mouse over them for a few seconds so that you aren't totally in the dark.

**FIGURE 18.2**
The main controls of the Script Debugger.

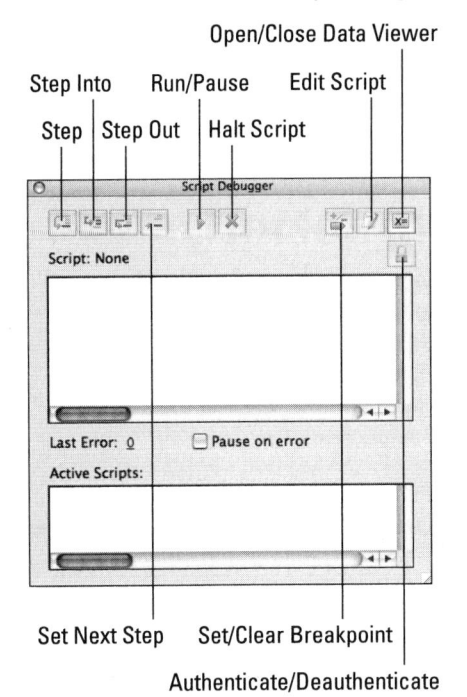

607

The buttons along the top of the Script Debugger window operate as follows:

- **Step:** Advances through the current script one line at a time, without stepping into (debugging) any subscripts.
- **Step Into:** Advances through the current script sequence line-by-line, stepping into and debugging any subscripts encountered as it goes.
- **Step Out:** Ceases debugging the current script or subscript, allowing it to run normally until its conclusion. (If you're debugging a subscript, you will be returned to the parent script at the line after the Perform Script[ ] command calling the subscript.) However, if the current script includes breakpoints, the step out button causes it to run until the next breakpoint is reached.
- **Set Next Step:** Allows you to designate a selected step as the next step to execute. Using this control lets you modify the execution sequence while debugging, either skipping over steps or repeating steps.
- **Run/Pause:** Sets the script running until the next break point (if any) or until its conclusion.
- **Halt Script:** Cancels all active scripts, regardless of state at the current step and exits the Script Debugger.
- **Set/Clear Breakpoint:** Adds or removes a marker (appearing as a red tag at the left) on the currently selected script step. When a breakpoint has been set, you can use the Run/Pause button to run the script through to the next breakpoint. (It will pause automatically when it reaches the tagged step.) You can also add or modify breakpoints in the Edit Script window by clicking in the gray band to the left of the script pane in FileMaker Pro Advanced.
- **Edit Script:** Opens the current script for editing or viewing in its Edit Script window. The current step of the script will be automatically pre-selected in the script when it opens for editing.
- **Open/Close Data Viewer:** Displays or hides the Data Viewer window, allowing you to see the values of fields, variables, or calculations as the script progresses.

**NEW FEATURE** Closing the Script Debugger does not halt execution of the active scripts. Instead, it sets them in motion for the remainder of their run without the Debugger. This behavior is a change from earlier versions of FileMaker Pro Advanced.

In addition, below the main script pane, the Script Debugger in FileMaker Pro 9 Advanced includes a checkbox option for Pause on Error. With this option enabled, running the script, either by clicking the Run/Pause button or closing the Script Debugger, results in the script pausing when an error code other than zero is encountered. If the Script Debugger has been closed, it reopens when an error is encountered.

# Data Viewer

The FileMaker Pro 9 Advanced Data Viewer lets you see your calculation results without having to add them to your solution or place them on a layout. You can test ideas — and get the calculation syntax right — by trying them out in the Data Viewer before adding them to your scripts or field definitions. Moreover, you can keep an eye on the values of variables and an assortment of application or system parameters, by adding calculations using selected Get ( ) functions to the Data Viewer.

You can access the Data Viewer — whether a script is running or not — by choosing Tools ➪ Data Viewer. As with the Script Debugger, the Data Viewer window permanently floats above other windows (with the exception the Script Debugger window), as shown in Figure 18.3.

**FIGURE 18.3**

Viewing the Data Viewer window floating over a solution window.

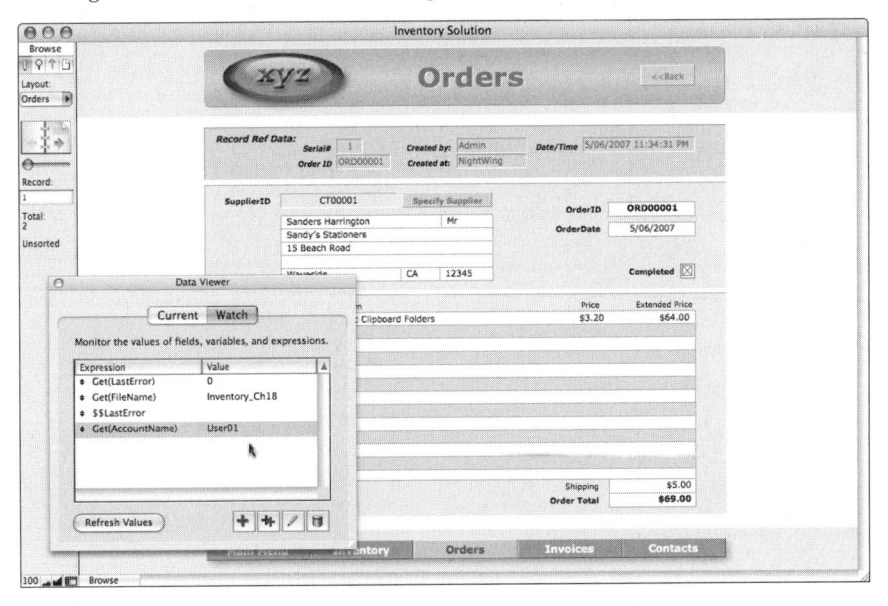

You can close and reopen the Data Viewer window at any time (except when viewing a modal dialog), and it will retain the calculations or values you manually added to it.

**Part V** Raising the Bar

## Current and Watch panels

**NEW FEATURE** The Data Viewer in FileMaker Pro 9 Advanced includes two tab panels, one automatically displaying variables in use and values referenced in the active script and the other enabling you to create calculations and monitor their results regardless of the current script context.

You can switch between the Current and Watch panels whenever the Data Viewer is open, providing you with access to two complementary modes of operation.

### The Current panel

Values tracked on the Data Viewer's Current panel update automatically to include current global variables (if no script is running) and current local and global variables (if a script is active). Moreover, when a script is in progress, fields referenced by the script are automatically added to the Current panel. As a script commences its run in the Script Debugger, the Data Viewer's Current panel performs a "pre-flight load" of all fields (including fields referred to by calculations) referenced by the script.

The Current panel is always available when you're logged in with an account that's assigned [Full Access] privileges. At other times, you're required to authenticate within the Data Viewer, as shown in Figure 18.4, to access the Current panel's display.

**FIGURE 18.4**

The Current panel requires authentication when you're logged in with a restricted access account.

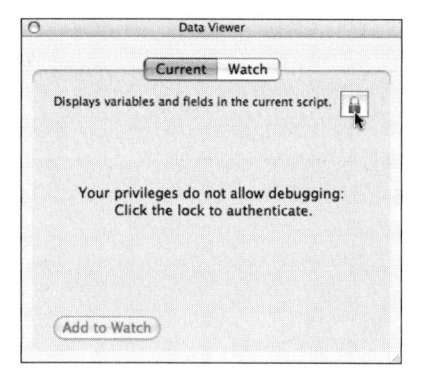

Authenticating with a [Full Access] account in the Data Viewer applies only to the Data Viewer and the Script Debugger in the current file; it has no effect on the login account for the rest of the file. If you have multiple files open with accounts assigned to restricted access privilege sets, you will need to authenticate the Data Viewer separately in each file in order to see script values in the Current panel in all the open files.

## FileMaker Pro Advanced Features

When you hold the mouse pointer over a selected line in the Current panel, a tooltip appears showing the result in its entirety. This tooltip is useful when the result is too long to appear fully in the limited space of the Value column—and especially if the value has multiple lines, as exemplified in Figure 18.5.

In addition, you view a line's values—and in the case of variables, directly edit them—by double-clicking the line in the Current panel. FileMaker displays the value in its entirety in a scrollable list in the Current Value dialog, as shown in Figure 18.6.

The Current Value dialog is resizable, so you can use it to display long values without truncation. Moreover, you can select values in the Current Value dialog and copy them to the clipboard.

**FIGURE 18.5**

The Current panel hover technique reveals long or multi-line viewer values.

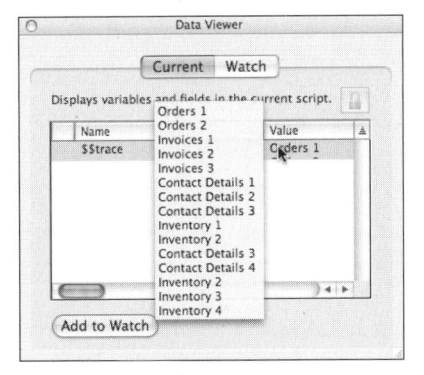

**FIGURE 18.6**

Viewing or editing a variable value in the Current Value dialog.

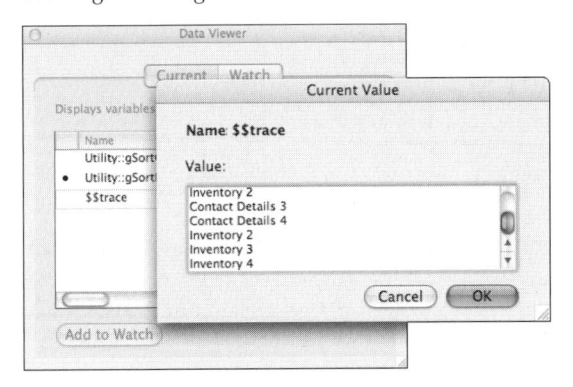

611

**Part V  Raising the Bar**

Where referenced fields have repetitions, the repetitions containing a value are loaded into the Data Viewer's Current panel. Repetitions (for either fields or variables) are shown in the Data Viewer using array notation, such as YourField[3] for the third repetition of YourField.

> **NOTE** You can copy fields or variables appearing in the Data Viewer's Current panel to the Watch panel by selecting them and clicking the Add to Watch button at the lower left of the Current panel.

### The Watch panel

The Data Viewer's Watch panel lets you specify calculation expressions and tracks their evaluation in the Value column, as shown in Figure 18.7.

The controls at the lower right of the Watch panel of the Data Viewer are as follows:

- **Add Expression:** Brings up an Edit Expression dialog (a variant of the Specify Calculation dialog) where you can enter a field, variable, or calculation formula to be monitored in the Watch panel.

- **Duplicate Expression:** Creates a copy of the selected expression in the list area of the Watch panel.

- **Edit Expression:** Opens the Edit Expression dialog for the currently selected expression in the Watch panel, allowing you to view a long calculation expression or copy or revise it.

- **Remove Expression:** Deletes the currently selected line from the Watch panel.

**FIGURE 18.7**

The controls of the Data Viewer's Watch panel.

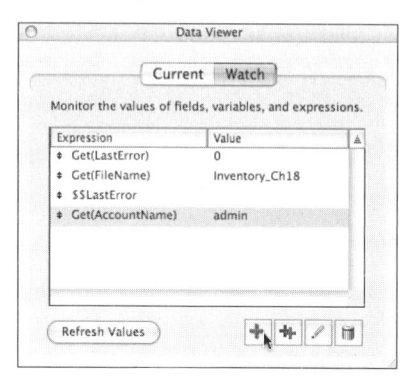

# FileMaker Pro Advanced Features

The values you enter into the Watch panel are retained until you delete them. They're not specific to the current file or files set, but apply to all files opened in the current copy of FileMaker Pro Advanced. However, expressions in the Watch panel are evaluated in the current context — so if they refer to fields in your solution, they only produce valid/meaningful results while those fields remain accessible.

> **TIP** You can sort either of the columns of the Data Viewer (in the Current panel as well as the Watch panel) by clicking the corresponding column heading.

## Using the Viewer with the Debugger

You can use the Data Viewer as a stand-alone feature by choosing it from the Tools ➪ Data Viewer. However, the Data Viewer is an invaluable adjunct to the Script Debugger, enhancing your ability to observe the results of scripts as you advance through them one step at a time. You can invoke or dismiss the Data Viewer from within the Script Debugger window by clicking the Open/Close Data Viewer button (bearing the "X=" symbol) in the upper-right corner of the Script Debugger window.

In particular, the Current panel automatically monitors the values of all the current variables and all fields referenced by the current script. Each value is updated with every line of the script as you step through it in the Debugger window.

> **NOTE** Global variables are listed in the Current panel while you're debugging a script, whether or not the current script references them.

## The Data Viewer sand pit

While the Data Viewer is a powerful adjunct to the Script Debugger, it has a variety of other uses in its own right. It is a very useful environment for building calculation expressions for use in your solution — either in scripts or field definitions — because it allows you to test the expression and view its result as you're writing it. In this way, the Data Viewer enables you to debug your calculation code in a safe sand-pit environment, copying the final expression and pasting it into your solution when you're satisfied with the result.

The Data Viewer's Edit Expression dialog, shown in Figure 18.8, includes a Result box below the Expression box, where the current expression's result appears when you click the Evaluate Now button.

> **NOTE** When you enter references to your solution's field and table occurrence structures into the Data Viewer via the Edit Expression dialog, FileMaker evaluates the references from the context of the current record and layout showing in the frontmost window of the active file.

**FIGURE 18.8**

The Edit Expression dialog accessible from the Watch panel of the Data Viewer.

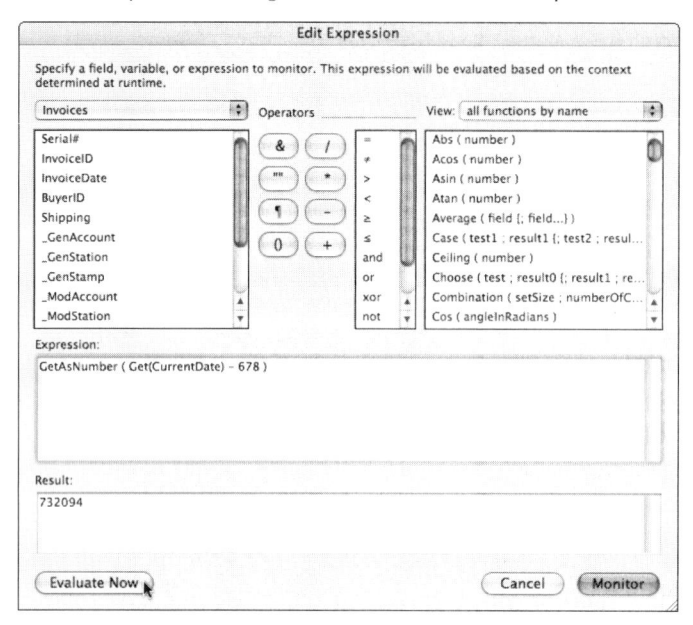

## The Data Viewer and variables

The Data Viewer is a convenient way to view the values assigned to variables in your solution, enabling you to keep track of their changing values as you test your scripts and calculations. Additionally, you can use the Data Viewer to modify a variable's value, either by editing it directly in the Current panel, or by including it in a Let ( ) expression in the Edit Expression dialog.

Bear in mind that anyone with a copy of FileMaker Pro Advanced can access the Data Viewer's Watch panel, even without a [Full Access] login, and can therefore modify the values assigned to variables in your solution. Keep in mind the following caveats regarding variables:

- Global variables are unsuitable for holding or handling sensitive or confidential information, including passwords, because a user who guesses the name of the variable can access its value using the Data Viewer (if they open your solution using a copy of FileMaker Pro Advanced).
- Variables aren't suitable for the storage of essential values your solution (and particularly your solution's security) depends upon because they can be edited directly by users who have access to the Data Viewer.

# FileMaker Pro Advanced Features

Concerns about the security of variable values with respect to the Data Viewer apply primarily to global variables because local variables are extant only while the script where they were declared is active (during which time a user without the ability to authenticate with a [Full Access] account is not able to use the Data Viewer). An exception to the normal expiration rules exists with respect to local variables associated with script zero.

**CROSS-REF** For a detailed discussion of variables, including variables associated with script zero, refer to Chapter 9.

## Database Design Report

Documenting your work is an important part of the professional development process. You can do some limited documentation in FileMaker Pro by printing scripts, tables, and layouts. However, FileMaker Pro Advanced substantially extends your ability to document the finer details of your solutions by including the Database Design Report (DDR).

To create a Database Design Report, follow these steps:

1. Open the file or file set you want to document.
2. Choose Tools ➪ Database Design Report. The Database Design Report dialog appears, as shown in Figure 18.9, enabling you to specify the files, tables, and kinds of detail to be included in the report, as well as the report's output format.

**FIGURE 18.9**

Selecting report options in the Database Design Report dialog.

615

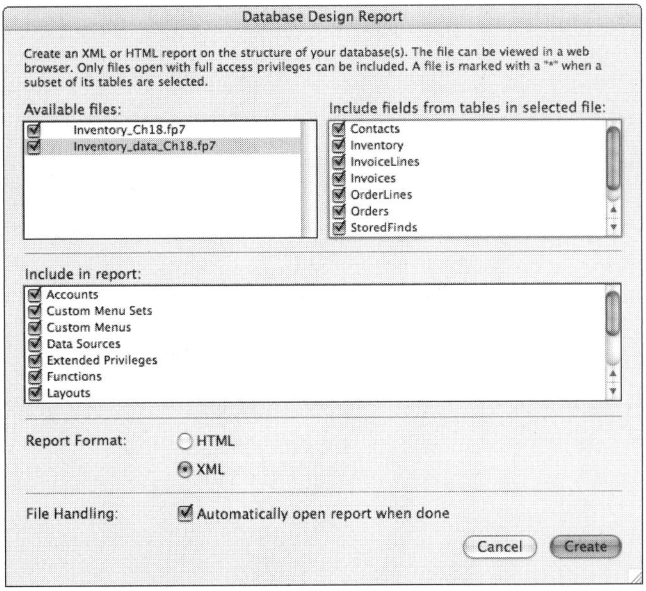

3. Select your desired options in the Database Design Report dialog.
4. Click the Create button and then choose a location to save the report files.
5. Click the Save button to accept the settings and commence creation of your Database Design Report.

**NOTE** If your solution is large and/or you choose to include most or all of the report detail options, be aware the report may take some time to compile. A coffee break may be in order while FileMaker prepares your report.

## DDR capabilities

A full DDR captures, in detail, almost every aspect of your solution's design, from scripts and script steps to tables, relationships, and calculation code. Data concerning all these elements and more are compiled into a structured and searchable document that defines and captures the current state of your solution files.

You can open the DDR in a Web browser — or any other HTML or XML compatible application — to peruse, search, or manipulate its contents, or to extract details for inclusion in other documents, archives, and so on. You can also use information in the DDR as a reference for further development or to build or repair parts of your solutions. For example, you can copy and paste the syntax of complex calculations, custom functions, and other code available in your DDRs into new field and function definitions in your solutions.

**TIP** Running a new DDR at intervals during your development work is one way of keeping track of your work, enabling you to refer back to the details of earlier versions of your data structure and code.

## Mining the DDR for information

At the most basic level, the DDR provides an index of organized data about your solution's structure and code, enabling you to browse and locate information in broad categories and giving you a useful overview of each file's contents. However, you can also call the DDR into service to solve problems.

The DDR provides a direct resource for locating specific references to elements in your solutions. For example, if you need to locate all the places where a particular field is referenced, you can generate a complete DDR and then search it for the name of the field in question. Similarly, to locate unresolved references such as missing fields (for example, a field has been referenced but subsequently deleted), you can search the HTML version of the DDR for the text string "Missing Field".

By performing HTML searches or by opening the DDR files in a text editor or other tool, you can perform various kinds of basic analysis of your solution content. If you want access to additional capabilities, use the optional XML output option and consider investing in one of the available tools for detailed analysis of your DDR's contents.

## Tools and techniques for interpreting DDR data

When you create DDR output in XML format, FileMaker generates a series of files containing the complete contents of the DDR, in a form you can readily convert into a variety of other formats (or upload into a database) for analysis.

You can create your own tools, such as a custom-built FileMaker database, to import DDR's XML version for analysis or to develop reports of your own using the data contained in one or more of your solution's DDRs. You can find more details about the XML Output Grammar used in the Database Design Report at the FileMaker, Inc., Web site to assist you in working with the XML content.

Additionally, a number of developers have created and published tools ready-made to perform a variety of analyses of DDR data. The best of these provide instant access to a wealth of information that can save you time and help you to produce better solutions.

**CROSS-REF** For additional details regarding the use of third-party tools, including tools for analysis of Database Design Report output, refer to Chapter 20.

## File Maintenance

FileMaker Pro Advanced provides you with three ways to compact or optimize your solution files. One is via the File ➪ Save a Copy As command (choosing the "compacted copy" option) — a method also available in FileMaker Pro. The other two methods are exclusive to FileMaker Pro Advanced, and you can access them by choosing Tools ➪ File Maintenance. When the File Maintenance dialog appears, as shown in Figure 18.10, you see two checkbox options and the briefest of explanations about what they do.

Despite the reassuring words below each checkbox option in the File Maintenance dialog, there is some confusion about the differences between the available methods of enhancing solution performance — and when to use them. It pays to tread carefully here.

**FIGURE 18.10**

The Compact and Optimize options in the File Maintenance dialog.

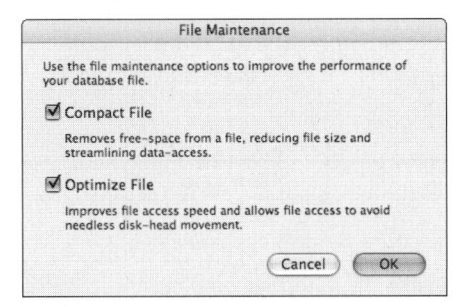

## Compact File

As you use your solution files, adding, editing, and deleting data, file blocks in various places become partially full in a process akin to disk fragmentation. The presence of partially full blocks increases overall file size and the amount of work your computer does when accessing data.

When you select the Compact File option, FileMaker Pro Advanced scans the file from end to end to locate opportunities to merge partially full adjacent blocks, resulting in a file with fewer blocks (and more data in each block). Because the procedure makes only a single pass over the file, a second Compact File procedure may further reduce the block count.

Don't use the Compact File procedure on a damaged file because it may damage it further — possibly beyond recovery. We recommend that you avoid using this procedure if you suspect file corruption and always first ensure that you have a current backup of your file.

## Optimize File

The Optimize File procedure isn't concerned with the number of blocks in your file, but with their sequence. It swaps the locations of blocks to bring information into a logical order, grouped with like elements and with data stored in creation order (the default presentation order, in many cases).

The Optimize procedure is not designed to reduce file size, as such, but may decrease the amount of disk activity required to read data for some database operations. Like the Compact File procedure, you shouldn't perform optimization when you suspect file damage, and otherwise should do so only when you have a current backup of the file.

## The Save a Copy As / Compacted alternative

The alternative procedure of saving a compacted copy of your file may have advantages in two important respects:

- Save a Copy As/Compacted copies the contents of your file, placing them into a new file in compacted and optimized form, in a process that generally results in a more compact file than can be produced via the File Maintenance/Compact procedure (for example, nearly all empty space in blocks is removed).
- When you use the Save a Copy As procedure, you're creating a new, separate file, leaving the original file intact. Thus, in the event anything goes amiss (for example,. because of anomalies in the block structure of your file), you have the original file to which to revert.

Given its advantages, we recommend the use of Save a Copy As in preference to the File Maintenance procedures, whenever convenient.

## FileMaker Pro Advanced Features

> **TIP** FileMaker minimizes the impact of anything but the most severe file fragmentation by using RAM cache for frequently accessed data. If you've been experiencing performance deterioration, you can expect increasing the FileMaker Pro and/or FileMaker Server cache allocation to provide more immediate and noticeable performance benefits than file optimization.

Solution design considerations such as reducing redundancy in your solution and optimizing field indexing are also likely to yield greater performance gains than file optimization in most cases.

The various optimization techniques place the data into a predictable and compact form ideal for efficient reading of data. However, you should consider that such a format is not necessarily ideal for a file in regular use. The lack of empty space in the file results in any additions being added at the end of the file, creating fresh fragmentation straight away. In general, therefore, compacting files is of greatest benefit when they're used for reference purposes (for example, as read-only archives).

## Defining Tooltips

FileMaker Pro can display *tooltips* (text flags associated with layout objects) in both Browse and Find modes; however, you need FileMaker Pro Advanced to define or edit tooltips.

To define a tooltip for an object, follow these steps:

1. Enter Layout mode and select the object.
2. Choose Format ➪ Set Tooltip. (You can also access the Set Tooltip command from the contextual menu by Ctrl+clicking/right-clicking with the mouse on the layout object.) The Set Tooltip dialog appears, as shown in Figure 18.11.
3. Type the tooltip text you want to use for a layout object and click OK. The relevant tip rectangle appears when the mouse pointer is stationary above the object (in Find or Browse mode) for a little more than a second, as shown in Figure 18.12.

> **TIP** To efficiently identify objects with tooltips attached when viewing your solution in Layout mode, choose View ➪ Show ➪ Tooltips. A small, colored note icon appears at the lower-right corner of objects with a tooltip defined.

**FIGURE 18.11**

Defining a tooltip for a selected object via the Set Tooltip dialog.

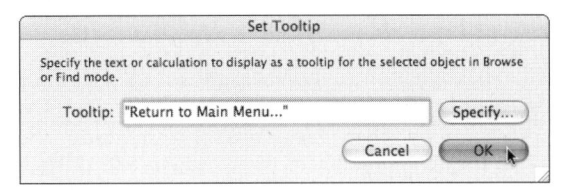

### FIGURE 18.12

A button tooltip displayed in Browse mode.

## Using conditional tooltips

In the preceding example, the tooltip was supplied as a literal text value. However, FileMaker Pro Advanced supports the use of calculation syntax when defining tooltips, enabling you to define different tooltips to display in different circumstances or to implement a method of turning tooltips on or off according to user preferences.

For example, if you have a script attached to a button that takes users to Find mode (if they are currently in Browse mode) or performs the Find if the solution is already in Find mode, you may want to vary the tooltip text according to the current window's mode. You can achieve mode-dependent tip text with a tooltip definition using a calculation expression along the lines of:

```
Choose(Get(WindowMode); "Go to Find mode..."; "Perform the current Find...")
```

**NOTE** The `Get(WindowMode)` function returns 0 in Browse mode and 1 in Find mode.

Similarly, if your solution keeps track of user preferences in a Users table, you can set your login script to store the user's tooltip preference (whether or not the user wants tooltips displayed during their sessions) in a global field, such as in a Utility table. With such a mechanism in place, you can determine whether your tooltips appear, based on the user's preference, by using a calculation expression such as

```
If(Utility::gTooltipPref = 1; "Your tooltip text here...")
```

## Keeping track of tooltips

If your solution is complex, you'll likely have many tooltips defined, and the same tooltip text may appear in multiple places. For example, when defining a tip such as the one shown in Figure 18.12, you're likely to want the same tip text appearing on all main menu navigation buttons throughout your solution — in other words, on most of the layouts.

When managing the text for a large number of tooltips, you should consider storing the tooltip content in a single location to facilitate managing it and updating it as needed. For example, if your solution has around 25 main menu buttons throughout, a better solution than defining (and subsequently managing) all the tooltip text separately is to create a global field called `gMainMenuButton` in a table called Tooltips in your solution and then specify the tooltip for the main menu buttons as

```
If(Utility::gTooltipPref = 1; Tooltips::gMainMenuButton)
```

With an approach of this kind, you can update the tooltip text for all the main menu buttons at once by editing the default value in the `Tooltips::gMainMenuButton` field.

To enhance the usefulness of a centralized tooltip management approach, we suggest that you store the reference text for each tooltip in your solution in separate records in the Tooltips table, loading the relevant values into the global field(s) referenced by your tooltip calculation expressions, as a sub-routine of your solution's start-up script. That way, when the solution is hosted, the current tooltip text is made available in the global fields in the Tooltips table at the commencement of each client session.

## Creating Custom Menus

The FileMaker Pro menu system provides users with access to all the basic application features and functions, but it does so in a generic way without reference to the particular needs, habits, preferences, or vocabulary of your users.

You can improve your solutions' usability by modifying the menus to remove commands not required by your users, to rename commands so that their meaning is specific to your solution (for example, "New Contact" instead of "New Record"), and/or to change the way commands operate, according to the needs of your users.

### Defining menus

The Custom Menu functionality in FileMaker enables you to define menu sets and then choose which menu set will be the default for each layout in your file, as well as changing the current menu set using the `Install Menu Set [ ]` script or button command.

**NOTE** The standard menus in FileMaker are always available as one of the options for you to assign to a layout or invoke via the `Install Menu Set [ ]` command.

To create a menu set for use in your solution, choose File ➪ Manage ➪ Custom Menus. The Manage Custom Menus dialog appears, as shown in Figure 18.13.

Creating a custom menu set requires you to configure elements at three levels:

- Setting the attributes — name and action to be performed — for the commands on each menu
- Naming and configuring each individual menu (groups of commands)
- Gathering a number of menus into a named set

To perform the first two tasks, select a menu in the Manage Custom Menus dialog's Custom Menus panel and click the Edit button at the bottom of the panel, causing the Edit Custom Menu dialog to appear.

## Part V  Raising the Bar

**FIGURE 18.13**

Selecting a menu for editing in the Custom Menus tab of the Manage Custom Menus dialog.

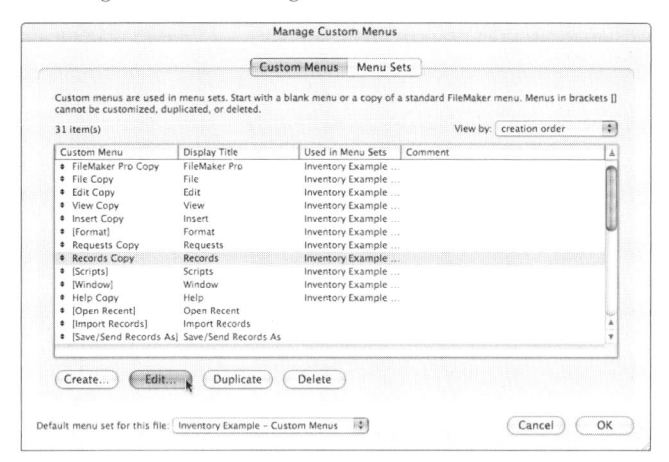

When building a custom menu, you can choose to modify an existing menu, make a copy of a menu and modify the copy, or start from scratch and build a whole new menu. These options correspond to the Create, Edit, and Duplicate buttons along the bottom of the Custom Menus panel shown in Figure 18.13.

You can't copy *default menus* (those with names enclosed in square brackets). However, copies of most menus are ready for editing or duplication when a file is first created. Because the menu copies originate at the point when you create a file, the menu configuration they reflect matches the configuration of the version of FileMaker used to create the file (so menu commands added in later versions are not included). For example, the Edit Copy custom menu available by default in a file created with a previous version of FileMaker includes a single Edit ➪ Undo command, whereas the Edit Copy custom menu in a file created with FileMaker Pro 9 includes Edit ➪ Undo and Edit ➪ Redo.

**TIP** When you create a menu, you can use it in multiple menu sets throughout your solutions — each menu set is made up of a collection of menus defined in the file — including FileMaker's default menus.

### Editing individual menus

The Edit Custom Menu dialog, shown in Figure 18.14, allows you to specify overall settings for the menu in the upper part of the dialog. These settings include the name of the menu, both as it appears in the Custom Menus dialogs and its *display title* (the name users will see when accessing it in your solution). You can also specify the platform(s) and mode(s) where the menu is to appear.

**NOTE** FileMaker's standard menu sets always appear in Layout mode.

## FileMaker Pro Advanced Features 18

**FIGURE 18.14**

Assigning a script to a menu command in the Edit Custom Menu dialog.

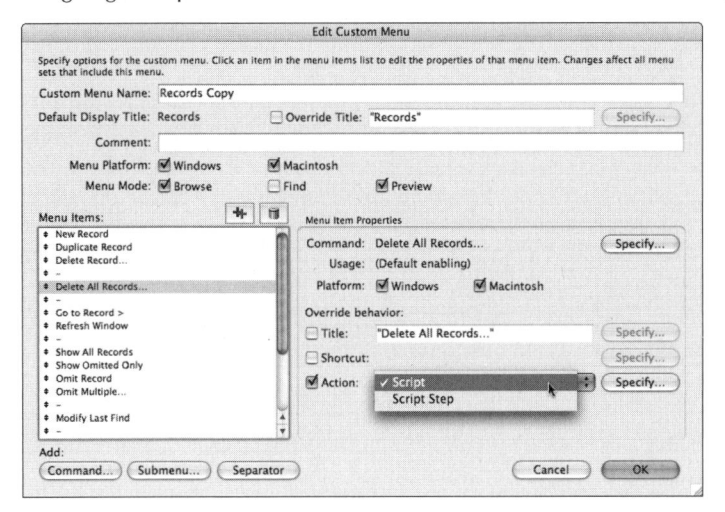

In the lower part of the Edit Custom Menu dialog, you edit the commands on the menu, configuring each to perform a default or custom (Script or Script Step) action, as well as setting the command's name, the platform(s) it is to be available on, and an associated keyboard shortcut. You can make each setting in the Menu Item Properties panel in the Edit Custom Menu dialog, after selecting the item in the Menu Items list.

### Benefits of the Script Step action

There is some benefit to assigning custom menu commands to the Script Step action rather than the Script action, even when your goal is to have the command you're configuring run a script. Using the Script Step option, you can select the `Perform Script[ ]` command to launch a script, with the advantage that you can then also configure the controls to manage any running scripts (selecting whether running scripts should Halt, Exit, Resume, or Pause when the script you attach to the command is triggered).

When configuring menus using the Edit Custom Menu dialog, you can add or remove items, submenus, and separators using the buttons immediately above and below the Menu Items list.

**TIP** When adding a menu item, you can base it on an existing FileMaker menu command or create it with No Command Assigned. The significance of the decision whether or not to repurpose an existing FileMaker command is that the command's availability is determined by the availability context of the command on which it is based.

For example, commands such as Duplicate Record and Delete Record aren't available (and therefore appear dimmed) when no records are in the current found set. If you want to create a command that is dimmed and unavailable when no records in the found set, you could choose to base it on one of these commands. (Its availability will be determined accordingly, even though you assign it a different name and a different action.)

623

### Benefits of window widgets

An important aspect of custom menu operation is that when you modify the actions associated with a standard menu command, window buttons and widgets performing the same task also acquire the new behavior. For example, if you reassign the Close Window command to run a script, clicking the Close button in the title bar of a database window also runs the assigned script.

When configuring the custom find log in the Inventory example in Chapter 9, we used custom menus to reassign the Perform Find command to run the Perform/Store Find script instead — so when users perform a Find (whether by using the menu command, clicking the Find button in the Status Area, or by pressing the Enter key) the script runs and the Find is logged.

In any situation where a command is associated with a window widget, you can employ custom menus to change the behavior of the widget by modifying the attributes of the associated command. The same is true regarding contextual menus and toolbar actions — like window widgets, their behavior is changed when the corresponding menu action is reassigned using custom menus.

## Adding menus to sets

Once you've created required menus and configured them with the menu commands you need, the next step is to assemble them into sets. You do so by navigating to the Menu Sets panel of the Manage Custom Menus dialog and using either the Edit (to modify an existing set) or Create (to assemble a new set) button to access the Edit Menu Set dialog, as shown in Figure 18.15.

In addition to adding or removing menus from the selected menu set, you can use the Edit Menu Set dialog to determine the order menus will appear (from left to right in the menu bar). To do so, drag the menus up and down by their handle icon in the Edit Menu Set dialog's Menus in <...> list.

## Assigning menu sets throughout your file

Once you have created one or more custom menu sets, you have several options available to you to specify when and where your users will have access to your custom menus.

### Setting the default menu set for a file

The simplest option for deploying your custom menu set is to assign it as the default menu set for the file where it is defined. You can do so via the pop-up menu setting on the bottom of the Manage Custom Menus dialog (see Figure 18.13). When you define a menu set, it appears in the pop-up list and can be selected as the file default.

### FIGURE 18.15
Assigning a menu to a Menu Set via the Edit Menu Set dialog.

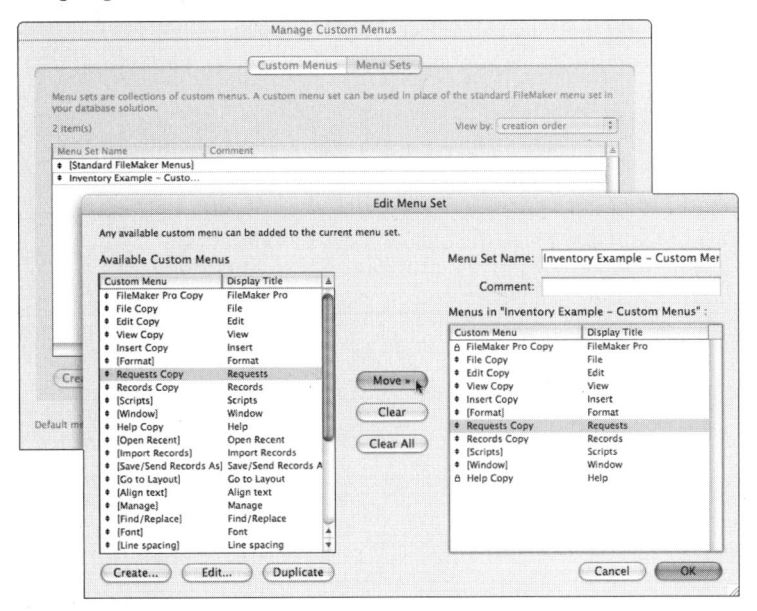

### Determining a menu set for each layout

You can also associate a default menu set with each layout in your file. To assign a default menu for a layout, proceed as follows:

1. Navigate to the layout in question.
2. Enter Layout mode
3. Choose Layouts → Layout Setup. The Layout Setup dialog appears, as shown in Figure 18.16.
4. Choose the desired menu set for the layout from the Menu Set pop-up menu near the bottom of the Layout Setup dialog's General panel.
5. Click OK to save the selection and dismiss the Layout Setup dialog.

FileMaker uses the term [File Default] to refer to a menu set assigned to the file via the pop-up menu setting at the bottom of the Manage Custom Menus dialog. The menu set specified as the file default applies everywhere in the file, except where you've chosen an alternative menu for a particular layout, or where your scripts have used the Install Menu Set[ ] command to change the current menu set.

### FIGURE 18.16
Setting the default menu set for the current layout via the General tab of the Layout Setup dialog.

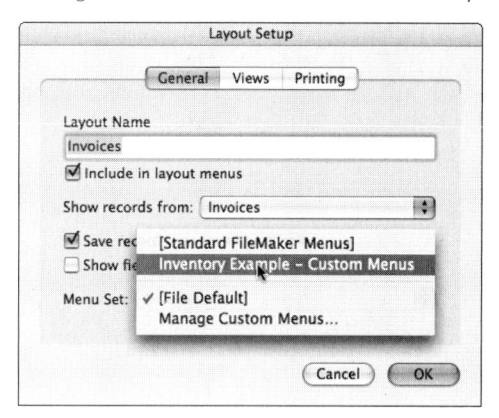

Conversely, the term [Standard FileMaker Menus] refers to the menu set that FileMaker uses when no custom menus have been created or selected. When a file is first created (and before any custom menu configuration changes have been made), [Standard FileMaker Menus] is set as the [File Default] menu set.

> **TIP** To quickly see which menu sets have been assigned as the defaults for each layout, go to Layout mode and choose Layouts ⇨ Set Layout Order.

The resulting dialog lists all the layouts in the file, showing in the right column the default menu set assigned to each layout.

Double-clicking a layout line in the Set Layout Order dialog invokes the Layout Setup dialog for that layout, allowing you to edit the layout's properties, including its assigned menu set.

### Controlling menu sets via script

Once you have set the default menu sets for the current file and/or for each layout in the file, you have established a basic operational environment for your users. You also have the option to further customize the user experience by providing access to alternative menus via script and button actions using the Install Menu Set [ ] command to vary the menus available on the current layout.

> **NOTE** A menu set invoked by a button or script normally remains in place only until the user switches to a different layout (when the default menu set for the new layout takes priority). If the user returns to the previous layout, the original menu set is reinstated until changed again by a script or button.

An exception is when you select the option on the Install Menu Set [ ] command to Use As File Default, in which case the selected menu set remains in place for all layouts configured to use the [File Default] menu set.

## Custom Functions

FileMaker Pro 9 provides you with a total of 243 calculation functions. However, you can extend that number in FileMaker Pro Advanced by defining your own functions using combinations of the original 243 functions as building blocks to assemble powerful new calculation functions of your own.

Custom functions are a great idea and should be part of your standard development toolkit for three compelling reasons:

- You can use custom functions to simplify the language of calculations, making your solution's code more readable and giving you shortcuts to commonly used code snippets.

- By encapsulating frequently repeated code (especially long or complex blocks of code) within a custom function, you can maintain the code in one place. When you change the custom function definition, calculations employing it throughout your solution automatically use the new function definition the next time they're evaluated.

- You can structure custom functions to produce *recursion* (repetition of a task until a condition is met), enabling them to tackle complex tasks beyond the scope of ordinary calculations.

**CROSS-REF** See Chapter 12 for a more complete discussion of the three advantages of custom functions.

### Defining custom functions

Custom functions are available only in the file where they are defined. If you want to have access to a particular custom function in multiple files, you will have to define it separately in each file.

Once defined, however, custom functions appear in the list of available functions in calculation dialogs throughout the field definitions, scripts, button commands, and everywhere else calculation formulae are accepted. Although custom functions can only be defined with FileMaker Pro Advanced, once defined they can be used in calculations created using FileMaker Pro.

To create a custom function:

1. Choose File ➪ Manage ➪ Custom Functions. The Manage Custom Functions dialog appears, as shown in Figure 18.17.
2. Click the New button. The Edit Custom Function dialog appears.
3. In the Function Name field, enter the custom function's name, as shown in Figure 18.18.

## Part V  Raising the Bar

**FIGURE 18.17**

Creating or editing a custom function via the Manage Custom Functions dialog.

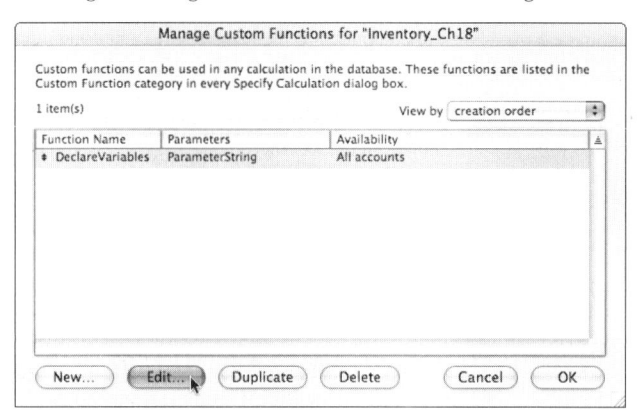

**FIGURE 18.18**

Specifying a Custom Function definition in the Edit Custom Function dialog.

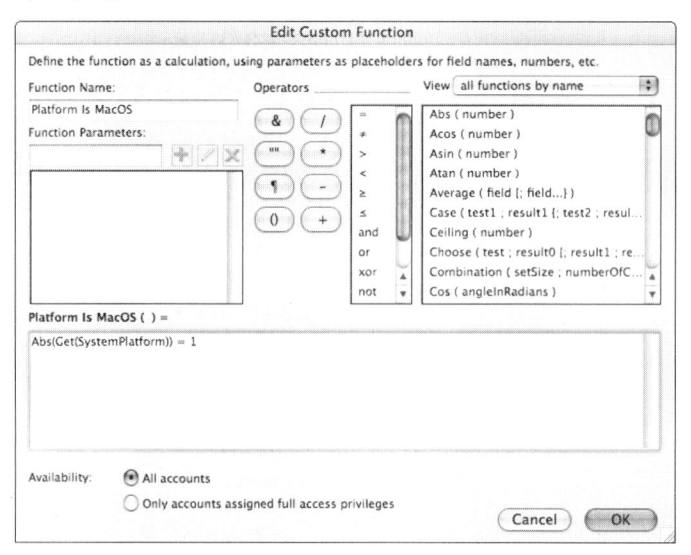

# FileMaker Pro Advanced Features

4. (Optional) After naming your custom function, add parameters in the Function Parameters field. *Parameters* enable you to pass values to your function when you reference it in calculations throughout your solution. Parameters are used as placeholders in the definition of your custom function, but are substituted with the values passed by your calculations when the custom function is evaluated.

5. Specify a calculation expression in the main text box occupying the lower area of the Edit Custom Function dialog. The function definition is created according to the same calculation syntax as used elsewhere in FileMaker, except that you can also refer to the parameters defined for the function, and to custom functions defined in the current file (including the current custom function).

6. Use the radio button options at the bottom of the Edit Custom Function dialog to determine whether the custom function you're creating will be available in calculations specified by users whose login account is not assigned to the Full Access privilege set. If you choose to limit the function's use to Full Access accounts in Step 6, calculations referencing the function will still work for all users, but will not be able to be defined or modified by users with restricted privileges. For example, if you have granted some users the ability to create or modify their own scripts, they will not be able to build calculations in their scripts using your custom function unless you have selected the All Accounts availability option for the function.

7. Click OK.

**NOTE** Custom functions operate and are available for use when defining calculations using FileMaker Pro, once they have been added to a file using FileMaker Pro Advanced.

## Custom functions as an aid to syntax readability

Custom functions offer an opportunity to simplify calculation syntax in your solutions. A simple but elegant example is provided by the custom function definition shown in Figure 18.18:

```
Abs(Get(SystemPlatform)) = 1
```

This somewhat arcane syntax .is specified as the definition of a custom function named Platform Is Mac OS, making it possible to use more easily scannable code in your solution. For example, with the preceding function installed in your file, a script requiring a different window width for each platform (to account for the difference in window borders between Macintosh and Windows) may use the expression

```
If(Platform Is MacOS; 865; 878)
```

instead of

```
If(Abs(Get(SystemPlatform)) = 1; 865; 878)
```

You can simplify many other commonly used expressions in your solutions — from tests for modifier keys to paths to shared directories to error results — making the resulting calculation code shorter and easier to read.

## Maximizing efficiency and ease of use

When you place long or complex calculation expressions into a custom function, you can use a single custom function name in your calculations in place of a much more convoluted expression. For an expression used only once in your solution, there may be little value in replacing it with a custom function because the complexity of the code is simply moved from the calculation definition to the custom function definition. However, if your solution references the expression in multiple places, defining its logic as a custom function provides a number of benefits.

The first and most obvious benefit of placing a complex calculation into a custom function is that it makes coding easier throughout the various occurrences of the logic in your solution. An added benefit is that if you need to update the logic of the calculation, a single update (to the custom function definition) propagates throughout your solution.

> **CAUTION** Previously calculated (and stored) values do not automatically update if the definition of a custom function used to calculate them changes. To apply a changed definition to stored values, you must separately prompt their recalculation — such as by updating the value of a referenced field.

For example, if your solution requires that a progressive (tiered) tax rate be applied in three salary bands to calculate net income, you can achieve the required result using a formula such as:

```
Let([Cap1 = 7500; Cap2 = 45000; Rate1 = 0; Rate2 = .33; Rate3 = .5];
Income::Gross -
(Min(Income::Gross; Cap1) * Rate1) -
If(Income::Gross > Cap1;
(Min(Income::Gross; Cap2) - Cap1) * Rate2) -
If(Income::Gross > Cap2;
(Income::Gross - Cap2) * .5)
)
```

An alternative technique, however, is to define the logic of the preceding calculation as a custom function where the rates and salary cap values are passed in as parameters, as shown in Figure 18.19.

With the `NetIncome()` custom function installed in your file, the previous calculation can be performed throughout your solution (in scripts and other calculations) with the new simplified syntax

```
NetIncome(Income::Gross; 7500; 45000; 0; .33; .5)
```

Moreover, should the rules for the application of progressive tax rates change in the future, a modification of the definition of the `NetIncome()` custom function implements the revised logic going forward.

# FileMaker Pro Advanced Features    18

### FIGURE 18.19
Defining a NetIncome custom function to apply a three-tiered tax structure.

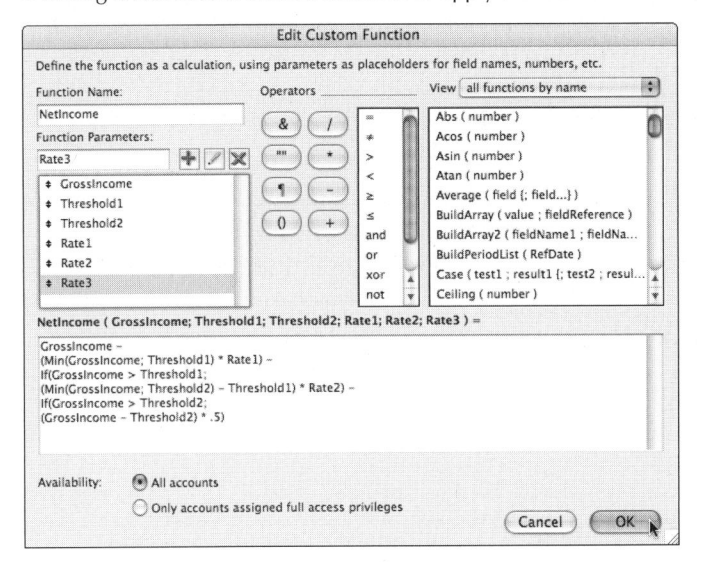

```
Edit Custom Function

Define the function as a calculation, using parameters as placeholders for field names, numbers, etc.

Function Name:                    Operators          View: all functions by name
NetIncome                                             Abs ( number )
Function Parameters:                                  Acos ( number )
  Rate3        + / X                                  Asin ( number )
    ♦ GrossIncome                                     Atan ( number )
    ♦ Threshold1                                      Average ( field {; field...} )
    ♦ Threshold2                                      BuildArray ( value ; fieldReference )
    ♦ Rate1                                           BuildArray2 ( fieldName1 ; fieldNa...
    ♦ Rate2                    and                    BuildPeriodList ( RefDate )
    ♦ Rate3                    or                     Case ( test1 ; result1 {; test2 ; resul...
                               xor                    Ceiling ( number )
                               not

NetIncome ( GrossIncome; Threshold1; Threshold2; Rate1; Rate2; Rate3 ) =

GrossIncome -
(Min(GrossIncome; Threshold1) * Rate1) -
If(GrossIncome > Threshold1;
(Min(GrossIncome; Threshold2) - Threshold1) * Rate2) -
If(GrossIncome > Threshold2;
(GrossIncome - Threshold2) * .5)

Availability:   ● All accounts
                ○ Only accounts assigned full access privileges       Cancel    OK
```

## Custom Functions and Recursion

Custom functions can do several tasks that regular FileMaker calculations cannot, because custom functions are capable of recursion.

*Recursion* is when a process explicitly and repetitively invokes itself until its work is accomplished. Recursion is analogous to a looping construction, excepting that a loop is explicitly iterative, whereas recursion achieves an equivalent logical outcome implicitly. Examples of recursion and iteration exist elsewhere in FileMaker Pro, such as when you define a script to loop until an exit condition is satisfied. Looping constructs (as well as requiring a script to implement them) tend to be longer and less efficient in operation, though they may sometimes be easier to read and interpret.

Elsewhere in FileMaker Pro, calculation expressions are evaluated only once, however you can define custom functions to call themselves, creating a looping effect. To successfully implement recursion in a custom function, you need to observe two simple rules:

- The function must call itself within its own syntax (supplying the appropriate parameter values).
- The function syntax must include an escape condition so that it will stop calling itself when the intended goal has been achieved.

Following these two basic rules, you can set up custom functions to perform a wide variety of tasks — including many not otherwise readily (or efficiently) accomplished within calculations.

## Things that only custom functions can do

Using the power of recursion, your calculation can perform operations in an extensible way, repeating a process until the required result is reached (according to the exit condition you build into its syntax).

Consider a very simple example, where you need to generate a series of numbers — say, for houses in a street, starting at one number and ending at another, where some streets may have many thousands of houses and the start and end numbers can be almost anything. This task is quite difficult, if not impossible, to do reliably for all cases using a conventional calculation, but achieved quite simply using the power of recursion, with the following function:

```
        //  SYNTAX:   NumRange ( From ; To )

If(From < To;
From & ", " & NumRange(From + 1; To);
From
)
```

When you define a custom function in this way and then employ it in a calculation expression, supplying the From parameter as, say, 52972 and the To parameter as, say, 53007:

```
NumRange ( 52972 ; 53007 )
```

FileMaker returns the result:

> 52972, 52973, 52974, 52975, 52976, 52977, 52978, 52979, 52980, 52981, 52982, 52983, 52984, 52985, 52986, 52987, 52988, 52989, 52990, 52991, 52992, 52993, 52994, 52995, 52996, 52997, 52998, 52999, 53000, 53001, 53002, 53003, 53004, 53005, 53006, 53007

Using this same function, you can generate number ranges starting anywhere and running for hundreds or even thousands of numbers, if need be. While this example is simple, you can perform much more complex tasks using the same essential principle, thanks to the power and flexibility recursion offers. In this case, the If ( ) function test provides an escape condition, while the work of the function is performed on the second line of the If ( ) expression:

```
From & ", " & NumRange(From + 1; To);
```

Here, on its first call, the function returns the From value, appends a comma and space, and then calls itself again with the From value incremented for the next iteration — so the expression continues to call itself until the If ( ) test fails (that is, until From is no longer less than To), at which point the accumulated sequence of From values is returned, spanning all the way from the original From value to the To value.

## The stack and the limits of recursion

To execute a procedure such as the one described in the previous section, FileMaker must hold the result of each call to the `NumRange()` function in memory until the process completes, and it can return the combined result of all the iterations. To do so, FileMaker uses an internal memory stack, where it stacks up each result in turn, in memory, until the task is complete, and then it retrieves each value in turn from the memory stack.

A potential risk when using a memory stack is that the process will continue until available memory is exhausted, resulting in an out-of-memory error that causes a problem for the application. To avoid this risk, FileMaker places an arbitrary limit on the depth of the stack at 10,000. If the process hasn't completed by the time the memory stack is 10,000 values deep, the process is aborted, and an error value ("?") is returned. This limit protects FileMaker from the possibility of an out-of-memory condition, but imposes an upper limit on recursive processes that make use of the memory stack.

In cases where 10,000 iterations is insufficient, you need a different approach. If you plan to use recursion, the conventional "stack-based" approach won't do, and you need to use an alternative calculation syntax known as *tail-end recursion*, or simply tail recursion.

## Tail recursion in practice

A custom function using tail recursion is designed to complete all its work at each call so that nothing need be held in memory while subsequent calls are evaluated. To do so, the function must be structured to pass its result to the next call (via the defined parameters or via a variable) rather than holding it on the stack.

For example, you can restructure the `NumRange()` function from the preceding discussion to no longer require use of the memory stack by changing its definition to

```
         //  SYNTAX:  NumRange ( From ; To )

Let(
pN = GetAsNumber(RightWords(From; 1));
If(pN < To; NumRange(From & ", " & (pN + 1); To); From)
)
```

Here, rather than each successive value being held in memory until the complete sequence has been compiled, the string of numbers is built within the From parameter and passed whole from each iteration to the next. Because nothing is left to be held in memory, the stack depth limit is not relevant, and this version of the function can return number ranges spanning more than 10,000 integers.

Tail recursion syntax enables functions to continue until FileMaker's limit of 50,000 total function calls for a single calculation operation is reached, so the revised (tail recursive) version of the `NumRange()` function can produce ranges containing up to 49,999 numbers before it, too, will fail.

**Part V  Raising the Bar**

> **NOTE** The 50,000 upper limit for sequential calls within a single calculation evaluation prevents you from locking your solution in an infinite loop, such as when you code your function with an invalid escape argument. Moreover, even with a powerful CPU, your computer will take a while to crunch through 50,000 nontrivial computations, so the limit is a good compromise between functionality and usability.

## Some useful examples

The example we provide in the preceding discussion is designed to help you comprehend the fundamentals of recursion, but in itself is of limited use. However, many other uses of recursive functions can become central and even essential components of your solution functionality, taking over where the built-in capabilities of the FileMaker calculation engine leave off.

While we'd love to provide many more examples (and we have enough of them to fill a book), the constraints of space are such that we limit ourselves to the ones described in the following sections.

### Creating an acronym from a supplied phrase

Producing an acronym by calculation is straightforward if you know in advance the maximum number of words occurring in the supplied text. You need not be concerned about that, however, if you use a recursion, as in this example:

```
// SYNTAX: Acronym ( Phrase )
Case(
WordCount(Phrase) > 1;
Upper(Left( Phrase; 1)) &
Acronym(RightWords( Phrase; WordCount( Phrase ) - 1));
Upper(Left( Phrase; 1))
)
```

This function accepts an input parameter such as "Your mileage may vary" and returns the acronym YMMV. It uses conventional (iterative) recursion. It is useful for generating initials from names, company acronyms from company names, and so on. Because it can also create very long acronyms, you can use it for generating an "imprint" of a longer block of text for quick identification. For example, using it, we've created the following imprint of this paragraph:

```
TFWAAIPSAYMMVARTAYIUCIRIIUFGIFNCAFCNESICACVLAICBUFGAIOALBOTFQIFEUIWCTFIOTP
```

### Extracting a character set from a supplied block of text

To establish the character domain of a text value (or a series of values), you need to be able to produce a list of all the characters used in the text — in other words, a character set. The following recursive function makes the task easy:

```
// SYNTAX: CharacterSet ( text )
Case(
Length ( text );
Let([
```

```
K1 = Left(Text; 1);
Kn = Substitute(text; K1; "")];
K1 & If(Length(Kn); CharacterSet(Kn))
)
)
```

The `CharacterSet ( )` function returns one of each character occurring in the text string you supply as input. Using it, you can develop appropriate collections of characters occurring in sample text, for use in filtering applications (where you need to constrain the character set to eliminate rogue or garbage content).

### Removing an unspecified number of leading carriage returns

Removing undesired characters from a text string is another task that's straightforward if you know how many characters to remove. If you use a recursive function, with an appropriately formed escape clause, the problem is solved, as in the following example:

```
// SYNTAX: TrimLeadingReturns ( text )

If(
Left(text; 1) = ¶;
TrimLeadingReturns(Right(text; Length(text) - 1));
text
)
```

The task of eliminating leading carriage returns is humble, yet practical and useful. We have selected this function as our third example because it provides another delightfully simple example of tail recursion — completing its task without invoking the memory stack.

**CROSS-REF** For links to resources containing a broad selection of documentation and examples of custom functions, refer to Appendix B

## Creating Runtime Applications

Complementing its wealth of customization options and developer tools, FileMaker Pro Advanced offers you the ability to generate royalty-free, stand-alone, runtime applications from your solutions. This ability means you can distribute stand-alone copies of your database solutions to users who don't own FileMaker Pro, and they'll be able to install them and use them as discrete applications.

Before generating a runtime application from your solution, it pays to give some thought to making your solution interface self-contained, adding appropriate branding and building in help and support information and contact details.

**NOTE** Apart from being good practice and basic professionalism, providing an "About" layout including your name and contact details for technical support is one condition of FileMaker, Inc.,'s license agreement permitting you to create and distribute runtime copies of your solution. Refer to the FileMaker Pro Advanced product documentation for full details.

## Generating a stand-alone solution

To create a self-contained application from your completed solution, open FileMaker Pro Advanced (leaving your solution files closed) and proceed as follows:

1. Choose Tools ➪ Developer Utilities. The Developer Utilities dialog appears.
2. Click the Add button and select all the database files required by your solution. These files will be added to the Solution Files list in the Developer Utilities dialog.
3. Ensure that the red arrow indicator at the left of the file list is pointing to your solution's primary file.
4. Choose a project folder by clicking the corresponding Specify button and making a selection.
5. Click the Specify button for Solution Options in the lower part of the Developer Utilities dialog. The Specify Solution Options dialog appears, as shown in Figure 18.20.

**FIGURE 18.20**

Specifying runtime solution options using Developer Utilities.

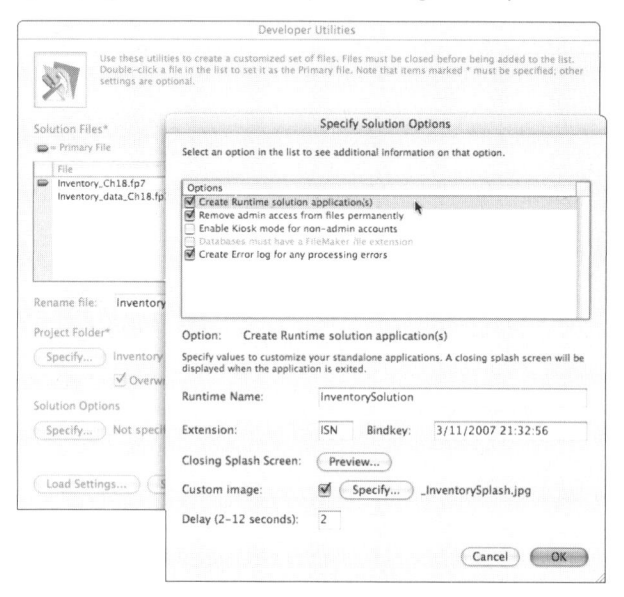

6. Select from the five available options in the Specify Solution Options dialog (you can select more than one) and, with the Create Runtime Solution application(s) option highlighted, enter an application name and unique extension. (*Note:* Runtime applications can't use the fp7 extension..

# FileMaker Pro Advanced Features

7. If desired, select a closing splash screen image and enter the preferred closing splash delay.
8. Enter a bindkey of your own choosing or make note of the bindkey value generated by FileMaker. You may need this value in the future.
9. Click OK to accept the Solution Options and dismiss the Solution Options dialog.
10. In the Developer Utilities dialog, click Create.

**NOTE** You can select the five options available in Developer Utilities in any combination—so you can use the procedure to permanently remove admin access accounts or enable kiosk mode, without choosing the option to create a runtime application.

Kiosk mode enables you to configure your files to run in a blacked-out screen with no menu bars or desktop visible or accessible. This mode is useful for computers that are available to the public for information purposes or for front-desk applications to log visitors and print name tags. However, the kiosk mode is less useful for general desktop productivity applications.

**TIP** When you apply kiosk mode to your solution files using Developer Utilities, your solution opens into kiosk mode whenever it's opened with a restricted access account, either in FileMaker Pro or with a runtime application engine.

## Binding for each platform

As part of the process of creating a runtime application, a simplified version of FileMaker Pro (without database design capabilities) is created and specifically bound to your solution files (so that it can only operate with the bound files). Because this version is an application in its own right, it is specific to the platform you create it on.

If you want a runtime to operate on Windows, you have to bind your files to the Windows runtime on the Windows operating system. If you require a runtime for the Mac OS PowerPC platform, you need to bind on PowerPC. A separate runtime is required to run natively on an Intel Macintosh computer.

When you need to produce multiple versions of your solution, to work on different operating systems, you need to bind the same files, using the same bindkey value, on each destination platform. The executable file from each bind procedure is required to run the solution on that platform.

## Hosting runtime files

Runtime applications are strictly single user. However, if you need to provide multi-user access to a runtime solution, you can configure FileMaker Server to open and host your runtime database files.

When runtime solution files are hosted by FileMaker Server, users will require full licensed copies of FileMaker Pro (or FileMaker Pro Advanced) to log in and use the solution. It can't be accessed over a network using the runtime application engine.

# Chapter 19

# Efficient Code, Efficient Solutions

FileMaker's reputation as a user-friendly database is legend — and, for the most part, well deserved. Users with no background in programming (but with self-motivation, good logical thinking, and some design sense) can make great progress from a standing start with FileMaker.

In fact, FileMaker draws you in with what it can do — leading the new user to try more complex and even daring feats only a short time after becoming familiar with the application. But FileMaker has a great deal more to it than you can see from the outset. FileMaker is a program with deep roots and hidden power — and it takes time and dedication to fully tap its potential.

A proportion of enthusiastic beginners, having had a ball making their first attempts at building a database, get serious and start looking for robust, fault tolerant, and efficient ways to code their solutions. They are the ones who make the transition to achieve professionalism as FileMaker developers (whatever their job title). If you fall into this group, this chapter is especially for you.

**IN THIS CHAPTER**

Designing your solutions for scalability

Finding ways to avoid redundancy

Seeking the most efficient ways to produce the desired outcomes

Building solutions around transactional principles

Keeping file sizes within limits

Working with images and media

## Designing for Scale: Size Considerations

One of the greatest problems you face — whether working with FileMaker or any other database application — is designing solutions so they continue to work well as they grow. Some designs succeed when modeled using only a small number of records and survive beta testing (also with moderate-sized record sets), but then founder in deployment, when encumbered with the accumulation of serious quantities of business data.

When a solution develops problems operating under load, many developers are tempted to blame the tool, but frequently such problems are a reflection of the design. What works well in small single-user databases does not necessarily translate well to situations calling for tens or hundreds of thousands of records in multi-user networked systems.

## The elephant in the cherry tree

Well, it's an old joke — and if you don't know it, you're not missing much — an elephant can't really hide in a cherry tree by painting his toenails red. However, elephants notwithstanding, while you can accommodate surprisingly large data sets in your FileMaker Pro solutions by paying heed to good design and avoiding bottlenecks and performance impediments, the qualities needed for scalability are fundamental, not cosmetic.

In itself, FileMaker is one of the most scalable development environments available, working with ease and elegance in the smallest of desktop solutions, yet capable of producing server-based solutions delivering large and complex functionality to hundreds of users simultaneously. Across this range, however, there are a variety of approaches you can use to produce viable solutions in high-volume, high-output deployments.

**CAUTION** Solutions need room to grow over time. Bear in mind that FileMaker Server supports up to a maximum of 250 client connections, so if a new solution's requirements already approach this number, it will have little scope for expansion.

Enterprise-wide solutions delivering data to thousands of users may still have a place for FileMaker as part of a larger mix of strategies, but not as a whole solution.

## Predicting what will scale well

Scale takes three main forms:

- Number of users
- Functional or logical complexity
- Volume of data.

Each form of scale brings its own issues and may be considered in isolation, though it is the combination of scale in multiple dimensions that presents the greatest challenge.

Some techniques are strictly single user — they break or cause problems when a solution is hosted. Notably, the use of global fields to store data across multiple sessions is a strictly single-user-only technique. Procedures depending on flag fields and record marking, or involving the use of the Replace Field Contents [ ] command, are also problematic in multi-user solutions. Finally, a lack of adequate error handling for record locking (and for a range of other conditions) becomes a serious impediment to functionality and data integrity when your solution is hosted.

When requirements are relatively simple, a variety of techniques can achieve the desired ends without unduly impacting performance. For example, a heavy dependence on unstored calculations to provide the solution interface, gather data across multiple tables, or pass data through an ungainly

# Efficient Code, Efficient Solutions

data structure is scarcely problematic while requirements remain relatively simple. However, such techniques become unsustainable, and their impact on performance increases exponentially as additional requirements are introduced and complexity increases.

In solutions with modest volumes of data (up to about a thousand records in each table), FileMaker is very forgiving:

- Finds performed on unindexed fields scarcely cause users to blink.
- Summary data calculated live in real time does not introduce unacceptable delays.
- Scripts looping through found sets do not take hours to complete.

Techniques depending upon real-time data summarization become problematic, though, when the volume of data is expected to become large. Similarly, many actions involving updating indexes and using unstored calculations (especially those aggregating data) and multi-predicate relationships encounter performance issues.

Conversely, solutions that are clean, simple, and concisely coded, with almost all values stored, indexing optimized, and with an efficient and unencumbered data model, scale well and can support tables with hundreds of thousands or even millions of records in FileMaker.

## Eliminating Redundancy

A first step toward the optimization of your solutions is avoidance or elimination of redundancy. The DRY (Don't Repeat Yourself) development principle should be at the forefront of your thinking. While eliminating redundancy makes sense from the point of view of speed and efficiency of development, its impacts are greatest in the fluency and responsiveness of the resulting solutions.

By consolidating similar elements and functions and repurposing solution components to serve multiple purposes, you can reduce bloated and ungainly solutions to a fraction of their size, with comparable performance benefits. You can recast awkward and suboptimal scripts that take hours to complete simple processes so that they complete in minutes or seconds.

Combining the techniques we suggest in this section and the following section throughout your solutions, you achieve a considerable reduction in file sizes and corresponding improvements in solution performance. Your solutions will be lean and powerful.

### Avoiding duplication of elements

Whenever two processes are similar in essentials, consider using a single script to serve both requirements (with a script parameter determining context-appropriate behavior, and internal branching to deal with variations). Before you begin, reflect on whether you really need 45 report scripts, or whether a single report controller script, with some additional lines and internal branching — plus a handful of small supporting sub-scripts for various special cases — will serve the same requirements. If so, when reporting requirements change, what would otherwise have been a week's work updating

641

each report and its associated script may be a task that you can complete in a couple of hours. In such a case, the reduction in size and complexity of your file has benefits that flow right through your solution, making your design tight, efficient, and powerful. Now, consider applying the same essential approach to layouts. We have seen files with several hundred layouts that, after some rethinking and repurposing, could achieve the same functionality with only a few dozen layouts — again, reducing complexity and overhead in every direction.

Your Relationships Graph is another area where duplication and redundancy produces a sub-optimal result. A solution design requiring more than the minimum number of table occurrences to achieve the desired functionality incurs performance penalties and complicates development and maintenance, because FileMaker must manage join results and concomitant cache updates across the Graph.

## Using portable and reusable code

While scripts are a key area where the reusability of code gives you many opportunities to increase efficiency and do more with less, relationship specifications and your calculation code's design provide scope for streamlining and introducing reusability.

### Appropriate use of sub-scripts

When you have a number of scripts where similar sequences of steps occur — even though those scripts may be substantially different in intent — consider placing those sequences into a sub-script and calling it from each of the main scripts. For example, error handling procedures for various conditions are apt to be repeated throughout many scripts. While we don't necessarily recommend having only a single, all-encompassing error handler script in your solutions, it certainly does make sense to consolidate the trapping and handling of certain errors or groups of errors. A single script to deal with record locking errors and another to deal with Perform Find [ ] errors (and so on) is a reasonable compromise between efficiency and manageability.

While sub-scripts enable you to consolidate code into a procedural model, reducing fragmentation and redundancy in your solution, the inappropriate use of sub-scripts can have the opposite effect. We recommend that you avoid breaking logically unified processes into multiple scripts without compelling reason to do so.

A good general rule is that unless a sub-script is called from multiple parent scripts in your solution, you should include its content in the body of the main script instead of making it a sub-script. We've been called in to troubleshoot lengthy processes where the logic is distributed across a dozen or more scripts, to no benefit. In fact, splitting a process into sub-scripts may introduce redundancy, since each script must separately instantiate and manage its own (local) parameters, variables, and so on. Exceptions to this rule are when

- One or more parts of an action are required to be performed with [Full Access] privileges, while the remainder of the process should be constrained by the privileges of the current user's account. In this situation, placing the part (or parts) of process requiring the Run Script with Full Access Privileges option enabled in a separate script makes good sense.

- Components of a process need to be performed in different files of a multi-file solution. This approach may be required so that a script can act on variables (all variables are scoped within the file where they are defined), logins, or access privileges (also specific to the file where they're defined).

You should limit your use of sub-scripts to occasions where they're necessary or where doing so significantly increases the efficiency of your code. In other cases, sub-scripts add needless clutter and complexity.

### Appropriate use of custom functions

One benefit of using custom functions in your solutions is the ability to avoid repetition of complex logic in your calculation code. By placing the essentials of calculation logic common to multiple scripts, schema calculations, or various other solution pieces (tooltips, button parameters, conditional formatting expressions, and so on) where calculations are used into a custom function, you can greatly simplify and streamline your solution's code.

As with script code, we counsel against separating calculation into custom functions unless you have a clear rationale for doing so. However, the benefits of using custom functions are several:

- A custom function's calculation logic is reusable and can be more efficiently managed in one place than if it were repeated throughout your solution's structures.
- Custom functions using recursion give access to functionality not available with calculation code elsewhere in FileMaker.
- Using custom functions enables you to make functionality available to end users without revealing proprietary or sensitive logic contained within the function definition.

Remember that custom functions are specific to the file where they're defined, so managing a large number of custom functions across all the files in a multi-file solution can itself become burdensome. Nevertheless, many situations arise where custom functions' benefits more than compensate for the time required to create and manage them.

**CROSS-REF** For detailed information about the design and use of custom functions, refer to Chapters 12 and 18.

## Designing for Flexibility and Adaptability

FileMaker, as a development environment, is notable for its flexibility, lending itself to innumerable ingenious and sometimes unexpected problem resolutions. One consequence of this flexibility is that you can approach almost any problem in several ways. If you can see only one path forward, chances are you aren't looking hard enough.

As a developer, your task is to choose the most effective method to address each requirement and provide each function point. However, some choices will lock you in, constraining subsequent design choices, while others leave your options relatively unencumbered. In most cases, choosing the paths offering greatest versatility is the wisest choice, even if doing so requires some additional work.

# Part V  Raising the Bar

In the preceding section, we suggest techniques for creating flexible and adaptable script and calculation code. However, other areas of your solution designs, including schema and interface, also benefit significantly from adopting design practices aimed at maximizing reusability and portability.

## Layouts and adaptable design

You can design layouts for flexibility and reusability using a variety of available techniques, several of which have been covered in preceding chapters.

Defining screen elements as nonprinting objects, positioning print-ready content behind them, supports combining print and screen versions of some layouts. Moreover, the ability to include multiple Sub-summary parts, invoking only those needed for a given report, according to the selected sort order lets you generate a variety of alternate reports from a single layout in your solution. Chapter 10 discusses examples of these techniques.

In addition, the FileMaker tab control layout object is well suited to circumstances where some screen or report elements should remain constant while others vary. Because tabs can be controlled either manually or via script, they also provide rich possibilities for condensing alternate interface and print content into single reusable layouts.

Combining tab control techniques with sliding objects, conditional formatting, and calculated interface elements, your interfaces can be dynamic and varied, while remaining compact and versatile.

## Concepts of reusability applied to the Relationships Graph

Another area where it pays you to minimize redundancy is FileMaker's Relationships Graph, because FileMaker must manage and update its cache of join results for every dependency affected by actions ranging from editing a key field (or a value upon which a key field depends) to creating or deleting a record. Any such change requires FileMaker to revisit all cached join results where dependencies may require that current cache contents be discarded. Consequently, where your Graph contains a large number of redundant connections, your solution is unnecessarily encumbered and its responsiveness degraded.

*Relationship joins*, where key fields on both sides of the join are indexed, are operable in both directions. We recommend that you avoid creating two or more essentially similar relationships where a single relationship may be repurposed (used in both directions) to provide the same functionality.

*Utility relationships* — such as those where a global field is used to establish temporary joins to related tables — should be designed to be reusable for various purposes where possible. To facilitate this goal, consider using a prefixed composite key (in other words, a calculation field combining multiple key values) in the targeted table so that you can reassign the global key used to filter the utility relationship by adding or alternating its prefix value.

# Traveling the Shortest Distance Between Two Points

A direct relationship exists between the ways you choose to structure your calculation code and the time it takes to execute. Lengthy and convoluted calculations tie up your workstation for many CPU cycles, unraveling their twisted logic. Calculations addressing related record sets require the retrieval of data from the host and carry a cost in network time, as well as processor cycles, on both server and client.

The unpleasant truth is that a single severely sub-optimal calculation can bring your solution to its knees, slowing users to a crawl and needlessly using vast computing resources. While this case is rare, a more common but equally problematic scenario is the solution where a number of calculations are sub-optimal and, while the effect of each is marginal, the combination is enough to severely impact performance. In either case, a few well-placed adjustments can yield significant and immediate gains.

## Optimal calculation syntax

The DRY principle, as it applies to calculations, mandates that you should structure expressions to calculate each value or logical unit of a computation only once. (For more on the DRY principal, see the section "Eliminating Redundancy," earlier in this chapter.)

Consider the seemingly inoffensive little calculation in the Customer table of an invoicing solution:

```
If(Sum(Invoices::BalancePayable) < 5; 0; Sum(Invoices::BalancePayable))
```

As a single line of code, it may hardly seem worthy of close attention. However, whenever the balance of amounts payable on related invoices equals or exceeds $5, the calculation must determine the balance twice over — first to evaluate the If ( ) test and again to deliver the result. When you consider that the number of related invoices involved in the computation may be large and, if the Invoices::BalancePayable is itself also an unstored calculation retrieving and reconciling related LineItems and Payments values for each Invoice record, several thousand values may be computed producing the result. The preceding line of code, requiring as it does that the task of summing balance payable amounts be done twice, carries a potentially heavy performance burden.

You can recast the calculation as follows:

```
Let(Bal = Sum(Invoices::BalancePayable); If(Bal < 5; 0; Bal))
```

The work required to evaluate the expression will be halved in many cases, because the values in the Invoices::BalancePayable field are summed only once for each record in the found set. If screen draws of list layouts including the original calculation were sluggish, this one small change increases its speed (up to doubling it, depending on the number of balances of $5 or more in the rows being listed).

> **NOTE** The `If( )`, `Case( )`, and `Choose( )` functions use short-circuit evaluation, so only those arguments required to be evaluated to return a valid result are processed. Consequently, in the original version of the preceding example, the second `Sum( )` function is not evaluated when the result of the first is less than 5.

In the preceding example, the Let ( ) function is used to avoid repetition of calculation syntax, while preserving the logical form of the original expression. The relatively minor adjustment has a marked effect on performance. Now consider a more profoundly sub-optimal calculation:

```
Case(
Sum(Invoices::BalancePayable) > 0 and Sum(Invoices::BalancePayable) < 50;
Sum(Invoices::BalancePayable) - Sum(Invoices::BalancePayable) * .05;
Sum(Invoices::BalancePayable) ≥ 50 and Sum(Invoices::BalancePayable) < 100;
Sum(Invoices::BalancePayable) - Sum(Invoices::BalancePayable) * .1;
Sum(Invoices::BalancePayable) ≥ 100 and Sum(Invoices::BalancePayable) < 150;
Sum(Invoices::BalancePayable) - Sum(Invoices::BalancePayable) * .15;
Sum(Invoices::BalancePayable) ≥ 150 and Sum(Invoices::BalancePayable) < 200;
Sum(Invoices::BalancePayable) - Sum(Invoices::BalancePayable) * .2)
Sum(Invoices::BalancePayable) ≥ 200;
Sum(Invoices::BalancePayable) - Sum(Invoices::BalancePayable) * .25)
)
```

This calculation is so poorly formed that you could be forgiven for thinking we made it up to illustrate a point. Not so; we copied both the examples in this section directly from a real (albeit poorly designed) solution. As you can see, the latter example requires evaluation of the `Sum(Invoices::BalancePayable)` expression a minimum of 4 times and up to a maximum of 11 times, depending on the cumulative amount owing for a given customer record.

In this instance, we re-cast the expression as:

```
Let([
Bal = Sum(Invoices::BalancePayable);
Rate = .95 - Min(4; Int(Bal / 50)) * .05];
Bal * Rate
)
```

Here, we eliminate redundancy, we no longer repeat the sum expression, and, after a single expression is used to calculate the discount rate, we apply it with the compact closing argument (`Bal * Rate`). The changes are twofold: The use of Let ( ) function's variables to avoid needless repetition, plus the reworking of the logic of the calculation to achieve a more straightforward formula. Not surprisingly, with this change, the client reported approximately 900 percent performance gains in the processes (screen draws and reports) where the calculation was used, after this one change was implemented.

Throughout your calculation code, considering alternative ways to structure each expression and also choosing syntax requiring fewer steps (and therefore fewer CPU cycles and/or disk or network calls) during evaluation confer many benefits. While optimizing a single calculation formula may yield tangible benefits — as in the preceding example — the cumulative effect of optimizations throughout your solutions will be considerably greater.

# Efficient Code, Efficient Solutions

## Alternative syntax examples

The examples discussed in the preceding section are calculations designed to act on related data sets. However, when you choose calculation syntax with care, your solution benefits in a number of ways. More compact and efficient calculations are frequently easier to read and understand (and therefore easier to maintain) and also provide improved performance.

When looking for opportunities to optimize calculation syntax, established methods such as eliminating repetition and eliminating redundant steps are a first step. However, a more radical rethink of approach will frequently take you further. For example, consider a situation where data imported into an Income table includes a delimited array of monthly balance amounts for the year, in the form:

1171|554|2034|943|1623|878|1340|2552|2154|3515|2091|3027|

Extracting the August income balance amount (the eighth value in the array) may lead you to first consider parsing the string using the pipe delimiter characters to break out the eighth value with an expression such as:

```
Middle(
Income::MonthBalances;
Position(Income::MonthBalances; "|"; 1; 7) + 1;
Position(Income::MonthBalances; "|"; 1; 8) −
Position(Income::MonthBalances; "|"; 1; 7) −1
)
```

A quick glance over this formula shows it is sub-optimal because the expression `Position(Income::MonthBalances; "|"; 1; 7)` occurs twice. A conventional approach to optimization, therefore, produces a slight improvement, as follows:

```
Let([
p1 = Position(Income::MonthBalances; "|"; 1; 7) + 1;
p2 = Position(Income::MonthBalances; "|"; 1; 8];
Middle(Income::MonthBalances; p1; p2−p1)
)
```

While the revised form of the calculation is a little more compact, a little quicker to evaluate, and perhaps a little more readable, the change is scarcely revolutionary. However, because we can be confident that the income amounts will all be numeric values, with some lateral thinking, we can adopt a quite different approach, arriving at the expression:

```
GetValue(Substitute(Income::MonthBalances; "|"; ¶); 8)
```

Each formulae in the preceding example produces the same result (2552), given the input string indicated. However, the last does so using considerably fewer steps.

> **NOTE** The method depending on the `GetValue( )` function works reliably in cases where the values in the delimited string being parsed will never include carriage returns, as in the case with an array of numeric values.

Elsewhere in the same solution, you may need to convert a text value representing the month into its corresponding numeric value (for example, a month number). We've seen various solutions set up to accomplish this using expressions like the lines of the following:

```
Let(
MonthName = Left(Income::IncomeMonthName; 3);
Case(
    MonthName = "Jan"; 1;
MonthName = "Feb"; 2;
MonthName = "Mar"; 3;
MonthName = "Apr"; 4;
MonthName = "May"; 5;
MonthName = "Jun"; 6;
MonthName = "Jul"; 7;
MonthName = "Aug"; 8;
MonthName = "Sep"; 9;
MonthName = "Oct"; 10;
MonthName = "Nov"; 11;
MonthName = "Dec"; 12
)
)
```

Consider, however, the fact that the same result can be returned using a strikingly different — and rather more compact approach — by employing FileMaker's `Position( )` function:

```
Position("xxJanFebMarAprMayJunJulAugSepOctNovDec";
Left(Income::IncomeMonthName; 3); 1; 1) / 3
```

These examples are selected somewhat arbitrarily to illustrate that you can bring a variety of techniques to bear to solve a given problem — and rarely is there only one viable approach. Our purpose here is to present you with the concepts so that you can apply them yourself to myriad calculation requirements, rather than to limit you to the specific approaches of the examples we are able to include here. Nevertheless, in the following sections, we include several additional examples to illustrate the ways alternate coding approaches may be beneficial.

## Working with modifier keys

A frequent calculation challenge — often associated with scripted procedures where different functionality is made available depending on whether the user holds down a keyboard modifier (such as Shift, Control, Option/Alt) while running the script — is to determine by calculation whether a particular modifier key is depressed.

When you hold down a modifier key, the FileMaker `Get(ActiveModifierKeys)` function returns a number representing the combination of modifier keys currently engaged. An issue arising when testing for a specific modifier, such as Shift, is the possibility that the Caps Lock key will be engaged, adding 2 to the value the function returns. So rather than testing for the Shift Key alone

```
Get(ActiveModifierKeys) = 1
```

# Efficient Code, Efficient Solutions

it's desirable to test for the Shift key both with and without the Caps Lock engaged, as in

```
Get(ActiveModifierKeys) = 1 or GetActivceModifierKeys) = 3
```

You can create an equivalent expression, however, evaluating as true when the `Get(ActiveModifierKeys)` function returns either 3 or 1, using the Abs( ) function as follows:

```
Abs(Get(ActiveModifierKeys) –2) = 1
```

To detect the presence of the Control key (on either Mac OS or Windows) regardless of the state of the Caps Lock, you can use

```
Abs(Get(ActiveModifierKeys) –5) = 1
```

In these examples, the expressions evaluate as true only if the Shift key or Control key (respectively) is the only modifier key (aside from Caps Lock) engaged. However, if you need to determine whether the Shift key is pressed regardless of the state of any of the remaining modifier keys, rather than using longhand and the pedestrian approach of testing against all 16 possible combinations (across both Mac and Windows), consider using

```
Mod(Get(ActiveModifierKeys); 2)
```

To test whether the Control key is pressed regardless of the state of any of the other modifier keys, consider using either of the two following expressions:

```
Mod(Get(ActiveModifierKeys); 8) > 3
```

or

```
Int(Mod(Get(ActiveModifierKeys); 8) / 4)
```

These more succinct methods arise from taking a step back and looking at the values returned by the `Get(ActiveModifierKeys)` function. Each of the five possible modifier keys (Shift, Caps Lock, Control, Option/Alt, ⌘) toggles a separate bit of a five-bit binary value. By isolating the relevant bit — by combined use of `Mod( )` and `Int( )` — you can efficiently read the state of a single key.

## Working with Boolean values

The Implementation of Boolean logic in FileMaker operates on the principle that nonzero numeric values are true, and zero and empty values are false. A basic understanding of this principle leads novice users to construct Boolean tests, such as the argument for the `If[ ]` step in a script, resembling the following:

```
If(Receipts::AmountPaid = 0 or IsEmpty(Receipts::AmountPaid); 0; 1)
```

Conversely, to toggle the state of a Boolean checkbox field, the novice may use

```
If(Receipts::ReceiptStatus = 0 or IsEmpty(Receipts::ReceiptStatus ); 1; 0)
```

While there is no denying these methods achieve their intent, they don't represent the shortest distance between points. In the case of the first example, the `If ( )` function is redundant, because the required Boolean result (0 or 1) is returned by the expression

```
Receipts::AmountPaid = 0 or IsEmpty(Receipts::AmountPaid)
```

However, a still more elegant (yet equally robust) way to meet the requirement is by using FileMaker's purpose-built (but remarkably under-utilized) function:

```
GetAsBoolean(Receipts::AmountPaid)
```

Similarly, the expression frequently used to set a Boolean checkbox to its alternate state is unnecessarily verbose and may instead be replaced by

```
not GetAsBoolean(Receipts::ReceiptStatus)
```

Or, depending on your mood,

```
Abs(Receipts::ReceiptStatus − 1)
```

Either of these alternatives is both more compact and more efficient in execution than the earlier method using the `If ( )` function. The first may be regarded as slightly more robust, as it still works even if the value in the `Receipts::ReceiptStatus` field is out of bounds (that is, neither empty, 0. nor 1), but both methods are viable alternatives.

## Avoiding dependency "spaghetti"

When you define a calculation field with an expression referencing a field of the same table in your solution, you are creating a *dependency;* when the referenced field is updated, FileMaker automatically re-evaluates the calculation. FileMaker manages these dependencies internally, so you don't have to set or manage them. However, it pays to be aware of them when designing your solutions' code architecture.

One consequence of dependencies is a predetermined sequence of calculation "events" when you update a value. For example, take the following steps:

1. Create a number field.
2. Create a calculation field adding 1 to the value in the number field.
3. Create an equi-join relationship using the calculation field (as defined in Step 2) as the match field.
4. Create a text field defined as an auto-enter lookup to copy a value from the related table via the relationship established at Step 3.
5. Create a calculation field performing a substitution on the looked-up value in the text field defined at Step 4.
6. Apply a conditional formatting formula to the field defined at Step 5, changing its color if it matches the value of another field in the current record.

## Efficient Code, Efficient Solutions

Each of the fields created in Steps 2, 4, and 5 depends on the resolution of the preceding steps, so you have set up an implicit chain of dependencies for FileMaker to manage. When you change the value in the number field created in Step 1, FileMaker must work its way down the dependency tree triggering consequent actions at every level. When updating the calculated key field (Step 2), FileMaker must dump the cached join results for the relationship at Step 3, re-establishing it (replacing the cached values), and then perform the lookup for the field created at Step 4. Only after the fresh looked-up value is written to the text field at Step 4 can FileMaker begin to re-evaluate the calculation field defined at Step 5—and only when the calculation has returned a result can FileMaker commence resolving the conditional formatting expression. Figure 19.1 illustrates this process.

What's significant about this dependency scenario is that it's entirely sequential. Each step commences after the preceding step has completed. No amount of parallel processing efficiency will improve the speed of execution of such a process; its inefficiency is inherent.

**NOTE** Sequential dependencies are most problematic when they involve unstored calculations (as they are re-evaluated each time they're displayed or referenced, using up large numbers of processor cycles as users work and hampering the responsiveness of your solution) and especially where unstored calculations are included in list views (requiring computation of the whole dependency chain multiple times over to draw a single screen).

**FIGURE 19.1**

The sequence of events required to resolve a chain of dependencies.

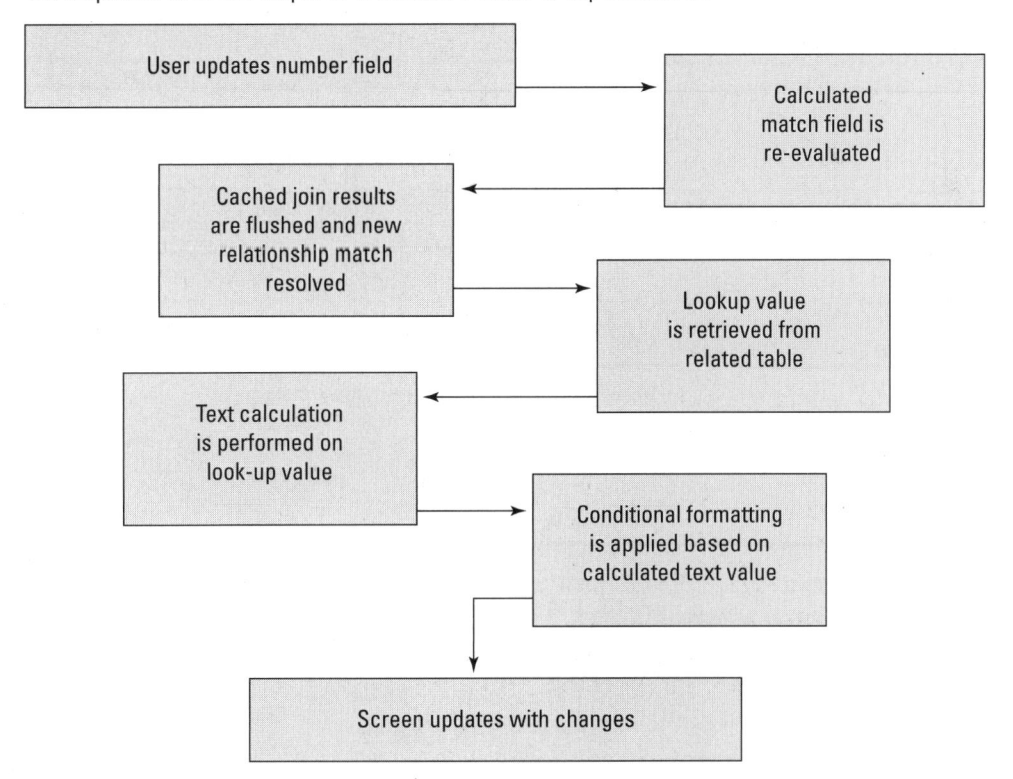

# Part V: Raising the Bar

It's likely when you define a series of dependent actions in the preceding steps that editing the value in the number field imposes a slight but perceptible pause before the conditional formatting at Step 6 is displayed. On a high-performance workstation running on a fast network, the delay may be minimal. You should, however, be aware of the performance implications when creating long chains of dependency. We have seen solutions where sluggish calculations followed dependency chains from table to table all over the solution and back (and therefore using unstored calculations at each step), sometimes 15 or more steps deep. Small wonder that the users experienced long pauses and mounting frustration!

You can do three things to avoid creating "logical spaghetti" throughout your solutions:

- Keep dependencies in view. Be aware of the implications of each dependency as you create it. If necessary, plot your dependency tree as part of your code design, updating it as you work.
- Aim to keep sequential dependencies at four levels or less in all cases, with most dependencies being either direct or dependent on only one other dependency. With most modern computer hardware, FileMaker can resolve two calculations concurrently more quickly than it can process two calculations in succession.
- When a sequential dependency chain arises, look for opportunities to break it or branch it to achieve the desired result with fewer tiers (successive stages) of dependency.

In the case of the preceding example, to reduce the length of the chain of sequential dependencies, consider two steps:

- Create a stored calculation field in the related table defined to subtract 1 from the value being used as the key for the equi-join and then use it as the match field for a relationship (Step 3) matching direct to the number field (Step 1). By doing so, you eliminate the need for the calculation field (Step 2), reducing the chain of dependencies from five to four.
- Create a stored calculation field in the related table defined to apply the required substitution (as at Step 5) to the text value looked up in Step 4 and then re-point the lookup to the field holding the calculated value. By doing so, you eliminate the dependent calculation in Step 5 from the dependency chain, further reducing the length of sequential dependencies.

With these changes in place, when you change the value in the original number field, FileMaker has to perform only the re-lookup and then apply conditional formatting to the result. Yet the outcome is functionally the same.

In this scenario, each of the calculations is still performed. However, the calculations in Steps 2 and 5 are performed separately when the values they reference in the related table are updated. When reevaluation of the calculations occurs, because they're directly dependent on fields in the related table, they introduce no perceptible delay. Yet the lengthy chain of dependencies has been significantly reduced.

Whether the specific techniques discussed in this example are appropriate for a given situation depends on what else you have in place in your solution. A variety of other strategies are possible. What matters is that you are aware of the dependency overhead as you work, taking opportunities to structure your solution design to minimize daisy-chain logic.

# 19 Efficient Code, Efficient Solutions

## Applying simplicity principles

The process of simplifying your code isn't as simple as it seems. That may be a great one-line jest, but it's nonetheless true.

A single line of code capable of replacing (and performing the same function as) half a page of code is obviously more powerful. The resulting solution, however, is cleaner and simpler, easier to maintain and use. Once you have taken the trouble to comprehend how and why the single line of code works, the solution containing it becomes easier to read and understand than the solution containing more verbose code. We doubt that the argument that longer code is preferable because it is "more explicit" or "easier to understand" is ever more than a rationalization.

One way you can view the concept of simplicity is in terms of elements. The elements are powerful. When you reduce your solution to its elemental properties, you remove extraneous and verbose material and invest a great deal in the remaining essentials. Mature computer applications such as FileMaker are inherently complex, permitting myriad paths toward any goal you identify. Your challenge is to find or create simplicity and harmony among the burgeoning complexity. If you succeed, your code and the solutions it supports will be powerful and elegant — as well as robust and scalable.

The following general principles govern the achievement of simplicity in solution development:

- **Simplicity doesn't simply happen.** In fact, if you have anything more than a shopping list to design, simplicity is frequently harder to achieve than complexity. Moreover, arriving at a set of simple principles requires a more profound understanding of both the solution requirements and the development environment.

  When you sketch out the design for a relational model, a challenging calculation, or a crucial screen design, you're probably approaching it from the wrong direction if it seems impressively complex. Take that complexity as a sign and look for an alternative way to conceptualize the problem.

- **The ideal solution is usually the simplest.** When you can achieve more with less, everybody wins. That's true whether you're talking about increased data accuracy with fewer error alerts, better system performance with more compact code, or more flexibility with less confusion.

  If your solution has 20 tables and you can build a fully functioning solution requiring only 50 table occurrences on the Relationships Graph, your achievement is superior — and will undoubtedly perform better (all other things being equal) than a comparable solution where there are 100 table occurrences on the Graph.

- **The deepest organizational model frequently is the simplest in operation.** Collapsing too many things together (when their fit is poor) leads to conflict and confusion, whether they're ideas, operational procedures, or entities and attributes in your relational model.

  By working from first principles and breaking the components down into their essential units, you establish clean lines of separation and workable models of the real world.

- **Simple for the user matters more than simple for the developer.** Avoid the temptation to rationalize with "If simple is good, then my job should be easy" — it just isn't so. Development is in part a process of creating order out of chaos, offering smooth and

653

streamlined paths where there were clutter and obstacles. The greater your thought and comprehension, the more likely it is your users will find the result simple to use and easy to like.

- **There is always room for improvement.** Perfection is unattainable, but improvement is not. However powerful and elegant a piece of code may be, remain open to the possibility of other ways and other ideas. Continually revisit design principles, removing the unnecessary, refining, condensing, and simplifying.

  Excellence arises from a continuous process of questioning and a sustained commitment to improvement.

A number of the principles in this list (along with others, perhaps) may aid you in a variety of pursuits, beyond the bounds of FileMaker development. However, when you're able to keep these five principles in mind throughout the development of your solutions, we are confident you (and your solution's users) will see direct benefits as a result.

# Transaction Modeling

Many database systems, especially those supporting large data sets and enterprise-wide network demands (perhaps serving up data to thousands of users concurrently), provide no equivalent for FileMaker's calculation and summary field types. All data, whether input data or derived data, is calculated on the spot (for example, using a stored procedure), verified, and then stored.

FileMaker's calculation and summary field capabilities are a convenience we would not have you forego, but they carry a price. As the size and complexity of your solutions grows, reliance on calculations and summaries becomes less desirable. In large and heavily loaded systems, data integrity and solution responsiveness is best served by adopting a transaction-based approach to use-case definition — that is, design and define the user experience and the solution's response to user inputs in terms of transactions.

## Live versus batch data

When your solution uses calculation and summary fields throughout, every action a user takes has flow-on consequences. Change the value of the quantity field in an invoice, and the change instantly propagates to the calculated totals and summaries showing on the user's screen. The automatic and immediate update of dependent values is the essence of live data interaction — as illustrated in Figure 19.2 — and many of the processes in FileMaker are built around this principle.

**FIGURE 19.2**

A dynamic international model where each user action produces a result.

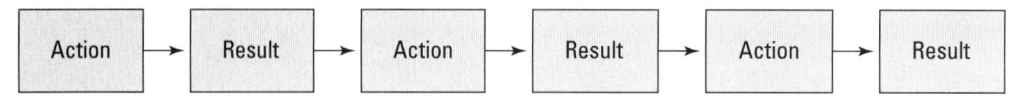

Action → Result → Action → Result → Action → Result

# Efficient Code, Efficient Solutions

An alternative way to conceptualize a data management process is to separate input actions from consequential actions. In such a process, you enter all the required information and then press a key or click a button, and all the resulting computations (along with validations and integrity checks) are performed. If the process is complete and all validation requirements are satisfied, the data is written to the database (committed) as a single transaction, as shown in Figure 19.3.

**FIGURE 19.3**

A transactional interaction model — the final user action precipitates a result (reflecting all the preceding actions).

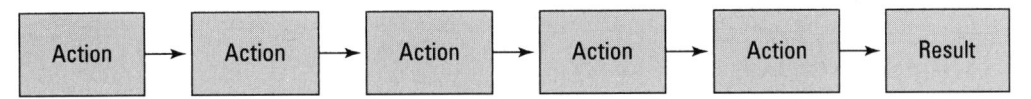

Action → Action → Action → Action → Action → Result

## Posting edits and propagating edits to related records

When you implement a transaction-based interaction model, a complete set of changes is committed as a whole, in a single action. At the time of that action, all interdependencies are resolved, validation checks performed, derived values are generated and stored, and data summaries are updated in a single closing procedure.

In FileMaker, the closing procedure for a transaction is best managed by a script, where the script commits the record and all related records updated as part of the transaction at the close of its process. Because a script manages the user's interaction with the stored data, you can use the script to generate and store derived (calculated) values and update summaries at the point where each change is committed.

With this type of interaction model in place, summary values are computed and stored at the conclusion of each transaction, rather than recalculating across vast record sets in real time (consuming CPU resources constantly as the user navigates the database and works with the data). Each time the user commits a record, such as by clicking a custom Save Changes button on each layout, a short delay occurs while FileMaker adjusts the summary data. However, summary re-computation, even at this point, is not required. The script can simply increment or decrement each stored summary value to reflect the current transaction's contribution. Because all calculations and summaries are stored, navigation, screen refresh, and reporting are instantaneous regardless of the size of your solution.

## Offline updates and processing

Another dimension of transactional systems is the potential for periodic data refresh using separate system processes not dependent on direct interaction between each client workstation and the host.

Overnight generation of updated summary data and reports is one implementation model for periodic processing. If you choose this approach, you schedule an extensive operation to occur during off-peak hours (overnight, for example) to generate queued reports, re-compute and store updated summary data (stock levels and so on), and perform various other batch processing tasks.

The strategic use of periodic updates (performed elsewhere — not on the client workstation) can relieve performance bottlenecks for a variety of non-time-critical requirements, freeing live computation or transactional updates to deal exclusively with immediate data requirements. For example, in a transaction process where the user records a customer payment and issues a receipt, the calculations generating the balance of account for the receipt and updating the customer balance record are required immediately, so you include them as part of the transaction work cycle. However, updates to the company profit and loss statements and general ledger are not required instantly and can occur in an overnight batch run gathering all receipts and payments in the preceding 24-hour period. In this way, you free user transactions of much of the burden of consequential processing, enabling the system to be deft and responsive for end users, yet all the required data is available according to appropriate timelines.

## Robots and batch automation

When you want to implement batch processing in a multi-user solution, several options are available. One of the most powerful and versatile options is deployment of a workstation dedicated to batch processing. Such a workstation is commonly termed a *robot,* as it self-regulates and performs a variety of preprogrammed tasks as an unattended client on the network.

A database robot has its own user account and remains logged in to the host database, as shown in Figure 19.4. Because its tasks are scheduled to occur without user intervention, you need to choose a late model or well-specified machine — providing it meets the requirements to run FileMaker Pro 9 and is robust enough to run 24/7, it will suffice. Its job is to work quietly in the background, relieving the client workstations of non-urgent process work and ensuring lengthy and process-intensive tasks are routinely completed.

Robot deployments need not be limited to overnight processing of lengthy batch jobs. They can be used as fax or database print managers, monitoring queues as users commit jobs for processing, generating the required documents throughout the daily work cycle, and then resuming routine batch processing outside scheduled work hours.

## Host/server script execution

With the introduction of FileMaker Server 9, you can schedule database scripts to run on the server at predetermined times. This approach provides you with a viable alternative to employing a robot workstation for some kinds of process work.

When you define a script to be executed on FileMaker Server, you're constrained to use the Web-compatible script step subset. You can view the available commands by selecting the checkbox labeled Indicate Web Compatibility in the lower left of the Edit Script window. Incompatible Script steps appear dimmed in the list of script commands at the left of the Edit Script window, as shown in Figure 19.5.

## Efficient Code, Efficient Solutions — 19

**FIGURE 19.4**

Overview of a server-based system incorporating a robot-processing station.

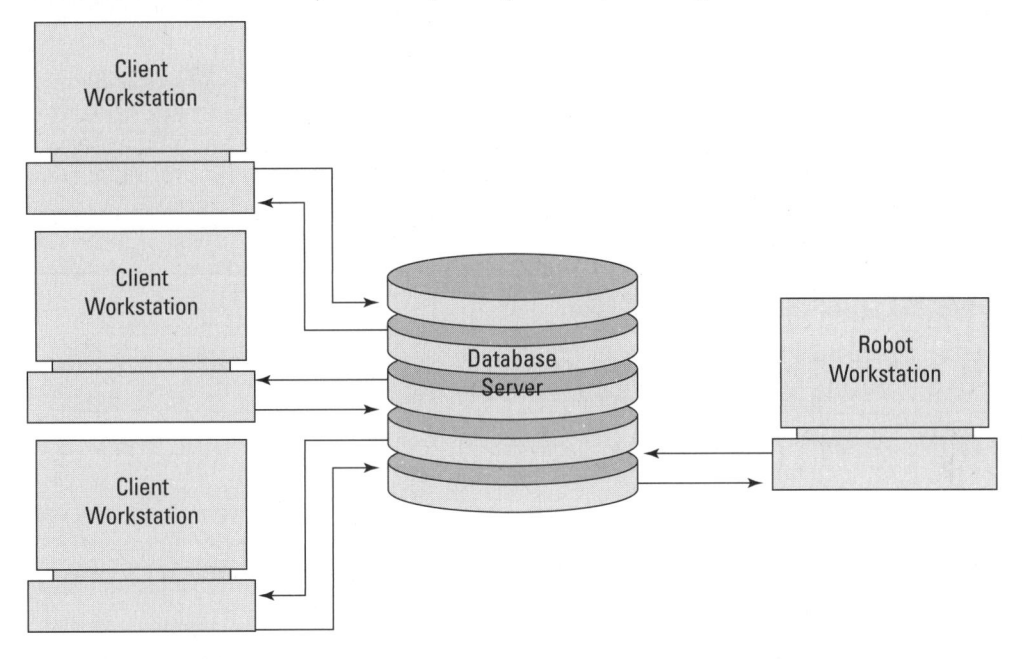

**FIGURE 19.5**

Viewing the Web-compatible script command subset available for use in scripts executed on FileMaker Server 9.

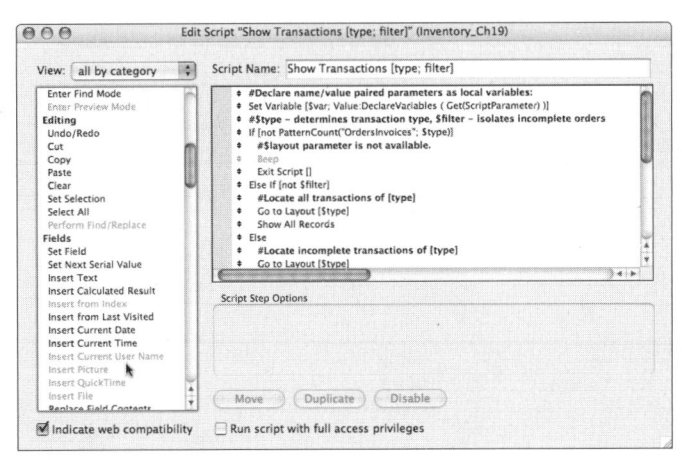

657

Despite the limited selection of commands available for use in scripts you want to schedule to run on FileMaker Server, you can address various operations using this mechanism. In general, we recommend that you schedule scripts to run during low-use times on FileMaker Server to minimize server load.

**CAUTION** Scripts scheduled to run on FileMaker Server fail if they include unsupported script steps (in other words, commands not indicated as Web compatible). A script containing incompatible steps either halts when the first such step is encountered (leaving the process incomplete and possibly leaving the solution of the data in an inappropriate state) or, if the Allow User Abort[ ] setting is on, continues, while skipping the incompatible step or steps.

# Managing File Size

A factor affecting both the manageability of your solution and its performance under load is the size of your database files. Large files are less efficient for several reasons.

One issue with very large files is that data segments are necessarily stored further apart on disk media, so more head movement is required to return nonsequential data sets, such as the results of a Find or records for display in a portal. FileMaker manages data caching to minimize performance impacts from this cause, but the performance you observe in a 200K file will outstrip your experience with a file approaching 5GB.

When files sizes become very large, a more profound impact arises because the backup process for the file takes considerably longer, which introduces periodic delays if your backups are frequent (and we recommend that they are)!

**NOTE** The storage of text and numeric data — especially where a majority of fields are not indexed — is very efficient and is not generally the primary cause of large file sizes. Images and files stored as data are the most frequent cause of large file sizes.

## Dealing with data in chunks

One way to mitigate the performance impact arising from large database files is to separate your data between two or more files. As part of this strategy, you can set separate backup schedules for each file. Because the files are smaller, performance impact when their backups occur will be less noticeable; moreover, you don't need to back up less used files, such as reference data that rarely changes, as frequently.

### Modularization strategies

If you need to address issues arising from file size, making modularization of your solution necessary, we suggest that you consider the following three approaches:

- Create separate database files to store container data — images, files, and multimedia content — using 1:1 relationships between records storing container data and the corresponding data records in your existing solution files.

# Efficient Code, Efficient Solutions

- Build files to store any large reference data sets and/or low-use data tables, because you don't need to back them up as frequently as other files. This strategy is of greatest use where you have very large reference sets of historical or geographic data that rarely changes.

- Define functional centers based on the operational requirements of different groups of users of your solution, separating the main data sets for each functional center into a different file. For example, accounts payable may be in a separate file from product inventory.

One or more of these strategies may enable you to adapt your solution's deployment strategy to improve performance and minimize storage and backup issues.

## Considering segmentation

An alternative approach to the management of large data sets is *segmentation*, where you subdivide data into ranges or subcategories, storing alternate blocks of data in separate "edition" files. For example, if your solution stores the content of newspaper articles spanning a century or so, you can consider segmenting data by decade, giving you ten files of manageable size, rather than one vast and unmanageable file.

Supporting segmentation requires an index file containing enough information, including keywords and titles, to let users search and summarize data across multiple segments. However, viewing a record's content in its entirety requires the user to navigate to the appropriate segment file. You can automate the navigation process, making the user's task a relatively straightforward one.

**CAUTION** Data segmentation is most useful for historical data sets where most segments are not expected to change or grow significantly.

## Data archiving

At some point in any solution's life, the question of archival storage of old or low-use data arises. If you're concerned about the impact of file size on your solution's performance, archiving aged data may present a viable option.

The simplest method of archiving is to create a copy of your solution structure and import records older than a given date into the copy. However, we recommend that you make significant changes to the interface and scripts to ensure the following:

- **Users can't mistake an archive file for the current file.** You don't want users mistakenly entering new data into the wrong file or searching in vain for current data in a file of ancient records.

- **Scripts, buttons, and screens associated with new record creation and other processes relevant only to current data are removed or disabled.** As part of this change, you should consider modifying all privilege sets assigned to user accounts to read-only in the archive file.

With an archive file established, build a scripted process in your solution to automate the process of locating candidate records for archiving and their transfer to the archive solution file.

**Part V**    Raising the Bar

**CROSS-REF**    For details of the processes of transferring data sets between files or alternate systems, refer to Chapter 17.

**NOTE**    When your solution includes an archive, all future changes of data structure should be replicated in the archive so that it is always able to accommodate data from the current solution structure without transformation.

## Images and Media in Databases

A significant cause of overly large database files is the storage of images and media content files, such as PDF or QuickTime, as part of your solution data. Be aware, however, of the range of options available to you for handling these content types.

If file size is the primary cause of performance issues, and that in turn is due to the storage of files and/or media content, one option you should consider is storing files separately, such as on a file server, and referencing them in your solution.

**CROSS-REF**    For techniques and procedures for handling images and stored files, refer to the details in the closing pages of Chapter 17.

By defining a media file as an external FileMaker data source for your solution, and selecting the Allow Creation of Related Records in This Table via This Relationship option, the location of the container content in a different file will not be evident to users.

When considering options for efficiently storing and handling container data, you should consider the capabilities of Web viewers as a means to present image and media content stored remotely.

To incorporate Web storage and viewer access and display of media data as a primary content strategy in your solution, you need to employ external scripting and/or third-party tools to aid in the transfer of files to and from online server locations. Even so, the merits of online content management, including the options for integrating database operations with Web support, make this option worthy of further consideration.

**CROSS-REF**    For additional details about external tools and products to assist in management of content via remote servers, refer to Chapter 20.

# Chapter 20

# Extending FileMaker's Capabilities

There is a great deal to know about FileMaker — so much that doing justice to its native capabilities, without providing coverage of the many related environments, technologies, products, and deployment options, in a book of this size is no small challenge. In this chapter, however, we provide you with a brief survey of products, tools, and techniques available to extend the reach of your solutions.

Many of the technologies we refer to here are the subject of a rich variety of books and other resources in their own right. We encourage you to consider the range of technologies available and choose appropriate resources for further exploration.

Because FileMaker's capabilities are extensive and provide support for wide-ranging functional requirements, you can create many solutions with FileMaker Pro without recourse to external tools or applications. When you reach the limits of the program's native capabilities, however, many options enable you to employ other technologies and push past those limits.

### IN THIS CHAPTER

Making use of external scripting calls

Rendering Web source code in FileMaker

Using Web viewer widgets

Getting acquainted with FileMaker plug-ins

Exploring Web deployment options

Reviewing available third-party tools

## External Scripting Calls

Among FileMaker's 134 ScriptMaker commands are two commands allowing you access to the repertoire of external capabilities made available via your computer's operating system and the scripting languages installed by default on your computer:

        Perform AppleScript [ ]

and

        Send Event [ ]

## Part V  Raising the Bar

These commands enable you to configure your FileMaker scripts to execute AppleScript code on Mac OS and VBScript code on Windows. These scripting languages, in turn, let your solution execute command-line (OS Shell) calls and control other applications running on the current workstation. Moreover, the `Send Event [ ]` command can pass messages (open application/document, print document) to other applications on Windows.

> **NOTE** `Send Event [ ]` also passes messages (called *AppleEvents*) on the Mac. However, the syntax of the messages differs between the platforms, and events that succeed on one platform may fail on the other. We strongly recommend that you ensure that you are on the correct platform for the event your solution is going to send. The `Get(CurrentPlatform)` function is extremely useful in this determination.

Despite the wealth of possibilities you can access via these commands, be aware of the following issues:

- Whereas FileMaker solutions are cross-platform, AppleScript, VBScript, and command-line syntax are specific to each platform. While there is overlap between the capabilities of these technologies, they work differently.

- When part of your script process occurs outside ScriptMaker via calls to external script languages, conventional FileMaker error handling is not available. Therefore, your solution cannot as readily determine if the external script process has completed or succeeded.

- Some variations exist in script capabilities and syntax between operating system versions, so what works in your test environment may not work (or may produce different results) on an end user's computer. Moreover, dependencies on the end user's computer configuration may make some scripts vulnerable.

For these reasons, we recommend that you use FileMaker's native script capabilities as far as possible, invoking alternative script capabilities only for requirements falling outside the scope of FileMaker's scripting vocabulary.

## Using Send Event and VBScript

On Microsoft Windows, you can execute either VBScript or command-line instructions from within your FileMaker scripts. Several methods are available for accessing external scripting capabilities. (We provide examples in the next two sections.) The process is relatively straightforward, giving you access to an immense vocabulary of instructions on the current workstation.

### Using VBScript with FileMaker Pro

The Microsoft Visual Basic Scripting engine (VBScript) installs by default on current versions of the Windows Operating System (including the versions FileMaker Pro 9 requires to operate)—making it a freely available resource for you to tap when your FileMaker solutions are deployed on Windows.

If you have a VBScript file already created and saved on your computer, you can run it using the `Send Event [ ]` script command. If desired, you can store a ready-made file containing VBScript code in a container field in your solution so that your script can export it and then run it as needed. For maximum flexibility, you can use FileMaker's calculation and scripting capabilities to create and run VBScript code dynamically.

## Extending FileMaker's Capabilities 20

In FileMaker 9, you can create a file containing a VBScript definition on a local disk drive and then have the Windows Script Engine run the file. You can efficiently accomplish this task by having your FileMaker script write the VBScript instructions into a global text field, then export them to a *.vbs file and open the file. The process requires a script sequence such as:

```
Set Variable [$vbs; Value:"file:" & Get(TemporaryPath) & "FMPmessage.vbs"]
Set Field [Utility::gVBS; "MsgBox \"You've run VBScript from FileMaker Pro.\""]
Export Field Contents [Utility::gVBS; "$vbs"; Automatically open]
```

In order to create the VBScript file and open it in a single step, select the Automatically Open File checkbox option in the Specify Output File dialog for the `Export Field Contents [ ]` command, as shown in Figure 20.1.

**FIGURE 20.1**

Setting the Exported .vbs file to open automatically.

The example script shown here uses a single line of code containing the VBScript MsgBox command to invoke a dialog on screen, as shown in Figure 20.2.

**FIGURE 20.2**

A VBScript dialog invoked from a FileMaker Pro script.

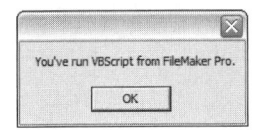

663

## Part V   Raising the Bar

While the one-line VBScript that produces the dialog in Figure 20.2 is a useful, albeit basic, demonstration of the technique, you can use VBScript's extensive capabilities to automate a great variety of processes.

> **CROSS-REF**   You can find links to resources containing thousands of ready-to-use VBScript examples in Appendix B.

### Calling Windows Command-Line scripts

You can also issue instructions to the Windows Command Line Interpreter using the FileMaker Send Event [ ] script command. For example, Figure 20.3 shows the options dialog for the Send Event [ ] script command configured with appropriate syntax to create a folder at an explicit path.

**FIGURE 20.3**

Using Send Event [ ] to call a command script creating a folder on the current workstation.

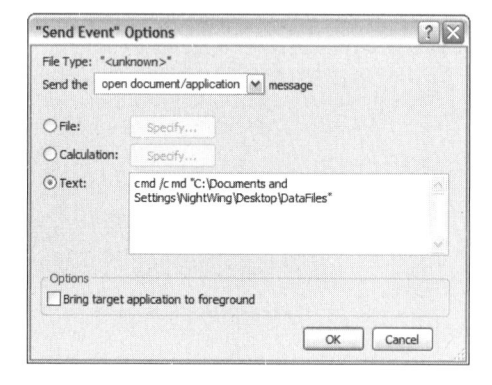

The example shown in Figure 20.3 provides a fixed text command-line instruction to create a new folder called DataFiles on the desktop of a user named NightWing on drive C:\ of the current workstation. The syntax of the code used in this example is formed as follows:

1. The instruction opens with cmd to invoke the Windows command-line interpreter (the cmd.exe application on the current computer).
2. The /c suffix is a command-line switch instructing the interpreter to exit after completion of the instruction.
3. The program call, md, is the command-line instruction for "make directory."
4. The closing argument
   "C:\Documents and Settings\NightWing\Desktop\DataFiles"
   provides the path (including the folder name) of the folder to create. The enclosing quotes are required only if (as in this case) the path contains spaces.

**Extending FileMaker's Capabilities** 20

> **NOTE** When you use `Send Event [ ]`, a scripted pause may be required before any subsequent step that depends on the outcome. In this case, for example, if your script's next action is to place a file in the newly created folder, a short pause of 1 to 2 seconds is required to give the command-line interpreter time to create the folder and exit.

While this example illustrates the technique, in practice, you will frequently find it more useful to determine paths dynamically. You can achieve the dynamic determination of paths using the option to employ a calculation specifying the `Send Event [ ]` command. For example, to build the path for creation of a folder named DataFiles, you can specify a calculation using as its basis the value returned by the built-in `Get(DesktopPath)` function, with an expression along the following lines:

```
Let([
UserDesk = Substitute(Get(DesktopPath); "/"; "\\");
MD_path = Right(UserDesk; Length(UserDesk) - 1)];
"Cmd /c md \"" & MD_path & "DataFiles\""
)
```

When you use a calculation to determine command-line syntax dynamically, as shown here, the procedure is more robust because it accurately reflects the extant environment on the user's computer.

> **CROSS-REF** The command-line instruction used in the preceding examples (md) is one of a large number of available Windows commands. For additional information about available commands and their uses, refer to the resources listed in Appendix B.

The Windows `Send DDE Execute [ ]` script step (*DDE* stands for Dynamic Data Exchange) provides added Windows-specific capabilities. In particular, it allows you to send service requests to other applications (such as requesting Internet Explorer to open a particular URL). The services available depend upon the application with which you're trying to communicate, so you need to examine that application's documentation for what it supports and the request syntax. While FileMaker Pro can send DDE requests, it isn't configured to respond to any DDE requests.

## Perform AppleScript

On the Macintosh Operating System, your FileMaker scripts can make use of the built-in AppleScript scripting language, providing extensive control over the operating system and many applications. Moreover, through AppleScript, you can gain access to Shell Scripts (UNIX command-line instructions).

Executing AppleScript code from within your FileMaker scripts is as simple as configuring the `Perform AppleScript [ ]` command with an appropriate AppleScript instruction. For example, to have AppleScript display a dialog similar to the one in the preceding section's example, you can configure the Perform AppleScript options to run a line of Native AppleScript, as shown in Figure 20.4.

When the script containing the Perform AppleScript instruction shown in Figure 20.4 executes, Mac OS presents a dialog displaying the specified message text, shown in Figure 20.5.

## Part V  Raising the Bar

Needless to say, the one-line AppleScript shown here does not do justice to AppleScript's expansive capabilities. However, it serves to illustrate the basic technique for integrating external script calls into your FileMaker scripts.

**FIGURE 20.4**

Running a line of Native AppleScript code with the `Perform AppleScript` command.

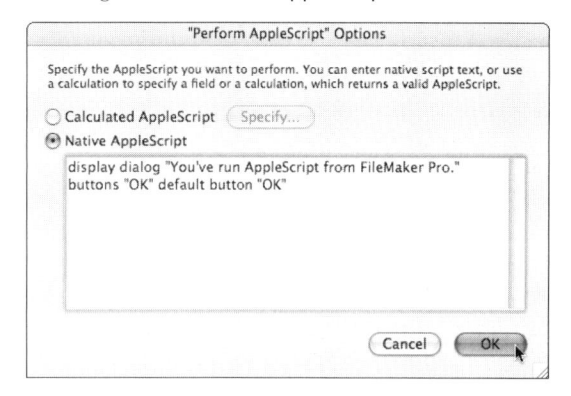

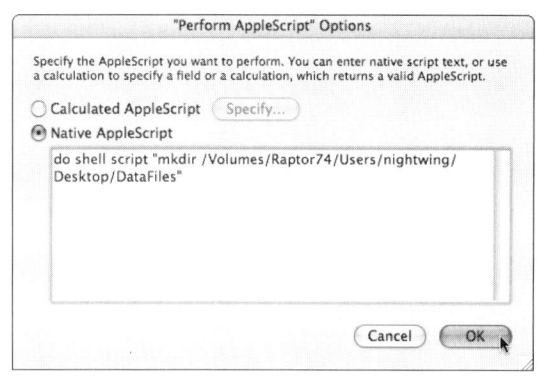

**FIGURE 20.5**

An AppleScript dialog invoked from a FileMaker Pro script.

**CROSS-REF** You can find links to resources containing detailed AppleScript syntax and a broad collection of useful examples in Appendix B.

## Extending FileMaker's Capabilities — 20

In addition to its native powers, AppleScript gives you access to the operating system's command-line capabilities.

For example, rather than using AppleScript instructions to create a folder (which is certainly possible), you can use it to execute a shell script. The example in Figure 20.6 shows an AppleScript call configured to run an OS script, hard-coded to create a new folder called DataFiles on the desktop of a user named nightwing on a volume named Macintosh HD on the current workstation.

**FIGURE 20.6**

Using AppleScript to call a Shell command creating a folder on the current workstation.

In practice, dynamically determining paths is frequently far more useful. You can, for example, use the shell syntax "`~/Desktop/DataFiles`" to determine the path to the DataFiles directory on the current user's desktop. Alternatively, you can employ the Calculated AppleScript option to specify the command syntax. For example, you can specify a calculation to build the required shell script instruction with an expression such as:

```
"do shell script \"mkdir '/Volumes" & Get(DesktopPath) & "DataFiles' \""
```

Because you can create both AppleScript and OS Shell commands via calculation and execute them using the `Perform AppleScript[ ]` command, you have a great deal of scope and flexibility.

**CROSS-REF** For information and examples of shell commands and their associated arguments, refer to the resources listed in Appendix B.

## Cross-platform solutions and external script calls

While the external script options differ between MacOS and Windows, there is significant overlap between the command-line and script engine capabilities, so many external scripting tasks can be accomplished on both platforms with the appropriate syntax.

667

To make best use of external script calls in your solutions, consider including a platform test and execute the external scripts according to the result. For example, to create a folder named DataFiles at the root directory of the boot drive, regardless of platform, you can use the following script code:

```
If [Abs(Get(CurrentPlatform)) = 1
  # Current Platform is MacOS-execute AppleScript/Shell Script:
  Perform AppleScript ["do shell script "mkdir 'DataFiles' ""]
Else
  # Current Platform is Windows - call Command-Line instruction:
  Send Event ["aevt"; "odoc"; "cmd /c md C:\DataFiles"]
End If
```

With strategic branching according to platform, your solution's scripts can respond appropriately wherever the files are opened. Using this technique, you can successfully incorporate a significant number of external script actions into your cross-platform solutions.

> **TIP** Because the `Perform AppleScript [ ]` command is not available on Windows, the third line of the preceding script must be tested with the file open on MacOS. Although the `Send Event [ ]` step is available on both platforms, we recommend that you create and test the external script calls for each platform on the appropriate operating system.

On Mac OS, the `Send Event [ ]` command provides you with the capability of directly sending AppleEvents to other applications (or even to your currently running copy of FileMaker Pro). When you install FileMaker Pro 9 (or FileMaker Pro 9 Advanced) on Mac, a FileMaker Pro database of AppleEvents is installed in the English Extras folder within the FileMaker folder within Applications.

On Windows, the `Send Event [ ]` command can be used to pass open or print events to designated applications, or to pass single lines of script or to invoke the command-line interpreter. A FileMaker database of script commands and code operable on Windows is available as a free download from the ConnectingData Web site (www.connectingdata.com).

## Third-party helpers and macros

Beyond FileMaker scripting, you can use a variety of external tools to automate common procedures, including repetitive FileMaker tasks.

Depending on the platform, you can use AppleScript or VBScript to initiate processes, opening files and setting scripts in motion (script calls require the use of ActiveX on Windows) and controlling your solution's interface.

Other third-party automation and scheduling tools are also worthy candidates for the automation of both developer and end user processes involving your solution (or your solution's interaction with other applications). For example, QuicKeys (available for both Mac OS and Windows) is a versatile macro environment providing user-configurable automation options for most sequences of keyboard and mouse input.

Other useful tools for enhancing productivity include TextExpander (Mac OS), As-U-Type (Windows), and AIM Keys (Windows) — each offering aids to the efficiency and accuracy of a wide variety of data-entry and computer management tasks — within and beyond your database solutions.

# Rendering HTML and JavaScript

FileMaker's Open URL [ ] script step and the Web viewer layout object give you direct access to content from a wide variety of sources, including Web services and output from a variety of applications capable of generating hypertext or Web-compliant content.

With the advent of FileMaker 9 and its increased support for Data URLs, FileMaker itself is now one of the applications you can use to generate Web viewer content. Calculations and stored data can be rendered directly in FileMaker Web viewers using the following syntax:

```
"data:text/html,"  & YourTO::YourHTMLcontent
```

In this example, the trailing field reference (or a calculation expression in its place) produces HTML and/or browser-compatible content (Flash, Javascript, and so on).

## Harnessing HTTP

When you produce Web content using any third-party tool, such as Dreamweaver, Netbeans IDE, or Eclipse, you can substitute placeholder flags for content or page rendering values (colors, sizes, coordinates). When you store the resulting content in FileMaker in a text field, your calculations can substitute values from the current record's fields (and its related data) for the embedded placeholder values.

This process's output is a dynamic rendering of your solution content. You can pass the result directly to a Web viewer for screen viewing or printing (or output to pdf, e-mail, and so on) or save the result to an external file, such as on a Web server for public access.

Using variations on the techniques described here, your solutions can incorporate the full depth of interface, data display, and dynamic visualization available using current Web and browser technologies.

## Bringing services to your solution

With a Web viewer pointed to any URL on the Internet, your solution can retrieve the page source using the following simple FileMaker calculation expression:

```
GetLayoutObjectAttribute ( "ViewerObjectName" ; "content" )
```

To reliably retrieve the source code from a designated Internet address, you must account for load times, pausing until the full content of the destination page has been recovered. You can do so with a scripted loop procedure.

**CROSS-REF** For a detailed description of script technique for scraping data from Web pages, refer to Chapter 10.

Using Web viewers in your solution lets you choose to render the content for screen or print output or to store the content as data in your solution. By combining the techniques discussed here with those described in previous sections, you can recover the source from a remote Internet address and then use it as a template or *wrapper*, interleaving or embedding data from your solution and rendering or printing the result.

Alternatively, these techniques allow you to draw source content from multiple sites, combining them and presenting them in a format of your choosing.

**CAUTION** Always ensure that your use of content not originating within your solution is in accordance with the terms of use and copyright provisions of its owners, authors, and publishers.

## Handling hypertext

Moving content between conventional data storage, such as text and number fields, and hypertext presents some challenges regarding formatting. By using FileMaker's native `GetAsCSS ( )` function, you can convert embedded text character formatting, including styles, sizes, fonts, and colors, to a tagged form appropriate for display in a Web viewer or browser environment.

For example, to display formatted text content from your database in a Web viewer, configure the Web viewer (in Layout mode, via the Web Viewer Setup dialog) to enclose the data URL content within the `GetAsCSS ( )` function, as shown in Figure 20.7.

**FIGURE 20.7**

Configuring a Web viewer to render embedded character formatting from content originating in data fields.

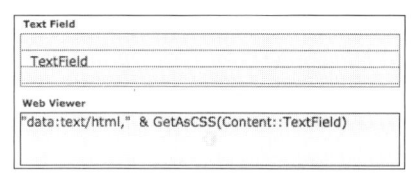

```
Text Field
  TextField

Web Viewer
  "data:text/html," & GetAsCSS(Content::TextField)
```

Using this technique, any character formatting applied to the text in the TextField field will be replicated in the CSS-tagged content the Web viewer renders. The rendering of styled field text in a Web viewer can be seen in the Browse mode image of the same layout reproduced in Figure 20.8.

**FIGURE 20.8**

Web viewer in Browse mode, displaying data formatting.

```
Text Field
  This is formatted text!

Web Viewer
  This is formatted text!
```

> **NOTE** A Web viewer renders unformatted text (that is, text without embedded character formatting) according to the default Web style — not necessarily matching the field box's display formatting. The application of default formatting applies separately to each aspect of formatting (font, size, style, and color).

# Web Viewer Widgets

Web viewers bring additional functionality to FileMaker. There is a world of innovation on the Web, much of it leaking into FileMaker layouts through Web viewers large and small.

With the gathering momentum of Web 2.0, dynamic and interactive content forms are appearing and evolving at an alarming rate — so we're resigned to anything we write here being old news almost before the words hit the page. You can assume that what we say here applies equally to a variety of technologies — including some not yet revealed.

## Charting with Flash

Data visualization tools are far more abundant with every passing year. Many of these tools cropping up in recent years are compact Shockwave Flash (SWF) files capable of receiving and rendering arrays of user data. The variety and quantity of this class of tools is steadily increasing, and a number of the tools are available free (and others are licensed for modest shareware fees).

The significance of this burgeoning technology for FileMaker lies in the opportunities you have to incorporate Flash charting into your solution. You can perform this feat by:

1. Storing the required Flash resource file in a container field.
2. Exporting the file to a known path on the user's workstation (for example, to the temp directory).
3. Setting a calculation to append arrays of solution data to the path to the Flash resource file.
4. Loading the resulting string into a Web viewer on your solution's layout.

Moreover, while this process requires a script to render your data in graphical form on your layout, by placing the required resources during your solution's start-up script and setting the path calculation as the default path for your Web viewer, you can make the process fully dynamic. Your solution's data will be charted "live" as users navigate records and edit field contents.

## Applets and servlets

The process outlined in the preceding section is not limited to data visualization. In addition to graphical and rendering widgets, a generation of calculation, communication, and analysis utilities is emerging in the form of miniature Web-capable, self-contained code snippets. Some of these emerging tools — commonly called *servlets* — are designed to operate in a fixed environment on a remote server, yet are accessible to anyone with a Web connection. Others are entirely portable, compatible with the models of use we've described for charting utilities, and are referred to as *applets*.

FileMaker is positioned to make full use of emerging technologies of this kind — and their continuing availability appears assured. Whatever the future of computing may hold, component technologies are set to be a significant part of it.

# FileMaker Plug-Ins

No survey of FileMaker's options for extensibility would be complete without mention of the plug-in API (Application-Program Interface) and the extraordinary variety of plug-in utilities (some so sophisticated they might be better thought of as ancillary applications) developers have made available as FileMaker plug-ins.

Although the plug-in interface was first envisaged (with the introduction of FileMaker 4) as an adjunct to the calculation engine — a way for developers to provide support for obscure computation functions — it rapidly became the base of wide-ranging innovation, with plug-ins emerging to serve such diverse purposes as script scheduling, systems integration, e-mail handling, and image manipulation.

As with almost every technology available for extending the program's scope, we could fill a book in its own right with detailed coverage of FileMaker plug-ins, their capabilities, and their use. We can't hope to do justice to even a fraction of the available tools here. However, we can provide you with an overview of the main techniques used to control plug-ins and some guidelines for their use.

## Installing and enabling plug-ins

To install and fully enable a plug-in on your client workstation installations of FileMaker Pro or FileMaker Pro Advanced, follow these steps:

1. Obtain the correct version of the plug-in for your computer's operating system. and place it in the Extensions folder inside the folder containing your copy of FileMaker Pro 9 (or FileMaker Pro 9 Advanced). Plug-ins on Mac OS have the file extension `.fmplugin`, whereas Windows plug-ins use the `.fmx` extension.

2. Launch FileMaker Pro 9 (if it was already running, quit and re-launch it to load the new plug-in) and choose FileMaker Pro ➪ Preferences (MacOS) or Edit ➪ Preferences (Windows). The Preferences dialog appears.

3. Navigate to the Plug-Ins tab, confirm the new plug-in appears in the list, and (if it is not already selected) select the checkbox next to its name, as shown in Figure 20.9.

   In your solution, configure the start-up script to call the plug-in's version function confirming its availability (and verifying the required version of the plug-in — or later — is installed). If the required plug-in version is not available, try the following:

   - If your solution is hosted and you're using auto-update to retrieve required plug-ins from the Server, have your script call the `FMSAUC_FindPlugIn( )` external function to search for the plug-in on the server and, if found, subsequently call the `FMSAUC_UpdatePlugIn( )` external function to retrieve and install the plug-in.

# Extending FileMaker's Capabilities    20

- If the plug-in is not available and your solution's functionality depends on it, post a dialog alerting the user to the problem and close your solution.

> **NOTE** Commercial and shareware plug-ins must be licensed and generally require that a valid license code be supplied by your solution before first use of the plug-in in each application session.

**FIGURE 20.9**
Enabling a plug-in via the Preferences Plug-ins tab.

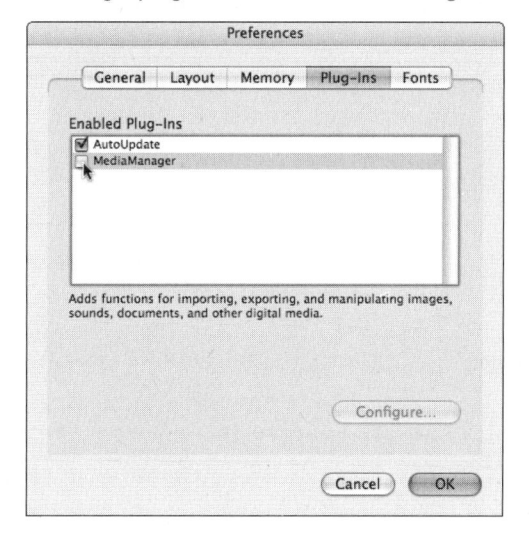

Passing a required license code to a plug-in is usually achieved by calling an external "register" function provided by the plug-in. Consult the documentation supplied by your plug-in vendor for details of the appropriate syntax for plug-in registration.

FileMaker Pro installs by default with a plug-in named AutoUpdate enabled. AutoUpdate enables you to configure your solutions to retrieve current versions of required plug-ins when they're stored in the designated plug-ins folder on the current FileMaker Server host computer.

To take advantage of plug-in auto-update capabilities, you must configure the following in accordance with the operational requirements of the auto-update process:

- FileMaker Server
- FileMaker Pro
- Your solution's start-up script

When each of these components are configured appropriately, the required plug-in versions are checked and, if necessary, are downloaded from FileMaker Server and enabled on the user's workstation, as your solution starts up.

**Part V** Raising the Bar

A notable change in the operation of the auto-update feature with FileMaker 9 is that plug-ins are automatically downloaded to new locations on the user's workstation. The target locations, depending on the user's operating system and platform, are

- On **Mac OS X**:

    Mac OS X: Macintosh HD/Users/User Name/Library/Application Support

- On **Windows XP**:

    C:\Document Settings\User Name\Local Settings\ApplicationData\FileMaker\Extensions

- On **Windows Vista**;

    C:\Users\User Name\AppData\Local\FileMaker\Extensions

The same plug-in folder locations are accessed by both FileMaker Pro 9 and FileMaker Pro 9 Advanced.

**NOTE** For additional information about the configuration requirements for automatic update of solution plug-ins, refer to the document named FileMaker Server 9 — Guide to Updating Plug-ins provided with the FileMaker Server 9 manuals and documentation. (It's also available from the Downloads section of the FileMaker, Inc., Web site.)

## Using external functions

Invoking plug-in capabilities requires you to call an external calculation function provided by the plug-in, supplying appropriate arguments to control the behavior of the plug-in, and pass it required data or parameters. The purpose of each external function — and its required syntax — is specific to the individual plug-in and should be detailed in documentation available from the plug-in vendor.

**TIP** Simply including an external function in a calculation is not sufficient. The function must be evaluated by FileMaker's calculation engine. For example, if you call the external function `zippScript_EnableTriggers` in the following calculation expression:

```
If(DayOfWeek(Get(CurrentDate)) = 5;
   zippScript_EnableTriggers)
```

the triggering capabilities of the zippScript plug-in will be enabled only on Fridays.

You can take advantage of this behavior by using calculation code to determine how and when external functions are evaluated.

Most plug-ins are designed to be called via calculations occurring in your solution's scripts (by including external functions in the formula for a Set Field [ ] or Set Variable [ ] command, for instance). However, you can include plug-in functions wherever calculations are supported, so you can add plug-in calls in schema calculations, access privileges calculations, conditional formatting expressions — wherever is appropriate for the plug-in functionality you require.

# Extending FileMaker's Capabilities    20

**NOTE** Ideal techniques for including external function calls in your solutions may vary according to a given plug-in's nature and functionality. Most plug-in vendors provide example databases showing a range of recommended techniques for calling the external functions provided by their plug-in. Such examples are indicative of the range of viable and supported triggering methods for the plug-in.

## Script triggering

One of the most ubiquitous plug-in capabilities is script triggering, which offers you the ability to trigger a script from a calculation in your solution. Script triggering capabilities can substantially extend and enhance your solution's capabilities. However, it can also lead to problems if not implemented expertly. For example:

- If your solution triggers a script from a schema calculation, and the script modifies the current record resulting in re-evaluation of the same calculation, your solution may become trapped in an infinite loop. The risk is no greater than pertains to the use of the FileMaker `Loop/End Loop` script commands (where failure to include a valid exit condition also results in an infinite loop) or the `Perform Script [ ]` command (where an inattentive developer can set a script to call itself). Nevertheless, you should be aware of the need to plan your implementation of script triggering with care.

- Calculations are evaluated when leaving a field or record, and you can use them to trigger a script (by inclusion of an external function call within the calculation expression). However, when you intend to have the script act upon the current record and the user exits the field by navigating to a different record, by the time your script commences, the current record is not the one where the trigger calculation was evaluated. Therefore, you must allow for this possibility and design your scripts accordingly, avoiding unintended outcomes from such uses of script triggering.

You can address both these issues by designing an appropriate framework for your script triggering plug-in calls, mindful of the potential issues, as we discuss in the next two sections.

### Robust triggering implementations

To ensure that your script triggers aren't activated by the actions of the script they call, becoming loop-locked, enclose schema (and schema-dependent) trigger calls within a condition preventing the evaluation of the external function if the script is already running. For example, to use the popular zippScript plug-in to call a script named `"Check"` in the current file (without the optional parameter or control settings), you can use the external function syntax:

```
zippScript_PerformScript(Get(FileName); "Check")
```

However, to ensure that the external function will not be evaluated if the Check script is already active, enclose the function in a conditional expression, as follows:

```
If(Get(ScriptName) ≠ "Check"; zippScript_PerformScript(Get(FileName); "Check"))
```

675

If the Check script calls other scripts that may in turn modify the field (or fields) used to trigger the external function call, you may need to guard against indirect recursion as well. To do so, extend the If( ) test in the preceding expression to forestall the trigger action while any of the implicated scripts are active.

By controlling the evaluation context of script triggering function calls as outlined in the preceding example, you can manage the external calls, determining the context when triggering occurs (also including other criteria if desired). This approach is appropriate in cases where the called script may have consequences leading to reevaluation of the external function activating the trigger, including schema calculations, privilege (Record Level Access) expressions, and layout calculations, such as Web viewer and conditional formatting expressions.

In cases where a triggered script is required to act on the record where the external function is evaluated, such as for data-entry validation, data updates, and other record-specific script processes, you need to capture the context where triggering originates. You can do so by using the external function call to pass a parameter to the called script, including the ID of the calling record in the parameter. In the following example, the zippScript function passes the primary ID of the current customer record to the Check script:

```
zippScript_PerformScript(Get(FileName); "Check"; CustomerID)
```

You should then structure your check script so that when run, it first confirms that the calling record is current and, if not, accesses it — for example, you can use one of the following methods:

- Structure your script to
    - Capture the current context (mode, layout, record, and window)
    - Freeze the screen, navigate to a utility layout, and enter Browse mode
    - Enter the script parameter value into a global field you've configured to establish a relationship to the relevant customer record

    The script can then proceed to perform its check procedure while accessing the appropriate record via the utility relationship, subsequently returning the user to the script's commencing context.

- Have your script create a new temporary database window out of the user's field of view (for example, off-screen), navigate to the customers layout and perform a Find to locate the relevant customer record, perform the required check, and then close the temporary window.

In either case, your script ensures that its actions are applied to the appropriate record, yet faithfully reinstates the context (active window, layout, found set, and current record) invoked by the user on leaving the field at the point the external function call triggers the Check script. With this implementation, the user can leave the current record by changing layouts, navigating to a different record, entering a different mode, or closing the current window, without compromising the script's ability to perform its intended function.

One further condition you should account for to ensure that your script triggering implementation is robust is the case where a user leaves the current record by closing the file or exiting the application. Because it's likely that your script trigger will not succeed in such a case, if it's essential that the script runs when data is edited, we recommend that you set the script trigger in an auto-enter calculation set to return a session ID value (for example, user login account and workstation ID) when triggered and have your script clear the value when it runs.

With this configuration, your file's closing script should check for the presence of the current session ID in the current table and, if found, call the check script before completing its run.

When you set in place a thoughtfully designed (and thoroughly tested) implementation along the lines set out in this example, you can be confident that your scripts will always run when triggered, will never lock your solution in a loop, and will always act on the appropriate record.

### Available script triggering plug-ins

A number of excellent script triggering plug-ins are available, and many provide triggering in addition to a variety of other features. The zippScript plug-in from zippTools (http://zipp-tools.com) is one of our favorites and, at the time of writing, is available free of charge. Other worthy offerings also available free of charge include EventScript from Softwares for Humans (www.softs4humans.com) and ScriptMaster from 360Works (www.360works.com).

Some additional script triggering plug-ins we have used and heartily recommend are the commercial plug-ins Troi Activator from Troi Automatisering (http://troi.com) and MenuMagic from New Millennium (http://newmillennium.com), both providing additional functionality (in the case of MenuMagic, an extensive suite of security and menu customization options).

**NOTE** An FMExample plug-in supplied on the FileMaker Pro Advanced installation CD includes script triggering capabilities. However, we advise against its use for most script triggering purposes because it does not include the ability to pass a parameter to the called script. Consequently, the FMExample plug-in is unsuitable as a trigger for any script where context is relevant to the actions the script performs.

## Dialog capabilities

The FileMaker Show Custom Dialog [ ] script step offers a core set of capabilities enabling you to perform two or three of the tasks commonly handled using dialogs in modern computer systems. Several leading third-party vendors — perhaps the best known being 24U Simple Dialog from 24U Software (www.24usoftware.com) and Troi Dialog Plug-in from Troi Automatisering (www.troi.com) — offer plug-ins with dialog capabilities.

Dialog plug-in capabilities include adding custom icons or graphics to your dialogs and altering the dialog's size or placement, including pop-up lists, checkbox options, radio buttons, fields of various sizes, and dynamically labeled buttons. Figure 20.10 shows an example of a dialog produced by calling an external function.

### FIGURE 20.10

A customized text display dialog produced using the Troi Dialog Plug-in.

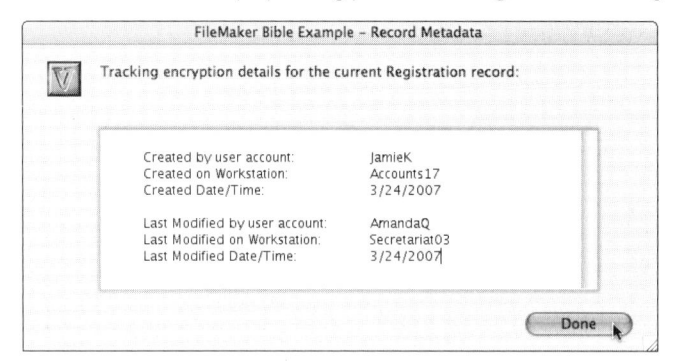

The customized dialog example shown in Figure 20.10 was created by calling three of Troi Dialog's external functions in succession, to specify the custom icon, the dialog title, and the parameters for the dialog to be displayed respectively. The syntax for the relevant script code is as follows:

```
Set Variable [$x; Value: Dial_IconControl("-SetCustomIcon"; I::gDialogIcon)]
Set Variable [$x; Value: Dial_SetDialogTitle( "" ; "FileMaker Bible Example -
    Record Metadata" )]
Set Variable [$x; Value: Dial_BigInputDialog( "-Width=600 -Height=280 -
    CustomIcon -DefaultButton1 -StopOnESC" ; "Tracking encryption details for the
    current Registration record:" ; "Done" ; "" ; "" ; "" ;
    Registrations::cRecordMetadata)]
```

**NOTE** Many other dialog formats and options are available. Full details of the syntax options for each external function — with examples of their use — are available from the vendors' sites.

While the example provided here gives you an indication of what is involved — and what results you can expect — from using a dialog plug-in, we have barely scratched the surface in an effort to point you in the right direction. We recommend that you download trial copies of plug-ins to determine the most appropriate options for your solution.

## File and media handling

One of several other areas of plug-in functionality worth highlighting is the broad range of file and media capabilities brought to FileMaker by a number of premier third-party providers — plug-ins such as CNS Image from CNS (www.cnsplug-ins.com), File Manipulator from Productive Computing (www.productivecomputing.com), MediaManager from New Millennium (www.newmillennium.com), and Troi File from Troi Automatisering (www.troi.com).

# Extending FileMaker's Capabilities 20

These plug-ins and others like them simplify the process of managing external content and extend your reach beyond what can readily be achieved with the combination of FileMaker Pro's native file management capabilities, and those available to you via the use of external scripting, as outlined in the "External Scripting Calls" section earlier in this chapter.

Also noteworthy with respect to content management tools is the SuperContainer plug-in from 360Works (www.360works.com), designed to provide coordinated access to remote server storage of files and media content using a Java servlet in conjunction with a Web viewer in your solution.

## E-mail, HTTP, and FTP

An ever-expanding selection of plug-ins providing support for online connectivity continues to emerge from established and new third-party vendors. Long-standing contenders such as mail.it (http://dacons.net), SMTPit, POP3it, FTPit (http://cnsplug-ins.com), and Troi URL Plug-in (http://troi.com) have been joined by the 360Works Email Plugin (http://360works.com) and the TCPdirect and SendMail offerings from Fusion (http://fusionplugins.com).

Recently, however, vendors are providing connectivity tools that combine broad-based and mixed capabilities in a single powerful plug-in. One of the difficulties these products face is their breadth and the potential to overlook them when targeting specific (and more traditional) niches. The relatively recent releases of Smart Pill from Scodigo (www.scodigo.com), the MBS FileMaker Plugin from Monkeybread Software (www.monkeybreadsoftware.de), and Fusion Reactor from Digital Fusion Ltd. (www.fusionplugins.com) — each exciting and ground-breaking in their own right — are equally hard to categorize in light of their versatility and breadth of applicability.

## Charting and other functionality

Another area of plug-in functionality with an established user base is charting and data visualization. Here the plug-in contenders include xmCHART from X2max Software (www.x2max.com), 24U SimpleChart Plugin from 24U Software (www.24usoftware.com), and the Charts Plugin from 360Works (www.360works.com). The breadth and depth of functionality varies between vendors, but continues to provide many users a viable alternative to more recent Web viewer–based charting options.

Also notable for the variety of options available are interapplication communication and data transformation plug-ins. Some of the many available options provide data conduits between FileMaker and established accounts, CRM, e-mail, address book, and organizer applications.

**NOTE** If you're interested in writing your own plug-ins, you can find an example plug-in project on the installation disk for FileMaker Pro Advanced. Moreover a plug-in development template and tutorial is available from 24U (www.24usoftware.com).

Suffice it to say, innovative plug-in developers around the globe cover an extraordinarily large number of bases, extending the uses of the API in every direction conceivable. A great deal more is on offer than we have been able to touch on here. If you have a problem, the chances are somebody has already solved it with FileMaker plug-in.

**CROSS-REF** For additional details regarding the broad range of third-party plug-ins, refer to the online resources listed in Appendix B.

# Web Deployment Options

In addition to its power and versatility as a desktop and client-server database system, FileMaker provides options for Web-deployment, enabling you to use your FileMaker data as the basis of Web site content. If your data includes schedules, catalogs, collections, facts, or figures, the chances are someone would like to look it up on the Web.

If you don't require users to enter data into your database (and if your data changes only infrequently), one option is to export your data as an html table (one of FileMaker's built-in data export formats) and incorporate it into an appropriate html framework by adding html frames, headers, and/or style sheets. But if your data requires two-way interaction or needs more than periodic updates, a live Web connection direct to your solution is preferable.

## Instant Web publishing

If the fmiwp extended privilege is enabled for one or more privilege sets in your solution, you can make your database available to up to five concurrent Web users in a matter of minutes by choosing File ➪ Sharing ➪ Instant Web Publishing and configuring the open databases for access, as shown in Figure 20.11.

**FIGURE 20.11**

Configuring your database for Web-browser access via the Instant Web Publishing dialog.

## Extending FileMaker's Capabilities

Once Instant Web Publishing (IWP) is enabled, users will be able to open your solution using a supported Web browser, by entering the IP address of your computer (preceded by http://) in their browser's address bar. Your solution's layouts are rendered in the user's browser and navigation, data entry, and limited scripts (those containing only Web-compatible script commands) are available.

Because of the nature of Web browsers — an inherently stateless user experience — FileMaker layouts are not as dynamic and responsive in IWP. The user experience is less suited to the FileMaker interface model than the FileMaker client application, and some layout objects exhibit different behavior when accessed via a Web browser. Nevertheless, IWP is a remarkable technology and serves a range of purposes well.

**NOTE** To access your solutions via Instant Web Publishing, the user's browser is required to provide full support for Cascading Style Sheets (CSS). That limits users to Internet Explorer 6.x (or later) or Firefox 1.x (or later) on Windows and Safari 1.2.x, Safari 2.0.x, Safari 3.x or Firefox 1.x (or later) on Mac OS.

If you can work within the IWP format's functional constraints, but require more than five simultaneous users, you should consider hosting your solution on FileMaker Server Advanced to make your solution available to up to 100 simultaneous Instant Web Publishing users.

**TIP** When using IWP, you can use the Web folder in your FileMaker Pro folder to store external files, such as images and referenced container files, to share via Instant Web Publishing. You can also include a customized entry page of HTML using the filename iwp_home.html, plus other pages of static HTML if required.

## Custom Web publishing

If you require more than 100 simultaneous Web-based users, if you require support for a larger selection of Web browsers, or if you require greater flexibility and control over the Web-browsing experience than is achievable within the constraints of Instant Web Publishing, FileMaker Server provides support for other forms of Web access to your solutions.

Custom Web Publishing enables you to build an alternative Web-specific interface to your solution, reading and writing directly to your solution's data structure in real time. Support is available for Web-publishing strategies based on XML/XSLT or PHP.

### Working with XML and XSLT

When your solution is hosted using FileMaker Server, you can make data access (for both read and write) available via XML (Extensible Markup Language) and XSLT (Extensible Stylesheet Language Transformation). By using XSLT, you can extract and transform your data into appropriate presentation formats for a variety of applications, such as Web forms, news feeds, or special-purpose downloads from your Web site.

## Part V  Raising the Bar

Similarly, using XML with XSLT can also dynamically generate the source and content for your Web pages, including data from FileMaker and, if desired, from other sources as well. To generate Web content using XML, you require an appropriate XSLT style sheet as the intermediary between FileMaker Server and its Web-publishing engine.

### The FileMaker PHP API

If you host your solution using FileMaker Server, you can make use of its built-in PHP support, making content from your solution available directly to external Web sites, receiving input from Web users. The support for PHP's open source standards for the Web enables you to rapidly assemble Web-based applications to access your FileMaker data via live, real-time connections with FileMaker Server.

With your installation of FileMaker Server, you receive a standard install of the PHP engine, the FileMaker API for PHP and sample code, and documentation. Once the server is operational, you have everything you need to begin publishing your FileMaker data via PHP.

> **NOTE** To prepare your solution for use with the PHP API, first activate the fmphp extended privilege for privilege sets in your solution files, as shown in Figure 20.12.

**FIGURE 20.12**
Activating the fmphp extended privilege in your solution files.

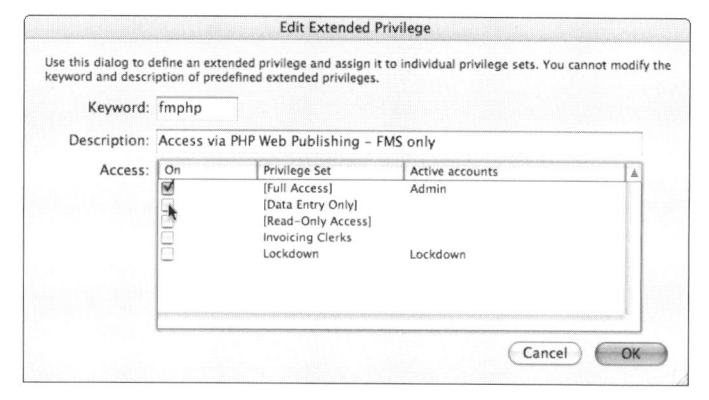

### FileMaker's PHP Site Assistant

FileMaker Pro 9 includes a PHP Site Assistant to walk you through the processes required to produce PHP-based Web pages, replicating a range of common Web design elements and formats such as data collection forms, list searching, and database record editing. You can take the resulting pages and place them directly on your Web server or open them in the Web-design environment of your choice (such as Dreamweaver, RapidWeaver, or GoLive) to edit and further refine the html.

By using the PHP Site Assistant, along with FileMaker's PHP API, you achieve an efficient method of creating direct links between your FileMaker solution and a new Web application forming the basis of your Web site. If you're an experienced PHP developer, you can bypass the Site Assistant and work directly with the FileMaker API for PHP. By doing so, you gain direct access to the broad range of capabilities PHP provides in conjunction with the functionality of your existing FileMaker solution.

**CROSS-REF** Refer to the documentation provided with your installation of FileMaker Server for additional detail and instructions about the use of the PHP Site Assistant and the FileMaker PHP API.

# Finding Third-Party Tools

The catalog of third-party tools you can find a use for in your FileMaker development is well beyond the scope of the advice we can offer here. It is an ongoing adventure for us, as it will be for you. However, several FileMaker-specific third-party tools are so useful or particularly suited to use with FileMaker that they deserve a mention here.

## Developer tools

When you're confronted with a challenging development task involving extensive manual updating of complex FileMaker solution files, you'll be relieved to know that powerful third-party automation tools can reduce the labor and increase the accuracy of your work. FMRobot from New Millennium (www.newmillennium.com) re-creates field definitions, custom functions, value lists, and privilege sets in a new FileMaker Pro 9 file, based on the structure and content of a source file, which can be in any version from FileMaker 6 onward.

Also from New Millennium is Security Administrator, which enables you to manage passwords and privileges centrally across a multi-file FileMaker solution. This tool lets you automate multi-file account management in FileMaker 9.

As an alternative or adjunct technology for generating PHP Web pages and developing and customizing Web applications that integrate closely with FileMaker data, FMStudio and FXForge from FMWebschool (www.fxforge.net) cover a lot of ground and help you to leverage multiple technologies to meet complex Web requirements.

For pure convenience and peace of mind when your solution is running on FileMaker Server, AdminAnywhere from 360Works (www.360works.com) lets you access Server administration features, monitor backups, and manage users remotely from a variety of devices via a browser interface you can run on a handheld device (e.g., iPhone or Palm Treo).

## Analysis and documentation

Beyond the capabilities of the DDR generated by FileMaker Pro Advanced, several third-party tools give you direct access to an abundance of detailed information about your solution files.

**Part V  Raising the Bar**

Foremost among the new breed of FileMaker analysis tools is FMDiff from Huslik Verlag GmbH (www.fmdiff.com), a deceptively simple tool capable of directly examining alternate versions of your FileMaker Pro files and detecting the differences between them. FMDiff also has a range of other useful capabilities, such as detecting and reporting possible structural anomalies and revealing embedded metadata, such as the version of FileMaker used to create your solution files, the versions used to open the file, and the number of times (if any) the file has been recovered.

Operating on different principles, yet no less impressive, is BaseElements from Goya (www.goya.com.au). When you generate a DDR from your solution, BaseElements can import, organize, and analyze the content, enabling you to rapidly detect errors, locate references to specific database objects, and identify unreferenced objects at all levels in your solution. Built in FileMaker, BaseElements massively extends the scope and value of the DDR, giving you the ability to comprehensively analyze and document your solution and to compare different versions of your solution.

As at the time of writing, other well-known and useful tools include MetaDataMagic from New Millennium (www.newmillennium.com) and Inspector from FMNexus (www.fmnexus.com). MetaDataMagic presently supports files in the .fp5 format and is an invaluable tool for use prior to and during the conversion of solutions from the .fp5 format. Inspector supports the .fp7 format and is a versatile and impressive analysis tool, although at the time of writing Inspector does not yet include support for features introduced in FileMaker 9. However, both tools remain invaluable for analysis of files created in previous versions, and we look forward to their support for FileMaker Pro 9.

## Shared information

Undoubtedly the most powerful tool of all is the information shared generously among members of the international developer community. Developers at all levels of expertise from countries on all continents willingly solve problems and exchange knowledge and expertise. Rather than jealously guard trade secrets and nurse competitive advantage, FileMaker developers have a long history of collegiality, where problems are shared and solutions debated in open forums.

We encourage you to build your skills and share them with others that you in turn may benefit from the collective expertise of FileMaker developers across the globe.

**CROSS-REF** A variety of resources, including Web links to community-sponsored forums and online archives of FileMaker-related information, are available in Appendix B.

# Part VI

# Appendixes

Although the human appendix is thought by some to be a useless, unnecessary, and vestigial organ, we consider this book's appendixes to be useful references that just don't quite fit in elsewhere in the book.

The material in this part provides a glossary of terms used in database and FileMaker discussion and the obligatory Index, allowing you to quickly locate where topics are covered. We also point you to a sampling of supplementary references (many Web-hosted) that enhance your FileMaker development experience and expertise. Finally, Appendix C collects all the On the Web references to the materials located at the book's companion Web site (primarily the example files demonstrating the techniques covered throughout the book). Enjoy!

**IN THIS PART**

Appendix A
Glossary

Appendix B
Expanding Your Knowledge with Additional Resources

Appendix C
About the Web Site

Index

# Appendix A

# Glossary

We assume throughout this book that you're familiar with your computer's operation as well as the user interface elements provided by your computer's operating system, be it Mac OS X or Windows (XP or Vista). What we don't assume is a background with Relational Database Management Systems and, in particular, with FileMaker Pro. As a result, we introduce a number of terms and concepts particular to data processing, databases, and FileMaker. This glossary collects those terms and named concepts, accompanied by definition and/or explanation.

**access privileges** delineate the records, fields, layouts, value lists, and scripts an account (or group of accounts) can access and the operations the accounts users are able to perform.

**account** An identifier, with associated password (*Note:* the password may be null, or the account may be configured for external authentication), allowing access to a database. Each account has associated access privileges (including extended privileges). See also *external authentication* and *security*.

**active ~** Used to refer to a window, record, or layout object, active means currently having focus. For example, the active field is the one that is currently holding the cursor; the active window is the frontmost window.

**ActiveX** A Windows scripting and programming protocol allowing external control of specified operations in FileMaker Pro, including running scripts and opening or closing files.

**Admin** The default account name associated with a newly created database (initially, the password is empty). Admin accounts come with Full Access privileges.

**algorithm** Th]e sequence of steps or codified instructions required to complete a task and achieve a determined result. An algorithm, given an initial state, terminates in a predictable (though variable) end-state.

**alphanumeric data** Data consisting of a combination of alphabetic characters and numeric digits.

**API** (Application Programming Interface) A set of software tools, including data structures, procedures, functions, and variables, available for use in the integration of programs or technologies.

**AppleEvents** The messages Macintosh applications send and receive to interact. An application can send AppleEvents to itself. See also *AppleScript*.

# Part VI  Appendixes

**AppleScript**  A purportedly English-like programming language from Apple Computer (Macintosh only) enabling intra- and interapplication communication via AppleEvents. FileMaker includes extensive support for AppleScript. See also *AppleEvents*.

**archive**  A copy, typically stored offline, of one or more files; frequently compressed. Archives are created for various reasons: to save disk space, to remove rarely accessed data and speed performance, and to serve as a backup copy, (a personal safety net) being common examples.

**argument**  A value (or an expression or reference producing a value) supplied to a function that the function uses to calculate its return value. Sometimes called a *parameter*. See also *expression, function,* and *operand*.

**ascending sort**  An ordering whose first values are the smallest or oldest and whose final values are the largest or most recent. Numeric values begin with the smallest value and proceed in numerical order. Text values are arranged according to the specified language's collating sequence, such as alphabetically. Dates and times are arranged chronologically. See also *descending sort*.

**ASCII**  Abbreviation for *American Standard Code for Information Interchange;* a code associating numerical values (0–255) with character or control code. Control codes, letters, punctuation, and numbers are found in codes 0–127. Codes 128–255 (commonly referred to as *Extended* or *High ASCII*) correspond to symbols and foreign language characters and are dependent upon the font in use. See also *Unicode*.

**auto-entered value**  A value, either literal or calculated, that is automatically entered into a particular field when a new record is created. You specify auto-entry options in the Options for Field dialog when defining a data field.

**auto-entry field**  A database field defined to acquire an auto-entered value.

**back up** *v*  To create a duplicate of one or more files — generally as a security measure to avoid or minimize the risk of data loss in a subsequent operation.

**backup** *n*  An exact copy of a file, folder, or disk.

**base table**  The underlying table with which a FileMaker table occurrence (TO) is associated. Because multiple TOs can point to a single table, and because all interaction with a table must occur via one of its TOs, there is an important distinction between table occurrences and the base tables they point to.

**binding**  Creating an association between a FileMaker solution and an instance of a FileMaker runtime application, as a preparation for distributing the solution as a royalty-free runtime. A solution can be bound using the Developer Utilities functionality of FileMaker Pro Advanced.

**body part**  A FileMaker Pro layout part used to present the content of an individual record and used to contain the fields and other elements that will be present for each record, in screens and reports.

**book icon**  A FileMaker Status Area icon employed to "page" through records in Browse mode, Find requests in Find mode, layouts in Layout mode, and report pages in Preview mode.

**Boolean**  A type of variable that allows for only two values — true and false. In FileMaker, the value true has the value 1, and false has the value 0. Fields, variables, or strings containing a zero value, no data, or text data are evaluated as false, while those containing any nonzero numeric value are evaluated as true.

**bound solution**  A database solution that has been configured to operate with a FileMaker runtime application (and may therefore be opened in single-user mode by end users who don't own a copy of FileMaker Pro). See also *binding* and *Developer Utilities*.

# Glossary    A

**break field**  A field used to group sorted records for the purpose of printing them separately, calculating summary data for each group separately, or to control the presence (and location) of a sub-summary part when previewing or printing. Whenever the value of the break field changes, a new group begins.

**browse mode**  The FileMaker viewing mode in which you enter, edit, or review information in records. Browse mode is the default mode.

**browsed records**  FileMaker Pro database records that are currently visible (not hidden). See also *found set*.

**button**  (1) A FileMaker Pro database layout object with an associated script or command. Clicking the button in Browse mode or Find mode invokes the script or command. (2) A user interface element found in many dialogs and windows that you click to select, confirm, or cancel an action.

**cache**  A block of computer memory dedicated to temporary storage of data intended for imminent or repeated access. Caching can greatly improve performance because RAM is much faster to access than a disk.

**calculation field**  A field type used to generate its value programmatically rather than via user input. Calculation field formulæ can reference other fields in the current record or related records, can reference variables and literal constants, and can use FileMaker Pro's built-in functions and custom functions created in FileMaker Pro 9 Advanced.

**calculation variable**  A variable with an unprefixed name (that is, not commencing with a dollar sign) created within a calculation via the use of the `Let( )` function. Calculation variables' scope is constrained to the function you use to define them.

**Cartesian product**  A type of relationship (denoted by an × between the table occurrences in the FileMaker Edit Relationship dialog) where every record in one table is related to every record in the other table. In classic database theory, a Cartesian product results when two joined tables lack a defining join condition.

**checkbox**  (1) A small box in a dialog allowing a Boolean value (selected is true, deselected is false). (2) A field format option in a FileMaker Pro layout that allows selection of one or more values from a value list. Clicking the box changes the state of the option (for the associated value) from selected to deselected (and vice versa). You can select multiple checkboxes, and for each selected checkbox the corresponding value resides in the associated field.

**child**  (1) A script called from within another script using the `Perform Script[ ]` command (also known as a sub-script). (2) A related record (child record), especially where the relationship is one-to-many and the related records are spawned from or enumerate a subset entity of the entity in the current or main table. See also *parent*.

**client**  Any user who opens a shared database after the host has opened it. The client is identified by the workstation he's using.

**clone**  An exact copy of a FileMaker database, but without records and containing no data (including in global fields). A clone may be used as the basis for a new, empty database. Clones are sometimes called *templates*.

**command**  A single defined action performed by a script or button. Because FileMaker uses the same set of commands for buttons and scripts, the term script step is frequently used interchangeably with command (although less than apt when the action is performed directly by a button rather than as part of a script). See also *script step*.

689

**commit** Save changes to one or more records you have modified in the current database solution. Records are committed when you exit them by navigating to another record, by changing modes, by navigating to a different layout, by pressing the Enter key, by clicking in an area of the layout not containing any fields, or by closing the current window.

**condition** Also sometimes referred to as a test or conditional test. An evaluation that determines different values to be returned (calculation) or operations to be performed (script), dependent upon the evaluation's result.

**constant** An invariant value. The function Pi returns the constant value 3.1415926535897932, while supplied values such as "Monday" and 274 are also examples of constants. A text constant in FileMaker Pro 9 may be up to 29,998 characters in length.

**constrain** To narrow (or refine) the found set by adding additional Find criteria. Performing a find using the Constrain Found Set command is the most common constraint method. See also *extend*.

**container field** FileMaker Pro fields used to store graphics, QuickTime movies (and audio), OLE objects (Windows only), sound clips, or other files.

**contextual menu** See *shortcut menu*.

**current field** The database field that presently has focus (contains the cursor). While you can modify fields other than the current field in many ways (such as via script or button actions), text entry or deletion via the keyboard (or from the clipboard) affect only the current field. See also *active ~*.

**current record** The active (or selected) record on a layout. While you can modify other records via relationships, scripts, or buttons, the current record provides the context for all user and script actions.

**Custom function** A calculation function created and installed into a FileMaker database file using FileMaker Pro Advanced. (Once created, custom functions can be used and accessed in FileMaker Pro.)

**Custom menu** A menu with content or behavior not part of the default FileMaker Pro menu sets. In FileMaker Pro Advanced, you can create and install or apply custom menus, menu items, and menu sets.

**data entry** (1) The process of typing values into data fields on a database layout. (2) The [Data Entry Only] privilege set — one of the three default privilege sets in a new FileMaker database file. An account assigned to the [Data Entry Only] privilege set can do the following: create, view, edit, and delete records; execute scripts; print; export; and access menu commands. However, it doesn't have design access (for example, to modify scripts, layouts, or value lists).

**Data Source** A named reference providing access to an external database (either a FileMaker database or a supported ODBC database).

**Data Source Name (DSN)** The collection of data an ODBC driver needs in order to connect to a specific remote database in a supported (ODBC compliant) format. The stored data include the location of the database, its name, the login details, and other defaults for the connection.

**Data Viewer** A FileMaker Pro Advanced window that displays the results of values, variables, and calculations used in running scripts or entered directly into the Data Viewer.

**database** An organized collection of information comprising one or more tables and stored in one or more files. In FileMaker, a database may include associated scripts, layouts, privilege sets, menus, and so on.

# Glossary

**Database Design Report (DDR)** A detailed report regarding the specifications, structure, code, and configuration of a FileMaker Pro database solution. Database Design reports are created using FileMaker Pro Advanced.

**database program (or database management program or DBMS)** A computer application for entering, editing, and otherwise managing data records.

**DDE** Abbreviation for Windows' *Dynamic Data Exchange*; instructions and data sent from one program to another, which direct the target to perform one or more specific commands. FileMaker Pro can send DDE commands (via the DDE Execute script step) on a Windows system but doesn't respond to them.

**default** An initial setting for a variable value. A default setting determines a return value or how an option or preference behaves if you never change the setting, such as an initial field value when a new record is created. Specifying a default value saves typing time and ensures that information is entered consistently.

**dependency** A value that references another value and therefore automatically changes when the referenced value changes. See also *trigger field*.

**descending sort** An ordering whose first values are the largest or most recent and whose final values are the smallest or oldest. Numeric values begin with the largest value and proceed in reverse numeric order. Text values are arranged according to the selected language's collating sequence (for example, reverse-alphabetical) with high ASCII values appearing before low ASCII values. Dates and times are arranged in reverse chronologic order. See also *ascending sort*.

**Developer Utilities** A collection of features in FileMaker Pro Advanced enabling you to generate license-free runtimes, set files to operate in Kiosk mode, permanently remove [Full Access] accounts, or automate the renaming of sets of files (updating internal links and references).

**dialog** A window-type employed by system software and applications to present information and instructions, as well as elicit additional information.

**drop-down list** One of the essential building blocks of FileMaker interfaces, available as a standard layout object you can assign to fields in a FileMaker solution. Drop-down menus allow you to type in a text box or click an adjoining button to choose from a list of options. See also *pop-up menu*.

**equi-join** The default relationship type, represented by an = sign, where records in one table are matched based upon an exact match between values in the specified join fields.

**export** To create a file of data from one file or program that other files or programs can read or use. See also *import*.

**expression** A combination of variables, constants, operators, and functions that can be evaluated to a single result. A calculation formula may be made up of one or more expressions. See also *argument*, *constant*, *function*, and *variable*.

**extend** (1) Adding additional Find criteria to increase the found set's size. (Expanding the found set is equivalent to performing an OR search in some other programs.) See also *constrain*. (2) A calculation function used to make a value from a non-repeating field (or a field with fewer repetitions) available to successive repetitions of other fields.

**extended privileges** A set of values defining the methods by which a database can be accessed. Examples are Network, Web, and Mobile.

**external** (1) Data located outside the current solution file. (2) A function class/group used to access the features of installed plug-ins. External functions such as FMSAUC_FindPlugIn( ) do not appear in the External Functions list (in the Specify Calculation dialog) unless the plug-in with which they're associated is installed and enabled.

**external authentication** A security configuration where login accounts are verified at the domain level (rather than against passwords stored in each database file of a solution). See also *security*.

**external script** A script residing in another FileMaker Pro database file, executed via the Perform Script[ ] command. The file containing the script automatically opens (if it's not already open) when the script executes.

**External SQL Data Source (ESS)** A supported ODBC database (designated versions of Oracle, Microsoft SQL Server, and MySQL) configured for live read/write access from your FileMaker solution. Access to an ESS requires an appropriately configured DSN on the host computer. You can add tables from an ESS to the Relationships Graph of a FileMaker solution and integrated into the solution's data design. See also *Shadow table* and *supplemental field*.

**field** An atomic constituent of a table's record structure. Each field in a record stores a single attribute or element of information, such as a name or date of birth. See also *field type* and *record*.

**field type** Specifies the class of information a particular field is designed to store and display. Some common field types are Text, Number, Date, and Time. The field type you select in the Manage Database dialog's Fields tab determines the kinds of operations FileMaker Pro can perform with the data. FileMaker warns you if, for example, you enter something other than a time in a Time field.

**file format** A program (or standards organization) specification for data storage and interpretation within a file. FileMaker supports a range of data interchange and data encapsulation formats, enabling it to interact with other systems and applications.

**File Maintenance** A feature exclusive to FileMaker Pro Advanced that enables you to compact and/or optimize the current database file. *Note:* The Save a Copy As (Compacted Copy) command is safer and more effective.

**FileMaker Network** The built-in network communication method built into FileMaker Pro (and FileMaker Server) that enables you to share FileMaker Pro files with other FileMaker Pro users over a network.

**filter** (1) To refine a data subset. One such example is to extract the digits in a phone number, removing all non-numeric formatting characters. Another is to modify the match value for a relationship to define the scope of related records. (2) The name of a calculation function used to perform filtering on text strings.

**find criteria** The comparison criteria used when performing Find operations.

**Find mode** The FileMaker Pro mode for entering criteria with which to locate a record or group of records. FileMaker Pro, like most other database systems, lets you specify multiple criteria when performing a Find. See also *find request*.

**find request** A group of search criteria entered on one or more FileMaker Pro layouts in Find mode. A Find request can consist of a single search criterion (entered into one field) or multiple criteria (an AND search, which involves several fields simultaneously). Conducting an OR search requires creating multiple Find requests. See also *Find mode*.

# Glossary

**flat-file database** A database comprising a single data table with no relationships. The table must contain every field necessary for the operation of the solution (*Note:* Flat file databases are non-optimal). See also *relational database program*.

**footer part** The FileMaker Pro layout part appearing at the bottom of every record or report page. Title footers appear on only the first page of a report. See also *Header part*.

**foreign key** A unique identifier from another (related) table, stored in the current table for the purposes of establishing a match between the current record and a corresponding record in the related table. See also *primary key*.

**form view** A layout display format that shows one record at a time in the current database window. You can invoke Form view (when available for the selected layout) by choosing View ➪ View as Form. See also *List view* and *table view*.

**formula** A set of instructions (comprised of calculation functions, field and variable references, and literal values) used by FileMaker Pro to determine a value used in a field, as the criteria for matching database records or to control the behavior of a variety of commands.

**found set** A found set is used to isolate a subset of the records in the current table to view, summarize, print, export, or edit them. A found set is created by performing a Find operation, such as a Find request, or an Omit operation, such as the Omit, Omit Multiple, or Find Omitted commands. *Note:* When a found set is in place, one or more records are temporarily omitted, but you can reinstate them by choosing Records ➪ Show All Records. See also *browsed records* and *Find mode*.

**[Full Access]** A predefined FileMaker Pro privilege set providing complete access to a FileMaker Pro database. See also *Admin* and *privilege set*.

**function** A named operation taking zero or more input values (also termed arguments or parameters) that yields a unique result for the supplied parameter set. You can combine one or more functions into expressions to produce a formula. See also *argument*, *expression*, and *formula*.

**function separator** The punctuation character (a semicolon) used to delineate parameters in a calculation function. For backward compatibility, if you enter a comma, FileMaker Pro automatically substitutes a semicolon when you exit the Specify Calculation dialog.

**global field** A field used to hold the same value for every record in the table. Any value that must be constant throughout the table is a candidate for Global storage. You specify Global storage for a field in the Options for Field dialog's Storage tab). Global fields have the advantages of being accessible from unrelated tables and being specific to each client in a hosted solution.

**global variable** A memory variable that a calculation or script anywhere in a file can reference for the duration of the current file session. Global variables are those assigned names commencing with $$. The value of a global variable persists until it is cleared or until the file is closed.

**Grand summary part** A layout part you can use to display summary information (total, average, and so on) pertaining to all records in the current found set. Grand summary parts can appear above or below the body part of the layout (or both).

**group** A set of layout objects to which you have applied the Group command so that you can treat them as a single object rather than as a collection of objects. Use the Ungroup command to change the group back into individual objects. Groups can nest (contain other groups).

**guest** A predefined user account, disabled by default, that can open a (shared or local) database. By default, the guest account is assigned the [Read-Only Access] privilege set. See also *client, host,* and *privilege set.*

**handle** (1) A square black dot appearing at each corner of selected Layout mode objects. You can drag a handle to resize the object. (2) A double-arrow icon you can use to drag list entries to new positions in the list (for example, Scripts in the ScriptMaker window, Fields in the Import and Export dialogs, and so on).

**Header part** The optional FileMaker Pro layout part appearing at the top of every record or report page. New blank layouts have a header by default. Title Header parts appear on only a report's cover page. See also *footer part.*

**header record** A special first record frequently included in exported tab or comma-delimited text files. The header specifies the name and order of the fields present in the file. See also *export.*

**host** (1) The user who first opens a FileMaker Pro database and turns on FileMaker Network Sharing, letting other networked FileMaker Pro users share that database. In subsequent sessions, other users may become the host. (2) A workstation or server designated to make a database available for client access (using either FileMaker Pro or FileMaker Server). See also *guest.*

**HTML** Abbreviation for *HyperText Markup Language,* the simple language used to create pages for the World Wide Web, enabling the display of formatted text and images in Web browsers (and a basis of various other Web and browser-based technologies). See also *XML.*

**import** To bring data in the format of another program or file into the current program or file. By importing data, you reduce or eliminate the need to retype data. See also *export.*

**index** An internal list of data, including the contents of specified Text, Number, Date, Time, Timestamp, and Calculation fields. Indexing lets FileMaker Pro execute Find requests efficiently. Indexing is optional and may be specified individually for desired fields on the Storage tab panel of the respective Options for Field dialog. See also *sort.*

**Instant Web Publishing** A FileMaker Pro database usage methodology, IWP makes a solution available on the Internet or a company intranet for viewing and interaction via a Web browser. Some script steps and operations are not supported when a solution is hosted via IWP.

**invalid data** Information that deviates from a field's acceptable input formats or that fails a field's validation criteria. This term also refers to data of the wrong type, such as character data in a Number field.

**JDBC** Abbreviation for *Java Database Connectivity,* a Java API that uses SQL statements to exchange data with hosted databases (using either FileMaker Pro or FileMaker Server Advanced as the data source). See also *ODBC.*

**join** See *relationship.*

**Key** (1) A field used for join matching as part of a relationship between two table occurrences. (2) A field defined to hold a value unique to a particular record in a table (also known as a *primary key*).

**Kiosk** A format for running a FileMaker solution without toolbars or menus and with the solution layout being the only thing visible to the user. (Other parts of the screen are blacked out.) In a kiosk, you must provide comprehensive on-screen navigation because users will not have access to any menu commands or keyboard shortcuts. Kiosk-based solutions are ideal for touch-screen implementations, and you can configure them for distribution as runtime solutions.

**layout** An arrangement of fields, graphics, portals, buttons, tab objects, Web Viewer objects, and static text used to produce a screen or report in FileMaker Pro. You can design an unlimited number of layouts, each with a different purpose, for each database. For example, you can use some layouts for data entry and others for generating printed or onscreen reports.

**layout mode**  The operational mode you use to create and modify the appearance and arrangement of screens, reports, and documents for a solution file.

**layout parts**  A database layout's constituent pieces or sections. Depending on the purpose of the layout, it may contain a body, header, footer, and summary, for example.

**List view**  A continuous scrolling list of records as opposed to the one record per screen shown in Form view. You can invoke List view (when available for the selected layout) by choosing View ⇨ View as List. See also *form view* and *table view*.

**literal value**  A text string (enclosed within quotation marks) or constant operand supplied as part of a calculation expression.

**local variable**  A memory variable with scope limited to the script that is active (at the top of the script stack) when the variable is defined. Local variables are those assigned names commencing with $. You can access the value of a local variable anywhere in the file while the current instance of the current script is in progress, expiring with the conclusion of the script.

**lock**  A Layout mode option where you can prevent selected fields, labels, graphics, and other layout objects from being moved, deleted, or their formatting or properties modified.

**lookup**  A field definition option instructing FileMaker Pro to fill a field from the specified field in the first record of another specified table that matches the data entered in the current table's key field.

**lookup table**  A reference table in which data is looked up in response to data being entered or edited in the current table's trigger field. See also *lookup*.

**mail merge**  Combining address and other personal or business information (usually from a database) with a form letter to generate a series of personalized letters.

**many-to-many relationship**  A correspondence between data in two database tables where more than one record in one table is related to more than one record in the other (related) table.

**match fields**  (1) The fields that are used to establish a data relationship. (2) The Fields aligned or associated when performing a selective data import into a FileMaker solution table.

**menu**  A list of choices from which you can choose an action, value, or setting. A menu opens when you click its title in the menu bar or, in the case of pop-up menus, on a layout or in a dialog.

**menu set**  A comprehensive set of menus and associated commands that installs as the FleMaker application menu on Mac OS or in Windows. You can use FileMaker Pro Advanced to create and install custom menu sets. See also *Custom menu*.

**Merge field**  A layout text object that enables you to insert database information directly into a text string on a FileMaker layout to produce a merged document, such as for a form letter. A merge field contracts or expands to accommodate the amount of data in the referenced field in the current record.

**mode**  FileMaker Pro's four operational modes are *Browse, Find, Layout,* and *Preview.* Each mode circumscribes the operations that can be performed.

**modifier key**  Keyboard keys comprising Shift, Caps Lock, Control, Option (Mac OS), Alt (Windows) and ⌘ (Mac OS), that, while pressed, make a value to FileMaker Pro. You can retrieve the value of the current combination of modifier keys by using the `Get(ActiveModifierKeys)` function to expressions controlling (modifying) the behavior of calculations and scripts throughout your solutions.

**Multi-key field** A match field that contains more than one value, each on a separate line. A multi-key field in one table matches to multiple corresponding values on different records in the match field of the related table.

**object** A FileMaker Pro layout contains discrete entities (buttons, graphical lines and shapes, fields, portals, imported graphics, text blocks, tab controls, and Web viewers) as objects that you can select and, when selected, modify, delete, move, or name.

**ODBC** Acronym for *Open Database Connectivity,* a standardized software API for interacting with database management systems. FileMaker Pro 9, FileMaker Pro 9 Advanced, and FileMaker Server 9 Advanced can act as an ODBC host program client program and request data from other sources, such as Oracle or Sybase databases for which you have installed ODBC drivers. FileMaker can also respond to ODBC queries from other applications. See also *External SQL Data Source (ESS)* and *JDBC.*

**OLE** Acronym for Microsoft's *Object Linking and Embedding* technology, which enables objects to be inserted into OLE-compliant programs, including FileMaker Pro. Using Windows, you can insert and edit OLE objects. When using a Macintosh, however, OLE objects can only be viewed, cut, copied, or pasted; they can't be inserted or edited in any manner.

**omit** Removal of a record (or group of records) from a found set. Selecting the Omit checkbox in the Status Area when specifying a Find request tells FileMaker Pro to find the records that do *not* match the search criteria. You can also manually omit records from the found set by choosing the Records ⇨ Omit Record or Records ⇨ Omit Multiple commands.

**one-to-many relationship** A correspondence between data in two database tables where one record in the first table is related to more than one record in the other (related) table.

**operand** A component of a calculation expression providing input and acted upon by adjacent operators. For example, in the calculation expression `Total > Threshold`, Total and Threshold are operands. See also *argument*, *expression, function,* and *operator.*

**operator** Symbols indicating how two or more calculation expressions are to be combined, including (1) Syntax and text operators, such as comment markers, reserved name operators, quote marks, and parentheses. (2) Standard arithmetic operators (+, –, /, *, and ^). (3) Logical operators used to set up conditions to be met to determine a value as true or false (and, or, xor, and not). (4) Find operators (<, =, @ *, and so on) that help you limit the records defined in a find request. (5) Relationship operators that define the match criteria between one or more pairs of fields in two tables, including =, ≠, >, <, ≤, ≥ and ×.

**operator precedence** See *order of operations.*

**options** See *preferences.*

**order of operations** Defines the sequence in which calculation expressions are evaluated. FileMaker has ten levels of precedence among calculation operators. When operators are of equal precedence, they're evaluated from left to right. Including parentheses in an expression can alter the order of operations. (Expressions in the innermost set of parentheses are evaluated first.) See also *expression* and *operator.*

**parent** (1) A script that calls another script using the `Perform Script[ ]` command (referred to as the parent script). (2) A related record (parent record), especially where the relationship is many-to-one and the current record is spawned from or part of a subset entity of the entity in the related table. See also *child.*

**password** A character sequence (associated with an account name) that a user must enter, to authenticate when opening a secured FileMaker Pro database. See also *external authentication* and *security.*

# Glossary

**platform**  A particular computer/operating system combination. Mac OS X (Tiger 10.4 and Leopard 10.5) on Macintosh and in Windows (XP and Vista) are the operating systems on which FileMaker Pro 9 will run.

**plug-in**  A software component that provides FileMaker Pro with additional or extended capabilities. For example, Auto-Update is a FileMaker Pro plug-in provided with the product by FileMaker, Inc., and it facilitates version control of other (third-party) plug-ins via a FileMaker Server installation. Plug-ins are typically specific to the application for which they were created: For example, FileMaker Pro will not recognize Photoshop plug-ins and vice versa.

**pop-up menu**  A user interface element typically appearing as a button that displays its current value, permitting you to click it to expose and select from a list of alternative values. You can format layout objects as pop-up menus when space is a consideration. Pop-up menus allow only one choice from a list.

**portal**  A rectangular layout area created with the Portal tool and used to display one or more records from a related table.

**precedence**  See *order of operations*.

**preferences**  Application- or document-specific options governing how various features of a program behave. Preferences are sometimes referred to as *options*.

**Preview mode**  A FileMaker Pro operational mode that enables the user to see (on-screen) what a printed report or other document will look like prior to committing it to paper. Sub-summary parts appear only in Preview mode.

**primary file**  The solution file in a runtime application created by FileMaker Pro Advanced that opens by default when the runtime is launched and contains references to (and navigation to) auxiliary files of the solution.

**primary key**  A field containing a unique identifying value for a table, suitable for use (or used) as the match key for relationships to other tables.

**privilege set**  A collection of permissions defined to determine the extent of user access to a FileMaker database file, for one or several user accounts. Privilege sets are file-specific, and you can create as many as are required to accommodate the needs of users of the file. By default, all FileMaker files contain three pre-defined privilege sets: [Full Access], [Data Entry Only], and [Read-Only Access].

**QuickTime**  An Apple-created cross-platform API that supports the creation, editing, and presentation of time-based data (audio, video, graphics, and VR) and sound data on any Mac OS X or Windows XP or Vista system. You can place QuickTime video and audio streams in Container fields.

**radio button**  On layouts and in dialogs, radio buttons present a series of mutually exclusive options or settings. You can format layout fields as radio buttons in FileMaker Pro in order to present a set of distinct choices. (Pop-up menus provide a similar capability, but you have to open the menu to see what the choices are.) *Note:* Making a new selection in a radio button field normally overrides any preceding selection. However, users can make multiple selections in a radio-button field in FileMaker by holding the Shift key while making second and subsequent selections.

**range validation**  A form of field validation that verifies that input data values fall within a prescribed range.

**record**  A database table's basic unit, which contains a set of fields. All tables are composed of records, each storing information for an instance of an entity or type of object. See also *field*.

**relational database program**  A program in which key fields can be used to link information contained in multiple tables, enabling you to generate reports and display information based on data from more than one table. See also *flat-file database*.

**697**

**relationship** The definition of a link between separate tables in a solution, allowing access to data from corresponding records. The most common relationship is based upon matching equal values in key fields of the two tables (an *equi-join*). However, FileMaker also allows relationships based upon other criteria, including less-than, not-equal-to, and greater-than.

**Relationships Graph** The diagrammatic representation of data structure appearing in the Relationships tab of the Manage Database dialog. The Relationships Graph optionally includes occurrences of tables in the current file and from any external database tables, showing joins between them. You can join tables by dragging a line between fields in different table occurrences in the Relationships Graph. See also *table occurrence*.

**Relookup** A command in FileMaker's Records menu (Browse mode) that causes all lookups (for every record in the found set) depending on relationships based on the currently active field (and in the current table) to be refreshed. Invoking this command ensures that all lookup fields dependent on the active field contain current data.

**repeating field** A field option that lets a single field store and display multiple values, thus providing limited support for data arrays.

**report** A display or printout of selected information from a database, often presented in sorted order and including summary data.

**required field (not empty)** A field validation option specifying that the field must hold a valid value before the record can be committed. The record's required fields are checked when you press Enter; attempt to switch to a different record, layout, or mode; close the database; or try to quit FileMaker Pro while the database is still open.

**resources** The layouts, value lists, scripts, custom menus, and fields of a FileMaker Pro database. The database designer or administrator can prevent users from modifying or even seeing particular resources through the use of access privileges.

**runtime solution** A database solution configured using FileMaker Pro Advanced so that users will not require FileMaker Pro or FileMaker Pro Advanced to use it. The Developer Utilities in FileMaker Pro Advanced are used to bind the solution's primary file and any auxiliary files to produce a stand-alone runtime solution. *Note:* FileMaker runtimes are single-user solutions. However, the database files forming part of a runtime solution may be hosted using FileMaker Server.

**schema** The organization or structure of the data elements, objects, and attributes within a database. The schema comprises tables, table occurrences, fields, and relationships throughout a database solution.

**script** A sequence of automated actions that can perform FileMaker Pro tasks (frequently used for complex or repetitive operations). A script consists of one or more script steps associated with a specific database that FileMaker executes either automatically (for example, on file open or file close) or upon user invocation.

**Script Debugger** A developer feature in FileMaker Pro Advanced that enables you to step through scripts one line at a time watching their effects and observing the error result code for each step.

**script step** An individual ScriptMaker command that you include in a script. See also *command*.

**ScriptMaker** The FileMaker Pro feature used to design, edit, and manage scripts.

**security** Controls used to restrict access to database files. FileMaker provides a granular role-based security system that permits the use of external authentication. The FileMaker security system is based on the allocation of individual password-protected user accounts to privilege sets defined within each file.

# Glossary

**self-join** A relationship in which a data table is related to itself. In FileMaker, because circular references aren't permitted in the Relationships Graph, you must create two TOs of the same table and specify a join between them to create self-join functionality. See also *relationship*.

**separator** A line included within a menu or list (for example, the scripts or layout menus) to delineate groups of menu items.

**serial number field** A field for which Auto-Entry options are set to the Serial Number option. Such fields acquire an automatically incrementing value. (Incrementation operates on the trailing numeric portion of text values.)

**Shadow table** A table sourced from an External SQL Data Source and that appears within a FileMaker File for the purpose of referencing it within the Relationships Graph, within calculations, or for adding supplemental fields (calculation and summary fields) drawing on the SQL data. See also *External SQL Data Source (ESS)* and *supplemental field*.

**shortcut menu** On a Macintosh or Windows PC, you can Control+click/right-click database fields and layout elements to display a menu of commands relevant to the item clicked. These context-sensitive menus are also available in many other programs, as well as on the Desktop and within open document folders. Historically, Mac users may see them referred to as *contextual menus*.

**slider** A graphical navigation control appearing immediately below the flip-book icon in the FileMaker Status Area in each database window. The slider shows the current location in the file and can be dragged to the left or right to navigate to a different location. In Browse mode, the slider enables you to navigate among records in the current table. In Layout mode, the slider enables you to navigate among layouts. In Find mode, the slider takes you between find requests, and in Preview mode, you can use the slider to move between pages of the current previewed document.

**sliding objects** Layout objects configured to move upwards and/or to the left to close gaps remaining beside or below the entries in adjacent fields. Sliding is invoked only when a layout is previewed or printed. To configure an object to slide, enter Layout mode, select the object, and choose Format ➪ Sliding/Printing.

**solution** One or more database files configured to interact together to provide self-contained functionality, meeting a set of defined objectives or business requirements.

**sort** To reorder a table's records into a sequence other than data entry order. FileMaker Pro, like most database programs, can sort on multiple fields, allowing for "tie-breaking" when the primary sort field contains multiple equal values. See also *index*.

**sort order** The setting that defines in what order a field's values are displayed or returned. You can sort a FileMaker Pro database field in one of three sort orders: ascending, descending, or according to the entries in a value list.

**Status Area** The area at the far left of a FileMaker Pro window. The Status Area displays tools and controls appropriate to the current FileMaker mode.

**step** A single command in a FileMaker Pro script. See also *script step*.

**sub-script** A FileMaker Pro script that is invoked by another script. See also *child*.

**Sub-summary part** A layout part you can use to view and display information from one or more records when the data is sorted and previewed or printed. A summary part displays information for each group of records sorted on the break field. You can add one or more sub-summary parts above (leading) or below (trailing) the layout's body part.

## Part VI  Appendixes

**summary field**  A FileMaker Pro field type used to summarize the information in a specified field across all records in the found set. You can configure summary fields to provide a total, running total, count, minimum, maximum, standard deviation, or fraction of total for records in the found set or for grouped records in a sub-summary.

**supplemental field**  A calculation field or summary field that you can append to tables sourced via ESS from a SQL database and integrated into your FileMaker solution schema. Such calculations are automatically defined as unstored and do not impact the structure of the SQL table. (They're visible only within FileMaker.) See also *External SQL Data Source (ESS)* and *Shadow table*.

**tab control**  A layout element used to group fields and other layout objects on separate panels. Tabs conserve screen space and avoid having to maintain separate layouts when the objects on the different tab panels do not have to be simultaneously available. You also frequently encounter tabbed dialogs in FileMaker Pro and other programs, particularly for setting preferences.

**tab order**  The sequence in which keyboard navigation moves you from object to object in a layout when in Browse or Find modes. In Layout mode, you can define a custom tab order to include fields, buttons, tab controls, and Web viewers in the navigation sequence.

**tab panel**  A component of a tab control, a tab panel is the rectangular area displayed when one of a tab control's tabs is selected. Tab panels can contain any combination of layout objects, including tab controls. (Tab controls can be nested.)

**table**  A collection of data that consists of fields and records applicable to a specific subject or entity (such as contact information or current inventory). A database consists of one or more tables although FileMaker Pro 9 allows you to create a database file with no tables—just layouts that are based on tables in other files.

**table occurrence (TO)**  An instance of a table in the Relationships Graph. All interactions with a table take place through TOs, which provide context for the interaction. The use of TOs eliminates circular references, yet provides support for multiple joins (and relationship paths) between tables.

**table view**  A spreadsheet-like data display. Each row corresponds to a record and each column to a field. You can invoke Table view (when available for the selected layout) by choosing View ⇨ View as Table. See also *form view* and *List view*.

**target file**  The file into which data is loaded during an import procedure

**TCP/IP**  Abbreviation for *Transmission Control Protocol/Internet Protocol*; a networking protocol used to connect to the Internet and manage intranets. TCP/IP is the only networking protocol supported by FileMaker Pro 9.

**text box (or text-edit box)**  A rectangular area on a layout or in a dialog used to enter or edit information in a designated field in the current or a related table. A common dialog example is the space provided for a filename in Save dialogs.

**text file (also called text-only file)**  A file saved without formatting (a single font and no style or size options). Tab-delimited and comma-separated-value files are examples of text files.

**timestamp**  A data format that represents both date and time. Timestamp values are stored in a form that represents the number of seconds elapsed since midnight on the morning of 1st January 0001. In

# Glossary

data, timestamps are represented by a date followed by a time, both represented according to the prevailing operating system defaults (or custom file or layout formats where specified).

**tooltip** A disclosure rectangle that appears below the mouse pointer when it hovers over an object, displaying relevant data or help text. Using FileMaker Pro Advanced, you can define tooltips for layout objects that will be displayed in FileMaker Pro when the mouse is held over the objects in Browse and Find modes.

**trigger field** (1) A field in the current table that initiates a lookup when data is entered or its contents are modified. (2) A field referenced by a calculation such that when the field is modified, the calculation is reevaluated. See also *dependency*.

**Unicode** An international character-encoding standard that provides a unique value for every character in known human languages, regardless of platform or application. FileMaker uses Unicode as the basis of its text handling.

**unique validation** A field validation option that specifies that the field can't contain the same value in two records. Unique validation is activated on record commit. See also *validation*.

**unstored calculation** A calculation field that is evaluated only when the field is referenced, either by another calculation, a script, or for display on a layout or inclusion in printed output. Unstored calculations save storage space, but consume additional processor resources because they're reevaluated frequently. Overdependence on unstored calculations can therefore impact solution performance.

**URL** Abbreviation for *Uniform Resource Locator;* an Internet standard expression specifying a protocol and address for communicating with another computer and accessing files or applications on the remote computer.

**validation** The process of verifying a particular field's contents for allowable and unacceptable data per the field definition. Typical validation criteria include range checking and that a field be non-empty, for example.

**value list** A list of choices or values. FileMaker value lists may be entered manually or based on the contents of a field (all values or related values only). Using value lists can help speed data entry and ensure the consistency of information presentation. You can use value lists as the basis of pop-up lists, pop-up menus, radio buttons, or checkboxes, as well as for data-entry validation.

**variable** A value, usually indicated by a letter or name, in an expression that holds a declared value for the duration of its scope.. Prepending a single dollar sign ($) to a variable's name constrains the variable's scope to the duration of the currently executing script. Prepending a double dollar sign ($$) grants the variable global scope (throughout the file where it is defined), allowing the variable to be referenced by scripts and calculations for the duration of the current file session.

**view** The presentation format for onscreen display of data in a FileMaker layout. You can view each layout as a form, list, or table. You can change the view format of the current layout by choosing View ➪ View As Form, View ➪ View As List, or View ➪ View As Table.

**Web page** A page on the World Wide Web accessed via HTTP (the HyperText Transport Protocol). You can load Web pages into a Web viewer for display on a FileMaker layout or invoke them in the current computer's default Web browser application via the Open URL [ ] command.

**Web viewer object** A FileMaker Pro layout object capable of rendering Web pages, HTML or other Web-compatible content 47 (however sourced) within a FileMaker layout.

## Part VI  Appendixes

**XML** Abbreviation for *eXtensible Markup Language,* a standard for document delivery via the Internet and for document interchange. (For example, Microsoft Office's new document formats are all XML-based.) You can find additional information about the XML standard at *XML.com: XML From the Inside Out* (www.xml.com) and at the *W3C Architecture Domain* XML page (www.w3.org/xml).

**XSLT** Abbreviation for *eXtensible Stylesheet Language Transformation,* a technology employed to repurpose (transform) data in XML format for use in applications where a different format (data structure) is required. For example, XSLTs are used to import XML data sets into FileMaker Pro.

**zoom** A FileMaker command and user operation to change the magnification level of a layout in the active database window, enlarging or reducing your view of all elements on the displayed layout. You can change magnification levels manually via the zoom buttons at the lower left of each FileMaker window or via the Set Zoom Level [ ] script or button command.

# Appendix B

# Expanding Your Knowledge with Additional Resources

This book and the documentation accompanying your FileMaker Pro 9 software provide a solid foundation for using FileMaker Pro 9 and leveraging its power. However, a worldwide community of FileMaker users and developers exist, and many of them share useful information, tips, and examples of both general and specific nature.

In this appendix, we describe and enumerate many of these other useful FileMaker information sources. These sources include consulting and development services, FileMaker technical support, online and published periodicals, and references to online discussion groups and mailing lists. You can find links to this appendix's references on the book's companion Web site for those sources with an Internet presence (see Appendix C).

### IN THIS APPENDIX

**Finding accurate and current information**

**Locating professional support and services**

**Sourcing examples and technique demos**

**Discussing FileMaker online**

**Using FileMaker printed and periodical resources**

## From the Horse's Mouth

The FileMaker, Inc., Web site (www.filemaker.com) is your contact point for online product support. But, more than just providing a technical and customer support contact point, the site is a repository of information, including links to tutorials, sample files, a directory of consultants, and compendium of various FileMaker add-ons, plug-ins, and developer tools (some freeware, some shareware, and some commercial).

In addition to these general categories, the FileMaker Web site includes viewable *Webinars* (recorded Web seminars); access to a broad online Knowledge Base of product issues; solutions and answers to specific questions; PDF copies of the various product manuals; and links to purchasing books (including this one) and magazines devoted to FileMaker. You can find a treasure trove of these and a wealth of other downloadable resources at www.filemaker.com/support/downloads/index.html.

**Part VI**    Appendixes

> **NOTE**    While FileMaker's Web site provides online support access, talking to a person is sometimes beneficial. The Product Technical Support number of (800) 325-2747 ((408) 727-8227 if outside North America) fills that bill. Be aware that, unless you purchase an extended support option (FileMaker calls it *Priority Support*), this phone support is limited to one call related to installing the software and one call related to usage problems. Priority Support offers single-case, five-case, and annual options.

Beyond the resources available from the FileMaker, Inc., Web site, resources and mailing lists are available via the membership-based programs (TechNet and the FileMaker Business Alliance) offered to developers and businesses working with FileMaker. Through these resources, users and developers around the globe stay abreast of news, changes, updates, and new releases of the software and exchange notes with each other and the Developer Relations contacts at FileMaker, Inc. Other resources, such as white papers and technical briefs, are available exclusively to members of FileMaker developer organizations.

> **NOTE**    Membership in TechNet and the FileMaker Business Alliance includes significant benefits in addition to providing access to a communication network dedicated to improving the state of the FileMaker development art. Ancillary software, access to prerelease versions, and even copies of FileMaker applications are included, based upon the membership chosen. See the FileMaker Web site for further details.

As an annual event, the FileMaker Developers Conference provides four days of intense information, resources, and exchange between attendees from many parts of the globe. At the time of publication, the next such event is scheduled to take place in Phoenix in July 2008 and will attract speakers and delegates from all major continents. In addition, regional conferences and special-purpose events (colloquia, briefings, meetings, and the like) are conducted in other cities with either sponsorship or involvement of FileMaker, Inc.

For the first time, a FileMaker Masters colloquium is scheduled. The 2008 event will occur over two days in Newport Beach, California, and will focus on providing high-level expertise and advice across a range of topics of interest to FileMaker developers. For additional information about the colloquium, visit www.filemakermasters.com.

# Professional Consulting and Development Services

A global network of professional FileMaker developers exists, many of whom provide and support complex applications for clients in a vast range of industries and in many countries of the world. FileMaker provides a certification program through a network of external test centers worldwide as a step toward the assurance of the knowledge and skill of professionals working in the field. Because FileMaker has been in use since 1985, professionals with extensive experience are available.

For those located in Canada and the United States, FileMaker, Inc., publishes a *FileMaker Resource Guide* listing individuals and companies providing FileMaker-based solutions and consultancy

# Expanding Your Knowledge with Additional Resources   B

services. The current edition is available online from the FileMaker Web site at `www.filemaker.com/downloads/pdf/resource_guide.pdf`.

Regrettably, the community is heavily shortchanged by the Resource Guide's exclusive focus on businesses located in the North American continent, as it excludes much of the worldwide network of developers. For example, the most recent edition of the guide makes no reference to a number of the key resources mentioned in this book, including Troi Automatisering in Holland, Digital Fusion in New Zealand, Goya in Australia, Huslik Verlag GmbH in Germany, and many other world-class companies and FileMaker resource providers. With the ready availability of the Internet, you need not be limited to one region or country when looking for the best support or solutions.

To access information about developers the world over, visit the FileMaker, Inc., regional Web sites listing consultants and developers in many other countries. These sites are available separately and managed by their respective regional offices of FileMaker, Inc. For example, FileMaker in France is represented at `/www.filemaker.fr`, FileMaker in the Asia Pacific region is represented at `www.filemaker.com.au`, in the United Kingdom FileMaker's Web site is `www.filemaker.co.uk` in Japan FileMaker's Web address is `www.filemaker.co.jp` and so on. You can find a full list of international Web locations at `www.filemaker.com/company/intl/index.html`.

You can find alternative sources of information about professionals working with FileMaker on public resource Web sites such as FMPug.com and FMPro.org and FileMaker forums or via the ubiquitous Internet search engines. For example, a search for "FileMaker Pro developers" on Google.com presently produces more than 1.2 million hits.

**NOTE** Due to the dynamic nature of the Internet and technology companies, we don't include a comprehensive list of URLs because they frequently become out of date. Instead, we encourage you to use the directories and resources outlined in this section to locate the help you need. In the following sections, we do, however, provide URLs for a few sites of particular interest.

## Online Design and Development Tips and Tricks

While we provide you with a broad base of design principles and techniques, as well as more than a modicum of examples and tips for developing your solutions, a book this small (yes, we said "small") can't begin to cover the breadth and depth of specific approaches you can employ, problems and solutions you may encounter, nor all the specific challenges you will face.

Fortunately, in addition to the professional FileMaker consultants referenced in this appendix and the publications listed in the upcoming section "Print Periodicals," other resources also provide high-quality examples, tips and tricks, and developer techniques. Foremost among these are the collections of example files freely available from Database Pros in California (`www.databasepros.com`); NightWing Enterprises in Australia (`www.nightwing.com.au/FileMaker`); Six Fried Rice in Arizona (`www.sixfriedrice.com`); and from commercial providers, such as

ISO FileMaker Magazine (www.filemakermagazine.com) and FMWebschool (www.fmwebschool.com). Specialist FileMaker Custom Function resources are available from Cleveland Consulting (www.clevelandconsulting.com) and BrianDunning.com (www.briandunning.com). Information, tips, and techniques are also plentifully available among innumerable blogs including those from The FileMaker Collective (www.fmcollective.com), Tokerud's FileMaker Fever (http://tokerud.typepad.com/FileMaker), and topics of interest are regularly placed under the microscope (or at any rate, in front of the microphone) on the periodic Adatasol FileMaker Podcasts (http://podcast.adatasol.com).

An international network of FileMaker Pro user groups operates and is coordinated from the FMPug.com Web site (www.fmpug.com). FMPug provides a vast collection of other useful resources, including a desktop compendium of code and other resources called "The Everything Reference for FileMaker Developers"; online directories of trainers, developers, and consultants from the world over; a database of feature and enhancement requests; and reviews of books and third-party products for FileMaker Pro users and developers.

In addition, innumerable professional development companies offer tips and examples of their work, sometimes giving generally applicable insights or approaches to problems encountered in a variety of contexts. Many of these resources are available free of charge, for the trouble of seeking them out!

> **TIP** A search for "FileMaker demos" produces more than a million hits each on both Yahoo! and Google's search engines.

## Online Forums and Mailing Lists

The Internet is teaming with mailing lists and online forums, many of which are free, publicly accessible, and full of rich and varied content about many facets of FileMaker Pro programming and use. A selection of the more targeted FileMaker-specific mailing lists and forums are provided at www.filemaker.com/support/mailinglists.html and http://www.filemaker.com/support/forums.html. If you have Usenet access, a newsgroup, comp.databases.filemaker, is an active discussion group covering FileMaker topics.

> **TIP** You can also use Google Groups (http://groups.google.com) interface to access Usenet groups.

Foremost among online forums for all things FileMaker is FMForums.com, boasting more than 40,000 members and approaching a decade online. The largest single online community of FileMaker users and developers, FMForums attracts a diverse group of participants representing all levels from the merest of beginners to the most accomplished professionals.

Also worthy of mention is the RealTech list operated for members of FMPug and dealing with a broad range of technical issues and challenges relating to FileMaker and FileMaker-related products and solutions. In addition, a number of the user groups listed on the FMPug site sponsor their own mailing lists, wiki Web sites, or online resource pages.

# Expanding Your Knowledge with Additional Resources

## Books and Periodicals

Numerous books are available about FileMaker Pro and related technologies, some repeating material available among the resources mentioned in the preceding sections, or offering little that is not amply covered in this book. We would, however, like to recommend several volumes that provide explorations or detail on matters that go beyond the scope of this book:

- *The Everything Reference for FileMaker Developers* by Andy Gaunt and Stephen Dolenski (FMPug.com)
- *FileMaker 9 Developer Reference* by Bob Bowers, Steve Lane and Scott Love (Que Publishing)
- *FileMaker Security: The Book* by Steven H. Blackwell (New Millennium)
- *Web Publishing with PHP and FileMaker 9* by Jonathan Stark (Sams Publishing)

Each of these publications offers a wealth of additional information that will prove useful to the professional developer and serious amateur alike. We recommend these titles for the accuracy, quality, and depth of information they provide.

Additionally, although you can occasionally find articles about FileMaker Pro usage in general computer print magazines, such as *Macworld* or *PCWorld*, but the following publications contain more concentrated coverage:

- *FileMaker Pro Advisor* is dedicated to FileMaker and related subjects. ADVISOR MEDIA, Inc.; PO Box 429002; San Diego, CA 92142. Web site: `http://my.advisor.com/pub/filemakerAdvisor`.
- *Databased Advisor* covers database issues and includes FileMaker among the database management systems covered (although Access, xBase, and other platforms consume the bulk of the ink). ADVISOR MEDIA, Inc.; PO Box 429002; San Diego, CA 92142. Web site: `http://my.advisor.com/pub/DataBasedAdvisor`.
- *MacTech Magazine* covers popular Macintosh technologies from the perspective of the "serious" user (and FileMaker is one of the many technologies covered). MacTech Magazine; PO Box 5200; Westlake Village, CA 91359-5200; (877) 622-8324 (805-494-9797 outside US/Canada); `http://www.mactech.com`.

# Appendix C

# About the Web Site

This appendix describes what you can find on this book's companion Web site at www.wiley.com/compbooks/filemakerpro9bible. While you can use any relatively current Web browser and operating system to peruse the site's pages, using much of the available content will impose additional requirements. For example, using the sample files will necessitate running FileMaker Pro 9 or FileMaker Pro 9 Advanced, with their consequent Mac OS and Windows requirements.

**IN THIS APPENDIX**

Locating resources accompanying the book

Taking steps to solve any problems that arise

**TIP** You can download a free 30-day trial copy of FileMaker Pro 9 from www.filemakertrial.com.

In addition to the preceding requirements, you need an Internet connection and appropriate computer hardware to access the Web site and run the required operating systems and other software.

## What's on the Web Site

The following list provides an overview of what the book's Web site contains:

- **Author-created materials:** We' include copies of all the referenced example files used in this book, in the corresponding chapter link in the Author section. In particular, we have made each iteration of our Inventory example solution available so that you can look at it in various stages of evolution, comparing it to experiments you may have created while working through the book's examples. Additionally, we offer a few referenced special examples.

- **Application and documentation links:** Exhaustive coverage of FileMaker's capabilities would require a book far larger than this one, and the ancillary information grows daily. Consequently, we avoid including reference data that is readily available elsewhere. For example, comprehensive lists of calculation functions and script commands for FileMaker Pro 9 are available as PDF downloads from the FileMaker Web site. Rather than include this extensive material as part of the text of this book, we use the space otherwise and encourage you to download the companion documents from the links we provide on the companion Web site.

In this section of the Web site, we include links to the trial version of FileMaker Pro 9 provided as a free download by FileMaker, Inc., as well as links to a variety of documents FileMaker, Inc., makes available that we believe to be particularly useful as an adjunct to the information we have collected in this volume.

We also provide links to useful utilities, including plug-ins, from a variety of third-party vendors such as 360Works, New Millenium, 24U Software, Troi Automatisering, Digital Fusion, and others, and utilities from companies such as FM::Nexus, FXForge FMDiff, and Goya. Finally, we include links to groups and periodicals devoted to the FileMaker development community, including FMPug user group resource, FileMaker TechNet, FileMaker Forums, the ISO FileMaker Magazine, FileMaker Advisor, and significant providers of demo and example files such as Database Pros and NightWing Enterprises.

# Troubleshooting

If you have difficulty accessing the Web site or downloading any of the provided materials (not including items downloaded from other sites to which we provide links), please contact the Wiley Technical Product Support Center at (800) 762-2974 (outside the United States, call 1-317-572-3993) or online at www.wiley.com/techsupport.

Additionally, if you have trouble installing or using software from any of the linked sites:

- Check to ensure that you have the requisite system software version, disk space, and memory required for that software.
- Ensure that the files or applications have been extracted from archives (.dmg or .zip and so on) in which they are provided for download.
- Disable any virus-protection software during the installation. Many viruses mimic the actions necessary for an installer to function, and the virus-protection software is prone to confuse the two. (Remember to re-enable your virus-protection software after completing the installation.)
- Quit other programs you have running. In addition to freeing up memory for the installation to proceed, the absence of other running programs removes any conflict as to files the installer may need to access, update, or replace.

Should you experience ongoing problems after following each of these steps, contact the site from which you obtained the software to seek advice or assistance. Note that some sites may require a purchase or fee to provide you with personal support.

# Index

## Symbols and Numerics

& (ampersand), changing to "and", 207–208
@ (at sign), as Find wildcard character, 120–121
' (apostrophe), as word separator, 417
\ (backslash), for escaping reserved characters, 202
, (comma), as word separator, 417
<< and >> (double angle brackets), for merge fields, 328
$ (dollar sign), in variable name, 297, 411
... (ellipsis), as Range operator, 120
> (greater than) character, for theta joins, 368
≥ (greater than or equal to) character
   testing for, 265
   for theta joins, 368
# (hash), for script comments, 255
- (hyphen), as word separator, 417
< (less than) character
   for Find, 120
   for theta joins, 368
≤ (less than or equal to) character
   testing for, 265
   for theta joins, 368
"" (null), setting variable to, 296
. (period), as word separator, 417
¶ (pilcrow)
   as carriage return indicator, 202
   as word separator, 417
# (pound sign), as Find wildcard character, 120–121
" " (quotes), for text literals in functions, 403
; (semicolon), to separate function arguments, 201
/ (slash), as word separator, 417

// (slashes), for comments, 448
/* and */ (slash asterisk), for comments, 448
1 error code, 456, 552
3-D embossed effect, 154
4th Dimension, 12
9 error code, 456
24U Simple Dialog, 677
24U SimpleChart plugin, 679
100 error code, 552
101 error code, 456, 552
209 error code, 456
301 error code, 552–554
360Works, 677, 679, 683
400 error code, 456
401 error code, 456
508 error code, 552

## A

"About" layout, 635
About menu command, 354
abstraction, layers of, 431–433
Access, 12
access, defining and constraining, 508–509
access privileges
   for cascading deletion, 541
   extended, 513–514
   granular, 511–513
   and scripts, 460–462
   term defined, 687
accounts, 687. *See also* user accounts
Accounts steps in script, 228
accuracy, in data modeling, 362
Acos ( ) function, 64
acronym, creating from phrase, 634
actions, buttons for, 130
Activate/Deactivate command, 61
activating software license, 31
activation code, 32

active, 687
active objects, 450–451
active tool, locking tool as, 135
active window, command for setting, 331
ActiveX, 687
Actual Technologies, 215
adaptability, model of, 398
Adatasol FileMaker Podcasts, 706
Add Fields to Portal dialog, 165, 267
Add Relationship dialog, 211
Admin account
   basics, 125, 687
   password for default, 126
AdminAnywhere, 683
AFIS (Automated Fingerprint Identification System), 3
aggregate functions, 425–426
aggregating calculations, 111–112
AIM Keys (Windows), 668
algorithm, 687
alias on desktop (Mac), 33
Align toolbar, in Layout mode, 76–77
alignment, of objects, 156–157
All Modifiable access level, 509
All No Access access control, 509
All View Only access control, 509
Allow User Abort (Off) command, 464, 519
alphabetical order, 4
alphanumeric data, 687
Always Lock Layout Tools setting, 52
American National Standards Institute (ANSI), letter format, 175
American Standard Code for Information Exchange (ASCII), 688
ampersand (&), changing to "and", 207–208
analysis tools Inspector (FMNEXUS), 29
anchor-buoy, 377, 378

# A Index

anchor points
    basics, 334
    changing for layout object, 71
    for enclosing objects, 338
AND operator, 275–276, 369
angle brackets, double (<< and >>), for merge fields, 328
ANSI (American National Standards Institute), letter format, 175
API (Application Programming Interface), 687
apostrophe ('), as word separator, 417
AppleEvents, 687
AppleScript, 25, 661–662, 665–667, 688
applets, 671–672
Application Programming Interface (API), 687
application verification, in start-up script, 464
"apply-if-different" rule, 292
archive, 688
archiving
    backups, 548
    data, 659–660
    log data, 575
arguments (parameters)
    basics, 629, 688
    in Data Viewer, 609
    for functions, 200, 400, 402
        basics, 200, 402
        supplying, 402–403
    passing and retrieving multiple, 470–472
    for scripts, 230, 466
    term defined, 197
arithmetic operators, 405, 407
Arrange menu
    ➪ Bring to Front, 156
    ➪ Group, 155
    ➪ Send to Back, 147, 157, 162
arrays
    basics, 15, 374, 427
    collapsing and expanding, 374–375
arrow keys, for object positioning on layouts, 137
As-U-Type (Windows), 668
ascending sort, 688

ASCII (American Standard Code for Information Exchange), 688
`Asin( )` function, 64
association table, 363
at sign (@), as Find wildcard character, 120–121
attributes
    assigning to command, 241–243
    basics, 12
audio, binary objects for, 16
audit trail, 564, 571
authentication
    for debugger, 83, 86
    internal and external, 516–517
    for SQL Host, 220
    of users, 514–517
auto-entered value, 688
Auto-Entry
    basics, 187–188
    for calculation field, and storage, 438
    calculations
        basics, 294
        calculation fields, compared to, 436–439
        for default values, 15
        formatting fields with, 137
        lookups for, 543–544
        and user needs, 123–125
auto-entry field, 688
Auto-Update utility, for loading plug-ins, 53
Automated Fingerprint Identification System (AFIS), 3
automatic notification of updates, disabling, 62
automation. *See also* scripts
    basics, 462–465
    of security, 517–518
`Average( )` function, 425
`Average of` function, 195
Avery label formats, 77

# B

Back button, 340–341
back end of solution, 385–386
background color, of Header part, 148

backslash (\), for escaping reserved characters, 202
backup copies of solution, script for, 251
backups of files
    alternatives to, 584
    basics, 36, 688
    hosted files, 551
    strategies, 548–549
base table, 688
base36 format, 536
BaseElements (Goya), 29, 546, 684
batch processing of data updates
    robots and, 656, 657
    scripts for, 250
Bento, 20
binary objects, FileMaker support for storing, 16
binding, 688
bindkey, 637
black box, 400
Body part of layout, 135, 136, 145–146, 688
bold text, 148, 294–295
book icon, 688
books, 707
Boolean operations, 408–409, 649–650
Boolean variable, 688
bound solution, 688
branching script according to state, 467–468
break fields, 322–323, 689
BrianDunning.com, 706
Browse mode
    basics, 38, 689
    multiple windows, 264
    record data entry in, 115
    Status Area controls in, 39
browsed records, 689
business layer, 386
Button Setup dialog, 61–62, 168, 269
buttons
    adding to layout, 269–270
    assigning attributes to objects, 43
    basics, 152, 167–171, 689
    defining and creating, 168–170
    executing, 171
    Mac and Windows differences, 312

712

# Index

multi-state, 319
scope, and commands, 170
setting as non-printing, 325
for static and dynamic actions, 130
for style, 294–295
style for, 169
to switch layouts, 163
for text formatting, 420–421

## C

cache
  and backup, 550
  of join results, 304–306
  managing, Relationships Graph and, 379
  and performance, 619
  size of, 52
  term defined, 689
  writing to disk, 35
Calculated Value checkbox, auto-entry, 188
calculation engine, 15, 28–29
calculation fields
  Auto-Entry calculations, compared to, 436–439
  basics, 11, 15, 186, 192–193, 689
  creating, 198–200
  dependencies on fields referenced, 193
  for SQL tables, 222–223
Calculation Result Is menu, 111
calculation variables, 296, 410–411, 689
calculations. *See also specific function names*
  abstraction layers, 431–433
  aggregating, 111–112
  Auto-Entry, 294
  basics, 386
  boolean operations, 408–409
  cascading operations, 303
  code formatting, 447–448
  compound expressions, 400–406
  conditional expression for, 105
  dates and times, 422–424
  disallowing deletion of referenced field, 184
  documentation for, 447–448
  examples, 206–208
  formulas for, 201–202
  functions, 204–206
  global, 307, 439–442
  for ID field, 99–100
  leading zero in, 111
  logic, 401–402
  nesting functions, 407
  online help for functions, 399–400
  operators, 405–406
  order of operations, 201, 406–408
  for phone number format, 565–566
  providing parameters for functions, 402–403
  setting up simple, 103–105
  summary data, 424–427
  supported by table of dependencies, 304–305
  terminology, 197–198
  text processing, 412–418
  triggering script from, 675–677
  unstored, 434–436
  using custom functions, 444–447
  variables, 410–412
calendar quarter, sorting records on, 207
Calendar View Demo, Information layout, 22–23
calling script, 473
camel case format, for field names, 95, 382
Cantor, Georg, 360
carriage return
  in data entry, 566
  as delimiter between exported records, 600
  in field content, 158
  removing leading, 635
  as word separator, 417
  `xValues` functions return of, 428–429
Cartesian joins, 369, 372–373
Cartesian product, 346, 689
cascading calculation operations, 303
cascading deletion, 539–540
  controlling at runtime, 542
  privilege requirements for, 541
`Case` function, 246, 646

case sensitivity
  in equi-join, 368
  of functions, 202
  of passwords, 126
`Case` statement, 201
`Ceiling` function, 207
centering objects, 339
certification program, by FileMaker Inc., 29–30
character-level formatting, 291–292
characters
  defining permissible set, 592
  extracting set from text block, 634–635
  out-of-range, 592–593
  rejecting out-of-scope, in data entry, 567
charting
  with Flash, 671
  plug-ins for, 679
checkboxes
  grouping, 187
  term defined, 689
child, 689
`Choose( )` function, 646
chronological roll-back, 576–577
chunks of data, 658–659
circles/ellipses, 151
circular references, avoiding, 210–212, 366
clarity in data modeling, 362
cleansing data, for import and export, 589–593
Cleveland Consulting, 706
click-sort columns, for sorting, 284–288
client
  basics, 689
  malware as risk, 525
clone, 689
closing
  database, data loss from improper, 35
  FileMaker, 32–33
  files
    basics, 35
    scripts running on, 465
  records, alternatives, 561–564

713

# Index

clutter, avoiding in layout, 149
CNS Image, 678
Codd, E.F., 6, 359–360
code, portable and reusable, 642
code comment braces, for reference in imported files, 183
Cognito, accounting software suite, 28
collapsing fields, 326
color
　basics, 343
　controlling programmatically, 293
　impact of, 150
　Mac and Windows differences, 311
　and printing, 141
color palette, 52, 138
columns
　click-sort, for sorting, 284–288
　width, in Manage Database dialog Tables panel, 179
comma (,), as word separator, 417
comma-separated values (CSV), importing and exporting, 27, 46–47
commands
　attaching to layout object, 167
　basics, 689
　selecting and duplicating multiple, 252
`Comment` function, 255
comment operators, 405, 406
comments
　in calculation code, 448
　as documentation, 382–384
　in scripts, 254–255
Comments field, 363
commit, 690
commitment of records, 45, 561–564
Compact File option, 617, 618
companion Web site
　database available on, 129
　overview, 709–710
　troubleshooting, 710
comparative operators (theta joins), 368
comparison operators, 405, 407, 409
compound interest, calculating, 207
compound join criterion, 346
compound keys, 372

computers
　retrieving network address, 535
　time savings from, 5
concatenated keys, 372
condition, 690
conditional execution, 246
conditional formatting
　basics, 65–66, 292
　hidden power of, 318–319
　for object visibility, 317
　`Self` function for calculations, 63
Conditional Formatting dialog, 153
conditional statements, in scripts, 246–247
conditional tooltips, 620
consolidated report, 9–10
constants
　in functions, 402
　term defined, 197, 690
constellations, in Relationships Graph, 377–378
constrain, 690
consulting services, 704–705
contact details, visibility in layout, 123–124
container fields
　basics, 16, 186, 690
　in Boolean operations, 408
　export and, 586–587
　as external data sources, 597
　importing file into, 587
container objects
　external storage, 598
　script for loading and unloading, 496–497
context
　basics, 209
　disappearing/reappearing objects based on, 314–317
　importance of, 50
　managing, 130
　for scripts, 232
　table occurrences and, 192
context variables, script-specific, 571
Control category of script commands, 468
control characters, 592–593

Control key, and running script, 648–649
control steps in script, 228
controls
　adding to layout, 269–270
　in Debugger, 607–608
　in ScriptMaker, 475–480
`Copy All Records/Requests[ ]` command, 277
copy and paste
　to move tables, 180
　script steps, 253
copying
　open files, risk of, 549–550
　records, 44
　script commands, 252
copyright, information in About dialog, 354
correspondence (letters)
　generating, 329–330
　information as basis of, 10–11
`Count( )` function, 204
`Count of` function, 195
crash, file corruption from, 585
Create a New Data Source to SQL Server dialog, 217–218
Create Database icon, 32, 59
cross-join, 369
cross-platform capability
　basics, 26, 310–313
　and external script calls, 667–668
"crows foot" terminator, 364–365
cues, spatial, for added meaning, 342
currency symbol, 140
current date
　placeholder for, 329
　retrieving, 205
current fields, 690
current mode, 50
Current panel, in Data Viewer, 610–612
current record
　and context, 50
　term defined, 690
current time, 329, 535

714

# Index

## D

custom dialog
    configuration to prompt for user input, 260
    dynamic attributes, 334
    as interface tool, 332–334
custom functions
    to avoid repetition, 643
    basics, 627–630, 690
    calculations using, 444–447
    merge feature, 632
    for name/value pairs, 472
    and recursion, 631–635
    syntax, 446
Custom Layout Privileges dialog, 511
custom menus
    creating, 621–626
    term defined, 690
    user access to, 624–626
Custom Record Privileges dialog, 511, 512
Custom Script Privileges dialog, 510
custom Web publishing, 681–683
cyclic relationships, preventing, 21

## D

damaged files, after recovery, 583
data
    avoiding need for duplication, 121–125
    basics, 7–8
    as basis of correspondence, 10–11
    editing, 43–45
    editing or deleting, 118–119
    forms to view subset, 8–9
    importing and exporting, 46–47
    salvaging, 583–584
    screen to display, 8
    storing and accumulating, 474–475
    viewing and interacting with, 113–121
data architecture, 8
data arrays, 374–377
data cleansing, 589–593
data domain, 592
data end of solution, 385–386

data entry
    applying standard formations, 565–566
    automatic adjustment of, 438
    automatic for serial number, 97–100
    basics, 43–45, 114–118, 690
    capturing edits, 571–575
    default values in, 11
    dialogs for, 332–334
    double-blind entry systems, 563–564
    formula for overriding, 566
    input fields, color to differentiate, 139
    modifying to requirements, 565
    pausing for script for, 248–249
    portals for, 375–376
    rejecting out-of-scope characters, 567
    scripts for, 250, 260
    styled source text in, 567
    trailing spaces and carriage returns in, 566
[Data Entry Only] privilege set, 125
Data field type, 185
data loss
    causes, 35
    costs of, 548
data management, with relationship-based techniques, 375–377
Data Merge (Word), 10–11
data modeling
    delineating fields in, 363
    guiding principles for, 362–364
    relational, 363
data modification, on paper, 5
data redundancy, in flat-file database, 6
data relationships, 223–225
data sets, synchronization, 594–597
Data Source, 690
Data Source Name (DSN), 496, 690
data sources, named and unnamed, 212–213
data storage decisions, 544
data structure compared to file architecture, 388–393

data transfer, migration utility for, 392
data types. *See* field types
data URLs, Web viewer object support for, 74
Data Viewer
    authentication, 86
    basics, 609–615, 690
    FileMaker Pro 9 Advanced enhancements
        Current panel, 85, 610–612
        Watch panel, 86, 612–613
    using with Script Debugger, 613
    and variables, 614–615
database
    advantages of computerized, 5
    basics, 3, 690
    creating, 92–112
    data loss from improper close, 35
    definition, 4
    flat-file, 6
    limitations of paper-based, 4–5
    practical examples, 7
    relational, 6–7
    Send e-mail link for sharing, 67–68
    value of, 17–18
Database Design Report, 88, 615–617, 691
database management program (DBMS), 691
Database Management Systems, 4
Database Pros, 30, 705
database solution, 7–12. *See also* solutions in FileMaker
database structure, documentation of, 380–384
*Databased Advisor*, 707
`DatabaseNames` function, 402, 443
date, placeholder for current, 329
date fields
    in Boolean operations, 408
    management, 421–422
date formats, precedence of, 293
`Date( )` function, 204–205, 401
`DayOfWeek( )` function, 424
days overdue for item, 206
dBASE, 12, 27

715

# D Index

DDE (Dynamic Data Exchange), 691
DeclareVariables( ) custom function, 472, 474
declaring variables, 297
default error dialog, 457–458
default [Full Access] account, 507
default layout
　basics, 131–132
　FileMaker creation of, 112
default menus, 622, 624
default privilege set names, square brackets for, 507
default settings
　for Auto-Entry, 187
　for Date field format, 185
　fonts, 54, 133
　formats and attributes for objects, 155–156
　for front tab, 72
　password for Admin account, 126
　for privilege set, 128–129
　term defined, 691
default table, for new database, 34
default user account, setting, 128–129
default values
　Auto-Entry for, 15
　in data entry, 11
deleted records, in recovered files, 583
deleting
　data, 118–119
　fields, 184–185
　Footer part of layout, 266
　Header part of layout, 266
　redundant records, 539–542
　tables, 178–180
　text formatting, 419–420
　value from list, 430–431
delimiters for import and export, 589, 600
dependencies
　avoiding "spaghetti", 650–652
　for calculation field, on fields referenced, 193
　between fields, 44
　global, 440–442
　limits of, 303
　managing, 544–546
　sequential, 652
　term defined, 691

dependency triggering, 193
dependent value, 44
dependent variables, 15
deployment, 398
derived values, 15
descending sort, 691
design
　approach to, 22–23
　of calculation expressions, 645
　External SQL Data Sources support and, 81
　for flexibility and adaptability, 643–644
　online tips and tricks, 705–706
　redundancy elimination, 641–643
　simplicity issues, 653–654
　size considerations, 639–641
design functions, 443–444
destroying variables, 296–297
Developer Utilities, 691
Developer Utilities dialog, 636
diagnostic tools, third-party, 546
dialogs. *See also* custom dialog
　capabilities, 677–678
　displaying for user prompt, 452–453
　Mac and Windows differences, 313
　term defined, 691
Digital Fusion Ltd., 679
dimensions of window, 488–489
disk drive. *See* hard disk drives
Display Progress Bar checkbox, for Web viewer object, 72
documentation
　of calculation expressions, 447–448
　of database structure, 380–384
　with field comments, 382–384
　with script comments, 254–255
　table for notes, 384
　third-party tools for, 683–684
Dolenski, Stephen, *The Everything Reference for FileMaker Developers*, 707
dollar sign ($), in variable name, 297, 411
domain controller, for authentication, 516
double-blind entry systems, 563–564

drag-and-drop text editing, 51
drag-to-layout tools, 136
drawing environment, 154–157
drill-downs, windows as, 331
drop-down lists
　basics, 40, 691
　for field control options, 117
DRY (Don't Repeat Yourself) principle, 641, 645
DSN (Data Source Name), 690
　defining, 496
duplicated records
　basics, 44
　in recovered files, 583
duplicating data, avoiding need for, 121–125. *See also* copying
dynamic actions, buttons for, 130
dynamic array, 375
Dynamic Data Exchange (DDE), 691
dynamic objects, 151–152

# E

e-mail, plug-ins for handling, 679
Edit Account dialog, 126, 515
Edit Custom Function dialog, 628, 629
Edit Custom Menu dialog, 622–624
Edit Data Source dialog, 220, 394
Edit Expression dialog, in Data Viewer, 613–614
Edit Extended Privilege dialog, 514
Edit Group dialog, 255
Edit menu
　➪ Copy, to duplicate buttons, 170
　➪ Duplicate, 169
　➪ Export Field Contents, 587
　➪ Paste, to duplicate buttons, 170
　➪ Preferences, 51, 132
　➪ Redo, 75
　➪ Select All, 134
　➪ Undo, 75
Edit Privilege Set dialog, 126, 508
Edit Relationship dialog
　alternative relationship operators, 367
　basics, 109, 266
　Delete Related Records In This Table When..., 539–540

716

# Index  E

Edit Script dialog, 69, 230–231, 236, 251
Edit Value List dialog, 101, 116
editing
    data, 118–119, 479–480
    posting, and propagating to related records, 655
    related data, 49–50
    steps in script, 228
efficiency
    custom functions for, 630
    in data modeling, 362
electronic form, index and documentation storage in, 176
element groups, 342
ellipsis (...), as Range operator, 120
`Else If`, 246–247, 481
embedded formatting, 291
embedded images, 597–600
embossing effect, 154, 342
empty fields, preventing, 190
empty values, in Boolean operations, 408
Enable Account command, 517
encryption, with Secure Sockets Layer, 527
`End If`, 246, 481
`End Loop` statement, 247, 481–482
Engraved effect, 137–138, 147, 342
`Enter Browse Mode[ ]` command, 237
Enter key, 158
entering data. *See* data entry
entities
    separate by type, 362–363
    term defined, 361
Entity Relationship Diagram (ERD), 21, 209
environment
    data returned by `Get( )` functions, 390
    functions to retrieve information about, 442–444
EOL markers, for import and export, 589
`.eps` file format, 151
equi-join, 16, 108–109, 225, 366–368, 691

ERD (Entity Relationship Diagram), 21, 209
ergonomics, 149–150
error capture, turning on, 458
error-check sequence, for potential command failure, 458–459
error codes
    basics, 552
    meaning of, 456
    retrieving, 455
    in Script Debugger, 84
    storing cumulative log, 474–475
error dialog, for calculation, 100
error handling
    adding to process, 457–459
    detecting and reversing, 576
    need for, 456–457
    sub-script for, 642
    trapping
        basics, 551–555
        in script, 454–459
        in sub-script, 485
errors, privilege-based, 461
escape character, for reserved characters, 202
ESS (External SQL Data Source), 692
ETL (Extraction, Transformation and Loading) process, 497, 589–590
`Evaluate( )` function, 202, 432–433
evaluation, short-circuited, 202
EventScript, 677
*The Everything Reference for FileMaker Developers* (Gaunt and Dolenski), 707
Excel files
    creating, 49
    importing and exporting, 27, 46–47
    paper output, compared to, 176
Excelisys, 30
Existing Value option, for fields, 190
exit conditions for loops, 482–484
`Exit Loop If` statement, 247, 481–482
`Exit Script[ ]` command
    basics, 473, 483
    error handler and, 455
exiting. *See* closing

explicit Boolean coding, 409
exploded keys, 371
Explorer (Windows), limitation for duplicating files, 36
`Export Field Contents[ ]` command, 491, 496, 600–601
`Export Records[ ]` command, 491
Export Records to File dialog, 47
exporting data
    basics, 46–47, 585–589, 691
    custom process, 601
    data cleansing, 589–593
    field contents, script for, 490–491
    file formats, 26–27, 491, 586–587
    selecting fields for, 492–493
    table data, script for, 491–492
expressions, 691
    compared to formulas, 400
    Data Viewer for developing, 613
    entry in formula box, 200
    in functions, 403
    term defined, 198
extend, 691
extended privileges, 513–514, 691
extensibility of FileMaker, 28
eXtensible Markup Language (XML)
    basics, 681–682, 702
    as DDR output option, 616, 617
    FileMaker Server use of, 24
    importing and exporting, 27, 495
eXtensible Style Language Transformation (XSLT) style sheets, 27, 681–682, 702
external, 692
external authentication, 692
external calls, in scripts, 661–668
external data, references to, 386
External Data Sources
    basics, 16
    field changes, 184
    for interface files, 389
    SQL (ODBC)
        basics, 77–79, 214–223
        and separation of data, 393–395
external functions, 404, 674–675

717

# Index

external resources, refreshing in startup script, 465
external script, 692
external scripting protocols, 25
External SQL Data Source (ESS), 692
Extraction, Transformation and Loading (ETL) process, 497, 589–590

## F

fatigue, avoiding visual, 149–150
feedback, to users for processing, 350
Field Behavior dialog
    basics, 139, 158, 269
    spell-checking options, 74–75
field boxes, 42, 151, 152
Field/Control Setup dialog, 115, 117, 166
field controls, 151
Field Options dialog
    Auto-Enter panel, 187
    basics, 97–103
field-specific spell-checking
    disabling, 160
    enabling, 74–75
Field tool, 136, 151
field types
    basics, 185–186, 692
    keyboard shortcuts for, 94
    and keys, 536–537
    and sort, 281
<FieldMissing> placeholder, 185
fields. *See also* container fields; global fields; indexes; text fields
    access privileges, 511–513
    adding, 183–185
    auto-entry, 187–188
    basics, 42, 692
    behavior settings for group, 140
    calculation, 15
    comments as documentation, 382–384
    convention for referring to, 101
    creating, 34, 44–45, 94–97
    definition, 4
    deleting, 184–185
    delineating in data modeling, 363
    dependencies between, 44
    editing data on the fly, 479–480
    enabling spell-check for specific, 74–75
    in FileMaker, 12
    formatting, 137–141
    multi-key, 370–371
    names
        changes, and formula update, 203
        Hungarian notation, 200
        limitations, 203
    optimizing index configurations, 302–303
    preventing empty, 190
    rectangle around group, 147–148
    referencing
        in formulas, 203
        in functions, 403
    resizing boxes, 136
    selecting for export, 492–493
    sorting by multiple, 119
    in SQL, 222
    supplemental, in External SQL Data Source table, 80–82
    Tab key to move between, 34
    trapping changes, 572–573
    validation options, 188–190
fields steps in script, 228
FieldType( ) function, 443
file architecture compared to data structure, 388–393
[File Default], for menu set, 625
File dialog, 33
file formats, 692
    delimiters and EOL markers, 589
    earlier, conversion, 36–37
    for import and export, 26–27, 491, 586–587
File Maintenance, 692
File Maintenance dialog, 617–619
File Manipulator, 678
File menu
    ➪ Close, 35
    ➪ Exit, 33, 37
    ➪ Export Records, 47
    ➪ File Options, 54, 128
    ➪ Import ➪ Folder, 587
    ➪ Import Records ➪ File, 46, 180, 181, 595
    ➪ Manage
        ➪ Accounts & Privileges, 126, 507
        ➪ Custom Functions, 627
        ➪ Custom Menus, 621
        ➪ Database, 44, 97, 219, 572
        ➪ External Data Sources, 212, 213, 395
        ➪ Scripts, 234, 237
        ➪ Value Lists, 116, 538
    ➪ New Database, 33, 91, 92, 181
    ➪ Page Setup (Mac), 142
    ➪ Print, 48
    ➪ Print Setup, 48, 142
    ➪ Recover, 581
    ➪ Save a Copy As, 36, 550, 617
    ➪ Save/Send Records As
        ➪ Excel, 49
        ➪ PDF, 49
    ➪ Send Link, 67
    ➪ Sharing
        ➪ FileMaker Network, 556
        ➪ Instant Web Publishing, 680–681
File Options dialog
    basics, 54
    Graphics tab, 57
    Open/Close tab, 55, 463
    Spelling tab, 55–56
    Text tab, 56
file paths, dynamic, with variables, 477–478
File References, 16
file session, 411
file sharing, risks, 558
File Transfer Protocol (FTP), plug-ins for handling, 679
FileMaker
    certification program, 29–30
    compared to other database development tools, 20–23
    exiting, 32–33
    flexibility, 24–25
    history, 19
    as integrated environment, 387
    language versions, 25, 26

# Index F

limitations as SQL front end, 393
navigation icon, 17
plug-ins and extensibility, 28
product family, 23–24
relational model, 225
scalability, 24–25
starting, 32–33
window, 38
FileMaker, Inc.
    Development Conventions paper, 382
    license agreement for runtime copies, 635
    Technical support, 704
    Web resources, 703–704
        on migrating legacy solutions, 37
FileMaker 9
    components, 24
    features, 12–18
*FileMaker 9 Developer Reference*, 707
FileMaker Business Alliance, 30, 704
FileMaker Collective, 706
FileMaker developer community, 29
FileMaker Developers Conference, 704
FileMaker Fever, 706
FileMaker Masters colloquium, 704
FileMaker Network, 692
FileMaker Network Settings dialog, 556–557
FileMaker Network Settings, enabling solution for, 558
FileMaker PHP API, 682
FileMaker Pro 9 Advanced
    compared to other versions, 24
    copying and pasting fields, 105
    custom functions, 627–630
    custom menu creation, 621–626
    Data Viewer, 609–615
    Database Design Report, 179, 615–617
    file maintenance, 617–619
    moving tables between files, 180
    new features, 82–88
    runtime application creation, 635–637
    Script Debugger, 605–608
    tooltips definitions, 619–621
*FileMaker Pro Advisor*, 707

FileMaker Pro menu (Mac)
    ⇨ Preferences, 51, 132
    ⇨ Quit FileMaker Pro, 33, 37
*FileMaker Resource Guide*, 704–705
*FileMaker Security*, 707
FileMaker Server
    automatic logging, 527
    basics, 24
    configuring as host for runtime files, 637
    scheduling scripts to run on, 656, 657
    security for, 526–527
FileMaker Suplog demo, 574
FileMaker TechNet, 30
files
    closing, 35
    closing, scripts running on, 465
    corruption, 584–585
    filtered display based on user account, 526
    list of recently opened, 32
    localization settings for, 56
    moving tables between, 180
    plug-ins for handling, 678–679
    references, 545
    saving, 33–35
    script to run on open, 463
    scripts for printing and managing, 251
    security for, 524–526
    size management, 658–660
    stored, 597–600
    warning of integrity problems, 585
Files steps in script, 228
Fill tool, for rectangle, 147
filter, 692
`Filter( )` function, 567, 593
filtering
    for import and export, 592–593
    portals, 264–270
    by script groups, 257–258
filtering relationship, 265
financial data, 7
Find
    AND for compound Find, 275–276
    basics, 12, 119–120

capturing criteria with script, 278–279
dynamically building criteria, 478–479
with OR, 276
on results of previous, 276–277
saving, 277–280
scripts for, 259, 279–280
special symbols for, 120
find criteria, 692
Find mode
    basics, 38, 40–41, 692
    Status Area controls in, 41
Find request, 14–15, 692
Finder (Macintosh), limitation for duplicating files, 36
flagging records, 555
Flash
    basics, 347–348
    charting with, 671
flashing, reducing or eliminating, 312
flat-file database, 6, 693
flexibility, 23, 24–25
fmapp extended privilege, 513
FMDiff, 29, 684
FMExample plug-in, 677
FMForums, 30, 706
fmiwp extended privilege, 680
FMNexus, Inspector, 29, 546, 684
`.fmplugin` file extension, 672
FMPug, 30
FMPug.com Web site, 706
FMPXMLRESULT encoding format, 495
FMRobot, 683
`FMSAUC_FindPlugIn( )` function, 672
`FMSAUC_UpdatePlugIn( )` function, 672
FMStudio, 683
FMWebschool, 683, 706
focus, objects with, 450–451
Folder of Files Import Options dialog, 587–588
folders
    exporting to and importing from, 587–588
    for scripts, 255

719

# Index

fonts
  for cross-platform development, 310–311
  differences in rendering, 311
  for printed output, 174–175
  setting preferences, 54
Footer part of layout
  basics, 135, 145–146, 693
  deleting, 266
foreign key, 366, 693
form letter, 10–11
Form view, 144–145, 335, 693
Format menu
  ⇨ Align Text ⇨ Center, 139
  ⇨ Button, 167
  ⇨ Button Setup, 269
  ⇨ Conditional, 65, 153
  ⇨ Field/Control
    ⇨ Behavior, 158, 269
    ⇨ Setup, 166
  ⇨ Font ⇨ Verdana, 134
  ⇨ Line Spacing ⇨ Custom, 325
  ⇨ Number, 140
  ⇨ Set Sliding/Printing, 143, 320, 325, 326, 327
  ⇨ Set Tooltip, 619
  ⇨ Size, 148
  ⇨ Style, 148
    ⇨ Italic, 155
  ⇨ Text Color, 139, 148, 155
formatting. *See also* conditional formatting
  basics, 290–291
  character-level, 291–292
  controlling programmatically, 293–294
  fields and text objects, 137–141
  layout filters, 292–293
  paragraph-level, 292
  pasting process and, 291–292
  text strings, 419–421
forms, 8–9
formulas
  for calculations, 104–105, 201–202
  compared to expressions, 400
  literal values in, 202–203
  referencing fields and tables in, 203
  term defined, 198, 693

forums, 706
found set
  basics, 12, 41, 693
  constraining and extending, 276–277
  inverting, 119
  multiple open, 264
  reducing size, 276
  saving, 277–280
  tracking, 489
  of unique records, 499
Found Sets steps in script, 228
4th Dimension, 12
.fp3 file format, 36
.fp5 file format, 36
.fp7 file format, 33, 77, 93, 388
.fpx file format, 151
Fraction of Total function, 195
fragmentation, 344
Freeze Window command, 237, 490
freezing screens, 489–490
frequency of backup, 548
FTP (File Transfer Protocol), plug-ins for handling, 679
[Full Access] privilege set, 125, 517, 525, 693
full access privileges, running script with, 461–462
function separator, 693
functions
  basics, 400
  for calculations, 204–206
  custom, 444–447
  external, 674–675
  structured syntax and nesting, 404–405
  term defined, 197, 693
  text literals in, quotes (" ") for, 403
Fusion Reactor, 679
FXForge, 683

# G

Gaunt, Andy, *The Everything Reference for FileMaker Developers*, 707
Georgia font, 310
Get (CurrentDate) function, 400

Get( ) functions
  basics, 208, 294, 404, 442–443
  environment data returned by, 390
Get (HostApplicationVersion) function, 64
Get (TemporaryPath) function, 64
Get(AccountName) function, 517
Get(ActiveModifierKeys) function, 648–649
GetAsBoolean( ) function, 409
GetAsCSS( ) function, 421, 670
GetAsDate( ) function, 200
GetAsNumber( ) function, 422, 423, 442–443, 535
GetAsText( ) function, 200, 599
GetAsTimestamp( ) function, 200, 404
Get(CurrentDate) function, 205, 206
Get(CurrentHostTimestamp) function, 535
Get(CurrentPlatform) function, 662
Get(DesktopPath) function, 478, 568
Get(DocumentsPath) function, 478
Get(ExtendedPrivileges) function, 517
GetField( ) function, 283, 431–432
Get(FilemakerPath) function, 478
Get(FilePath) function, 478
Get(Last Error) function, 455
Get(LastMessageChoice) function, 260
GetLayoutObjectAttribute( ) function, 669–670
GetNextSerialValue( ) function, 533
GetNthRecord( ) function, 278, 403, 428
Get(PreferencesPath) function, 478
Get(PrivilegeSetName) function, 462, 517
Get(RecordID) function, 534, 535
GetRepetition( ) function, 428

# Index

`GetSummary( )` function, 427
`Get(SystemNICAddress)` function, 535
`Get(TemporaryPath)` function, 478
`GetValue( )` function, 429, 470, 647
`Get(WindowMode)` function, 620
`Get(WindowName)` command, 486
.gif file format, for graphic in layout, 17, 151, 157
global calculations
    basics, 307, 439–442
    creating field, 265
global dependencies, 440–442
global fields
    basics, 196–197, 306–307, 555, 640, 693
    and indexes, 372
global text fields
    basics, 454
    for dialog input, 333
    exporting from, 601
global variables
    basics, 296, 410, 411, 693
    for colors, 294
    destroying, 297
    importance of tracking, 297–298
    in start-up script, 465
    and user accounts, 614
`Go to Field[ ]` command, 497
`Go to Layout[ ]` command, 237, 475
`Go to Object[ ]` command, 233, 451, 479–480
`Go to Related Record` function
    basics, 50, 231, 270–273, 331, 339–340
    New Window Options configuration, 273
Go to Related Record Options dialog, 273
`Go to Related Records[ ]` command, 552
Goya, BaseElements, 29, 546, 684
Grand summary part, 693
granular security, 510–514
graphical effects, 137
graphical environment, 154–157
graphical progress indicator, 352

graphics. *See* images
graphs, creating separate, 397–398
groups
    of layout elements, white space between, 149
    for organizing scripts, 69–70, 244
    of scripts, 257
        filtering by, 257–258
    term defined, 693
guest, 694

## H

`Halt Script` command
    basics, 231, 245, 483
    error handler and, 455
handle, 694
hard disk drives
    local compared to network drive, benefits, 35
    writing cache to, 35
hardware failure, and data loss, 585
hash (#), for script comments, 255
Header part of layout
    basics, 135, 145–146
    deleting, 266
    setting background color, 148
    term defined, 694
header record, 694
help for users
    basics, 354
    text in layouts, 22–23
Help menu, 60–61
hidden objects, selecting, 156
hidden state, file opened in, 463
hierarchy of scripts, 69
holding table, for double-blind entry system, 563–564
horizontal dimension parameters, in Object Info palette, 169
host, 694
hour value, in Time field, 186
HTML (Hypertext Markup Language)
    basics, 16, 669–671, 694
    manipulating source via calculation, 348
    searches in DDR files, 616
    tables, 680

HTTP (Hypertext Transfer Protocol), plug-ins for handling, 679
Hungarian notation, 104, 200, 382
Huslik Verlag GmbH, 29, 684
hypertext, 670–671
Hypertext Transfer Protocol (HTTP), plug-ins for handling, 679
hyphen (-), as word separator, 417

## I

ID field, and serial number field, 99
ideal database structure, 8
IDs
    for fields, 184
    for records, 534–535
`If( )` function
    basics, 105, 246, 632
    nesting, 481
    parameters, 402
    short-circuit evaluation, 646
images
    binary objects for, 16
    in databases, 660
    formats supported, 151
    imported, and performance, 342
    importing to layout, 17
    from other applications, 157
implicit Boolean coding, 409
import field map, for XML data, 496
Import Field Mapping dialog, 46–47, 181, 494–495, 588, 595–596
import matching, 595
Import Options dialog, 182
importing data
    basics, 46–47, 585–589, 694
    data cleansing, 589–593
    data matching for, 494–496
    file formats, 26–27, 491, 586–587
    scripts for, 493
    selectively, 596–597
    tables, 180–183
In Range option, setting for data entry, 190
indexes
    basics, 191–192
    creating on demand, 191

721

# Index

indexes *(continued)*
    field types and, 186
    for key fields, 224
    myths, 299–300
    numeric compared to text, 301
    optimizing field index configurations, 302–303
    roles, 298
    and storage, 300
    term defined, 694
    for text fields, 298–299
    Unicode and alternate language, 301–302
indirect objects, references, 545
infinite loops, risk of, 485
information. *See also* data
    editing via scripts, 250
    giving meaning to, 150
    logical flow of, 122–123
    organizing presentation of, 136–137
initial layouts, 131–146
initials, calculating from person's name, 206
`Insert File[ ]` command, 496
Insert menu
    ⇨ From Index, 191, 298
    ⇨ Merge Field, 328
    ⇨ Picture, 157, 343
`Insert Picture[ ]` command, 496, 497
`Insert QuickTime[ ]` command, 496
inserted graphics, 151
inserting value in list, 430
Inspector (FMNexus), 29, 546, 684
`Install Menu Set[ ]` command, 621, 625, 626
Instant Web Publishing, 680–681, 694
instantiating variables, 296–297
instructions in layouts, 22–23
integrated environment, FileMaker as, 387
integrity of backups, 549
intercapping, 95, 382
interface files, 386, 389–391
interface for database
    basics, 8–11
    dependence, and script commands, 239

elements, 353–354
importance of, 131
multi-lingual, 356–358
internal ID
    for layouts, 444
    for scripts, 253
International Standards Organization, A4 page standard, 175
Internet location. *See* URL (Uniform Resource Locator)
invalid data, 694
inverting found set, 119
investment, protecting, 504–505
invisible characters, 593
IP address of user, capturing in log, 568
ISO FileMaker Magazine, 706
isolating relationship, 376–377
italic text, 155
`iwp_home.html` page, 681

## J

Java Database Connectivity (JDBC), 694
JavaScript, 347–348
JDBC (Java Database Connectivity), 694
join table, 363, 373
joins
    basics, 13
    caching results, 304–306
    compound criterion, 346
    fields to define, 16
    naturally occurring, 373
    non-equal and equi-, 367–368
`.jpg` file format, for graphic in layout, 17, 151, 157

## K

key fields, 16, 224, 366
keyboard, for tab navigation, 344, 345
keyboard shortcuts
    for field options, 94, 98
    for operating modes, 38–39
    for undo and redo, 75
keys
    basics, 694
    compound, 372
    and data type, 536–537

    for referential integrity, 530–536
    retrofitting, 537–539
keystroke logging software, 525
keywords, associating with privilege sets, 513
kiosk, 637, 694

## L

label formats, Avery, 77
labels in layout, 136
language
    for indexes, 301–302
    versions of FileMaker, 25, 26
laptop computer, synchronizing data set with server, 594
last day of current month, `Date` function to return, 401
late fees, calculations for evaluating, 206
launching
    FileMaker, 32–33
    scripts from Script Debugger, 82. *See also* start-up script
layers
    of abstraction, 431–433
    basics, 385–387
    business or procedural, 386
    Mac and Windows differences, 312
    of protection, 524–525
layout buttons, 42–43
Layout context, 130
layout ID, 444
Layout mode
    basics, 39, 131, 695
    color palette in, 52
    font changes in, 134
    and relationships, 121
    tools and features, 134–136
    vertical dotted line in, 142
layout objects, 71, 450
Layout Setup dialog
    basics, 271–272
    General tab, 114, 626
    Printing tab, 142
    Views tab, 145
layout window, 33, 38
layouts
    access to, 511
    adaptable design, 644

Align toolbar, 76–77
for Avery labels, 77
basics, 13–14
centering objects, 339
data visibility in, 123–124
default front tab, 72
displaying summary data on, 146
editing tab order, 159
elements in, 42–43
in FileMaker, 12, 13
FileMaker creation of default, 112
format filters, 292–293
help text or instructions in, 22–23
keyboard control of, 158
managing complex resizing, 336–338
menu of viewable, 39
menu set for, 625–626
multiple, for composite report, 176, 500
multiple uses of, 114
objects
    automatic resizing, 70–71
    basics, 150–151
    static and dynamic, 151–152
parts, 42, 145–146, 695
for printing, 141–143, 325
for selection window, 266–267
toolset for, 17
views, 144–145
visual structure importance, 146–150
WYSIWYG for, 48
Layouts menu
    ➪ Layout Setup, 114, 145, 271
    ➪ New Layout/Report, 145
    ➪ Set Tab Order, 159
Leading Grand Summary part of layout, 146
leading zero
    in calculation, 111
    for numeric value sort as text, 281
Learn More icon, 32, 59, 61
Learning Center, pointer to, 61
left coordinate, in Object Info palette, 170
Left( ) function, 206, 294, 414–415
LeftValues( ) function, 428, 430, 431

LeftWords( ) function, 417–418
Length( ) function, 205, 404
less-than character (<), for Find, 120
Let( ) commands, for declaring multiple variables, 469–470, 471
Let( ) function
    for avoiding calculation repetition, 646
    basics, 410–411
    benefits for variable declaration, 412
    for calculation variable, 296
letters (correspondence)
    generating, 329–330
    information as basis of, 10–11
LexisNexis, 3
license
    activating, 31
    controlling assignment of, 61
line breaks, in calculation code, 448
line height, specifying, 325
Line Pattern tool, 147
lines, 151
List( ) function, 204, 428
list separators, for scripts, 254
List view, 144–145, 335, 695
lists
    adding or inserting value, 430
    basics, 8, 427
    data entry based on, 11
    extracting value from, 429
    portals for, 345
    removing value from, 430–431
    retrieving values as, 427–428
    xValues functions for managing, 428–429
literal text, references, 545
literal values
    in calculations, 200
    in formulas, 202–203
    in functions, 402
    locating references for update, 546
    term defined, 197, 695
live Web connection, 680
local disk drives, compared to network drive, 35
local file
    backup of, 550–551
    basics, 32

local variables
    basics, 296, 410, 411, 468–469, 695
    creating, 297
localization settings for files, 56
location coordinates of window, 488
Location information, display on Web viewer, 73
lock, 695
lock icon, for Web viewer object, 73
locked-down database, 520
locked record, 45, 563
locked scripts, 69
logging out, solution structure for, 521–522
logic, nonlinear, scripts with, 480–484
logical flow of information, 122–123
logical operators, 405
login account for record creation, capturing, 106–107
login procedures, in start-up script, 464
login prompt, for debugging restricted access script, 83
login script, 525, 568
logout, creating custom option, 520–523
logs
    alternative approaches, 578–579
    built-in capabilities, 567–569
    managing accumulation of data, 575–576
    of record deletions, 574–575
    to roll forward, 578
    of scripts, 569–571
    for security, 522–523
    in start-up script, 464
    of user navigation, 340–341
Lookup for Field dialog, 112
lookup table, 695
lookups, 19, 543–544, 695
Loop/End Loop structure, 485
Loop statement, 247, 481–482
looping. *See* recursion

# M

Mac OS
    AppleScript, 25, 661–662, 665–667, 688
    cross-platform capability of FileMaker, 26

# Index

Mac OS (continued)
  development for Windows and, 310–313
  Finder, limitation for duplicating files, 36
  ODBC driver for, 215
macros, 16, 668. See also scripts
*MacTech Magazine*, 707
mail merge, 695
mailing lists, 706
main menus, for solutions, 354
Manage Accounts & Privileges dialog
  basics, 507, 515, 517
  Extended Privileges panel, 513
Manage Custom Functions dialog, 627–628
Manage Custom Menus dialog
  basics, 621–622
  Custom Menus tab, 622, 624
Manage Data Sources dialog, 78
Manage Database dialog
  basics, 572
  Field Name box, 34
  Fields tab
    basics, 21
    for creating fields, 34, 93, 94
    for External SQL Data Source, 80
    for field changes, 184
    Type pop-up menu, 185
  opening, 34
  Relationships tab, 108, 178
  SQL table in, 80
  Tables tab, 95, 96, 178, 265
Manage External Data Sources dialog, 213
Manage Scripts window
  basics, 234, 237, 244, 268
  folders in, 69
  list separators in, 254
  parts, 235
Manage Value List dialog, 116, 166
many-to-many relationship, 373, 695
margins, for printing, 142
marking records, 555
match fields, 16, 366, 695
`Max( )` function, 408, 426
`Maximum` function, 195

MBS FileMaker Plugin, 679
media
  in databases, 660
  plug-ins for handling, 678–679
MediaManager, 678
Member of a Value List, for validating entry, 190
memory stack, and recursion limits, 633
memory variables, 296, 410
menu commands, for specific tabs, 344
menu set, 695
MenuMagic, 677
menus
  basics, 40, 695
  creating custom, 621–626
  for layouts, 625–626
  scripts for controlling sets, 626
  for solutions, 354
Merge Field placeholder, formatting, 329
Merge fields, 328–329, 695
message, for validation failure, 101, 190
metadata
  capturing, 106–107
  capturing and extending standard, 568–569
  fields for logs, 567–568
  functions to retrieve, 442–444
  preventing printing, 143–144
MetaDataMagic, 684
Microsoft SQL Server, 27
Microsoft Visual Basic Scripting engine, 662
`Middle( )` function, 294, 350, 414–415
`MiddleValues( )` function, 428, 429
`MiddleWords( )` function, 417–418
migrating legacy solutions, Web resources on, 37
migration utility, for automating data transfer, 392
`Min( )` function, 408, 425–426
Mini Mode menu, 37, 38
Minimal index indicator, 300
`Minimum` function, 195

mining Database Design Report, 616
minute value, in Time field, 186
Miscellaneous steps in script, 229
modal window, simulating, 332
modeling. See data modeling
modes of operation, 38–39, 695
modifier key, 648–649, 695
modifying data, on paper, 5
modular approach, to solution development, 389
modular-centric approach, to Relationships Graph, 378
modularization strategies, 658–659
Monkeybread Software, 679
`Month( )` function, 400
`Move/ResideWindow[ ]` command, 488
`Move/Resize[ ]` script command, 331
movies, binary objects for, 16
moving
  objects based on window size, 334–336
  tables between files, 180
  windows, 488–489
moving between records. See navigating
multi-criteria relationships, 369
multi-file solutions, 388–389
multi-key fields, 224, 370–371
multi-lingual interface, implementing, 356–358
multi-part PDF report, scripts for, 499–500
multi-predicate relationships, 224, 369–370
multi-purpose relationships, 372
multi-user environment
  basics, 25
  record locking in, 563
  techniques to avoid, 554–555
multi-window environment, techniques to avoid, 554–555
MultiKey fields, 16, 696
multiple fields, sorting by, 119
MySQL, 27, 214

# Index

## N

name/value pairs, 471–472
named data sources, 212–213
names
    of button object, 171
    of calculation field, 104
    conventions, 382
    of fields
        basics, 95, 200
        length of, 382–384
    of layout objects, 450–451
    of objects
        assigning, 160
        in scripts, 233
    personal, calculating initials from, 206
    of scripts
        basics, 252, 253–254
        search by, 258
    for SQL Server connection, 216
    of tables
        changing, 179–180
        editing, 95
    of user accounts, 515
    of variables, 469
    of windows, 331, 486–488
    of workstation, 51
navigating
    constraining, 452
    data, 39–40
    portals for, 346
    records, 129
    scripts for, 249–250
    shortcut, 270–274, 339–341
    between Tab control, 162
navigation steps in script, 228
nesting
    functions, 404–405
    group summaries, 322–323
    `If/Else` conditions, 481
network address, retrieving for computer, 535
network drives, compared to local drive, 35
networks
    FileMaker capabilities, 25
    restricting access to, 525
    solutions available over, 45

New Layout/Report dialog, 61
New Millennium Communications, 28, 677, 678, 683, 684
New Record/Request step, in scripts, 231
`New Window[ ]` command, 330, 487
New Window Options dialog, 488
NightWing Enterprises, 22–23, 30, 574, 705
nonlinear logic, scripts with, 480–484
nonprinting objects, 143–144, 320, 325–326
not operator, 407
Notes field, 363
null ("")
    in Boolean operations, 409
    setting variable to, 296
Number field type, 185
Number Format for selected objects dialog, 140
number formats, precedence of, 293
numeric data
    custom function to generate ranges, 632
    indexing, 192, 301
    sorting, 281
Nutshell, 19

## O

Object Effects palette, Embossed effect, 154, 156
Object Info command, 169
Object Info palette, 70–71, 334
Object Linking and Embedding (OLE), 696
Object Selection tool, 151
objects
    alignment of, 156–157
    buttons as, 171
    centering, 339
    conditional format attributes, 152–154
    default formats and attributes, 155–156
    disappearing/reappearing based on context, 314–317
    fine tuning layout position of, 137
    font changes in, 134
    in layouts, 158–160
    moving based on window size, 334–336
    multi-state, 319
    names
        basics, 160
        in scripts, 233
    properties, 152
    resizing behavior of enclosing, 338
    in scripts, 16
    size changes, 336
    sliding, 326–328
    stacking, 156–157
    term defined, 696
ODBC (Open Database Connectivity), 696
    adding data source to solution, 78
    basics, 25
    configuring drivers, 214–219
    importing from data sources, 496
ODBC Administrator (Mac OS), 215–216
ODBC Data Source Administrator, 215
ODBC Data Source Administrator control panel (Windows XP), 215
off-screen windows, creating, 489
offline updates, 655–656
OLE (Object Linking and Embedding), 696
omit, 696
`Omit Record` command, 479
omitted record sets, displaying, 41
one-to-many relationship, 373, 696
one-way relationships, 372–373
Onegasoft, 30
online help for users, 354
Open Database Connectivity (ODBC), 696
Open Database icon, 32, 59
Open Menu Item steps in script, 229
Open Remote File dialog, 557
`Open URL` script step, 669
opener files, for remote connection, 559–560
opening files
    from default or different account, 129
    script to run on, 463

725

# Index

operands, 400, 696
operating systems
    capturing in log, 568
    for runtime application, 637
operators in calculations
    basics, 400
    order of operations, 406–407
    term defined, 197, 696
Optimize File procedure, 618
Option/Alt key, and running script, 648–649
Options for Field dialog
    Auto-Enter tab, 98
    Do Not Replace option, 439
    Storage tab, 191, 196
    Validation tab, 101–102, 189–190
Options for Summary Field dialog, 194
OR Find, 276
Oracle, 27, 214
order of operations, 201, 696
organization of data
    for database creation, 5–6
    for import and export, 590
orientation of printed page, 142
out-of-memory error, 633
out-of-range characters, 592–593
out-of-scope characters, rejecting in data entry, 567
Oval tool, 154

# P

page breaks, 324–325
page number, placeholder for current, 329
page orientation, 142
pagination of reports, 324–325
paper-based database, limitations of, 4–5
Paragraph dialog, line height controls, 325
paragraph-level formatting, 292
parameters (arguments)
    basics, 629, 688
    in Data Viewer, 609
    for functions, 200, 400, 402
    supplying, 402–403

passing and retrieving multiple, 470–472
for scripts, 230, 466
term defined, 197
parent script, 473, 696
parentheses, and order of operations in calculations, 406–407
parsing
    practical aspects, 418
    text as whole words, 417
    XSLT style sheets for, 27
Part Definition dialog, 321
Part tool, 136, 146
parts of layout
    basics, 42
    reducing when printing, 326–328
passwords
    case sensitivity of, 126
    for default Admin account, 126
    script collection of, 519
    term defined, 696
    for users, 515, 525
Paste[No Style] script step, 292
pasting, and formatting, 291–292
path
    for file in container field, 599
    to temporary folders, function returning, 64
PatternCount( ) function, 202, 415–417, 429
pause in scripts, 245, 453
Pause on Error, in Script Debugger, 84
Pause/Resume-Script-[Indefinitely] command, 248
PDF files
    appending to, 66–67
    composite, from multiple layouts, 176
    generating, 49
    for images, 151
    paper output, compared to, 176
    print settings for, 142
    scripts for multi-part, 499–500
peer-to-peer hosting, 556–557
Perform AppleScript [ ] command, 661–662, 665–666

Perform Script[ ] command, 244, 245, 473, 483, 623
    and access privileges, 460
performance
    cache and, 619
    cascading calculations and, 303
    design and, 81–82
    file size and, 658–660
    for hosted databases, 555
    and imported graphics, 342, 343
    periodic updates and, 656
    as variable benefit, 412
PerformFind[ ] command, storing Find criteria in, 277
period (.), as word separator, 417
periodicals, 707
phone numbers, calculation formula for, 565–566
PHP, 24
PHP Site Assistant, 87, 682–683
phrase, creating acronym from, 634
Pi function, 402
pilcrow (¶), 202, 417
pivoting data between tables, 497–498
placeholders, for system and contextual information, 329
platform
    for runtime application, 637
    term defined, 697
plotting time, 422–423
plug-ins for FileMaker
    basics, 28, 672–679, 697
    installing and enabling, 672–674
.png file format, 17, 151, 157
pop-up menus, 40, 697
pop-ups, windows as, 331
portability of solution, fonts and, 310
Portal Setup dialog, 164–165, 290
Portal tool, 267
portals
    basics, 15, 43, 151, 345–347
    for data entry of new record, 375–376
    dynamically sorted, 346
    filtering, 264–270
    invisibility, 314–316
    resizing, 71, 338
    script commands moving cursor to, 233

# Index    R

setting up, 164–167
sorting, 290
in tab control, 163
term defined, 697
`Position( )` function, 350, 415–417, 648
pound sign (#), as Find wildcard character, 120–121
power outage, and data loss, 35, 585
precedence order of operations, 201, 696
preferences
    term defined, 697
    for tooltip display, 620
Preferences dialog
    basics, 51–54
    Fonts tab, 54, 133
    General tab, 51, 62–63
    Layout tab, 52, 132–133
    Memory tab, 52–53
    Plug-Ins tab, 53, 673
prefix character, for reserved characters, 202
presentation of data, for import and export, 591
Preview mode
    basics, 39, 697
    for printing, 48
primary file, 697
primary key, 366, 375, 697
`Print [ ]` command, 238
`Print Setup [ ]` command, 237
printable area
    basics, 142
    positioning objects outside, 143
printed output
    basics, 48
    considerations, 174
    fonts for, 174–175
    page size and setup, 175
    paper compared to PDF or Excel, 176
printer, choosing, 142
printer driver, 48
printing
    design for, 325–330
    layouts for, 141–143
    scripts for, 259

privilege sets
    basics, 125, 518, 697
    creating and configuring, 508–509
    default, 128–129
    restricted lockout, 521–522
    for user groups, 514
procedural layer, 386
process management, 11–12
Product Documentation menu, 60–61
Productive Computing, 678
progress bar
    basics, 350–353
    script to display, 485
    for Web viewer object, 73
Prohibit Modification of Value during Data Entry option, 187
properties of objects, 152

## Q

Query, in SQL, 14. *See also* Find
Quick Launch toolbar (Windows), FileMaker, 33
Quick Start screen
    basics, 33
    options on, 32, 59–60, 92
    preference settings for, 51
    Starter solutions on, 91, 181
QuicKeys, 668
QuickTime, 697
quitting. *See* closing
`Quote` function, 202
quotes (" "), for text literals in functions, 403

## R

RAD (rapid application development), 177
radio button, 697
`Random` function, 402
Range operator (...), 120
range validation, 697
rapid application development (RAD), 177
RDMS (Relational Database Management Systems), 359–360

`Re-login[ ]` command, 520
[Read-Only Access] privilege set, 125
readability of formulas, 201
real world modeling, 360–362
RealTech list, 706
recently opened files, list of, 32
record commit, 45
record navigation text, 208
record number, placeholder for, 329
record zero, global storage fields as, 196
records
    access privileges, 511–513
    basics, 12, 13, 697
    commitment of, 45
    creating
        basics, 44, 114–118
        capturing login account for, 106–107
    current, and context, 50
    definition, 4
    deleting redundant, 539–542
    duplicating, 44
    exiting and commitment, alternatives, 561–564
    IDs, 534–535
    locating unique, 499
    locking, 45, 552–554, 563
    logging deletions, 574–575
    moving between. *See* navigating
    propagating edits to related, 655
    saving, 34
    sorting
        basics, 280–281
        dynamic techniques, 281–284
        multiple keys, 281
Records menu
    ➪ Duplicate Record, 44
    ➪ Go to Record, 40
    ➪ New Record, 44, 115
    ➪ Omit Multiple, 41
    ➪ Omit Record, 41
    ➪ Replace Field Contents, 534, 538
    ➪ Revert Record, 44, 45
    ➪ Show All Records, 41, 119
    ➪ Show Omitted Only, 41, 119
    ➪ Sort Records, 119

727

# Index

records steps in script, 228
Recover command, 581, 582–583
rectangles, adding for group of fields, 147–148
recursion
    custom functions and, 446, 631–635
    in scripts, 481–482, 485
    stack and limits of, 633
    tail-end, 633–634
recursive relationships, preventing, 21
redo capabilities, multilevel, 75
redundancy, eliminating, 641–643
redundant data in flat-file database, 6
redundant records, deleting, 539–542
references
    avoiding circular, 210–212
    to files, 598
    in imported tables, 183
    to other FileMaker files, creating, 213
referential integrity. *See also* keys
    common causes of problems, 529–530
    configuring relationships for, 540–541
    costs and benefits, 530
    unique keys for, 530–536
refreshing screens, 489–490
`RefreshWindow[ ]` command, 304–305, 490
relation, 13
relational data modeling, 363
relational database, 6–7
Relational Database Management Systems (RDMS), 359–360
relational database program, 697
relational theory, background, 359–364
relationship joins, 644
relationship operators, 366–370
relationships
    alternative techniques, 370–373
    basics, 49–50
    caching, 489
    creating, 108–110
    data display, without context, 163–164

    multi-predicate, 369–370
    one-way, 372–373
    problem solving with, 224–225
    purpose of, 50
    techniques for data management, 375–377
    term defined, 698
    visual cues for, 121–122
Relationships Graph
    accessing, 108
    adding notes, 381
    basics, 20–21, 22, 208, 364–366, 377, 698
    common misconceptions, 209–210
    duplicating TOs in, 109–110
    reusability concepts in, 644
    SQL databases in, 77, 79
Relookup, 698
remote files
    basics, 32
    opener files for connection, 559–560
    opening, 555–560
remote storage of backup, 549
removing. *See* deleting
repeating fields
    basics, 15, 374, 698
    summarizing, 194
repetitions, 15
`Replace Field Contents[ ]` command
    basics, 591, 593
    in multi-user solutions, 640
    risk of errors, 554
Replace Field Contents dialog, 538
`Replace( )` function, 208, 407–408, 413–414, 430, 438
report generator, FileMaker as, 27
reports
    consolidated, 9–10
    controlling pagination, 324–325
    segmentation for, 380
    term defined, 698
Requests menu
    ↪ Constrain Found Set, 276
    ↪ Extend Found Set, 276–277
required field (not empty), 698

reserved characters, in text in calculations, 202
`Reserved Name` operator, 405, 406
reserved words, 203
resizing
    layout objects, automatic, 70–71
    windows, 488–489
resources
    availability to Web viewers, 347–348
    basics, 698
restore process for backups, 549
restricted-access scripts, debugging, 83, 607
result, term defined, 197
Return key, for going to next field, 158
reversing sort order of column, 284
`RextSizeRemove( )` function, 419–420
`RGB( )` function, 293, 420
`Right( )` function, 294, 414–415
`RightValues( )` function, 428, 430, 431
`RightWords( )` function, 400, 417–418
risks
    evaluation, 523
    identifying, 504
robots, 656, 657
role-based security, 507–508
roll-back, implementing, 576–578
Rolodex icon, for FileMaker navigation, 17
`Round( )` function, 205
"rule of multiples", 325
rules, for Conditional Formatting dialog, 66
running total, 194
runtime applications, 635–637
runtime, controlling cascading deletes at, 542
runtime solutions, 24, 698. *See also* solutions in FileMaker

# S

satellite-based graph, 379, 380
Save a Copy As procedure, 618–619

728

# Index  S

Save Layout Changes Automatically option, 52
`Save Records as Excel[ ]` command, 477
`Save Records as PDF[ ]` command, 477
    Append to Existing PDF option, 66–67
saving
    data, 34
    files, 33–35
    Finds and found sets, 277–280
    records, 34, 45
scalability, 24–25, 639–641
scheduled check for updates, 62
schema, 698
schema privilege controls, 509–510
Scodigo, 679
scope of variables, 411
screen elements, 42–43
screens
    adaptable screens with, 320
    basics, 8
    dynamic elements, 314–319
    freezing and refreshing, 489–490
    layout considerations, 174
    Mac and Windows differences in rendering, 311–312
    window location coordinates, 488
script commands, 16
Script Debugger
    basics, 82–84, 605–608, 698
    using Data Viewer with, 613
script engine, single-threaded, 244–245
script stack, 245
Script Step action, benefits of assigning custom menu command to, 623
Script Step Options area, 241, 242
script steps, 16, 698
script variables, 410, 411
scripting protocols, external, 25
ScriptLog table, 569–570
ScriptMaker
    basics, 16, 227–233, 698
    dynamic and indirect controls, 475–480
    editing, 251–253

ScriptMaster, 677
scripts
    and access privileges, 460–462
    access to, 510
    for account management, 517–520
    to act on user input, 260
    assigning attributes to command, 241–243
    to audit logging, 579
    basic setup, 237–239
    basics, 16, 228, 386
    branching according to state, 467–468
    capturing Find criteria with, 278–279
    changing command order, 239–241
    commands process, 239
    comments in, 254–255
    conditional statements, 246–247
    container objects loading and unloading, 496–497
    context for, 232
    controlling execution, 245–249
    for controlling menu sets, 626
    for data entry to custom dialog, 333
    for data import and export, 490–497
    debugging restricted privilege, 607
    declaring variables, 468–470
    defining and editing, 234–243
    dynamically building Find criteria with, 478–479
    editing information via, 250
    exit conditions for loops, 482–484
    external calls, 661–668
    for file management and printing, 251
    for Find, 259
    groups for organizing, 69–70, 255–257
    and layout object names, 450–451
    list separators, 254
    locked, 69
    logging, 569–571
    for modal window effect, 332
    modular code, 484–485. *See also* sub-scripts

    for multi-part PDF report, 499–500
    multiple parameters, 470–472
    with nonlinear logic, 480–484
    notable uses, 249–251
    operation in separated solution, 390
    organizing, 253–258
    parameters, 230, 466
    pause in, 245, 248–249, 453
    for printing, 259
    for process monitors, 351–352
    recursion, 485
    to reinstate Find, 279–280
    reordering and grouping, 257
    repetitions, 247–248, 481–482
    for retrieving data from HTML content, 350
    running on file close, 465
    running on file open, 463
    searching by name, 258
    and security, 519–520
    for selection window, 268–269
    sequence in, 232–233
    for solution backup, 550–551
    specifying and retrieving result, 473–474
    steps
        categories, 228–229
        creating, 230–232
    term defined, 698
    testing for errors, 552
    for toggling storage state of container field, 599–600
    tracking execution, 570–571
    trapping for errors, 454–459
    triggering, 244, 675–677
    for window management, 485–490
Scripts menu
    ➪ Revert Script, 252
    ➪ Save Script, 238
    ➪ ScriptMaker, 234, 268
    using, 243–245
searches. *See also* Find
    AND for compound Find, 275–276
    with OR, 276
    for scripts by name, 258

# Index

seconds value, in Time field, 186
Secure Sockets Layer, 527
SecureFM, 28
security
    appearance or reality, 505–506
    automation of, 517–518
    basics, 125–129
    concepts, 503–506
    determining level, 523–524
    extended privileges, 513–514
    for FileMaker Server, 526–527
    global variables and, 614–615
    granular, 510–514
    logs for, 522–523
    for multi-file solutions, 391
    multi-file solutions, 518–519
    for physical files, 524–526
    procedures in start-up script, 464
    role-based, 507–508
    schema privilege controls, 509–510
    and scripts, 519–520
    term defined, 698
    UID (unique identification) values, 535–536
    user authentication, 514–517
Security Administrator (New Millennium), 683
segmentation
    of large data sets, 659
    in Relationships Graph, 379–380
    for reports, 380
Select Field dialog, 121
SELECT statement, 14
Select Window[ ] command, 331
selected objects, formatting for multiple, 156
selected text, bold text for, button creation for, 294–295
selecting
    hidden objects, 156
    multiple objects, 136
    multiple script steps, in Script Debugger, 84
    script commands, 252
Selection tool, 135
selection window
    basics, 264
    layouts for, 266–267

selective formatting of text, 420
Self function, 63, 294, 402
self-join portal, highlighting current record in, 346
self joins, 376, 699
semicolon (;), to separate function arguments, 201
Send DDE Execute [ ] script step, 665
Send e-mail link for database sharing, 67–68
Send Event [ ] command, 661–662, 664
Send Us Your Feedback command, 61
separation anxiety, 387
separation model, 386
separation of data
    approaches to, 391–392
    costs and benefits, 392–393
    in existing solution, 395–398
    and External SQL Sources, 393–395
separator, 699
sequential dependency, 652
Serial Number checkbox, auto-entry, 188
serial numbers
    automatic data entry, 97–100
    field for, and ID field, 99
    generating for keys, 532–534
    term defined, 699
SerialIncrement( ) function, 533
servlets, 671–672
session table, 568
Set Field[ ] command, 294, 350, 437
Set Next Serial Value[ ] command, 533
Set Sliding/Printing dialog, 143–144, 325
Set Tab Order dialog, 159
set theory, 6, 13, 360
Set Tooltip dialog, 619
Set Variable[ ] command, 297, 411, 469–470, 599
Set Web Viewer command, 173, 349, 482

Set Window Title command, 486
"Set Window Title" Options dialog, 486
Set-Error-Capture [On] command, 458
shadow tables, 222, 699
Shift key, and running script, 648–649
short-circuited evaluation, 202
shortcut menu, 699
shortcut navigation, 270–274, 339–341
shortcuts on desktop (Windows), 33
Show All Records command, 237, 319
Show Custom Dialog [ ] command, 452–453, 459
Show Custom Dialog Options dialog, Input Fields tab, 332
Show Custom Dialog [ ] script step, 677
Show Transactions [Type] script, 249–250, 478
Show/Hide Status Area[ ] command, 520
simplicity
    custom functions to provide, 445
    in data modeling, 362
    of FileMaker Pro, 20
single-threaded script engine, 244–245
Six Fried Rice, 705
size
    of files, 658–660
    of fonts, screen vs. print, 174–175
    of layout objects, automatic, 70–71
    of objects, 336
    of printed page, 175
    of windows, 488–489
slash (/), as word separator, 417
slider, 699
sliding objects, 699
Smart Pill, 679
software license, activating, 31
Softwares for Humans, 677
solutions in FileMaker
    back end, 385–386
    backup of code, 549
    basics, 12, 24, 699

# Index S

converting single-file architecture, to separated architecture, 395
cross-platform capability, and external script calls, 667–668
documentation, 354
interaction model for interface, 129
interface vulnerabilities, 505–506
main menus for, 354
modular approach to development, 389
multi-file
    basics, 388–389
    security for, 391, 518–519
multi-lingual interface, 356–358
portability, fonts and, 310
runtime applications from, 635–637
script for backups, 251
separation issues, 387
separation of data in existing, 395–398
structure for logging out, 521–522
value of, 505
Web services in, 669–670
sort order, 699
`Sort Records[ ]` command, 237, 534
Sort Records dialog, 119
sorting
    click-sort columns for, 284–288
    data, 119–120
    open-ended three-tier, 282–284
    portals, 290, 346
    records
        basics, 280–281
        dynamic techniques, 281–284
        multiple keys, 281
    related data, 288–290
    term defined, 699
sounds, binary objects for, 16
spaces
    in data entry, 566
    in field names, 95
    in text, discarding, 414
spatial cues, for added meaning, 342
special symbols, for finding data, 120

Specify Calculation dialog
    basics, 20, 21, 111, 192–193, 197, 404
    Custom Functions category, 445
    for ID field, 99–100
    Learn More icon, 61–62
    parts, 198–200
    for simple calculations, 103–105
    storage options, 307
    for trapping field changes, 572
Specify Field dialog, 164, 328
Specify Field list dialog, 123–124, 209
Specify Field Order for Export dialog, 48, 492–493
Specify Fields for Value List dialog, 116
Specify File dialog, 213
Specify Output File dialog, 663
Specify Script Options dialog, 269, 466, 467
Specify Table dialog, 214, 219
spell-checking, field-specific
    disabling, 160
    enabling, 74–75
Spelling steps in script, 229
spider graphs, 377
splash screens, 353
spreadsheet as flat-file database, 6. *See also* Excel files
spyware, 525
SQL (Structured Query Language)
    behavior differences with FileMaker, 80
    data views, primary key values for, 394
    database in Relationships Graph, 79
    FileMaker limitations as front end, 393
    integrating tables with FileMaker data, 219–222
    queries, 14
    support as External Data Source, 77–79
    terminology, 12
SQL Server (Microsoft)
    basics, 27, 214
    name for connection, 216
square brackets, for default privilege set names, 507

squares/rectangles, 151
squid graph, 377
stacking multiple Sub-summary parts, 320–322
stacking objects, 156–157, 312
`Standard Deviation Of` function, 195
`[Standard FileMaker Menus]`, 626
Standard System Palette (256 colors), 133
Standard toolbar, new buttons for version 9, 76
Start menu
    ➪ All Programs, 32
    ➪ Control Panel ➪ Additional Options ➪ Data Sources (ODBC), 215
Starter solutions, selecting, 181
starter templates, 32
starting FileMaker, 32–33
start-up script, 463, 464–465, 525, 559
state
    script branching according to, 467–468
    user capture of, 355–356
state variables, 469
state-aware button objects, 319
static actions, buttons for, 130
static array, 374
static data, 11
static objects, 151–152
Status Area
    basics, 37, 38
    in Browse mode, 39
    Button tool, 167
    contents, 37, 38
    in Find mode, 41
    hidden and locked, 520
    in Layout mode, 52
    Portal tool, 164
    record count on, 113
    Symbols menu, 120
    Tab Control tool, 161
    term defined, 699
    Web Viewer tool, 172
status bar, in Windows application, 312–313

731

# Index

steps buttons, in Script Debugger, 84
steps in scripts, 228, 699
storage
    of files, 597–600
    and indexes, 300
Storage Options dialog, 439
stored procedures, 16. *See also* scripts
style buttons, 294–295
sub-scripts, 245, 473, 484–485, 642–643, 699
Sub-summary part
    basics, 320, 699
    stacking multiple, 320–322
    When Sorted By field for, 146, 321
subset of data, forms to view, 8–9
substantive privileges, 462
Substitute( ) function, 202, 208, 413, 430–431
substituting fonts, 310
Sum( ) function, 425
summaries, nesting group, 322–323
summary fields
    basics, 15, 186, 192–193, 194–196
    definition, 700
    disallowing deletion of referenced field, 184
    overview, 424–427
    part for, 146
    referencing, 426–427
    in report, 9–10
    for SQL tables, 222–223
super-users, scripts as, 460
supplemental fields
    in External SQL Data Source table, 80–82
    term defined, 700
The Support Group, 30
Sync button, 80
synchronization of data, 494–495, 594–597
syntax
    basics, 401, 404–405
    custom functions for readability, 629
    custom functions to simplify, 445
    term defined, 197
system failure, reasons, 547–551

# T

tab character, as word separator, 417
Tab control
    basics, 43, 71, 152, 160–161, 343–344
    concealed and remotely operated, 316–317
    default front tab, 72
    defining and creating, 161–162
    limitations, 163
    navigating between, 162
    resizing behavior of, 338
    scripts for, 344
    term defined, 700
    width of, 72
Tab Control Setup dialog, 72, 161, 316–317
Tab key, to move between fields, 34
tab order, 158, 159, 700
tab panel, 700
tab-delimited files, importing and exporting, 27, 589
tab-separated data, importing and exporting, 46–47
Table Occurrence Groups (TOGs), 130
Table Occurrences (TOs)
    basics, 108, 178, 209, 364–365
    duplicating in Relationships Graph, 109–110
    including in function parameter, 403
    line terminators, 365
    multiple, pointing to single table, 211
    as pointer, 365–366
    re-pointing, 396–397
    tables, compared to, 210
    term defined, 700
table of dependencies, 15, 304–305
table relationships, 20. *See also* Relationships Graph
Table view, 144–145, 335, 700
tables
    access privileges, 511–513
    adding fields to, 96–97
    basics, 700
    creating additional, 95
    default, for new database, 34
    definition, 4
    deleting, 178–180
    importing, 180–183
    moving between, and context change, 130
    moving between files, 180
    for notes as documentation, 384
    pivoting data between, 497–498
    placing multiples in separate, 363
    referencing, in formulas, 203
    table occurrences, compared to, 210
Tahoma font, 310
tail-end recursion, 633–634
target file, 700
TCP/IP (Transmission Control Protocol/Internet Protocol), 556, 700
TechNet, 704
templates, starter, 32
temporary edit interface, 561–564
temporary folders, function returning path to, 64
testing
    cross-platform scripts, 668
    database setup, 118
    for errors, in scripts, 552
text arrays, 375
text box, 700
text fields
    basics, 16, 185
    calculation formula for constraining, 593
    global, 333, 454
    indexing, 192, 298–299
        compared to numeric indexing, 301
    as keys, 536
text files
    importing and exporting, 46–47
    term defined, 700
text literals in functions, quotes (" ") for, 403
text objects
    basics, 151
    conditional formatting, 318
    formatting, 137–141
text operators, 405, 407

# Index U

text placeholders, 329
text strings
   in Boolean operations, 408
   Format button creation for, 420–421
   formatting, 419–421
   processing
      discarding spaces, 414
      extracting parts, 414–415
      Position and PatternCount, 415–417
      Replace( ) function, 413–414
      Substitute( ) function, 413
      xWords functions, 417–418
   selective formatting, 420
Text StyleRemove( ) function, 419–420
Text tool, 148
TextColor( ) function, 419, 420
   color value for, 293
TextColorRemove( ) function, 419–420
TextExpander (Mac OS), 668
TextFont( ) function, 419
TextFontRemove( ) function, 419–420
TextFormatRemove( ) function, 419–420, 438, 567
TextSize( ) function, 419
TextStyleAdd( ) function, 419
theta joins (comparative operators), 368
third-party products
   for automation, 668
   finding, 683–684
   plug-ins in start-up script, 464
   for security, 526
threats to data
   balanced view of, 523–524
   identifying, 504
3-D embossed effect, 154
thumbnail image, importing, 587
tiers of dependency, 304
.tif file format, 151
time
   current, 535
   placeholder for current, 329
   plotting, 422–423

time fields
   basics, 186
   in Boolean operations, 408
time formats, precedence of, 293
time savings, from computers, 5
timed pauses, 248
Times font, 175, 310
timestamp, 107, 423, 700
timestamp fields, 186, 408
Timestamp( ) function, 423
Title Footer part of layout, 146
Title Header part of layout, 146
TOGs (Table Occurrence Groups), 130
Tools menu
   ⇨ Database Design Report, 615
   ⇨ Developer Utilities, 636
   ⇨ File Maintenance, 617
   ⇨ Launch PHP Assistant, 87–88
   ⇨ Script Debugger, 605
tools, retaining active setting, 52
tooltips, 619–621, 701
top coordinate, in Object Info palette, 170
TOs. *See* Table Occurrences (TOs)
Total of function, 195
Trailing Grand Summary part of layout, 146
trailing spaces, in data entry, 566
training partners, 30
transaction modeling, 654–658
transformation script, 498
Transformations table, 601
translucency, in imported graphics, 343
transparency
   conditional formatting for objects, 319
   in imported graphics, 343
Trebuchet font, 175, 310
trigger field, 701
triggering scripts, 675–677
Trim( ) function, 414, 566
TrimAll( ) function, 414
Troi Activator, 677
Troi Automatisering, Troi File, 28
Troi Dialog plug-in, 677, 678

tuple, 13
type-conversion functions, 200

# U

UID (unique identification) values, 535–536
underscore prefix, for metadata fields, 106
undo capabilities
   multilevel, 75
   and roll-back, 577
Undo/Redo command, in scripts, 231
Unicode
   basics, 25, 701
   for indexes, 301–302, 368
Uniform Resource Locator (URL), 701
   loading in Web Viewer, 349
   term defined, 701
   in Web Viewer Setup dialog, 172
unindexed fields, 434
unique ID, 375
unique records, locating, 499
unique validation, 701
Unique Value option, for fields, 190
unnamed data sources, 212–213
unstored calculations, 434–436, 701
Update Records in Found Set import, 596–597
updates
   to global calculations, 440–441
   scheduled check for, 62
Upper( ) function, 405
URL (Uniform Resource Locator)
   loading in Web Viewer, 349
   term defined, 701
   in Web Viewer Setup dialog, 172
usability, 129–130
user accountability, 564
user accounts
   creating, 515
   filtered file display based on, 526
   obtaining name of, 568
   scripts for managing, 460, 517–520
   setting default, 128–129
   support for multiple, 125
user input. *See* data entry

733

# Index

user license. *See* license
user preferences
    basics, 355–358
    in start-up script, 464
user prompt, displaying dialog for, 452–453
user sessions table, 522–523
users
    anticipating, 123–125
    authentication, 514–517
    controlling views available to, 145
    global field values for each, 197
    logs to track activity, 522–523
    managing interaction, 452–454
    online help for, 354
    overwriting data, 436–438
    pausing for script for input, 248–249
    requiring response from, 452
    support for, 394–395
users table, 355–356
utility relationship, 376–377, 497–498, 644
utility table, 520, 596–597

## V

validation
    basics, 15, 701
    rules for fields, 101–102
Value from Last Visited Record checkbox, auto-entry, 188
value index for text fields, 299
value lists
    access to, 510
    creating, 116–117
    term defined, 701
ValueCount ( ) function, 428
ValueListItems ( ) function, 427–428, 545
values
    basics, 16
    calculation of, 11
    reference in script, 85
~Values ( ) functions, 375
variables
    basics, 295, 410–412
    benefits in calculation, 411
    comparing to global fields, 307

and Data Viewer, 609, 614–615
declaring, 297, 468–470
declaring in start-up script, 465
dependent, 15
destroying, 411
for dynamic file paths, 477–478
instantiating and destroying, 296–297
kinds, 296
and memory usage, 296
scope, 390, 411
setting to null, 296
term defined, 197, 701
tracking, 297–298
.vbs file extension, 663
VBScript, 25, 661–665
vendors, information in About dialog, 354
Verdana font, 133, 175, 310, 311
versions, information about, 354, 568
vertical dimension parameters, in Object Info palette, 169
vertical dotted line, in Layout mode, 142
view controls, scripts for, 249–250
View Index dialog, 191
View menu
    ⇨ Browse Mode, 141
    ⇨ Find Mode, 119, 120
    ⇨ Layout Mode, 114, 134
    ⇨ Object Info, 70, 152, 169
    ⇨ Preview Mode, 143
    ⇨ Show
        ⇨ Non-Printing Objects, 326
        ⇨ Sliding Objects, 326
        ⇨ Tooltips, 619
    ⇨ View as Form, 144
    ⇨ View as List, 144
    ⇨ View as Table, 144
Viewer Setup dialog, 61
views of data. *See also* screens
    data, 39–40
    multiple, 330–332
    related data, 49–50
    term defined, 701
    using and changing, 130
visibility of objects
    based on context, 314–317
    conditional formatting for, 317

visual cues for state, 314
visual fatigue, avoiding, 149–150
visual spell-checking, 74–75, 160
visual structure, importance for layouts, 146–150

## W

Watch panel in Data Viewer, 612–613
Web-based Learning Center, pointer to, 61
Web browser, opening Database Design Report in, 616
Web Compatibility steps in script, 229
Web pages
    basics, 701
    deployment, 680–683
    scraping data from, 349–350
Web publishing, custom, 681–683
*Web Publishing with PHP and FileMaker 9*, 707
Web resources
    companion Web site, 709–710
    design tips and tricks, 705–706
    on FileMaker, 30
    help on calculation functions, 399–400
    migrating legacy solutions, 37
    FileMaker, Inc. Web site, 703–704
    online forums and mailing lists, 706
Web scraping, 349
Web services, in solutions, 669–670
Web viewer objects
    advanced techniques, 347–350
    alternative for progress indicators, 352–353
    applets and servlets, 671–672
    basics, 16, 43, 152, 701
    charting with Flash, 671
    complementary data concepts, 174
    controlling, 173
    enhancements, 72–74
    FileMaker verson for, 36
    rendering internally calculated content, 348–349
    setup, 172–173
    in solutions, 669–670
Web Viewer Setup dialog, 73, 172

# Index

Webinars, 703
what-you-see-is-what-you-get (WYSIWYG), for layouts, 48
white space
    in formulas, 201
    in layouts, 149
wildcard operators, in Find, 120–121
Window menu ⇨ New Window, 264
window title, 486
window widgets, 624
`WindowNames` function, 402
windows
    addressing by name, 486–488
    controlling one from other, 274–275
    creating off-screen, 489
    moving and resizing, 488–489
    multiple
        basics, 330–332
        techniques to avoid, 554–555
    placement and size, 330–331
    placement in start-up script, 464
    platform-specific behavior, Windows or Mac, 312–313
    as pop-ups and drill-downs, 331
    resizing, and layout object change, 70
    resizing components of, 334
    simulating modal, 332
    zoom controls for, 37

Windows (Microsoft)
    application window, 313
    cross-platform capability of FileMaker, 26
    development for Mac and, 310–313
    executing VBScript code, 661–662
Windows command-line scripts, calling, 664–665
Windows Explorer, limitation for duplicating files, 36
Windows steps in script, 228
word index, 298–299
word processing, form letter, 10–11
word separators, characters acting as, 417
`WordCount( )` function, 417–418
workstations
    dedicating to batch processing, 656
    placeholder for user name, 329
    preference settings for, 51–54
WYSIWYG (what-you-see-is-what-you-get), for layouts, 48

## X

X2max Software, 28
xmCHART, 28, 679
XML (eXtensible Markup Language)
    basics, 681–682, 702
    as DDR output option, 616, 617

FileMaker Server use of, 24
    importing and exporting, 27, 495
XSLT (eXtensible Style Language Transformation) style sheets, 27, 681–682, 702

## Y

`Year( )` function, 400
years, converting 2-digit to 4-digit, 591

## Z

zero
    in Boolean operations, 408
    leading
        in calculation, 111
        for numeric value sort as text, 281
zero record, global storage fields as, 196
`zippScript` plug-in, 677
"zoning" approach, to resizing management, 336–338
zoom
    controls for windows, 37, 38
    term defined, 702
Zoom Percentage, in FileMaker window, 38

735